Lecture Notes in Computer Science 11334

Commenced Publication in 1973
Founding and Former Series Editors:
Gerhard Goos, Juris Hartmanis, and Jan van Leeuwen

More information about this series at http://www.springer.com/series/7407

Jaideep Vaidya · Jin Li (Eds.)

Algorithms and Architectures for Parallel Processing

18th International Conference, ICA3PP 2018
Guangzhou, China, November 15–17, 2018
Proceedings, Part I

Editors
Jaideep Vaidya
Rutgers University
Newark, NJ, USA

Jin Li
Guangzhou University
Guangzhou, China

ISSN 0302-9743 ISSN 1611-3349 (electronic)
Lecture Notes in Computer Science
ISBN 978-3-030-05050-4 ISBN 978-3-030-05051-1 (eBook)
https://doi.org/10.1007/978-3-030-05051-1

Library of Congress Control Number: 2018962485

LNCS Sublibrary: SL1 – Theoretical Computer Science and General Issues

This Springer imprint is published by the registered company Springer Nature Switzerland AG
The registered company address is: Gewerbestrasse 11, 6330 Cham, Switzerland

Preface

Welcome to the proceedings of the 18th International Conference on Algorithms and Architectures for Parallel Processing (ICA3PP 2018), which was organized by Guangzhou University and held in Guangzhou, China, during November 15–17, 2018.

ICA3PP 2018 was the 18th event in a series of conferences devoted to research on algorithms and architectures for parallel processing. Previous iterations of the conference include ICA3PP 2017 (Helsinki, Finland, November 2017), ICA3PP 2016 (Granada, Spain, December 2016), ICA3PP 2015 (Zhangjiajie, China, November 2015), ICA3PP 2014 (Dalian, China, August 2014), ICA3PP 2013 (Vietri sul Mare, Italy, December 2013), ICA3PP 2012 (Fukuoka, Japan, September 2012), ICA3PP 2011 (Melbourne, Australia, October 2011), ICA3PP 2010 (Busan, Korea, May 2010), ICA3PP 2009 (Taipei, Taiwan, June 2009), ICA3PP 2008 (Cyprus, June 2008), ICA3PP 2007 (Hangzhou, China, June 2007), ICA3PP 2005 (Melbourne, Australia, October 2005), ICA3PP 2002 (Beijing, China, October 2002), ICA3PP 2000 (Hong Kong, China, December 2000), ICA3PP 1997 (Melbourne, Australia, December 1997), ICA3PP 1996 (Singapore, June 1996), and ICA3PP 1995 (Brisbane, Australia, April 1995).

ICA3PP is now recognized as the main regular event in the area of parallel algorithms and architectures, which covers many dimensions including fundamental theoretical approaches, practical experimental projects, and commercial and industry applications. This conference provides a forum for academics and practitioners from countries and regions around the world to exchange ideas for improving the efficiency, performance, reliability, security, and interoperability of computing systems and applications.

ICA3PP 2018 attracted over 400 high-quality research papers highlighting the foundational work that strives to push beyond the limits of existing technologies, including experimental efforts, innovative systems, and investigations that identify weaknesses in existing parallel processing technology. Each submission was reviewed by at least two experts in the relevant areas, on the basis of their significance, novelty, technical quality, presentation, and practical impact. According to the review results, 141 full papers were selected to be presented at the conference, giving an acceptance rate of 35%. Besides, we also accepted 50 short papers and 24 workshop papers. In addition to the paper presentations, the program of the conference included four keynote speeches and two invited talks from esteemed scholars in the area, namely: Prof. Xuemin (Sherman) Shen, University of Waterloo, Canada; Prof. Wenjing Lou, Virginia Tech, USA; Prof. Witold Pedrycz, University of Alberta, Canada; Prof. Xiaohua Jia, City University of Hong Kong, Hong Kong; Prof. Xiaofeng Chen, Xidian University, China; Prof. Xinyi Huang, Fujian Normal University, China. We were extremely honored to have them as the conference keynote speakers and invited speakers.

ICA3PP 2018 was made possible by the behind-the-scene effort of selfless individuals and organizations who volunteered their time and energy to ensure the success of this conference. We would like to express our special appreciation to Prof. Yang Xiang, Prof. Weijia Jia, Prof. Yi Pan, Prof. Laurence T. Yang, and Prof. Wanlei Zhou, the Steering Committee members, for giving us the opportunity to host this prestigious conference and for their guidance with the conference organization. We would like to emphasize our gratitude to the general chairs, Prof. Albert Zomaya and Prof. Minyi Guo, for their outstanding support in organizing the event. Thanks also to the publicity chairs, Prof. Zheli Liu and Dr Weizhi Meng, for the great job in publicizing this event. We would like to give our thanks to all the members of the Organizing Committee and Program Committee for their efforts and support.

The ICA3PP 2018 program included two workshops, namely, the ICA3PP 2018 Workshop on Intelligent Algorithms for Large-Scale Complex Optimization Problems and the ICA3PP 2018 Workshop on Security and Privacy in Data Processing. We would like to express our sincere appreciation to the workshop chairs: Prof. Ting Hu, Prof. Feng Wang, Prof. Hongwei Li and Prof. Qian Wang.

Last but not least, we would like to thank all the contributing authors and all conference attendees, as well as the great team at Springer that assisted in producing the conference proceedings, and the developers and maintainers of EasyChair.

November 2018   Jaideep Vaidya
                                                                           Jin Li

Organization

General Chairs

Albert Zomaya   University of Sydney, Australia
Minyi Guo   Shanghai Jiao Tong University, China

Program Chairs

Jaideep Vaidya   Rutgers University, USA
Jin Li   Guangzhou University, China

Publication Chair

Yu Wang   Guangzhou University, China

Publicity Chairs

Zheli Liu   Nankai University, China
Weizhi Meng   Technical University of Denmark, Denmark

Steering Committee

Yang Xiang (Chair)   Swinburne University of Technology, Australia
Weijia Jia   Shanghai Jiaotong University, China
Yi Pan   Georgia State University, USA
Laurence T. Yang   St. Francis Xavier University, Canada
Wanlei Zhou   Deakin University, Australia

Program Committee

Pedro Alonso   Universitat Politècnica de València, Spain
Daniel Andresen   Kansas State University, USA
Cosimo Anglano   Universitá del Piemonte Orientale, Italy
Danilo Ardagna   Politecnico di Milano, Italy
Kapil Arya   Northeastern University, USA
Marcos Assuncao   Inria, France
Joonsang Baek   University of Wollongong, Australia
Anirban Basu   KDDI Research Inc., Japan
Ladjel Bellatreche   LIAS/ENSMA, France
Jorge Bernal Bernabe   University of Murcia, Spain
Thomas Boenisch   High-Performance Computing Center Stuttgart, Germany

George Bosilca   University of Tennessee, USA
Massimo Cafaro   University of Salento, Italy
Philip Carns   Argonne National Laboratory, USA
Alexandra Carpen-Amarie   Vienna University of Technology, Austria
Aparicio Carranza   City University of New York, USA
Aniello Castiglione   University of Salerno, Italy
Arcangelo Castiglione   University of Salerno, Italy
Pedro Castillo   University of Granada, Spain
Tzung-Shi Chen   National University of Tainan, Taiwan
Kim-Kwang Raymond   The University of Texas at San Antonio, USA
  Choo
Mauro Conti   University of Padua, Italy
Jose Alfredo Ferreira Costa   Federal University, UFRN, Brazil
Raphaël Couturier   University Bourgogne Franche-Comté, France
Miguel Cárdenas Montes   CIEMAT, Spain
Masoud Daneshtalab   Mälardalen University and Royal Institute
                                    of Technology, Sweden
Casimer Decusatis   Marist College, USA
Eugen Dedu   University of Bourgogne Franche-Comté, France
Juan-Carlos Díaz-Martín   University of Extremadura, Spain
Matthieu Dorier   Argonne National Laboratory, USA
Avgoustinos Filippoupolitis   University of Greenwich, UK
Ugo Fiore   Federico II University, Italy
Franco Frattolillo   University of Sannio, Italy
Marc Frincu   West University of Timisoara, Romania
Jorge G. Barbosa   University of Porto, Portugal
Chongzhi Gao   Guangzhou University, China
Jose Daniel García   University Carlos III of Madrid, Spain
Luis Javier García Villalba   Universidad Complutense de Madrid, Spain
Paolo Gasti   New York Institute of Technology, USA
Vladimir Getov   University of Westminster, UK
Olivier Gluck   Université de Lyon, France
Jing Gong   KTH Royal Institute of Technology, Sweden
Amina Guermouche   Telecom Sud-Paris, France
Jeff Hammond   Intel, USA
Feng Hao   Newcastle University, UK
Houcine Hassan   Universitat Politècnica de València, Spain
Sun-Yuan Hsieh   National Cheng Kung University, Taiwan
Chengyu Hu   Shandong University, China
Xinyi Huang   Fujian Normal University, China
Mauro Iacono   University of Campania Luigi Vanvitelli, Italy
Shadi Ibrahim   Inria, France
Yasuaki Ito   Hiroshima University, Japan
Mathias Jacquelin   Lawrence Berkeley National Laboratory, USA
Nan Jiang   East China Jiaotong University, China
Lu Jiaxin   Jiangxi Normal University, China

Contents – Part I

Distributed and Parallel Computing

High Performance Computing

Distributed and Parallel Computing

Network-Aware Grouping in Distributed Stream Processing Systems

Fei Chen, Song Wu$^{(\boxtimes)}$, and Hai Jin

Services Computing Technology and System Lab, Cluster and Grid Computing Lab,
School of Computer Science and Technology,
Huazhong University of Science and Technology, Wuhan 430074, China
{fei_chen_2013,wusong,hjin}@hust.edu.cn

Abstract. *Distributed Stream Processing* (DSP) systems have recently attracted much attention because of their ability to process huge volumes of real-time stream data with very low latency on clusters of commodity hardware. Existing workload grouping strategies in a DSP system can be classified into four categories (i.e. raw and blind, data skewness, cluster heterogeneity, and dynamic load-aware). However, these traditional stream grouping strategies do not consider network distance between two communicating operators. In fact, the traffic from different network channels makes a significant impact on performance. How to grouping tuples according to network distances to improve performance has been a critical problem.

In this paper, we propose a network-aware grouping framework called Squirrel to improve the performance under different network distances. Identifying the network location of two communicating operators, Squirrel sets a weight and priority for each network channel. It introduces *Weight Grouping* to assign different numbers of tuples to each network channel according to channel's weight and priority. In order to adapt to changes in network conditions, input load, resources and other factors, Squirrel uses *Dynamic Weight Control* to adjust network channel's weight and priority online by analyzing runtime information. Experimental results prove Squirrel's effectiveness and show that Squirrel can achieve 1.67x improvement in terms of throughput and reduce the latency by 47%.

Keywords: Stream processing · Load balancing · Grouping Network distance

1 Introduction

DSP systems such as Storm [18], Naiad [9], Flink [4], Heron [8] model a streaming application as a *directed acyclic graph* (DAG), where vertices are called processing elements (i.e. operator) and edges are called streams. A processing element (or operator) receives data tuples from input queue, performs computation logics on the tuples, and emits the output to output queue. Edges represent the data

© Springer Nature Switzerland AG 2018
J. Vaidya and J. Li (Eds.): ICA3PP 2018, LNCS 11334, pp. 3–18, 2018.
https://doi.org/10.1007/978-3-030-05051-1_1

streaming directions. For scalability, each processing element can have a set of instances running in parallel called processing element instance. Upstream processing element instances partition the streams into sub-streams using different grouping strategies and balance these workloads among multiple downstream instances.

Existing workloads grouping strategies in a DSP system can be classified into four categories (i.e. raw and blind, data skewness, cluster heterogeneity, and dynamic load-aware). Shuffle grouping, which forwards messages typically in a round-robin way to achieve load balancing, is a raw and blind method. The second kind of grouping is developed for dealing with data skewness. For example, PKG [11–13] adopts the power of two choices to dispatch tuples in the presence of bounded skew. Consistent Grouping [10] partitions tuples to each downstream operator according to node's capacity in heterogeneous clusters. The last category is a dynamic load-aware manner. OSG [15] keeps track of tuple execution times and adopts a greedy online scheduling mechanism to assign tuples to operators dynamically. We show an example of shuffle grouping in Fig. 1.

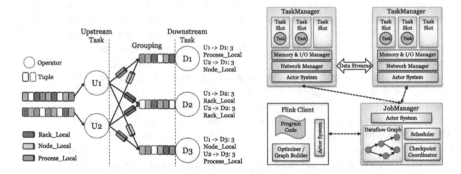

Fig. 1. An example of shuffle grouping   **Fig. 2.** Architecture of Flink

However, these traditional stream grouping strategies do not consider network distance between two communicating operators. In fact, the traffic from different network channels makes a significant impact on performance [2,19]. Intra-process communication (i.e. Process_Local), where two operators locate in the same *Java Virtual Machine* (JVM) process, delivers messages in shared-memory way. Inter-process communication (i.e. Node_Local), where two operators locate in different JVM processes but in the same host, uses socket but loopback device to pass messages. Inter-node communication (i.e. Rack_Local), where two operators locate in different hosts but in the same rack, forwards messages via *Network Interface Card* (NIC) and one-hop router. Inter-rack communication (i.e. Any), where two operators locate in different racks, sends and receives messages through at least two-hop routers. The performance of different communication modes differ greatly. It has been a critical problem how to grouping messages according to network distances to improve performance.

In this paper, we propose a network-aware grouping framework called Squirrel to assign tuples to different network channels. By locating the resource location (TaskManager, Host, Rack) of two communicating operators, we set a weight and priority for each network channel. *Weight Grouping* decides the number of tuples sent to each network channel according to channel's weight and priority. In order to adapt to changes in network conditions, input load, resources, and other factors, *Dynamic Weight Control* adjusts network channel's weight and priority online by periodically analyzing runtime information such as tuple execution time. In summary, this paper makes the following contributions:

- We analyze distinctions of different network distances and identify differentiated performance for stream applications under different network channels. We find that the performance gets worse while two operators locate further in network distances.
- We present Squirrel, a network-aware grouping framework for assigning tuples to different network channels. By locating the network distances between two communicating operators, we introduce *weight grouping* to distribute tuples to downstream operator instances. We adopt *dynamic weight control* to adjust the weight of each network channels online based on runtime information.
- We have implemented Squirrel on Flink and conducted a comprehensive evaluation with various benchmarks. Experimental results show that Squirrel can achieve 1.67x improvement in terms of throughput and reduce the latency by 47%.

The rest of this paper is organized as follows. In Sect. 2, we introduce the architecture of Flink and clarify traditional stream grouping strategies. Section 3 explains the motivation of network-aware grouping. In Sect. 4, we describe our network-aware grouping strategy and the design of Squirrel. Section 4.1 presents the implementation of Squirrel based on Flink. We evaluate the performance of our system in Sect. 5. Section 6 surveys the related works briefly. Finally, Sect. 7 concludes this paper.

2   Background

In this section, we first introduce the architecture of Flink. Then we classify traditional stream grouping strategies into four categories and describe their representative strategy respectively.

2.1   Architecture of Flink

Flink is a typical open-source stream processing framework for low-latency streaming applications [1,4]. As depicted in Fig. 2, a Flink cluster consists of three kinds of processes: the Client, the JobManager, and the TaskManager. The Client receives and parses the program code, transforms it to a dataflow graph (i.e. DAG), and submits this graph to the JobManager. The JobManager is responsible for the distributed execution of the dataflow. It monitors the state and progress of each operator and stream, schedules and deploys new operators, and conducts checkpointing and recovery when failures occur. The TaskManager launches each operator as a task instance, and reports operator's status and progress to the JobManager. It also manages the buffer pools to buffer the streams data, and maintains the network connections to transmit messages between operators.

2.2   Stream Grouping Strategies

We classify traditional stream grouping strategies into four categories.

Raw and Blind. Many default grouping strategies of open-source distributed stream processing systems are raw and blind. They adopt either a round-robin fashion or a hashing manner. Shuffle grouping forwards messages typically in a round-robin way. Messages are distributed across the downstream tasks one by one such that each task can receive the same number of messages. Key grouping is usually implemented through hashing and allows each upstream task route each message via its key. This ensures the messages which have the same key are processed by the same downstream task.

Data Skewness. Real-world stream workloads are usually with skewed distribution. *Partial Key Grouping* (PKG) [11–13] uses the classical power of two choices to achieve nearly perfect load balance when data skew occurs. DStream [5] adopts different partitioning mechanisms for different keys. It groups the popular keys using shuffle grouping and handles unpopular keys with key grouping. DKG [16] monitors the incoming stream to identify skewed keys and estimate their frequency. It uses these estimated frequencies and the buckets' size as parameters to run a greedy scheduling algorithm in order to obtain a one-to-one mapping of elements to target instances.

Cluster Heterogeneity. Heterogeneities are very common in current clusters. [17] uses the TCP blocking rate per connection as the metric of heterogeneous workers' service rate and models the load balancing problem as a minimax separable resource allocation problem. [10] proposes *Consistent Grouping* (CG) to group tuples to each processing element instance according to its capacity. CG borrows the concept of virtual workers from the traditional consistent hashing and can handle both the potential skewness in input data distribution, as well as the heterogeneity in resources.

Dynamic Load-Aware [7]. proposes to partition workload by using a mixed strategy. It first assigns some keys to the specified target worker threads and handles all other keys with the hash function. The system can update the routing table which has the chosen keys adaptively when incoming data stream has short-term distribution fluctuations. OSG [15] leverages sketches to monitor tuple execution time at operator instances, assign tuples to operator instances by applying a greedy online multiprocessor scheduling algorithm at runtime. [3] collects and analyzes the application's traces online to identify correlations between the keys. It distributes correlated keys to the instances which are located on the same server to reduce network traffic.

3 Motivation

In this section, we first introduce distinctions of four different network distances, and then conduct experimental analysis under different network distances. Finally, we present the key idea of Squirrel.

3.1 Network Distances

In current deployment of stream application topology, there are four network distances between two communicating operators. They are intra-process (i.e. Process_Local), inter-process (i.e. Node_Local), inter-node (i.e. Rack_Local), and inter-rack (i.e. Any). Different network distances have different communication modes, accompany with different performance impacts. Table 1 summarizes the characteristics of each network distance.

Table 1. Comparison of different network distance

Location	Communication	Manner	Serialization	Latency	Bandwidth
Process_Local	Inter-thread	Shared memory	No	100 ns	20 GB/s
Node_Local	Inter-process	Loopback device	Yes	20 us	2.5 GB/s
Rack_Local	Inter-node	1-hop router	Yes	200 us	100 MB/s
Any	Inter-rack	N-hop router	Yes	350 us	10 MB/s

Intra-process communication, where two operators locate in the same JVM process, delivers messages in shared-memory way. These two operators work in the same memory address space of one JVM. Upstream task only needs to pass a pointer of messages to downstream task. Messages do not need to be serialized and deserialized. Intra-process communication is the fastest with the latency of memory access (about 100 ns) and has the largest bandwidth as high as 20 GB/s. Inter-process communication, where two operators locate in different JVM processes but in the same host, uses socket but loopback device to pass messages. Network packets are forwarded by loopback device in network layer, and they do not need to go through a NIC and a router. Messages need to be serialized and deserialized. Inter-process communication is fast with the latency of 20 us and has large bandwidth of 2.5 GB/s. Inter-node communication, where two operators locate in different hosts but in the same rack, forwards messages via NIC and one-hop router. Messages need to be serialized and deserialized. Inter-node communication is slow with the latency of 200 us and has small bandwidth of 100 MB/s. Inter-rack communication, where two operators locate in different racks, sends and receives messages through at least two-hop routers. Messages need to be serialized and deserialized. Inter-rack communication is the slowest with the latency of 350 us and has the smallest bandwidth of 10 MB/s.

3.2 Experimental Analysis

In order to clarify the motivation, we conduct some experiments to show differentiated performance under different network distances. Experimental setup is listed in Sect. 5. We use classic wordcount as the workload.

Performance Under Different Network Distances. Figure 3 shows the performance when running wordcount under different network distances. We measure the tuples' average processing time in Fig. 3(a) and throughput in Fig. 3(b) respectively. Process_Local where two slot sharing groups are deployed in the same JVM (i.e. taskManager in Flink) can achieve average processing time as low as 0.47ms and throughput as high as 33000 tuples/s. The performance get worse as two operators locate further in network distances. Average processing time in Node_Local increases by 3.5x than in Process_Local. Throughput in Rack_Local decreases about 2.5x than in Process_Local. Performance under inter-rack communication are the worst of all, where average processing time increases by 8.8x and throughput decreases up to 3.6x comparing with Process_Local.

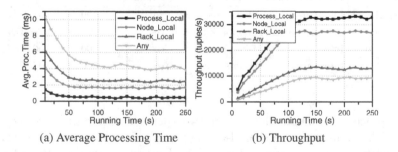

(a) Average Processing Time   (b) Throughput

Fig. 3. Performance under different network distances

Performance Between Two Communicating Operators. We measure the performance between two communicating operators in Fig. 4. Average transmission time is from the time when a tuple enters into *FlatMap* to the time when the tuple reaches to *Keyed Aggregation*. From Fig. 4, we can see that different network channels show great performance differences. Tuples' average transmission time in Process_Local can be as low as 0.032ms and throughput can be as high as 180000 tuples/s. However, performance degrades significantly when two operators have further network distances. It shows the similar tendency with the whole topology's performance in Fig. 3. Average transmission time in Node_Local increases by 5.8x than in Process_Local. Throughput in Rack_Local decreases about 2.3x than in Process_Local. Performance under inter-rack communication is the worst of all, where average processing time increases by 19.5x and throughput decreases up to 3.8x comparing with Process_Local.

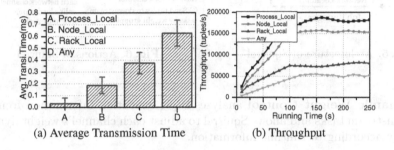

(a) Average Transmission Time   (b) Throughput

Fig. 4. Performance between two communicating operators

In summary, different network channels can achieve differentiated performance. When two operators locate further in network distances, applications' performance will get much worse. How to grouping tuples according to network distances has great impacts on applications' performance.

4 System Design

In this section, we describe the system design of Squirrel. We begin with an overview of Squirrel's architecture, followed by introducing the system details.

4.1 System Overview

Figure 5 overviews the architecture of Squirrel. Being aware of resource location of each task, Network Locator identifies network distance of two communicating tasks. Load Monitor collects and analyzes runtime information to adapt to changes of network conditions and other factors. Squirrel centers on the design of *weight grouping* and *dynamic weight control* to enable efficient network-aware grouping.

– **Weight Grouping** assigns different weights and priorities for different network channels. *Weight Grouping* chooses a target channel for tuples according to channel's weight and priority.

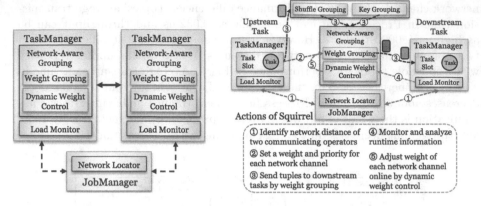

Fig. 5. Architecture of Squirrel   **Fig. 6.** Actions of Squirrel

– **Dynamic Weight Control** analyzes tuple execution information from all downstream tasks and allows Squirrel to adjust each channel's weight dynamically according to runtime information.

We present Squirrel's actions in Fig. 6. Squirrel works as follows: (1) when a task is deployed and begins running, Network Locator in JobManager records the resource location (such as TaskManagerID, HostID, RackID) and broadcasts the location to all upstream tasks. Upstream tasks compare this location with its own location and decide the network distances of these two tasks. (2) Squirrel sets initial weight and priority for each network channel according to network distance. The closer the network distance is, the greater the weight and the higher priority (Process_Local > Node_Local > Rack_Local > Any). (3) Squirrel sends tuples to downstream tasks by weight grouping. (4) Load Monitor collects and analyzes runtime information to be aware of the changes of network conditions, input load, resources. (5) Dynamic weight control adjusts each network channel's weight according to runtime information from downstream tasks such as tuple waiting time, tuple execution time.

4.2   Network and Load Aware

Network Aware. Considering about pipelined deploying mode in distributed stream processing systems, a task instance of upstream operator is likely to be deployed and scheduled after downstream tasks. If there is one downstream task deployed and running, JobManager records its resource location and broadcasts the location to all alive upstream tasks. If there is one upstream task deployed after downstream tasks, it will not receive these location information. However, it notifies pipelined consumers (i.e. downstream tasks) when its result partition is ready. This will trigger the deployment of consuming tasks. If one downstream task has been deployed and is running, JobManager sends this downstream task's location to the upstream task. Upstream tasks compare these locations with their own locations and decide the network distances of these two tasks. If they have the same TaskManagerID, they are Process_Local. Otherwise if they have the same HostID, they are Node_Local. If they have the same RackID, they are Rack_Local. If they have completely different resource locations, they are Any.

Load Aware. Squirrel collects runtime information dynamically to be aware of the changes in network conditions, input load, and resource contention. Flink outputs metric reports to log file or web console periodically. In Squirrel, these metric reports including latency, length of input queue, and other metrics are sent to JobManager through heartbeat messages. Squirrel tracks the latency of records traveling through the system by emitting a special record, called Latency Marker. The marker contains a timestamp from the time when the record has been emitted at the sources and does not include any logical operations. Squirrel analyzes these metrics to decide whether load are balanced among downstream tasks.

4.3   Weight Grouping

Identifying the network distances between two communicating tasks, Squirrel assigns an initial weight and priority for each network channel according to different network distances. The closer the network distance, the greater the weight and the higher priority. Squirrel sends tuples to downstream tasks by weight grouping. Algorithm 1 shows the procedure of weight grouping.

Line 1–2 assigns an initial weight and priority for each network channel. When choosing a channel for a tuple, Squirrel prefers the channel selected by the default channel selection strategy (such as shuffle grouping, key grouping). If the default selected channel has sufficient weight share (emitTimes[channel] < weight[channel]), then the tuple is sent to this channel (line 3–6). Otherwise, if the default selected channel has used up all its weight share, Squirrel traverses from the channel of highest priority and looks for channel with enough weight share (line 7–15). If all channels have used up their weight shares, Squirrel begins to assign a new round of weight shares to each channel (line 16–18). Squirrel adjusts each channel's weight dynamically according to tuple execution information (line 19).

4.4   Dynamic Weight Control

Although weight grouping can distribute tuples among downstream tasks in a static manner efficiently, it is not robust enough in case of data skewness and cluster heterogeneity. Besides, considering how to set ideal initial weight for each channel depends on application developers' experience, Squirrel needs dynamic weight control to correct the error of initial weight. Squirrel adopts a mechanism similar with TCP congestion control (i.e., AIMD, *additive increase/multiplicative decrease*) to adjust each channel's weight dynamically. By comparing average tuple execution time in each downstream task, Squirrel checks whether the

---

Algorithm 1. Weight Grouping

Input: t: input tuple, n: total channels, *locations*: network locations of channels, *emitTimes[channel]*: times of tuples through each channel

Output: targetChannel

1: $weight[channel] \Leftarrow initializeWeight(n, locations)$
2: $priority[channel] \Leftarrow sortChannel(n, locations)$
3: $selectedChannel \Leftarrow defaultGrouping(t, n)$
4: **if** $emitTimes[selectedChannel] <$
    $weight[selectedChannel]$ **then**
5:     $targetChannel \Leftarrow selectedChannel$
6:     $emitTimes[targetChannel] + +$
7: **else**
8:     **for** $priorityChannel \Leftarrow priority[channel]$ **do**
9:         **if** $emitTimes[priorityChannel] <$
            $weight[priorityChannel]$ **then**
10:             $targetChannel \Leftarrow priorityChannel$
11:             $emitTimes[targetChannel] + +$
12:             $break$
13:         **end if**
14:     **end for**
15: **end if**
16: **if** $usedUpWeight(weight, emitTimes[], n)$ **then**
17:     $reassignWeight(weight, emitTimes[], n)$
18: **end if**
19: $dynamicWeightControl(n, locations)$
20: **return** $targetChannel$

---

weight share of a channel is appropriate. If average tuple execution time in one channel is further longer than in other channels, it shows that the channel is congested. Squirrel lowers the weight of congested channel with an exponential reduction. If average tuple execution time in one channel is further shorter than in other channels, it shows that the channel is underloaded. Squirrel grows the weight of underloaded channel linearly. Algorithm 2 presents the procedure of dynamic weight control.

5   Experimental Evaluation

In this section, we evaluate Squirrel's performance under various workloads. First, we describe the experimental setup and workloads, then present the experimental results.

5.1   Experimental Setup

Our evaluations are conducted on a cluster of 5 commodity machines. Each machine is comprised of two dual-core Intel Xeon E5-2670 2.6 GHz CPUs, 16 GB

Algorithm 2. Dynamic Weight Control

Input: $initialWeight[channel]$: initial weight of each channel, $executionTime$
$[Channel]$: average tuple execution time in each channel, n: total channels
Output: dynamicWeight[channel]
1: $dynamicWeight[channel] \Leftarrow initialWeight[channel]$
2: $timeList \Leftarrow sort(executionTime[channel])$
3: $medianTime \Leftarrow median(timeList)$
4: **for** $channel\ i = 1 \rightarrow n$ **do**
5:     **if** $executionTime[i] > \alpha * medianTime\ (\alpha > 1)$ **then**
6:         $dynamicWeight[i] \Leftarrow dynamicWeight[i]/2$
7:     **else if** $executionTime[i] < \alpha * medianTime$ **then**
8:         $dynamicWeight[i] \Leftarrow dynamicWeight[i] + \delta$
9:     **end if**
10: **end for**
11: **return** $dynamicWeight[channel]$

---

memory, and 210 GB disks. All computers are interconnected with 1 Gbps Ethernet cards. We use Flink-1.4.0 as the distributed computing platform and Redhat
Enterprise Linux 6.2 with the kernel version 2.6.32 as the OS. One machine in the
cluster serves as the master node to host the JobManager. The other machines
run Flink TaskManagers.

5.2 Workloads

We use word count topology (stream version) and advertising topology to evaluate Squirrel's performance. Wordcount is a classic application for benchmarking distributed engines. It splits a sentence into words and counts the number
of each word in the input stream. Advertising topology is a typical streaming
benchmark which simulates an advertisement analytics pipeline [6]. This pipeline
consists of six operations including receive, parse, filter, join, window count, and
store back. We set buffer timeout to control latency and throughput. *setBuffer-
Timeout(0)* triggers buffer flushing after every record thus minimizing latency.
setBufferTimeout(-1) triggers buffer flushing only when the output buffer is full
thus maximizing throughput.

5.3 Latency

In performance test (including latency and throughput), for wordcount, we use
a large-scale trace collected from real-world systems as the dataset. This trace
is a set of records which represent the usage of each machine and contains 1
billion records associated with 300 thousand unique keys. For advertising, the
source dataset is generated from its own *EventGeneratorSource*. In all grouping phases, Squirrel adopts *Weight Grouping* no matter the default grouping is
shuffle grouping or key grouping. However, Flink uses a combination of shuffle
grouping and key grouping. For example, in wordcount, the map stage which

rebalances words among downstream tasks uses shuffle grouping. The reduce stage which aggregates keys by a hash operation uses key grouping.

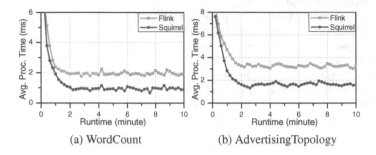

(a) WordCount   (b) AdvertisingTopology

Fig. 7. Processing latency in wordcount and advertising

Figure 7 shows the processing latency (i.e., average tuple execution time) in wordcount and advertising. We compare Squirrel with the original Flink. In Squirrel, the average tuple execution time of wordcount and advertising is 1.03 ms and 1.62 ms, respectively. However, in Flink, the average tuple execution time of wordcount and advertising is 1.91 ms and 3.26 ms, respectively. The experimental results show that Squirrel can improve average tuple execution time by up to 47%.

5.4   Throughput

Figure 8 compares the throughput of Squirrel with Flink in wordcount and advertising. In Squirrel, the average throughput of wordcount and advertising is 91624 tuples/s and 127209 tuples/s, respectively. However, in Flink, the average throughput of wordcount and advertising is 57162 tuples/s and 76173 tuples/s, respectively. The experimental results show that Squirrel achieves 1.67x improvement of the average system throughput compared to Flink.

We presents the performance improvements for batch processing in Fig. 9. Although Flink is a streaming computation engine, it embraces batch processing model through treating a bounded dataset as a special case of an unbounded one. Optimizations on Flink engine can also improve the performance of batch processing. We compare the performance of Squirrel with Flink when running wordcount as a batch job on them. We vary the size of input files from 160 MB to 2560 MB. The experimental results show that Squirrel improves the job completion time by 29%–41%.

5.5   Dynamic Weight Control

In order to evaluate the performance of *Dynamic Weight Control*, we conduct extended experiments with generated synthetic dataset with 100 million tuples

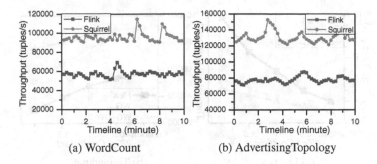

(a) WordCount   (b) AdvertisingTopology

Fig. 8. Throughput test in wordcount and advertising

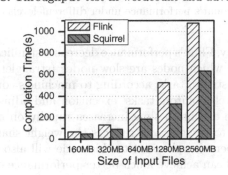

Fig. 9. Improvements for batch processing running WordCount

and 1 million keys at different levels of skewness using the Uniform distribution and Zipfian distributions. We vary the zipf coefficients of the dataset from 0.5 to 2.0. With higher zipf coefficient, the data distribution is more skewed. We also test Squirrel's performance under cluster heterogeneity. We turnoff some CPU cores and lower the frequency of the remaining cores to produce heterogeneous machines which have different computational capabilities. The ratio of physical resources (represented by cores*frequency) between the fastest machine and the slowest machine varies from 1 to 8.

Data Skewness. Figure 10 plots the system performance when running word-count under data skewness. The results show that Flink's performance decreases when the coefficient increases. The default key grouping can not balance those tuples with high levels of skewness very well. WG (*Weight Grouping*) amortizes the impacts of skewed keys by limiting the number of tuples in each channel according to its weight share. DWC (*Dynamic Weight Control*) can be aware of the overloaded downstream tasks and adjusts their weight shares. So, the performance of Squirrel (WG+DWC) does not decrease significantly.

Cluster Heterogeneity. Figure 11 evaluates the performance of Flink and Squirrel in the case of heterogeneous machines. With the exacerbation of

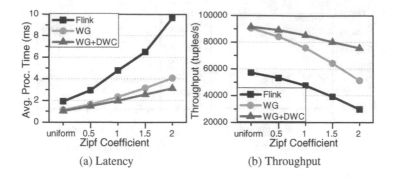

Fig. 10. Wordcount's performance under different levels of skewness

machines' heterogeneity, Flink's performance decreases significantly. It is because Flink can not identify which nodes are slow nodes (stragglers). It can not distribute tuples to downstream tasks according to machine's computational capability. However, Squirrel monitors tasks' execution and adjusts weight dynamically. If average tuple execution time increases rapidly on one node, Squirrel identifies this node as a straggler and reduces the weight share of tasks on this node. Thus, the number of tuples sent to this node will also be reduced in the next time. So, Squirrel can achieve much better performance even under heterogeneous environments.

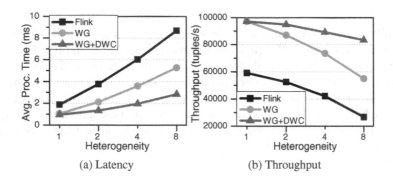

Fig. 11. Wordcount's performance under different levels of heterogeneity

6   Related Work

Distributed Stream Processing Systems. Many systems have been developed to process real-time streaming data. Storm [18] models an application as a topology that defines operators (i.e. Spouts and Bolts) and the stream (i.e. the way which tuples flow between operators). Naiad [9] is a distributed streaming system which can execute cyclic dataflow programs. Twitter's Heron [8] addresses several issues in Storm but with the same API with Storm.

Operator Scheduling. T-Storm [19] proposes a traffic-aware online scheduler and minimizes inter-process and inter-node traffic by re-assigning tasks dynamically according to traffic-aware scheduling. R-Storm [14] presents a resource-aware scheduling algorithm within Storm. This algorithm traversals the topology graph according to improved breath-first strategy and conduct task assignment.

7   Conclusion

This paper proposes a network-aware grouping framework called Squirrel to assign tuples to different network channels. Different from traditional grouping strategies, Squirrel takes the locations of downstream tasks into account when grouping tuples. By identifying the network distance of two communicating operators, Squirrel decides the number of tuples sent to each network channel by *weight grouping*. In response to data skewness and cluster heterogeneity, Squirrel adopts a mechanism similar with TCP congestion control (i.e., AIMD) to adjust each channel's weight dynamically. Squirrel has been implemented on the top of Flink. Our evaluation with various benchmarks demonstrates that Squirrel can improve throughput by 1.67x and reduce latency by 47%.

Acknowledgment. This work was supported by National Key Research and Development Program under grant 2018YFB1003600 and Pre-research Project of Beifang under grant FFZ-1601.

References

1. Apache flink. http://flink.apache.org/
2. Aniello, L., Baldoni, R., Querzoni, L.: Adaptive online scheduling in storm. In: Proceedings of DEBS 2013, pp. 207–218 (2013)
3. Caneill, M., El Rheddane, A., Leroy, V., De Palma, N.: Locality-aware routing in stateful streaming applications. In: Proceedings of Middleware 2016, pp. 1–13 (2016)
4. Carbone, P., Ewen, S., Haridi, S.: Apache flink: stream and batch processing in a single engine. Bull. IEEE Comput. Soc. Tech. Comm. Data Eng. **36**(4), 28–38 (2015)
5. Chen, H., Zhang, F., Jin, H.: Popularity-aware differentiated distributed stream processing on skewed streams. In: Proceedings of ICNP 2017, pp. 1–10 (2017)
6. Chintapalli, S., et al.: Benchmarking streaming computation engines: storm, flink and spark streaming. In: Proceedings of IPDPSW 2016, pp. 1789–1792 (2016)
7. Fang, J., Zhang, R., Fu, T., Zhang, Z., Zhou, A., Zhu, J.: Parallel stream processing against workload skewness and variance. In: Proceedings of HPDC 2017, pp. 15–26 (2017)
8. Kulkarni, S., et al.: Twitter heron: stream processing at scale. In: Proceedings of SIGMOD 2015, pp. 239–250 (2015)
9. Murray, D., McSherry, F., Isaacs, R., Isard, M., Barham, P., Abadi, M.: Naiad: a timely dataflow system. In: Proceedings of SOSP 2013, pp. 439–455 (2013)
10. Nasir, M.A.U., et al.: Load balancing for skewed streams on heterogeneous clusters. CoRR abs/1705.09073 (2017). http://arxiv.org/abs/1705.09073

11. Nasir, M.A.U., Morales, G.D.F., Garcia-Soriano, D., Kourtellis, N., Serafini, M.: The power of both choices: practical load balancing for distributed stream processing engines. In: Proceedings of ICDE 2015, pp. 137–148 (2015)
12. Nasir, M.A.U., Morales, G.D.F., Garcia-Soriano, D., Kourtellis, N., Serafini,M.: Partial key grouping: load-balanced partitioning of distributed streams. CoRR abs/1510.07623 (2015). http://arxiv.org/abs/1510.07623
13. Nasir, M.A.U., Morales, G.D.F., Kourtellis, N., Serafini, M.: When two choices are not enough: balancing at scale in distributed stream processing. In: Proceedings of ICDE 2016, pp. 589–600 (2016)
14. Peng, B., Hosseini, M., Hong, Z., Farivar, R., Campbell, R.: R-storm: resource-aware scheduling in storm. In: Proceedings of Middleware 2015, pp. 149–161 (2015)
15. Rivetti, N., Anceaume, E., Busnel, Y., Querzoni, L., Sericola, B.: Online scheduling for shuffle grouping in distributed stream processing systems. In: Proceedings of Middleware 2016, pp. 11–22 (2016)
16. Rivetti, N., Querzoni, L., Anceaume, E., Busnel, Y., Sericola, B.: Efficient key grouping for near-optimal load balancing in stream processing systems. In: Proceedings of DEBS 2015, pp. 80–91 (2015)
17. Schneider, S., Wolf, J., Hildrum, K., Khandekar, R.: Dynamic load balancing for ordered data-parallel regions in distributed streaming systems. In: Proceedings of Middleware 2016, pp. 21–34 (2016)
18. Toshniwal, A., et al.: Storm @twitter. In: Proceedings of SIGMOD 2014, pp. 147–156 (2014)
19. Xu, J., Chen, Z., Tang, J., Su, S.: T-storm: traffic-aware online scheduling in storm. In: Proceedings of ICDCS 2014, pp. 535–544 (2014)

vPlacer: A Co-scheduler for Optimizing the Performance of Parallel Jobs in Xen

Peng Jiang[1], Ligang He[1(✉)], Shenyuan Ren[1], Zhiyan Chen[1], and Rui Mao[2]

[1] Department of Computer Science, University of Warwick, Coventry CV4 7ES, UK
Ligang.He@warwick.ac.uk
[2] College of Computer Science and Software Engineering, Shenzhen University,
Shenzhen, China
mao@szu.edu.cn

Abstract. Xen, a popular virtualization platform which enables multiple operating systems sharing one physical host, has been widely used in various fields nowadays. Currently, the existing schedulers of Xen are initially targeting at serial jobs, which achieves a remarkable utilization of computer hardware and impressive overall performance. However, the virtualized systems are expected to accommodate both parallel jobs and serial jobs in practice, and resource contention between virtual machines results in severe performance degradation of the parallel jobs. Moreover, the physical resource is vastly wasted during the communication process due to the ineffective scheduling of parallel jobs.

This paper aims to optimize the performance of the parallel jobs in Xen using the co-scheduling mechanism. In this paper, we statistically analyze the process of scheduling parallel jobs in Xen, which points out that the credit scheduler is not capable of properly scheduling a parallel job. Moreover, we propose vPlacer, a conservative co-scheduler to improve the performance of the parallel job in Xen. Our co-scheduler is able to identify the parallel jobs and optimize the scheduling process to satisfy the particularity of the parallel job. The prototype of our vPlacer is implemented, and the experimental results show that the performance of the parallel job is significantly improved and the utilization of the hardware resource is optimized.

Keywords: Xen · Virtualization · Parallel job · Scheduler

1 Introduction

Virtualization, which enables multiple operating systems to be hosted on one single machine by establishing a resource sharing environment, has become a primary power to accelerate the growth of various computing services. In a virtualized system, each operating system is running inside a virtual machine (VM) which abstracts the hardware components to provide virtualized interfaces. Each VM has several virtual CPUs (vCPU), and these vCPUs are assigned to execute

© Springer Nature Switzerland AG 2018
J. Vaidya and J. Li (Eds.): ICA3PP 2018, LNCS 11334, pp. 19–33, 2018.
https://doi.org/10.1007/978-3-030-05051-1_2

on physical CPUs (pCPU). In practice, virtualization provides flexible management of physical resource by effectively allocating vCPUs to vCPUs, which satisfies the requirement of execution of the hosted operating system. Moreover, the potential of the multicore system is vastly exploited by virtualization. Comparing with the traditional use of the multicore system, virtualization efficiently utilizes the physical resource of the multicore system by hosting multiple operating systems simultaneously. Furthermore, virtualization introduces an additional layer between the physical layer and the system layer, which improves the security of the entire system by strictly control the access to the hardware. Finally, the virtualized environment delivers an isolated environment of execution, which minimizes the various interference to a dedicated OS. Due to the significant advantages, virtualization has been widely adopted as a solution of resource management by industry. For example, Amazon EC2 [2] uses the virtualization technology to provide economical and reliable cloud computing service across the world.

Despite virtualization technology has significant advantages, recent studies [8,10,12,14,16] have pointed out that the parallel job is not well supported. Existing schedulers are initially designed for the assignment of serial jobs. The serial jobs are generally considered to be isolated, while a parallel job requires internal communications among these parallel job nodes to exchange intermediate results. However, the parallel job is likely to co-exist with serial jobs on the same host in the real world. Lacking awareness of parallel job in current schedulers results in the parallel job VMs (PVMs) being treated as regular serial job VMs (SVMs), which causes dramatic performance degradation of performance of the parallel job. Furthermore, the utilization of the physical resource, which is the core advantage of virtualization, will be negatively affected due to unnecessary waiting time between PVMs.

In this paper, we present vPlacer, a conservative co-scheduler to improve the performance of the parallel job in a virtualized environment. In our solution, VMs with parallel workload are explicitly labeled by the user, and the co-scheduler identifies the presence of parallel workload by examining VMs during execution. Once a parallel job has been discovered, the co-scheduler adjusts the run queues maintained by pCPUs and places related PVMs at the synchronous positions to increase the possibility of the parallel job being synchronously scheduled. The prototype of vPlacer is implemented in Xen 4.4.2. The main contributions of this paper are as follow:

- We model the scheduling behavior of Credit scheduler [1] of Xen to simulate the process of scheduling the parallel job, which proves the downsides of the credit scheduler of Xen.
- A co-scheduling solution is proposed to alleviate the performance degradation of the parallel job. Our approach enables Xen Virtualization system to identify the parallel workload, and a proper allocation of resource can also be coordinated. With help from our co-scheduler, the overall utilization is also improved as a side effect.

– We have implemented a prototype of co-scheduler in Xen. Our co-scheduler works with Credit scheduler of Xen without brother and provide effective support to deal with the parallel workload. Extensive experiments have been made to evaluate the performance of our co-scheduler.

The rest of the paper is organized as follows: Sect. 2 introduces the technical background of Xen. Section 3 states the problem and statistically analyses the scheduling process of the credit scheduler. The design of co-scheduler is described in Sect. 4. In Sect. 5, we explain the implementation details of vPlacer in Xen. Section 6 presents the experimental results and evaluation. We discuss related works in Sect. 7. Finally, a conclusion is given in Sect. 8.

2 Background

Xen is an open source software developed by Cambridge University in 2003, and it has become one of the most popular virtualization platforms in this field. It supports paravirtualization, which requires a modified OS kernel to be installed in VMs to provide multiple VMs executing concurrently and each VM is allowed to have maximum 32 vCPUs. An additional layer called Virtual Machine Monitor (VMM or Hypervisor) is introduced directly on top of the hardware layer to separate hardware management and software management. VMs are running above the hypervisor known as domains. A privileged domain (dom0) is created at boot time and is given access to the hypervisor's controlling interface, which makes dom0 a key role in managing all other domains (called guestdomains or domUs), for example, creating VM, deleting VM, and terminating VM. Xen uses a credit scheduler to allocate the computing resource to vCPUs, which achieves outstanding performance overall.

2.1 The Communications in Xen

In Xen, the communications between domains fall into two categories according to where the communicating parties are hosted. Inter-node communication refers to the communication that is established between domains hosted by different physical machines. This type of communication requires the native network device to be part of the communicating process, where the hosts are supposed to run within the same network. Intra-node communication indicates the communicating parties are placed on the same host, in other words, the communicating domains co-exist on one physical machine, which is commonly seen in modern clusters.

2.2 The Credit Scheduler

The credit scheduler is a proportionally fair sharing scheduling algorithm, is the default scheduler of Xen. Each domain has two values weight and cap, which defines the share of execution time the domain will be given. Weight indicates the relative proportion of CPU time, and cap defines the upper limit of execution time. Each domain is given credits decided by its weight value, and a domain's credits are evenly assigned to its vCPUs. Credits will be consumed as long as the vCPU gets executed on a pCPU and subtracted according to the execution time of the vCPU. Each scheduled vCPU has a *timeslice* of maximum 30 ms to run, and a global value called *ratelimit* indicates the minimum time to occupy the pCPU. A vCPU is set to *UNDER* if there are remaining credits, and *OVER* priority is given to vCPU with negative credits. The credit scheduler re-calculate and replenish credits every 30 ms.

Credit scheduler allows each pCPU to have a run queue of vCPUs, and pCPU maintains its run queue based on the priority of vCPU. The vCPUs with *UNDER* priority are in front of the run queue and get scheduled only in a round robin fashion. Notably, the credits do not affect the scheduling order of vCPUs with the same priority, Those vCPUs with *OVER* priority are behind vCPUs with *UNDER* priority and wait for replenishment of credits. The vCPU's priority can be changed between *UNDER* and *OVER* during the replenishment, and the run queue is re-sorted accordingly. *IDLE* priority is lower than *OVER*, hence the vCPU with *IDLE* is placed at the end of the run queue. vCPUs with *IDLE* priority are usually used to create the run queue at boot time and keep queues existing.

The earlier version of credit scheduler essentially targets at computation-intensive workloads which merely employ the CPU resource. However, I/O intensive applications have become prevalent in recent year, and Xen introduces *BOOST* priority to catch up the new trend. *BOOST* priority is the highest priority among these four priorities, therefore, the vCPUs with *BOOST* priority are placed in the head of the run queue. The vCPU which is expected to respond I/O request are set to *BOOST*, and the *BOOST* vCPU is permitted to preempt other current executing vCPUs. A vCPU is woke up when a request is incoming, and the vCPU is boosted to *BOOST* priority and get scheduled immediately. If there is a vCPU running on the pCPU, it will be preempted by the boosted vCPU. By introducing BOOST mechanism, the I/O request can be processed without too much delay.

3   Problem Analysis

In the virtualized environment, a pCPU is proportionally shared among several vCPUs, and each vCPU in the local job queue is scheduled for a certain length of time periodically. Therefore, the nodes of a parallel job are not guaranteed to be scheduled simultaneously, where the execution of the parallel application is severely compromised. In this section, We first list assumptions based on practical experience and common sense. Then we statistically analyze the problem of scheduling a parallel job in Xen.

3.1   Assumptions

- Firstly, the number of nodes of a parallel job should be smaller to that of the physical nodes of a virtualized system. Essentially, the virtualized system should have enough CPU resource to host a parallel job in the real world, especially for the server providers.
- Secondly, non-parallel domains are assumed to be in busy running status. In a virtualized system, vCPUs proportionally share a pCPU, and each vCPU is given a certain time to occupy the pCPU.
- Thirdly, the nodes of a parallel job are considered to be only committed to the assignment of a parallel job. If serial jobs co-exist inside a parallel node, its identity of a parallel workload cannot be confirmed.
- Finally, we assume that each VM has only one vCPU, namely, a Uni-Processor machine. In the traditional cluster, each node of the parallel job is normally allocated a dedicated core for executing the sub-task of a parallel job to prevent from being interfered.

3.2   Discussion

In a virtualized environment, each VM shares the use of pCPU with other VMs of the same run queue, which results in performance degradation of execution of a serial job comparing with the performance of a job on a dedicated core. Suppose a pCPU's run queue consists of n VMs, then each VM of the queue will be allocated $1/n$ of the pCPU resources. Consequently, the performance of running a serial job on VM is $1/n$ of running a serial job on a standalone machine, i.e., the execution time will be n times longer than that of a standalone machine as each job in the queue is only given $1/n$ use of the pCPU. A parallel job is divided into sub-tasks, and each of these sub-tasks will be executed on different nodes (or pCPUs). Therefore, the best performance of running a parallel job in a virtualized system should be $1/n$ of the parallel job's native performance on dedicated cores, which can be achieved by synchronously scheduling the nodes of a parallel job.

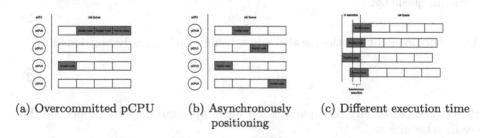

(a) Overcommitted pCPU   (b) Asynchronously positioning   (c) Different execution time

Fig. 1. Three problems in scheduling the parallel job

The synchronous execution of the parallel nodes, which decides the performance of a parallel job in Xen, is affected by three problems. First of all, the pCPUs are overcommitted to serve vCPUs. As we indicated before, the credit scheduler has no knowledge about the parallel job, therefore, multiple parallel nodes may be allocated to the same pCPU as illustrated in Fig. 1(a). Secondly, the nodes of a parallel job may not be scheduled simultaneously. The parallel nodes are expected to be online at the same time to process the internal communications among the parallel nodes, however, the parallel nodes are placed in the asynchronous positions of there run queues, which causes that the parallel nodes are scheduled asynchronously. Figure 1(b) shows the parallel nodes are asynchronously positioned. Finally, each node of the parallel job has different execution time. By default, the vCPU in Xen is allowed to run on pCPU for a time slice every time it gets scheduled. However, this varies depending on runtime situation. Figure 1(c) shows the problem of the different execution time of parallel nodes. Unfortunately, the credit scheduler of Xen is not aware of the existence of the parallel job.

3.3   Efficiency Analysis of Scheduling Parallel Job in Xen

As we discussed above, to achieve a high performance of a parallel job in Xen, we need to overcome three problems. Since the execution time varies all the time during execution, we only assess the scheduling efficiency of credit scheduler in the parallel job from two perpectives and give an overall evaluation of scheduling a parallel job in Xen. Let p be the number of cores in a Xen host, s be the number of nodes of a parallel job and j be the total number of VMs running on the host. We know that the credit scheduler, and all VMs are treated as serial jobs in Xen. Therefore, we know the possibility of the parallel nodes being distributed to different pCPUs is:

$$P_A = \frac{\prod_{j=0}^{j<s} p - i}{p^s} \tag{1}$$

To avoid asynchronous positioning of parallel nodes, we need to place the parallel nodes in the synchronous positions of their run queues so that the synchronous execution of a parallel job can be improved. We can obtain the size of each run queue by:

$$q = j/p \tag{2}$$

Thus, the possibility of the parallel nodes being synchronously positioned is:

$$P_B = \frac{1}{q^{s-1}} \tag{3}$$

Hence, the probability of a parallel job being appropriately positioned by the credit scheduler is:

$$P'_C = \frac{\prod_{j=0}^{j<s} p - i}{p^s} \cdot \frac{1}{q_{min}^{s-1}} \tag{4}$$

Due to $dom0$ processes the I/O request in Xen, it is compulsory to schedule $dom0$ along with the parallel nodes. Therefore, the formula becomes:

$$E_{overall} = \frac{\prod_{j=0}^{j<s+1} p - i}{p^s + 1} \cdot \frac{1}{q_{min}^s} \qquad (5)$$

The formula describe the chance of a parallel job being properly scheduled by credit scheduler, and the chance is extremely low in practice. Therefore, a co-scheduler is required to assist the credit scheduler to make the appropriate decision on scheduling the parallel job.

4 Design of the vPlacer

By analyzing the native scheduling behavior of credit scheduler, the shortcomings of executing a parallel job in Xen have been identified. In this section, we introduce our co-scheduler to mitigtate the negative influence and improve the performance of the parallel job in a virtualized environment.

4.1 The Design Principles

Our co-scheduler can assist the credit scheduler to provide additional support to properly schedule the parallel job in Xen. The design of our co-scheduler follows the principles given below:

- The co-scheduler should be a light-weighted module. Our co-scheduler should not bring too much overhead in both identifying a parallel job and assisting the primary scheduler.
- The co-scheduler has minimum impact on the credit scheduler and the scheduling policy of credit scheduler should be respected by the co-scheduler.
- The probability of synchronous scheduling of the parallel nodes can be improved by the co-scheduling.

4.2 Design of Co-scheduler

The co-scheduler is an independent scheduling module running along with the credit scheduler, and it will perform an additional check after the credit scheduler has made a general scheduling decision. Notably, the scheduling process of credit scheduler will not be affected by the co-scheduler, which minimizes the impact on credit scheduler.

The co-scheduling process consists of three steps to support the parallel job. Firstly, it identifies the parallel job in Xen. In practice, the user must have the knowledge of nodes of a parallel job because the parallel job is set up by the user. For example, an MPI job requires the user to deploy the job on several nodes, and the user must know which nodes are used to execute the job. The co-scheduler will identify parallel workload via checking the given label of each VM. If a parallel job exists, then it will start the co-scheduling process to coordinate the resource allocation. The co-scheduler firstly re-assign the parallel nodes to different pCPUs. As stated in the previous section, the PVMs of a parallel job

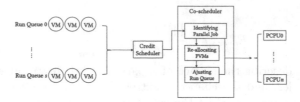

Fig. 2. Workflow of Co-scheduler

need to be executed on different pCPUs to guarantee that the parallel job has the chance to he scheduled online at the same time. The co-scheduler will check if a pCPU's run queue has morc than one parallel node waiting to be scheduled. If there is, then the latter parallel node in the run queue will be migrated to other pCPU to avoid overcommitted use of pCPU. Thirdly, the position of each PVM of a parallel job in the run queue will be examined and adjusted. Because the nodes of a parallel job should be in the synchronous positions in the run queues, we can choose one parallel node as the flag to indicate if the parallel job is awaiting. When the flag vCPU is about to be scheduled, the co-scheduler adjusts the positions of other nodes of a parallel job correspondingly. Because the boosted VM may preempt the pCPU resource from the currently running VM, the parallel node's position can be affected when it is waiting in the queue. Preemption of pCPU is not allowed once the repositioning process starts until the parallel nodes have been scheduled off. Moreover, the scheduled PVMs will be forced to execute for a fixed time to avoid preemption by setting minimum execution time. The workflow of the vPlacer is illustrated in Fig. 2.

5   Implementation

Our co-scheduler is an independent light-weighted module, which only requires a few modifications to the credit scheduler of Xen. In this section, we introduce how we implement the co-scheduler in detail.

5.1   Modifications to Xen

Firstly, the struct *parallel_job* is defined for storing the information of a parallel job, and we use five attributes to describe a parallel job in Xen as can be seen from Algorithm 1 (1) The *job_id* is the job number of a parallel job. (2) Attribute *number_of_nodes* indicates how many nodes are involved in a parallel job. (3) The *doms* is an array of domain IDs which can be used to retrieve the nodes of a parallel job, and each parallel job can have up to 50 domains In practice, each parallel job is allowed to have maximum $p-1$ domains. (4) The attribute *active* points out if the parallel is currently active. (5) Attribute *reallocated* indicates if the parallel job has been reallocated by the co-scheduler. Secondly, we add new attributes to the existing domain struct of credit scheduler *csched_dom* to

---

Algorithm 1. Co-scheduling Algorithm

Input: sVCPU eVCPU
Output: co-scheduling decision

```
1  if eVCPU is a parallel VCPU then
2  |    if eVCPU is flag VCPU then
3  |    |    eVCPU.dom.pjob.active = FALSE;
4  |    |    resetting();
5  |    end
6  end
7  if sVCPU is a parallel VCPU then
8  |    if parallel job not reallocated then
9  |    |    cosched_reallocate(sVCPU);
10 |    |    sVCPU.dom.pjob.reallocated = TRUE;
11 |    end
12 |    if sVCPU is flag VCPU then
13 |    |    sVCPU.dom.pjob.active = TRUE;
14 |    |    cosched_adjust(sVCPU);
15 |    |    return sVCPU;
16 |    else
17 |    |    if sVCPU.dom.pjob.active then
18 |    |    |    return sVCPU;
19 |    |    else
20 |    |    |    bypass_parallel_vCPU(csVCPU, sVCPU);
21 |    |    |    return csVCPU;
22 |    |    end
23 |    end
24 else
25 |    return sVCPU;
26 end
```

---

save the information of a parallel job. The *flag* variable indicates if the VM is the flag node of a parallel job. The *pjob* variable stores the details of the parallel job. Finally, we also modified *csched_private* which stores global parameters of credit scheduler. Specifically, we add some new attributes to control the co-scheduler globally. The $is_coscheduling\_activated$ attribute indicates the state of co-scheduler. The *jobs_count* is the number of the parallel jobs running on the host, and *jobs* holds an array of existing parallel jobs.

5.2 The Co-scheduling Algorithm

The Algorithm 1 shows the pseudo-code of the *co_sched()* function. Due to Xen has provided functions to retrieve the domain of a vCPU, we only use vCPU to illustrate the co-scheduling process. The function takes two VCPUs as the arguments: sVCPU and eVCPU. The sVCPU is the job selected by credit scheduler and about to be put on pCPU to execute. The eVCPU is the previous job which has been moved to the tail of the job queue. The algorithm begins with setting previous parallel job to be inactive (line 1–6), all changes for execution of the parallel job are reset to default. Then, the currently selected job will be examined by the co-scheduler. The sVCPU is returned straightway if it is not a parallel job, otherwise the co-scheduling process starts. The co-scheduler first re-allocates the nodes of the parallel job by calling the *cosched_reallocate*() function (line 8–11), and the re-allocation status will be changed accordingly, all parallel nodes will be pinned to new allocated pCPUs. After reallocation, the co-scheduler will adjust the job queue if the selected vCPU is the flag of the parallel job (line 12–15). Meanwhile, the running status of the parallel job is changed to active. In *coshed_adjust*(), boosting is disabled to prevent the nodes of the parallel job from being preempted. Additionally, the *ratelimit* of credit scheduler is also set to be equal to the length of *timeslice* of credit scheduler to stop the parallel nodes from yielding the pCPUs. The vCPUs of an active parallel job will be moved to the head of the job queue. The nodes of inactive parallel job will be bypassed and next available vCPU of the same run queue will be chosen (line 19–22), which is done by calling *bypass_parallel_vCPU*().

6   Performance Evaluation

6.1   Experimental Setup

We conduct the experiments on a host which has a quad-core CPU (Intel Core I7-3820 CPU @ 3.60 GNz) and 16 GB RAM. The Xen 4.4.2 is adopted as the virtualization platform, and the guest operating system is Ubuntu 14.04. We create total of 32 uniProcessor virtual machines for the experiment.

6.2   Evaluations on Repositioning the Parallel Job

As the main function of our co-scheduler is to adjust the positions of parallel nodes, we first observe if the nodes of a parallel job are correctly placed in the positions for synchronous scheduling, we use Synchronous Position Rate (SPR) to measure the influence of vPlacer, which means the percentage of the parallel nodes being correctly placed. The previous sections have depicted the expected positions of the parallel nodes, we know that all parallel nodes should be put in the head of the queues. Therefore, the SPR can be obtained by tracing one node and checking if other parallel nodes are in the expected positions. We generate serial workload on all VMs using bash and randomly select several a number of VMs as the targeting VM (assuming they are executing parallel nodes), and the SPRs of both credit scheduler and vPlacer can be obtained. Notably, we arrange some periodic communications between non-targeting VMs. We run the test for five times, and the average value will be used to for evaluation. Figure 3 shows the comparison of SPR between the credit scheduler and vPlacer.

   The result shows that vPlacer effectively places all specified parallel job nodes, which increases the possibility of the parallel node being scheduled together. This is due to the large parallel job urgently needs vPlacer's coordination of computational resource. The parallel job nodes are not guaranteed

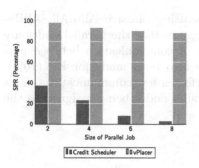

Fig. 3. The synchronous positioning rate

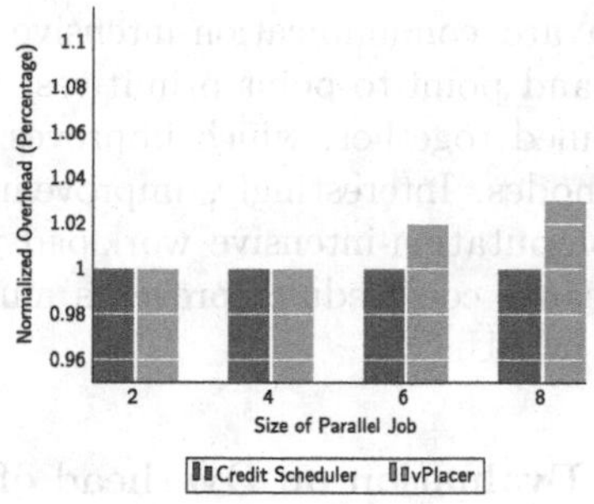

Fig. 4. The overhead of co-scheduling process

to be placed in synchronous positions and the SPR of vPlacer decreases as the parallel job size becomes bigger, which may be caused by some parallel nodes are inserted to the over queue due to out of credits.

6.3 Evaluations on Performance of Parallel Job

In this experiment, the NAS Parallel Benchmark Suite is used to evaluate the performance of vPlacer. NPB [3], developed by NASA Advanced Supercomputing Division, is a application which concentrates on benchmarking the performance of the parallel system. This benchmark suite contains 8 different types of workloads for evaluating the parallel system from different angles. Additionally, NPB provides six different problem sizes to choose for different parallel systems. We set the problem size to C and run all benchmark programs introduced in the Figure using 4 nodes for five times. The average results are normalized to native performance are shown in Fig. 5.

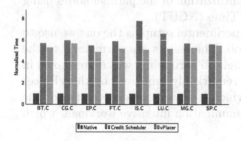

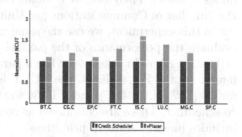

Fig. 5. NPB performance of a four nodes parallel job

Fig. 6. The number of communications per uni time

The evaluation shows that vPlacer is able to improve the performance of the parallel job in all benchmarks as expected. As can be seen from the figure, vPlacer dramatically reduces the execution time for IS (30%) LU(21%) FT (12%)

which are communication-intensive programs using massive AlltoAll, AllReduce and point-to-point primitives. This is because that the parallel nodes are
scheduled together, which improves efficiency of communication between parallel nodes. Interestingly, improvements have also been made for EP (10%),
an computation-intensive workload which performs few communications. This
is because co-scheduler prevents multiple parallel nodes being assigned to the
same pCPU.

6.4   Evaluation on Overhead of vPlacer

In this experiment, we evaluate the overhead incurred by the co-scheduling process. We adopt the same experimental setup as the one we used in evaluating the
re-positioning performance. We calculate the average time spent on producing a
scheduling decision for both credit scheduler and vPlacer and compare between
them. The results are normalized to the average decision time of credit scheduler
for better illustration. The results are shown in Fig. 4.

The overhead of the vPlacer is consider to be negligible overall. For a small
parallel job (below 4 nodes), the overhead of vPlacer remains the same level as
that of credit scheduler. The scheduling time increases as the size of the parallel
job grows, and this is because the co-scheduler needs to loop a longer array of
the parallel nodes and more re-positioning operations need to done during the
co-scheduling process of vPlacer.

6.5   Evaluation on Utilization

When parallel node is in a pending state and waiting for the intermediate result,
it still consumes the cpu cycle due to the busy-pulling mechanism, which is
considered as utilization of resource by Xen. To observe the real utilization of
the parallel nodes, monitor the frequency of communications between the parallel
nodes in *dom*0. Therefore, we evaluate the utilization of the parallel nodes using
the Number of Communications per Unit Time (NCUT).

In this experiment, we use the same experimental setup as the one we use to
evaluate the performance of the parallel job. The results are normalized to the
utilization of credit scheduler when a parallel job is running, which are shown in
figure. As the Fig. 6 shows, the NCUT is remarkably improved by the vPlacer
for IS (59%) LU (41%) and FT (30%), which is under our expectation of the
co-scheduler. These are considered as communication intensive workload, which
includes massive AlltoAll primitives.

7   Related Work

Effectively scheduling a parallel job on a multicore system has been well studied
in the past. Among various scheduling methods, Backfill and Gang are the two
main strategies. In Backfill strategy, each job is given a reserved starting time
and an estimated execution time. The small jobs are moved forward and utilized

the node during the time gap between now and reserved starting time of the head of the job queue. The primary goal of backfill is to achieve the best utilization of the resource without causing any delay in scheduling other jobs. The Gang scheduling approach [6] aims to improve the performance of the parallel job by scheduling relevant process or thread on different processors at the same time. The strategy requires pre-knowledge of the parallel job, when a process or thread of a parallel job is scheduled, then all related parts will be scheduled accordingly so that the internal communications of a parallel job can be completed without waiting for transmitting data from each other. Unlike the backfill approach, the gang method tries to accomplish the best performance of a parallel job.

As virtualization is widely adopted to serve HPC job, the influence of virtualized environment on the performance of HPC job is concerned by both industry and academia. Many performance studies [8,10,12,16] focus on benchmarking the HCP applications and try to evaluate the impact of virtualized environment on HPC workloads. Youseff et al. evaluate the influence of Xen on HPC workload in a different way from others in their study, they perform experiments on three non-Xen kernels (RHEL4 Build2.6.9, RHEL4 Build 2.6.12 and LLNLCHAOS) to compare three different Linux configurations with the Xen-based kernel [15]. The result shows that Xen paravirtualization does not impose noticeable overhead to other Linux. However, the reasons behind the performance degradation of parallel job are not explicitly revealed.

Many efforts have been made to mitigate the impact of virtualization on the performance of the parallel job. Chen and et al. indicate that the performance of the concurrent job and I/O intensive jobs are suffering from overcommitted VMs in their work [4]. They propose to mitigate the performance penalty by applying various time slices to VCPUs according to their behaviour. Similarly, Shao and et al. discover the same problem in his research and analyze the potential penalty on the performance of the parallel job when the virtualized system becomes overcommitted [11]. In contrast to Chen and et al., they choose to alleviate the negative impact of the overcommitted virtualized environment by exposing the scheduling information of the guest OS to the hypervisor, their work focuses on separating the high-throughput job and concurrent job, and then use different scheduling strategy to allocate different types of jobs. Huang and et al. try to achieve native performance in a VM-based environment for HPC by implementing VM-aware HPC framework [7]. Kang and et al. present a MapReduce Group Scheduler (MRG) which improves performance of MapReduce by grouping the scheduling of VMs belonging to the same MapReduce job [9]. They use two-level scheduling mechanism to reduce the impact of I/O blocking, which achieves proportional fair sharing in both two-level (MapReduce job group and VMs). Later on, Chen and et al. present a locality-aware scheduling algorithm (LaSA) for Hadoop workload [5]. RT-Xen [13] is the first real-time hypervisor scheduling framework for Xen, which connects the gap between real-time theory and Xen.

8 Conclusion

The parallel job works in a different way from the serial job, which requires more considerations to be taken when designing a schedule. In this paper, we review the scheduling logic of credit scheduler, then we investigate problem of appropriately scheduling a parallel job. We proved that the performance of the parallel job can be improved by job re-positioning. Therefore, we present vPlacer, a co-scheduler, which assists the credit scheduler in handling the parallel application. Our co-scheduler first identifies the parallel job in the system, reallocates the related VCPU to avoid overcommitted problem and adjusts the job queues to achieve synchronous scheduling of the parallel job. Moreover, we implemented a prototype of the co-scheduler in Xen. Finally, we conduct a series of experiments to test co-scheduler. The evaluation indicates that the performance of the parallel job and the utilization are significantly improved.

Acknowledgement. This work is partially supported by the National Key R&D Program of China 2018YFB1003201 and Guangdong Pre-national Project 2014GKXM054.

References

1. Ackaouy, E.: The Xen credit Cpu scheduler. In: Proceedings of (2006)
2. Amazon EC2: Amazon web services (2015). http://aws.amazon.com/es/ec2/. Accessed Nov 2012
3. Bailey, D.: The NAS parallel benchmarks. Int. J. Supercomput. Appl. **5**(3), 63–73 (1991). https://doi.org/10.1177/109434209100500306
4. Chen, H., Jin, H., Hu, K., Huang, J.: Scheduling overcommitted VM: behavior monitoring and dynamic switching-frequency scaling. Futur. Gener. Comput. Syst. **29**(1), 341–351 (2013). https://doi.org/10.1016/j.future.2011.08.006, http://www.sciencedirect.com/science/article/pii/S0167739X11001452, including Special section: AIRCC-NetCoM 2009 and Special section: Clouds and Service-Oriented Architectures
5. Chen, T.Y., Wei, H.W., Wei, M.F., Chen, Y.J., Hsu, T., Shih, W.K.: LaSA: a locality-aware scheduling algorithm for hadoop-mapreduce resource assignment. In: 2013 International Conference on Collaboration Technologies and Systems (CTS), pp. 342–346, May 2013. https://doi.org/10.1109/CTS.2013.6567252
6. Gorda, B., Brooks, E.I.: Gang scheduling a parallel machine, p. 3 (1991)
7. Huang, W., Koop, M.J., Gao, Q., Panda, D.K.: Virtual machine aware communication libraries for high performance computing. In: Proceedings of the 2007 ACM/IEEE Conference on Supercomputing, SC 2007, pp. 9:1–9:12. ACM, New York (2007). https://doi.org/10.1145/1362622.1362635
8. Huang, W., Liu, J., Abali, B., Panda, D.K.: A case for high performance computing with virtual machines. In: Proceedings of the 20th Annual International Conference on Supercomputing, ICS 2006, pp. 125–134. ACM, New York (2006). https://doi.org/10.1145/1183401.1183421
9. Kang, H., Chen, Y., Wong, J.L., Sion, R., Wu, J.: Enhancement of Xen's scheduler for mapreduce workloads. In: Proceedings of the 20th International Symposium on High Performance Distributed Computing, HPDC 2011, pp. 251–262. ACM, New York (2011). https://doi.org/10.1145/1996130.1996164

10. Mergen, M.F., Uhlig, V., Krieger, O., Xenidis, J.: Virtualization for high-performance computing. SIGOPS Oper. Syst. Rev. **40**(2), 8–11 (2006). https://doi.org/10.1145/1131322.1131328
11. Shao, Z., Wang, Q., Xie, X., Jin, H., He, L.: Analyzing and improving MPI communication performance in overcommitted virtualized systems. In: 2011 IEEE 19th Annual International Symposium on Modelling, Analysis, and Simulation of Computer and Telecommunication Systems, pp. 381–389, July 2011. https://doi.org/10.1109/MASCOTS.2011.27
12. Vallee, G., Naughton, T., Engelmann, C., Ong, H., Scott, S.L.: System-level virtualization for high performance computing. In: 16th Euromicro Conference on Parallel, Distributed and Network-Based Processing (PDP 2008), pp. 636–643, February 2008. https://doi.org/10.1109/PDP.2008.85
13. Xi, S., Wilson, J., Lu, C., Gill, C.: RT-Xen: towards real-time hypervisor scheduling in Xen. In: Proceedings of the Ninth ACM International Conference on Embedded Software, EMSOFT 2011, pp. 39–48. ACM, New York (2011). https://doi.org/10.1145/2038642.2038651
14. Ye, K., Jiang, X., Chen, S., Huang, D., Wang, B.: Analyzing and modeling the performance in Xen-based virtual cluster environment. In: 2010 IEEE 12th International Conference on High Performance Computing and Communications (HPCC), pp. 273–280, September 2010. https://doi.org/10.1109/HPCC.2010.79
15. Youseff, L., Wolski, R., Gorda, B., Krintz, C.: Evaluating the performance impact of Xen on mpi and process execution for HPC systems. In: Proceedings of the 2nd International Workshop on Virtualization Technology in Distributed Computing, p. 1. IEEE Computer Society, Washington, D.C. (2006). https://doi.org/10.1109/VTDC.2006.4
16. Youseff, L., Wolski, R., Gorda, B., Krintz, C.: Paravirtualization for HPC systems. In: Min, G., Di Martino, B., Yang, L.T., Guo, M., Rünger, G. (eds.) ISPA 2006. LNCS, vol. 4331, pp. 474–486. Springer, Heidelberg (2006). https://doi.org/10.1007/11942634_49

Document Nearest Neighbors Query Based on Pairwise Similarity with MapReduce

Peipei Lv[1,2], Peng Yang[1,2(✉)], Yong-Qiang Dong[1,2], and Liang Gu[1,2]

[1] School of Computer Science and Engineering, Southeast University, Nanjing, China
[2] Key Laboratory of Computer Network and Information Integration,
Southeast University, Ministry of Education, Nanjing, China
{lvpp,pengyang,dongyq,guliang}@seu.edu.cn

Abstract. With the continuous development of Web technology, many Internet issues evolve into Big Data problems, characterized by volume, variety, velocity and variability. Among them, how to organize plenty of web pages and retrieval information needed is a critical one. An important notion is document classification, in which nearest neighbors query is the key issue to be solved. Most parallel nearest neighbors query methods adopt Cartesian Product between training set and testing set resulting in poor time efficiency. In this paper, two methods are proposed on document nearest neighbor query based on pairwise similarity, i.e. *brute-force* and *pre-filtering*. *brute-force* is constituted by two phases (i.e. copying and filtering) and one *map-reduce* procedure is conducted. In order to obtain nearest neighbors for each document, each document pair is copied twice and all records generated are shuffled. However, time efficiency of *shuffle* is sensitive to the number of the intermediate results. For the purpose of intermediate results reduction, *pre-filtering* is proposed for nearest neighbor query based on pairwise similarity. Since only first top-k neighbors are output for each document, the size of records shuffled is kept in the same magnitude as input size in *pre-filtering*. Additionally, detailed theoretical analysis is provided. The performance of the algorithms is demonstrated by experiments on real world dataset.

Keywords: Nearest neighbors query · Pairwise similarity
Time efficiency

1 Introduction

People are flooded by plenty of information from the Internet, and how to retrieval information needed is a challenge problem nowadays. Document classification is one of the typical technologies that has been employed by search engines for information management. And nearest neighbors query is one of the key issues to be addressed.

© Springer Nature Switzerland AG 2018
J. Vaidya and J. Li (Eds.): ICA3PP 2018, LNCS 11334, pp. 34–45, 2018.
https://doi.org/10.1007/978-3-030-05051-1_3

K-Nearest Neighbor (*KNN*) query is a representative technology on nearest neighbor search [1,12]. In order to obtain the nearest neighbors, similarity computation should be conducted between all training samples (*T*) and testing samples (*S*). Obviously, the corresponding time complexity is $O(|T|*|S|)$. More seriously, dynamic Web sites have increased exponentially over the past several years, and emerging issues related to Big Data are beyond the computing capability of centralized methods in serial mode (including nearest neighbors query).

Fortunately, these issues are alleviated by Hadoop cluster [15]. MapReduce framework of Hadoop introduces a kind of programming paradigm, in which problems to be solved are partitioned and each subtask shares nothing. *shuffle* procedure is invoked between *map* and *reduce*, which is going to group intermediate results by *key*. *shuffle* is a time consuming process that affects efficiency of MapReduce jobs obviously, and there is some research on parallel nearest neighbors query. However, the approaches related introduce complicated samples partitioning strategies or adopt Cartesian Product, which is not reasonable.

In this paper, two algorithms based on pairwise similarity, *brute-force* and *pre-filtering*, are proposed for document nearest neighbors query on MapReduce. *brute-force* is implemented in every detail based on common sense as a baseline. Since all document pairs sharing term(s) are output twice and sorted by similarity during *shuffle* procedure, *brute-force* results in high time complexity. In order to further improve the time efficiency, *pre-filtering* is proposed. Since records are ordered in sorting phase, nearest neighbors of each document are more likely to locate at the beginning of the pairwise similarity results. And only first top-*k* neighbors are output for each document due to the restriction on quantify, records shuffled are reduced greatly. What's more, detailed theoretical analysis is introduced on both *brute-force* and *pre-filtering*.

The rest of the paper is organized as follows: related works are briefly reviewed in Sect. 2; Sect. 3 presents two algorithms proposed; comprehensive experimental results are proposed in Sect. 4; Sect. 5 concludes the paper.

2   Related Work

The task of nearest neighbors query is a fundamental primitive in computer science, with applications ranging from text classifying to network monitoring [1,12]. *K-Nearest Neighbor* (*KNN*) is a typical method on nearest neighbor query. Since similarity computation is conducted between all training samples (*T*) and testing samples (*S*), high time complexity ($O(|T|*|S|)$) is one of the fatal defects of *KNN*. Strategies on time efficiency improvement are very essential and they can be realized with similarity computation reduction [2,3,5,8,24,26,30] or structurization [4,16,17,19,21,23,25,29,33,34].

Early contributions in computation reduction can be organized as follows: dimension reduction [24], sample reduction [8,26] and computation reduction with the index [2,5]. The main goal of dimension reduction is to improve time efficiency with the help of minimized number of relevant features selected by methods proposed in [24]. Familiar with the procedure of the dimension reduction, [26] and [8] suggested that better time efficiency could also be obtained with condensed (grouped) samples, and samples that did not add extra information were eliminated from training set. As samples were ordered with the index, neighbors selection was faster in methods of computation reduction [30]. [3] introduced various-widths clustering before nearest neighbors query.

In order to further improve the time efficiency, k-d tree with the significant advantage of handling many types of queries efficiently by a single data structure was proposed, which is used for associative searching [4,25]. One disadvantage on dividing of k-d tree is that boundary is not reasonable. For the purpose of overcoming the disadvantage, ball-tree reducing distance computation remarkably emerged [19,23], in which boundary is determined by hypersphere, not hyperrectangle any more. Furthermore, [16] and [34] divided the sample set according to planes. Principal axis search tree was proposed based on detailed analysis of ball tree in [21], and the sample set was partitioned along the direction of maximum variance. [17] summarized the most previous methods, including ball tree and k-d tree, then a new tree-like algorithm was provided based on PAT [14]. [13] taken both time efficiency and accuracy of neighbors query into consideration. [33] constructed k*Tree with a subset of the training samples to improve the time efficiency of nearest neighbors query.

With the development of MapReduce, the focus shifted to exploit parallel framework advantages as much as possible, such as distributed computing [7, 22,32]. To our knowledge, [32] introduced a representative parallel *KNN* Join based on sample split, afterward, space decomposition techniques was proposed for processing the classification procedure in a parallel manner in [22].

Document similarity is a widely used technology on document nearest neighbors query and it has attracted the researcher's attention extensively [11,28]. [27] analysed the factors that affected documents similarity and pointed out that combination of different factors might perform better. Similar to [6,31] provided another document similarity model based on the summary of STD (Suffix Tree Document) and VSD (Vector Space Document), better time efficiency and accuracy were achieved. [20] and [18] both discussed the document nearest neighbors query based on Cartesian Product, which resulted in poor time efficiency.

Generally, all the previous works can be divided into two categories: the centralized and the paralleled [9]. The centralized methods can be subdivided into the structure less and the structure based. The structure less is time consuming due to the whole samples handling and the structure based obtains time efficiency improvement based on global data structure resulting in poor scalability.

3   Methodology

Nearest neighbors query for each document inner document collection is constituted by stages of *Document Similarity* and *Neighbors Query* (Fig. 1). Two algorithms are proposed in *Neighbors Query*, i.e., *brute-force* and *pre-filtering*.

brute-force is constituted by phases of copying and filtering and one *mapreduce* procedure is needed. In order to obtain nearest neighbors for each document, each pairwise similarity is copied twice and all records generated are

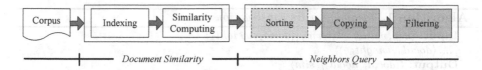

Fig. 1. Document nearest neighbors query procedure

shuffled. Compared with the methods that Cartesian Product adopted between training set and testing set, a considerable amount of intermediate results are filtered in the phase of *shuffle* in *brute-force*. For the purpose of further intermediate results reduction, *pre-filtering* is proposed, in which extra sorting procedure is conducted. Thus potential neighbors are more likely to locate at the beginning of the output generated by the previous phase, and only top-k records are emitted. Hence, the intermediate results are reduced greatly.

3.1 Preliminary

Each document is represented as $d_i = (t_{i1}, t_{i2}, ..., t_{in})$, t_{in} denotes the term in the document and "bag of words" model is employed. w_{t,d_i} denotes the weight of the term t in d_i (i.e. frequency of t in d_i). Equation 1 denotes the similarity.

$$sim(d_i, d_j) = \sum_{t \in d_i \land t \in d_j} w_{t,d_i} \cdot w_{t,d_j} \tag{1}$$

Pairwise document similarity [10] (Fig. 2) itself is consisted of two main phases too, indexing and pairwise similarity calculating. And two *map-reduce* procedures are needed. In addition, class labels of documents are all omitted in related figures and algorithms for simplicity's sake.

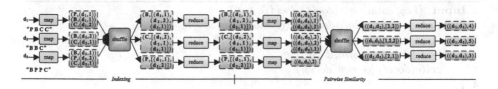

Fig. 2. Pairwise document similarity

Each term in document is emitted as the key, and a tuple consisting of the document identification and term weight is emitted as the value during *map* phase. Records are output into disk during *reduce* and "*posting*" is generated.

In the course of similarity computing, all "*posting*" are processed in *map*, and key tuples are associated with the corresponding term weights product. All results are grouped in the phase of *shuffle*. Then *reduce* sums up all individuals and the similarity is generated. An algorithm is proposed to guarantee the uniqueness of document pair generated (Algorithm 1).

Algorithm 1. *document pairs construction*

Input: $\langle key, value \rangle = \langle term, \langle \langle docid_1, weight_1 \rangle$
$, ..., \langle docid_n, wieght_n \rangle \rangle \rangle$
Output: $\langle \langle docid_i, docid_j \rangle, sim \rangle$
1 **for** $i = 1; i < n; i + +$ **do**
2 | **for** $j = i + 1; j < n; j + +$ **do**
3 | | $sim = weight_i * weight_j$;
4 | | **if** $docid_i >= docid_j$ **then**
5 | | | $write(docid_i \mid docid_j, sim)$;
6 | | **else**
7 | | | $write(docid_j \mid docid_i, sim)$;

In the second phase of pairwise similarity (Fig. 2), the output is constituted by class identification (*classid*), document identification (*docid*) and similarity. Since the front *classid* (*docid*(s)) is no less than the later one, the uniqueness of document pair is guaranteed ($<classid_i\_docid_i \mid classid_j\_docid_j, sim>$, *classid* is omitted in both Algorithm 1 and Fig. 2, as previously discussed).

3.2 *brute-force* Algorithm

brute-force algorithm is consisted of copying and filtering phases of *Neighbors Query* as a baseline (Fig. 1), and one *map-reduce* procedure is needed (copying and neighbor query in Fig. 3). Besides, it is self-described for its copying of all pairwise similarity generated, and more details are presented next.

Algorithm 2. *brute-force*

Input: $\langle key, value \rangle = \langle \langle docid_i, docid_j \rangle, sim \rangle$
Output: $\langle \langle docid_i, sim \rangle, docid_j \rangle, \langle \langle docid_j, sim \rangle, docid_i \rangle$
1 $map(key, value)\{$
2 | $write(docid_i \mid -sim, docid_j)$;
3 | $write(docid_j \mid -sim, docid_i)$;
4 $\}$
5 $reduce(key, value)\{$
6 **for** $i = 0; i < k; i + +$ **do**
7 | $context.write(docid_i \mid -sim, docid_j)$;
8 $\}$

In order to ensure all neighbors are shuffled and sorted, each record obtained from the previous pairwise similarity stages is copied twice in *map* phase of Algorithm 2. And each newly-generated record is a pair of *key* and *value*, in which *key* is consisted of document identification and similarity, and *value* is another document identification corresponded.

There is an implicit phase, *shuffle*, whereas it is very important for our method. After *map*, partitioning (grouping) and ordering are implemented during *shuffle* period, and all records are grouped by document identification and ordered by similarity respectively. Actually, opposite number of *sim* is used for sorting during *shuffle*, which is combined with document identification as a combination *key* (e.g., $docid_i \mid sim$). In addition, we discuss the opposite number of similarity in sorting phase of *pre-filtering* algorithm deeply next.

3.3   *pre-filtering* Algorithm

Figure 3 displays the procedure of the *pre-filtering*, which can be organized as sorting, copying and neighbors query. And extra sorting is conducted for similarity ordering compared with *brute-force*. Two *map-reduce* procedures are needed in total. One is for sorting and the other is for copying and neighbors query.

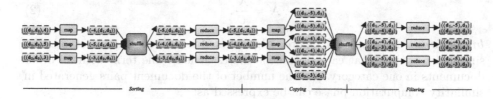

Fig. 3. Sorting and nearest neighbors query procedure

During sorting phase (Algorithm 3), document pairs are sorted by similarity. With the help of *shuffle* ordering, newly generated records composed of pairwise similarity and document identifications are sorted by *key* in descending order by default. In this phase, pairwise similarity is emitted as *key*, and all records are sorted in descending order by pairwise similarity in *shuffle*. Our approach attempts to ensure that all potential neighbors are located at the very beginning of the input (*posting*). Therefore, opposite number of similarity is applied for sorting, and "*-sim*" is emitted as *key*. Shuffled sequence is in ascending order of similarity, and one *map-reduce* procedure is needed (Fig. 3).

Since results of pairwise similarity are ordered, nearest neighbors are more likely to locate at the beginning of the results. Only potential neighbors are copied for *shuffle* based on the ordered results emitted in the previous phase in the phase of copying. In addition, a counter is constructed, with which the approach restricts top-k occurrence of each document identification for the next step. And filtering phase is conducted based on Algorithm 2.

3.4   Theoretical Analysis

The section analyses the time complexity of *brute-force*, *pre-filtering* and two other algorithms used as benchmarks (i.e. *MR_KNN* [20] and *BF_J* [18]).

Algorithm 3. *Sorting phase*

Input: $\langle key, value \rangle = \langle \langle docid_i, docid_j \rangle, sim \rangle$
Output: $\langle -sim, \langle docid_i, docid_j \rangle \rangle$
1 $map(key, value)\{$
2 $write(-sim, (docid_i, docid_j));$
3 $\}$
4 $reduce(key, value)\{$
5 **for** $i = 0; i < value.length; i + +$ **do**
6 $\quad\lfloor\ write(-sim, (docid_i, docid_j));$
7 $\}$

Suppose that the number of documents is $\mathcal{N}$ and all documents can be divided into $\mathcal{C}$ categories with equal size. Thus the number of the documents in each class can be formally stated as:

$$\tilde{\mathcal{N}} = \frac{\mathcal{N}}{\mathcal{C}}. \tag{2}$$

brute-force. As discussed before, Algorithm 2 is a brute-force method. For simplicity, assume that each document shares at least one term with all other documents in one category, and the number of the document pairs generated in similarity computation phase can be expressed as:

$$P = \binom{\tilde{\mathcal{N}}}{2} * \mathcal{C} = \frac{\frac{\mathcal{N}}{\mathcal{C}} * (\frac{\mathcal{N}}{\mathcal{C}} - 1)}{2} * \mathcal{C}. \tag{3}$$

In order to obtain objective neighbors for each document, all records should be copied twice in copying stage. Hence the number of records shuffled can be expressed by formulation 4. Furthermore, records shuffled are all pulled from *map* and pushed toward *reduce* through the network, and it is time consuming.

$$P_{brute\_force} = \binom{\tilde{\mathcal{N}}}{2} * \mathcal{C} * 2 = \mathcal{N} * (\frac{\mathcal{N}}{\mathcal{C}} - 1). \tag{4}$$

pre-filtering. Compared with *brute-force*, *pre-filtering* algorithm needs extra sorting procedure. The number of the records sorted is the same with the number of the records generated in *brute-force* (formulation 4). Since only *top-k* neighbors are emitted, records shuffled are greatly reduced during the procedure of neighbors query in Algorithm 4. The number of the records can be stated as:

$$P_{pre\_filtering} = \mathcal{N} * k * \mathcal{B}. \tag{5}$$

$\mathcal{B}$ denotes the number of the *map*. Obviously, the number of the records shuffled could be kept in the same order of magnitude with the input size.

MR_KNN and BF_J. Both *MR_KNN* and *BF_J* adopt Cartesian Product between training set and testing set. Obviously, the time complexity of similarity computation of the algorithms is $O(\mathcal{N}^2)$ (in *map*). Additionally, *MR_KNN*

Algorithm 4. *Copying and neighbors query phases*

Input: $\langle -sim, \langle docid_i, docid_j \rangle \rangle$
Output: $\langle \langle docid_i, -sim \rangle, docid_j \rangle$, $\langle \langle docid_j, sim \rangle, docid_i \rangle$

1   $map(key, value)\{$
2   **if** $HashMap.get(docid_i) == null$ **then**
3     $write(docid_i \mid -sim, docid_j);$
4     $HashMap.put(docid_i, 1))$

5   **else if** $HashMap.get(docid_i) < k$ **then**
6     $write(docid_i \mid -sim, docid_j);$
     $HashMap.put(docid_i, HashMap.get(docid_i) + 1))$

7   $\}$
8   **if** $HashMap.get(docid_j) == null$ **then**
9     $write(docid_j \mid -sim, docid_i);$
10   $HashMap.put(docid_j, 1))$

11   **else if** $HashMap.get(docid_j) < k$ **then**
12   $write(docid_j \mid -sim, docid_i);$
     $HashMap.put(docid_j, HashMap.get(docid_j) + 1))$

13   $\}$
14   $reduce(key, value)\{$
15   **for** $i = 0; i < k; i + +$ **do**
16   $write(docid_i \mid -sim, docid_j);$

17   $\}$

---

summarizes all intermediate results as one record set in each *map* and *BF_J* emits all neighbors in corresponding *map*, the records shuffled can be denoted as $\mathcal{B}$ and $(\mathcal{N} * k)$ respectively.

Theoretically, *pre-filtering* obtains the best time complexity.

4 Result Analysis

Performance comparison is conducted between *pre-filtering*, *brute-force*, *MR_KNN* [20] and *BF_J* [18]. Firstly, we test the time efficiency improvement of our approach on datasets with different sample sizes; then we do experiments on the same dataset with different numbers of the nearest neighbors; thirdly, we focus on the key procedure (i.e. *map*) that affects the time efficiency greatly; lastly, we analyse the time efficiency of pairwise similarity calculating.

Cluster is equiped with three *datanodes*, among which one of them is *namenode*. Each is equiped with 64GB memory and Intel Xeon E5-2620. The edition of Hadoop is 2.6 and Spark is with the version of 1.2. Sogou corpus[1] is the dataset.

Figure 4a displays the time efficiency of the algorithms. *pre-filtering* obtains the best performance. Time taken is consisted of "sorting" and "neighbors query" for *pre-filtering* algorithm displayed in Fig. 3. When the sample size is small,

---

[1] http://www.sogou.com/labs/dl/c.html.

time efficiency of *pre-filtering* is worse than *brute-force*'s, which is reasonable. "sorting" is excess, and extra time is needed for ordering. Though additional "sorting" is needed and excess time is consumed, more and more records are reduced with increment of the sample size during copying phase, which makes use of the ordered sequence emitted by "sorting". And more time is saved during *shuffle* in neighbors query stage. Better time efficiency is obtained.

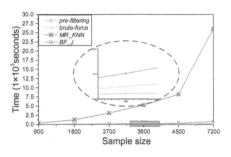

(a) Run time of nearest neighbors query

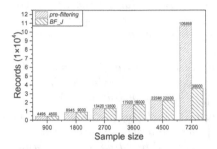

(b) Records that *map* emitted during neighbors query procedure

Fig. 4. Performance of the algorithms with different input sizes

Figure 4b illustrates the number of the records that *map* emitted in the procedure of nearest neighbors query. Since *MR_KNN* summarizes all records in one set and *brute-force* generates more reords than *pre-filtering* obviously, we just conduct comparison between *BF_J* and *pre-filtering*. In most scenarios, the number of records emitted in *pre-filtering* is less than that in *BF_J* as expected. With the increment of the document collection size, more *map*s are invoked ($\mathcal{B}$) and more duplicates are emitted. Thus the number of records generated by *pre-filtering* (106898) is greater than that *BF_J* generated (36000) (Theoretical value is 2876400, $\widetilde{N}*(\widetilde{N}-1)/2*\mathcal{C}$) (Formulation 5). The time complexity of *BF_J* (and *MR_KNN*) is $O(n^2)$, while the time complexity of *pre-filtering* is $O(n)$.

The number of the neighbors is another key feature that affects the time efficiency. Figure 5a demonstrates the performance of the algorithms with different ks. Obviously, better time efficiency is obtained by *pre-filtering*. As discussed in theoretical analysis section, *MR_KNN* and *BF_J* adopt the Cartesian Product. From Fig. 5b, when sample size is not big enough, *map* time difference between all algorithms is not prominent. With the increment of the sample size, more time is saved in *map* phase of *pre-filtering*.

As both *pre-filtering* and *brute-force* depend on document pairwise similarity, some research is conducted on the time cost to illustrate its performance. Figure 6 shows that the time cost of the pairwise similarity computing (including indexing procedure) is increasing with the increment of the dataset size. Thus a interesting future work direction is to improve the time efficiency of the pairwise similarity computation.

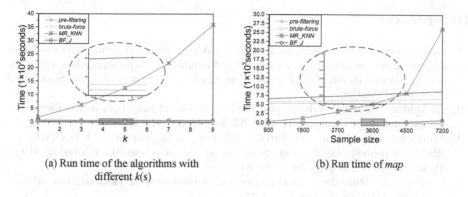

(a) Run time of the algorithms with different k(s)

(b) Run time of *map*

Fig. 5. Time efficiency of the algorithms with different k(s) and the phase of *map*

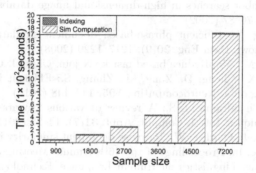

Fig. 6. Run time of pairwise similarity computation

5   Conclusion

In this paper, two novel algorithms on document nearest neighbors query inner document collection are presented based on pairwise similarity on MapReduce framework, i.e. *brute-force* and *pre-filtering*, that can be applied on "more like this" in many websites. Each record output by the phase of pairwise similarity is copied twice in *brute-force*, resulting in huge *shuffle* input. Time efficiency of the *shuffle* is sensitive to the number of the intermediate results. Thus an improved algorithm *pre-filtering* is proposed, which is more applicable for huge sample size. Furthermore, detailed analysis is provided. And experiments on real world dataset verify our work. Future work is to improve the time efficiency of the pairwise similarity computation.

Acknowledgment. This work is supported by the National Science Foundation of China under grants No. 61472080, No. 61672155, No. 61272532, the Consulting Project of Chinese Academy of Engineering under grant 2018-XY-07, National High Technology Research and Development Program (863 Program) of China under grant No. 2013AA013503 and Collaborative Innovation Center of Novel Software Technology and Industrialization.

References

1. Ahmed, O.S., Franklin, S.E., Wulder, M.A., White, J.C.: Extending airborne lidar-derived estimates of forest canopy cover and height over large areas using knn with landsat time series data. IEEE J. Sel. Top. Appl. Earth Observ. Remote Sens. $9(8)$, 3489–3496 (2016)
2. Al Aghbari, Z.: Array-index: a plug&search K nearest neighbors method for high-dimensional data. Data Knowl. Eng. $52(3)$, 333–352 (2005)
3. Almalawi, A.M., Fahad, A., Tari, Z., Cheema, M.A., Khalil, I.: k NNVWC: an efficient k-nearest neighbors approach based on various-widths clustering. IEEE Trans. Knowl. Data Eng. $28(1)$, 68–81 (2016)
4. Bentley, J.L.: Multidimensional binary search trees used for associative searching. Commun. ACM $18(9)$, 509–517 (1975)
5. Cha, G.H., Zhu, X., Petkovic, D., Chung, C.W.: An efficient indexing method for nearest neighbor searches in high-dirnensional image databases. IEEE Trans. Multimed. $4(1)$, 76–87 (2002)
6. Chim, H., Deng, X.: Efficient phrase-based document similarity for clustering. IEEE Trans. Knowl. Data Eng. $20(9)$, 1217–1229 (2008)
7. Dai, J., Ding, Z.M.: MapReduce based fast kNN join. Chin. J. Comput. (2015)
8. Deng, Z., Zhu, X., Cheng, D., Zong, M., Zhang, S.: Efficient kNN classification algorithm for big data. Neurocomputing 195, 143–148 (2016)
9. Dhanabal, S., Chandramathi, S.: A review of various k-nearest neighbor query processing techniques. Int. J. Comput. Appl. $31(7)$, 14–22 (2011)
10. Elsayed, T., Lin, J., Oard, D.W.: Pairwise document similarity in large collections with MapReduce. In: Proceedings of the 46th Annual Meeting of the Association for Computational Linguistics on Human Language Technologies: Short Papers, pp. 265–268. Association for Computational Linguistics (2008)
11. Fier, F.: Distributed similarity joins on big textual data: toward a robust cost-based framework (2017)
12. Ghiassi, M., Fa'al, F., Abrishamchi, A.: Large metropolitan water demand forecasting using DAN2, FTDNN, and KNN models: a case study of the city of Tehran, Iran. Urban Water J. $14(6)$, 655–659 (2017)
13. Kibanov, M., Becker, M., Mueller, J., Atzmueller, M., Hotho, A., Stumme, G.: Adaptive kNN using expected accuracy for classification of geo-spatial data. arXiv preprint arXiv:1801.01453 (2017)
14. Lai, J., Liaw, Y.C., Liu, J.: Fast k-nearest-neighbor search based on projection and triangular inequality. Pattern Recognit. $40(2)$, 351–359 (2007)
15. Lee, K.H., Lee, Y.J., Choi, H., Chung, Y.D., Moon, B.: Parallel data processing with mapreduce: a survey. AcM sIGMoD Rec. $40(4)$, 11–20 (2012)
16. Li, S.Z., Chan, K.L., Wang, C.: Performance evaluation of the nearest feature line method in image classification and retrieval. IEEE Trans. Pattern Anal. Mach. Intell. 11, 1335–1349 (2000)
17. Liaw, Y.C., Leou, M.L., Wu, C.M.: Fast exact k nearest neighbors search using an orthogonal search tree. Pattern Recognit. $43(6)$, 2351–2358 (2010)
18. Lin, J.: Brute force and indexed approaches to pairwise document similarity comparisons with MapReduce. In: Proceedings of the 32nd International ACM SIGIR Conference on Research and Development in Information Retrieval, pp. 155–162. ACM (2009)
19. Liu, T., Moore, A.W., Gray, A.: New algorithms for efficient high-dimensional nonparametric classification. J. Mach. Learn. Res. 7, 1135–1158 (2006)

20. Maillo, J., Triguero, I., Herrera, F.: A MapReduce-based k-nearest neighbor approach for big data classification. In: Trustcom/BigDataSE/ISPA, 2015 IEEE. vol. 2, pp. 167–172. IEEE (2015)
21. McNames, J.: A fast nearest-neighbor algorithm based on a principal axis search tree. IEEE Trans. Pattern Anal. Mach. Intell. **23**(9), 964–976 (2001)
22. Nodarakis, N., Sioutas, S., Tsoumakos, D., Tzimas, G., Pitoura, E.: Rapid AkNN query processing for fast classification of multidimensional data in the cloud. Eprint Arxiv (2014)
23. Omohundro, S.M.: Five balltree construction algorithms. International Computer Science Institute Berkeley (1989)
24. Schiaffino, L., et al.: Feature selection for KNN classifier to improve accurate detection of subthalamic nucleus during deep brain stimulation surgery in Parkinson's patients. In: Torres, I., Bustamante, J., Sierra, D. (eds.) VII Latin American Congress on Biomedical Engineering CLAIB 2016, Bucaramanga, Santander, Colombia, October 26th -28th, 2016. IP, vol. 60, pp. 441–444. Springer, Singapore (2017). https://doi.org/10.1007/978-981-10-4086-3_111
25. Sproull, R.F.: Refinements to nearest-neighbor searching in k-dimensional trees. Algorithmica **6**(1–6), 579–589 (1991)
26. Tan, S.: An effective refinement strategy for KNN text classifier. Expert Syst. Appl. **30**(2), 290–298 (2006)
27. Tombros, A., Ali, Z.: Factors affecting web page similarity. In: Losada, D.E., Fernández-Luna, J.M. (eds.) ECIR 2005. LNCS, vol. 3408, pp. 487–501. Springer, Heidelberg (2005). https://doi.org/10.1007/978-3-540-31865-1_35
28. Velásquez, J.D., et al.: Docode 5: building a real-world plagiarism detection system. Eng. Appl. Artif. Intell. **64**, 261–271 (2017)
29. Wang, Y., Wang, Z.O.: A fast KNN algorithm for text categorization. In: 2007 International Conference on Machine Learning and Cybernetics, vol. 6, pp. 3436–3441. IEEE (2007)
30. Yu, C., Ooi, B.C., Tan, K.L., Jagadish, H.: Indexing the distance: an efficient method to KNN processing. In: VLDB, vol. 1, pp. 421–430 (2001)
31. Zamir, O., Etzioni, O.: Web document clustering: a feasibility demonstration. In: Proceedings of the 21st Annual International ACM SIGIR Conference on Research and Development in Information Retrieval, pp. 46–54. ACM (1998)
32. Zhang, C., Li, F., Jestes, J.: Efficient parallel KNN joins for large data in MapReduce. In: Proceedings of the 15th International Conference on Extending Database Technology, pp. 38–49. ACM (2012)
33. Zhang, S., Li, X., Zong, M., Zhu, X., Wang, R.: Efficient knn classification with different numbers of nearest neighbors. IEEE Trans. Neural Netw. Learn. Syst. **29**(5), 1774–1785 (2018)
34. Zhou, Y., Zhang, C., Wang, J.: Tunable nearest neighbor classifier. In: Rasmussen, C.E., Bülthoff, H.H., Schölkopf, B., Giese, M.A. (eds.) DAGM 2004. LNCS, vol. 3175, pp. 204–211. Springer, Heidelberg (2004). https://doi.org/10.1007/978-3-540-28649-3_25

Accurate Identification of Internet Video Traffic Using Byte Code Distribution Features

Yuxi Xie, Hanbo Deng, Lizhi Peng$^{(\boxtimes)}$, and Zhenxiang Chen

Shandong Provincial Key Laboratory of Network Based Intelligent Computing,
University of Jinan, Jinan 250022, People's Republic of China
plz@ujn.edu.cn

Abstract. Video traffic, the most rapidly growing traffic type in Internet, is posing a serious challenge to Internet management. Different kinds of Internet video contents, including illegal and adult contents, make it necessary to manage different video traffic using different strategies. Unfortunately, there are few research work concerning Internet video traffic type identification. In this paper, we propose a new effective feature extraction method, namely byte code distribution (BCD), for Internet video traffic type identification. The BCD method first counts the times of each byte code value (0 to 255) from a video flow, and then computes the ratio between each count and the total byte count. Such that the 256 ratios are used as the features. Comparing with traditional packet-level features, the BCD features contain more video type information, and are able to make identification more accurately. To test the performance of our proposal, we collect a set of video traffic traces containing two typical video types, romance and action. We conduct a set of comparing experiments on the collected data. The results show that the BCD method can hit extremely high identification accuracies (higher than 99%), far higher than those of the traditional packet-level feature extracting methods. The empirical studies show that the BCD method is promising for Internet video traffic identification.

Keywords: Byte code distribution · Feature extraction
Video traffic identification · Machine learning

1 Introduction

Recent years, Internet has witnessed an explosion of video traffic. According to Cisco's report [1], 82% Internet traffic is generated by video applications. Rapidly emerged video contents greatly enhance Internet users experiences while impose heavy burden on Internet. At the same time, lots of abnormal videos, such as pornographic and violent videos, are widely spread on the Internet. Such videos carry high risks for both of the security and the mental health of Internet users. Therefore, how to effectively identify and manage Internet video

© Springer Nature Switzerland AG 2018
J. Vaidya and J. Li (Eds.): ICA3PP 2018, LNCS 11334, pp. 46–58, 2018.
https://doi.org/10.1007/978-3-030-05051-1_4

traffic has become an urgent problem to be resolved. Video content analysis is an important research topic in computer vision area [18]. Generally, such researches first extract key frames from the original videos. Then, global image features and local object features, such as image colors, textures, and shapes are extracted to identify the video contents [11]. Most video content analysis methods process static and complete data. That is to say, such methods analyze video contents using complete video or image data, leading to poor real-time processing ability. Additionally, on the Internet, real time video streams make it difficult to collect complete image or video data on network devices. Therefore, from the view point of engineering, it is infeasible to apply traditional video content analysis techniques to Internet video traffic identification. Internet traffic identification research provides a possible solution for this problem. In fact, observing the video stream packets on a network device, and extracting features on the packet level or the flow level, and identifying the video content types using these features, such a process is a typical traffic identification process. Unfortunately, as far as we know, there are so few researchers concern on this problem. Most research work related to Internet video traffic was carried out to identify whether a network flow is a video flow or not [4,10], but not the video traffic content type. Schuster et al. [17] made a preliminary attempt for Internet video traffic content type identification in 2017. They use the burst pattern, together with other traditional packet level features, e.g. packet length, and byte rate, to identify the video streams. Their experimental results show that both of the traditional packet level features and the burst pattern feature can hit accuracies higher than 90% for most cases. However, in this research, the video content level features were completely ignored, in contrast of the emphasis of the packet level features, resulting the low identification accuracies for some cases. Therefore, to explore more complex and effective features, and build accurate identification models is the feasible way for Internet video traffic identification.

To address this problem, in this paper, we set out to find content related Internet video traffic features, which can be applied to identify video traffic accurately. Such features should be extracted from video flows efficiently. Driven by this motivation, we make the following contributions in this paper:

- We first collect a set of video traffic data in a real campus network environment, which contain romance and action types. Different from the work in [17], we use the video content types as the instance labels. We consider romance and action videos in our study, as they are the most two representative Internet video types.
- A video content related feature extraction method, namely "Byte code distributions(BCD)", is proposed. We first extract the byte codes of each video flow, and then calculate the occurrence frequency of each code based on the observation of the flow. The observation can be the early section or any fraction of the video flow. Finally, all the byte code frequencies form a vector, that is the feature vector. BCD features can be efficiently extracted from video traffic data. Moreover, they contains more information of different video types than traditional packet level features do.

To test the performances of our proposal, a set of empirical studies are conducted. Three typical supervised learning algorithms are applied for the identification in our studies, they are C4.5 decision trees, support vector machine (SVM), and BP neural networks (BPNN). The experimental results show that video flow BCD features are extremely effective for the identification of the romance and action movies. Our method hits a high identification accuracy of 99.9%, significantly higher than those of using the traditional packet level features. Empirical studies show that our proposal is promising for Internet video content type identification.

The rest of the paper is organized as follows. In Sect. 2, we review the related work. Section 3 introduces our study framework. Section 4 gives the technical details of our data collection method and the data set. The feature extraction and identification methods are presented in Sect. 5. The experimental evaluation details, including the settings, the results, and the analysis are given in Sect. 6. Finally, we conclude the paper in Sect. 7.

2 Related Work

2.1 Network Traffic Identification

From the technical view point, network traffic identification methods fall into three categories: port-based identification, deep packet inspection (DPI), and machine learning (ML) based identification. Port-based identification, the most antique network traffic identification method, simply identifies the application layer protocol types by the source/destination port number of a TCP or UDP flow. DPI techniques are able to achieve extremely high identification accuracies under the conditions that the packet payloads can be inspected. However, these techniques have two fatal drawbacks: firstly, they cannot cope with encrypted traffic; secondly, these techniques are not able to be deployed in high-speed networks because of their high computation and storage costs.

Machine learning based methods, with fine generalization and intelligent capabilities, have become the dominant methods for traffic identification. Generally, ML-based methods extract traffic features from the packet level, flow level, or session level, and then use a set of labeled feature data to train a ML model. Finally, the trained ML model is applied to predict unknown traffic instances. Feature extraction is the basic and vital step for ML-based methods. Moore et al. [9] use 248 statistical features to describe the flow, such as the length of flow duration, packet arrival time interval and packet size, etc. Peng et al. [12] studied effectiveness of statistical features for early stage Internet traffic identification. By using statistical packet and flow level features, different machine learning techniques, including supervised machine learning [3,19], unsupervised machine learning [15], and semi-supervised machine learning [21] were widely applied for traffic identification.

Gong et al. [6] proposed an improved incremental SVM learning algorithm to identify P2P traffic. Preprocessed incremental data and trained SVM model are brought into incremental learning algorithm to obtain a new prediction model.

Qiao et al. [14] proposed a method using the time window to generate simple and effective features from the header of the network stream packets. Zhang et al. [22] introduced a new scheme of Robust statistical Traffic Classification (RTC) by combining random forest and k-means to address the problem of zero-day applications. Peng et al. [13] used IDGC model to identify imbalanced traffic.

The above methods about network traffic identification is identification of application type instead of the type of video. The granularity of recognition is coarser.

2.2 Video Content Identification

In fact, a lot of research work have been done to identify video content using computer vision techniques. However, most of these methods process static and complete data, which leads to poor real time processing ability. Yuan et al. [20] proposed a new method that using a hierarchical Support Vector Machines to distinguish the different video genres based on ten computable spatio-temporal features. Rasheed and Shah [16] put forward that through the visual disturbance feature and average shot length of every movie, the movie genre has been successfully classified. A transductive learning framework for robust video content analysis based on feature selection and ensemble classification was presented by Ewerth et al. [5]. Liu et al. [8] proposed a method that applying a (wavelet-based) analysis to extract the long and short range dependencies within the video traffic for generation of the robust and efficient traffic fingerprint. Chaisorn et al. [2] presented a hybrid signature along with a hierarchical filtering approach for similar content identification. Li et al. [7] proposed to extract robust video descriptor by training deep neural network to automatically capture the intrinsic visual characteristics of digital video.

In terms of video traffic recognition, a consistency-based feature analysis and selection method was presented by Dong et al. [4] to systematically find some new and effective features for video traffic classification. And a hierarchical k-Nearest Neighbor (KNN) classification algorithm is then developed based on the combinations of these statistical features. Mu et al. [10] studied a parallel network flow classification method based on Markov's model. These small amounts of research just identify the traffic generated by video applications in numerous network traffic. In terms of Internet video content recognition, the method presented by Israeli scholars have opened the door to identify the content and types of the video at the traffic level. A relatively good results have been obtained through the burst pattern feature of data packets and the methods of convolution neural network in their work. More specifically, the identified object is the title of the video.

3   Study Framework

The study framework of this paper contains three main stages: data collection, feature extraction, and classification.

Firstly, raw video traffic data is captured and stored in the server. Then a set of preprocessing steps, e.g. noise data filtering and TCP flow converging, are conducted on the raw data. As most Internet video streams are transmitted using the TCP protocol, we only consider TCP flows in our study. After the preprocessing operations, a processed original video traffic data set is generated.

At the second stage, a set of video traffic feature extraction studies are carried out. There are two main steps in this stage. First, three types of packet sampling operations are executed on the original video traffic data, including early stage sampling, fraction sampling, and regular interval sampling. The reason of applying sampling operations is easy to be understood: it makes non sense in real scenarios to extract feature data on a complete flow. Second, we extract BCD features as the video content features based on the sampled packets. The extracted feature data forms the feature data set, which can used for the training and testing of the machine learning models. In addition to the BCD features, we also extracted two traditional packet level features, packet size and packet inter-arrival time, for comparisons.

Finally, we applied three classical machine learning models, C4.5, SVM, and BPNN for the identification and validation of the extracted features. It should noticed that we do not care the machine learning models. Instead, we focus on the applying of these machine learning models on our video traffic data. That means we can choose the most effective learning model for the real video traffic identification problem according to the evaluation results.

4   Data Collection and Preprocessing

4.1   Data Collection

The data collection test bed is deployed in our campus network environment, which is shown in Fig. 1. We deployed seven user computers as the collection clients. Each client computer equips two Intel Pentium G620 CPUs, and runs Windows 7. We deploy the Wireshark packet capturing tool on the client computers to collect the raw video traffic data. The collected data are then sent to a centralized server, and preprocessed on the server.

In this study, two typical video content types are considered, romance and action. During October 2017 to March 2018, the users of the client computers visited Internet video sites and played the two types of videos from time to time. When a client computer was playing target videos, all other network applications were stopped to avoid generating non-video traffic, and the Wireshark tool was started for capturing. Many Internet videos begin with advertisement videos, which were manually skipped in our studies.

The Internet video sites we visited cover Youku, Tudou, iQIYI, Sohu video, and Tencent video. For each video site, we selected 100 romance movies and 100 action movies. The first 15 min of each movie were played and its packets were captured. Considering the storage limitation, we did not collect the complete video of each movie. In fact, we consider that the 15 min section is enough to contain the unique network characters of an Internet video. Table 1 shows the details of the collected video traffic data.

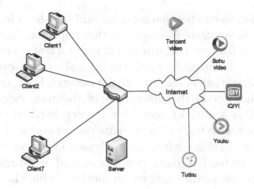

Fig. 1. The architecture of data collection

Table 1. Collected video traffic data

Video site	Video type	# instances	# bytes (GB)
Youku	Romance	100	2.3
	Action	100	5.1
Tudou	Romance	100	1.9
	Action	100	4.9
iQIYI	Romance	100	2.1
	Action	100	4.9
Sohu video	Romance	100	1.8
	Action	100	4.8
Tencent video	Romance	100	2.2
	Action	100	5.2

4.2 Data Preprocessing

The raw data is saved in standard .pcap format files. As most Internet video sites using the TCP protocol for video stream transmission, we first picked up all TCP packets in the preprocessing operations. Then all the packets were converged into distinguished TCP flows (connections). In some TCP flows, the SYN packet, or the FIN packet, or RST packet are missed, because we just captured the first 15 min of each movie instance. Therefore, we use the timeout strategy to determine the beginning and ending of the incomplete TCP flows. In addition, flows that contain less than 1000 packets were discarded. The underlying fact is that such "short" flows are usually generated by background applications, and should be filtered as noise data.

5   Feature Extraction

It is well known that feature extraction is vital for machine learning tasks, as the learning results greatly depend on the qualities of the extracted features.

In traffic identification researches, packet-level and flow-level features are widely used, such as packet size, packet inter-arrival time, up/down byte rate, up/down byte volume, etc. Such features perform well in general traffic identification tasks. However, for video traffic identification, traditional packet-level and flow-level features that are just statistical features at the network level, not at the content level obviously cannot reveal the differences of different video content types. On the other hand, as stated in Sect. 1, it is very hard to extract computer vision features from the living video streams on networks. They analyze and process the complete video file while we analyze and process the data packet. In comparison, our method is more convenient and real-time. Therefore, we propose fast video traffic feature extraction method using the BCD features of packet payloads, which will be introduced in details in Subsect. 5.1. We also use two basic packet-level features, packet size and packet inter-arrival time, in our study for comparison.

5.1   Byte Code Feature

It can be easily and intuitively concluded that each video content type has its unique scene style. For example, romance movies have smooth and mild scenes, in contrast with the violent and fast-paced scenes of action movies. Similarly, different video content types also have different patterns for the sound, the emotional expression, and so forth. When the videos are packed into network packets, and transmitted on the network, such different patterns can be mapped to the byte coding styles of the network packets. If we observe these packets on the network, and extract the features with right ways, we can identify different video types by finding their unique patterns.

Let's observe a fraction of a video flow, for example 2 min. Suppose there are n packets in this fraction, all the packets in this fraction form a sequence $P_1, P_2, ..., P_n$. The payload size of the ith packet is S_i. If we extract each byte of the packet, and get its values (varying from 0 to 255), then all the byte values can be illustrated as Table 2. If we sum up the byte values of each row in the table, then we get 256 counts $c_1^i, c_2^i, ..., c_{256}^i$ for the ith packet. We conduct the counting procedure on each packet of the packet sequence $P_1, P_2, ..., P_n$, and get a count matrix

Table 2. Byte values of the ith packet

	$Byte1$	$Byte2$	...	$ByteS_i$
0	0	0	...	1
1	1	0	...	0
⋮	⋮	⋮	⋮	⋮
255	0	1	...	0

$$C = \begin{bmatrix} c_1^1 & c_2^1 & \cdots & c_{256}^1 \\ c_1^2 & c_2^2 & \cdots & c_{256}^2 \\ \vdots & \vdots & \vdots & \vdots \\ c_1^n & c_2^n & \cdots & c_{256}^n \end{bmatrix} \quad (1)$$

Finally, we sum up each column of this matrix, and get 256 count numbers. Then compute the proportion of the jth count number as follows.

$$f_j = \frac{\sum_{i=1}^n c_j^i}{\sum_{k=1}^{256} \sum_{i=1}^n c_k^i}, \quad j = 1, 2, ..., 256. \quad (2)$$

So we get a vector containing 256 components $F = \{f_1, f_2, ..., f_{256}\}$. That is the feature vector.

It can be observed these features show the distributions of the 256 byte codes in the video flow fraction. Such simple statistical features have two significant advantages. First, these features can be easily extracted with low computation and storage costs. Second, such features depend on the contents of the original videos to some extent. That is to say, they can show the patterns of the original videos.

5.2   Feature Extraction Algorithm

Algorithm 1 describes the feature extracting procedure. In which the input is the preprocessed data set D. That is to say, in D, we have filtered the noise data and all the flows have been converged as illustrated in Sect. 4. We go through the whole data set, and compute a feature vector F containing 256 components for each video flow. Therefore, a feature data set is formed, and each instance is a video flow instance. Finally, the video type labels, 0 for romance and 1 for action, are added to each instance. This feature data set can be used for the training and testing of the learning models, which will be introduced in the next section.

Algorithm 1. BCD features extraction

Input: Preprocessed data set D;
Output: Feature data set FD(BCD features data set);
  1: **for** each flow $FLOW_k$ in D **do**
  2:    Initialize the count matrix C using zero elements;
  3:    **for** each packet P_i in $FLOW_k$ **do**
  4:      **for** each byte b_j in P_i **do**
  5:        $c_{b_j}^i$ ++;
  6:      **end for**
  7:    **end for**
  8:    Compute the feature vector F_k according to Eq. (2);
  9:    Add the video type label of the flow y_k to the end of F_k;
 10: **end for**

---

6   Experiments

6.1   Performance Measures

We use accuracy and f-measure as the performance measures in our empirical evaluations. Without lose of generality, we consider binary classification tasks. For such tasks, the accuracy acc can be defined as follows.

$$acc = (TP + TN)/(TP + TN + FP + FN) \tag{3}$$

Where, true positive (TP) is the number of the correctly classified positive instances, true negative (TN) is the number of the correctly classified negative instances, false positive (FP) is the number of the negative instances those be incorrectly classified as positive ones, false negative (FN) is the number of the positive instances those be incorrectly classified as negative ones. Precision p and recall r are two typical measures, which are defined as:

$$p = TP/(TP + FP) \tag{4}$$

$$r = TP/(TP + FN) \tag{5}$$

Both precision and recall are able to show the prediction performance of a learning model from different points. F-measure, the harmonic mean of precision and recall, is a complicated measure which is defined as follows.

$$F - measure = (2 * r * p)/(r + p) \tag{6}$$

6.2   Classifier Parameter Settings

Three classification algorithms are used to classify the feature data sets in our experiments. Including C4.5 decision trees, SVM and BPNN. Table 3 shows the parameter settings of the classifiers.

Table 3. Classifier parameter settings

C4.5	SVM	BPNN
confidenceFactor:0.25	kernel function:linear	Transfer function of ith layer
minNumObj:2	method:SMO	hidden layers:'tansig' 'logsig'
seed:1	polyorder:3	output layer:'purelin'
splitCriterion:IGR	rbf sigma:1	training function:'traingd'
		learning function:'learngdm'
		number of iterations:15000
		learning rate:0.01

6.3   Results and analysis

Table 4 shows the accuracies and f-measures the three classifiers got using BCD features.

Table 4. Comparison of experimental results

	Accuracy	F-measure
C4.5	0.9992	0.9992
SVM	0.9950	0.9950
BPNN	0.9942	0.9942

As can be seen from the results, all the three classifiers output extremely high values (higher than 99%) for both of accuracy and f-measure. These results strongly imply that the BCD features are really effective for video traffic type identification.

Comparisons Between Packet-Level Features and BCD Features. To further validate the effectiveness of the BCD features, we carry out a set of comparing experiments between the packet-level features and the BCD features. This time, we extract the packet sizes and IATs of the original video flow, and then use C4.5, SVM and BPNN for the identification. Finally, the results are compared with those of the BCD features, as Figs. 2 and 3 show. The significant differences between the results of the BCD features and the results of the two types of packet-level features can be easily observed. For both of accuracy and f-measure, all the three selected learning models output result values no more than 0.9, far lower than the high values of the BCD features. The comparison results strongly suggests the BCD features are far more effective than the traditional packet-level features in video traffic identification.

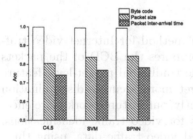

Fig. 2. Comparison results of accuracy

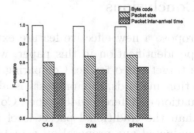

Fig. 3. Comparison results of F-measure

Identification Results of the Sampled Data. We use three packet sampling strategies to validate the real application effectiveness of the BCD features. First, we randomly select a 10 min fraction from each video flow for the feature extraction, and we call such strategy as the fraction sampling. For the second strategy, we select the packets in the first 2 s of each flow to extract the features, and we call it as early stage sampling. The third sampling method, namely regular interval sampling, selects the packets of each video flow every 3 s. We then extract the BCD features from the sampled video data, and put the feature data into C4.5, SVM and BPNN for identifications. Again, we use histograms to show the identification results, as shown in Figs. 4 and 5.

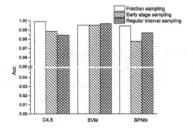   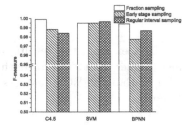

Fig. 4. Results of classification accuracy   **Fig. 5.** Results of classification F-maesure

As can be seen from the results in Figs. 4 and 5, all the three packet sampling strategies can get high classification performance. Most of the result values of the three learning models are higher than 0.98. The differences between them are negligible. In other words, the two video types can be accurately identified using both the stream's early features and equal interval sampling features. Regarding these results, two conclusions can be drawn. First, the BCD features are proved to be effective for either the complete traffic data or the sampled data. Second, it is possible to accurately identify video content types in real network traffic environment.

7   Conclusions

We propose a new effective feature extraction method for Internet video traffic type identification in this paper, which computes the BCD of the packets of the target video traffic. Comparing with the traditional packet-level feature extraction methods, our proposal is able to get more accurate discrimination information of different video types. Consequently, our features work more effective than the traditional packet-level features for video traffic identifications. We conducted our proposal on a real collected video traffic data, using three classic machine learning algorithms. The experimental results provide empirical evidences that the BCD features are able to get extremely high identification performance, which are far higher than that of the traditional packet-level features. Our experimental results also show that the BCD features work well with packet sampling techniques, which is important for high speed networks. However, we only investigated two typical types of videos: romance and action. In our future work, more video traffic types should be studied, and that will be a big challenge.

Acknowledgement. This research was partially supported by the National Natural Science Foundation of China under grant No. 61472164, No. 61573166, No. 61572230, and No. 61672262, the Doctoral Fund of University of Jinan under grant No. XBS1623, and No. XBS1523.

References

1. Baranyi, P.: Visual network index (VNI) complete prediction. https://www.cisco.com/c/zh_cn/solutions/service-provider/visual-networking-index-vni/index.html
2. Chaisorn, L., Fu, Z.: A hybrid approach for image/video content representation and identification. In: Industrial Electronics and Applications, pp. 966–971 (2012)
3. Dong, S., Li, R.: Traffic identification method based on multiple probabilistic neural network model. Neural Comput. Appl. **1**, 1–15 (2017)
4. Dong, Y.N., Zhao, J.J., Jin, J.: Novel feature selection and classification of internet video traffic based on a hierarchical scheme. Comput. Netw. **119**, 102–111 (2017)
5. Ewerth, R., Mühling, M., Freisleben, B.: Robust video content analysis via transductive learning. ACM Trans. Intell. Syst. Technol. (TIST) **3**(3), 41 (2012)
6. Gong, J., Wang, W., Wang, P., Sun, Z.: P2P traffic identification method based on an improvement incremental SVM learning algorithm. In: International Symposium on Wireless Personal Multimedia Communications, pp. 174–179 (2015)
7. Li, Y.N., Chen, X.P.: Robust and compact video descriptor learned by deep neural network. In: IEEE International Conference on Acoustics, Speech and Signal Processing, pp. 2162–2166 (2017)
8. Liu, Y., Sadeghi, A.R., Ghosal, D., Mukherjee, B.: Video streaming forensic-content identification with traffic snooping. Asian J. Agric. Rural Dev. **2**(10), 39–45 (2010)
9. Moore, A.W., Zuev, D.: Discriminators for Use in Flow-Based Classification. Intel Research, London (2005)
10. Mu, X., Wu, W.: A parallelized network traffic classification based on hidden markov model. In: International Conference on Cyber-Enabled Distributed Computing and Knowledge Discovery, pp. 107–112 (2011)
11. Peng, L., Xue, Y., Wang, C.: Survey on recognition and filtering of network video content. Comput. Eng. Des. **10**, 048 (2008)
12. Peng, L., Yang, B., Chen, Y., Chen, Z.: Effectiveness of statistical features for early stage internet traffic identification. Int. J. Parallel Program. **44**(1), 181–197 (2016)
13. Peng, L., Zhang, H., Chen, Y., Yang, B.: Imbalanced traffic identification using an imbalanced data gravitation-based classification model. Comput. Commun. **102**(1), 177–189 (2017)
14. Qiao, M., Ma, Y., Bian, Y., Liu, J.: Real-time multi-application network traffic identification based on machine learning. In: International Symposium on Neural Networks, pp. 473–480 (2015)
15. Rao, Z., Niu, W., Zhang, X., Li, H.: Tor anonymous traffic identification based on gravitational clustering. Peer-to-Peer Netw. Appl. **11**(3), 592–601 (2018)
16. Rasheed, Z., Shah, M.: Movie genre classification by exploiting audio-visual features of previews. In: Proceedings of the International Conference on Pattern Recognition, vol. 2, pp. 1086–1089 (2002)

17. Schuster, R., Shmatikov, V., Tromer, E.: Beauty and the burst: remote identification of encrypted video streams. In: Proceedings of the 26th USENIX Security Symposium, pp. 1357–1374 (2017)
18. Shinkar, T., Hanchate, D.B.: Video content identification using video signature: survey. Int. Res. J. Eng. Technol. (IRJET) **4**, 746–751 (2017)
19. Ye, Z., Wang, M., Wang, C., Xu, H.: P2P traffic identification using support vector machine and cuckoo search algorithm combined with particle swarm optimization algorithm. In: Zhang, S., Xu, K., Xu, M., Wu, J., Wu, C., Zhong, Y. (eds.) ICoC 2014. CCIS, vol. 502, pp. 118–132. Springer, Heidelberg (2015). https://doi.org/10.1007/978-3-662-46826-5_10
20. Yuan, X., Lai, W., Mei, T., Hua, X.S., Wu, X.Q., Li, S.: Automatic video genre categorization using hierarchical SVM. In: IEEE International Conference on Image Processing, pp. 2905–2908 (2006)
21. Zhang, J., Chen, C., Xiang, Y., Zhou, W., Vasilakos, A.V.: An effective network traffic classification method with unknown flow detection. IEEE Trans. Netw. Serv. Manage. **10**(2), 133–147 (2013)
22. Zhang, J., Chen, X., Xiang, Y., Zhou, W., Wu, J.: Robust network traffic classification. IEEE/ACM Trans. Netw. **23**(4), 1257–1270 (2015)

RISC: Risk Assessment of Instance Selection in Cloud Markets

Jingyun Gu$^{(\boxtimes)}$, Zichen Xu$^{(\boxtimes)}$, and Cuiying Gao$^{(\boxtimes)}$

Nanchang University, Nanchang, China
{jgu,arry}@email.ncu.edu.cn, xuz@ncu.edu.cn

Abstract. Cloud markets provide instances as products in Infra-structure-as-a-Service (IaaS). Users usually underprovision instances while risking the possible failure of SLOs, or overprovision resources by suffering higher expenses. The underlying key nature of user behavior in purchasing instances can be essential for maximizing cloud market profits. However, for cloud service providers, there is little knowledge on assessing the risk of user choices on cloud instances. This paper proposes one of the first studies on the risk assessment in IaaS cloud markets. We first provide a modeling process to understand user and violations of SLOs, from server statistics. To understand the risk, we propose RISC, a mechanism to assess the risk of instance selection. RISC contains an ana-lytic hierarchy process to evaluate the decisions, an optimization process to expose the risk frontier, and a feedback approach to fine-tuning the instance recommendation. We have evaluated our approach using simu-lations on real-world workloads and cloud market statistics. The results show that, compared to traditional approaches, our approach provides the best tradeoff between SLOs and costs, as it can maximize the overall profit up to 5X for the cloud service provider. All users achieve their SLOs goals while minimizing their average expenses by 34.6%.

1 Introduction

The worldwide public cloud market is projected to \$186.4 billion in 2018, with more than 22% from Infrastructure-as-a-Service (IaaS) Cloud [24]. The IaaS exposes high-level APIs to provide instant computing infrastructure, or *instance*, provi-sioned and leased over the Internet. The cloud service providers (CSPs) can over-sell their physical resources by scaling-out the number of loaded instances. Thus, the leasing price of a cloud instance is usually low, compared to physical machines. CSPs have to market to sell as many as possible to make the maximum profit from such products. Successful cloud markets include Amazon Web Services [9], Google Cloud [19], Microsoft Azure Cloud [27], Tencent Cloud [23], etc.

The pricing for the cloud instance is positively correlated to the number of assigned resources. For example, a *n1-standard* instance with one virtual CPU, is usually cheaper than a *n1-highCPU* instance with two or four virtual CPUs in Google Cloud [2]. Thus, customers can scale up and down the instance(s) based on their workload, and pay on demand. However, studies [30,31] show that it is

© Springer Nature Switzerland AG 2018
J. Vaidya and J. Li (Eds.): ICA3PP 2018, LNCS 11334, pp. 59–74, 2018.
https://doi.org/10.1007/978-3-030-05051-1_5

very hard to project the correct amount of resources for future workloads, and customers can lose their revenues from bad selections. Customers suffer from (1) paying for missing the service-level objective (SLO) from resource underprovision and workload misprediction; (2) paying for exclusively accessing computing resources but leaving such resource idle from overprovisioning. The instance selection can be a risky decision. Although CSPs do provide some pricing tools and workload profilers, they are not sufficient to provide possible risk assessment for each decision [26, 28].

The selection risk problem is more challenging since CSPs provide different pricing models. There are many different kinds of pricing cloud markets, auction-based bidding pricing [32], fine-grained pricing [13], perpetual pricing [12], etc. Customers can choose their desired pricing methods, for example, if the SLO for the workload is loosely constrained, the bidding model might be a better choice. For risk assessment, multiple pricing models on multiple instances lead to many possible decisions, which makes the selection risk problem hard to solve.

Unlike previous research [8, 17, 25] that infer there may exist one best solution for the instance selection optimization, risk is a factor that changes on different selections. Meanwhile, customers may have different expectation on the selection. It is plausible to find a mean-to-variation efficiency frontier that plots the tradeoff between risk and profit. This frontier works as the portfolio management in the bond market. The customer can purchase a low-risk bond or high-risk stock. Depending on the expected return (i.e., profits), there exist a list of possible selections with different risk (e.g., instance fails) curving in the solution space. Finding these risks and possible combinations of profit and risk of different selections performs the risk assessment on cloud instance markets.

In this paper, we propose a mechanism, RISC, to perform **R**isk assessment on **I**nstance **S**election in **C**loud markets. RISC presents an Analytic Hierarchy Process (AHP) to evaluate metrics from the instance leasing. AHP is a decision-making method that models a list of choices based on selections and pricing models. RISC optimizes the decision based on this combination of choices with the tradeoff between risk and profit. Thus, a curve of risk frontier is provided for the decision process. The runtime performance of past decision is considered as historical metadata in RISC, and it feeds back into the RISC loop to enhance the performance of the modeling and optimization process. In this way, RISC provides the risk assessment from CSPs to customers.

We evaluate our RISC using real workload Google Cluster [3]. All pricing metrics are obtained from the top cloud service providers, like Amazon Web Services, Google Cloud, etc. The results show that, compared to traditional approaches, our approach provides the best tradeoff between SLOs and expenses, such that it maximizes the overall profit by 5X for the cloud service provider. All users achieve their SLOs goals while minimizing their expenses by 34.6%.

In summary, this paper makes the following contributions:

- We find the problem of revenue loss due to complex IaaS cloud markets and bad instance selection choices.

- We formulate such problem as a risk assessment problem in cloud instance selection, and design a mechanism, RISC to solve it.
- We provide a closed-loop design of RICS, including the risk modeling, the AHP analysis, and the target risk frontier.
- We show that RISC benefits both customers and service providers. Our simulation results show that RISC provides the best tradeoff between SLOs and costs, such that it maximizes the overall profit by 5X.

The follow part of this manuscript is organized as follows: Sect. 2 introduces the background of IaaS clouds and the AHP process. Section 3 illustrates the design and implementation of RISC. Section 4 explains our setup for evaluation, and Sect. 5 illustrates RISC can greatly reduce the cost of the system. We compares our RISC with related work in Sect. 6. Section 7 concludes the paper.

2 Background

Risk assessment quantifies the scene to which an event or thing can be impacted or lost. In traditional market analysis, the risk assessment is performed by identifying threats and vulnerabilities of the product, and recommending possible fixes [16,18]. In cloud markets, most computer scientists focus on identifying the privacy and security leak in cloud services [11,21]. In RISC, we believe violating the SLOs of running workloads can be treated as threats and vulnerabilities in the market as well. In this case, it is very important to expand the research on identifying and assessing risks in choosing the right services in clouds.

AHP is a simple, flexible and practical multi-criteria decision making method for qualitative analysis and qualitative problems. It is an effective tool for dealing with complex decision making, and may aid the decision maker to set priorities and make the best decision [1]. The AHP is suitable for multi-objective decision making and used to evaluate each solution when there are multiple criteria. AHP selects when a decision is influenced by multiple factors, and there is a hierarchical relationship or a clear classification between the elements and the degree of influence of each indicator when final evaluation cannot be directly calculated.

ANP is a networked form of AHP in multi-criteria decision analysis. ANP is used to deal systematically with all kinds of dependence and feedback in the performance system. However, in our cloud market, AHP is sufficient and effective to establish a model to manage enterprise economic information. In the comprehensive evaluation of the quality of economic growth, AHP can find the most important evaluation factor simply and effectively. AHP can find the main factors affecting economic efficiency to improve economic efficiency. In addition, AHP is also applied to user selection of suppliers and market researches.

Our model established in the cloud market is a one-way hierarchical relationship between decision-making layers. AHP emphasizes the one-way relationship between decision-making layers, as the influence of the next layer on the upper layer. As a more generalized process, we choose AHP to be our model in our cloud market.

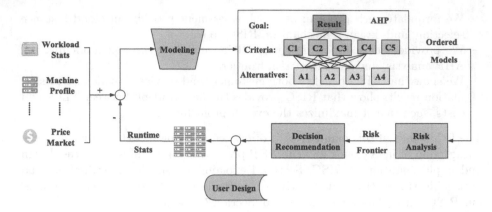

Fig. 1. The system diagram of RISC

3   Design

RISC is the framework on assessing risks of instance selection. By analyzing sets of server-side statistics, RISC can provide the comparison between different instance selections. The whole process of RISC can be illustrated in Fig. 1. RISC collects information about workloads, machines, prices, etc., as the input to model risk-profit metrics. Given the set of metrics, AHP in RISC calculates the weight and priority for each instance selection combined *per se*. Then, AHP outputs an ordered of selections. Based on the order of different selections and modelled weights, RISC calculates the risk of each selection and draws the risk-profit efficiency frontier. The frontier can be used to understand the possible risk and profit of their instance(s) selection. At last, in the next decision period, all runtime statistics will be collected to re-assess the risk/profit from previous decisions, thus, altering the risk frontier in the next epoch.

3.1   Selection Profiles

As aforementioned in Sect. 1, it is difficult to quantify a realistic SLOs from users. As a service provider, it is easy to collect workload profiles, such as response time, waiting time, and job status (Fig. 2(a)); machine profiles, such as CPU/memory resource and utilization (Fig. 2(b)); and the price market, (Fig. 2(c), $/h for each instance). We believe these profiles are essential to infer the risk of users' decision, indirectly. However, it is a challenge work to find the best profile model. It is a harder challenge when such workload, machine, and price profiles are dynamic, as shown in Fig. 2.

  Figure 2(a) shows runtime stats from two workloads: intensive *workload1* and skewed *workload2* in Google Clusters [3]. Both workloads fluctuate along with time. However, these two workloads from two different users never be peaked or valleyed at the same time. This may cause higher utilization on one instance, which is good, or they may race for resources, which is bad. Understanding the

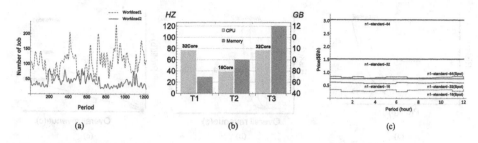

Fig. 2. Dynamics in instance selection profiles: (a) workload dynamics; (b) instance resources; (c) pricing.

statistics of workloads can be essential to analyze the risk. Similarly, although resources assigned in each instance are static (Fig. 2(b)), choosing different instances combined is an optimization problem, which is usually considered as the classic bin-packing problem [10]. For the price, given one location, the price for on-demand instances are static, as in Fig. 2(c). However, if one wants to use spot instances, he/she may suffer from a much higher risk of failure. In the design of RISC , we consider all these issues in the modeling process.

3.2   Modeling

After understanding the dynamics and schemes of variables, we begin to establish decision models for workload, machine, and price market, labeled as *criteria* and *alternatives*. Criteria are standards for decision making. Criteria should be closely connected to each alternatives, and be able to depict some features from elapsed alternatives. In RISC , collected profiles are considered as the criteria, as, CPU capacity (*cores*), memory capacity (*memory*), utilization (μ), unit price (*price*), and average response time (*time*). We collect ratios of each instance type from different criteria as weights. Then, we begin to establish the initial pairwise comparison, in order to obtain the priority of each alternative.

Workload Criteria: We assume jobs, i.e., workloads, arrive in the system following a G/GI/m model, which means the generic distribution of arrival rate, generic independent distribution for average processing time in each window, and we have m instances to serve these workloads in this period. Using the well-known Allen-Cunneen approximation [5] for the GI/G/m model, the response time and the number of servers needed to satisfy a given demand are related as follows:

$$\bar{t} = \frac{1}{\mu} + \frac{\rho}{\mu(1-\rho)}\left(\frac{C_A^2 + C_B^2}{2}\right) + \frac{2E[I] + \lambda E[I^2]}{2(1 + \lambda E[I])} \tag{1}$$

where $\bar{t}$ is the mean response time, $\frac{1}{\mu}$ represents the mean service time of a server, λ is the mean request arrival rate, $\rho = \frac{\lambda}{\mu}$ represents the average utilization of a server, C_A^2 and C_B^2 represent the squared coefficient of variation of request

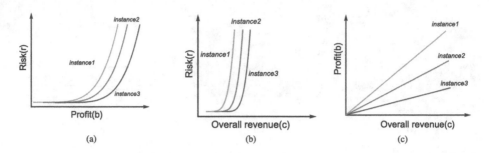

Fig. 3. Risk-profit-revenue curves using three different instances: (a) risk-profit; (b) profit-revenue; (c) risk-revenue.

inter-arrival times and request sizes, respectively, and $E[I]$ represents the mean initial set-up time for the exceptional first service.

Cost Model. Selection policies can decrease revenue by assigning highly priced instances. Also, policies that increase the frequency of adapting spot instances that increase risks of violating SLOs. We model the total revenue as a weighted function of (1) expense to lease instances and (2) risks of picking certain instances. Equations 2–6 show the model:

$$\vartheta_i \triangleq \frac{\zeta}{\ell_i^{k_i}} \tag{2}$$

$$k_i \triangleq \begin{cases} 1, & \zeta \leq \varpi \\ \infty & \zeta > \varpi \end{cases} \tag{3}$$

$$\ell_i \triangleq \sum p_j T \tag{4}$$

$$r_i \triangleq (1 - \tau)\iota_i \cdot \varepsilon + \tau \iota_i \cdot \kappa \tag{5}$$

$$\complement \triangleq \text{MAX}\{c_1, c_2, \ldots, c_{(m,n)}\} \tag{6}$$

$$c_i \triangleq r_i^\alpha \vartheta_i \tag{7}$$

In these equations, i indexes the ith selection of combined instances and j indexes the jth instance. $\complement$ is the possible maximum revenue when examining a vector of possible selections, i.e., $\{c_1, c_2, \ldots, c_{(m,n)}\}$, where m is the number of selected instances and n is the total number of instances available. c_i is the total revenue from serving workloads from selection i. The total revenue is a nonlinear combination of financial profit (ϑ_i) and correspondent risk factor (r_i). Parameter α is the weight coefficient.

The profit ϑ_i captures gaining from the possible SLO (ζ) while spending (ℓ_i) for leasing the ith selection. Noting that we use k_i as the weight coefficient when SLO ζ violates certain threshold ϖ. Usually, we set $\varpi = 99.999\%$. In our current setup, we do not want any SLO violations in RISC . Thus, violating the threshold ϖ can lead to infinitely large expense, thus a zero revenue. The parameter (ℓ_i) calculates the total expense from the ith selection in the period T. For the ease of our analysis, we set $T = 1$.

We define the risk factor r based on successful/failure rate, $(\kappa)/(\varepsilon)$, respectively. (ι) is the impact of an ordered criteria, produced from our AHP process. τ is a weight coefficient on successes and failures in one decision period.

Figure 3 shows the relationship between, the revenue c_i, the profit ϑ_i, and the risk factor r. Our simulation shows the converging from three different instance selection. These curves could be much wider and unexpected when multiple users selecting more instances combined to serve their request.

3.3 Analytic Hierarchy Process

AHP can be implemented in three simple consecutive steps: Computing the vector of criteria weights, computing the matrix of option scores, ranking the options [1]. The three hierarchies in AHP are set as clusters and elements of each cluster are called nodes. The first step after setting clusters and nodes is computing the weights for the different criteria. AHP would create a pairwise comparison matrix A. The matrix A is a $l \times l$ real matrix, where n is the number of nodes in criteria.

$$
\begin{array}{cccc}
 & A_1 & A_2 & ... & A_l \\
A_1 & a_{11} & a_{12} & ... & a_{1l} \\
A_2 & a_{21} & a_{22} & ... & a_{2l} \\
 & \cdot & \cdot & \cdot & \cdot \\
A_l & a_{l1} & a_{l2} & ... & a_{ll}
\end{array}
$$

Each entry a_{ij} of the matrix A denotes the importance of ith criterion relative to the jth criterion. If ith criterion is more important than jth criterion, then $a_{ij} > 1$, while if ith criterion is less important than ith criterion, then $a_{ij} < 1$. If the two criteria have the same importance, then a_{ij} has value of 1. The entries satisfy the following constraint:

$$a_{ij} \cdot a_{ji} = 1, a_{ij} > 0, a_{ii} = a_{jj} = 1 \tag{8}$$

Then, AHP computes the maximum feature root using $(\lambda)_{max}$ and its normalized feature vector $W = (w_1, w_2, ..., w_l)^T$ in Eq. 9;

$$AW = \lambda_{max} \times W \tag{9}$$

$W = (W_1, W_2, ..., W_l)^T$ represents vectors for weights of each node. Then, we have to conduct consistency check for matrix A, if each entry $a_{ij} = \frac{a_{ih}}{a_{jh}}$, then matrix A is consistency matrix. The steps are: (a) Compute consistency index (C.I.): $C.I. = \frac{\lambda_{max} - l}{l - 1}$, n stands for the judgement for order of the matrices. (b) Compute average random consistency index R.I.. R.I. is obtained as the arithmetic mean of calculation of the eigenvalues of the judgement matrix repeatedly. (c) Compute consistency ratio C.R.: $C.R. = C.I./R.I.$. When $C.R. < 0.1$, the consistency of the judgement matrix is acceptable.

Giving an example, RISC sets CPU, memory, price, response time, number of jobs as criteria and six different instance types as alternatives. Then RISC has the matrix A as a 6×6 matrix. $a_{11} = 1$ which represents the ratio of importance for CPU and itself, while a_{12} represents the ratio of importance for CPU and for memory. Finally, after a series of computation, we would obtain a priority among the alternatives with a value attached to each one of them.

3.4 Risk Analysis

After AHP, we are able to obtain the results of the priority among a list of choices and their weights. We use (ι) to represent the impact of the different choices and the product of impact and success/failure rates to represent risk factors (r). Therefore, we are able to obtain the results of relation between risk and profit with different selection. The curve is the fitting a list of possible choices for users under their preference. The value of curvature F can be presented:

$$F = \int_{\vartheta_m}^{\vartheta_1} r^2(\vartheta)d\vartheta \tag{10}$$

Then, the fitting value can be presented:

$$F_n = \int_{\vartheta_m}^{\vartheta_1} r^2(\vartheta)d\vartheta \tag{11}$$

The value of profit is within the range $[\vartheta_1, \vartheta_m]$. Generally, risk and profit are positively related. The choices of low risk and high profits in Fig. 3 are the ones we try to recommend in our results, while the opposite ones are not. More discussion will be presented in Sect. 5.

Table 1. Instance profiles

Label	Instance type	Cores	Memory	Pricing type	Price($/H)
T1	n1-standard-64	64	240 GB	On-demand	3.0400
				Spot	[0.5760,0.7040]
T2	n1-highmem-64	64	416 GB	On-demand	3.7888
				Spot	[0.7200,0.8800]
T3	n1-highcpu-32	32	28 GB	On-demand	1.1344
				Spot	[0.2667,0.3259]
T4	n1-standard-32	32	120 GB	On-demand	1.5200
				Spot	[0.2880,0.3520]
T5	n1-highmem-32	32	32 GB	On-demand	4.5600
				Spot	[0.8640,1.0560]
T6	n1-highmem-16	16	16 GB	On-demand	0.9600
				Spot	[0.1800,0.2200]

4   Setup

As aforementioned, RISC is designed to find the risk-benefit frontier for instance selections. In this section, we provide our simulation setup for evaluating RISC using Google Cluster Traces [3]. The trace contains data from 12.5k-machine cell over about a month-long period in May 2011. To further illustrate the benefit of using RISC , we perform multiple tests of running RISC with many baselines, using workloads with different distributions.

Table 1 shows profiles of different types of Google instances. For their spot instances, we report 0.4751$/H on average across all instances. Spot instances were 68% cheaper than their regular on-demand instances. The average lifetime of a spot instance was 36 min and prices between sites were not correlated, as previously shown in Fig. 2(c).

Simulation Setup: We built a testbed to first illustrate the runtime performance of RISC using Google traces. The simulation testbed contains AHP simulator based on real-world user traces. *Super Decisions* [4] is our decision support software that implements the Analytic Hierarchy Process (AHP). *Super Decisions* help to simulate different decision-making methods that decompose the factors involved into the different hierarchy: machine profiles, workload statistics, and alternatives. Based on different criteria, we are able to obtain the sets of reduced choices among the alternatives to achieve the target benefit. Our Matlab application simulates the whole loop of RISC, while calculating all metrics during the simulation.

Software Setup: The operating system is built as CentOS 7 (kernel version 3.10.0). The experiments are built based on a client-server model, as shown in Fig. 1. The client sends batched workloads periodically or continuously to show the functionality of RISC and other baselines. In this paper, we mainly evaluate RISC with the following baselines:

- **Original** shows the original decision and its impact from traces;
- **Simple RISC** is our RISC without the AHP process;

Workloads and Traces: We verify the performance of RISC using real world workloads and traces. We use the popular cluster trace: Google [3]. Workloads are simple reads/writes, with different CPU/memory demand, arrived in Poisson distribution, as intensive workload (*Workload1) and skewed workload (*Workload2). We define customers' decision patterns as follows:

- *Aggressive* users always choose the highest risk decision along the frontier.
- *Conservative* users always choose the lowest risk decision along the frontier.
- *Random* users choose selection randomly.

Next, we provide our analysis of running RISC with over 1 million queries.

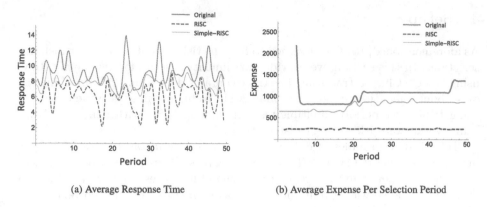

(a) Average Response Time   (b) Average Expense Per Selection Period

Fig. 4. 50 h performance snapshots between RISC and alternatives in Google traces.

5 Evaluation

We evaluate RISC on Google traces that lease both spot/on-demand instances. The simulation allows us to study RISC while spot prices change. Noting that, we do not control the spot price change but use the spot price history instead. We have already shown the candidate node profiles in Table 1. We compare RISC to other systems to show that (1) RISC costs less than widely used alternatives and (2) RISC contributes to both customers and cloud service providers (CSPs). Below, we describe baseline systems associated with each category above. For the remainder of this paper, we will refer to each baseline using italicized words.

A 50-H Performance Analysis. In Fig. 4, we highlight the performance of RISC , we compare it to *Simple-Risc* and *Original*, using a continuous 50 h trace data, (5th to 7th May 2011, to be exact). In Fig. 4(a), we observe that RISC shifts the selected instances significantly. Sometimes, RISC can have a much lower response time than *Simple-Risc* and *Original* (e.g., around period 4 and 18), due to the performance boost from serving queries on more spot instances. However, if spot instances fail, jobs are routed to other on-demand instances, causing the sharp response time increase (e.g., around period 18 to 20). By carefully selecting the variable leasing number of spot instances. Illustrated in Fig. 4(b), RISC can significantly reduce expenses. RISC cuts the cost up to 83.7% when selecting good spot candidates under certain risk during period 1–4. The average per-period expense of RISC is 2.41\$/H per selected instance set. While *Simple-Risc* and *Original* cost about 7.89\$/H and 11.33\$/H per selected instance set, respectively. In another word, given the same budget, RISC can scale up 70% to 80% more nodes, than *Simple-Risc* and *Original*, respectively.

Expense/Performance Comparison. Figure 5 shows statistical expense and performance comparison between RISC and both baselines. On the performance side, we examine the mean, 25th-percentile, and 75th-percentile response time of all queries as the latency metric. Figure 5(a) shows that RISC has lowest

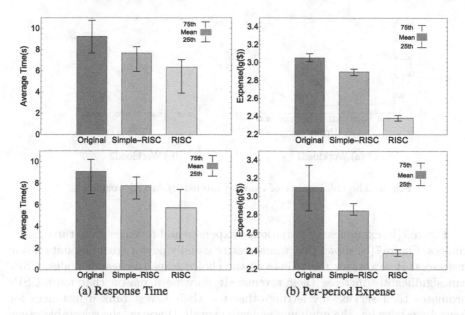

Fig. 5. Performance/Expense comparison in *Workload1* (first row) and *Workload2* (second row)

response time on both workloads, but with higher variance in the collected data, which is within 21% and 10% of *Original* and *Simple-RISC*, respectively.

As shown in Fig. 5(b), RISC is 36% lower than *Original* and 24% lower than *Simple-Risk* under the skewed *Workload1*. The cost savings increase under the intensive *Workload2*. In both cases, we observe that workload misprediction causes significant impact on expenses of instance selection.

User Decision Impact. Figure 6 describes the output of our AHP model. Every dot represents a candidate of instance selection in the solution space running *Workload1* and *Workload2*, as Fig. 6(a) and 6(b), respectively. We created the frontier from the collected AHP outputs. The x-axis captures the possible gain from satisfying SLOs while minimizing the expense. The y-axis captures the mean risk factors. Points along the frontier maximize the mean-to-variation, thus are all good indicators for instance configuration.

Based on the analyzed frontier, we evaluate behavior from different user patterns, like *Conservative, Random,* and *Aggressive.* Figure 7(a) describes curves of different choices made by all three types of users in term of risks and total revenues. As it is shown, the possible revenue gain from *Conservative* is rather limited. Meanwhile, it is evident that *Aggressive* can provide highest revenues to CSPs by 5X and 3X, as compared to *Conservative* and *Random,* respectively. However, he or she must sustain the possible high risk of failures and violation of SLOs.

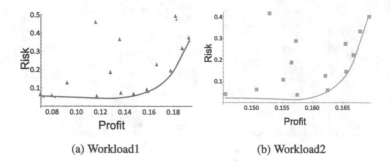

Fig. 6. The risk frontier of running intensive/skewed workloads.

Figure 7(b) examines the variation of expenses and revenues from three users' choices. Figure 7(b) shows that *Conservative* usually pays a great amount on safe instances. However, for most times, if the choice leans to cheaper nodes, CSPs can significantly increase their revenue. It may be a reason that most CSPs promotes their services by letting other use their lowest ranked instances for free. *Aggressive* has the minimum expense overall. However, the selectable range is rather small, as compared to *random*. Our results suggest CSPs shall advise customers to be more aggressive during the selection, even with a higher risk to fail.

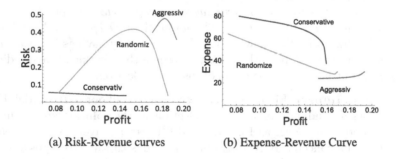

Fig. 7. Impact of different user decision patterns.

Overall Server-Side Statistics. Figure 8 demonstrates the number of instances leased and the job distribution onto these instances under RISC. RISC prefers instances with larger memory and the medium number of cores, and medium price among all six types of instances. As jobs are fairly distributed among all selected instances, the job distribution almost converges to the distribution of instance selections. As shown in Fig. 8(b), although some instances are rarely selected, jobs assigned to these nodes are fit based on their resource capacity. Thus, the average response time from all six types of instances is fairly close. RISC can provide a fair selection with a good tradeoff between expense

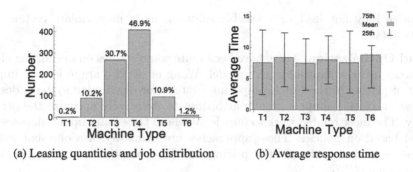

(a) Leasing quantities and job distribution   (b) Average response time

Fig. 8. Server-side statistics under RISC .

and risk. If (1) the underline machine statistics are correct or predictable, such as queuing theory analysis, and (2) users can tolerate the certain range of risks when processing their jobs onto the cloud. Better workload prediction algorithms could lead to increased resource utilization, thus a better selection suggestion to users.

6   Related Work

Risk assessment in cloud markets is a relatively new topic in the cloud pricing market. It is hard to evaluate the users' perspective from the cloud service provider side. Our work tries to fill the gap in-between. Although there is no closely related work, this is a inter-disciplinary research across several topics:

Risk Assessment in Cloud: International Organization for Standardization (ISO) published the ISO 31000 [22] on Risk Management Standard for data centers. This standard mainly describes the risk of building a data center for cloud services, and privacy/security concerns. All incidents, including the level of risk on the basis of the likelihood of a risk scenario mapped against the estimated negative impact, are widely discussed in [6,14,15]. Compared with these related work, our work focuses on the runtime instance selection. By analyzing the impact from selecting certain cloud instances, RISC can obtain the risk and profit frontier for all possible decisions.

Pricing in Cloud: Pricing is the process of determining what a service provider will receive from an end user in exchange for their services [7,17,20]. When it comes to cloud business, pricing strategies could be affected by many factors, such as the average usage, the total time of usage, the user demand, and many other. Research on pricing in cloud markets started arguably from the work of Wang's Hotcloud work [25]. The majority price modelling and optimization work are contributed in research, starting from Li [29]. There is certainly much prior work on pricing in computer networks [7]. The survey by Gohad et al. [12] provides a useful overview of the field. Our work considers pricing dynamics, as a significant impact on the users' selections. However, judging solely on optimizing the price may not lead to a feasible solution, as it may violate certain risk constraints.

Cloud Optimization: There have been quite some studies on optimizing cloud resources using a multi-objective model. Wang et al. [25] argue for the importance of pricing in the cloud computing context for distributed systems design. Macias et al. [17] adopt a genetic algorithm to iteratively optimize the pricing policy. The most related work to ours is [8] where they build up a risk assessing model based on policies. These approaches are primarily of a one-shot nature without considering the effect of pricing and SLO adaptivity on future demand and revenue [?,?,?].

7   Conclusion and Future Work

In cloud markets, computing resources are selling as products to fill users' computation requirement. In IaaS, users may under-provision or over-provision instances, which would lead to either the risk of failing in SLOs or the reduction in profits. Our work puts forward a new approach to evaluate user choices while satisfying SLOs and expenses reduction to the utmost extent. We use server-side statistics to analyse user choices on purchasing the products. In our system, RISC, we use the AHP method to analyze the selection-related criterion, and provide the priority order, based on runtime statistics. Together with a feedback system, RISC forms a mechanism to build the risk assessment in cloud markets. We evaluate RISC with datasets from Google Clusters, and find that RISC can increase the overall revenue for cloud providers by 5X while reducing the expenses from users down by 83.7%. Some immediate future work would be deploy RISC on top of a real cloud platform, such as Tencent Cloud, Amazon AWS services, or Google Cloud. Meanwhile, we will prototype the system onto a real physical testbed, to verify the impact from more workloads and collect underline profiles.

Acknowledgement. This research was supported by the grant from the Tencent Rhino Grant award (11002675), by the grant from the National Science Foundation China (NSFC) (617022501006873), and by the grant from Jiangxi Province Science Foundation for Youths (708237400050).

References

1. Analytic hierarchy process. https://www.dii.unisi.it/~mocenni/Note_AHP.pdf
2. Google cloud. https://cloud.google.com/compute/pricing
3. Google cluster. https://github.com/google/cluster-data
4. Super decisions. https://www.superdecisions.com
5. Ahmad, F., Vijaykumar, T.N.: Joint optimization of idle and cooling power in data centers while maintaining response time. In: Architectural Support for Programming Languages and Operating Systems, vol. 45, no. 3, pp. 243–256 (2010)

6. Brender, N., Markov, I.: Risk perception and risk management in cloud computing: results from a case study of swiss companies. Int. J. Inf. Manag. **33**(5), 726–733 (2013)
7. Cao, X.R., Shen, H.X., Milito, R., Wirth, P.: Internet pricing with a game theoretical approach: concepts and examples. IEEE/ACM Trans. Netw. **10**(2), 208–216 (2002)
8. Cayirci, E., Garaga, A., Santana, A., Roudier, Y.: A cloud adoption risk assessment model. In: 2014 IEEE/ACM 7th International Conference on Utility and Cloud Computing (UCC), pp. 908–913. IEEE (2014)
9. Cloud, A.E.C.: Amazon web services (2011). Accessed 9 Nov 2011
10. Coffman, G.E., Garey, M.R., Johnson, D.S.: An application of bin-packing to multiprocessor scheduling. SIAM J. Comput. **7**(1), 1–17 (1978)
11. Drissi, S., Houmani, H., Medromi, H.: Survey: risk assessment for cloud computing. Int. J. Adv. Comput. Sci. Appl. **4**(12), 143–148 (2013)
12. Gohad, A., Narendra, N.C., Ramachandran, P.: Cloud pricing models: a survey and position paper. In: 2013 IEEE International Conference on Cloud Computing in Emerging Markets (CCEM), pp. 1–8. IEEE (2013)
13. Jin, H., Wang, X., Wu, S., Di, S., Shi, X.: Towards optimized fine-grained pricing of IaaS cloud platform. IEEE Int. Conf. Cloud Comput. Technol. Sci. **3**(4), 436–448 (2015)
14. Kaplan, S., Garrick, B.J.: On the quantitative definition of risk. Risk Anal. **1**(1), 11–27 (1981)
15. Latif, R., Abbas, H., Assar, S., Ali, Q.: Cloud computing risk assessment: a systematic literature review. In: Park, J., Stojmenovic, I., Choi, M., Xhafa, F. (eds.) Future Information Technology. LNEE, vol. 276, pp. 285–295. Springer, Berlin (2014). https://doi.org/10.1007/978-3-642-40861-8_42
16. Luko, S.N.: Risk assessment techniques. Qual. Eng. **26**(3), 379–382 (2014)
17. Macías, M., Guitart, J.: A genetic model for pricing in cloud computing markets. In: Proceedings of the 2011 ACM Symposium on Applied Computing, pp. 113–118. ACM (2011)
18. Miller, L., Mcelvaine, M.D., Mcdowell, R.M., Ahl, A.S.: Developing a quantitative risk assessment process. Rev. Sci. Tech. OIE **12**(4), 1153–1164 (1993)
19. Mishra, A.K., Hellerstein, J.L., Cirne, W., Das, C.R.: Towards characterizing cloud backend workloads: insights from google compute clusters. ACM SIGMETRICS Perform. Eval. Rev. **37**(4), 34–41 (2010)
20. Paschalidis, I.C., Tsitsiklis, J.N.: Congestion-dependent pricing of network services. IEEE/ACM Trans. Netw. **8**(2), 171–184 (2000)
21. Peiyu, L., Dong, L.: The new risk assessment model for information system in cloud computing environment. Procedia Eng. **15**, 3200–3204 (2011)
22. Purdy, G.: Raising the standard-the new ISO risk management standard. In: Wellington Meeting (2009)
23. Scaling, A.A.: Auto scaling. Amazon Web Services Inc. (2013)
24. Susan Moore, R.v.d.M.: Gartner forecasts worldwide public cloud revenue to grow 21.4 percent in 2018, April 2018. https://www.gartner.com/newsroom/id/3871416
25. Wang, H., Jing, Q., He, B., Qian, Z., Zhou, L.: Distributed systems meet economics: pricing in the cloud (2010)
26. Ward, B.T., Sipior, J.C.: The internet jurisdiction risk of cloud computing. Inf. Syst. Manag. **27**(4), 334–339 (2010)
27. Wilder, B.: Cloud Architecture Patterns: Using Microsoft Azure. O'Reilly Media Inc, Cambridge (2012)

28. Xie, F., Peng, Y., Zhao, W., Chen, D., Wang, X., Huo, X.: A risk management framework for cloud computing. In: 2012 IEEE 2nd International Conference on Cloud Computing and Intelligent Systems (CCIS), vol. 1, pp. 476–480. IEEE (2012)
29. Xu, H., Li, B.: Maximizing revenue with dynamic cloud pricing: the infinite horizon case. In: 2012 IEEE International Conference on Communications (ICC), pp. 2929–2933. IEEE (2012)
30. Zhao, H., Pan, M., Liu, X., Li, X., Fang, Y.: Optimal resource rental planning for elastic applications in cloud market. In: 2012 IEEE 26th International Parallel & Distributed Processing Symposium (IPDPS), pp. 808–819. IEEE (2012)
31. Zhao, H., Pan, M., Liu, X., Li, X., Fang, Y.: Exploring fine-grained resource rental planning in cloud computing. IEEE Trans. Cloud Comput. **3**(3), 304–317 (2015)
32. Zheng, L., Joewong, C., Tan, C.W., Chiang, M., Wang, X.: How to bid the cloud. In: ACM Special Interest Group on Data Communication, vol. 45, no. 4, pp. 71–84 (2015)

Real-Time Data Stream Partitioning over a Sliding Window in Real-Time Spatial Big Data

Sana Hamdi[1]([⊠]) [iD], Emna Bouazizi[2], and Sami Faiz[3]

[1] Tunisia Polytechnic School, University of Carthage, BP 2078, La Marsa, Tunisia
hamdisana@gmail.com
[2] MIRACL Laboratory, University of Sfax, BP 1088, 3018 Sfax, Tunisia
emna.bouazizi@gmail.com
[3] LTSIRS Laboratory, BP 37, Le Belvedere, 1002 Tunis, Tunisia
sami.faiz@insat.rnu.tn

Abstract. In recent years, real-time spatial applications, like location-aware services and traffic monitoring, have become more and more important. Such applications result in dynamic environments where data, as well as queries, are continuously moving. As a result, there is a tremendous amount of real-time spatial data generated every day. The growth of the data volume seems to outspeed the advance of our computing infrastructure. For instance, in real-time spatial Big Data, users expect to receive the results of each query within a short time period without holding into account the load of the system. But with a huge amount of real-time spatial data generated, the system performance degrades rapidly, especially in overload situations. To solve this problem, we propose the use of data partitioning as an optimization technique. Traditional horizontal and vertical partitioning can increase the performance of the system and simplify data management. But they remain insufficient for real-time spatial Big data; they can't deal with real-time and stream queries efficiently. Thus, in this paper, we propose a novel data partitioning approach over a sliding window in real-time spatial Big Data named VPA-RTSBD (Vertical Partitioning Approach for Real-Time Spatial Big data). This contribution is an implementation of the Matching algorithm for traditional vertical partitioning. We find, firstly, the optimal attributes sequence by the use of the Matching algorithm. Then, we propose a new cost model used for database partitioning, for keeping the data amount of each partition more balanced limit and for providing a parallel execution guarantee for the most frequent queries. VPA-RTSBD aims to obtain a real-time partitioning scheme and deals with stream data. It improves the performance of query execution by maximizing the degree of parallel execution. This affects QoS (Quality Of Service) improvement in real-time spatial Big Data especially with a huge volume of stream data. The performance of our contribution is evaluated via simulation experiments. The results show that the proposed algorithm is both efficient and scalable and that it outperforms comparable algorithms.

© Springer Nature Switzerland AG 2018
J. Vaidya and J. Li (Eds.): ICA3PP 2018, LNCS 11334, pp. 75–88, 2018.
https://doi.org/10.1007/978-3-030-05051-1_6

Keywords: Real-time spatial Big Data · Vertical partitioning
Horizontal partitioning · Matching algorithm · Hamming distance
Stream query

1   Introduction

The demand for real-time spatial data has been increasing recently. Nowadays, we are talking about a real-time spatial Big Data that process a large amount of heterogeneous data (may be in the size of terabyte). As a result, the real-time spatial Big Data can be overloaded and many transactions may miss their deadlines because data retrieval processes are time consuming. In order to speed up query processing, several works have proposed many optimization techniques as data partitioning. Therefore, breaking a large table into several smaller units is a necessity.

Data partitioning [23] is a fragment of a logical database into distinct independent units. It is applied in large-scale databases to improve responsiveness, scalability and availability of data. Several works have shown the importance of this approach. But traditional partitioning approaches are not a real time process. Thus, in real-time spatial Big Data, the traditional partitioning technologies have encountered as many problems:

- Traditional partitioning technologies are based on known table structure. They don't have the ability to partition for unknown database in real-time spatial Big Data;
- Traditional partitioning technology can only deal with persistent and stable workload. But the real time spatial Big Data can be overloaded and many transactions may miss their deadlines, or real-time spatial data can be violated.
- Traditional partitioning technologies are unable to adapt to high-throughput in real-time spatial Big Data.

In this paper, we research on the limitations of traditional partitioning technologies. Then, we propose a novel approach to process stream queries in real-time spatial Big Data. This contribution is an implementation of the matching algorithm for traditional vertical partitioning. It uses Hamming distance to produce clusters.

The remainder of this paper is organized as follows: In Sect. 2, we introduce some related works. In the Sect. 3, we introduce our contribution. The simulation model and the results of simulation experiments are given in Sect. 4. The last Section consists of conclusions and some future research directions.

2   Related Works

In this section, we give an overview of real-time spatial Big Data and we discuss pertinent works related to data partitioning approaches.

2.1 System Overview

Real-time spatial applications have a great importance. Such applications continuously receive a huge amount of heterogeneous data from mobile objects (e.g., moving vehicles in road networks). The streaming nature of real-time spatial data poses new challenges that require combining real-time spatial Big Data and data stream management systems.

In this section, we give an overview of heterogeneous real-time spatial data model and transaction model.

Heterogeneous Real-Time Spatial Data Model. Stored data in real-time spatial applications are from heterogeneous sources and are maintained under heterogeneous formats and structures. These data can be divided into two types: the structured data and unstructured data:

– Structured data: can be processed automatically by machines.
– Unstructured data: no common pattern can be used to process for this type of data which come from different sources and have a different format as text, pictures, multimedia content or numeric traces, etc.

Real-time spatial data must be integrated. Structured data and unstructured content are simultaneously accessed via an integrated user interface. The issue of real-time and heterogeneity is extremely important for taking effective decision. As a solution we propose the use of ETL (Extract-Transform-Load) process as follows:

– Data extraction: extracts data from heterogeneous data sources.
– Data transformation: transforms the data for storing it in the proper format or structure for the purposes of querying and analysis.
– Data loading: loads it into the final target (data warehouse).

A real-time spatial data stream distinguishes itself from a traditional real-time data stream in the following: real-time spatial data have the ability to change their locations continuously. Thus, the arrival of a new location information about the data, say p, at some time t_2 ($t_2 > t_1$) may result in expiring the previous location information of p at time t_1. This is in contrast to traditional data where data are expired only after its deadline as it becomes in the system [19].

Transaction Model. Spatial real-time transactions can be classified into two classes: update transactions and user transactions.

– Update transactions: update the values of real-time spatial data in order to reflect the state of the real world.
– User transactions (continuous queries): user requests arrive aperiodically and may read real-time data and non-real-time data. This type of transaction can be executed several times or continuously during a period as required by the user.

2.2   Data Partitioning Approaches

Several surveys on data partitioning algorithm classify them into horizontal and vertical data partitioning methods:

- Horizontal partitioning [2,3,8,9] divides a table into disjoint sets of rows. There are three techniques of horizontal partitioning based on values of data sets (Round-Robin partition, Range partition and Hash partition). Range partitioning is the most popular approach, especially when there is a periodic loading of a new data.
- Vertical partitioning [7,20,21,25–27] divides a table into vertical and disjoint sets of columns. There are two major classes of vertical partitioning:
  - cost-based approach [1,5,13,22]: During this approach, a cost model is constructed to predict the performance of the system for any given configuration. Then, an algorithm enumerating the configuration space is used.
  - procedural approach [17,21,24]: During this approach, there is not a cost model. Procedural approach proposes some kind of a procedure which will result in a good configuration.

Both of these strategies (horizontal partitioning and vertical partitioning) have a significant impact the performance of the database systems, especially with respect to responsiveness, storage and processing cost. But, they still static (they are not able to adapt to dynamic environments) i.e. a configuration is selected once. In case of changes in the workload (new transaction) or the data (new data) the algorithm has to be re-run. Our goal is to adapt the partitioning scheme to a constantly changing workload in real-time spatial Big Data.

In [8], Curino et al. proposed a workload-driven approach named Schism for database partitioning. Schism creates a graph and uses a method called METIS [16] to divide this graph into K balance parts. Schism has a significant impact the performance of the database systems. But it can't deal with the large volume of stream data and with large-scale dynamic queries.

To solve the problem associated with dynamic data partitioning, Liroz-Gistau et al. in [18], have proposed a dynamic workload-based partitioning algorithm for continuously growing databases (like databases used in scientific applications where the data is continually growing to the database). This algorithm defines a mathematical model of dynamic partitioning. This definition is designed with heuristics that considers the affinity of data with queries and fragments. In fact, this approach is quite interesting because the execution time of this algorithm depends only on newly arrived data and not on entire size of the database. But, it is not able to get real-time results after every query.

In this paper [15], Jindal et al. have presented an efficient O^2P (One-dimensional Online Partitioning) algorithm. The main idea of this algorithm is computing the affinity between every pair of attributes and clustering them [6,7,14,20]. Then, it uses a greedy strategy to calculate the cost of every possible split line to get the best partitioning scheme. Actually, the importance of this approach appears clear. But, it must know the table structure in advance which is not available in real-time spatial Big Data. Besides, it can't deal with stream queries and can't get real-time result after every query.

In this paper [10], Guo et al. present a workload-driven stream partitioning system named WSPS to solve the above problems by the integration of partitioning technology and streaming framework. WSPS constructs a dynamic data model, cluster and merge nodes according to the node affinity, then get the optimal partitioning scheme according to a cost model. WSPS can deal with stream data and obtain real-time partitioning scheme. But, it uses distributed queries; a query accessed attributes on different partitions and on several nodes. This costs more resources and the transactions risk to miss their deadlines while waiting for its validation.

3   A Data Partitioning Approach for Real-Time Spatial Big Data

In this Section we describe our contribution. We propose a novel data partitioning approach for real-time spatial Big data; the implementation of the Matching algorithm [4] for vertical partitioning. This algorithm uses Hamming distance to produce clusters.

This approach is divided into three steps that are detailed in the following sections:

- Data model initialization
- Implementation of Matching algorithm
- Data Partitioning.

3.1   Data Model Initialization

Given a query workload W_t which is a stream of queries seen till time t $W_t = \{q_0, q_1, q_2, .., q_t\}$.

Step 1: Assuming that the query q accesses the attribute a, we begin with the definition of the access function as follow:

$$\text{Access(q, a)} = \left\{ \begin{array}{l} 1 \; q \, access \, a \\ 0 \; otherwise \end{array} \right\} \tag{1}$$

Then, we define a matrix M. Rows in the matrix are the attributes accessed by query q $(0 < i < t)$ in the workload W_t and columns are the queries. Each element in the matrix $M[i, j] = $ Access(q_i, a_j) where $i \in [1, t], j \in [1, m]$ and m is the number of attributes accessed by t queries.

Let us consider an example. Suppose that we have five queries accessing six attributes:

q1: SELECT a FROM T WHERE a = 10;
q2: SELECT b, f FROM T WHERE b = f;
q3: SELECT c, d FROM T WHERE a $\geq$ c;
q4: SELECT f FROM T WHERE f $\leq$ 100;
q5: SELECT e FROM T;

In this case, $W_t = \{q_1, q_2, q_3, q_4, q_5\}$ and

$$M = \begin{bmatrix} & a\ b\ c\ d\ e\ f \\ q1 & 1\ 0\ 0\ 0\ 0\ 0 \\ q2 & 0\ 1\ 0\ 0\ 0\ 1 \\ q3 & 0\ 0\ 1\ 1\ 0\ 0 \\ q4 & 0\ 0\ 0\ 0\ 0\ 1 \\ q5 & 0\ 0\ 0\ 0\ 1\ 0 \end{bmatrix}$$

When the sliding window continues, some existing transactions are deleted from the sliding window and some new transactions arrive. Thus, M is dynamically updated at every window. If a new query accesses to attributes already exist in M, only a new row will be added at the end. If the query accesses to new attributes not exist in M, a new row will be added at the end and new columns will be added to the matrix on the right. If an existing query is deleted from the sliding window, the row of this query and the attributes acceded only by this query have to be deleted.

3.2 Implementation of Matching Algorithm

This algorithm is developed to reorganize data and to identify clusters [4]. We start with mentioning the different steps of the Matching algorithm:

Step 1: From an m x t matrix array M compute the m x m array $B = M^T * M$

Step 2: Select one of the m rows of $M^T * M$ arbitrarily; set i = 1.

Step 3: Select j = i + 1.

Step 4: Try placing the jth row in each of the (i + 1) positions. Compute the sum $\phi = \sum_{i=1}^{m-1} b_{i,i+1}$ where $b_{i,i+1}$ is the element in the intersection fo the ith row and the $(i+1)^{th}$ column of the matrix array B

Step 5: j = j + 1 and repeat Step 4 until j = m.

Step 6: Place the row k in the position where the maximum value of ϕ is obtained, i + 1 $\leq$ k $\leq$ m,

Step 7: i = i + 1 and repeat steps 3, 4, 5, 6 and 7 till $i = m$

We use the same matrix M in our previous example and we apply the different steps of the Matching algorithm as follow:

$$
B = \begin{bmatrix}
 & q1 & q2 & q3 & q4 & q5 \\
a & 1 & 0 & 0 & 0 & 0 \\
b & 0 & 1 & 0 & 0 & 0 \\
c & 0 & 0 & 1 & 0 & 0 \\
d & 0 & 0 & 1 & 0 & 0 \\
e & 0 & 0 & 0 & 0 & 1 \\
f & 0 & 1 & 0 & 1 & 0
\end{bmatrix}
\begin{bmatrix}
 & a & b & c & d & e & f \\
q1 & 1 & 0 & 0 & 0 & 0 & 0 \\
q2 & 0 & 1 & 0 & 0 & 0 & 1 \\
q3 & 0 & 0 & 1 & 1 & 0 & 0 \\
q4 & 0 & 0 & 0 & 0 & 0 & 1 \\
q5 & 0 & 0 & 0 & 0 & 1 & 0
\end{bmatrix}
=
\begin{bmatrix}
 & a & b & c & d & e & f \\
a & 1 & 0 & 0 & 0 & 0 & 0 \\
b & 0 & 1 & 0 & 0 & 0 & 1 \\
c & 0 & 0 & 1 & 1 & 0 & 0 \\
d & 0 & 0 & 1 & 1 & 0 & 0 \\
e & 0 & 0 & 0 & 0 & 1 & 0 \\
f & 0 & 1 & 0 & 0 & 0 & 2
\end{bmatrix}
$$

Initially, $\phi = \sum_{i=1}^{5} b_{i,i+1} = 1$

The final reordering given through the application of the algorithm is:

$$
B = \begin{bmatrix}
 & d & c & f & b & a & e \\
d & 1 & 1 & 0 & 0 & 0 & 0 \\
c & 1 & 1 & 0 & 0 & 0 & 0 \\
f & 0 & 0 & 2 & 1 & 0 & 0 \\
b & 0 & 0 & 1 & 1 & 0 & 0 \\
a & 0 & 0 & 0 & 0 & 1 & 0 \\
e & 0 & 0 & 0 & 0 & 0 & 1
\end{bmatrix}
\qquad \phi = \sum_{i=1}^{5} b_{i,i+1} = 2
$$

The optimal attributes sequence $Oas = \{d, c, f, b, a, e\}$. Every time a new query comes, the matrix M is calculated, then the new OaS is dynamically created.

3.3 Data Partitioning

The main objective of the vertical partitioning approach in real-time spatial Big Data is to improve the performance of query execution and the system throughput. The high performance of query execution is related to minimizing the access cost of data partitions. Especially that the frequency of accessing data on different partitions is a major factor to affect the query execution cost. Thus, it is very important to minimize this frequency for the high performance of query execution.

The improvement of the system throughput can be achieved by maximizing the degree of parallel execution. We can improve this degree if we can minimize the frequency of interfered accesses between data queries.

As a result, we can define the cost model that reflects both objectives of vertical partitioning mentioned above as follow:

$$
\text{Cost}(q_i, P(W_t, Oas_t)) = \left| \sum_{L(q_i) \subseteq L'} (\alpha C(q_i) + I(q_i)) \times |L'| - \sum_{L(q_i) \subseteq L - L'} (\alpha C(q_i) + I(q_i)) \times |L - L'| \right|
$$

(2)

where:

- $P(W_t, Oas_t)$ is a partitioning scheme over OaS of workload W on the time t.

- $L(q_i$ is a collection of attributes the query q visited.
- A partition line splits the OaS into two sets L' and L-L'.
- $C(q_i)$ is the access number of q_i.
- $I(q_i)$ is the interfered access number of q_i.
- α is a proportional constant between $C(q_i)$ and $I(q_i)$, $\alpha > 1$.

Our objective is to find the split vector SV that minimize the execution cost, which is defined as follows:

$$SV = \arg\ \min(\mathrm{Cost}(q_i, P(W_t, Oas_t)) \tag{3}$$

3.4 Algorithm Analysis

The characteristics of $VPA - RTSBD$:

- it deals with stream data; there is no need to have all queries before partitioning.
- it improves the performance of query execution.
- it improves the system throughput by maximizing the degree of parallel execution.
- it can get real-time result after every query: a real-time partitioning scheme.

We compare the following properties: best time complexity, worst time complexity, real-time processing, workload type, table structure of $VPA - RTSBD$ with $WSPS$, $Schism$ and O^2P (Table 1).

Table 1. Algorithm comparison.

	VPA-RTSBD	WSPS	Schism	O^2P
Real-time processing	Yes	Yes	No	No
Stream processing	Yes	Yes	No	No
Workload type	Dynamic/static	Dynamic/static	Static	Static
Table structure	Unknown/known	Unknown/known	Known	Known
Best time complexity	O(n)	O(n)	-	O(n)
Worst time complexity	O(n)	O(n)	-	$O(n^2)$
Optimize queries processing	Yes	Yes	-	-
Optimize system throughput	Yes	No	-	-

Although VPA-RTSBD is the best in its comparison with $WSPS$, $Schism$ and O^2P, the split vector calculation becomes time-consuming especially when the number of partitions grows.

4   Simulation Results

In this section, we give our simulation model. Then, we compare the result of VPA-RTSBD and the result of the traditional partitioning approaches like $WSPS$, $Schism$ and O^2P.

4.1   Simulation Model

In order to access the performance of our proposed approach, we have implemented a simulator in Java, which describes the architecture FCSA-RTSBD (Feedback Control Scheduling Architecture for Real-Time Spatial Big Data) [11] as shown in Fig. 1.

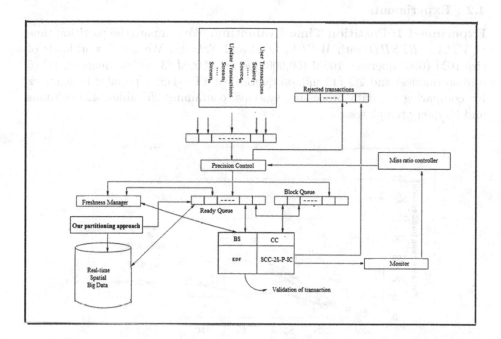

Fig. 1. Simulation model.

In our system, a transaction T_i is associated with a deadline D_i, period P_i, start time R_i, end time E_i and Execution Time Estimation ETE_i. Update transactions arrive periodically and the arrival of user transactions is defined using the Poisson distribution given by the following formula:

$$F_x(t) = \left\{ \begin{matrix} e^{-t} & x > 0 \\ 0 & otherwise \end{matrix} \right\} \tag{4}$$

T_i is continually evaluated for stream data belonging to a window whose size is defined by either the period P_i or number of the data received most recently.

Real-time spatial transactions have scheduled transactions, according to the Earliest Deadline First (EDF) algorithm. Transaction handler consists of a concurrency controller (CC) by the use of the algorithm SCC-2S-P-IC [12], a freshness manager (FM) and a basic scheduler. A transaction can be aborted and restarted by CC. Freshness manager (FM) checks the freshness of real-time data before the initiation of a user transaction. If the accessing data is currently stale,

FM blocks the corresponding transaction will be transferred from the block queue to the ready queue as soon as the corresponding data is put up to date.

Simulation results are measured by the monitor periodically. Miss ratio Controllers and precision control compute the miss ratio and utilization control signals based on the obtained results.

4.2   Experiments

Experiment 1: Partition Time Evaluating. We compare the partition time of $VPA - RTSBD$ with $WSPS$, O^2P and $Schism$. We use 5 workloads of size 10M (6000 queries), 100M (60,000 queries), 500M (3 million queries), 1G (6 million queries) and 2G (12 million queries) of TPC-DS; a popular benchmark for comparing big data processing systems, containing 25 tables, 429 columns and 99 query templates.

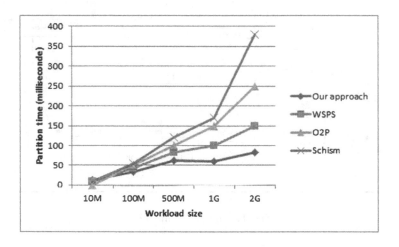

Fig. 2. Partition time of TPC-DS.

By analyzing the result in Fig. 2, we can find, firstly, that when the workload size is increasing, the partition time is increasing also for all algorithms. In other hand, although $VPA - RTSBD$ keeps a query window which means partitioning is done after every N queries contrarily $WSPS$ partitioning is done after every query, $VPA - RTSBD$ and $WSPS$ have the same computing complexity and the partition time of our approach is significantly lower than $WSPS$.

Schism and O^2P can't deal with the large volume of stream data and with large-scale dynamic queries. So, they have the worst partition time.

Experiment 2: High-Throughput Adaption. We use a workload size of 500M and we generate data at different rates (from 0.5G/s to 5G/s). The objective of this experiment is to evaluate the ability of the high-throughput adaption. The result is as shown in Fig. 3.

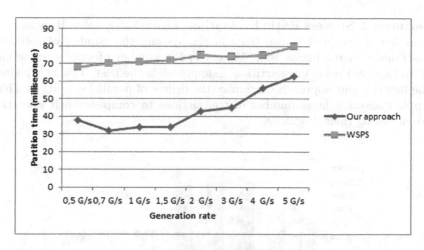

Fig. 3. High-throughput control.

By analyzing the result, we can find that the rate of generating data affects the partition time for both algorithms $WSPS$ and $VPA - RTSBD$. But our approach has the ability to adapt to high-throughput better than $WSPS$. So, the importance of $VPA - RTSBD$ appears clear; it can deal well when facing with large-scale stream queries.

Experiment 3: Total Running Time Evaluating. Figure 4 presents the total running time of our simulator on all 20 queries of the benchmark TPC-DS with a dataset size fixed to 1 TBytes. For all queries, FCSA-RTSBD with partitioning approach outperforms FCSA-RTSBD with partitioning approach for all types of queries. The importance of our partitioning approach appears clear because partitioning algorithm improves responsiveness, scalability and availability of data.

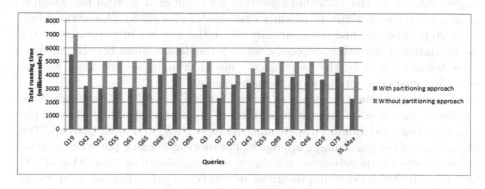

Fig. 4. Evaluation on all queries using 1 TB data.

Experiment 4: Success Ratio Evaluating. Figure 5 shows that If we increase the number of accepted transactions in the system, the number of validated transactions is increasing as well. Moreover, the number of valid transactions (user and update) using our partitioning approach is the best. This is explained by the fact that our approach maximizes the degree of parallel execution. Thus, this policy allows a large number of transactions to complete their execution before achieving their deadlines.

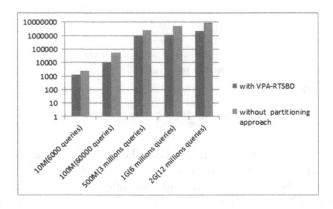

Fig. 5. Success ratio evaluating.

5   Conclusion

In this paper, we have researched on the limitations of traditional partitioning technologies. Then, we have proposed $VPA - RTSBD$ a novel approach to process stream queries in real-time spatial Big Data. This contribution is an implementation of the Matching algorithm for traditional vertical partitioning. It uses Hamming distance to produce clusters. $VPA - RTSBD$ is divided into three steps: first, we find automatically the initial number of partitions by the use of Matching algorithm. Secondly, we keep the data amount of each partition more balanced limit by the use of a cost model. Finally, we provide a parallel execution guarantee for the most frequent queries.

A simulation study is shown to prove that $VPA - RTSBD$ can achieve a significant performance improvement in terms of success ratio, high-throughput adaption and total running time compared to $WSPS$, O^2P and $Schism$. The importance of our partitioning approach appears clear because partitioning algorithm improves responsiveness, scalability and availability of data. This affects QoS (Quality Of Service) improvement in real-time spatial Big Data especially with a huge number of data and transactions.

As follow, we have to find more policies for QoS improvement in a large-scale real-time spatial data. The most important requirements for these data structures are the ability of providing fast access to the large volumes of data. Thus, we shall find new techniques for the data indexing. Another future work consists of relaxing transaction real-time constraints (ACID) by allowing the loss of some invocations.

References

1. Agrawal, S., Narasayya, V., Yang, B.: Integrating vertical and horizontal partitioning into automated physical database design. In: Proceedings of the 2004 ACM SIGMOD International Conference on Management of Data, pp. 359–370. ACM, June 2004
2. Ahirrao, S., Ingle, R.: Scalable transactions in cloud data stores. J. Cloud Comput.: Adv. Appl. **4**, 1–14 (2015). SpringerOpen
3. Bernstein, P.A., et al.: Adapting microsoft SQL server for cloud computing. In: 2011 IEEE 27th International Conference on Data Engineering (ICDE), pp. 1255–1263. IEEE, April 2011
4. Bhat, M.V., Haupt, A.: An efficient clustering algorithm. IEEE Trans. Syst. Man Cybern. **1**, 61–64 (1976)
5. Chu, W.W., Ieong, I.T.: A transaction-based approach to vertical partitioning for relational database systems. IEEE Trans. Softw. Eng. **19**(8), 804–812 (1993)
6. Comer, D.W., Philip, S.Y.: A vertical partitioning algorithm for relational databases. In: 1987 IEEE Third International Conference on Data Engineering, pp. 30–35. IEEE, February 1987
7. Cornell, D.W., Yu, P.S.: An effective approach to vertical partitioning for physical design of relational databases. IEEE Trans. Softw. Eng. **16**(2), 248–258 (1990)
8. Curino, C., Jones, E., Zhang, Y., Madden, S.: Schism: a workload-driven approach to database replication and partitioning. Proc. VLDB Endow. **3**(1–2), 48–57 (2010)
9. Das, S., El Abbadi, A., Agrawal, D.: ElasTraS: an elastic transactional data store in the cloud. HotCloud **9**, 131–142 (2009)
10. Guo, M., Kang, H.: The implementation of database partitioning based on streaming framework. In: 2016 13th Web Information Systems and Applications Conference, pp. 157–162. IEEE, September 2016
11. Hamdi, S., Bouazizi, E., Faiz, S.: A new QoS management approach in real-time GIS with heterogeneous real-time geospatial data using a feedback control scheduling. In: Proceedings of the 19th International Database Engineering & Applications Symposium, pp. 174–179. ACM (2015)
12. Hamdi, S., Bouazizi, E., Faiz, S.: A speculative concurrency control in real-time spatial big data using real-time nested spatial transactions and imprecise computation. In: 2017 IEEE/ACS 14th International Conference on Computer Systems and Applications (AICCSA), pp. 534-540. IEEE, October 2017
13. Hammer, M., Niamir, B.: A heuristic approach to attribute partitioning. In: Proceedings of the 1979 ACM SIGMOD International Conference on Management of Data, pp. 93–101. ACM, May 1979
14. Hoffer, J.A., Severance, D.G. : The use of cluster analysis in physical data base design. In: Proceedings of the 1st International Conference on Very Large Data Bases, pp. 69–86. ACM, September 1975
15. Jindal, A., Dittrich, J.: Relax and let the database do the partitioning online. In: Castellanos, M., Dayal, U., Lehner, W. (eds.) BIRTE 2011. LNBIP, vol. 126, pp. 65–80. Springer, Heidelberg (2012). https://doi.org/10.1007/978-3-642-33500-6_5

16. Karypis, G., Kumar, V.: METIS-unstructured graph partitioning and sparse matrix ordering system, version 2.0. (1995)
17. Lin, X., Orlowska, M., Zhang, Y.: A graph based cluster approach for vertical partitioning in database design. Data Knowl. Eng. **11**(2), 151–169 (1993)
18. Liroz-Gistau, M., Akbarinia, R., Pacitti, E., Porto, F., Valduriez, P.: Dynamic workload-based partitioning for large-scale databases. In: Liddle, S.W., Schewe, K.-D., Tjoa, A.M., Zhou, X. (eds.) DEXA 2012. LNCS, vol. 7447, pp. 183–190. Springer, Heidelberg (2012). https://doi.org/10.1007/978-3-642-32597-7_16
19. Mokbel, M.F., Xiong, X., Aref, W.G., Hambrusch, S.E., Prabhakar, S., Hammad, M.A.: PALACE: a query processor for handling real-time spatio-temporal data streams. In: Proceedings of the Thirtieth International Conference on Very Large Data Bases-Volume 30, VLDB Endowment, August, pp. 1377–1380 (2004)
20. Navathe, S., Ceri, S., Wiederhold, G., Dou, J.: Vertical partitioning algorithms for database design. ACM Trans. Database Syst. (TODS) **9**(4), 680–710 (1984)
21. Navathe, S.B., Ra, M.: Vertical partitioning for database design: a graphical algorithm. In: ACM Sigmod Record, vol. 18, no. 2, pp. 440–450. ACM, June 1989
22. Papadomanolakis, S., Ailamaki, A.: An integer linear programming approach to database design. In: 2007 IEEE 23rd International Conference on Data Engineering Workshop, pp. 442–449. IEEE, April 2007
23. Phansalkar, S., Ahirrao, S.: Survey of data partitioning algorithms for big data stores. In: 2016 Fourth International Conference on Parallel, Distributed and Grid Computing (PDGC), pp. 163–168. IEEE, December 2016
24. Rodríguez, L., Li, X.: A support-based vertical partitioning method for database design. In: 2011 8th International Conference on Electrical Engineering Computing Science and Automatic Control (CCE), pp. 1–6. IEEE, October 2011
25. Shraddha Phansalkar, D.A.: Transaction aware vertical partitioning of database (TAVPD) for responsive OLTP applications in cloud data stores. J. Theor. Appl. Inf. Technol. **59**(1), 73–81 (2014)
26. Son, J.H., Kim, M.H.: An adaptable vertical partitioning method in distributed systems. J. Syst. Softw. **73**(3), 551–561 (2004)
27. Zhao, W., Cheng, Y., Rusu, F.: Workload-driven vertical partitioning for effective query processing over raw data. (2015)

A Priority and Fairness Mixed
Compaction Scheduling Mechanism
for LSM-tree Based KV-Stores

Lidong Chen[1,2], Yinliang Yue[1,2(✉)], Haobo Wang[1,2], and Jianhua Wu[3]

[1] Institute of Information Engineering, Chinese Academy of Sciences, Beijing, China
yueyinliang@iie.ac.cn
[2] School of Cyber Security, University of Chinese Academy of Sciences,
Beijing, China
[3] Tencent TEG, Shenzhen, China

Abstract. Key-value (KV) stores have become a backbone of large-scale applications in today's data centers. Write-optimized data structures like the Log-Structured Merge-tree (LSM-tree) and their variants are widely used in KV storage systems. Conventional LSM-tree organizes KV items into multiple, successively larger components, and uses compaction to push KV items from one smaller component to another adjacent larger component until the KV items reach the largest component. Unfortunately, LSM-tree has severe file retention phenomenon. File retention phenomenon means that lots of SSTables locate in one component and then too many SSTables are involved in one compaction, which causes one compaction occupies long time and causes front-end writing pauses or even stops frequently. We propose a new compaction scheduling scheme called Slot, and implement it on LevelDB. The main idea of Slot is to combine score centric priority based compaction scheduling with time-slice centric fairness based compaction scheduling to alleviate the file retention and then decrease the write amplification of LSM-tree based key/value stores. Slot avoids too many files involved in one compaction and decreases the frequency of write pause or write stop. We conduct extensive evaluations and the experimental results demonstrate that Slot keeps the writing procedure more smoothly and outperforms LevelDB by 20–210% on write throughput without sacrificing the read latency.

Keywords: LSM-tree · KV-Stores · Compaction

1 Introduction

For write-intensive workloads, key-value stores based on Log Structured Merge Trees (LSM-trees) [15] have become the state of the art. Various distributed and local stores built on LSM-trees are widely deployed in large-scale production environments, such as LevelDB [9] at Google, HBase [8] at Facebook and PNUTS

J. Vaidya and J. Li (Eds.): ICA3PP 2018, LNCS 11334, pp. 89–105, 2018.
https://doi.org/10.1007/978-3-030-05051-1_7

[3] at Yahoo. The main advantage of LSM-trees over other indexing structures (such as B-trees) is that they maintain sequential access patterns for writes. Small updates on B-trees may involve many random writes, and are hence not efficient on either solid-state storage devices or hard-disk drives.

To deliver high write performance and decrease the write latency, LSM-tree adopts the lazy-update scheme. LSM-tree batches key-value pairs and writes them sequentially. Subsequently, to enable efficient lookups (for both individual keys as well as range queries), LSM-trees continuously read, sort, and write key-value pairs in the background, thus maintaining keys and values in sorted order. LSM-tree organizes the sorted key/value pairs as fixed size SSTables (Sorted String Table) to facilitate the management and compaction. As a result, one key value pair is read and written multiple times throughout its lifetime and I/O amplification in typical LSM-trees can reach a factor of 20x or higher [13,14].

Several designs have been proposed to solve the write amplification problem of LSM-tree based KV stores. Skip-tree [23] makes the KV items top-down moving much faster via skipping some components. dCompaction [16] is based on the postponement strategy to reduce the write amplification and then speed up the write operations. VT-tree [18] and LWC-tree [22] use the stitching technique to avoid unnecessary data movement. PCP [24] adopted a pipelined compaction procedure to fully utilize both CPUs and I/O devices, in order to speed up the compaction procedure.

LSM-tree based KV-Stores usually have multiple components. In each component, the key/value pairs are organized into multiple SSTables. For example, there are seven levels L0, L1,... L6 in one typical LSM implementation LevelDB. The procedure to merge and sort key/value pairs is called Compaction. We conduct extensive experiments to observe the detailed compaction behaviors. We found that LSM-tree based KV-Stores' score centric priority based compaction scheduling is always concentrated on the first few levels, so it leads to file retention of low levels, and thereby sacrifices the overall write throughput and stability. Although lots of works have been done to decrease the write amplification via various approaches, none of them conclude the file retention problem and optimize the performance of LSM-tree from this view.

In this paper, in order to alleviate the file retention of LSM-tree based KV-Stores, we propose a new compaction scheduling scheme called Slot and implement it on LevelDB which is the representative LSM-tree based KV-Store. The main idea of Slot is to combine score centric priority based compaction scheduling with time-slice centric fairness based compaction scheduling to alleviate the file retention and then decrease the write amplification of LSM-tree based key/value stores. By adopting Priority and Fairness Mixed Compaction scheduling mechanism, compactions do not concentrate on a limited number of low-level components, such as L0 and L1 in the typical key/value store implementation LevelDB. By doing so, Slot avoids too many SSTables involved in one compaction and decreases the frequency of write pause or stop and finally achieves the goal that Slot keeps the write procedure more smoothly and outperforms LevelDB by 20–210% on write throughput without sacrificing the read latency.

The rest of this paper is organized as follows. Section 2 describes the background and motivation, and the overview of our solution is presented in Sect. 3. Section 3 describes the priority and fairness mixed compaction scheduling mechanism which combines score centric priority based compaction scheduling with time-slice centric fairness based compaction scheduling. We show extensive evaluation experiments of Slot in Sect. 4 and investigate related work in Sect. 5. At last, we conclude this paper in Sect. 6.

2 Background and Motivation

In this section, we first explain the design of one typical LSM-tree based KV-Store LevelDB and write pause/stop phenomenon. Secondly, we investigate the serious write amplification of LSM-tree. Then, we describe the file retention problem and score centric priority based compaction scheduling mechanism in LSM-tree based KV-Stores.

2.1 LSM-tree Based KV-Store and Write Pause/Stop Phenomenon

The overall architecture of LSM-tree based KV-Stores is shown in Fig. 1. The main data structures in LSM-tree based KV-Stores are an on-disk log file, two in-memory sorted skiplists (memtable and immutable memtable), and seven levels (L0 to L6) of on-disk Sorted String Table (SSTable) files. LSM-tree organizes KV items into multiple, successively larger components. In the typical LSM-tree implement LevelDB, one level represents one component.

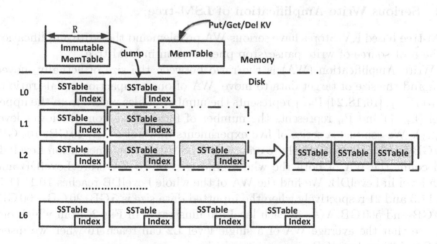

Fig. 1. LSM-tree based KV-Store architecture.

LSM-tree based KV-Stores initially store inserted key-value pairs in a log file and the in-memory memtable. Once the memtable is full, LSM-tree based KV-Stores switches to a new memtable and log file to handle further inserts from the user. The previous memtable is converted into an immutable memtable. In the background, one compaction thread flushes the immutable memtable to the disk and forms a new SSTable file at level 0 (L0). Then the previous log file can be discarded. For the on-disk multiple components, LSM-tree uses compaction to push KV items from one smaller component to another adjacent larger component until the KV items reach the largest component. To make a better description of our experiments and design, we define some symbols in Table 1.

Table 1. Symbols.

Symbol	Meaning
Ln	The nth level of LSM-tree based KV-Stores on disk
Nn	The files number of Ln
Tn	The threshold of file number on Ln
Sn	Sn = Nn/ Tn
RAn/WAn	Read/Write amplification on Ln

We conduct extensive experiments on typical LSM-tree based KV-store LevelDB, and find that there are frequent front-end write pause and write stop phenomena on it. We put 50 GB data into LevelDB, and the frequency of write pauses and stops is 76%.

2.2 Serious Write Amplification of LSM-tree

LSM-tree based KV-Stores have serious WA problem and the write amplification is the root source of write pause/stop phenomenon in LSM-tree.

Write Amplification (WA) is the ratio between the size of actually moved data and the size of target data to move. WA of one compaction equals ratio of P_n to P_{n-1}. [16,18,24] P_{n-1} represents the number of files picked from the upper level (L_{n-1}) and P_n represents the number of files picked from the lower level (L_{n-1}). We conduct a series of five experiments and put 5 GB, 20 GB, 100 GB, 200 GB to 500 GB respectively to one typical LSM-tree implementation LevelDB and count the WA of both the whole LSM-tree based KV-store LevelDB and each level in LevelDB. We find the WA of the whole LevelDB reaches 10.1, 11.7, 14, 17.3 and 21 respectively when the inputted data size is 5 GB, 20 GB, 100 GB, 200 GB and 500 GB. WAs of each level are illustrated in Fig. 2, from which one can see that the average WA of a single level L2 can reach 16 when we insert 500 GB data to LevelDB.

On the one side, there are WA*P_{n-1} SSTables involved in one compaction (WA is a shorthand for Write Amplification). So bigger WA of a compaction means more SSTable files are involved in this compaction, and the compaction needs more time to deal with more files.

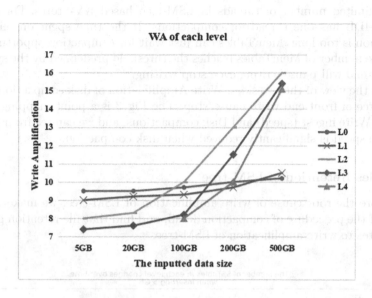

Fig. 2. WA of each level with different inputted data sizes

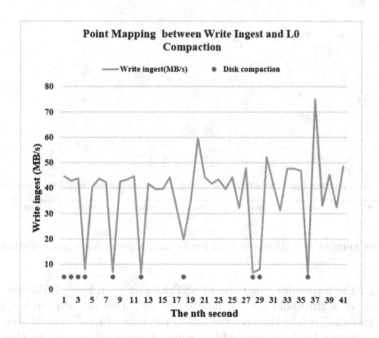

Fig. 3. Point mapping between Write ingest and Disk compaction.

On the other side, MemTables' and different levels' compactions together share a limited number of threads in LSM-tree based KV-Stores. For example, LevelDB has one thread for compactions. If the time spent on one disk compaction is too long, MemTables can just wait for compaction opportunities. When the number of MemTables reaches the threshold predefined by the system, the front-end will pause writing even stop writing.

From the view of the two sides, Write Amplification of disk compaction is the root source of front-end write pause/stop. The Fig. 3 is a point mapping figure between Write ingest (speed) and Disk compactions, and we can see from it that the write speed is significantly reduced when disk compaction.

2.3 Files Retention of LSM-tree

To explore the root cause of write amplification of LSM-tree, we make a deep survey of the procedure of compaction detail, and find that file retention greatly contributes to write amplification of LSM-tree.

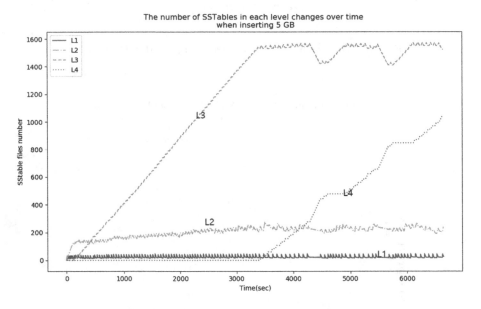

Fig. 4. The number of SSTables in each level changes over time when inserting 5 GB.

To limit the unbounded increase of SSTables on each level, LSM-tree based KV-Stores set a threshold for the number of SSTables of each level, which is listed in Table 2. Tn (the threshold of Ln) is 10* that of Ln-1 in LSM-tree based KV-Stores except for L1's threshold 5, which is nearly the same as the smallest threshold of L0. One can see that there are three thresholds 4, 8 and 12 of L0. When the number of SSTables reaches 4, the compaction between L0 and L1 is triggered. The front-end writes are paused when the number of SSTables increases up to 8, and the front-end writes are stopped when the number of SSTables increases up to 12. Note that the threshold of L0 is much fewer than that of the other levels. Due to the fact that the SSTables in L0 are generated directly from the immutable memtable flushing, the key ranges of all the SSTables are overlapped with each other, thus all the SSTables are involved in the compaction between L0 and L1. Based on this, the threshold of L0 is always set as a relatively small number to avoid the compaction involving too many SSTables. The compaction between L0 and L1 would be triggered once the number of SSTables surpasses the threshold 4 to aggressively push SSTables down to the lower levels. Note that the threshold of L1 is set as 5, which is almost equal to that of L0. The basic motivation of this design point is to avoid the write amplification between L0 and L1. But it contributes to file retention on the lower levels, and we explain the relationship between file retention and the settings of L0 and L1 in the next subsection. Besides, the 10x components' size increasing can lead to a TB-size key/value store.

However, the actual run-time LSM-tree based key/value stores can not reach the ideal aim. We find that the predefined threshold can not really work and can not limit the number of SSTables in the corresponding components.

We conduct experiments to demonstrate the change of the number of SSTables at each level when LevelDB V1.20 (the latest version) writes 5 GB, 20 GB and 100 GB data.

From the experimental results, which is shown in Figs. 4 and 5, one can get the following two conclusions. The one is that the thresholds of each level do not effectively limit the actual number of SSTables on corresponding levels, the other is that the average SSTable number involved in each level's compaction is much larger than the theoretical value 11 [15,16,23].

As one can see from Fig. 4, after the SSTables number of L3 (N3) exceeds T3 (500) at the time point of 1213th second, L3 delays the compaction more than 2250 s instead of immediately performing a compaction, which can be seen from the fact that L4 begins to have SSTables after the 3300th second. The number of SSTables in L3 reaches 1527 at the 3300th second, which is a serious file retention. The file retention in L3 results in serious write amplification of L2, and the reason is that lots of SSTables in L3 are involved in the compactions between L2 and L3. In detail, the average WA of L2 reaches 23.2 between the 3300th second and the 3400th second.

File retention leads too many SSTables involved in one compaction and contributes to WA.

Table 2. The threshold for the number of SSTables of each level.

The nth level	L0	L1	L2	L3	L4	L5	L6
The threshold Tn of Ln	4, 8, 12	5	50	500	5000	50000	500000

As shown in Fig. 5, one can see that the average SSTable number involved in each level's compaction is much larger than the theoretical write amplification

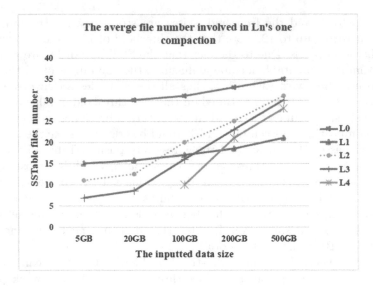

Fig. 5. The average file number involved in Ln's one compaction with different inputted data sizes.

value 11, and grow as the input data size grows greatly. For example, the average file number involved in L2's compactions grows from 11 to 31 when the inputted data size grows from 5 GB to 500 GB.

The reason of WA of compaction is that too many SSTables involve in a single compaction. WA of compaction contribute to the overall WA of the system.

2.4   Score Centric Priority Based Compaction Scheduling Mechanism

The compaction scheduling mechanism is the root source of the file retention of LSM-tree. After analyzing the default compaction scheduling mechanism of LevelDB, which is a typical implementation of LSM-tree, we find that score centric priority based compaction scheduling mechanism is adopted. In LevelDB, the score of each level is defined as $Sn = Nn/Tn$, in which Sn, Nn and Tn represent the score of Ln, the run-time number of SSTables of Ln and the threshold of the number of SSTables on Ln respectively. LSM-tree based KV-Stores' conventional compaction scheme always picks a level which has a biggest score to do a compaction.

Note that the priority of L0 is always the highest and the score of L0 is set as a default value 10000. As long as the number of SSTables on L0 reaches its first threshold of 4, L0 performs compaction at once. The priority privilege of L0 in LSM-tree causes serious write amplification. For the one side, the moving of SSTables from L0 to L1 can allow much more memtables flushed to disks and make the front-end writes continue. For the other side, the top priority of the moving of SSTables from L0 to L1 can also lead to the retention of lots of SSTables, and thus cause the huge write amplification between L0 and L1, which occupies much longer compaction time and then restrains the following front-end writes.

The imbalance of compaction opportunity is the side effects of score centric priority based compaction scheduling mechanism, and it motivates us to propose a much more balanced compaction priority scheduling mechanism named Slot.

Slot relieves file retention, so it reduces the file number picked up in one compaction, ensuring that more Disk I/O resources serve the front-end data inserting.

3 Design

The main idea of Slot is to combine score centric priority based compaction scheduling with time-slice centric fairness based compaction scheduling to alleviate the file retention and then decrease the write amplification of LSM-tree based key/value stores. Slot avoids too many files involved in one compaction and decreases the frequency of write pause or write stop.

The time-slice centric compaction scheduling is a kind of fair compaction scheduling, and is used to supplement origin score centric priority based compaction scheduling of LSM-tree based KV-stores. Our mixed mechanism not only takes into account the need for L0 and L1 to get more compactions, but also ensures the fairness that each level gets compaction opportunity, avoiding some low levels do not get a compaction for a long time when their files numbers are already much bigger than their thresholds.

Firstly, we describe the steps of score centric priority based compaction.

(1) The system starts to run.
(2) Do preparations for compaction, including calculating the scores of all levels.
(3) Choose the level with the highest score to do compaction.
(4) The current compaction finishes. Go back to step 2 to do preparations for the next compaction.

Secondly, we added time-slice centric fairness based compaction scheduling on the basis of the score centric priority based compaction scheduling.

(1) The system starts to run.
(2) Initialize Slot related data, including the threshold (length) of time slice.
(3) Calculate the scores of all levels and rank the levels in descending order of their scores.
(4) According to the level sequence of step 3, do compaction on these levels one by one until the time of compactions consumed by the sequence is greater than or equal to the threshold (length) of the time slice. L0 and L1 can execute at most two consecutive compactions, and the other levels can be executed at most once. We will elaborate on the reason for this setting in the next paragraph.
(5) Update Slot related data, including updating the time slice threshold based on historical compaction data.
(6) A time slice ends. Returns to step 3.

Then, we supplement the Slot algorithm. In the actual implementation, we dynamically adjust the time slice threshold (length) based on compaction data including each level's average time to finish one compaction and the number of levels which own at least one file. Unlike origin LSM-based KV-stores, in a time slice, a certain level except L0 or L1 does compaction for at most one time. But in origin LSM-based KV-stores, L0 or L1 do compactions continuously with no limit as shown in Sect. 2.4. After L0 or L1 completes a compaction, if their scores are still greater than 1, they can do compaction once again, but not more than twice totally in a time slice. The remaining levels can continuously do compaction for at most once in a time slice. It not only ensures more opportunities of L0 and L1 from both priority and continuous execution rights, but also takes into account the fairness that each level gets compaction opportunity. Slot avoids that the remaining levels get no chance of compaction because the priority of L0 and L1 compaction is too high.

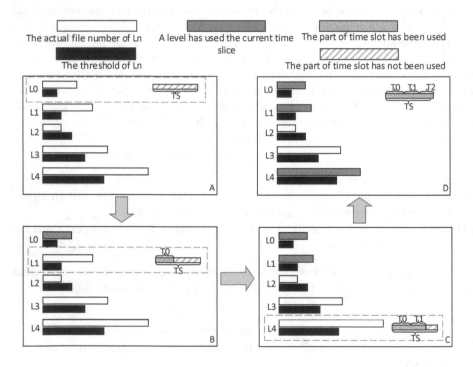

Fig. 6. One time slice life cycle

To describe SLOT more vividly, we illustrate 4 representative phases of one time slice life cycle in Fig. 6. The 'TS' in the Fig. 6 means the length of a time slice. It should be noted that this figure is a schematic figure. In the actual LSM-tree, the threshold of the files number in each level (component) is incremented by 10 times level by level.

During A phase, the system has started to run. The system counts the scores of all levels whose file number is bigger than its threshold, and the result sequence in descending order is S0, S1, S4, S3, S2. (Sn represents the score of Ln.) According to compaction schedule rule, L0 occupies the time slice and starts to do one compaction. L0's compaction uses T0 time and T0 is smaller than TS.

During B phase, the time slice flows to the L1, which means the time slice is occupied by L1 now. L1's compaction uses T1 time during B phase and the sum of T0 and T1 is smaller than TS.

During C phase, the time slice flows to the L4. And the compaction on L4 costs T2 time.

During D phase, the time slice has been used up, that means the sum of T0, T1 and T2 is greater than or equal to TS. Thus, the system counts the scores of all levels again and phase D will start a new time slice life cycle.

By combining score centric priority based compaction scheduling with time-slice centric fairness based compaction scheduling, Slot controls the number of files on each level and alleviates the file retention. Then Slot decreases the write amplification of LSM-tree based key/value stores and improves overall system throughput.

4   Evaluation

In this section, we conduct extensive experiments by YCSB benchmark [4] and LevelDB's own microbenchmark dbbench to compare the write performance and write performance of Slot with that of LevelDB, which is a representative LSM-tree implementation distributed by Google. We also examine compaction details and the impacts of request distribution.

4.1   Evaluation Tools

The YCSB benchmark provides a framework and a standard set of six workloads for evaluating the performance of key-value stores. We use YCSB, whose settings are listed in Table 3 to compare the performances of LevelDB and SLOT. Besides, we get compaction details with LevelDB's own microbenchmark (dbbench), which can generate LevelDB LOG.

4.2   Write Performance

We show the put (write) throughput of LevelDB and Slot in Fig. 7(a). With the increase of the input data size, the performance improvement of Slot compared with LevelDB gets larger and larger gradually as well. Slot improves the write throughput by 25%–370% compared to LevelDB, especially when the data size is large. As the data size grows, the throughput of LevelDB decreases sharply and it is only 312 ops of 100 GB. The reason is that the big data size leads longtime compactions, causing write stop, even write stop. However, Slot relieves this problem.

Table 3. Base YCSB workload configurations.

Parameter	Value
Operation count	5000000
Read proportion	0.05
Update proportion	0
Scan proportion	0
Insert proportion	0.95
Request distribution	Uniform

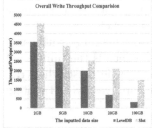 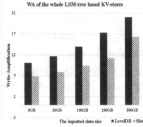 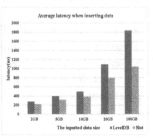

(a) Overall Write Throughput

(b) Write Amplification of the whole KV-Stores

(c) Write latency when inserting data

Fig. 7. Write performance comparison

As one can see from Fig. 7(b), the WA gets an optimization of 27% to 45% for Slot avoids picking up too many SSTables in one compaction. As shown in Fig. 7(c), the insert latency of Slot is only 57%–80% of that of LevelDB. As data size grows, the optimization ratio of the average latency of data inserting grows. The reason is that Slot reduces the number of SSTables involved in one compaction. Thus the LevelDB can serve front-end writing first. With the increase of data volume, the growth rate of the number of SSTables selected by Slot per compaction is much smaller than that of LevelDB. Slot can always provide more system resources for front-end writing.

4.3 Read Performance

Due to trade-offs in design, read amplification has been a major issue for LSM-Tree based system.

To serve a lookup operation, LSM-tree based KV-Stores search the memtable first, immutable memtable next, and then SSTables L0 to L6 in order. The number of file searches required to locate a random key is bounded by the maximum number of levels, since keys do not overlap between SSTables within a single level, except in L0. Since SSTables in L0 can contain overlapping keys, a lookup may search multiple SSTables at L0. To avoid a large lookup latency, LSM-tree based KV-Stores slow down the frontend write traffic if the number of SSTables at L0 is bigger than eight, in order to wait for the compaction thread to compact some SSTables from L0 to L1.

Read amplification happens in two phases. On the one hand, the system searches through multi-levels for the KV entry with the inputted key. When the target key is on the bottom level, the SSTables needed to be searched are up to 10 SSTables (4 on L0, and 1 for each of the other levels). On the other hand, in order to find a KV entry in the SSTable, the LevelDB needs to read three blocks of metadata in the SSTable on the second phase. Specifically, the three metadata blocks are an index block (16 KB), a bloom-filter block (4 KB) and a block (4 KB) storing KV data.

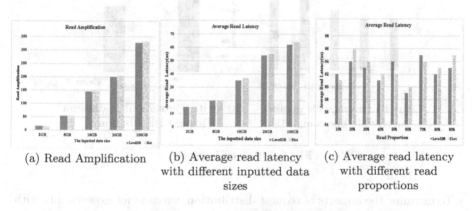

(a) Read Amplification   (b) Average read latency   (c) Average read latency
with different inputted data   with different read
sizes   proportions

Fig. 8. Read performance comparison

Experiments show that Slot has almost no read performance decrease. As shown in Fig. 8(a), the excess part of Slot's Read Amplification compared LevelDB's is only −1%–4% of LevelDB's Read Amplification. According to the last two paragraphs, Read Amplification is mainly caused by looking up KV item level by level. However, Tn is far bigger than the sum of T1 to Tn-1. As one can see from Fig. 4, if we move all SSTables between L0 and Ln-1 to Ln, the SSTables of Ln will not exceed Tn, except that the SSTables number of Ln has reached 90% of the threshold of Ln.

Figure 8(b) represents that the read performance of Slot is slightly worse than that of LevelDB, with the average read latency about 0.3%–4.1% higher than that of LevelDB. We conduct further experiments on YCSB dataset to evaluate the read latency of Slot compared with LevelDB under mixed put/get workloads. In YCSB dataset, we set the data size as 100 GB. We use the mixed put/get workloads and vary the read proportion from 10% to 90%. As shown in Fig. 8(c), the increase ratio of Slot's average read latency compared with LevelDB's is about −2% to 3.1% and reaches an average value of 0.7%.

4.4   Other Evaluation

Through Fig. 9(a), we compare the average number of compaction-selected SSTables with the increase of data volume before and after system optimization. As one can see from the figure, the average file number involved in one compaction of Slot grows slower than that of LevelDB. It ensures that the Slot can provide more resources serving for user writing than LevelDB.

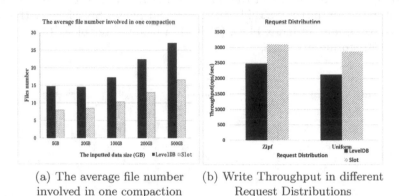

(a) The average file number   (b) Write Throughput in different
involved in one compaction   Request Distributions

Fig. 9. Other evaluations

To examine the impacts of request distribution, we conduct experiments with request distribution of Zipf and Uniform respectively. As shown in Fig. 9(b), the throughput of LevelDB and Slot under uniform distribution is lower than that under Zipf distribution. The reason is that there are many duplicate KV items under Zipf distribution, and only the KV item of the newest version can be retained if the KV items with the same key meet in the compaction procedure, so the output data size of one compaction is usually smaller than the input data size of this compaction under Zipf distribution, which means the write amplification would be smaller. However, there is no duplicate KV item under uniform distribution, so the output data size of one compaction is the same as the input data size of this compaction under uniform distribution, and the write amplification would be larger. As a result, the throughput under Zipf distribution is higher than that under uniform distribution.

4.5   Conclusion

In general, Slot outperforms LevelDB under YCSB dataset and dbbench microbenchmark, especially in big data volume. Our experiments also prove that Slot performs well both in write performance and read performance and is friendly both to put-intensive workloads and get-intensive workloads. Meanwhile, as we expected, Slot's read performance is a little worse than LevelDB which can be nearly ignored. Besides, this defect can be easily solved by using multi-level cache, which has been widely used in practical applications, such as Facebook's photo-serving stack [6].

5   Related Work

5.1   KV Stores for Specific Storage Medium

Various key-value stores have been proposed for a specific storage medium. Wisckey [13] is a flash-optimized key-value store. Its main idea is to separate keys from values to reduce I/O amplification by mitigating the migration of values. NVMKV [14] is an FTL-aware lightweight KV store which leverages native FTL capabilities to provide high performance. SkimpyStash [6] is RAM space skimpy key-value store on flash-based storage, which moves a part of the table to the SSD using a linear chaining. FlashStore [5] is a high throughput persistent key-value store using cuckoo hashing. LOCS [19] is an LSM-tree based KV store on SSD, which exposes its internal flash channels to applications to better work with the LSM-tree based KV store. SILT [12] combines the log-structure, hash-table, and sorted-table layouts to provide a memory-efficient KV store. Memcached [7] and Redis [2] are the popular memory KV implementations. GD-Wheel [11] provides a cost-aware replacement policy for memory based KV stores, which takes access recency and computation cost into account.

5.2   KV Stores for Specific Scenarios

Other researchers are dedicated to developing key-value stores for specific scenarios. zExpander [21] dynamically partitions the cache into two parts for high memory efficiency and low miss ratio, respectively, by compressing one of the partitions. ForestDB [1] addresses the performance degradation of large keys by employing a new hybrid index scheme. LSM-trie [20] constructs a prefix tree to store data in a hierarchical structure which helps to reduce the metadata and the write amplification. bLSM [17] proposes a spring and gear merge scheduler, which bounds write latency and provides high read and scan performance. Atlas [10] is a key-value storage system for cloud data, which stores keys and values on different hard drives. Among these Works, bLSM, LSM-trie, Wisckey, VT-tree, Altas, and LOCS are optimized for traditional LSM-tree based key-value stores.

6   Conclusion

KV-stores have become a fundamental building block in data-intensive applications. The core data structure of KV-store is LSM-tree. The LSM-tree incurs front-end write stalls and large write amplification when plenty of SSTables are involved in one compaction. To relieve this phenomenon, we propose Slot, a more reasonable Compaction Scheduling Mechanism, in this paper. Slot reduces the number of SSTables involved in one compaction by alleviating the file retention on disk levels. Extensive benchmark and real-world workloads drove experimental results demonstrated that compared with LevelDB, Slot has about 25%–370% write performance improvement and matchable read performance when handling write-intensive workloads (e.g., write-95% workload), and also has comparable read performance when handling read-intensive workload (e.g., read-90% workload).

References

1. Ahn, J.-S., Seo, C., Mayuram, R., Yaseen, R., Kim, J.-S., Maeng, S.: ForestDB: a fast key-value storage system for variable-length string keys. IEEE Trans. Comput. **65**(3), 902–915 (2016)
2. Carlson, J.L.: Redis in Action. Manning Publications Co., Shelter Island (2013)
3. Cooper, B.F., et al.: PNUTS: Yahoo!'s hosted data serving platform. Proc. VLDB Endow. **1**(2), 1277–1288 (2008)
4. Cooper, B.F., Silberstein, A., Tam, E., Ramakrishnan, R., Sears, R.: Benchmarking cloud serving systems with YCSB. In: Proceedings of the 1st ACM Symposium on Cloud Computing, pp. 143–154. ACM (2010)
5. Debnath, B., Sengupta, S., Li, J.: FlashStore: high throughput persistent key-value store. Proc. VLDB Endow. **3**(1–2), 1414–1425 (2010)
6. Debnath, B., Sengupta, S., Li, J.: SkimpyStash: RAM space skimpy key-value store on flash-based storage. In: Proceedings of the 2011 ACM SIGMOD International Conference on Management of data, pp. 25–36. ACM (2011)
7. Fitzpatrick, B.: Distributed caching with memcached. Linux J. **2004**(124), 5 (2004)
8. George, L.: HBase: The Definitive Guide: Random Access to Your Planet-size Data. O'Reilly Media Inc., Sebastopol (2011)
9. Ghemawat, S., Dean, J.: LevelDB (2011). https://github.com/google/leveldb, http://leveldb.org
10. Lai, C., et al.: Atlas: Baidu's key-value storage system for cloud data. In: 2015 31st Symposium on Mass Storage Systems and Technologies (MSST), pp. 1–14. IEEE (2015)
11. Li, C., Cox, A.L.: GD-Wheel: a cost-aware replacement policy for key-value stores. In: Proceedings of the Tenth European Conference on Computer Systems, p. 5. ACM (2015)
12. Lim, H., Fan, B., Andersen, D.G., Kaminsky, M.: SILT: a memory-efficient, high-performance key-value store. In: Proceedings of the Twenty-Third ACM Symposium on Operating Systems Principles, pp. 1–13. ACM (2011)
13. Lu, L., Pillai, T.S., Gopalakrishnan, H., Arpaci-Dusseau, A.C., Arpaci-Dusseau, R.H.: WiscKey: separating keys from values in SSD-conscious storage. ACM Trans. Storage (TOS) **13**(1), 5 (2017)
14. Marmol, L., et al.: NVMKV: a scalable and lightweight flash aware key-value store. In: HotStorage, p. 8 (2014)
15. O'Neil, P., Cheng, E., Gawlick, D., O'Neil, E.: The log-structured merge-tree (LSM-tree). Acta Informatica **33**(4), 351–385 (1996)
16. Pan, F., Yue, Y., Xiong, J.: dCompaction: delayed compaction for the LSM-tree. Int. J. Parallel Program. **45**(6), 1310–1325 (2017)
17. Sears, R., Ramakrishnan, R.: bLSM: a general purpose log structured merge tree. In: Proceedings of the 2012 ACM SIGMOD International Conference on Management of Data, pp. 217–228. ACM (2012)

18. Shetty, P., Spillane, R.P., Malpani, R., Andrews, B., Seyster, J., Zadok, E.: Building workload-independent storage with VT-trees. In: Usenix Conference on File and Storage Technologies, pp. 17–30 (2013)
19. Wang, P., et al.: An efficient design and implementation of LSM-tree based key-value store on open-channel SSD. In: Proceedings of the Ninth European Conference on Computer Systems, p. 16. ACM (2014)
20. Wu, X., Xu, Y., Shao, Z, Jiang, S.: LSM-trie: an LSM-tree-based ultra-large key-value store for small data. In: Proceedings of the 2015 USENIX Conference on Usenix Annual Technical Conference, pp. 71–82. USENIX Association (2015)
21. Wu, X., Zhang, L., Wang, Y., Ren, Y., Hack, M., Jiang, S.: zExpander: a key-value cache with both high performance and fewer misses. In: Proceedings of the Eleventh European Conference on Computer Systems, p. 14. ACM (2016)
22. Yao, T., et al.: A light-weight compaction tree to reduce i/o amplification toward efficient key-value stores. In: Proceedings of the 33rd International Conference on Massive Storage Systems and Technology (MSST 2017) (2017)
23. Yue, Y., He, B., Li, Y., Wang, W.: Building an efficient put-intensive key-value store with skip-tree. IEEE Trans. Parallel Distrib. Syst. **28**(4), 961–973 (2017)
24. Zhang, Z., et al.: Pipelined compaction for the LSM-tree. In: 2014 IEEE 28th International Parallel and Distributed Processing Symposium, pp. 777–786. IEEE (2014)

PruX: Communication Pruning of Parallel BFS in the Graph 500 Benchmark

Menghan Jia, Yiming Zhang, Dongsheng Li, and Songzhu Mei[⊠]

National University of Defense Technology, Changsha, China
{jiamenghan12,ymzhang,dsli,sz.mei}@nudt.edu.cn

Abstract. Parallel Breadth First Search (BFS) is a representative algorithm in Graph 500, the well-known benchmark for evaluating supercomputers for data-intensive applications. However, the specific storage model of Graph 500 brings severe challenge to efficient communication when computing parallel BFS in large-scale graphs. In this paper, we propose an effective method PruX for optimizing the communication of parallel BFS in two aspects. First, we adopt a scalable structure to record the access information of the vertices on each machine. Second, we prune unnecessary inter-machine communication for previously accessed vertices by checking the records. Evaluation results show that the performance of our method is at least six times higher than that of the original implementation of parallel BFS.

Keywords: Breadth First Search · Graph 500
Communication pruning

1 Introduction

Graph abstraction is playing an important role in social interaction data, e-mail and telephone network communication data, website linking related data and other data [17]. In these areas, we use graphs to describe the relationship between entities, and the data are processed with the algorithm related to the graph. With the continuous explosion of data in the world, the concept of distributed computing has been proposed. The key characteristic of distributed graph computing is that it brings extra inter-machine communication. In fact, the overhead of its inter-machine communication might be much higher than that of its computation.

In this paper, we focus on the inter-machine communication. Parallel Breadth First Search (BFS) is a common distributed graph traversal algorithm, which involves many aspects such as storage, computation, communication and synchronization. How to balance these costs is a problem worth exploring. There has been a series of optimization methods on parallel BFS (discussed in Sect. 2). On the one hand, it is the underlying optimization, such as multithreading, and graph storage, etc. Multithreading accelerates the execution of the algorithm by making full use of the computing resources of the computer. The graph storage

© Springer Nature Switzerland AG 2018
J. Vaidya and J. Li (Eds.): ICA3PP 2018, LNCS 11334, pp. 106–121, 2018.
https://doi.org/10.1007/978-3-030-05051-1_8

focuses on balancing the storage load, then balancing the computing load and reducing the inter-machine communication overhead. On the other hand, it is the optimization of the upper level, such as the direction optimization of BFS, and message compress, etc. The direction optimization accelerates the algorithm execution by reducing the number of inter-machine communication. And the message compress compresses inter-machine communication messages, thereby reducing inter-machine communication overhead. From the previous study, the inter-machine communication overhead is often greater than the computing overhead in parallel BFS. How to reduce the cost of inter-machine communication more effectively will be a crucial issue. As an upper optimization method, our method called Prux focus on cutting off unnecessary inter-machine communication to reduce the inter-machine communication overload. In fact, Prux is more effective than the existing upper level optimization, and it can be well combined with the underlying optimization.

In 2010, the international Graph 500 organizations proposed new benchmarks to rank supercomputers based on their performance on data-intensive applications [14]. And BFS is the most representative benchmark. The Graph 500 provides the original implementation of parallel BFS which defines the mode of communication between processes, the method of graph partitioning, and the way the BFS algorithm executes. Because of the characteristics of graph storage of Graph 500, it leads to a lot of inter-machine communication, which is the first challenge. Our Prux is applied to solve this problem, and we evaluate the performance of our Prux on a large scale graph with 1 billion edges. These graphs are all sparse graphs, that is, the number of edges m is a constant times the number of vertices n.

1.1 Our Contributions

We propose a method to PruX to reduce the inter-machine communication in parallel BFS. The following are our major contributions:

- We have improved the performance of the original implementation of parallel BFS at least 6 times over the one billion edges graph by PrunX. The source code of Prux is available at www.nicexlab.com/prux.
- We have briefly implemented the BFS for directional optimization and compared it to our method.
- Under the constraints of the experimental environment, we did not do experiments on a larger scale and more process. But we combine the 2D partitioning with our method and propose a method that can be applied to a larger scale.

This paper is organized as follows. In Sect. 1, we discuss the background of Graph 500 and BFS. In Sect. 2, we discuss the related work of parallel BFS algorithm. In Sect. 3, we discuss the underlying communication structure in parallel BFS algorithm, and introduce our contribution. In Sect. 4, we prove the effectiveness of our method by experiments. In Sect. 5, we summed up the work we did and put forward the future work.

2 Related Work

In this section, we will introduce the parallel Breadth First Search (BFS) algorithm [4,5]. Next, we will also introduce the recent breakthroughs in the parallel BFS algorithm of Graph 500 [16].

2.1 Parallel Breadth First Search

Here we focus on the implementation of the parallel BFS algorithm for Graph 500 [1,19,22]. The parallel BFS algorithm is the direct extension of the serial BFS algorithm [2]. Graph 500 implements a communication library, AML, based on MPI [11,21]. In fact, each process element runs the same code, and control the program through interprocess communication. The whole graph G is divided into several subgraphs G' and assigned to different process elements. The process element i is only responsible for dealing with the related calculations of the vertices and edges in the subgraph G'_i. Graph in Graph 500 is 1D partitioning, which is partitioned and sent to different processes by source vertex hash. As Fig. 1 shows, the edges with the same source will be assigned to the same process element.

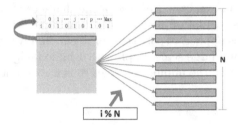

Fig. 1. 1D partition. Vertex and edges with the vertex as source vertex in graph data will be assigned to different process according to the source vertex hash.

Communication is another important aspect of expansion. Unlike the serial BFS algorithm for a single process element, parallel BFS algorithms have data communication between process elements. The AML library allows us to define *send ()* and *receive ()* functions for communication between process elements. In Graph 500, the data sent by the *send ()* function is an edge (v, u), which is sent from the process element where the vertex v is located to the process element where the vertex u is located. The *receive ()* function receives the data (v, u), and whether the vertex u is accessed at its own process element. If the vertex u is not accessed, the parent node of the vertex u is recorded as the vertex v, and the access state of the modified vertex u is accessed. In addition, the vertex u is added to the next processing queue Q_2. If the vertex u has been accessed, nothing will be done. Algorithm 1 gives the implementation of *receive ()* functions.

Different from the serial BFS algorithm, the parallel BFS algorithm has synchronization. The process elements will perform synchronization when the vertices in the current processing queue Q_1 in each process element are processed.

Algorithm 1. Receive Function

Require: G′ (V, E): local unweighted undirected graph
    v: the source vertex received from the function send
    u: the target vertex received from the function send
    Q_2: the local next processing queue
    visited: the local collection of visited vertex
Ensure: bfs_tree(): local parent map of BFS tree
 1: **if** u ∉ visited **then**
 2:    visited ← visited ⋃ {u}
 3:    Q_2 ← {u}
 4:    bfs_tree[u] ← v
 5: **end if**

When all the process elements execute synchronization, it is indicated that the vertices in this layer in the "Breadth First spanning tree" are all accessed, and the vertices in next layer can be accessed. Then the current processing queue Q_1 is updated and the next processing queue Q_2 is emptied. The program enters the next round of iterations. Parallel BFS must be executed as the Algorithm 2 shows.

Algorithm 2. Layer-synchronization Parallel BFS Algorithm

Require: G′ (V′, E′): local unweighted undirected graph
    root: root vertex in BFS
    Q_1: the local current processing queue
    Q_2: the local next processing queue
    visited: the local collection of visited vertex
    owner(): the mapping of the vertex and the process element to which it belongs
    myrank: the own process element
    send(): send data composed of source vertex and target vertex
Ensure: bfs_tree(): local parent map of BFS tree
 1: bfs_tree[v] ← -1, ∀ v ∈ V′
 2: **if** owner[root] = myrank **then**
 3:    bfs_tree[root] ← root
 4:    visited ← visited ⋃ {root}
 5:    Q_1 ← {root}
 6: **end if**
 7: **while** Q_1 ≠ null **do**
 8:    **for** each u ∈ Q_1 **do**
 9:     **for** w ∈ E(u) **do**
 10:      send(u,w)
 11:     **end for**
 12:    **end for**
 13:    Q_1 ← Q_2
 14:    Q_2 ← null
 15: **end while**

2.2   Breadth First Search Algorithm Optimization

Thread Level Parallelism. In the original implementation of parallel BFS of Graph 500, the use of a MPI based communication library can only achieve process level parallelism. Thread level parallelism can be implemented by multithreading [15]. Multithreading technology usually uses the idle time of CPU to accelerate program execution [3]. In fact, a physical core can handle only one thread at the same time, and multithreading technology only takes full advantage of the physical core free time. But research shows that only part of the physical core processing threads are involved in the operation. In order to make full use of the computing power of the physical core, the concept of hyper threading is proposed, which means to convert a physical core into two logical cores. In some cases, two different operations can be performed at the same time on a physical core. The program will be accelerated in this way. In order to further improve the computational performance, Intel's Many Integrated Core (MIC) processor architecture is proposed [12]. Each core can be handed over to MIC for execution of some of the threads belonging to it, which can perform more threads at the same time. There is also the concept of Graphics Processing Unit (GPU) acceleration [18]. In order to take advantage of the many core features on the GPU, the physical core on the Central Processing Unit (CPU) assigns some GPU capable threads to the GPU. Precisely, this way improves the number of threads that each process can handle at the same time, and accelerates the execution of the program. All in all, thread level parallelism is by making full use of computing resources, improving computing power, and accelerating the execution of the algorithm.

Direction Optimization. *Checconi et al.* proposed direction optimization of the parallel BFS algorithm, which means that use a mixed BFS instead of top-down BFS used in Graph 500 [6]. The BFS tree is divided into several layer [20]. For top-down BFS, search is always from parent to child. But mixed BFS means that, in some cases, top-down BFS will switch to bottom-up BFS, and search starts from all vertices that are not accessed. Unvisited vertices will validate whether his neighbor vertices have been visited. We introduce two parameters, P_d, P_u, in the bottom-up BFS algorithm. P_d represents the estimate of the number of vertices that can be accessed at the vertex of the current processing queue at an iteration. P_u represents the estimate of the number of vertices that can be accessed at vertices that have not been accessed at a certain iteration. Before each iteration, we will predict the P_d in the next iteration according to the updated Q_1, and count the number of vertices that have not been visited after the iteration to predict the P_u in the next iteration. If P_d is less than P_u, we use the top-down BFS algorithm, and if P_u is less than P_d, we use the bottom-up BFS algorithm. And after each iteration, P_d and P_u are detected. The algorithm uses the top-down BFS algorithm by default. This method can reduce a lot of communication when the number of vertices that can be accessed at vertices that have not been accessed at a certain iteration is less than the number of vertices that can be accessed at the vertex of the current processing queue at an iteration. In other word, it accelerates the parallel BFS algorithm by reducing the amount of communication.

Compressed Communication Message. *Checconi et al.* proposed a method of compressing communication messages [9]. They notice that there are a lot of communication message between the process elements. Suppose that the vertex v is the source vertex of an edge *(v, u)*, u is the target vertex of the edge. In fact, the format of the communication message is arbitrary type, *data*. In Graph 500, the format of the communication message between the process elements that store the vertex v and the process elements that store the vertex u is (v,u). If there are multiple communication messages *(v, u_i)* $(1 < i \leq n)$, and u_i is stored in the same process element, the communication message compression will transform all u_i into an array *u[]*. Compared to the total amount of communication messages in the original implementation of parallel BFS, communication message compression can reduce the amount of communication to $\frac{i+1}{2\times i}$ for i communication messages in this format. In fact, the process element of the storage vertex v sending i communication messages needs to be prepared i times, and the process element of the storage vertex u receiving communication messages also need to be prepared i times. These operations only need to be executed once by communication message compression. In fact, the communication overhead is smaller than the $\frac{i+1}{2\times i}$ for i communication messages of the previous communication overhead.

2D Partitioning. *Chow et al.* put forward a 2D partitioning method instead of 1D-Partition method applied to Graph 500 [10]. 2D partitioning can balance storage overhead and computing overhead [8,23]. Edges with the same source vertex will be assigned to several process elements, and then all computation of these edges will be undertaken by several process elements.

In summary, the advantage of 2D partitioning is to balance the computing load and speed up the speed of each iteration, thus accelerating the BFS algorithm.

All these optimization can work effective on parallel BFS of Graph 500, but in fact, they all have some common shortcomings. We divide communication into valid communication and invalid communication. Invalid communication means the BFS program can work without them, otherwise it is valid communication. As seen in Fig. 2, A is the first visitor of D. For BFS algorithm, $A{\rightarrow}D$ means valid communication, and $B{\rightarrow}D$ as well as $C{\rightarrow}D$ are called invalid communication. For a certain graph, the edges of BFS tree can be regarded as valid communication of the parallel BFS algorithm. Our optimization accelerates the algorithm by reducing invalid communication, called PruX.

PruX and direction optimization are similar, and we all adjust the BFS algorithm to reduce the communication. But our optimization is more effective. And our optimization can be combined with other optimizations, such as multithreading, 2D partition, communication message compression, and so on, to achieve better optimization results. The detailed optimization will be introduced as follows.

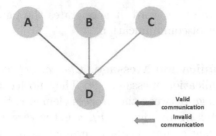

Fig. 2. Valid communication and invalid communication

3   Parallel Breadth First Search Algorithm Optimization

In this section, we will introduce our optimization of parallel Breadth First Search (BFS) algorithm on Graph 500. First of all, we will give a brief introduction to Graph 500.

The standard of the graph 500 benchmark is *TEPS* (Traversed edges per second). We defines num_traval_i as the number of traversed edges for BFS on i-th iteration, and bfs_time_i as the runtime of BFS on i-th iteration. Then *TEPS* for i-th iteration means:

$$TEPS_i = \frac{num\_traval_i}{bfs\_time_i} \tag{1}$$

We will generate 64 unique root vertices, and then run 64 times BFS and take the mean value of *TEPS* (*mean_TEPS*) as the final standard.

$$mean\_TEPS = \frac{\sum_{i=1}^{64} TEPS_i}{64} \tag{2}$$

When the number of traversing edges is almost constant, the performance of the BFS algorithm can only be boosted by reducing the BFS time. BFS time consists of computation time and communication time. In order to promote the performance of BFS, we focus on reducing inter-machine communication time. Through previous experiments, we found that there is a large number of invalid communication in the original implementation of parallel BFS for Graph 500. We modify the communication mode of parallel BFS to reduce the amount of invalid communication.

3.1   Graph Storage

The implementation of the PruX is based on the original implementation of parallel BFS of Graph 500. Graph partition is carried out according to the method of 1D partitioning. The graph data is stored as the adjacency matrix and then converted into a compressed sparse row (CSR) matrix [13]. The process of transforming the adjacency matrix into a CSR matrix is shown in Fig. 3.

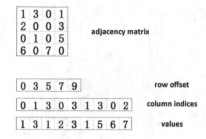

Fig. 3. Transformation of adjacency matrix into CSR matrix.

It is assumed that the adjacency matrix is a sparse matrix of $n' \times n'$, where the number of stored edges is m. So the length of the array *row offset* is $n'+1$, the length of the array *column indices* is m, and the length of the array *values* is m. The $i+1$ element of the array *row offset* subtracts the i element of the array *row offset* to indicate the number of edges stored in the i-th line of adjacency matrix. The array *column indices* continuously stores the target vertices of the edge in adjacency matrix row by row. The array *values* continuously stores the values of the edge in adjacency matrix row by row. If you want to take the data from line i of the adjacency matrix in the CSR matrix, you need to take out the i element d_i and the $i+1$ element d_{i+1} of the row offset array first. Then the d_{i+1}-d_i elements are read at the location of the d_i of the *column indices* array to represent the target vertices of the edge in the i-th line of adjacency matrix. Finally, the d_{i+1}-d_i elements are read at the location of the d_i of the *values* array to represent the value of the edge in the i-th line of adjacency matrix.

In parallel BFS, the array *values* can be omitted because it is calculated in the unweighted graph. In fact, only $n+m+1$ vertices can be used to represent all the edges, while the directly storing edge requires $2 \times m$ vertices.

3.2 Breadth First Search Communication

Before introducing the method of communicating pruning, we first introduce the communication mode in the original implementation of parallel BFS provided by Graph 500 in Fig. 4.

There are K process elements that store the edges like (v, u). Each process element stores I_k edges $(0 \leq k < K)$. Edges stored on process element k can be represented as (v_{ki}, u) $(0 \leq i < I)$. And (v_{k0}, u) represents the first edge of the K process element to access the vertex u. Valid communication in BFS means the first access to the target vertex. So valid communication to vertex u in parallel BFS must belong to the set of (v_{k0}, u). Then we can cut off all edges like (v_{ki}, u) $(0 < i < I)$ in each process element.

In fact, we follow the idea that the global optimal is bound to be local optimal. In the parallel BFS algorithm, valid communication is the global optimal communication. In each process element, we can ensure that the global optimal communication is not pruned as long as we retain the local optimal communication. So we put forward the implementation of the PruX as follows.

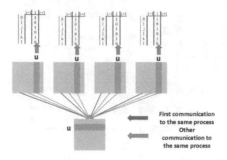

Fig. 4. Communication mode of Graph 500.

Recording Access State of Vertex. We set up an array *flagv[]* on each process element whose length is equal to the number of vertices. The *flagv[u]* records whether the vertex *u* has been accessed by the process element. The initial value of each element in *flagv[]* is 0, and when vertex *u* is accessed, the corresponding element *flagv[u]* value is set to 1.

Communication Mode. Before communicating to other process, we will test the local *flagv[]*. The process will communicate with other process for vertex *u*, if and only if vertex *u* has not been accessed on this process. In this way, we can reduce a lot of invalid communication. As Fig. 5 shows, only the first access to other vertices can be communication, others are cut off. A number of invalid communication will be reduced by this way. Lower communication overhead brings a higher TEPS.

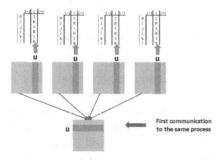

Fig. 5. Communication mode of PruX.

If the communication message from the vertices of the process elements to vertex u are represented as v_k, u $(0 \leq k < the number of process elements)$. The number of communication messages sent to vertex u for each process element is recorded as I_k. Then after using the PruX, the number of communication messages sent to u for each process element is recorded as I'_k. The relationship between I'_k and I_k is shown in Eq. (3).

$$I'_k = \begin{cases} I_k & 0 \le I_k \le 1 \\ 1 & I_k > 1 \end{cases} \tag{3}$$

We found that in any case, the parallel BFS using the Prux will not lead to more communication than the parallel BFS implemented by the original implementation of parallel BFS of Graph 500. And the execution flow of the optimized parallel BFS algorithm will be performed strictly in accordance with Algorithm 3. Compared with the parallel BFS algorithm provided by Graph 500, the parallel BFS algorithm of PruX has maintained an extra array *flagv*. It asks whether vertex w has been accessed in the local process element before asking whether the vertex w has been visited in the owner process element of vertex w.

Algorithm 3. Parallel BFS Algorithm with PruX

Require: G' (V', E'): local unweighted undirected graph
       root: root vertex in BFS
       Q_1: the local current processing queue
       Q_2: the local next processing queue
       visited: the local collection of visited vertex
       owner(): the mapping of the vertex and the process element to which it belongs
       myrank: the own process element
       flagv(): the mapping of the vertex and the access state of the vertex
       send(): send data composed of source vertex and target vertex
Ensure: bfs_tree(): local parent map of BFS tree
1: bfs_tree[v] ← -1, $\forall$ v $\in$ V'
2: flagv[v] ← 0, $\forall$ v $\in$ V'
3: **if** owner[root] = myrank **then**
4:     bfs_tree[root] ← root
5:     visited ← visited $\bigcup$ {root}
6:     Q_1 ← {root}
7: **else**
8:     flagv[root] = 1
9: **end if**
10: **while** Q_1 $\ne$ null **do**
11:     **for** each u $\in$ Q_1 **do**
12:         **for** w $\in$ E(u) **do**
13:             **if** flagv[w] = 0 **then**
14:                 send(u,w)
15:                 flagv[w] ← 1
16:             **end if**
17:         **end for**
18:     **end for**
19:     Q_1 ← Q_2
20:     Q_2 ← null
21: **end while**

In fact, when the size of the graph is small, we use an array to store whether the local process element has visited each vertex. As the size of the graph increases, we use bit storage instead of array storage to save storage space. But by analyzing, we find that on a larger scale, the storage overhead in each process element to record whether each vertex has been accessed in local process element is not affordable. In this way, we put forward a parallel BFS algorithm which combines the method of PruX and the 2D partition method.

4   Experiment

In this section, we regard reference code as baseline. And we simply implement the direction optimization of parallel Breadth First Search (BFS) algorithm[1]. In order to demonstrate the effectiveness of PruX, we have done a lot of experiments on the parallel BFS algorithm implemented by three methods based on 1D partitioning. If there is no special description, the default experiment condition is the parallel environment of the 8 node and 32 process.

First of all, we will introduce some necessary information related to the graph data. In fact, the graph is generated by the Kronecker graph generator which is provided by Graph 500. The input parameter of the generator is only one, $SCALE$, which indicates that the graph contains 2^{SCALE} vertices. Another important default parameter is *edgefactor*, which represents the ratio of the edge to the vertex in the graph, with the default value of 16. In practice, we found that the graph generated by the generator is actually a pseudo random graph, and the same graph will be generated for the same input $SCALE$. In addition, this graph contains a lot of isolated vertices and some subgraph. Almost all edges are in a subgraph, and BFS algorithm runs on this subgraph. We count up the ratio of vertices in the subgraph to total vertices and edges in the subgraph to total edges under different $SCALE$ at Fig. 6. In fact, because there are a large number of points that have not been accessed, we can only record the access state of the vertices that exist in this subgraph in the actual calculation. But considering that we need to query the access status of every vertex in the subsequent iteration, we sacrifice some extra storage space to improve the efficiency of the algorithm.

This shows that with the increase of $SCALE$, the ratio of the edge to the vertex is increasing in the actual running graph of the BFS algorithm. This ratio is the average degree of the vertex, and it also indicates the average number of times each vertex is actually accessed. As shown in Eq. (4), the average degree acc of the vertex is the ratio of the number of total access com' to the number of vertices in the subgraph n'.

$$acc = \frac{com'}{n'} \tag{4}$$

---

[1] The PruX and direction optimization are all optimized by modifying the algorithm execution mode to implement the parallel BFS algorithm. So we choose direction optimization as a contrast.

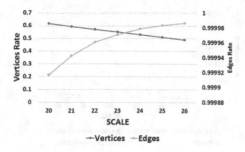

Fig. 6. The ratio of vertices in the subgraph to total vertices and edges in the subgraph to total edges under different *SCALE*.

For each vertex, only one access is a valid access, and the rest of *acc*-1 accesses is invalid. In Fig. 7, we show the *acc* values of three different implementations under the various $SCALE^2$. Obviously, the *acc* of the PruX is not only much smaller than the *acc* of the original implementation of parallel BFS, but also smaller than the *acc* of the direction optimization. The experimental result shows that Prux is the most effective method in communication optimization of parallel BFS.

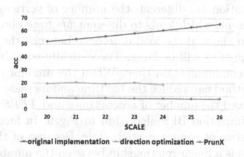

Fig. 7. The *acc* of three different implementations of BFS algorithm under different *SCALE*.

Here, we also show in Fig. 8 the number of access for each method and the number of valid access under different *SCALE*.

The three methods have different sizes of invalid access. But relatively, the method of PruX brings the least invalid access. In particular, as the size of the graph increases, the difference between different methods of invalid access is more obvious. As you can see in Fig. 7, even if the size of the graph is increasing, the *acc* of the PruX remains stable, not a linear increase in the *acc* of the original implementation of parallel BFS. This also illustrates the scalablity of the PruX.

---

[2] We only implement the direction optimization at the algorithm level, and do not optimize its storage and computation, which results in breakdown when *SCALE* is too large.

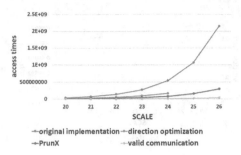

Fig. 8. The valid access times and access times of three different implementations of BFS algorithm under different *SCALE*.

In fact, as Eq. (1) shows, the number of traversed edges is determined when the input *SCALE* is determined, so *TEPS* is mainly determined by BFS runtime. The BFS runtime is made up of the following parts.

$$bfs\_time = computation\_time + communication\_time + \bigtriangledown \tag{5}$$

$\bigtriangledown$ is a small random value that varies from the actual state of the process elements. In fact, it represents the synchronization cost. Because the root vertices of each computation are different, the number of vertices involved in each iteration is also different, which leads to different *bfs_time* obtained from the 64 BFS computation. In short, if the load difference between the process elements is too large, the value of $\bigtriangledown$ will be large. Theoretically speaking, reducing communication reduces communication time. When the amount of computation is not changed, this method can reduce the bfs time and increase the *TEPS*. When *SCALE* is 20, we record the number of access times and *TEPS* for each iteration of the direction optimization BFS algorithm in Fig. 9. In fact, it is difficult to make accurate statistics of *communication_time*. Because of the randomness of the graph data, there is a linear relationship between the number of access times and the *communication_time*, so the number of access times is used instead of the *communication_time*.

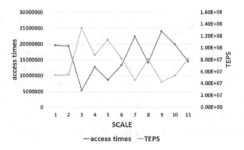

Fig. 9. Comparison of the number of access times and *TEPS* of directional optimization

Limited to the size of the statistical graph, we randomly selected 11 sets of data from 64 iterations to make up Fig. 9. It is clear that the *TEPS* value is always reduced as the number of access times increases, which also fully illustrates that reducing access times can reduce *bfs_time* and increase *TEPS*. When access times is larger, the inter-machine communication overhead is larger, and the entire *bfs_time* will become larger, resulting in a smaller *TEPS*.

In Fig. 10, we show the great advantage of the implementation of PruX relative to other implementations under different *SCALE*[3]. As *SCALE* gets bigger, we find that the Prux method is getting better and better, far more than the other methods. This shows that the Prux method is a scalable method, and its effect does not discounted with the increase of the *SCALE*.

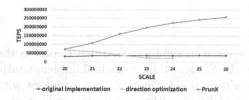

Fig. 10. Comparison of three methods in *TEPS*

In fact, it can be seen that the method of PrunX has great advantages in speeding up the parallel BFS algorithm, whether it is relative to original implementation of parallel BFS or direction optimization. In order to more accurately show the number of accesses and *TEPS* changes after using the pruning method, we recorded in Table 1 the ratio of PruX methods to original implementation of parallel BFS on access times and *TEPS* under different *SCALE*. With the increasing of *SCALE*, the optimization effect is more obvious. On the one hand, this shows the scalability of the PruX method, and the optimization effect is better when the *SCALE* is larger. On the other hand, this shows that communications will reach a bottleneck when *SCALE* is large enough. The reduction of communication will be more effective in accelerating the execution of the algorithm.

In a word, we have proved by a series of experiments that reducing the number of access can effectively accelerate the execution of the parallel BFS algorithm. PruX that reduces the number of access times without many extra computation overhead can bring more than 6 times the performance improvement under experimental conditions. And performance improvement will increase with the increase of *SCALE*. This fully illustrates the excellent effect of PruX.

---

[3] Because there are still a lot of isolated vertices in the graph, the direction optimization will compute these vertices in the bottom-up BFS algorithm, which will bring a lot of computation cost and lead to the performance degradation of large-scale graphs.

Table 1. The ratio of our optimization to reference code on communication and *TEPS*.

SCALE	Communication	TEPS
20	16.50%	2.329×
21	15.56%	3.079×
22	14.86%	4.360×
23	14.11%	5.260×
24	13.41%	5.948×
25	12.74%	6.348×
26	12.11%	6.720×

5   Conclusion

In this paper, we propose a method PruX, which improves the performance of Breadth First Search (BFS) algorithm of original implementation by at least six times under the experimental environment, and increases with the increase of experimental scale. The BFS algorithm is only an application, and more importantly, the idea of Prux inclusion. This is a general guiding rule, that is, reducing the invalid communication of distributed algorithm, thus reducing the communication load and speeding up the execution of distributed algorithm. Following this criterion, a good optimization effect can also be achieved in Graph 500 another standard Single-Source Shortest Paths (SSSP) [7]. We start from this criterion, continue to solve the problems encountered, the final implement a scalable distributed optimization algorithm BFS, and more importantly, it can be combined with other optimization such as multithreading, communication message compression, 2D partitioning, etc. to achieve better optimization results. This is also our future work.

Acknowledgment. This work is sponsored in part by the National Basic Research Program of China (793) under Grant No. 2014CB340303 and by National Natural Science Foundation of China (NSFC) under Grant No. 61772541.

References

1. Agarwal, V., Petrini, F., Pasetto, D., Bader, D.A.: Scalable graph exploration on multicore processors. In: High Performance Computing, Networking, Storage and Analysis, pp. 1–11 (2010)
2. Ajwani, D., Meyer, U., Osipov, V.:. Improved external memory BFS implementation. In: The Workshop on Algorithm Engineering & Experiments (2007)
3. Akkary, H., Driscoll, M.A.: A dynamic multithreading processor. In: 1998 Proceedings of ACM/IEEE International Symposium on Microarchitecture, Micro-31, pp. 226–236 (1998)
4. Awerbuch, B., Gallager, R.: A new distributed algorithm to find breadth first search trees. IEEE Trans. Inf. Theory **33**(3), 315–322 (2003)

5. Bader, D.A., Madduri, K.: Designing multithreaded algorithms for breadth-first search and st-connectivity on the Cray MTA-2, vol. 34, no. 2, pp. 523–530 (2006)
6. Beamer, S., Patterson, D.: Direction-optimizing breadth-first search. In: International Conference on High Performance Computing, Networking, Storage and Analysis, p. 12 (2012)
7. Bidstrup, S.M., Grady, C.P.L.: SSSP: simulation of single-sludge processes. Journal 60(3), 351–361 (1988)
8. Bulu, A.: Parallel breadth-first search on distributed memory systems, pp. 1–12 (2011)
9. Checconi, F., Petrini, F.: Traversing trillions of edges in real time: graph exploration on large-scale parallel machines. In: IEEE International Parallel and Distributed Processing Symposium, pp. 425–434 (2014)
10. Chow, E., Henderson, K., Yoo, A.: Distributed breadth-first search with 2-D partitioning. Lawrence Livermore National Laboratory (2005)
11. Dongarra, J., et al.: Special issue - MPI - a message passing interface standard. Int. J. Supercomput. Appl. High Perform. Comput. 8, 165 (1994)
12. Duran, A., Klemm, M.: The Intel® many integrated core architecture. In: International Conference on High Performance Computing and Simulation, pp. 365–366 (2012)
13. Greathouse, J.L., Daga, M.: Efficient sparse matrix-vector multiplication on GPUs using the CSR storage format. In: High Performance Computing, Networking, Storage, pp. 769–780 (2015)
14. Jose, J., Potluri, S., Tomko, K., Panda, D.K.: Designing scalable graph500 benchmark with hybrid MPI+ OpenSHMEM programming models (2013)
15. Leiserson, C.E., Schardl, T.B.: A work-efficient parallel breadth-first search algorithm (or how to cope with the nondeterminism of reducers). In: SPAA 2010: Proceedings of the ACM Symposium on Parallelism in Algorithms and Architectures, Thira, Santorini, Greece, June, pp. 303–314 (2010)
16. Lu, H., Tan, G., Chen, M., Sun, N.: Reducing communication in parallel breadth-first search on distributed memory systems, pp. 1261–1268 (2015)
17. Lumsdaine, A., Gregor, D., Hendrickson, B., Berry, J.: Challenges in parallel graph processing. Parallel Process. Lett. 17(01), 5–20 (2007)
18. Luo, L., Wong, M., Hwu, W.M.: An effective GPU implementation of breadth-first search. In: Design Automation Conference, pp. 52–55 (2010)
19. Malewicz, G., et al.: Pregel: a system for large-scale graph processing. In: ACM SIGMOD International Conference on Management of Data, pp. 135–146 (2010)
20. Sallinen, S., Gharaibeh, A., Ripeanu, M.: Accelerating direction-optimized breadth first search on hybrid architectures. In: Hunold, S., et al. (eds.) Euro-Par 2015. LNCS, vol. 9523, pp. 233–245. Springer, Cham (2015). https://doi.org/10.1007/978-3-319-27308-2_20
21. Snir, M.: MPI : The Complete Reference, pp. 4038–4040 (2010)
22. Su, B.Y., Brutch, T.G., Keutzer, K.: Parallel BFS graph traversal on images using structured grid, pp. 4489–4492 (2010)
23. Yoo, A., Chow, E., Henderson, K., Mclendon, W., Hendrickson, B., Catalyurek, U.: A scalable distributed parallel breadth-first search algorithm on BlueGene/L. In: Proceedings of the ACM/IEEE SC 2005 Conference on Supercomputing, p. 25 (2005)

Comparative Study of Distributed Deep Learning Tools on Supercomputers

Xin Du[1,2], Di Kuang[1,2], Yan Ye[1,2], Xinxin Li[1,3], Mengqiang Chen[1,3], Yunfei Du[1,3], and Weigang Wu[1,2(✉)]

[1] School of Data and Computer Science,
Sun Yat-sen University, Guangzhou, China
{duxin5,kuangd}@mail2.sysu.edu.cn,
yunfei.du@nscc-gz.cn, wuweig@mail.sysu.edu.cn
[2] Guangdong Province Key Laboratory of Big Data Analysis and Processing,
Guangzhou, China
[3] Key Laboratory of Machine Intelligence and Advanced Computing,
Ministry of Education, Guangzhou, China

Abstract. With the growth of the scale of data set and neural networks, the training time is increasing rapidly. Distributed parallel training has been proposed to accelerate deep neural network training, and most efforts are made on top of GPU clusters. This paper focuses on the performance of distributed parallel training in CPU clusters of supercomputer systems. Using resources at the supercomputer system of "Tianhe-2", we conduct extensive evaluation of the performance of popular deep learning tools, including Caffe, TensorFlow, and BigDL, and several deep neural network models are tested, including Auto-Encoder, LeNet, AlexNet and ResNet. The experiment results show that Caffe performs the best in communication efficiency and scalability. BigDL is the fastest in computing speed benefiting from its optimization for CPU, but it suffers from long communication delay due to the dependency on MapReduce framework. The insights and conclusions from our evaluation provides significant reference for improving resource utility of supercomputer resources in distributed deep learning.

Keywords: Distributed deep learning · Tianhe-2 · Speedup
Performance evaluation · Parallel processing

1 Introduction

Deep learning has been widely applied in various fields, but it is still facing many challenges. Among others, increasing training time, due to the increase of data set and neural network depth, is becoming more and more serious. Traditional single-node multi-thread acceleration method is far from enough to train large-scale neural networks. Such a problem stimulates the paradigm of distributed parallel training, which can employ large clusters of computing nodes.

Most existing distributed parallel training systems are designed for GPU clusters [1]. GeePS [2] proposed accelerating parallel training through hybrid of CPU and GPU resources. There are also some works on benchmarking deep learning tools [3, 4], but

© Springer Nature Switzerland AG 2018
J. Vaidya and J. Li (Eds.): ICA3PP 2018, LNCS 11334, pp. 122–137, 2018.
https://doi.org/10.1007/978-3-030-05051-1_9

most of them consider only parallelization inside one node. There are indeed some real deployment of parallel deep learning on cluster of multiple nodes, but, to the best of our knowledge, there are usually no results are publicly published.

In this paper, we consider distributed parallel training using CPU clusters at supercomputers. The supercomputer system has sufficient computing resources and can help accelerate distributed deep learning. We can use up to millions of cores if needed to deploy deep learning tasks, and the communication optimization and consistency mechanisms among the clusters are well established. Besides, the nodes in super-computer are connected by Gigabit Ethernet, which makes less communication delay. It can be foreseen that deploying a distributed deep learning system in a supercomputing platform can achieve better performance both on computation and scalability.

There are many popular deep learning tools, such as BigDL [5], Caffe [6], Tensorflow [7, 8], CNTK [9], MXNet [10], Torch [11] and so on. Among them, BigDL is the only one that specially designed for CPUs clusters. TensorFlow and Caffe perform well on both CPUs and GPUs. CNTK, MXNet and Torch are mainly focused on acceleration via GPUs.

Since we consider supercomputer systems, which is rich in CPU resources, we choose Caffe, TensorFlow and BigDL to conduct evaluation of distributed parallel training. Since the native version of Caffe does not support distributed computing, we choose Caffe-oMPI [12], a distributed extension of Caffe.

The experiment in this paper uses resources of the high-performance partition in Tianhe-2 supercomputer. Tianhe-2 is currently ranked the No. 2 in Top500 list [13, 26]. We choose several representative and popular convolutional neural network models, such as AutoEncoder [14], LeNet [15], ResNet [16] and AlexNet [17] for the experiments. Major performance metrics include forward and backward propagation time, communication time, data loading time, accuracy rate, speedup and so on. Experiment results show that Caffe is the best in terms of scalability, while BigDL is the best in terms of computation efficiency. TensorFlow has the most complete library and functionalities, so it is easy to program.

The rest of the paper is organized as follows. Section 2 presents the background and related work. Section 3 introduces our experimental methods. Experimental results are presented in Sect. 4, followed by our discussion in Sect. 5. We conclude the paper and introduce our future work in Sect. 6.

2 Deep Learning Models and Tools

2.1 Deep Neural Networks

Different from fully-connected neural networks before, deep neural networks are mostly convolutional neural networks (CNN) [18–20]. Convolutional neural network (CNN), as illustrated in Fig. 1, is a multi-layer neural network, each layer consists of multiple 2D planes, and each plane includes multiple independent neurons. CNNs use a set of kernels to build a convolutional layer, and each kernel's parameters are shared across the entire field, effectively reduces the amount of parameters.

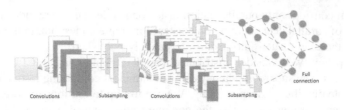

Fig. 1. The structure of convolution neural network

The training process of CNNs also follows the BP neural network scheme [21] and consists of forward and backward propagations. Forward propagation abstracts high-level semantic information from the original data input via a series of operations of convolution, summary, and non-linear activation function mapping, etc. The backward propagation refers to calculating the gradient of each parameter in each convolution kernel. The training process is carried out in an iterative way until the convergence of model is achieved.

Based on CNN, researchers also propose different types of deep neural networks for different requirements and applications, such as AutoEncoder [14], LeNet [15], ResNet [16], AlexNet [17], GoogleNet [22], VGGNet [23], FCN [24], LSTM [25] and so on. In our experiments, we choose four representative models for distributed traning evaluation: AutoEncoder, LeNet, ResNet and AlexNet. AutoEncoders is mainly used for data reduction or feature extraction [14]. LeNet [15] is one of the most representative solutions in hand-writing recognition systems. ResNet [16], which consists of residual units, can protect information integrity and accelerate the training of ultra-deep neural networks. AlexNet [17] is a representative of complex neural networks, which contains a total amount of 60 M or more parameters, and is suitable for examining efficiency of distributed training.

2.2 Popular Strategies and Deep Learning Tools

There are quite a number of popular deep learning tools that include major neural network models and programming/running libraries. BigDL [5] is a distributed deep learning framework specially designed for CPU resources. It relies on Apache Spark to realize distributed training across computing nodes. Caffe [6] is a lightweight deep learning tool implemented by C++/CUDA. The code is clear and easy to read and modular programming makes it easy for users to modify. Tensorflow [7, 8] is the most fully-featured deep learning tool, which can be divided into stand-alone implementation and distributed implementation. CNTK [9] is a unified computational network toolkit developed by Microsoft research, which supports the most popular network. MXNet [10] is a multi-language supported deep learning framework for providing more flexible programming interfaces to improve efficiency. Torch [11] is a general-purpose digital computing framework and machine learning library, which aims to provide a flexible environment for designing and training learning machines. In this paper, considering the characteristics of the supercomputing platform, Caffe, BigDL, and Tensorflow are selected to conduct evaluation experiments.

3 Experimental Methods

3.1 Hardware Platform

The experiment uses CPU resources of high-performance partition in the Tianhe-2 supercomputer system. The partition has a total of 17,920 computing nodes. Each node is equipped with two 12-core Intel Xeon E5-2692 v2 CPUs whose frequency is up to 2.2 Ghz. Single-CPU double-precision floating-point peak performance up to 211.2GF, computing node peak performance up to 3.432TF. The memory capacity of each node is 64 GB, the total memory capacity of cluster is 1.4 PB, and the external storage is a 12.4 PB hard disk array. Nodes are connected through PCI-E 2.0 built in Intel's Ivy Bridge microarchitecture, with a single lane bandwidth of 10 Gbps, providing powerful speed support for data communication across nodes.

3.2 Evaluation Metrics

People usually use the time duration of an iteration that processes a mini-batch of input data to effectively measure the performance of a deep learning tool. However, in data parallel, as the degree of data parallelism changes, the amount of data and tasks of a single node and the communication time between nodes will also change. Therefore, we insert the statistical code to refine the processing time into forward and backward propagation time, communication time, and data loading time. By observing the change trend with different degrees of data parallelism, we can infer the main factor that slows down the task. In terms of convergence rate. The speed of convergence is judged by the slope of the curve, and the convergence of the model is judged by the magnitude of the accuracy rate at the task. Different deep learning tools are implemented in different ways, which results in that specific evaluation metrics and their definitions may vary in different tools.

The methods of time measurement for each tool are as follows:

- Caffe-oMPI [12]: Because Caffe-oMPI implements cross-node communication through the MPI protocol and the data loading process is abstracted as a data layer, it is easy to separate computing time, communication time, and data load time.
- TensorFlow [7, 8]: Insert time points before and after the function body representing a specific process, such as forward propagation and backward propagation.
- BigDL [5]: The communication and data loading process are implemented based MapReduce functions. The calculation process is implemented across the nodes through the InvokeAndWait function. The code can be inserted at the corresponding position to obtain the relevant time.

Lots of flexible programming APIs and configuration options are available for users to achieve better performance. For example, in BigDL, the total training time can be controlled by modifying the configuration item "MaxIteration" Changing the configuration item "InitialMethods" can change the method of parameter initialization. It is necessary to state that the setting of training parameters in this paper is based on our limited understanding of the network model structure and deep learning tools, not the best performance that can be achieved.

The version of each tool is shown as the following Table 1:

Table 1. The version of tools

Deep learning tools	Version
Caffe-oMPI	0.1.0
TensorFlow	1.0.1
BigDL	0.3.0

3.3   Neural Networks and Data Sets

The conducted experiments select AutoEncoder, LeNet and ResNet for testing. AutoEncoder, with 3 layers, is mainly used for data dimension reduction and feature extraction. LeNet is the first convolutional neural network successfully applied to handwriting recognition, which contains all the components of a modern convolutional neural network. ResNet protects the integrity of information by passing the input information directly to the output, which simplifies the learning process and ultimately eliminates the problem of gradient disappearance as the number of layers continues to increase. As for data sets, AutoEncoder and LeNet are constructed for MNIST, while ResNet is used for Cifar-10.

3.4   Data Parallelism and Mini-Batch

In Caffe and BigDL, the degree of data parallelism refers to the number of nodes and the number of cores used in one training task, and it requires that the number of cores in each node are the same. In TensorFlow, due to the introduction of parameter servers and the inability to define the number of used cores, the degree of data parallelism is the number of parameter server nodes and work nodes.

According to previous work, it can be found that when the size of the Mini-batch takes a certain value, the best computing performance can be achieved. In the evaluation experiment of this paper, we choose the size of mini-batch as the following Table 2:

Table 2. The size of mini-batch

Networks	Mini-batch size
AutoEncoder	64
LeNet	128
ResNet	128
AlexNet	128

4 Experimental Results

Comparing the performance of them running in supercomputer system, we present the results of conducted experiments in three aspects: Caffe-oMPI, TensorFlow, and BigDL.

4.1 Caffe-oMPI

Accuracy Rate. Figure 2 shows that for LeNet and AlexNet, data parallelism does not significantly change the accuracy of model, and it can even be assumed that the effects of between them are equivalent after ignoring floating-point errors. When ResNet reaches 16,000 iterations, the convolutional layer computing time is skyrocketing, which seriously affects the collection of detailed metrics. Moreover, the maxIteration is too small to make the network convergent, thus accuracy rate oscillates dramatically.

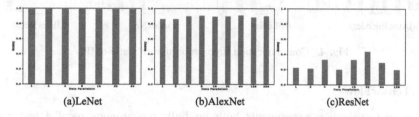

|(a)LeNet|(b)AlexNet|(c)ResNet|

Fig. 2. Accuracy rate of Caffe-oMPI

Speedup. Figure 3 shows that speedup, which is serial training time divided by parallel training time, significantly improves with the parallelism except for AutoEncoder.

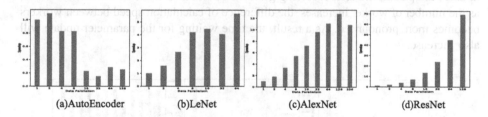

|(a)AutoEncoder|(b)LeNet|(c)AlexNet|(d)ResNet|

Fig. 3. Speedup of Caffe-oMPI

When the increase in the communication time is greater than the reduction in the calculation time, the speedup decreases. For LeNet, when the data parallelism is increased from 16 to 32, the speedup slightly decreases because all communication processes occur within one node. And the multi-thread synchronization within the node using shared memory access and parallel segment processing, so communication latency is extremely low. When data parallelism is up to 32 or more, the multi-node training process brings about extra communication between nodes. AlexNet's speedup has an extreme value when data parallelism is 128. Due to ResNet's high computational complexity, the decrease in the computation time is much larger than the increase in the communication time, thus the speedup is continuously increasing. The network size of AutoEncoder is so small that training time of network is always lower than the communication time.

Communication Time Proportion. It can be seen from Fig. 4 that for any model, the increase of data parallelism leads to an increase in the communication time and directly affects the proportion of communication time in distributed parallel training, which directly explains the phenomenon that speedup is not strictly positively correlated with data parallelism.

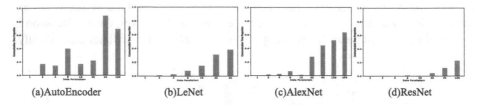

(a)AutoEncoder   (b)LeNet   (c)AlexNet   (d)ResNet

Fig. 4. Communication time proportion of Caffe-oMPI

4.2   TensorFlow

We conduct evaluation experiments both on bulk synchronous parallel and asynchronous parallel about TensorFlow, the results are as follows.

Average Total Training Time. As Fig. 5 shows, the total training time will show an increasing trend as the number of worker increases in synchronous parallel. The workload that each worker shares is the same, and the parameter server uniformly updates the parameters after receiving gradient information from all worker. However, as the number of worker increases, the difference of calculation speed between workers becomes more pronounced. As a result, the time waiting for the parameter update will also increase.

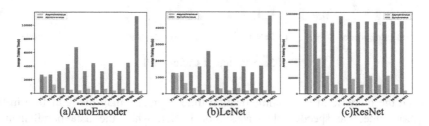

(a)AutoEncoder   (b)LeNet   (c)ResNet

Fig. 5. Average total training time of TensorFlow

While in asynchronous parallel, as the number of parameter servers remains unchanged, the total training time of the model decreases significantly with the increase of workers. Because in the asynchronous mode, each worker completes an iteration separately and can immediately interact with the parameter server to update parameters. In addition, regardless of the synchronous or asynchronous parallel, the total training time remains the same as the number of parameter servers varies.

Average Forward Propagation Time. The forward propagation time in TensorFlow refers to using parameters and input training data to calculate the predicted value.

Figure 6 shows that both AutoEncoder and LeNet have a forward propagation time of approximately 0.02 s, while that of ResNet is about 0.78 s. Because the structure of ResNet is far more complex, the forward propagation time is much longer. Meanwhile, it can be seen that forward propagation time is significantly related to neither the number of parameter servers and workers nor parameter update mode.

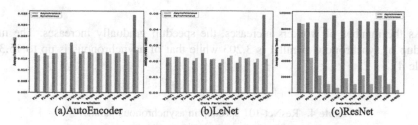

(a)AutoEncoder　　　　　　(b)LeNet　　　　　　(c)ResNet

Fig. 6. Average forward propagation time of TensorFlow

Average Backward Propagation Time. The backward propagation time in TensorFlow refers to time when the model calculates gradients layer by layer reversely according to loss and sends gradients to the parameter server and then obtain the latest parameters. As Fig. 7 shows, the backward propagation time increases with the number of working nodes. For that the asynchronous update reduces the waiting time between nodes when parameters are updated, its backward propagation time is shorter.

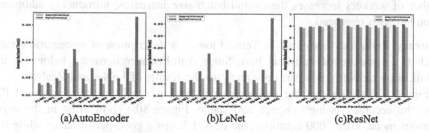

(a)AutoEncoder　　　　　　(b)LeNet　　　　　　(c)ResNet

Fig. 7. Average backward propagation time of TensorFlow

We can find that when increasing the waiting time, there is an apparent increase in backward propagation time in AutoEncoder and LeNet. However, for ResNet, the back propagation time is as long as 5.9 s. The main time-consuming is gradient calculation instead of applying gradients.

Speedup. The speedup reflects the actual acceleration effect of distributed parallel training. We use ResNet to reflect the changes in the speedup with the data parallelism. The time used in P2-W1 is the reference time. The results are as following (Table 3):

Table 3. ResNet-101 speedup in synchronous parallel

PS-workers	Accuracy	Time(s)	Speedup
P2-W1	0.692	87547.6	1
P2-W2	0.695	61436.6	1.425
P2-W4	0.694	55408.7	1.58
P2-W8	0.695	36126.6	2.423
P2-W16	0.698	27335.4	3.203

As the number of workers increases, the speedup gradually increases. The max speedup of synchronous parallel is 3.203 while that of asynchronous is up to 15.393 (Table 4).

Table 4. ResNet-101 speedup in asynchronous parallel

PS-workers	Accuracy	Time(s)	Speedup
P2-W1	0.656	86344.4	1
P2-W2	0.652	33166.5	2.603
P2-W4	0.656	16765.3	5.15
P2-W8	0.658	11934.4	7.235
P2-W16	0.654	5609.0	15.393

Workers share the same size of mini-batch in synchronous mode, so when the number of workers increases the overall batch size increases, introducing additional communication overhead.

Accuracy Rate. Accuracy rate in TensorFlow is a description of systematic errors, which is a measure of statistical bias. Since AutoEncoder does not belong to the classification problem, this part only analyzes the results of LeNet and ResNet.

Figure 8(a) shows that the performance is best in synchronization mode of P2-W16, the accuracy is high enough and stable. Figure 8(b) shows that in the asynchronous mode, after 1000 iterations, the P2-W1 keeps a good performance while P2-W16 fluctuates a lot. In asynchronous mode, stale gradient negatively affects the update of parameters, so that parameters cannot always be changed in the optimal direction.

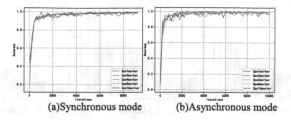

(a)Synchronous mode   (b)Asynchronous mode

Fig. 8. Accuracy rate of LeNet

As shown in Fig. 9(a), in ResNet, the accuracy curve under data parallelism has a significant stratification phenomenon in the synchronous mode. Since there is no stale gradient, with more workers, the larger amount of samples being trained per iteration, the higher accuracy rate can be achieved. In the asynchronous mode of Fig. 9(b), because the stale gradient has negative effects on the descent direction, the accuracy is in a jittery state, where the amplitude of the fluctuation in the P2-W16 parallelism is the largest and the final accuracy is the lowest.

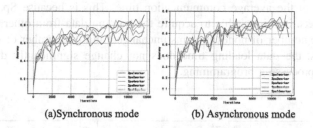

(a)Synchronous mode   (b) Asynchronous mode

Fig. 9. Accuracy rate of ResNet

4.3   BigDL

BigDL relies on Apache Spark to realize distributed training across computing nodes. When using multiple nodes to accelerate computing tasks, the number of CPU cores started in each node is required to be the same.

Average Communication Time. The average communication time refers to the average time required for driver to summarize and update parameters in one interation. The longer the average communication time, the greater the communication overhead and the worse the scalability of distributed parallel training.

Figure 10(a), (b) and (c) shows that when the number of nodes is constant, the communication time decreases slightly with the increase in the total number of cores. However, when the number of cores in a node is constant, the communication time increases with the number of nodes in exponential growth.

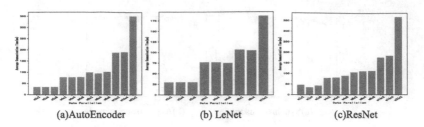

Fig. 10. Average communication time of BigDL

Because in synchronous mode, workers are required to wait until all the gradient information is uploaded, so as data parallelism rises, the waiting time increases and the communication time becomes longer. The difference from three models is the communication volume. As a result, LeNet has fewer model parameters and thus the communication time is shorter.

Average Data Loading Time. The data loading process refers to the process that each worker obtains their data to be trained.

From Fig. 11(a), (b) and (c), it can be seen that the trend of the data loading time is similar to that of the average communication time. This is because Spark store distributed data sets, it is inevitable to acquire the training data from other nodes. However, when the number of nodes remains unchanged and the number of cores in each node increases, the data loading time does not change significantly due to shared memory multiprocessing programming.

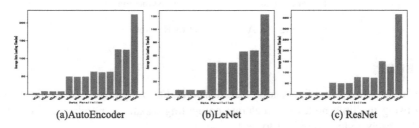

Fig. 11. Average data loading time of BigDL

Single Iteration Time. The single iteration time in BigDL refers to the time from the creation of the driver and worker processes to the completion of the training. For the same model, the shorter the single iteration time, the better the acceleration effect that can be achieved. The results about three models are as Fig. 12.

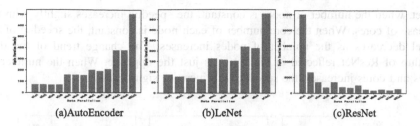

(a)AutoEncoder	(b)LeNet	(c)ResNet

Fig. 12. Single iteration time of BigDL

As can be seen in Fig. 12(a) and (b), when the number of cores per node is fixed, the single iteration time increases exponentially with the number of nodes; when the number of nodes is constant, as the number of cores increases, the single training time of AutoEncoder was almost unchanged while that of LeNet was significantly reduced. ResNet in Fig. 12(c) shows that as the number of nodes and cores increase, the single iteration time decreases significantly.

As mentioned earlier, when the number of nodes increases, the average communication time and average data loading time will increase significantly, but the average calculation time will decrease. For LeNet and AutoEncoder, the reduction in calculation time is much less than the increase in communication and data loading time. However, ResNet's structure is so difficult to calculate that the calculation time is much longer than the communication time and data loading time. Therefore, as the number of nodes increases, the reduction of the calculation time will have a greater impact.

Average Calculation Time. In BigDL, the calculation time refers to the time required to complete one forward propagation and backward propagation process under the single iteration, that is, the sum of both. From Fig. 13(a), (b) and (c), it can be seen that when data parallelism increases, the average calculation time of the three models decreases proportionally. This is because the size of mini-batch in synchronous mode is constant, and the higher data parallelism, the fewer data samples each core needs to process, the less time it will take.

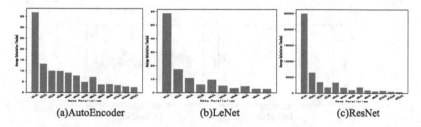

(a)AutoEncoder	(b)LeNet	(c)ResNet

Fig. 13. Average calculation time of BigDL

Speedup. The speedup in BigDL refers to the ratio of total time of single-core single-core training to that of parallel training, which indicates the acceleration of network in parallel mode. Figure 14(a) and (b) shows that during the training of AutoEncoder and

LeNet, when the number of nodes is constant, the speedup increases slightly with the increase of cores. When the core number of each node is constant, the speedup of the model decreases as the number of nodes increases. The change trend of the data speedup of ResNet reflected in Fig. 14(c) is just the opposite. When the number of nodes and cores increases, the speedup will increase significantly.

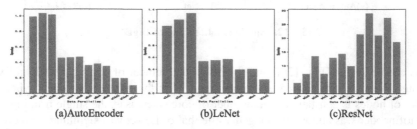

(a)AutoEncoder   (b)LeNet   (c)ResNet

Fig. 14. Speedup of BigDL

The specific reason is similar to the previous one. The model structure of Auto-Encoder and LeNet is simple and does not require too many computing resources. The extra communication overhead in multi-node parallelism slows down the overall computational speed; ResNet has deep hidden layers and high computational complexity, so the calculation time is much greater than communication time. Therefore, as the number of nodes increases, the speedup greatly increases.

Accuracy Rate. During the operation of BigDL, the validation data set is input into the existing model every certain iterations, and calculate the ratio of the correctly identified sample, which is the accuracy of the model. Figure 15(a) shows that in synchronous mode, the accuracy rate of LeNet changes roughly with the increase of data parallelism, tends to stabilize around 1000 iterations, and the final accuracy can reach over 97%. In contrast, Fig. 15(b) shows that the accuracy of the ResNet will be significantly jittery due to ResNet's model structure and data set are relatively complex. After 16,000 iterations, the accuracy of the model is stable at less than 70%.

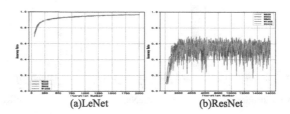

(a)LeNet   (b)ResNet

Fig. 15. Accuracy rate of BigDL

5   Comparison

5.1   Communication

In terms of communication, with the increase in the number of nodes and cores, the communication time of the BigDL increases the fastest, TensorFlow followed by and Caffe-oMPI is the slowest. This is because the MapReduce programming framework adopted by BigDL has long waiting time between nodes while updating parameters thus the communication time is the longest. Caffe-oMPI uses MPI to achieve inter-node communication. Although it is more difficult to program, it is closer to the bottom of the network, with less overhead.

By observing the performance of TensorFlow, we found that the communication time in asynchronous parallel is shorter, more iterations can be performed within the same time, and the calculation efficiency is higher. However, when a more complex model structure is encountered, the asynchronous parallel has poor convergence and convergence oscillation phenomenon may occur.

5.2   Computation

In terms of numerical computation performance, BigDL's computation speed is significantly better than Caffe-oMPI and TensorFlow when the number of samples for a single iteration calculation is the same. In the backward propagation propagation time, the backward propagation time of TensorFlow and Caffe is about 2–3 times of the forward propagation time. The backward propagation time of BigDL is only about 1.5 times of the forward propagation time, and the forward propagation time is also significantly shorter than the other two deep learning tools.

5.3   Speedup

In terms of speedup, with the number of nodes and cores expands, the speedup of Caffe-oMPI is the fastest, and BigDL is the slowest. When the data parallelism gradually increases, the communication time will increase sharply, and when the increase of communication time is greater than the decrease of computing time, the speedup will decrease.

5.4   Discussion and Open Problems

In terms of the variety of parallel modes, TensorFlow is far better than Caffe-oMPI and BigDL. There are not only traditional bulk synchronous parallel, but also asynchronous parallel and N-Soft synchronous and staleness synchronous parallel for users to choose.

According to the experiments, we found that in the distributed deep learning task under the supercomputing platform, the communication time that increases dramatically as the number of nodes increases will become the performance bottleneck of the entire system, resulting in poor scalability. And because the VPN connecting Tianhe-2 is unstable, it will cause shutdown of the computing task by the foreign host frequently, and a better failure recovery mechanism is needed to ensure the successful implementation of distributed deep learning tasks.

6   Conclusion

The main purpose of this paper is to use the high-quality CPU resources to test different neural network models and different distributed deep learning tools on the Tianhe-2 supercomputing platform, and to collect its calculation time, communication time, data loading time, and model accuracy. Then we comprehensively analyze the experimental data, which provides data support for researchers who use the supercomputing platform for deep learning. The experimental results show that the performance of the three deep learning tools, Caffe, TensorFlow, and BigDL, are mutually superior in bulk synchronous parallel.

There are two main directions for future research. At first, we plan to add more models for testing, such as VGG, GoogleNet, etc. Secondly, based on the results of this evaluation experiment and the comparative analysis among the three tools, we will seek appropriate improvements and implement them.

References

1. Cong, G., Kingsbury, B., Gosh, S., et al.: Accelerating deep neural network learning for speech recognition on a cluster of GPUs. In: Proceedings of the Machine Learning on HPC Environments, pp. 1–8. ACM, New York (2017)
2. Cui, H., Zhang, H., et al.: GeePS: scalable deep learning on distributed GPUs with a GPU-specialized parameter server. In: Proceedings of the Eleventh European Conference on Computer Systems, pp. 1–16. ACM, New York (2016)
3. Shi, S., Wang, Q., Xu, P., et al.: Benchmarking state-of-the-art deep learning software tools. In: 7th International Conference on Cloud Computing and Big Data, pp. 99–104. IEEE, Macau (2016)
4. Bahrampour, S., Ramakrishnan, N., Schott, L., et al.: Comparative study of deep learning software frameworks Computer Science (2015)
5. BigDL. https://github.com/intel-analytics/BigDL
6. Jia, Y., Shelhamer, E., Donahue, J., et al.: Caffe: convolutional architecture for fast feature embedding. In: Proceedings of the 22nd ACM International Conference on Multimedia, pp. 675–678. ACM, New York (2014)
7. Tang, Y.: TF.Learn: TensorFlow's high-level module for distributed machine learning. CoRR 1612(04251) (2017)
8. Abadi, M., Barham, P., Chen, J., et al.: TensorFlow: a system for large-scale machine learning. In: OSDI 2016 Proceedings of the 12th USENIX Conference on Operating Systems Design and Implementation, pp. 265–283. USENIX Association, Savannah (2016)
9. Yu, D., Eversole, A., Seltzer, M., et al.: An Introduction to computational Networks and the Computational Network Toolkit. Microsoft Research, Bangalore (2014)
10. Chen, T., Li, M., Li, Y., et al.: MXNet: a flexible and efficient machine learning library for heterogeneous distributed systems, CoRR 1512(01274) (2015)
11. Collobert, R., Kavukcuoglu, K., Farabet, C.: Torch7: a matlab-like environment for machine learning. Biglearn, Nips Workshop, pp. 1–6 (2012)
12. Caffe-oMPI. https://github.com/RickLee26/Caffe-oMPi
13. Liao, X., Xiao, L., Yang, C., et al.: MilkyWay-2 supercomputer: system and application. Front. Comput. Sci. 8(3), 345–356 (2015)

14. Baldi, P.: Autoencoders, unsupervised learning, and deep architectures. In: Proceedings of the 2011 International Conference on Unsupervised and Transfer Learning Workshop, Washington pp. 37–50 (2011)
15. Lecun, Y., Bottou, L., Bengio, Y., et al.: Gradient-based learning applied to document recognition. Proc. IEEE **86**(11), 2278–2324 (1998)
16. He, K., Zhang, X., Ren, S., et al.: Deep residual learning for image recognition. In: 2016 IEEE Conference on Computer Vision and Pattern Recognition (CVPR), pp. 770–778. IEEE, Las Vegas (2016)
17. Deng, J., Dong, W., Socher, R., et al.: ImageNet: a large-scale hierarchical image database. In: Computer Vision and Pattern Recognition, pp. 248–255. IEEE, Miami (2009)
18. Krizhevsky, A., Sutskever, I., Hinton, G.E.: ImageNet classification with deep convolution neural networks. In: Advances in Neural Information Processing Systems, Lake Tahoe, Nevada, pp. 1097-1105 (2012)
19. Orozco, C.I., Iglesias, F., Buemi M.E., Berlles, J.J., et al.: Real-time gender recognition from face images using deep convolutional neural network. In: 7th Latin American Conference on Networked and Electronic Media (LACNEM) IET, Valparaiso, pp. 7–11 (2017)
20. Zbontar, J., LeCun, Y., et al.: Stereo matching by training a convolutional neural network to compare image patches. J. Mach. Learn. Res. **17**(1), 2287–2318 (2016)
21. Hecht-Nielsen, R.: Theory of the backpropagation neural network. In: International 1989 Joint Conference on Neural Networks, pp. 593–605. IEEE, Washington (1989)
22. Szegedy, C., Liu, W., Jia, Y., et al.: Going deeper with convolutions. In: 2015 IEEE Conference on Computer Vision and Pattern Recognition (CVPR), pp. 1–9. IEEE, Boston (2015)
23. Simonyan, K., Zisserman, A.: Very deep convolutional networks for large-scale image recognition. Comput. Sci. **1409**(1556) (2014)
24. Shelhamer, E., Long, J., Darrell, T.: Fully convolutional networks for semantic segmentation. IEEE Trans. Pattern Anal. Mach. Intell. **39**(4), 640–651 (2014)
25. D'Informatique, D.E., Ese, N., Esent, P., et al.: Long short-term memory in recurrent neural networks. EPFL **9**(8), 1735–1780 (2001)
26. November 2017 top500 list. https://www.top500.org/lists/2017/11/

Noncooperative Optimization of Multi-user Request Strategy in Cloud Service Composition Reservation

Zheng Xiao[1](✉), Yang Guo[1], Gang Liu[1], and Jiayi Du[2](✉)

[1] College of Computer Science and Electronic Engineering, Hunan University,
Hunan 410082, China
{zxiao,guoyang,liug}@hnu.edu.cn
[2] School of Computer and Information Engineering,
Central South University of Forestry and Technology, Hunan 410004, China
dujiayi@csuft.edu.cn

Abstract. With the maturity of virtualization technology and service-oriented architecture, single cloud services have been difficult to satisfy cloud users' increasingly complex demand. Cloud service composition has become a hot topic. Nevertheless, few researches consider the problem of competition of service compositions among multiple users and interaction between the user and the cloud provider. Aiming at this problem, a service composition reservation model of a cloud provider, a cloud broker and multiple users is provided in this paper. A utility function related to revenue, payoff and performance of service compositions is designed and each user expects to maximize it. We consider this optimization problem from the perspective of game theory, and model it as a non-cooperative game. The existence of Nash equilibrium solution of the game is proved and an iterative proximate algorithm (IPA) is proposed to compute it. A series of simulation experiments are conducted to verify the theoretical analysis and the performance of IPA algorithm. The results show IPA algorithm quickly converge to a relatively stable state, and improve the utility of the user and the resource utilization of the cloud provider.

Keywords: Service composition · Non-cooperative game
Nash equilibrium

1 Introduction

With the maturity of virtualization technology and service-oriented architecture, cloud computing has gained increasingly attention in recent years. Cloud computing has become an effective means of storing and managing data, improving the utilization of computing resources, and providing various computing and IT services via the Internet. IaaS, PaaS and SaaS are three main cloud service models, and service market is gradually formed.

© Springer Nature Switzerland AG 2018
J. Vaidya and J. Li (Eds.): ICA3PP 2018, LNCS 11334, pp. 138–152, 2018.
https://doi.org/10.1007/978-3-030-05051-1_10

Due to the diversification of users' requests, single services, such as scientific computing and network storage, have been unable to satisfy their demands. Service composition tries to deliver a value-add composite service to meet users' requests [12]. Forming a composite service is a NP-hard problem, and there are a larger number of researches working on how to quickly find the optimal solution. Fanjiang [6] used the optimal solution search to solve the semantic-based automatic service composition problem. Based on skyline [20], Wang [18] applied particle swarm optimization algorithm to find it, whose optimal solution space is high-dimensional. However, most current researches mainly focus on finding the optimal composite service for single users, ignoring multiple concurrent requests for services compositions [19]. As each user seeks the optimal solution without considering the performance of the entire service system, it may cause users to compete for limited resources and results in a decline in the user's utility of service composition.

When competition occurs among multiple users, game theory is an effective way to solve the problem of interaction and decision-making [14]. There is few researches about multi-user competing for service compositions. In [8], Kang proposed a service selection optimization algorithm based on integer programming for multiple users. Li [9] modeled a non-cooperative game model for multiple users under QoS constraints and tries to maximize the utility of each user by selecting appropriate service. Aiming at different users with different service quality levels (SLA) of service composition, Shen [16] modeled a game for users to negotiate on resource reallocation. However, these works ignore the SLA of service composition changes with others' request strategies in a multi-user dynamic environment. Meanwhile, they only consider the utility of the user, ignoring the impact of interaction between users and the cloud provider on the performance of them.

In a multi-user cloud environment, the user expects to maximize his utility under QoS constraints, while the cloud provider wants to improve resource utilization, thus increasing his utility. In order to collaborate users and the cloud provider, they can negotiate SLA of service composition and the request strategy of the user in advance. Similar to [10,17], a reservation model can be used, where users submit their request strategies according to their demands and the cloud provider determines the SLA of service according to the total user request strategies. In order to motivate users to transfer requests from peak time to non-peak time, a dynamic pricing similar to [11] is considered and the response time is calculated by queue theory like [2]. Due to the selfishness of users, each user is devoted to maximizing his own utility but it is influenced by other users' strategies. Therefore, the optimization problem can be modeled as a game and solved by finding Nash equilibrium solution.

In this paper, a multi-user cloud service composition request reservation model is studied and our contributions are as follows:

(a) Provide a system model composed of a cloud provider, a cloud broker, and multiple users. A utility function of users related to revenue, payoff and

performance of service composition is designed, and each user expects to maximize its own utility.
(b) Model the optimization problem as a non-cooperative game, and its existence of Nash equilibrium solution is proved.
(c) Propose an iterative approximation algorithm to find a Nash equilibrium solution, and conduct a series of experiments to verify its convergence and effectiveness.

The rest of this paper is organized as follows. Section 2 describes the detail about system model and the optimization problem. Section 3 models the problem as a non-cooperative game problem and proves its existence of Nash equilibrium solution. IPA algorithm is proposed to find Nash equilibrium solution in Sect. 4. Section 5 verify the convergence and effectiveness of IPA through experiments. The summary and future work is shown in Sect. 6.

2   Model Formulation and Analysis

To begin with, we present our system model consisting of a cloud provider, a cloud broker and multiple competing cloud users. The cloud provider provides $M = \{1, \ldots, M\}$ types different services for reservation, represented as $S = \{s_1, \ldots, s_M\}$. The cloud broker combines different types or numbers of services to form $D = \{1, \ldots, D\}$ types service compositions, denoted as $SC = \{sc_1, \ldots, sc_D\}$. We denote the set of users as $N = \{1, \ldots, N\}$, and they compete for reservation of service composition. Similar to [1,13], we assume the request strategy of each user is determined in advance for future $H = \{1, \ldots, H\}$ time slots. Each time slot represents different time horizons, like one hour of a day.

2.1   Architecture Model

The architecture model is systematically introduced and is shown as Fig. 1. Its work process is described as follows:

(1) According to single services provided by the cloud provider, the cloud broker forms a series of service compositions combining with different types or numbers of services and publish them on the information exchange module.
(2) The user $n(n \in N)$ selects appropriate service compositions and submits its service request strategy to the cloud broker.
(3) Then the cloud broker integrates the service composition requests of all users and decompose them into service aggregated requests according to the type of services and submits them to the cloud provider.
(4) The cloud provider models service $s_m(m \in M)$ as $M/M/c$ queue to process users' requests, and send the information about the pricing parameters and response time of each service according to service aggregated requests. Then the broker calculates publish them on the information exchange module.
(5) The user calculates its utility function of current request strategy and if the user is not satisfied with it, he can send new request strategy to the broker and cycle steps (2–5) until all users keep current request strategy.

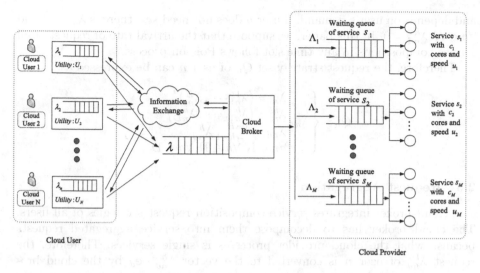

Fig. 1. Architecture model

2.2 Request Strategy Model

According to M types services of the cloud provider, the cloud broker combines D types service compositions, denoted as SC, where sc_d consists of multiple services such as $sc_d = \{s_1, s_2, s_3\}$. Each service in sc_d has a certain relationship such as serial, parallel and hybrid. Therefore, there are some restrictions on the amount of request of each service in sc_d in the same time slot, such as linear and polynomial.

In this paper, we consider there is a proportional relationship between request of each service in sc_d. Assume $k_d^m (k_d^m \geq 0, m \in M)$ is the scale factor of s_m in sc_d. So if the user requests for unit request of sc_d, the need of $s_m(m \in sc_d)$ is k_d^m. And there is $k_d^m = 0$ when sc_d does not need s_m. Therefore unit request of sc_d can be represented as

$$\mathbf{e}_d = \left(k_d^1, \cdots, k_d^M\right). \tag{1}$$

We consider a user request model similar to [4], where user $n's(n \in N)$ request strategy of service composition in future H time slot is represented as

$$\lambda_n = \left(\lambda_n^1, \cdots, \lambda_n^H\right)^T, \tag{2}$$

where $\lambda_n^h(h \in H)$ is request strategy of user n in time slot h. Because user n requests multiple service compositions at the same time, λ_n^h can be denoted as

$$\lambda_n^h = \left(\lambda_{n1}^h, \cdots, \lambda_{nD}^h\right), \tag{3}$$

where λ_{nd}^h is the amount of request of sc_d in time slot h. And it is subject to the constraint $\sum_{h=1}^H \lambda_{nd}^h = \lambda_{nd}$, where λ_{nd} is the total request of user $n's$ in sc_d

and depends on user's demand. If user n does not need sc_d, there is $\lambda_{nd} = 0$ and $\forall h \in H, \lambda_{nd}^h = 0$. In this paper, we suppose that the arrival rate of request of all service compositions in any time slot follows Poisson process.

Therefore, the request strategy set Q_n of user n can be expressed as:

$$Q_n = \left\{ \lambda_n \middle| \begin{array}{l} \lambda_n = \left(\lambda_n^1, \cdots, \lambda_n^H\right)^T \\ \lambda_n^h = \left(\lambda_{n1}^h, \cdots, \lambda_{nD}^h\right) \\ \lambda_{nd} = \sum_{h=1}^{H} \lambda_{nd}^h \\ \forall n \in N, \forall h \in H, \forall d \in D \end{array} \right. . \tag{4}$$

2.3 Request Aggregation

The cloud broker integrates service composition request strategies of all users. The cloud broker has to decompose them into service aggregated requests because what the cloud provider processes is single services. Therefore, the request λ_{nd}^h of user n is converted to the vector $\lambda_{nd}^h \cdot \mathbf{e}_d$ by the cloud broker and the aggregated request of sc_d in time slot h is $\sum_{n=1}^{N} \lambda_{nd}^h \cdot \mathbf{e}_d = \sum_{n=1}^{N} \lambda_{nd}^h \left(k_d^1, \cdots, k_d^M\right)$.

Because different service compositions may all contain service s_m, the aggregated request of s_m in time slot h is

$$\Lambda_m^h = \sum_{d=1}^{D} \sum_{n=1}^{N} k_d^m \lambda_{nd}^h, \tag{5}$$

and the total aggregated request of s_m in H future time is

$$\Lambda_m = \sum_{h=1}^{H} \Lambda_m^h = \sum_{h=1}^{H} \sum_{d=1}^{D} \sum_{n=1}^{N} k_d^m \lambda_{nd}^h. \tag{6}$$

After service compositions are decomposed by the cloud broker, the service aggregated request strategy is submitted to the cloud provider and denoted as

$$B = \left\{ \Lambda \middle| \begin{array}{l} \Lambda = (\Lambda_1, \cdots, \Lambda_M) \\ \Lambda_m = \sum_{h=1}^{H} \Lambda_m^h \\ \Lambda_m^h = \sum_{d=1}^{D} \sum_{n=1}^{N} k_d^m \lambda_{nd}^h \\ \forall m \in M, \forall n \in N, \forall h \in H, \forall d \in D \end{array} \right. . \tag{7}$$

2.4 Service Model

When involved in SLA in service composition, the most common term is QoS, which includes not only price but also response time. In this subsection, we present how the cloud provider deals with this two indicators.

Service Charge. In order to effectively encourage users to transfer their requests during peak periods and reasonably charge users, the cloud provider adopts a price mechanism similar to [4]. The unit price of s_m in a certain time slot is set as an increasing and smooth function of the total request in that time slot. The unit request charge of s_m in time slot h is:

$$C(\Lambda_m^h) = a_m(\Lambda_m^h)^2 + b_m, \tag{8}$$

where parameters a_m and b_m are constant parameters with $a_m, b_m > 0$, and $\Lambda_m^h = \sum_{d=1}^{D} \sum_{n=1}^{N} k_d^m \lambda_{nd}^h$ is the aggregated request of s_m of all users in all service compositions in time slot h. The unit price increases with the total request, which can encourage users to transfer the request from the peak periods to the non-peak periods.

Service Response Time. Service s_m with c_m homogeneous server of the cloud provider is modeled by a $M/M/c$ queue to process users' requests, where users' request is placed in a common request queue. Assume that processing capacity of each server in s_m is u_{m0}, so the total processing capacity of s_m is $u_m = u_{m0} \cdot c_m$. Let p_{ni} denote the probability that there is i service requests (including waiting and processing requests) in s_m request queue. The total request in s_m is Λ_m, so the service efficiency of s_m is $\rho_m = \Lambda_m / u_m$. With reference to [4,5], we have

$$p_{mi} = \begin{cases} p_{m0} \dfrac{(c_m \rho_m)^i}{i!}, i < c_m \\ p_{m0} \dfrac{(c_m)^{c_m}(\rho_m)^i}{c_m!}, i \geq c_m \end{cases}, \tag{9}$$

where

$$p_{m0} = \left\{ \sum_{j=0}^{c_m - 1} \frac{(c_m \rho_m)^j}{j!} + \frac{(c_m \rho_m)^{c_m}}{c_m!} \cdot \frac{1}{1 - \rho_m} \right\}^{-1}. \tag{10}$$

The average number of service request on the service s_m is

$$\bar{N}_m = \sum_{i=0}^{\infty} j p_{mi} = c_m \rho_m + \frac{\rho_m}{1 - \rho_m} P_{mq}, \tag{11}$$

where P_{mq} is the probability that the incoming requests of s_m needs to wait in queue. In this paper, we assume all servers of s_m is highly likely to keep busy. Otherwise, the cloud provider may turn off some servers to reduce the energy consumption, therefore $P_{mq} = 1$.

Applying Little's conclusion, the average response time of s_m is

$$\bar{R}_m = \frac{\bar{N}_m}{\Lambda_m} = \frac{c_m}{u_m} + \frac{1}{u_m - \Lambda_m}. \tag{12}$$

The average response time of s_m in time slot h is

$$\bar{R}_m^h = \frac{c_m}{u_m} + \frac{1}{u_m - \Lambda_m^h}, \tag{13}$$

where $\Lambda_m^h < u_m$, that is, the aggregated request of s_m in time slot h will not exceed the processing capacity of its all servers, ensuring the cloud provider can process all requests in unit time slot.

2.5   Utility Function

It is natural for a rational user to expect to maximize his utility through a reasonable request strategy, where the utility is the difference among revenue and payoff and performance of his request λ_n.

Suppose the user is rewarded sr_m by using unit service s_m to complete task. Therefore, the benefit factor of sc_d is a function l_d of its contained services, namely $r_d = l_d(sr_m), m \in sc_d$. According to the provided a_m, b_m, the payoff of unit sc_d in time slot h is $P_d^h = \sum_{m \in sc_d} k_d^m C(\Lambda_m^h) = \sum_{m \in sc_d} k_d^m \left(a_m (\Lambda_m^h)^2 + b_m \right)$. The response time is $R_d^h = \sum_{m \in sc_d} \bar{R}_m^h = \sum_{m \in sc_d} \left(\frac{c_m}{u_m} + \frac{1}{u_m - \Lambda_m^h} \right)$. As the user wants to complete requests as soon as possible, so performance will deteriorated with the delay of time slot [10]. Hence, in this paper, we assume the deteriorating rate of response time is $\delta (\delta > 1)$, then in time slot h it becomes δ^h, which grows exponentially. The performance of sc_d in time slot h is denoted as $T_d^h = \delta^h R_d^h$.

In summary, user $n's$ utility of sc_d in time slot h is

$$U_{nd}^h(\lambda_{nd}^h, \lambda_{-nd}^h) = r_d \lambda_{nd}^h - P_{nd}^h(\lambda_{nd}^h, \lambda_{-nd}^h) - w_{nd} T_d^h(\lambda_{nd}^h, \lambda_{-nd}^h), \qquad (14)$$

where $\lambda_{-nd}^h = (\lambda_{11}^h, \ldots, \lambda_{n(d-1)}^h, \lambda_{n(d+1)}^h, \ldots, \lambda_{ND}^h)$ represents the vector of all users request strategies in time slot h except sc_d of user n. In the paper, we consider that different users may have different urgency for requesting sc_d, so $w_{nd}(w_{nd} > 0)$ is waiting cost factor. When users are more concerned with response time, w_{nd} should be a larger value. To simplify writing, we use P_{nd}^h, T_d^h instead of $P_{nd}^h(\lambda_{nd}^h, \lambda_{-nd}^h), T_d^h(\lambda_{nd}^h, \lambda_{-nd}^h)$ respectively.

Since user n requests multiple service compositions at the same time, his utility in time slot h is

$$U_n^h(\lambda_n^h, \lambda_{-n}^h) = \sum_{d=1}^{D} U_{nd}^h(\lambda_{nd}^h, \lambda_{-nd}^h). \qquad (15)$$

The utility of user n in H future time slots is

$$U_n(\lambda_n, \lambda_{-n}) = \sum_{h=1}^{H} U_n^h(\lambda_n^h, \lambda_{-n}^h) = \sum_{h=1}^{H} \sum_{d=1}^{D} U_{nd}^h(^d\lambda_n^h, {}^d\lambda_{-n}^h). \qquad (16)$$

Due to all users are selfish and trying to maximize their own utilities in future H time slots, i.e., each user $n(n \in N)$ tries to find a solution to the following optimization problem(OPT_n):

$$\begin{aligned} maxmize \quad & U_n(\lambda_n, \lambda_{-n}) \\ s.t. \ \lambda_n & \in Q_n \end{aligned} \qquad (17)$$

3   Game Formulation and Analysis

In this section, the optimization problem is modeled as a non-cooperative game model, and its existence of Nash equilibrium solution is proved.

3.1   Game Formulation

It is obvious that a user's utility not only depends on his own request strategy, but also related to those of others from Eq. (16). Users are mutually dependent but selfish to maximize their own utilities, therefore we can model the optimization problem as a non-cooperative game.

Game theory is an effective approach to study how agents maximize their own utilities or minimize their own negative utilities. A non-cooperative game model usually consists of a set of participants, a set of strategies, and utility functions. In this paper, each user is a participant, so participant set is the set N. The strategy set is composed of all users' request strategy Q_n, and the joint strategy set is $Q = \prod_{n=1}^{N} Q_n$. Since all users are selfish, the optimization problem of user n can be converted from Eq. (17) to

$$\begin{aligned} minimize\ f_n(\lambda_n, \lambda_{-n}) = \sum_{h=1}^{H} \sum_{d=1}^{D} \left(\lambda_{nd}^h P_d^h + w_{nd} \delta^h R_d^h - r_d \lambda_{nd}^h \right) \\ s.t.(\lambda_n, \lambda_{-n}) \in Q_n \end{aligned} \tag{18}$$

which constitutes utility functions.

Therefore, the optimization problem can be modeled as a non-cooperate game, and formally defined by the tuple $G = <Q, \mathbf{f}>$, where $\mathbf{f} = (f_1, \dots, f_N)$. Given the request strategies of other users λ_{-n}, the goal of user n is to choose an appropriate strategy $\lambda_n \in Q_n$ to make $f_n(\lambda_n, \lambda_{-n})$ reach its minimum. The optimal requests strategy is

$$\lambda_n^* \in \arg\min_{\lambda_n \in Q_n} f_n(\lambda_n, \lambda_{-n}^*), \lambda^* \in Q. \tag{19}$$

To solve game G problem, it is necessary to find its Nash equilibrium solution. That is, when the other users' request strategies are unchanged, each user cannot obtain less negative utility by choosing other strategy. When each user's strategy is an optimal response to other users' strategies, it is a Nash equilibrium solution.

3.2   Nash Equilibrium Analysis

In this subsection, we analyze the existence of Nash equilibrium solution of the non-cooperative game $G = <Q, f>$.

Theorem 1. *Given the game $G = <Q, f>$, suppose that the following conditions hold*

(a) *For each user $n(n \in N)$, strategy set Q_n is a convex and also a tight set, and his negative utility function $f_n(\lambda_n, \lambda_{-n})$ is continuously different in λ_n.*
(b) *For each fixed tuple λ_{-n}, the negative utility function $f_n(\lambda_n, \lambda_{-n})$ is convex in λ_n subjected to Q_n.*

The game G has a nonempty and compact solution set.

Proof. It is obvious that statements in (a) of above theorem hold. We only need to prove the convexity of function $f_n(\lambda_n, \lambda_{-n})$ in λ_n for every fixed λ_{-n}. This can be achieved by proving the Hansen matrix of $f_n(\lambda_n, \lambda_{-n})$ is positive semi-definite [7,15].

Since $f_n(\lambda_n, \lambda_{-n}) = \sum_{h=1}^{H} \sum_{d=1}^{D} \left(\lambda_{nd}^h P_d^h + w_{nd} \delta^h R_d^h - r_d \lambda_{nd}^h \right)$, so we have

$$\nabla_{\lambda_n} f_n(\lambda_n, \lambda_{-n}) = \left[\frac{\partial f_n(\lambda_n, \lambda_{-n})}{\partial \lambda_{nd}^h} \right]_{h=1,d=1}^{h=H,d=D} = \left(\frac{\partial f_n(\lambda_n, \lambda_{-n})}{\partial \lambda_{n1}^1}, \cdots, \frac{\partial f_n(\lambda_n, \lambda_{-n})}{\partial \lambda_{nD}^H} \right),$$

and the Hessian matrix can be expressed as

$$\nabla_{\lambda_n}^2 f_n(\lambda_n, \lambda_{-n}) = diag \left\{ \left[\frac{\partial^2 f_n(\lambda_n, \lambda_{-n})}{\partial (\lambda_{nd}^h)^2} \right]_{h=1,d=1}^{h=H,d=D} \right\}$$

$$= diag \left\{ \left| \sum_{m \in sc_d} \left(4a_m \left(k_d^m\right)^2 \Lambda_m^h + \sum_{d'=1}^{D} \left(2a_m \left(k_d^m\right)^3 \lambda_{nd}^h + \frac{2w_{nd}\delta^h \left(k_d^m\right)^2}{\left(u_m - \Lambda_m^h\right)^3} \right) \right) \right|_{h=1,d=1}^{h=H,d=D} \right\}.$$

$$(20)$$

Obviously, all diagonal elements of matrix in Eq. (20) are positive. Therefore, the Hansen matrix of $f_n(\lambda_n, \lambda_{-n})$ is positive semi-definite. Theorem 1 is proved.

4   Algorithm

Once proved the existence of Nash equilibrium solution of game G, we are interested in designing a suitable algorithm to find it. In this section, we propose algorithms to solve the problem.

4.1   The Iterative Proximal Algorithm

In order to reduce communications between users and the cloud provider, we rewrite the optimization problem into the following form

$$minimize\ f_n(\lambda_n, \lambda_\Sigma) = \sum_{h=1}^{H} \sum_{d=1}^{D} \left(\lambda_{nd}^h P_d^h + w_{nd} \delta^h R_d^h - r_d \lambda_{nd}^h \right), \quad (21)$$
$$s.t.\lambda_n \in Q_n$$

where λ_Σ represents the aggregated request strategies of all users in future H time slots, namely $\lambda_\Sigma = \sum_{n=1}^{N} \lambda_n$. Therefore, the user only needs his own request strategy and the aggregated request strategy (λ_Σ), which does not involve each user's individual request strategy (λ_{-n}).

Since all users are selfish, at each iteration, each user $n(n \in N)$ updates his request strategy to minimize his own negative utility. However, according to Theorem 4.2 in [14], if all users are allowed to update their own strategies simultaneously, the convergence of the game may not be guaranteed. In order to overcome this shortcoming, according to the Proximal Decomposition Algorithm 4.2 in [14], an iterative approximation algorithm (IPA) is proposed. Each user $n(n \in N)$ tries to solve the following optimization problems

$$minimize\ f_n(\lambda_n, \lambda_\Sigma) + \frac{\tau}{2} \left\| \lambda_n - \bar{\lambda}_n \right\|^2.$$
$$s.t.\lambda_n, \bar{\lambda}_n \in Q_n$$
$$(22)$$

Algorithm 1. Iterative Proximal Algorithm (IPA)

Input: : Strategy set of all users: Q,ε.
Output: : Request configuration: λ.
1: *Initialization*: Each cloud user $n(n \in N)$ randomly chooses a $\lambda_n^{(0)} \in Q_n$ and set
  $\bar{\lambda}_n \leftarrow 0$. Set $S_c \leftarrow N$, $S_l \leftarrow \emptyset$, and $t \leftarrow 0$.
2: **while** $(S_c \neq S_l)$ **do**
3:   Set $S_l \leftarrow S_c$.
4:   **while** $(\left\|\lambda^{(t)} - \lambda^{(t-1)}\right\| \geq \varepsilon)$ **do**
5:     **for** (each cloud user $n \in S_c$) **do**
6:       Compute $\lambda_n^{(t)}$ as follows (by Algorithm 2):
         $$\lambda_n^{(t+1)} \leftarrow \underset{\lambda_n \in Q_n}{\arg\min} \left(f_n(\lambda_n, \lambda_{\sum}^{(t)}) + \frac{\tau}{2} \left\|\lambda_n - \bar{\lambda}_n\right\|^2 \right)$$
7:     **end for**
8:     Set $t \leftarrow t + 1$
9:   **end while**
10:   Each user $n \in S_c$ updates his Nash equilibrium strategy $\bar{\lambda}_n \leftarrow \lambda_n^{(t-1)}$
11:   **for** (each user $n \in S_c$) **do**
12:     **if** $(U_n(\lambda_n^{(t)}, \lambda_{\sum}^{(t)}) < 0)$ **then**
13:       Set $\lambda_n^{(t)} \leftarrow 0$ and $S_c \leftarrow S_c - \{n\}$
14:     **end if**
15:   **end for**
16: **end while**
17: **return** λ.

That is, given the aggregated request strategy, we need to find a strategy vector λ_n^* for user n satisfying

$$\lambda_n^* \in \underset{\lambda_n \in Q_n}{\arg\min} \left(f_n(\lambda_n, \lambda_{\sum}) + \frac{\tau}{2} \left\|\lambda_n - \bar{\lambda}_n\right\|^2 \right), \tag{23}$$

where $\tau(\tau > 0)$ is a regularization parameter, and if the value of τ is large enough, the convergence of the algorithm can be guaranteed.

A more formal description is shown in Algorithm 1. Steps 4–9 calculate the Nash equilibrium solution and record it at step 10. If the user's utility is below 0 at Nash equilibrium, we treat it as a non-participator in next iteration and remove it as shown in steps 11–15. S_l denotes the set of users participating in this iteration, while S_c denotes the set of users participating in next iteration. Repeat the above process until S_l is equal to S_c as step 2.

4.2 Sub-algorithm Based on Lagrange Multiplier

Now focusing on the calculation of Eq. (22), it can be rewritten as follow

$$L_n(\lambda_n, \lambda_{\sum}) = f_n(\lambda_n, \lambda_{\sum}) + \frac{\tau}{2} \left\|\lambda_n - \bar{\lambda}_n\right\|^2. \tag{24}$$

We must minimize $L_n(\lambda_n, \lambda_{\sum})$, and the only variable for user n is λ_n, so it can be denoted as

$$L_n(\lambda_n, \kappa) = f_n(\lambda_n, \kappa) + \frac{\tau}{2} \left\|\lambda_n - \bar{\lambda}_n\right\|^2, \tag{25}$$

Algorithm 2. $Calculate\_\lambda_n(\varepsilon, u_m, a_m, b_m, r_d, \tau, \lambda_n, \Lambda, \lambda_{nd})$

Input: : $\varepsilon, u_m, a_m, b_m, r_d, \tau, \lambda_n, \Lambda, \lambda_{nd}$.
Output: : λ_n.
1: *Initialization*: Let *inc* be a relative small positive constant. Set $\lambda_n \leftarrow 0$.
2: **for** (each service composition $d \in D$) **do**
3:     **while** $(\lambda_{nd}^1 + \cdots \lambda_{nd}^H < \lambda_{nd})$ **do**
4:         Set $\phi_d \leftarrow \phi_d + inc$, and $inc \leftarrow 2 \times inc$.
5:         $\forall h \in H, \lambda_{nd}^h \leftarrow Calculate\_\lambda_{nd}^h(\varepsilon, u_m, a_m, b_m, r_d, \tau, \kappa_d^h, \phi_d)$;
6:     **end while**
7:     Set $lb \leftarrow 0$ and $ub \leftarrow \phi_d$.
8:     **while** $(ub - lb > \varepsilon)$ **do**
9:         Set $\phi_d \leftarrow (lb + ub)/2$.
10:       $\forall h \in H, \lambda_{nd}^h \leftarrow Calculate\_\lambda_{nd}^h(\varepsilon, u_m, a_m, b_m, r_d, \tau, \kappa_d^h, \phi_d)$;
11:       **if** $(\lambda_{nd}^1 + \cdots \lambda_{nd}^H < \lambda_{nd})$ **then**
12:           Set $lb \leftarrow \phi_d$.
13:       **else**
14:           Set $ub \leftarrow \phi_d$.
15:       **end if**
16:     **end while**
17:     Set $\phi_d \leftarrow (lb + ub)/2$.
18:     $\forall h \in H, \lambda_{nd}^h \leftarrow Calculate\_\lambda_{nd}^h(\varepsilon, u_m, a_m, b_m, r_d, \tau, \kappa_d^h, \phi_d)$;
19: **end for**
20: **return** λ_n

---

where $\kappa = \lambda_\sum - \lambda_n$,$\kappa = \{\kappa_1 \cdots \kappa_D\}, \kappa_d = \{\kappa_{dm} | m \in sc_d\}$ and $\kappa_{dm} = \Lambda_m^h - \lambda_{nd}^h k_d^m$. Meanwhile, there are some restriction in user n's request strategy

$$\lambda_{nd}^1 + \cdots + \lambda_{nd}^{II} = \lambda_{nd}, \forall d \in D.$$

Minimize Eq. (25) by means of Lagrangian multiplier, for all $1 \leq h \leq H$ there is

$$\frac{\partial L_n}{\partial \lambda_{nd}^h} = \phi_d \frac{\partial \lambda_{nd}}{\partial \lambda_{nd}^h} = \phi_d,$$

where $\phi_d(1 \leq d \leq D)$ represents the Lagrangian multiplier. We obtain

$$\frac{\partial L_n}{\partial \lambda_{nd}^h} = \sum_{m \in sc_d} \sum_{d'=1}^{D} \left(2\lambda_{nd}^h \left(k_d^m\right)^2 a_m \left(\kappa_{dm}^h + k_d^m \lambda_{nd}^h\right) + \frac{w_{nd}\delta^h k_d^m}{\left(u_m - \kappa_{dm}^h - k_d^m \lambda_{nd}^h\right)^2} \right)$$

$$\sum_{m \in sc_d} \left(k_d^m \left(a_m(\kappa_{dm}^h + k_d^m \lambda_{nd}^h)^2 + b_m\right) \right) - r_d + \tau(\lambda_{nd}^h - \bar{\lambda}_{nd}^h) = \phi_d. \tag{26}$$

The second-order of $\frac{\partial L_n}{\partial \lambda_{nd}^h}$ is

$$\frac{\partial^2 L_n}{\partial \left(\lambda_{nd}^h\right)^2} = \sum_{m \in sc_d} \sum_{d'=1}^{D} \left(2a_m \left(k_d^m\right)^3 \lambda_{nd}^h + \frac{2w_{nd}\delta^h \left(k_d^m\right)^2}{\left(u_m - \kappa_{dm}^h - k_d^m \lambda_{nd}^h\right)^3} \right) +$$

$$\sum_{m \in sc_d} 4a_m \left(k_d^m\right)^2 \left(\kappa_{dm}^h + k_d^m \lambda_{nd}^h\right) + \tau > 0. \tag{27}$$

Therefore $\frac{\partial L_n}{\partial(\lambda_{nd}^h)}$ is a monotonically increasing function in λ_{nd}^h, we can increase the value of ϕ_d continuously from 0 until the right one is found. With reference of [3], we proposed an algorithm to find a suitable strategy $\lambda_n (n \in N)$ and the pseudo code is in Algorithm 2. In steps 3–6, we use the increasing inc to find the right border of ϕ_d which satisfies $\lambda_{nd}^1 + \cdots \lambda_{nd}^H \geq \lambda_{nd}$. In steps 7–16, we use binary search approach to approximate the right ϕ_d. In steps 17–18, we calculate the request strategy λ_n according to the approximated ϕ_d. In this algorithm, a sub-algorithm is used, which is used to calculate the temporary λ_{nd}^h and the pseudo-code is shown in Algorithm 3. The temporary λ_{nd}^h can be found in a certain interval $[lb, ub]$ through the binary search approach according to temporary ϕ_d.

Algorithm 3. $Calculate\_\lambda_{nd}^h(\varepsilon, u_m, a_m, b_m, r_d, \tau, \kappa_d^h, \phi_d)$

Input: : $\varepsilon, u_m, a_m, b_m, r_d, \tau, \kappa_d^h, \phi_d$.
Output: : λ_{nd}^h.
1: *Initialization*: Set $lb \leftarrow 0, ub \leftarrow \max\left\{\left((1-\varepsilon)u_m - \kappa_{dm}^h\right)/k_d^m\right\}$.
2: **while** $(ub - lb > \varepsilon)$ **do**
3:     Set $mid \leftarrow (lb + ub)/2$, and $\lambda_{nd}^h \leftarrow mid$.
4:     **if** $(\frac{\partial L_n}{\partial \lambda_{nd}^h} < \phi_d)$ **then**
5:         Set $lb \leftarrow mid$.
6:     **else**
7:         Set $ub \leftarrow mid$.
8:     **end if**
9: **end while**
10: **return** λ_{nd}^h.

---

5   Evaluation of Algorithm

In this section, we conduct a series of simulation experiments to verify the performance of IPA algorithm. To begin with, we set the experimental parameters. Suppose that the cloud provider has $M = 5$ types services with benefit factor sr_m randomly generated from 40 to 60. The charge parameters are set as $a_m = 0.001$ and $b_m = 0$. For the sake of simplicity, the cloud broker froms $D = 10$ types service compositions according to service types, where each service composition contains 3 types services. k_d^m is randomly generated from 1 to 5 and the benefit factor of sc_d is $r_d = \sum_{m \in sc_d} k_d^m \cdot sr_m$. Let us consider a service composition reservation model consisting of $N = 50$ users, where H is set to 24 and each time slot is assumed to be an hour. Each user randomly selects 3 types service compositions with $\lambda_{nd} = \sum_{h=1}^{H} \lambda_{nd}^h = 60$, and w_{nd} is randomly selected. The initial value of $\lambda_n (n \in N)$ is chosen randomly from Q_n, ε is set to 0.001 and the deterioration rate δ is 1.2.

We first prove the convergence of IPA algorithm. As shown in Fig. 2, it presents users' utility during iteration, in which we randomly select 4 users

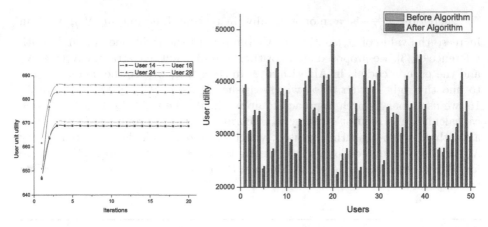

Fig. 2. User utility vs. iterations

Fig. 3. Changes in user utility

(user 14, 18, 24, and 29). It is obvious users' utilities increase with iterations
and eventually quickly reach a relatively stable within 10 iterations. In other
word, the entire system reaches a Nash equilibrium, verifying the convergence
of IPA algorithm. Figure 3 shows the utilities of all users before and after IPA
algorithm. It can be seen that the vast majority users' utilities have increased. It
demonstrates the effectiveness of IPA algorithm, which can effectively encourage
users to use the service composition reservation model to improve their utilities.

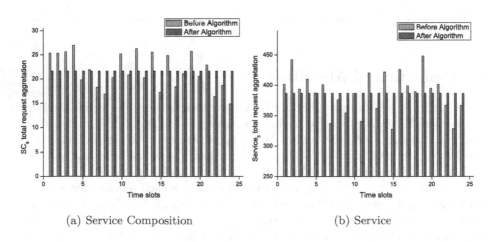

(a) Service Composition

(b) Service

Fig. 4. Aggregated load

Meanwhile, IPA algorithm can effectively improve the resource utilization
of the cloud provider, and the results is shown in Fig. 4. Service composition aggregated requests in different time slots are shown in Fig. 4(a), and

service aggregated requests are presented in Fig. 4(b), where the aggregated requests come from all service compositions requests of all users. The result of *BeforeAlgorithm* is the result of the initial request strategies, and the *AfterAlgorithm* is the result of Nash equilibrium solution after using IPA algorithm. It can be clearly seen that our proposed model can encourage users to transform their service composition requests from peak periods to non-peak periods, resulting in a more balanced result in aggregated service composition requests as well as in service requests. The aggregated request of different time slots is almost the same, which confirms that IPA algorithm can effectively reduce idle servers' costs and improve resource utilization of the cloud provider.

6   Conclusion

In this paper, we first present a service composition reservation model for multiple users. A utility function related to revenue, payoff and performance of service compositions is designed and each user expects to maximize it. Next, we consider the optimization problem from the perspective of game theory and model it as a non-cooperative game. Then the existence of Nash equilibrium solution of game is proved and IPA algorithm is proposed to compute it. Finally, we do a series simulation experiments to verify our theoretical analysis. The experimental results show that IPA algorithm can quickly converge to a relatively stable state, and it can improve the utilities of users and the resource utilization of the cloud provider.

The reservation model in this paper is mainly beneficial to users, although it enables the cloud provider to improve resource utilization, it does not maximize its utility as the pricing parameters are fixed. Therefore, on the one hand, our future work is to design a more appropriate dynamic pricing mechanism, enabling users and providers to negotiate appropriate pricing parameters and achieve the bilateral utility maximum. On the other hand, we hope to establish a more complete theoretical system to prove the feasibility of the reservation model and the convergence of IPA algorithm.

Acknowledgments. This work is partially supported by Natural Science Foundation of China (No. 61872129 and No. 61802444) and Doctoral Scientific Research Foundation of Central South University of Forestry and Technology (No. 2016YJ047).

References

1. Atzeni, I., Ordóñez, L.G., Scutari, G., Palomar, D.P., Fonollosa, J.R.: Demand-side management via distributed energy generation and storage optimization. IEEE Trans. Smart Grid **4**(2), 866–876 (2016)
2. Cao, J., Kai, H., Li, K., Zomaya, A.Y.: Optimal multiserver configuration for profit maximization in cloud computing. IEEE Trans. Parallel Distrib. Syst. **24**(6), 1087–1096 (2013)

3. Cao, J., Li, K., Stojmenovic, I.: Optimal power allocation and load distribution for multiple heterogeneous multicore server processors across clouds and data centers. IEEE Trans. Comput. **63**(1), 45–58 (2014)
4. Chen, H., Li, Y., Louie, R.H.Y., Vucetic, B.: Autonomous demand side management based on energy consumption scheduling and instantaneous load billing: an aggregative game approach. IEEE Trans. Smart Grid **5**(4), 1744–1754 (2013)
5. Fadlullah, Z.M., Quan, D.M., Kato, N., Stojmenovic, I.: GTES: an optimized game-theoretic demand-side management scheme for smart grid. IEEE Syst. J. **8**(2), 588–597 (2014)
6. Fanjiang, Y.Y., Yang, S.: Semantic-based automatic service composition with functional and non-functional requirements in design time: a genetic algorithm approach. Inf. Softw. Technol. **56**(3), 352–373 (2014)
7. Foster, I., Zhao, Y., Raicu, I., Lu, S.: Cloud computing and grid computing 360-degree compared. In: Grid Computing Environments Workshop GCE 2008 (2008)
8. Kang, G., Liu, J., Tang, M., Liu, X., Fletcher, K.K.: Web service selection for resolving conflicting service requests. In: IEEE International Conference on Web Services, pp. 387–394 (2011)
9. Li, H., Zhu, Q., Ouyang, Y.: Non-cooperative game based QoS-aware web services composition approach for concurrent tasks. In: IEEE International Conference on Web Services, pp. 444–451 (2011)
10. Liu, C., Li, K., Xu, C., Li, K.: Strategy configurations of multiple users competition for cloud service reservation. IEEE Trans. Parallel Distrib. Syst. **27**(2), 508–520 (2016)
11. Mardukhi, F., Nematbakhsh, N., Barati, A., Barati, A.: QoS decomposition for service composition using genetic algorithm. Appl. Soft Comput. **13**(7), 3409–3421 (2013)
12. Pan, L., An, B., Liu, S., Cui, L.: Nash equilibrium and decentralized pricing for QoS aware service composition in cloud computing environments. In: IEEE International Conference on Web Services, pp. 154–163 (2017)
13. Samadi, P., Mohsenian-Rad, H., Schober, R., Wong, V.W.S.: Advanced demand side management for the future smart grid using mechanism design. IEEE Trans. Smart Grid **3**(3), 1170–1180 (2012)
14. Scutari, G., Palomar, D.P., Facchinei, F., Pang, J.S.: Convex optimization, game theory, and variational inequality theory. Signal Process. Mag. IEEE **27**(3), 35–49 (2010)
15. Scutari, G., Palomar, D.P., Facchinei, F., Pang, J.S.: Monotone Games for Cognitive Radio Systems. Springer, London (2012). https://doi.org/10.1007/978-1-4471-2265-4_4
16. Shen, Y., Yang, X., Wang, Y., Ye, Z.: Optimizing QoS-aware services composition for concurrent processes in dynamic resource-constrained environments. In: IEEE International Conference on Web Services, pp. 250–258 (2012)
17. Simhon, E., Starobinski, D.: Game-theoretic analysis of advance reservation services. In: Information Sciences and Systems. pp. 1–6 (2014)
18. Wang, S., Sun, Q., Zou, H., Yang, F.: Particle swarm optimization with skyline operator for fast cloud-based web service composition. Mob. Netw. Appl. **18**(1), 116–121 (2013)
19. Yang, Y., Mi, Z., Sun, J.: Game theory based Iaas services composition in cloud computing environment. Adv. Inf. Sci. Serv. Sci. **4**(22), 238–246 (2012)
20. Zhou, X., Li, K., Zhou, Y., Li, K.: Adaptive processing for distributed skyline queries over uncertain data. IEEE Trans. Knowl. Data Eng. **28**(2), 371–384 (2016)

Most Memory Efficient Distributed Super Points Detection on Core Networks

Jie Xu[1(✉)], Wei Ding[2], and Xiaoyan Hu[2]

[1] School of Computer Science and Engineering, Southeast University, Nanjing, China
xujieip@163.com
[2] School of Cyber Science and Engineering, Southeast University, Nanjing, China
wding@njnet.edu.cn

Abstract. The super point, a host which communicates with lots of others, is a kind of special hosts gotten great focus. Mining super point at the edge of a network is the foundation of many network research fields. In this paper, we proposed the most memory efficient super points detection scheme. This scheme contains a super points reconstruction algorithm called short estimator and a super points filter algorithm called long estimator. Short estimator gives a super points candidate list using thousands of bytes memory and long estimator improves the accuracy of detection result using millions of bytes memory. Combining short estimator and long estimator, our scheme acquires the highest accuracy using the smallest memory than other algorithms. There is no data confliction and floating operation in our scheme. This ensures that our scheme is suitable for parallel running and we deploy our scheme on a common GPU to accelerate processing speed. Experiments on several real-world core network traffics show that our algorithm acquires the highest accuracy with only consuming littler than one-fifth memory of other algorithms.

Keywords: Super points detection · Distributed computing
GPU computing · Network measurement

1 Introduction

With the developing of the network, thousands of Gigabytes data pass through the Internet every second [6]. It is too expensive to monitor every host in the network. An efficient way is to focus on special ones which have great influence on the network security and management. The super point, a host which communicates with lots of others, is one of such special hosts playing important roles in the network, such as Web servers [14][19], P2P spreaders [4,16], DDoS victims [21,24], scanners [3,8] and so on. Detecting super point can help us with network management and security. It is also a foundation module of many instruction detection system [15].

For example, DDoS (Distributed Denial of Service) attack is a heavy threat to the Internet [9,11]. It appears at the beginning of the Internet and becomes complex with the rapid growth of the network technology. Although many defense

© Springer Nature Switzerland AG 2018
J. Vaidya and J. Li (Eds.): ICA3PP 2018, LNCS 11334, pp. 153–167, 2018.
https://doi.org/10.1007/978-3-030-05051-1_11

algorithms have been proposed, most of them are too elaborate to deploy in the high-speed network. The peculiarity of a victim under DDoS attack is that it will receive huge packets with different source IP addresses in a short period. A DDoS victim is a typical super point. Super point only accounts for a small fraction of the overall hosts. If we detect super points first and spend more monitoring resource to them, we can defense DDoS much more efficiently. Real-time super points detection on the core network is an important step of these applications.

The speed of nowadays network is growing rapidly. For a core network, it always contains several border routers which locate at different places. How to detect overall super points from all of these distributed routers is more difficult than from a small single router. A distributed super points detection algorithm should satisfy following criteria:

1. High accuracy.
2. Small memory requirement.
3. Real-time packets processing time.

A high accuracy algorithm should detect out all super points and does not report normal hosts as super points by mistake. Many researchers try to use small and fast memory, such as static random accessing memory SRAM [12,13], to detect super point. These algorithms used estimating method to record hosts' cardinalities, the opposite hosts number during a time period. But the accuracy of these algorithms will decrease with the reduction of memory. Parallel computation ability of GPU (Graphic Processing Unit) is stronger than that of CPU because of its plenty operating cores. When using GPU to scan packets parallel, we would get a high throughput and that is what we do in this paper.

To overcome previous algorithms' weakness, we devise a novel distributed super points detection algorithm which has the highest accuracy but consumes smaller than one-fifth memory used by other algorithms. The contributions of this paper are listed following:

1. A tiny super points detection algorithm is proposed in this paper.
2. A high accuracy super points filtering algorithm is proposed.
3. We design the most memory efficient scheme for distributed super points detection.
4. We implement our algorithm on GPU for real-time super point detection on core network traffic.

In the next section, we will introduce other super point detection algorithms and analyze their merit and weakness. In Sect. 3, our novel memory efficient algorithm will be represented in detail. How to deploy our algorithm in GPU is described in Sect. 4. Section 5 shows experiments of our algorithm compared with other ones. And we make a conclusion in the last section.

2   Related Work

Super point detection is a hot topic in network research field. Venkataraman et al. [20] proposed an algorithm that did not keep the state of every host so this algorithm can scale very well. Cao et al. [4] used a pair-based sampling method to eliminate the majority of low opposite number hosts and reserved more resource to estimate the opposite number of the resting hosts. Estan et al. [7] proposed two bits map algorithms based on sampling flows. Several hosts could share a bit of this map to reduce memory consumption. All of these methods were based on sampling flows which limited their accuracy.

In these previous algorithms, only a few were suitable for running in distributed environment [12,17,22].

Wang et al. [22] devised a novel structure, called double connection degree sketch (DCDS), to store and estimate different hosts cardinalities. They updated DCDS by setting several bits to one simply. In order to restore super points at the end of a time period, which bits to be updated were determined by Chinese Remainder Theory (CRT) when parsing a packet. By using CRT, every bit of DCDS could be shared by different hosts. But the computing process of CRT was very complex which limited the speed of this algorithm.

Liu et al. [12] proposed a simple method to restore super hosts basing on bloom filter. They called this algorithm as Vector Bloom Filter (VBF). VBF used the bits extracted from IP address to decide which bits to be updated when scanning a packet. Compared with CRT, bit extraction only needed a small operation. But VBF would consume much time to restore super point when the number of super points was very big because it used four bit arrays to record cardinalities.

Most of the previous works only focused on accelerating speed by adapting fast memory but neglected the calculation ability of processors. Shin et al. [17] first used GPU to estimate hosts opposite numbers. They devised a Collision-tolerant hash table to filter flows from origin traffic and used a bitmap data structure to record and estimate hosts' opposite numbers. But this method needed to store IP address of every flow while scanning traffic because they could not restore super points from the bitmap directly. Additional candidate IP address storing space increased the memory requirement of this algorithm.

To reduce transmission data in the distributed environment, we devise a novel super point opposite number estimator which can tell if a host is a super point with only 8 bits. Base on this memory efficient estimator, a smart super point restoring algorithm is devised. We will describe our novel algorithm in the following section.

3 Super Point Detection

The Super point is a host which contacts with many others in a time period T. "Other host" here has different means under different cases. When monitoring opposite IP at a host's network card, other host means every one that sends packets to or receives packets from this host. But this kind of opposite IPs could only be counted by each host self. Generally, a host is locating in a network managed by some Internet Service Providers (ISP). The managers of this subnetwork hope to get information about the traffic between their network and others. From the inspection of ISP, opposite host represents one that being watched at the edge of ISP's subnetwork. Edge of a network means a set of routers forwarding packets between this network and other networks. When monitoring traffic between different network, a router could be regarded as a watch point (WP).

Let SNet represent the subnetwork managed by an ISP and ONet represent the set of other network communicating with SNet through its edge routers. When detecting the super point at the edge of SNet, the set of a host's opposite IP addresses is defined as below.

Definition 1 (Opposite IP Set/Opposite IP Number). *For a host h in SNet or ONet, its Opposite IP set is the set of IP addresses communicating with it over a certain time period T through the edge of SNet written as $OP(h)$. h's opposite IP number is the number of elements in $OP(h)$ denoted as $|OP(h)|$.*

Then we can give the definition of the super point used in this paper.

Definition 2 (Super Point). *In a certain time period T, if a host h in SNet or ONet has no less than θ opposite IPs, $|OP(h)| \geq \theta$, h is a super point.*

Super points may be located in *SNet* or *ONet*. Both of these super points could be found out by the same algorithm with changing the order of IP addresses. In the rest of this paper, super point means SNet's super point briefly. Opposite IP number estimation is the foundation of super point detection. In this paper, we proposed two novel estimators: short estimator and long estimator.

3.1   Short Estimator

In order to judge if a host is a super point, we should record its opposite IP addresses while scanning packets sending to it or it receives. The estimation accuracy is related to the size of memory using to record opposite number. The bigger the size of allocating memory, the more accuracy the result will be. One of the most memory efficient algorithms is OPT proposed by Kane et al. [10]. But the computing complex of OPT is very complex. In this paper, we proposed a more memory efficient algorithm derived from OPT to judge if the opposite IP's number is more than a threshold θ. We call this method as Short Estimator (SE) because it uses only 8 bits, much shorter than other algorithms consumed.

Suppose that SE consists of g bits. 8 is big enough for g when host's IP address is version 4. Every bit of SE is initialized to 0 at the begin of a time period. When receiving a packet related to host h, h's opposite IP address *oip* in this packet will update a bit of SE if the least significant bit of *oip*'s randomly hashed value is bigger than an integer τ. *oip* is firstly hashed by a random hash function [5] H_1 to make sure that the hashed value is uniform distribution. H_1 will map an integer between 0 and $2^{32} - 1$ to another random value in the same range.

If $lsb(H_1(oip)) \geq \tau$, one bit in SE, seleted by another hash function H_2, will be set to 1. H_2 map an integer between 0 and $2^{32} - 1$ to a random value between 0 and $g - 1$.

τ is an integer derived from θ by the following equation:

$$\tau = ceil(log_2(\theta/8)) \tag{1}$$

Function ceil(x) returns the smallest integer no less than x. After scanning all h's relevant packets, we can judge if $|OP(h)|$ is bigger than θ by counting the number of "1" bits in SE. The number of "1"bits in SE is also called the weight of SE, written as $|SE|$. If $|SE| \geq 3$, $|OP(h)|$ is judged as bigger than θ.

We have introduced how to judge if a single host is a super point by SE. But there are millions of host in the network and it's not reasonable to allocate a SE for each of them because of the following two reasons:

1. Too many memory is required. A core network always contains millions of host. For an IP address of version 4, it will consume 4 bytes. Together with 8 bits used by an SE, each host requires 5 bytes. For a core network containing 100 millions of hosts, we will allocate more than 500 millions of bytes. Such big size of memory is a heavy burden for both memory allocation on server and transmission in the distributed environment.
2. The memory location is very difficult for huge hosts. IP addresses of hosts are widely distributed between 0 and $2^{32} - 1$, especially for IP addresses of ONet. How to store and access these randomly hosts efficiently is a hard task. No matter storing these IP addresses in a list or hash table, we have to spend much time in memory accession.

To overcome previous questions, we design an SE sharing structure which can use a fixed number of SE to judge and restore lots of hosts. In the next section, we will introduce super point restoring algorithm based on SE.

3.2 Restoring Super Points by Short Estimator

Without allocating an SE for each host, we won't know the IP address of super point. In order to detect super points at the end of a time period, we have to reconstruction IP address from our data structure. This requires that our data structure will contain enough IP address information when updating. Based on this requirement, we design a novel structure called Short Estimator Array, written as SEA, which can avoid keeping huge SE instances but can restore super point easily.

From the name of the SEA, we can see that it is an array of SE. SEA has SR rows and the ith row contains $SC(i)$ SEs. When receiving a packet, we extract an IP pair with format $< hip, oip >$ from it where hip is the IP address of the host that we want to monitor and oip is its opposite IP address. An SE in each row of the SEA will record oip. hip decides which SE of each row is chosen. Because there are huge hosts in the network, using a single SEA would cause that its SEs is overshared by many hosts. "Overshare" means there are too many hosts map to the same SE. So we use 2^r SEAs and each SEA record a part of traffic. We call these 2^r SEAs as SEA Vector (SEAV). Using which SEA to record and estimate a host's opposite IP number is decided by the rightest r bits of the host. We call the right r bits of a host as Right Part (RP) and the rest left 32-r bits as the Left Part (LP). Figure 1 shows how to choose SEA to record opposite IP number.

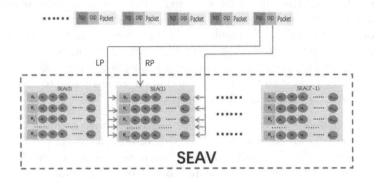

Fig. 1. Short estimarot arrays vector

For a certain SEA in SEAV, RP of a host is clear and only LP is unknown. When choosing a SE to update, we extract several successive bits from hip's LP as the index of SE in each row. SE's index, written as $Idx(i, LP(h))$, means the ith row's column identifier of SE relating to a host h whose LP is $LP(h)$. If every bit of LP is contained in one or more SEs' indexes, we can restore LP by extracting and concatenating bits in all these indexes. To explain how to get $Idx(i, lp)$ of each row, we give the following declaration:

Definition 3 (Index Starting Bit). *For the ith row in a SEA, its index starting bit $ISB(i)$ is a bit in the LP from which we begin to extract sub bits of the LP.*

Definition 4 (Index Bits Number). *For the ith row in a SEA, its index bits number $IBN(i)$ is the number of bits that we would extract from the LP.*

$IBN(i)$ decides the number of SE, which is written as $SC(i)$, in the ith row. We can acquire $Idx(i, LP(h))$ by $IBN(i)$ and $ISB(i)$. Let $Idx(i, LP(h))[j]$ point to the jth bit of $Idx(i, LP(h))$ and $LP(h)[j]$ represent the jth bit of $LP(h)$. Every bit of $Idx(i, LP(h))$ could be determined by the following equation.

$$Idx(i, LP(h))[j] = LP(h)[(ISB[i] + j) mod (32 - r)] \qquad (2)$$

where $0 \leq j \leq IBN(i) - 1$ and $0 \leq i \leq SR - 1$. The value of $IBN(i)$ and $ISB(i)$ should obey two constraints.

1. Every bit of $LP(h)$ locates in at least one index. This constraint makes sure that $LP(h)$ could be reconstructed from the SR indexes. In another word, for $j \in [0, 31 - r]$, there is at least a $i \in [0, SR - 1]$ that let $ISB[i] \leq j \leq ISB[i] + IBN[i] - 1$.

2. One index should have several bits same to its next index part. These duplicating bits could help us to remove fake candidate IP addresses efficiently. For $i \in [0, SR - 1]$, $(ISB[i] + IBN[i])mod(32 - r) \leq ISB[(i+1)modSR]$.

The rows number SR will affect $ISB(i)$ and $IBN(i)$. When SR choose a bigger number, the first condition could be matched even all $IBN(i)$s are small. For example, we can set the value of $IBN(i)$ equal to $ceil(\frac{32}{SR}) + a$ and $ISB(i) = i * ceil(\frac{32}{SR})$, where $i \in [0, SR - 1]$ and a is a positive integer. When a is fixed, $IBN(i)$ will decrease with the increasing of SR. Small $IBN(i)$ causes small memory consumption of SEA. Because each packet will be updated by SR SEs, when SR is very big, the updating time will increase too. Considering that the memory requirement of a single SE is very small, only one byte, we can set SR to a small value such as 3 or 4.

At the end of a time period, super points will be restored from SEVA. By Eq. 2, we can see that each bit of $LP(h)$ could be recovered from the set of $Idx(LP(h)) = \{Idx(i, LP(h))|0 \leq i \leq SR - 1\}$ by a reverse equation as shown below.

$$LP(h)[j] = Idx(i, LP(h))[j - ISB(i)] \tag{3}$$

where $0 \leq j \leq 31$, $0 \leq i \leq SR - 1$, $ISB(i) \leq j$ and $j - ISB(i) \leq IBN(i)$.

But when update SEAV, we do not record $Idx(LP(h))$. We can derive that if a host h is a super point, $SE(i, Idx(i, LP(h))$ will contain no less than 3 '1' bits. We call these SE whose weight is no less than 3 as Hot SE (HSE). Let $HSE(i)$ represent the set of HSE in the ith row.

By picking SR HSEs from every $HSE(i)$, we can get a candidate index set $CIdx =< c[0], c[1], \cdots , c[SR - 1] >$ where $SE(i, c[i]) \in HSE(i)$ and $0 \leq i \leq SR - 1$. Supposing there are $|HSE(i)|$ elements in the ith row, there would be total $\prod_{i=0}^{SR-1} |HSE(i)|$ different $CIdx$. The set of all $CIdx$ is denoted by CIS. If h is a super point, $Idx(LP(h)) \in CIS$. By test each $CIdx$ in CIS we can reconstruct all super points.

In order to reduce this influence of bit sharing, we test if the union SEU, acquiring by the bit-wise "AND"of all these SR SEs, still contains more than θ opposite hosts. When its weight is no less than 3, we will return the restored LP as a super point's LP. Together with RP, the index of this SEAV, a super point will be restored. But some normal hosts, whose opposite number is littler than θ, maybe detected as super points too. To reduce the number of these normal hosts, we apply a more precise estimation method, long estimator, together with the short estimator.

3.3 Long Estimator

Long estimator are used to improve the accuracy of detection result. It uses more bits to estimate host's opposite number. Our long estimator is based on linear distinct counting algorithm (LDC) [23]. LDC is a bit vector of k bits initialized with 0. When recording an opposite host oip, one bit in LDC, chosen by a random

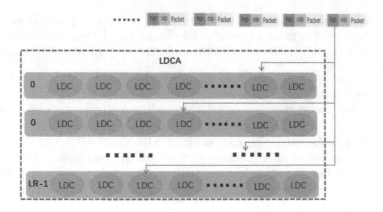

Fig. 2. Structure of LDCA

hash function $H_3(oip)$, will be set. LDC has the simplest updating process. The opposite hosts number could be estimated by the following equation:

$$Est' = -k * ln(\frac{z_0}{k})$$ (4)

z_0 is the resting zero number in LDC after recording all opposite hosts. LDC has a good accuracy performance in estimating opposite host number, but its memory consumption is very large. So it's too expensive to allocate an LDC for every host. Like SEA, we construct an array of LDC, written as $LDCA$, with LR rows and LC columns. Figure 2 describes the structure of $LDCA$ and how to update it.

We use LR random hash functions LH_i to map a host to LR different LDC in each row. No need to restore super points, the updating algorithm is much simpler than SEAV. For a given host at the end of a time window, its opposite hosts number is acquired from the union LDC related with it in each row by Eq. 4. Two LDC is merged by bit-wise "AND" operation.

LDCA improves the accuracy of detection result. Both $SEAV$ and $LDCA$ can be updated parallel without any data accessing conflict which ensures the success deploying on GPU. In the next section we will introduce how to detect super points in parallel and distributed environment.

4   Distributed Super Points Detection on GPU

In a high speed network, such as 40 Gb/s, there are millions of packets passing through the edge of the network. To scan so many packets in real time requires plenty computing resource. Graphic processing unit (GPU) is one of the most popular parallel computing platform in recent years. For these tasks that have no data accessing conflict and processing different data with the same instructions (SIMD), GPU can acquire a high speed up [2, 18]. Every packet will update SEAV and LDCA. Both these processes just set several bits and every bit could be set by different threads concurrently without introducing any mistakes. Our algorithm has great potential of scanning packets parallel on GPU. When detecting super points on different WPs, there are three critical stages: scanning packets on every WP; merging $SEAV$ and $LDCA$ of every WP into global ones; restoring super points from global $SEAV$ and $LDCA$.

4.1   Packets Scanning

Edge routers transmit packets between SNet and ONet. IP addresses of every packet could be acquired directly at these edge routers. But GPU has its own memory and it can only access its graphic memory directly. So we have to copy IP addresses from WP to GPU's global memory. It's not efficient to copy these IP addresses one by one because the copying processing requires additional starting and ending operations. In order to reducing copying time, we allocate two buffers on WP and GPU separately. When the buffer on WP is full, we will copy it to buffer on GPU and clear it for storing other IP addresses.

GPU has hundreds of cores and can launch thousands of threads to coping with different data parallel. After receiving IP addresses buffer from WP, we will start plenty threads to cope with these IP pairs parallel.

Each WP will only cope with IP pairs of packets passing through it. But a host's opposite hosts may pass through different WPs. It's not possible to get the accuracy opposite number from one WP. So we should gather all $SEAV$ and $LDCA$ from distributed WPs together for global super points restoring.

4.2   Data Merging and Super Points Restoring

At the end of a time period, we will merge all $SEAV$ and $LDCA$ together. In order to relieve the pressure of WP, we set another server as the global server (GS) to restore super points. All WP will send their $SEAV$ and $LDCA$ to GS. $SEAV$ and $LDCA$ in different WPs have the same size and all of them are very small. So communication delay between WPs and GS will not cause congestion.

On GS, we acquired the global $SEAV$ and $LDCA$. Super points will be acquired from global $SEAV$ and opposite hosts number of super points could be calculated from global $LDCA$.

Our algorithm requires small memory and has simple operation, no floating operation. A cheap GPU can acquire a high speed up as showed in our experiment.

5   Experiment and Analysis

In order to evaluate the performance of our algorithm, we use six real world core network traffic to compare the accuracy and consumption time of our algorithm with others. These traffics could be downloaded from Caida [1]. Caida's OC192

Table 1. Traffic information

Taffic	#SNet IP	#ONet IP	#Flow	Packet speed (kpps)	#Super points
Caida 2015_02_19	2500423	1536625.4	6608075	917.8962	228.1667
Caida 2015_05_21	1374198	562558.5	2994325	668.8070	146.2500
Caida 2015_09_17	1192966	758124.7	2884065	700.1335	173.1667
Caida 2016_01_21	2437770	746176.6	4800712	1100.5775	393.0833
Caida 2016_02_18	2185536	863207.2	4440282	959.5180	327.5833
Caida 2016_03_17	2164777	638812.5	4349516	976.4834	334.2500

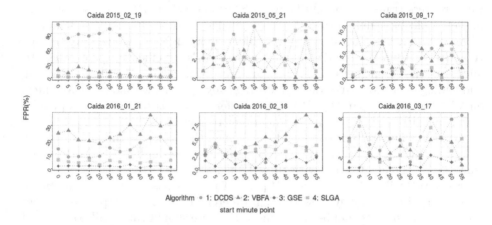

Fig. 3. FPR of different algorithms

data monitors an hour-long trace starting from 13:00. Table 1 shows the detail information of every experiment traffic.

We use a common and low cost GPU, Nvidia GTX 650, to run every algorithm. There are total 1 GB of graphic memory in this GPU card and it communicates with computer through PCIe bus. We compare the performance of different algorithms: DCDS [22], VBFA [12], GSE [17] and SLGA. SLGA is the one proposed in this paper.

5.1   Accuracy and Memory

False positive rate (FPR) and false negative rate (FNR) are two important criteria of detection accuracy. FPR means the ratio of the number of detected fake host to the number of super points. FNR is the ration of the number of these super points that failed be detected by an algorithm to the number of super points. For an estimating algorithm, we hope that its FPR and FNR are small at the same time because FPR shows a negative correlation with FNR. Figures 3 and 4 illustrate the FPR and FNR of different algorithms. In our algorithm, the time window is set to 300 s and each one-hour traffic is split into 12 sub traffics according to the time window.

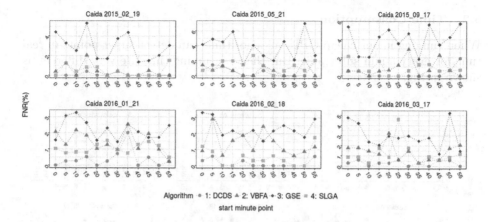

Fig. 4. FNR of different algorithms

GSE has a smaller FPR than other algorithms have. SLGA's FPR is a little higher than that of GSE but much smaller than that of DCDS and VBFA.

Although GSE has a small FPR, its FNR is higher than other algorithms'. A high FNR will let GSE fail to detect some important super points. DCDS's FNR is the lowest at the cost of its high FPR. SLGA's FNR is between DCDS's and VBFA's. In order to have an overall detection accuracy, we use the sum of FPR and FNR, called false total rate (FTR), as the accuracy criterion. SLGA's FTR is the smallest in all of these algorithm. Table 2 shows the memory consumption and average result of different algorithms.

Table 2. Average result of different algorithms

Algorithm	Memory (MB)	avgFNR (%)	avgFPR (%)	avgFTR (%)	avgSpeed (Mpps)
DCDS	192.00	0.2963153	15.700018	15.996334	11.74924
VBFA	80.00	1.0239972	8.013012	9.037009	14.16054
GSE	128.00	3.0326514	1.381296	4.413948	27.11616
SLGA	16.25	0.8896756	2.918181	3.807857	24.13770

Both DCDS and GSE use more than 100 MB memory and DCDS uses nearly 200 MB memory. VBFA uses smaller memory than DCDS and GSE. But SLGA consumes the smallest memory in all of these algorithm, only one-fifth memory that VBFA uses. Small memory requirement let SLGA has a small communication latency in a distributed environment than other algorithms. False rates listing in Table 2 are acquired by calculating the average value of an algorithm at all these time windows. From Table 2 we can see that SLGA not only has the smallest memory requirement, but also the smallest overall false rate. Its processing speed is fast enough for deal with this traffic in real time.

5.2   Time Consumption

When running in our cheap GPU, all algorithms can detect super points in real time for every 5-min sub traffic. But their consuming time are very different as shown in Fig. 5.

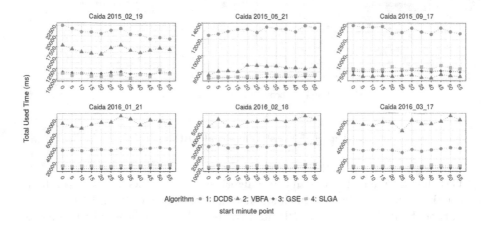

Fig. 5. Total used time of different algorithms for every sub traffic

DCDS uses much more time than GSE and SLGA because it employs CRT to restore super points which requires more complex operation than a hash function does. In the first three traffics, VBFA uses littler time than DCDS does. This is because VBFA can locate column index by extracting sub bits of hosts's IP addresses. But when reconstructing super points, VBFA will generate huge candidate IP addresses. The number of candidate IP addresses increases sharply with the number of super points. In the last three traffic, which all contain more than 300 super points, VBFA uses much more time than all the other algorithms.

SLGA uses a little more time than GSE. When scanning traffic, GSE only needs to set one bit while SLGA will set several bits in SEA and $LDCA$. But GPU can hide the memory accessing delay by launching plenty threads parallel. So SLGA is slower than GSE a little. In this paper, we divide the total packets number in a time window by the processing time to get the speed. The unit of algorithm's speed is million packets per seconds, written as Mpps. Speeds of different algorithms listed in Table 2 is the mean value of different algorithms's speeds of all 5-min sub traffics.

SLGA and GSE have faster speed than VBFA and DCDS. The experiment traffics have an average bandwidth of 4.5 Gb/s [1]. Suppose that 900 MB memory of GPU are available for different algorithms' kernel structures and the rest 100 MB memory are used for IP addresses buffer and other running parameters. For a higher bandwidth traffic, more memory will be required. Suppose that the memory requirement grows linearly with the bandwidth which could be realized by splitting IP addresses by their right bits. From the memory perspective, our algorithm can deal with network traffic with bandwidth as high as 249 Gb/s, while the highest traffic bandwidth for DCDS, VBFA and GSE are 21.1 Gb/s, 50.6 Gb/s and 31.6 Gb/s. Note that the GPU used in our experiment is a cheap one which costs only 30 dollars. A more advanced GPU, such as GTX 1080 with 11 GB graphic memory, could be brought with 1000 dollars to deal with a faster and bigger network.

6 Conclusion

In this paper we introduce a memory efficient distributed super points detection algorithm. Super point plays important roles in network management and security. How to find them out in real time is the foundation of super points application. Unlike other algorithms, we use two kinds of opposite number estimation algorithms in our scheme: short estimation and long estimation. SE consumes very small memory and has a fast processing speed. Based on SE, we design a novel super point restoring structure SEAV. From SEAV we can get a candidate super points lists. In order to improve the accuracy of the detection result, we introduce LE. LE consumes more memory than SE but has a higher accuracy. Using SE and LE together makes our algorithm get the highest accuracy with the smallest memory.

References

1. The Center for Applied Internet Data Analysis: The caida anonymized internet traces (2017). http://www.caida.org/data/passive. Accessed 2017
2. Bernaschi, M., Bisson, M., Rossetti, D.: Benchmarking of communication techniques for GPUS. J. Parallel Distrib. Comput. **73**(2), 250–255 (2013). https://doi.org/10.1016/j.jpdc.2012.09.006. http://www.sciencedirect.com/science/article/pii/S0743731512002213
3. Bhuyan, M.H., Bhattacharyya, D., Kalita, J.: Surveying port scans and their detection methodologies. Comput. J. **54**(10), 1565–1581 (2011). https://doi.org/10.1093/comjnl/bxr035
4. Cao, J., Jin, Y., Chen, A., Bu, T., Zhang, Z.L.: Identifying high cardinality internet hosts. IEEE INFOCOM **2009**, 810–818 (2009). https://doi.org/10.1109/INFCOM.2009.5061990
5. Carter, J., Wegman, M.N.: Universal classes of hash functions. J. Comput. Syst. Sci. **18**(2), 143–154 (1979). https://doi.org/10.1016/0022-0000(79)90044-8. http://www.sciencedirect.com/science/article/pii/0022000079900448
6. Cisco: Global IP traffic forecast (2017). http://www.cisco.com/c/en/us/solutions/collateral/service-provider/visual-networking-index-vni/vni-hyperconnectivity-wp.pdf
7. Estan, C., Varghese, G., Fisk, M.: Bitmap algorithms for counting active flows on high-speed links. IEEE/ACM Trans. Netw. **14**(5), 925–937 (2006). https://doi.org/10.1109/TNET.2006.882836
8. Harang, R.E., Mell, P.: Evasion-resistant network scan detection. Secur. Inf. **4**(1), 4 (2015). https://doi.org/10.1186/s13388-015-0019-7

9. Jonker, M., Sperotto, A., van Rijswijk-Deij, R., Sadre, R., Pras, A.: Measuring the adoption of DDoS protection services. In: Proceedings of the 2016 Internet Measurement Conference, IMC 2016, pp. 279–285. ACM, New York (2016). https://doi.org/10.1145/2987443.2987487

10. Kane, D.M., Nelson, J., Woodruff, D.P.: An optimal algorithm for the distinct elements problem. In: Proceedings of the Twenty-Ninth ACM SIGMOD-SIGACT-SIGART Symposium on Principles of Database Systems, PODS 2010, pp. 41–52. ACM, New York (2010). https://doi.org/10.1145/1807085.1807094

11. Krotofil, M., Cárdenas, A.A., Manning, B., Larsen, J.: CPS: driving cyber-physical systems to unsafe operating conditions by timing dos attacks on sensor signals. In: Proceedings of the 30th Annual Computer Security Applications Conference, ACSAC 2014, pp. 146–155. ACM, New York (2014). https://doi.org/10.1145/2664243.2664290

12. Liu, W., Qu, W., Gong, J., Li, K.: Detection of superpoints using a vector bloom filter. IEEE Trans. Inf. Forensics Secur. **11**(3), 514–527 (2016). https://doi.org/10.1109/TIFS.2015.2503269

13. Liu, Y., Chen, W., Guan, Y.: Identifying high-cardinality hosts from network-wide traffic measurements. IEEE Trans. Depend. Secure Comput. **13**(5), 547–558 (2016). https://doi.org/10.1109/TDSC.2015.2423675

14. Moraes, D.M., Duarte, Jr, E.P.: A failure detection service for internet-based multi-as distributed systems. In: 2011 IEEE 17th International Conference on Parallel and Distributed Systems, pp. 260–267, December 2011. https://doi.org/10.1109/ICPADS.2011.5

15. Roesch, M.: Snort - lightweight intrusion detection for networks. In: Proceedings of the 13th USENIX Conference on System Administration, LISA 1999, pp. 229–238. USENIX Association, Berkeley (1999). https://dl.acm.org/citation.cfm?id=1039834.1039864

16. Rossow, C., et al.: SoK: P2PWNED - modeling and evaluating the resilience of peer-to-peer botnets. In: 2013 IEEE Symposium on Security and Privacy, pp. 97–111, May 2013. https://doi.org/10.1109/SP.2013.17

17. Shin, S.H., Im, E.J., Yoon, M.: A grand spread estimator using a graphics processing unit. J. Parallel Distrib. Comput. **74**(2), 2039–2047 (2014). https://doi.org/10.1016/j.jpdc.2013.10.007. http://www.sciencedirect.com/science/article/pii/S0743731513002189

18. Silber-Chaussumier, F., Muller, A., Habel, R.: Generating data transfers for distributed GPU parallel programs. J. Parallel Distrib. Comput. **73**(12), 1649–1660 (2013). https://doi.org/10.1016/j.jpdc.2013.07.022. http://www.sciencedirect.com/science/article/pii/S0743731513001603. Heterogeneity in Parallel and Distributed Computing

19. Snyder, P., Ansari, L., Taylor, C., Kanich, C.: Browser feature usage on the modern web. In: Proceedings of the 2016 Internet Measurement Conference, IMC 2016, pp. 97–110. ACM, New York (2016). https://doi.org/10.1145/2987443.2987466

20. Venkataraman, S., Song, D., Gibbons, P.B., Blum, A.: New streaming algorithms for fast detection of superspreaders. In: Proceedings of Network and Distributed System Security Symposium (NDSS), pp. 149–166 (2005)

21. Wang, B., Zheng, Y., Lou, W., Hou, Y.T.: DDoS attack protection in the era of cloud computing and software-defined networking. Comput. Netw. **81**, 308–319 (2015). https://doi.org/10.1016/j.comnet.2015.02.026. http://www.sciencedirect.com/science/article/pii/S1389128615000742

22. Wang, P., Guan, X., Qin, T., Huang, Q.: A data streaming method for monitoring host connection degrees of high-speed links. IEEE Trans. Inf. Forensics Secur. **6**(3), 1086–1098 (2011). https://doi.org/10.1109/TIFS.2011.2123094

23. Whang, K.Y., Vander-Zanden, B.T., Taylor, H.M.: A linear-time probabilistic counting algorithm for database applications. ACM Trans. Database Syst. **15**(2), 208–229 (1990). https://doi.org/10.1145/78922.78925

24. Xiao, P., Qu, W., Qi, H., Li, Z.: Detecting DDoS attacks against data center with correlation analysis. Comput. Commun. **67**, 66–74 (2015). https://doi.org/10.1016/j.comcom.2015.06.012. http://www.sciencedirect.com/science/article/pii/S0140366415002285

Parallel Implementation and Optimizations of Visibility Computing of 3D Scene on Tianhe-2 Supercomputer

Zhengwei Xu[1,2], Xiaodong Wang[1], Congpin Zhang[1(✉)], and Changmao Wu[2(✉)]

[1] School of Computer and Information Engineering, Henan Normal University, Henan, China
zhangcongpin@139.com
[2] Laboratory of Parallel Software and Computational Science, Institute of Software, Chinese Academy of Sciences, Beijing, China
changmao@iscas.ac.cn

Abstract. Visibility computing is a basic problem in computer graphics, and is often the bottleneck in realistic rendering algorithms. Some of the most common include the determination of the objects visible from a viewpoint, virtual reality, real-time simulation and 3D interactive design. As one technique to accelerate the rendering speed, the research on visibility computing has gained great attention in recent years. Traditional visibility computing on single processor machine has been unable to meet more and more large-scale and complex scenes due to lack parallelism. However, it will face many challenges to design parallel algorithms on a cluster due to imbalance workload among compute nodes, the complicated mathematical model and different domain knowledge. In this paper, we propose an efficient and highly scalable framework for visibility computing on Tianhe-2 supercomputer. Firstly, a new technique called hemispheric visibility computing is designed, which can overcome the visibility missing of traditional perspective algorithm. Secondly, a distributed parallel algorithm for visibility computing is implemented, which is based on the master-worker architecture. Finally, we discuss the issue of granularity of visibility computing and some optimization strategies for improving overall performance. Experiments on Tianhe-2 supercomputer show that our distributed parallel visibility computing framework almost reaches linear speedup by using up to 7680 CPU cores.

Keywords: Visibility computing · Performance optimization
Parallel implementation

1 Introduction

As a basic problem in computer graphics, visibility computing is a center in many computer graphics applications such as virtual reality, real-time simulation and

© Springer Nature Switzerland AG 2018
J. Vaidya and J. Li (Eds.): ICA3PP 2018, LNCS 11334, pp. 168–183, 2018.
https://doi.org/10.1007/978-3-030-05051-1_12

3D interactive design. Research on visibility computing has been one of the most important problems since the birth of computer graphics [18]. Especially with the development of graphics, 3D scenes are increasingly large and complex, which usually consists of millions of triangles. Although the graphics have got great support on hardware, it still can't meet the requirements of efficient rendering of large-scale scenes. One of the reasons is that visibility computing is often the bottleneck in realistic rendering algorithms. Therefore, research on visibility computing has attracted more and more attention.

There are many researches on visibility computing in the world, and the literatures [18, 24] have a good overview. In general, a primitive in the 3D scene is visible, which must meet the following conditions: First of all, it's in the field of imaging. Then, it does not deviate from the point of view and it's not obscured by other primitives closer to the point of view. The mainstream methods about visibility computing are as follows: It [13] offers a method with visibility processing based on bounding box testing and normal detection to improve the performance by Rohlf et al. The method proposed by [7, 14] provides a compact set of meeting sets for each subspace in the scene. It only needs to deal with each local meeting set to speed up the visibility computing, but its preprocessing is generally complex and time-consuming. According to the internal structure of the building, the scene is divided into some areas, and the set of visible surfaces they share is calculated for the viewpoints in each area [16]. Bittner and his colleagues proposed an algorithm allowing efficient culling of the invisible portion through occlusion tree that is used to determine the viewpoint-to-region visibility efficiently [6].

At present, most work on visibility computing for large scale scenes are still running on single processor ma?chines, which usually require many hours or even days to compute. Through many algorithms are proposed to speed up the visibility computing, it still can't meet the actual needs. Therefore, how to accelerate visibility computing in parallel becomes urgent. However, there remain the following challenges to design a distributed parallel framework for visibility computing:

- Imbalanced calculation time. The visibility computing in each triangle is different, which may result in severe imbalance.
- Tremendous amount of computation. As the request for photorealistic images becomes a common trend, the amount of visibility computing in 3D scenes is growing accordingly.
- Necessary domain knowledge. It needs professional knowledge in different fields for visibility computing, such as accelerating structure (BVHs, Grid, Kd-trees), Monte Carlo sampling methods.

As a result, visibility computing on the cluster is still very less to be seen. In this paper, we focus on developing an efficient and scalable framework and an optimization algorithm for visibility computing on Tianhe-2 supercomputer. The main contributions of this work are listed as follows:

– A novel hemispheric sampling model is proposed for visibility computing, which overcomes the problem that some triangles will be lost in the visibility computing.
– A distributed parallel framework for visibility computing is implemented.
– The issue of granularity of visibility computing is discussed and some optimization strategies for improving overall performance are offered.
– Performance evaluations on the Tianhe-2 supercomputer are presented.

The remainder of the paper is organized as follow: In Sect. 2, we provide a short overview of the visibility computing and corresponding mathematical model. And in Sect. 3, we design parallelization strategies for the visibility computing in a cluster. Then, the framework of implementation and the optimization for load balancing are discussed in Sects. 4 and 5. The Sect. 6 will give the test results for the large-scale scene on the Tianhe-2 supercomputer. We conclude the paper in Sect. 7.

2   Global Illumination and Visibility Computing

With people's demand for photorealistic rendering is growing increasingly, global illumination as an important component has been widely concerned. Global illumination includes not only direct illumination but also reflection and refraction of rays, which is divided into direct illumination and indirect illumination. Computer-generated images which use global illumination are more realistic and natural than just applying direct illumination [17]. The commonly used algorithms for calculating global illumination include Monte Carlo ray tracing methods, photon mapping, point-based global illumination algorithm etc.

At present, there are many algorithms for visibility computing, some of which improve the computational efficiency and the realism of the entire scene by reducing the number of primitives that need to be calculated [19]. As shown in Fig. 1, the triangle formed entirely by the dotted lines does not need to be calculated since it is completely obscured by the preceding primitives. However, visibility computing is not only just a simple problem of occlusion judgment in practical application. And the traditional HSR (hidden surface removal) algorithm is difficult to meet the actual application requirements since many factors affect the visibility judgment such as the sensitivity of scene size, the inaccuracy of visibility judgment results and so on [3,12].

The problems of visibility computing can be divided into 3 types: visibility judgment based on cones, visibility judgment of entities themselves and occlusion relationship among entities [12]. We usually build the perspective camera to get the cone which is mainly to judge whether the primitives are in sight or obscured for fast culling unnecessary drawings elements to save time. To quickly eliminate objects that are completely out of sight, the intersection operations of bounding box of objects and view in space are often carried out. Further investigation is made by stepwise refinement, when bounding box of object intersects with view boundary [5,12]. Literature [15] proposes that replacing the frustum of the cone with the cuboid through coordinate transformation due to the time-consuming

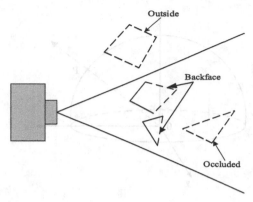

Fig. 1. Perspective camera is built to compute visibility of the scene. The dotted line refers to the invisible portion, and the solid line indicates the region that can be seen.

computation of the intersection with the frustum of the cone, which can reduce overhead by parallel projection for intersection. However, these methods have a common drawback that they can't completely cover the entire hemisphere space, which may miss some visible primitives. As shown in Fig. 1, the visibility of quadrilateral primitive formed by the dotted line is omitted since it is outside the scope of cone.

We design a new method called hemispheric visibility computing to overcome the loss of some visible primitives, see Fig. 2. Main steps are as follow:

- Set a hemispheric space with a radius of one. The barycentric coordinates of the given triangle is considered as sphere centered O and the triangle normal is viewed as direction.
- Unbiased random sampling on the surface of hemispheric space. For example, we get a point $P(x, y, z)$ by random sampling on hemispheric space, then we can obtain a ray which project to scene through connecting O and P. The nearest one is the visibly triangle when the ray intersects with triangles in 3D scene.
- Next, repeat the above steps to get the set of visibility of whole scene.

Then, we should consider how to sample evenly on the hemispherical surface in all directions. This is a mathematical problem. Next we will deduce the corresponding mathematical formulas.

First, uniform sampling means that probability density is a constant, so we can get the formulas as follow:

$$\int_0^{2\pi} p(\omega)d\omega = 1 \Rightarrow c \int d\omega = 1 \Rightarrow c = \frac{1}{2\pi} \tag{1}$$

$$p(\omega) = \frac{1}{2\pi} \quad or \quad p(\theta, \varphi) = \frac{\sin\theta}{2\pi} \tag{2}$$

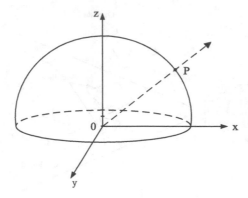

Fig. 2. O is at the barycentric coordinates of the given triangle. And P is a random point on the surface of the hemisphere. Through connecting O and P, we can get a ray cast to the scene.

Considering sampling in θ direction, we need to calculate its directional boundary probability density. Then, the probability density function of the φ direction can be calculated.

$$p(\theta) = \int_0^{2\pi} p(\theta, \varphi)d\varphi = \int_0^{2\pi} \frac{\sin\theta}{2\pi}d\varphi = \sin\theta \tag{3}$$

$$p(\varphi, \theta) = \frac{p(\theta, \varphi)}{p(\theta)} = \frac{1}{2\pi} \tag{4}$$

In addition, we can calculate the probability density function of θ direction and φ direction in turn since the probability density of the φ direction is homogeneous. Then, replace $1 - \xi$ with ξ since they are uniform random variables in $[0, 1]$ for getting a uniform random sampling formulas in θ, φ direction.

$$p(\theta) = \int_0^\theta \sin\theta d\theta = 1 - \cos\theta \tag{5}$$

$$p(\varphi, \theta) = \int_0^\varphi \frac{1}{2\pi}d\varphi = \frac{\varphi}{2\pi} \tag{6}$$

$$\theta = \cos^{-1}\xi_1 \qquad \varphi = 2\pi\xi_2 \tag{7}$$

The above is the random sampling formulas on hemispheric surface. Next, we need convert them from spherical coordinates to Cartesian coordinates.

$$x = \sin\theta\cos\varphi = \cos 2\pi\xi_2 \sqrt{1 - \xi_1^2} \tag{8}$$

$$y = \sin\theta\sin\varphi = \sin 2\pi\xi_2 \sqrt{1 - \xi_1^2} \tag{9}$$

$$z = \cos\theta = \xi_1 \tag{10}$$

ξ_1 and ξ_2 are random variables that are distributed in $[0, 1]$. We can randomly sample on hemispheric surface through above formulas to compute visibility of triangles in 3D scenes, and according to [10], it has good stability that will only have a theoretical repetition in $2^{64} - 1$ times. One of the best test algorithms for intersecting straight lines with planes (triangles) is given in [8, 20], which we used in this paper. These are the formulas for the hemispheric visibility computing, which can overcome the loss of some visible primitives. Next, we will show the visibility of a simple 3D scene consists of 48 triangles to further illustrate our method, as shown in Fig. 3.

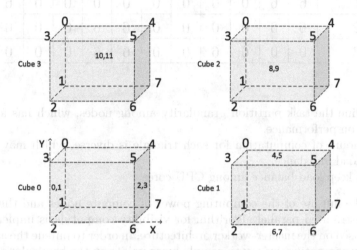

Fig. 3. A simple scene consists of four cubes which have six geometric planes that composed by two triangles i.e. this scene consists of 48 triangles.

As shown in Fig. 3, the visibility of triangle 0 and triangle 1 in *cube*0 is zero since they can't see any other triangles. Triangle 2 and 3 in *cube*0 can see triangle 0 and 1 from *cube*1 and triangle 0, 1, 6 and 7 from *cube*2 i.e. they can see that the number of other triangles is 6, and so on. In this way, the visibility of the 48 triangles (some triangles have a visibility of zero) constitute the visibility of the whole scene. Table 1 shows the set of visibility of whole scene. In practical work, the scene may be composed of millions even more triangles, which has brought great challenges to our work.

3   Parallelization Strategies

Complex scenes may be modeled using millions of triangles to have a good level of detail [11]. In general, the visibility computing of each triangle can be used as a basic parallel task unit since this process is independent. It is generally called the demand-driven method, also known as the output-based partitioning method. Our aim is to quickly and efficiently compute the visibility of a given scene on a cluster. The main problems we need to solve are as follow:

Table 1. The first column and the first row refer to the identifier of the cube and corresponding triangles respectively. The number inside cells is the value of triangle's visibility. For example, the cell in the fourth column, the second row means visibility of the No. 2 triangle in $cube0$ is 6.

Vis \ $nTri$ nCu	0	1	2	3	4	5	6	7	8	9	10	11
0	0	0	6	6	0	0	0	0	0	0	6	6
1	6	6	0	0	0	0	0	0	0	0	6	6
2	6	6	0	0	0	0	6	6	0	0	0	0
3	0	0	6	6	0	0	6	6	0	0	0	0

- Determine the task partition granularity among nodes, which has a crucial impact on performance.
- The amount of computation for each triangle is diverse, which may lead to severe load imbalance.
- How to keep load balance among CPU cores.

To make full use of the computing power of compute nodes and their CPU cores, a distributed parallel algorithm for visibility computing is implemented, which is based on the master-worker architecture. In order to pursue the accuracy of visibility computing, we try to sample more points on the hemisphere surface i.e. each triangle launch rays as many as possible. The number of samples can even reach millions, which will spend a lot time especially when the scene consists of a large number of triangles. We make further improvements to the parallel strategy which can still maintain a near-linear speedup by using 7680 CPU cores on the Tianhe-2 supercomputer.

A prerequisite for parallel visibility computing is how to carry out the distribution of assignments among compute nodes in a cluster, which is significant for the performance. We divide assignment allocation into two types. One of the types is responsible for allocating assignment among compute nodes, which is called primary assignment. The other is secondary task that divides the primary assignment into some basic task units that are executed by the CPU cores.

In general, the primary assignment consists of some triangles and the visibility computation of each triangle is a basic task unit. Since the number of triangles in the scene is constant, the more primary assignments, the fewer triangles each primary assignment contains. In order to speed up the visibility computing with the distribution of parallel, it is necessary to adjust the number of triangles contained in each primary task [21]. On the one hand, we hope that the number of primary assignments is not less than the total number of compute nodes and as much as possible for making full use of the computing power of each compute node. The more the number of primary assignment, the smaller the difference in the amount of computing among compute nodes, which is easier to achieve good efficiency. On the other hand, it will lead to increased communication overhead between compute nodes if the number of primary assignments is too large, which also influence its performance. After comprehensive consideration, the number of triangles contained in each primary assignment is controlled between eight and sixty-four times the number of CPU cores of a compute node.

Each secondary task is a process of visibility computing of a single triangle in the scene. In other words, some secondary tasks make up a primary assignment so that the division of primary assignment directly affects secondary task. It divides primary assignment into smaller task units (triangles) executed by CPU cores.

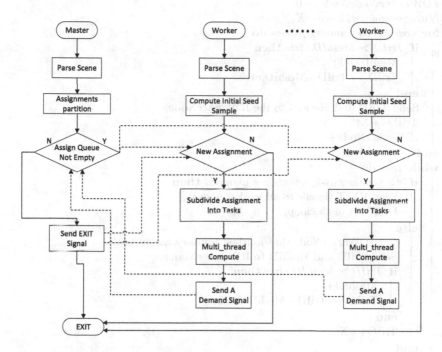

Fig. 4. Framework based on parallelism for visibility computing. It divides the compute nodes into one master node and some worker nodes. The dashed arrows represent the exchange of information between master node and worker nodes. And there is no information interchange among worker nodes. The solid line represents the workflow of each compute node.

4   Framework and Algorithm

In our algorithm, we divide the compute nodes into one master node and some worker nodes. The master node and the worker nodes in a cluster are responsible for different functionality during the process of visibility computing. The master node is connected to all worker nodes and responsible for allocating primary assignments and EXIT signal. The worker nodes are responsible for splitting the received primary assignments into secondary tasks, which are then executed by the CPU cores. There is no exchange of information among worker nodes, as shown in Fig. 4.

Algorithm 1. Algorithm on the master node

---

1 Parse scene data;
2 $MeshID \leftarrow 0$;
3 $TriID \leftarrow 0$;
4 $IDWorkerNodeNode \leftarrow 0$;
5 $NumSecondaryTask \leftarrow X$;
6 **for** $node=1$ **to** $numberOfNodes$ **do**
7 | **if** $TriID > MeshID.ntris$ **then**
8 | | MeshID++;
9 | | TriID $\leftarrow$ TriID - MeshID.ntris;
10 | **end**
11 | Send TriID and MeshID to the IDWorkerNode;
12 | TriID+=X;
13 | IDWorkerNode++;
14 **end**
15 **while** $true$ **do**
16 | **if** $All\ primary\ assignments\ are\ assigned$ **then**
17 | | Send EXIT signals to all worker nodes;
18 | | Drop out of the loop;
19 | **else**
20 | | Get IDWorkerNode that finished primary assignment;
21 | | Send TriID and MeshID to IDWorkerNode;
22 | | **if** $TriID > MeshID.ntris$ **then**
23 | | | MeshID++;
24 | | | TriID $\leftarrow$ TriID - MeshID.ntris;
25 | | **end**
26 | | TriID+=X;
27 | **end**
28 **end**
29 Clean up;

The MPI process on the master node knows the number of worker nodes at the beginning. Therefore, after distributing the initial primary assignments, the master node waits for requesting signal from the worker nodes that already finished the assignment [22]. Then, master nodes will send a new primary assignment to the worker node if there is still primary assignment remaining. Otherwise, it will send the EXIT signal to all worker nodes. The worker node divides the primary assignment into secondary tasks (triangles) and puts them in a sharing pool after they receive the primary assignment from master node. Each CPU core (thread) of the worker node concurrently requests a secondary task from the sharing pool and performs it independently [22]. The worker node sends a signal to the master node for a new primary assignment when all the secondary tasks in sharing pool are computed by CPU cores. The master node will assign the primary assignments to the worker nodes dynamically, and the worker nodes repeat the above steps to perform primary assignments until they receive the EXIT signal, see Fig. 4. Since communication is only required to distribute assignments and signals, idle time should be minimal [25]. The strategies we designed for master node and worker nodes are outlined in the Algorithms 1 and 2.

Algorithm 2. Algorithm on the worker nodes

---
1 Parse scene data;
2 Receive MeshId and TriID from Master node;
3 **while** *true* **do**
4   **if** *Receive EXIT signal* **then**
5 | Drop out of the loop;
6   **else**
7   Divide the primary assignment into secondary tasks and puts them in a sharing pool;
8   Perform the secondary tasks by CPU cores in parallel;;
9   Clean sharing pool up;
10   Send IDWorkerNode to master node;
11   Receive MeshId and TriID from Master node;
12   **end**
13 **end**
14 Clean up;

---

5   Optimization

5.1   Static Strategy

From Sect. 3, each secondary task (triangle) is a basic parallel unit. If we use the cluster with 10 nodes and 240 CPU cores to compute a scene that consists of 240k triangles, then each node is responsible for 1000 triangles. If we increase the number of compute nodes to 100 and the corresponding CPU cores up to 2400, each CPU core only needs to compute 100 triangles. As the number of compute nodes increases, each CPU core needs to compute fewer triangles. This method is called static algorithm, which assigns triangles to all compute nodes equally before executing. It has good performance when the scenes are simple. However, as the scenes are complex and contain more triangles, its performance has bottlenecks.

The main reason is that even though each primary assignment contains the same number of triangles, their amount of calculation is also very different. From the literature [22], each ray tasks a different amount of processor time to compute, depending on the complexity of the intersections that occur: ray can travel long distances as it is reflected by mirror surfaces, or can be rapidly attenuated by collisions with non-reflective surfaces. Even though all the lights could travel the same distance due to reflection and refraction over surfaces of objects in the scene, it will still lead to uneven workload and incoherent execution among light samples since light samples will be terminated randomly by Russia roulette [4, 22]. In other words, every triangle emitting the same number of rays also has a different amount of calculation. Therefore, some compute nodes would finish before others and keep idle while waiting for the slowest ones, which will cause the waste of resources.

As shown in Table 1, the triangles in the scene are divided into two categories, one with the visibility of 0 and the other with the visibility of 6. So we can conclude that the triangles in the same scene can see the number of other triangles is not identical. Seeing Fig. 5, two geometric figures similar to the sphere make up the scene. Geometric figure on the right contains more triangles than the one on the left. However, the triangle in left geometric figure (refers to the triangle that faces another geometric figure) can see more triangles than right. Therefore, as a fundamental parallel unit, the visibility computing for each triangle is different.

Through our test, the slowest compute node usually spends dozens of times, sometimes even more, than the fastest compute node. It can greatly reduce the overall performance according to buckets effect. Therefore, different compute nodes with the same computing power may need different time to compute the same number of triangles, which brings great challenges for the load balancing among compute nodes.

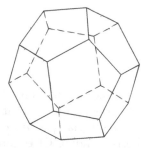
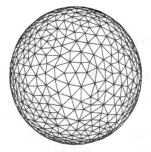

Fig. 5. The scene consists of two geometric figures similar to the sphere. Geometric figure in left contains fewer triangles than right. There is no doubt that the triangles (refers to the triangle that faces another geometric figure) that are located in left geometric figure can see more another triangles than right.

5.2   Optimization Strategy

From Sect. 4, we already described the general workflow and framework of optimization strategy, which is based on the master-worker architecture, seeing Fig. 4. In our optimization strategy, we divide the compute nodes into one master node and m worker nodes. And the master node will allocate primary assignments dynamically to the worker nodes after distributing the initial primary assignments. It dynamically allocates primary assignment among compute nodes instead of static allocation, which overcomes the problem of imbalance workload among compute nodes.

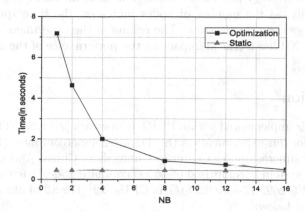

Fig. 6. A simple scene consists of 48 triangles (as shown in Fig. 3) we tested on PC with the value of NB increases from 1 to 16.

Granularity of assignment partition and the number of compute nodes used are the most important factors to control the performance of optimization algorithm. Granularity of assignment partition means the number of secondary tasks (triangles) in primary assignment. In our algorithm, master node allocates a primary assignment to the worker node each time i.e. granularity of assignment partition represents the number of triangles each time the master node is assigned to the worker node specified. For the rest of the article, we use NB to replace granularity of the assignment partition in order to facilitate our annotation and avoid redundancy. For example, if we set NB = 100 in our test, which means that each time master node will assign 100 triangles to the specified worker nodes. Now, we consider the extreme situation to further explain the impact of NB on overall performance. We set the value of NB equals one or increase NB continuously until it equals the total number of triangles divided by number of worker nodes where master node allocate all the triangles to worker nodes at a time. It will lead to maximum communication overhead between master node and worker node when NB = 1. In the latter case, its performance is almost equivalent to the static strategy that using one less compute nodes since master node does not participate in the calculation. When the scene is complex and the number of nodes used is large, this difference can be ignored. If the number of NB continues to increase, the phenomenon of load imbalance among compute nodes is further aggravated, which result in its performance worse than static strategy.

It's a waste of resource to test these extreme cases on Tianhe-2 supercomputer, which will also take a significant computational cost especially when NB = 1. Therefore, we chose a very simple scene (as shown in Fig. 3) that consists of 48 triangles and each triangle will launch 512 × 512 rays to test on the PC in this extreme case, as shown in Fig. 6. Although the experimental results will be slightly different due to the performance of PC, this does not affect the overall experimental results. We can draw a conclusion from Fig. 6: First of all, the optimization strategy takes much more time than the static algorithm when NB = 1. Secondly, as the number of nodes increases, the time spent by optimization strategy is on the decrease. The results of the experiment support our conclusion that NB has a crucial impact on the performance of the optimization algorithm.

6   Evaluation

The algorithm is implemented within PBRT framework [2, 11, 23]. The hardware platform used for our experiments is the Tianhe-2 supercomputer [1, 9], located in the National supercomputer Center in Guangzhou, China. And the Tianhe-2 supercomputer system is comprised of 16000 compute nodes, each of them consists of 2 Intel E5-2692 12-core 2.200 GHz CPUs [22]. For all of our experiments will be discussed below.

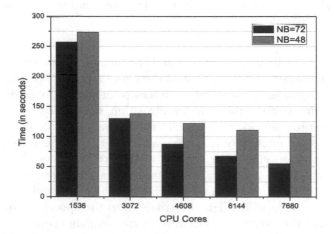

Fig. 7. The graph with costing time shows the time used as the number of CPU cores increases when NB equals 48 and 72 respectively. The test platform is Tianhe-2 supercomputer.

We select a typical scene consisting of 5 triangle meshes and 2605k triangles to compute its visibility by our optimization algorithm. Each triangle will launch

1024×1024 rays for interaction detection. The maximum number of compute nodes used is 320 and the corresponding number of CPU cores is 7680. Generally speaking, the value of NB is eight to sixty-four times that of CPU cores. However in actual tests, we found that this range is not applicable on Tianhe-2 supercomputer since the speed of information exchange among compute nodes in supercomputers is much faster than ordinary clusters. Therefore, we selected the values of NB are 48 and 72 respectively, which have good performance for testing results. The graphs with cost time and speedup are presented in Fig. 7 and Fig. 8 respectively.

As shown in Fig. 7, the black part represents the time spent when NB = 72 and the red part represents the time spent when NB = 48. The number of compute nodes used increased from 64 to 320 and corresponding CPU cores is 1536 up to 7680. We can easily observe that with the number of CPU cores increases, the time of visibility computing is significantly reduced, especially when NB = 72. When using the same number of cores, NB = 72 is less time-consuming than NB = 48. The difference in the time spent between NB = 48 and NB = 72 enlarge gradually as the number of CPU cores increases. We can preliminarily obtain that optimization algorithm has better performance when NB = 72.

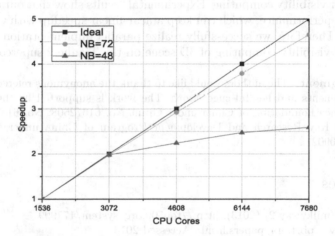

Fig. 8. The graph with speedup describes the performance and effectiveness of optimization algorithm when the value of NB is 48 and 72, respectively.

Figure 8 describes the speedup of optimization algorithm when the value of NB is 48 and 72, respectively. The black line in the Fig. 8 is the speedup under the ideal condition, and the red line and blue line respectively correspond to the speedup with NB = 72 and NB = 48. We can observe that the three lines basically overlap when the number of CPU cores is less than 3072. The growth of blue line has slowed, and red line still maintains linear speedup, when the value of NB is greater than 3072. Therefore, we can conclude that with the increasing number of compute nodes, the value of NB has a decisive influence on the performance of our algorithm. From the above analysis, there are three main factors that take effect to performance of optimization algorithm: the value of NB, the scale of scene, the number of compute nodes used. In a word, our algorithm successfully achieved parallelization of visibility computing on Tianhe-2 supercomputer and enables it to maintain a near-linear speedup.

7   Conclusion

In this paper, we design a novel algorithm to compute the visibility on Tianhe-2 supercomputer, which was rarely done by other researchers before. Firstly, we designed the new method called hemispheric visibility computing, which can compute the visibility of the scene more comprehensively than using the traditional algorithm with cone. Secondly, we propose a novel assignment partitioning algorithm for compute nodes and their cores, which is based on the master-worker architecture. Finally, we discussed the influence factors of the algorithm we designed, and other algorithms.

In Sect. 6, we carried out experiments on Tianhe-2 supercomputer with the CPU cores increase from 1536 to 7680 to test the performance of optimization algorithm for visibility computing. Experimental results show that our algorithm has superior performance, which can keep a near-linear speedup with CPU cores up to 7680. Therefore, we successfully realize parallel implementation and optimizations of visibility computing of 3D scene on the Tianhe-2 supercomputer.

Acknowledgment. The authors would like to thank the anonymous referees for their valuable comments and helpful suggestions. The work is supported by the National Natural Science Foundation of China under Grant No. 61672508, No. 61379048 and the National Key Research and Development Program of China under Grant No. 2017YFB1400902.

References

1. Tianhe-2(milkyway-2) (2013). http://top500.org/system/177999
2. http://www.pbrt.org/papers.html . Accessed 2018
3. Alipour, S., Ghodsi, M., Güdükbay, U., Golkari, M.: Approximation algorithms for visibility computation and testing over a terrain. Appl. Geom. **9**(1), 53–59 (2017)
4. Arvo, J., Kirk, D.: Particle transport and image synthesis. ACM SIGGRAPH Comput. Graph. **24**(4), 63–66 (1990)
5. Assarsson, U., Moller, T.: Optimized view frustum culling algorithms for bounding boxes. J. Graph. Tools **5**(1), 9–22 (2000)
6. Bittner, J., Havran, V., Slavik, P.: Hierarchical visibility culling with occlusion trees. In: Computer Graphics International, p. 207 (1998)
7. Durand, F., Drettakis, G., Thollot, J., Puech, C.: Conservative visibility preprocessing using extended projections, pp. 239–248 (2000)
8. Ericson, C.: Real-Time Collision Detection (The Morgan Kaufmann Series in Interactive 3-D Technology). Morgan Kaufmann Publishers Inc., Burlington (2004)

9. Li, D., et al.: Parallelizing and optimizing large-scale 3D multiphase flow simulations on the Tianhe-2 supercomputer. Concurr. Comput. Pract. Exp. **28**(5), 1678–1692 (2016)
10. O'Neill, M.E.: PCG: a family of simple fast space-efficient statistically good algorithms for random number generation. ACM Trans. Math. Softw. (2014)
11. Pharr, M., Jakob, W., Humphreys, G.: Physically Based Rendering: From Theory to Implementation. Morgan Kaufmann, Burlington (2016)
12. Jiantao, P., Zha, H.: Research on visibility for large-scale and complex scenes. J. Comput. Res. Dev. **42**(2), 236–246 (2005)
13. Rohlf, J., Helman, J.: Iris performer: a high performance multiprocessing toolkit for real-time 3D graphics. In: Proceedings of the 21st annual conference on Computer graphics and interactive techniques, pp. 381–394 (1994)
14. Schaufler, G., Dorsey, J., Decoret, X.: Conservative volumetric visibility with occluder fusion. In: Conference on Computer Graphics and Interactive Techniques, pp. 229–238 (2000)
15. Stamminger, M., Drettakis, G.: Perspective shadow maps. ACM Trans. Graph. (TOG) **21**(3), 557–562 (2002)
16. Teller, S.J., Séquin, C.H.: Visibility preprocessing for interactive walkthroughs. In: Conference on Computer Graphics and Interactive Techniques, pp. 61–70 (1991)
17. Wang, B.: Research on point based global illumination. Ph.D. thesis, Shandong University (2014)
18. Wang, W., Wei, F., Enhua, W.: Visibility determination for rendering large scale scenes. J. Comput.-Aided Des. Comput. Graph. **18**(2), 161–169 (2006)
19. Wang, Z., Shu, B., Qiu, X., Wang, Z.: Visibility culling for large dynamic crowds within buildings. J. Comput.-Aided Des. Comput. Graph. **21**(3), 331–338 (2009)
20. Woop, S., Feng, L., Wald, I., Benthin, C.: Embree ray tracing kernels for CPUs and the Xeon Phi architecture. In: ACM SIGGRAPH 2013 Talks, p. 44. ACM (2013)
21. Changmao, W., Zhang, Y., Yang, C.: Large scale satellite imagery simulations with physically based ray tracing on Tianhe-1a supercomputer. In: 10th IEEE International Conference on High Performance Computing and Communications (HPCC), pp. 549–556. IEEE (2013)
22. Wu, C., Zhang, Y., Yang, C., Lu, Y.: Physically based parallel ray tracer for the metropolis light transport algorithm on the Tianhe-2 supercomputer. In: 2014 20th IEEE International Conference on Parallel and Distributed Systems (ICPADS), pp. 444–453. IEEE (2014)
23. Zhang, C., Yue, D.: Distributed parallel algorithm of physically based ray tracing. J. Comput. Appl. **34**(6), 1591–1594 (2014)
24. Zhang, H., Manocha, D., Hudson, T., Hoff, K.E.: Visibility culling using hierarchical occlusion maps. In: Conference on Computer Graphics and Interactive Techniques, pp. 77–88 (1997)
25. Zhao, Y., Yoshigoe, K., Bian, J., Xie, M., Xue, Z., Feng, Y.: A distributed graph-parallel computing system with lightweight communication overhead. IEEE Trans. Big Data **2**(3), 204–218 (2017)

Efficient Algorithms of Parallel Skyline Join over Data Streams

Jinchao Zhang[1], JingZi Gu[1(✉)], Shuai Cheng[1,2], Bo Li[1], Weiping Wang[1], and Dan Meng[1]

[1] Institute of Information Engineering, Chinese Academy of Sciences, Beijing, China
{zhangjinchao,gujingzi,chengshuai,libo,wangweiping,mengdan}@iie.ac.cn
[2] University of Chinese Academy of Sciences, Beijing, China

Abstract. The issue of finding *skyline* tuples over multiple relations, more commonly known as the *skyline join* problem, has been well studied in scenarios in which the data is static. Most recently, it has become a new trend that performing skyline queries on data streams, where tuples arrive or expire in a continuous approach. A few algorithms have been proposed for computing skylines on two data streams. However, those literatures did not consider the inherent parallelism, or employ serial algorithms to solve the skyline query problem, which cannot leverage the multi-core processors. Based on this motivation, in this paper, we address the problem of parallel computing for *skyline join* over multiple data streams. We developed a *Novel Iterative* framework based on the existing work and study the inherent parallelism of the *Novel Iterative* framework. Then we propose two parallel skyline join algorithms over sliding windows, *NP-SWJ* and *IP-SWJ*.

To the best of our knowledge, this is the first paper that addresses parallel computing of *skyline join* over multiple data streams. Extensive experimental evaluations on real and synthetic data sets show that the algorithms proposed in this paper provide large gains over the state-of-the-art serial algorithm of *skyline join* over data streams.

Keywords: Skyline join · Sliding window · Data stream
parallel computing

1 Introduction

Skyline queries have been extensively studied since its introduction in the database context [3], and are widely used in applications, such as multi-criteria decision making [7], wireless sensor networks [13,18], and geographic based services [6,21]. Further more, skyline queries are related to some well-known issues, involving top-k queries [1,8], preference collection [2] and nearest neighbor search [12]. Let R denote a relation, and B denote the attribute set of R. Let τ and τ' denote tuples in R. We can claim that the tuple τ' is dominated by τ, denoted as $\tau \prec_B \tau'$, if the following conditions are satisfied simultaneously, (1) $\tau.a_i \leq \tau'.a_i$[1],

---

[1] Small values are preferable in this paper.

© Springer Nature Switzerland AG 2018
J. Vaidya and J. Li (Eds.): ICA3PP 2018, LNCS 11334, pp. 184–199, 2018.
https://doi.org/10.1007/978-3-030-05051-1_13

(2) $\exists a_j, \tau.a_j < \tau'.a_j$, where $a_i, a_j \in B$, and $\tau.a_i$ denotes the value of τ on the attribute a_i. The *skyline* query of R with respect to B is defined as $SKY_B(R)=$ $\{\tau_t| \nexists\tau_k$ s.t. $\tau_k \prec_B \tau_t, \tau_t, \tau_k \in R\}$. The attributes in B are termed as *skyline attributes*. For simplicity, we use $SKY(R)$ instead of $SKY_B(R)$ in this paper.

Most early works focused on the issue of performing skyline query on a single dataset. However, in some applications, *skyline attributes* belong to multiple datasets, and a variation of skyline query that is skyline join query has been proposed. The issue of *skyline join* query has been extensively studied, representative works include [4, 9–11, 15, 17, 19, 20, 22, 25–27]. Recently, there is a new trend in research of skyline query, which is computing skylines on data streams, representative works include [5, 16, 23, 24], among which [5, 23, 24] focuses on skyline query over a single data stream. By far, the literature [16] is the only work that studies the problem of skyline query over multiple data streams, which developed an algorithm *LSJ* based on the *Iterative* framework [22]. However, the *LSJ* algorithm uses a serial paradigm for skyline computing, and cannot utilize multi-core processors.

In this paper, we study the issue of parallel skyline join over multiple data streams. We improve the *Iterative* framework, and propose a *Novel Iterative* framework. Then we figure out the inherent parallelism of the *Novel Iterative* framework. Finally, we propose two parallel skyline join algorithms over sliding windows, *NP-SWJ* and *IP-SWJ*. The *IP-SWJ* algorithm uses the *Novel Iterative* framework, and performs skyline query over sliding windows in an incremental manner. While the *NP-SWJ* algorithm independently computes skylines over multiple pairs of windows. Extensive experiments illustrate that the *NP-SWJ* algorithm and *IP-SWJ* algorithm have a remarkable performance on both real datasets and synthetic datasets.

To the best of our knowledge, this is the first paper to address the issue of parallel skyline join over multiple data streams. The contributions of this paper are summarized as follows, a) we propose the *Novel Iterative* framework, which is an improvement of the *Iterative* framework, b) we propose two parallel skyline join algorithms, *NP-SWJ* and *IP-SWJ*. The rest of the paper is structured as follows: in Sect. 2, we review the existing work in the field of skyline join. Section 3 presents the preliminaries and the prerequisite knowledge about skyline join. In Sect. 4, we introduce the design and implementation of the proposed algorithms. Section 5 presents the extensive experimental evaluations of the proposed approaches. Finally, we conclude the paper in Sect. 6.

2 Related Work

2.1 Skyline Join over Static Datasets

The *skyline join* query was firstly studied by Jin *et al.* [9]. Inspired by this work, Sun *et al.* [22] presented a method to prune the join space, and proposed two algorithms for *skyline join* queries. Jin *et al.* [10] developed nonblocking algorithms for skyline queries on equi-joins. Raghavan and Rundensteiner [19] proposed a progressive algorithm which computes the *skyline join* queries at multiple levels of abstraction. Based on this work, a framework termed as *SKIN* [20] was proposed. Bhattacharya and Teja [25] developed several efficient algorithms, which try to perform the skyline query on local relations as much as possible before the join operation. *PrefJoin* [11] is a general framework for preference-aware join queries over multiple relations, which is suitable for *skyline join* queries as well. Vlachou et al. [26] proposed an algorithm *SFSJ* which is inspired by *SFS* algorithm [4]. Nagendra and Candan [15] introduced a concept of layer/region pruning (*LR-pruning*) for *skyline join* queries. Based on this pruning approach, the authors proposed S^2J algorithm and S^3J algorithm in the same literature.

All aforementioned algorithms are only applicable for *skyline join* on two relations. Nagendra and Candan proposed two algorithms S^2J-M and S^3J-M [17] for *skyline join* on more than two relations by extending S^2J and S^3J respectively. For M relations, they firstly generate an intermediate relation by joining M-1 datasets, and then perform S^2J or S^3J algorithm on the remaining relation and the intermediate relation. Zhang *et al.* [27] proposed an algorithm *Skyjog* for *skyline join* on two or more relations. *Skyjog* achieves a remarkable performance by leveraging the properties of *local skylines*.

Although these algorithms compute skyline results using different approaches and techniques, they try to improve performance by avoiding redundant computation and reducing intermediate datasets.

2.2   Skyline Join over Data Streams

Most recently, the problem of skyline queries on data stream attracts much attention. Substantial literatures focus on computing skylines over various kinds of data streams, which contains uncertain or uncomplete tuples. However, we only consider the data stream with certain and complete tuples in this paper, and revisit the most relevant work in the following. The algorithms of computing skylines over data streams are able to continuously monitor the changes in the skyline according to the arrival of new tuples and expiration of old ones.

Sun *et al.* [23] proposed an algorithm called *BOCS* for computing skylines over distributed data streams. The algorithm *BOCS* combines an centralized algorithm named *GridSky* and associated communication protocol to compute skylines in an incremental manner. Das Sarma *et al.* [5] proposed serval multi-pass algorithms for computing skylines on data streams with worst-case performance guarantees. The work demonstrates that one pass algorithms under the sliding window model are too restrictive, and proves that it is impossible to design an efficient skyline algorithm that reads each tuple only once.

To simplify the memory management, several literatures employ sliding window model to reduce memory consumption. The skyline result over sliding window may changes in two circumstances, one is new tuples append to the window, the other is old tuples expire. Since maintaining skyline result when new tuples appear is straightforward, it has become imperative to replace expired skyline objects with their proper successor(s) without having to compute from scratch among objects that are exclusively dominated by the expired ones. To tackle this problem, Tao *el al.* present the *Eager* algorithm [24] that employs an event list to track the successor(s) of current skyline tuples. While Lin *et al.* [14] propose the *StabSky* algorithm which leverages dominance graphs. Both these methods are derived by memorizing the relationship between a current skyline object and its successor(s). Once skyline objects expire, their successor(s) can be added to current skyline result without any extra computation.

The aforementioned algorithms focus on computing skylines on a single stream, which renders them inapplicable for *skyline queries* on multiple data streams. Nagendra *et al.* [16] proposed an algorithm *LSJ* which was the first algorithm of *skyline queries* on multiple data streams. The *LSJ* algorithm partitions the overall process into processing layers and maintains skyline-join results in an incremental manner by continuously monitoring the changes in all layers of the process.

3   Preliminaries

In this section, we introduce the preliminaries about our research. As it is known, there are two types of sliding window models, the *count-based* sliding window model and the *time-based* sliding window model. A tuple q in the *count-based* sliding window will expire when w subsequent tuples have been received after q, where w denotes the size of the *count-based* sliding window. In the *time-based* sliding window, a tuple q will expire after ts unit of time has passed since q has been received. In this paper, we focuses on skyline join over pairs of *count-based* sliding windows. Table 1 summarizes the notations used throughout the paper.

Table 1. Notations used in this paper

Notation	Description
T_i	Input table
W_i	Sliding window
w	Size of a *count-based* sliding window
σ	The number of tuples skipped from one window to the next
LSS	A dataset containing tuples that are both local skylines and global skylines
LSN	A dataset containing tuples that are both local skylines but not global skylines
LNN	A dataset containing tuples that are neither local skylines nor global skylines

3.1   Skyline Join Query

In some cases, the *skyline attributes* are distributed over multiple relations. For example, for a skyline query on 2 relations R_1, R_2, the set of *skyline attributes* consists of 2 disjoint sets, B_1, B_2, where B_i is the *skyline attribute* set of R_i. Intuitively, skyline query on these relations can be calculated by joining these two relations firstly, then performing the skyline query on the join result set with respect to the union set of B_1, B_2. This query is formalized as $SKY_{B_1 \cup B_2}(R_1 \bowtie R_2)^2$, and we name this query as *skyline join* query since the skyline query is performed on a join result set. This naive approach for calculating *skyline join* is inefficient, since it performs skyline query on a large intermediate dataset which is generated by joining all relations. Algorithms for *skyline join* should prune useless tuples before join operation, and reduce the skyline computation as much as possible.

As stated in [9], for *skyline join* on two relations, each relation is partitioned into groups in terms of the join attribute, i.e., tuple τ and tuple $\tau\prime$ are in the same group if the join attribute of them are the same. If τ is not dominated by other tuples of its group, then τ is a local skyline point. If τ is not dominated by other tuples of all groups, then τ is a global skyline point. Tuple τ belongs to one of three cases[3], (a) *LSS*, τ is both a local skyline point and a global skyline point. (b) *LSN*, τ is a local skyline point, but not a global skyline point. (c) *LNN*, τ is neither a local skyline point nor a global skyline point. Tuples belong to *LNN* are dominated by *LSN* tuples in the same group, and they cannot contribute to the finally skyline results. Thus, they should be pruned before the join operation. As illustrated in [9], tuples generated by $LSS(R_1) \bowtie LSS(R_2)$, $LSS(R_1) \bowtie LSN(R_2)$, and $LSN(R_1) \bowtie LSS(R_2)$, are guaranteed to be skyline points.

4   Algorithm Design and Implementation

In this section, we first develop a novel *iterative framework* for skyline join query. Based on this framework, we propose two parallel skyline join algorithms on sliding windows.

4.1   The Novel Iterative Framework for Skyline Join

Inspired by the *Iterative* framework [22], we propose a *Novel Iterative* algorithm for *skyline join* query with the optimized computing process. As stated in [22], the effectiveness of pruning downgrades as iterates 2 or more times. Thus, we use a loop counter l to limit the number of iterative process. The algorithm is described in Table 2.

The *Novel Iterative* algorithm starts with *PruneByJoinAttribute* (line 1), which prunes tuples that cannot generate join results from the two input tables T_1 and T_2. The algorithm runs the loop section (line 2–10) when both of T_1 and T_2 are not empty, and the loop counter l is not equal to 0. Then the algorithm generates partial skyline results based on the results of group skyline computation on T_1 and T_2, and put the partial skyline results into temporary result set T (line 5–6). During the process of group skyline computation, the algorithm records the outsiders for each tuple of the global skylines (*LSS*). The *outsiders*

---

[2] Join referred in this paper indicates equi-join operation.

[3] *LSS, LSN* and *LNN* are denoted as *LS(S), LS(N)* and *LN(N)* in original paper.

Table 2. The *Novel Iterative* algorithm

Input: Two tables, T_1 and T_2, for *skyline join* query,
l indicates the max number of iteration.
Output: Skyline result of $T_1 \bowtie T_2$.

1. $PruneByJoinAttribute(T_1,T_2)$
2. **while** T_1 is not *empty and* T_2 is not *empty and* l is not *equal to* 0
3. $(LSS(T_1),LSN(T_1))=GroupSkyline(T_1)$
4. $(LSS(T_2),LSN(T_2))=GroupSkyline(T_2)$
5. $G_1=LSS(T_1) \bowtie LSS(T_2)$, $G_2=LSS(T_1) \bowtie LSN(T_2)$, $G_3=LSN(T_1) \bowtie LSS(T_2)$
6. $T=T \cup G_1 \cup G_2 \cup G_3$
7. $T_1=OutsiderPrune(LSN(T_1),G_1 \cup G_2 \cup G_3)$
8. $T_2=OutsiderPrune(LSN(T_2),G_1 \cup G_2 \cup G_3)$
9. $l=l$-1
10. **end while**
11. **if** T_1 is *empty or* T_2 is *empty*
12.   *return* T
13. **else**
14. $T_m=Skyline(T_1 \bowtie T_2, T)$
15.   *return* $T_m \cup T$
16. **end if**

[22] of a skyline point, i.e. q, are those tuples that cannot be dominated by q, which can be used for pruning LSN tuples (line 7–8). We will describe more details about *outsiders* later. The loop ends when either one of the T_1 and T_2 is empty, or the loop counter l is equal to 0. If either T_1 or T_2 is empty, it indicates that all the skyline join results have been identified, and the temporary result set T is the final skyline join results. The algorithm outputs T and terminates (line 12). If the counter l is equal to 0, it indicates that the loop has already run l times, and the skyline results found so far are stored in T. In order to acquire the final skyline join results, the algorithm has to check tuples of $T_1 \bowtie T_2$ by comparing with T (line 14–15). As we notice that if l is set as a negative number, the limitation of iterative times is ineffective, then the iterative process proceeds until either T_1 or T_2 is empty.

As aforementioned, tuples generated by $LSN \bowtie LSN$ may be skyline points, and they will be the input tables for the next iteration. Before that, we prune LSN by *outsiders* to reduce the overhead of the following computation. As illustrated in Table 3, the *outsiders* are calculated in the process of group skyline computation. Firstly, the tuples belonging to LNN will be pruned by *localSkyline*[4] procedure (line 1). Then $GroupSkyline$ computes LSS, LSN and *outsiders* of each tuple in LSS and LSN by a variant of SFS [4]. For a tuple T_j that cannot dominated T_i, T_i is a outsider of T_j only when T_i belongs to LSN, which is different from the definition of *outsiders* in [22]. The new *outsiders* improve the

---

[4] Please refer to [22] for details of *localSkyline*.

Table 3. The *GroupSkyline* algorithm

Input: A table T
Output: LSS, LSN of table T
1. $T = localSkyline(T)$
2. $sort(T)$
3. **for** i from 1 to T.length-1
4.   tag=$false$
5.   add join attribute of each tuple in LSN to T_i's *outsider*
6.   **for** j from 0 to i-1
7.   **if** tag==$false$ *and* $T_j \prec T_i$
8.   put T_i to LSN
9.   tag=$true$
10.   add T_i's join attribute to $T_0, ..., T_{j-1}$'s *outsider*
11.   **else if** tag==$true$ *and* $T_j \not\prec T_i$
12.   add T_i's join attribute to T_j's *outsider*
13.   **end if**
14.   **end for**
15. **end for**
16. *return* T-LSN, LSN

prune efficiency since tuples of LSS in *outsiders* may increase the false-positive chance of T_i's domination, where T_i is a tuples in LSN.

Figure 1 illustrates the computing process of *Novel Iterative* algorithm. For two tables, T_1 and T_2, each of them contains one join attribute, A_1 and B_1, respectively, and the rest are skyline attributes. The *Novel Iterative* algorithm firstly computes group skyline for T_1 and T_2, then generates partial skyline results by combining $LSS(T_1) \bowtie LSS(T_2)$, $LSS(T_1) \bowtie LSN(T_2)$ and $LSN(T_1) \bowtie LSS(T_2)$. Then we use the partial skyline results generated in this step to prune $LSN(T_1)$ and $LSN(T_2)$. The tuple $(3, 40, 40)$ is removed from $LSN(T_1)$, since it is dominated by $(4, 20, 40, 5, 5)$ of G_2 on the skyline attributes A_2 and A_3, and the join attribute of tuple $(3, 40, 40)$ 3 is not in the outsider set of tuple $(4, 5, 5)$. Lastly, the pruned $LSN(T_1)$ and $LSN(T_2)$ will be the input tables for the next iterative step.

4.2   Parallel Processing Algorithm

In this section, we propose two parallel processing structures for skyline join on sliding window, which is Naive Parallel Sliding Window Join and Incremental Parallel Sliding Window Join (*IP-SWJ*).

A. Naive Parallel Skyline Window Join

Based on the *Novel Iterative* Framework, we design a parallel skyline join algorithm on sliding window, named Naive Parallel Sliding Window Join (*NP-SWJ*). As depicted in Fig. 2(a), tuples of streams within a window are taken as the input tables, then we can simultaneously calculate the results of skyline join on multiple windows by applying the *Novel Iterative* Algorithm. As we noticed, there is

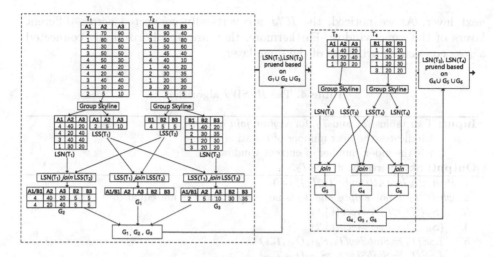

Fig. 1. The Novel Iterative framework

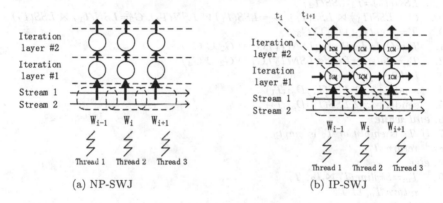

Fig. 2. Parallel skyline window join

no structural dependency or data dependency among the computation on adjacent windows, thus, threads for skyline join computation can run independently.

B. Incremental Parallel Skyline Window Join

Although *NP-SWJ* algorithm is easy to understand and implement, there may exist significant amount of redundant computations, since we observe that there are overlaps between consecutive windows of each layer. Intuitively, we need to figure out how to utilize the intermediate results of the previous window on the same layer, and avoid calculating results from scratch. As shown in Fig. 2(b), we propose the Incremental Parallel Skyline Window Join structure(*IP-SWJ*), which calculates skyline join on current window based on the results of the previous window. The circles in Fig. 2(b) are intermediate computing modules (*ICM*), which generate partial skyline join results and prepare the input tables for the next layer. As we noticed, the *ICM* are vertically connected across different layers of the same window. Furthermore, they are also horizontally connected across consecutive windows of the same layer.

Table 4. The *IP-SWJ* algorithm

Input: Two tables, T_1 and T_2, for *skyline join* query,
        l indicates the max number of iteration.
        i is the index number of current window.
Output: Skyline result of $T_1 \bowtie T_2$.

1. *PruneByJoinAttribute(T_1,T_2)*, j=0
2. **while** T_1 is not *empty and* T_2 is not *empty and* l is not equal to 0
3. (S_{n1}, D_{g1}, T_{p1})=*recv*(i,j,1)
4. (S_{n2}, D_{g2}, T_{p2})=*recv*(i,j,2)
5.   *LSS(T_1)=StabSky($T_1, S_{n1}, D_{g1}, T_{p1}$)*
6.   *LSS(T_2)=StabSky($T_2, S_{n2}, D_{g2}, T_{p2}$)*
7.   *LSN(T_1)=T_1-LSS(T_1)*
8.   *LSN(T_2)=T_2-LSS(T_2)*
9. G_1=*LSS(T_1)* $\bowtie$ *LSS(T_2)*, G_2=*LSS(T_1)* $\bowtie$ *LSN(T_2)*, G_3=*LSN(T_1)* $\bowtie$ *LSS(T_2)*
10. T=$T \cup G_1 \cup G_2 \cup G_3$
11. T_1=*OutsiderPrune(LSN(T_1)*,$G_1 \cup G_2 \cup G_3$)
12. T_2=*OutsiderPrune(LSN(T_2)*,$G_1 \cup G_2 \cup G_3$)
13. l=l-1,j=j+1
14.   send(i+1,j,1,*LSS(T_1)*D_{g1},T_1)
15.   send(i+1,j,2,*LSS(T_2)*D_{g2},T_2)
16. **end while**
17. **if** T_1 is *empty or* T_2 is *empty*
18.   *return* T
19. **else**
20. T_m=*Skyline($T_1 \bowtie T_2$, T)*
21.   *return* $T_m \cup T$
22. **end if**

As mentioned above, the *StabSky* [14] algorithm addresses skyline query on sliding window by an incremental manner, it calculates skylines of current window based on the information corresponding to the previous window, i.e., the expired tuple, the partial skyline result and the dominance graph. Thus, we implement *IP-SWJ* algorithm by combining the *StabSky* algorithm and the *Novel Iterative* algorithm, and it is shown in Table 4.

The *IP-SWJ* algorithm receives intermediate results generated by the procedure on W_{i-1} of jth layer (line 3–4), and uses *StabSky* algorithm to calculate the skyline results of T_1 and T_2 (line 5–6). T_{p1} and T_{p2} denote the tuple set of previous window, and S_{n1} and S_{n2} denote the skyline results of T_{p1} and T_{p2}. D_{g1} and D_{g2} denote the *dominance graph* [14] of T_{p1} and T_{p2}. Due to the limitation of length, we omit the implementation of *StabSky* in this paper. After generating essential results, *IP-SWJ* sends results to shared cache, which will be used for computation on the next window of the same layer. It is important that there exits data dependency for computation on consecutive windows of the same layer. As depicted in Fig. 2(b), the execution at time t_{i+1} starts only when it finishes at t_i, which is a pipeline style execution.

5   Performance Evaluation

In this section, we evaluate the performance of the proposed algorithms, *NP-SWJ* and *IP-SWJ*, on real and synthetic data sets by varying the parameters involved.

5.1   Experimental Setup

This is the first paper that we are aware of which targets parallel skyline join on data streams. Therefore, for evaluation purposes, we compare *NP-SWJ* and *IP-SWJ* with the serial algorithm *LSJ*. Experiments in this section are conducted on a server with an Intel Xeon 2.2 GHz CPU, 64 GB RAM. All algorithms in these experiments are implemented in Java.

Datasets. The evaluations are carried out on synthetic and real data sets. (1) The synthetic data sets are generated based on correlated, independent and anti-correlated distributions as described in [3]. (2) We use *Intel Berkeley Research (IBR)* lab sensor data stream[5] as the real data set, which contains about 2.3 million rows and was collected from 54 sensors. The data set contains 12 attributes and the schema is shown in Table 5. In this experiment, we only use five of these attributes, *moteid, temperature, humidity, light* and *voltage*, of which, *moteid* is used as the *join attribute*, and the rest are the *skyline attributes*. We eliminate incomplete or invalid records, i.e. value is negative, from the data set, and the cardinality of the purged data set is about 1.9 million. We then divide the data set into two equal-sized data sets.

Table 5. Schema of Intel Berkeley lab data set

date:yyyy-mm-dd	*time*:hh:mm:ss.xxx	*epoch*:int	*moteid*:int
temperature:real	*humidity*:real	*light*:real	*voltage*:real

Evaluation Parameters. On static data sets, execution time is recognized as the major evaluation metric for skyline algorithms. In this paper, we use *through-put* to evaluate the performance of the proposed algorithms. The *throughput* of a skyline join algorithm on data streams is the number of windows processed per second. We report the *throughput* after examining over 50 consecutive sliding windows.

---

[5] http://db.csail.mit.edu/labdata/labdata.html.

The parameters involved in this experiment include the size of sliding window (w), the shift length (σ), the depth of iteration (l), the number of dimensions (d), the number of threads for parallel computing (p), and the distribution of data sets. The default value for each variable is 1000 for w, 300 for σ, 4 for l, 4 for d, and 4 for p. We use independent distribution as the default data distribution.

5.2   Evaluation over Synthetic Streams

Effect of Data Distribution. Figure 3(a) illustrates the behavior of the proposed algorithms and *LSJ* on three typical data distributions [3], correlated distribution (*cor*), independent distribution (*ind*) and anti-correlated distribution (*ant*). We notice that all the three algorithms perform well on correlated distribution, with the worst performance on anti-correlated distribution. This phenomenon exists in almost all skyline related algorithms, since the size of skyline result on correlated distribution is smaller than that on independent distribution and anti-correlated distribution, and it needs less computation to obtain the final results. While the algorithms spend more time for computation on anti-correlated distribution, since the size of skyline result is much larger than that on correlated distribution and independent distribution. Of all the three algorithms, the *throughput* of *NP-SWJ* and *IP-SWJ* are about 4 times higher than that of *LSJ*, since we use 4 threads to run *NP-SWJ* and *IP-SWJ*. Compared with *NP-SWJ*, *IP-SWJ* has a better performance, which implies the incremental manner used by *IP-SWJ* is efficient for performance improvement.

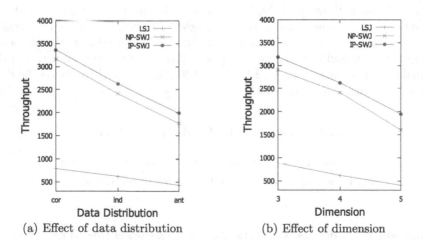

(a) Effect of data distribution   (b) Effect of dimension

Fig. 3. Effect of data distribution and dimension

Effect of Number of Dimensions. Figure 3(b) shows the effect of dimensionality. Although the *throughput* of *NP-SWJ* and *IP-SWJ* degrades with the growth of dimensionality, they still perform well on high-dimensional streams.

As we expected, the *NP-SWJ* and *IP-SWJ* are about 4 times faster than *LSJ*, and *IP-SWJ* has a better performance than *NP-SWJ*, which demonstrates that the incremental manner used by *IP-SWJ* is still effective on high-dimensional streams as well.

Effect of Window Size and Shift Length. The experiment reported in Fig. 4(a) studies the effect of the size of the sliding windows. It shows that *IP-SWJ* and *NP-SWJ* still have a better performance, about 3–4 times faster than *LSJ*. The *IP-SWJ* algorithm is better than *NP-SWJ* on all test cases. With the growth of the size of sliding windows, all of the three algorithms need much more computation for each pair of sliding windows. Thus, all the algorithms have a performance degradation.

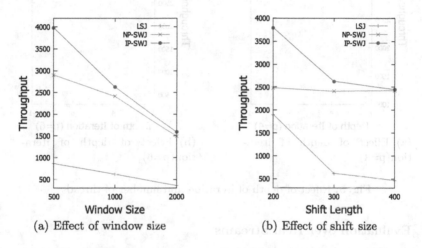

(a) Effect of window size   (b) Effect of shift size

Fig. 4. Effect of window size and shift length

Figure 4(b) examines the performance of the proposed algorithms as the shift length is changed. We notice that the shift length has a negligible effect on the performance of the *NP-SWJ* algorithm, since the *NP-SWJ* algorithm does not rely on the overlaps for skyline computing. For the *LSJ* algorithm and *IP-SWJ* algorithm, a larger shift size implies a smaller overlap of the consecutive sliding windows, which reduces the efficiency of incremental computation.

Effect of Depth of Iteration and Number of Threads. Figure 5(a) and (b) show the effect of the number of threads, and we do not take the serial algorithm *LSJ* as a counterpart in this experiments. As we have seen from the two figures, the *NP-SWJ* algorithm has a linear performance improvement when the number of threads changes from 4 to 6. With the increasing of the depth of iteration (from 2 to −1, −1 indicates the unlimited depth), the performance of *NP-SWJ* gradually degrades. This can be explained that the efficiency of pruning reduces as the depth of iteration grows, and the iteration will incur extra overhead. For the *IP-SWJ* algorithm, due to the data dependency, it can achieve full speed running only when the depth of iteration (l) is equal to or greater than the number of threads. That's the reason the *throughput* of IP-SWJ increases and then decreases. The performance of *NP-SWJ* is barely affected by the growth of shift length, as *NP-SWJ* does not use the incremental computing manner based on the overlaps.

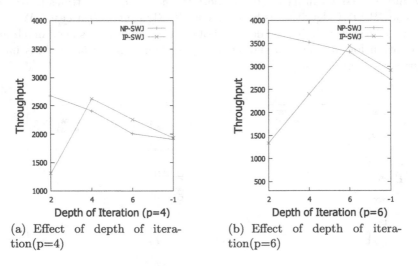

(a) Effect of depth of iteration(p=4)

(b) Effect of depth of iteration(p=6)

Fig. 5. Effect of depth of iteration and number of threads

5.3   Evaluation over Real Streams

Effect of Window Size and Shift Length. As illustrated in Fig. 6(a), with the growth of the size of sliding window, the proportion of overlaps over consecutive windows decreases, which reduces the efficiency of incremental computation, thus the performance of *LSJ* and *IP-SWJ* drops. For *NP-SWJ*, a larger size of sliding windows implies more skyline computation is required, therefore, the *throughput* of *NP-SWJ* drops as well.

Figure 6(b) shows the effect of shift size. As mentioned above, the proportion of overlaps decreases as the size of shift grows, which induces the performance degradation for *LSJ* and *IP-SWJ*.

Effect of Depth of Iteration and Number of Threads. As shown in Fig. 7(a) and (b), the performance of the *NP-SWJ* algorithm improves on all test cases when the number of threads increases. However, when the depth of iteration increases, the efficiency of data pruning decreases, more overhead is brought by the extra iterations. Due to the data dependency, the *IP-SWJ* behaves the best performance when the depth of iteration (l) is equal to or greater than the number of threads, thus the *throughput* of *IP-SWJ* increases and then decreases.

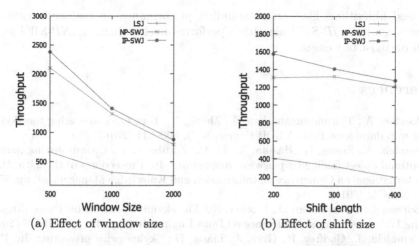

(a) Effect of window size

(b) Effect of shift size

Fig. 6. Effect of window size and shift length on real datasets

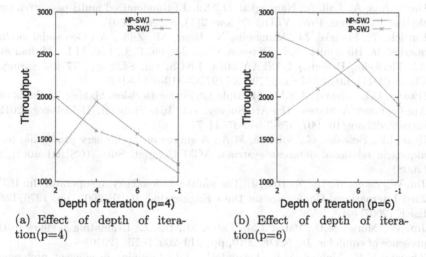

(a) Effect of depth of itera-
tion(p=4)

(b) Effect of depth of itera-
tion(p=6)

Fig. 7. Effect of depth of iteration and number of threads on real datasets

6 Conclusion

In this paper, we introduced and studied the problem of parallel computing of skyline join over data streams. We developed a *Novel Iterative* framework based on the existing work and study the inherent parallelism of the *Novel Iterative* framework. Then we propose two parallel skyline join algorithms over sliding windows, *NP-SWJ* and *IP-SWJ*. The *NP-SWJ* algorithm computes results of skyline join on multiple pairs of windows simultaneously, while the *IP-SWJ* algorithm employs an incremental computing manner based on the overlaps of consecutive windows. Extensive experiments demonstrate that both of the two proposed algorithms have an outstanding performance on real and synthetic datasets, and the *IP-SWJ* algorithm performs better than the *NP-SWJ* algorithm on most test cases.

References

1. Asudeh, A., Thirumuruganathan, S., Zhang, N., Das, G.: Discovering the skyline of web databases. Proc. VLDB Endow. **9**(7), 600–611 (2016)
2. Asudeh, A., Zhang, G., Hassan, N., Li, C., Zaruba, G.V.: Crowdsourcing pareto-optimal object finding by pairwise comparisons. In: Proceedings of the 24th ACM International on Conference on Information and Knowledge Management, pp. 753–762. ACM (2015)
3. Borzsony, S., Kossmann, D., Stocker, K.: The skyline operator. In: Proceedings of the 17th International Conference on Data Engineering, pp. 421–430. IEEE (2001)
4. Chomicki, J., Godfrey, P., Gryz, J., Liang, D.: Skyline with presorting. In: Proceedings of the 19th International Conference on Data Engineering, pp. 717–719. IEEE (2003)
5. Das Sarma, A., Lall, A., Nanongkai, D., Xu, J.: Randomized multi-pass streaming skyline algorithms. Proc. VLDB Endow. **2**(1), 85–96 (2009)
6. Emrich, T., Franzke, M., Mamoulis, N., Renz, M., Züfle, A.: Geo-social skyline queries. In: Bhowmick, S.S., Dyreson, C.E., Jensen, C.S., Lee, M.L., Muliantara, A., Thalheim, B. (eds.) DASFAA 2014. LNCS, vol. 8422, pp. 77–91. Springer, Cham (2014). https://doi.org/10.1007/978-3-319-05813-9_6
7. Hwang, C.L., Masud, A.S.M.: Multiple Objective Decision Making Methods and Applications: A State-of-the-Art Survey, vol. 164. Springer, Heidelberg (2012). https://doi.org/10.1007/978-3-642-45511-7
8. Ilyas, I.F., Beskales, G., Soliman, M.A.: A survey of top-k query processing techniques in relational database systems. ACM Comput. Surv. (CSUR) **40**(4), 11 (2008)
9. Jin, W., Ester, M., Hu, Z., Han, J.: The multi-relational skyline operator. In: IEEE 23rd International Conference on Data Engineering, ICDE 2007, pp. 1276–1280. IEEE (2007)
10. Jin, W., Morse, M.D., Patel, J.M., Ester, M., Hu, Z.: Evaluating skylines in the presence of equijoins. In: ICDE 2010, pp. 249–260. IEEE (2010)
11. Khalefa, M.E., Mokbel, M.F., Levandoski, J.J.: Prefjoin: an efficient preference-aware join operator. In: ICDE, pp. 995–1006. IEEE (2011)
12. Kossmann, D., Ramsak, F., Rost, S.: Shooting stars in the sky: an online algorithm for skyline queries. In: Proceedings of the 28th International Conference on Very Large Databases, VLDB 2002, pp. 275–286. Elsevier (2002)
13. Liang, W., Chen, B., Yu, J.X.: Energy-efficient skyline query processing and maintenance in sensor networks. In: Proceedings of the 17th ACM Conference on Information and Knowledge Management, pp. 1471–1472. ACM (2008)
14. Lin, X., Yuan, Y., Wang, W., Lu, H.: Stabbing the sky: efficient skyline computation over sliding windows. In: Proceedings of the 21st International Conference on Data Engineering, ICDE 2005, pp. 502–513. IEEE (2005)
15. Nagendra, M., Candan, K.S.: Skyline-sensitive joins with LR-pruning. In: Proceedings of the 15th International Conference on Extending Database Technology, pp. 252–263. ACM (2012)

16. Nagendra, M., Candan, K.S.: Layered processing of skyline-window-join (SWJ) queries using iteration-fabric. In: 2013 IEEE 29th International Conference on Data Engineering (ICDE), pp. 985–996. IEEE (2013)
17. Nagendra, M., Candan, K.S.: Efficient processing of skyline-join queries over multiple data sources. ACM Trans. Database Syst. (TODS) **40**(2), 10 (2015)
18. Pan, L.Q., Li, J.Z., Luo, J.Z.: Approximate skyline query processing algorithm in wireless sensor networks. J. Softw. **21**(5), 1020–1030 (2010)
19. Raghavan, V., Rundensteiner, E., et al.: Progressive result generation for multi-criteria decision support queries. In: ICDE 2010, pp. 733–744. IEEE (2010)
20. Raghavan, V., Rundensteiner, E.A., Srivastava, S.: Skyline and mapping aware join query evaluation. Inf. Syst. **36**(6), 917–936 (2011)
21. Shi, J., Lu, H., Lu, J., Liao, C.: A skylining approach to optimize influence and cost in location selection. In: Bhowmick, S.S., Dyreson, C.E., Jensen, C.S., Lee, M.L., Muliantara, A., Thalheim, B. (eds.) DASFAA 2014. LNCS, vol. 8422, pp. 61–76. Springer, Cham (2014). https://doi.org/10.1007/978-3-319-05813-9_5
22. Sun, D., Wu, S., Li, J., Tung, A.K.: Skyline-join in distributed databases. In: VLDB Workshop, pp. 176–181. IEEE (2008)
23. Sun, S., Huang, Z., Zhong, H., Dai, D., Liu, H., Li, J.: Efficient monitoring of skyline queries over distributed data streams. Knowl. Inf. Syst. **25**(3), 575–606 (2010)
24. Tao, Y., Papadias, D.: Maintaining sliding window skylines on data streams. IEEE Trans. Knowl. Data Eng. **18**(3), 377–391 (2006)
25. Teja, A.B.B.P.: Aggregate skyline join queries: skylines with aggregate operations over multiple relations. Manag. Data 15 (2010)
26. Vlachou, A., Doulkeridis, C., Polyzotis, N.: Skyline query processing over joins. In: Proceedings SIGMOD 2011, pp. 73–84. ACM (2011)
27. Zhang, J., Lin, Z., Li, B., Wang, W., Meng, D.: Skyline join query processing over multiple relations. In: Gao, H., Kim, J., Sakurai, Y. (eds.) DASFAA 2016. LNCS, vol. 9645, pp. 353–361. Springer, Cham (2016). https://doi.org/10.1007/978-3-319-32055-7_29

Air Flow Based Failure Model for Data Centers

Hao Feng[1], Yuhui Deng[1,2(✉)], and Liang Yu[1]

[1] Jinan University, Guangdong, Guangzhou, China
76020634@qq.com, tyhdeng@jnu.edu.cn
[2] The State Key Laboratory of Computer Architecture, Institute of Computing
Technology, Chinese Academy of Sciences, Beijing, China

Abstract. With the explosive growth of data, thousands upon thousands servers are contained in data centers. Hence, node failure is unavoidable and it generally brings effects on the performance of the whole data center. On the other hand, data centers with vast nodes will cause plenty of energy consumption. Many existing task scheduling techniques can effectively reduce the power consumption in data centers by considering heat recirculation. However, traditional techniques barely take the situation of node failure into account. This paper proposes an airflow-based failure model for data centers by leveraging heat recirculation. In this model, the spatial distribution and time distribution of failure nodes are considered. Furthermore, the Genetic algorithm (GA) and Simulated Annealing algorithm (SA) are implemented to evaluate the proposed failure model. Because the position of failures has a significant impact on the heat recirculation and the energy consumption of data centers, failure nodes with different positions are analyzed and evaluated. The experimental results demonstrate that the energy consumption of data centers can be significantly reduced by using the GA and SA algorithms for task scheduling based on proposed failure model.

Keywords: Energy efficiency · Data centers · Node failure
Task schedule

1 Introduction

With the rapid development of Cloud computing, a huge volume of data is being generated every day in various fields. In order to process these explosively incremental data, large-scale data centers have been built and played a significant role in various applications, such as Internet of Things (IOT) and Internet-based services [1,4,10,24,26,28]. In many data centers, due to the complexity of topology structure and the long-time running of IT equipment, the occurrence of node failure is inevitable [3,3,5,13,21,32]. Sahoo et al. [19] analyze the empirical and statistical properties of node failure from a data center with nearly 400 servers running a diverse workload over a year. Results reveal the problem of

© Springer Nature Switzerland AG 2018
J. Vaidya and J. Li (Eds.): ICA3PP 2018, LNCS 11334, pp. 200–214, 2018.
https://doi.org/10.1007/978-3-030-05051-1_14

hardware failure accounted for more than 50%, while software failure takes up about 20%. Failure rate depends mostly on system size and less on the type of hardware. There is evidence of a correlation between the failure rate of a machine and intensity of workload running on it [21,32,33]. IT equipment with heavy task load is easy to become a local hot spot and consequently faulted. Hence, the task schedule directly affects the rate of failures and the power consumption of the whole data center. In order to further study the related task scheduling problem in data center after node failure, a failure model is necessary.

Data centers can be modeled to explore the insight of energy consumption. The traditional way is using Computational Fluid Dynamic (CFD) model to describe heat recirculation. However, the model is computationally expensive to produce. Hence, it is not appropriate for real-time task scheduling. An analytical model designed by Wang et al. [25] can be used to describe the data center energy consumption with air transfer properties and thermal characters. This model leverages profiles between task and temperature, and designs the scheme of thermal-aware workload placement. Tang et al. [23] build a linear heat recirculation model to minimize peak inlet temperature of nodes by different task scheduling. Previous research about modeling data centers can effectively solve the energy saving issues. However, they neglect the situation of node failure in data centers.

Many researches have been conducted on energy-saving task scheduling in data centers. Lee and Zomaya [11] put forward two task consolidation strategies which are designed to maximize resource utilization and reduce energy consumption. Polverini and Wang et al. [17,25] propose some task distribution approaches by considering the inlet temperature of servers and reducing the energy consumption of cooling systems. Liu et al. [15] propose an integrated workload management system in data centers that develop renewable power supply, cooling supply and dynamic pricing of electricity. Besides, Moore et al. [16] design a temperature-aware workload placement algorithm which leverages a thermo dynamic formulation with information of the steady state of hot and cold spots to place tasks in data centers. Yang et al. construct a power model to correlate the task assignment, heat recirculation, inlet temperature, and cooling cost in the homogeneous and heterogeneous data centers with under-floor air supply [29]. Existing task scheduling methods can effectively reduce the power consumption in data centers. However, traditional techniques fail to take the situation of node failure into account.

Different from the existing work, this paper puts forward the model of node failure by taking heat recirculation into consideration. Specifically, with our proposed model, corresponding energy-saving task scheduling problem is considered. The major contributions of this paper are listed as follows:

1. A new failure model is proposed by taking the heat recirculation of data centers into account. In this model, the spatial distribution and time distribution of failure nodes are considered. Furthermore, the relevant change of the cross-interference matrix and the relationship between CPU use ratio and time grades needed is studied in this model.

2. Based on the proposed failure model, the Genetic algorithm (GA) and Simulated Annealing algorithm (SA) are implemented to construct the strategy of task scheduling for the sake of reducing energy consumption of the cooling system. Results of experiments demonstrate the effectiveness of the algorithms.
3. Experiments are carried out to find the relationship between energy consumption of the cooling system and positions of failure nodes. Experimental results prove that failure nodes close to the top of racks bring more energy consumption in data centers, in contrast to nodes close to the bottom of racks.

The remainder of this paper is organized as follows. Section 2 introduces the related work. The relevant introduction of power model of data centers is introduced in Sect. 3. Section 4 details the model of node failure. Section 5 presents the intelligent algorithms of task distribution by using the proposed failure model. The experiment and evaluation are introduced in Sect. 6. Section 7 concludes this paper.

2   Related Work

Traditional data centers are usually made of IT equipment (servers), power systems, Computer Room Air Conditioning unit (CRAC) and so on (light systems). Among them, IT equipment is the vital part of data centers. The energy consumption of IT equipment depends on hardware specifications and tasks required to perform. Statistics show that CRAC, as a key part of the data center, requires an army of cooling energy consumption, occupying almost 40% to 60% of the energy consumption of the entire data center [14, 22]. Hence, reducing the power consumption of CRAC has become an important challenge (Fig. 1).

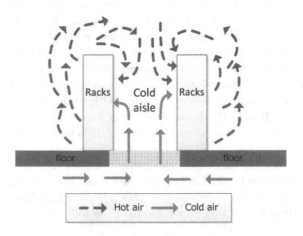

Fig. 1. The heat recirculation of airflow in data centers.

Data centers with vast nodes will cause plenty of energy consumption, as well as a higher emission of greenhouse gas. For example, an IBM data center consumes 20 MW, almost equivalent to 22,000 US building energy consumption [6]. A few works are dedicated to reducing energy consumption in data centers [2,8,9,18,20,30]. The energy consumed by the cooling system can reach up to more than 50% of the total energy used in a data center [11,22]. Thus, energy consumption of CRAC is still one determining factor of the total energy consumption in data centers. A key challenge in optimizing the operation of data centers is to minimize the cooling requirement and improve the overall energy efficiency [12]. Heat recirculation plays a vital role in a data center's power model. It compels the cooling system to supply cold air with a temperature much lower than the servers need, thus increasing the power consumption of cooling system. A scheme is investigated in [27] that dynamically "right-sizing" data centers by turning off servers during specific periods to save energy. With a further general model proposed and an on-line algorithm developed, significant cost savings are made possible. Effective power provisioning strategies proposed in [7] can be used to determine how much computing equipment can be safely and efficiently hosted within a given power budget. Besides, a modeling framework is presented to estimate the potential of power management schemes to reduce peak power and energy usage. A power-aware data replication strategy by leveraging data access behavior is proposed in [31]. This strategy can effectively reduce the resource and energy consumption of the whole data storage systems.

However, energy saving strategies mentioned above are based on normal and failure-free data centers or data storage systems. Considering the frequent occurrence of failure in the high-scale growing data center, research of this paper is aimed at reducing the energy consumption of data centers with node failure by promoting the efficiency of cooling system.

3   Power Model of Data Centers

IT equipment will be referred to as nodes below. The frequently used denotations in this paper are listed and explained in Table 1. Supposing $Node_1$ has an inlet temperature T_{in}^1, then T_{in}^1 is a mixture of the cool airflow offered by CRAC and the heat flow from other nodes. The cold airflow enters the nodes from the front side, picks up the heat from the circuitry, and exits the nodes into the heat flow. Part of heat flow from $Node_1$ will back into CRAC, while another part of it reaches the other nodes (include $Node_1$) by heat recirculation. On the other hand, $Node_1$ is also affected by heat recirculation of other nodes, as shown in Fig. 2. Inlet air temperature of $Node_1$ mainly consists of the air temperature T_{sup} from CRAC and the cross-interference coefficient (a_{11}, a_{31}, a_{21}). The recirculation of heat can be denoted by a cross-interference coefficient matrix $A = [a_{ij}]_{n \times m}$, which describes how much of its outlet heat each node contributes to the inlet of every other node. The outlet air temperature of $Node_1$ has two ways: one is back to CRAC and another one forms the cross-interference coefficient (a_{11}, a_{12}, a_{13}), a_{ii} represents the self-interference coefficient.

Table 1. The meaning of labels

Symbols	Meaning
u	CPU use ratio of the data center before node failure.
$Node_i$	One random node i
T_{in}^i	The inlet temperature of $Node_i$
T_{out}^i	The outlet temperature of $Node_i$
T_{sup}	Temperature of cool airflow offered by CRAC
D	The matrix of heat distribution
C_{tot}	Total task in the data center
m	Number of servers contained in each node
a	The energy consumption of one server of $Node_i$
b	The basic energy consumption of $Node_i$
D	The heat distribution matrix
c_i	Task for $Node_i$
a_{ij}	The interference coefficient form $Node_i$ to $Node_j$
Q_{out}^i	The total heat of outlet air of $Node_i$
A	The cross-interference matrix of all the nodes
P	The energy needed by each node in the data center
K	The diagonal thermodynamic matrix, $K_i = \rho f_i C_p$
C_p	The specific heat of air
ρ	The air density
f_i	The flow rate

3.1   The Airflow Distribution Model

Assuming a data center is given a task of size C_{tot} to run, and for simplicity, the size of task means the number of processors required. For example, a task of size 20 means the task requires 20 servers to run. For multiprocessor and multi-core systems, we can easily split the total task by the number of cores into each server. A scheduler assigns the task to n nodes, each node will run a "sub-task" of size c_i. Assuming each node contains m servers, the scheduling results should satisfy the constraints: $\sum_{i=1}^{n} c_i - C_{tot} = 0$, and $c_i \leq m$. The mathematical methods of minimizing temperature of inlet airflow by task scheduling are concluded in [23]:

$$minimize \max_i T_{in}^i, and \; \boldsymbol{t}_{in} = \boldsymbol{t}_{sup} + D\boldsymbol{b} + Dc\boldsymbol{a},$$

where a denotes the energy consumption of one server in $Node_i$ when executing task k (the utilization of CPU is 100%), $\boldsymbol{b}$ represents the basic energy consumption of node i, D is on behalf of the heat distribution matrix, it can be deduced from A, $D = [(K - A^T K)^{-1} - K^{-1}]$. Because $\boldsymbol{t}_{sup}$, $D\boldsymbol{b}$ and a can be obtained in one data center, we can calculate the most suitable subtask assignment vector $c = \{c_1, c_2, ...c_n\}$ to minimize the inlet airflow temperature of nodes.

3.2   Task Scheduling Methods

The algorithms used for task scheduling are divided into two groups: (a) the traditional non thermal-aware algorithms (*UT* and *Random* algorithms) and (b) the thermal-aware algorithms (*Genetic algorithm* and *Simulated Annealing* algorithm).

- *Uniform Task (UT)*: In this algorithm, all nodes are assigned the same amount of tasks: $c_i = C_{tot}/n, \forall i$.
- *Random*: It is a random allocation algorithm to uniformly distribute task.
- *Genetic algorithm (GA)*: A genetic algorithm is an iterative approach. Assuming given a pool of *genomes* (i.e. feasible solutions), and by mixing solutions (i.e. *mating*) and inserting random alterations (i.e. *mutating*), it will create new solutions and discard inefficient parts based on a *fitness function* (i.e. a metric). This algorithm can effectively explore the solution space to reach a near-optimal solution.
- *Simulated Annealing (SA)*: SA is a probabilistic algorithm for seeking the global optimum of a given function. Specifically, it is a heuristic algorithm to seek approximately global optimization in a large search space. It is typically used when the search-space is discrete.

3.3   Distribution of Failure Nodes

Schroeder et al. [21] compute six different time sequences for each node in a system. From their study, the failures mainly consist of hardware and software failure, environment, human error, network failure and unknown cause. They find that failure rates vary widely across systems, depending mostly on system size and less on the type of hardware. In addition, they also study the aging problem of computing data center software and point out that with the increase of nodes' running time, more and more errors will be accumulated inside the software, resulting in increasingly high node failure rate. The spatial distribution of failure nodes in data centers meets the *Zipf* distribution rule.

The *Zipf* distribution rule can be denoted as:

$$C = P(r) * r^{\alpha}. \tag{1}$$

where the product of $P(r)$ and r^{α} is one constant, and in log coordinates, α is one skewness parameter of *Zipf*. In fact, the study finds that if α is 0.01, the data center node failure tends to be evenly distributed. However, if α is 0.99, most of the failure nodes are concentrated in a relatively small area.

Besides, the time distribution of failure nodes is fit well by *Weibull* distribution. Assuming all nodes in the data center have not faulted within time t. The failure rate represents the probability of failure of all nodes in the data center from t to $t + \Delta t$. The failure rate is a function of t, which can be expressed as $\lambda(t)$, represents the reliability of all nodes in the data center during Δt. The failure rate can be expressed as follows:

$$\lambda(t) = \frac{pdf(t)}{1 - cdf(t)} = [\frac{shape}{scale}] \times [\frac{t}{scale}]^{shape-1}. \tag{2}$$

The rule shows that node which just faulted is likely to be faulted again, and when it comes back to run, the probability of failure will be lower and lower, but when it reaches the minimum value, it will rise with time going by.

4   The Air Flow Based Failure Model

From the above discussion, it can be obtained that the spatial distribution of failure nodes in data centers meets the *Zipf* distribution. In order to facilitate our study of the location and energy consumption of failure nodes, this paper sets the skewness parameter α of *Zipf* as 0.99. Therefore, if one node has the lowest r, then it has the maximal possibility to be failure node.

On the basis of the *Weibull* distribution of failure nodes in time distribution, nodes that just occur failure will be easy to fail again, hence the strategy of the failure model is shutting down this node directly. When this strategy is adopted, the cross-interference coefficient matrix A is changed accordingly. We will present the solution of A after one or more failure nodes occurred.

4.1   The Cross-Interference Matrix of Existing Failure Nodes

From Eq. (3), in order to get the matrix A, we should get n different energy distribution vector $\boldsymbol{P}_k$, $k = 1, 2...n$, and accordingly acquire different temperature distribution vector T_{out}^{new}. When $Node_k$ is is shut down after failing, it will not be affected by other nodes with the heat cycle. And meanwhile, node $Node_k$ will not execute task, hence the influence of heat cycle from $Node_k$ on other nodes can be regarded as 0. Through the above analysis, we can deduce the change of the cross-interference coefficient matrix A' within one failure $Node_k$, that is $a_{ik} = 0, i = 1...n$ and $a_{ki} = 0, i = 1...n$.

Assuming there are four nodes $Node_1$, $Node_2$, $Node_3$, $Node_4$ in one data center. The cross-interference coefficient matrix A of these four nodes can be denoted as:

$$A = \begin{bmatrix} a_{11} & a_{12} & a_{13} & a_{14} \\ a_{21} & a_{22} & a_{23} & a_{24} \\ a_{31} & a_{32} & a_{33} & a_{34} \\ a_{41} & a_{42} & a_{43} & a_{44} \end{bmatrix}.$$

If the $Node_2$ is a failure node, $Node_2$ will neither generate heat nor participate in the heat cycle among nodes. Hence, when we shut down $Node_2$, it will not be affected by heat cycle with other nodes, we have $a_{i2} = 0, i = 1...4$ and $a_{2i} = 0, i = 1...4$. The cross-interference coefficient matrix $A_{Node_2\ is faulted}$ can be shown as:

$$A_{Node_2\ is\ faulted} = \begin{bmatrix} a_{11} & 0 & a_{13} & a_{14} \\ 0 & 0 & 0 & 0 \\ a_{31} & 0 & a_{33} & a_{34} \\ a_{41} & 0 & a_{43} & a_{44} \end{bmatrix}.$$

4.2   The Failure Model

When a node failure occurs, the matrix for one node failure can be denoted as $X_1 = MZ_1$, where M represents the unit diagonal matrix: $M = diag(x_1, x_2, ...x_n), x_i = 1, i = 1...n$, and Z_1 denotes one n line and 1 column vector that $Z_1 = [y_1, y_2, ...y_n]^T, y_j = 0, j \in 1, 2, ...n$, and $y_i = 1, \{i \neq j\} \cap \{i = 1...n\}$.

Similarly, z failure nodes occur in one data center, the matrix for multiple node failure can be denoted as $X_z = MZ_z$. Vector $z = z_1, z_2...z_z$, where $z_1, z_2...z_z$ denote the number of failure nodes in the data center. Hence we have $y_z = 0, z \subset 1, 2, ...n$, and $y_i = 1, \{i \neq z\} \cap \{i = 1...n\}$.

Supposing one data center contains n nodes, m blades for each node with power characteristics a, b. Then the data center airflow distribution model for z failure nodes can be denoted as finding a task placement vector c to:

$$minimize \; \max_i \{T_{in}^i\},$$

such that:

$$C_{tot} - \sum_{j=1}^n c_j = 0,$$

$$t_{in} = t_{sup} + X_z DX_z b + X_z DX_z ca \; (z = 1...n),$$

with:

$$m \geq c_j \geq 0, j = 1...n - z \quad u \leq (1 - z/n) \times 100\%,$$

or

$$(z + 1)m \geq c_j \geq 0, j = 1...n - z \quad u \leq (1 - z/n) \times 100\%.$$

The meaning of each label is given in Table 1.

On account of t_{sup}, $X_z DX_z b$ and a can be obtained, minimum $\max_i \{T_{in}^i\}$ can be converted into minimum $\max_i \{t_{sup} + X_z DX_z b + X_z DX_z ca\}$. Hence, we can use the intelligent algorithm to obtain the approximately optimal solution of the model (the optimal task allocation vector).

5   Task Scheduling on Failure Model

We introduce the failure model based on heat recirculation of data centers in the preceding part of the text. As solving the optimal task allocation vector of the failure model is one NP-hard problem, in this paper, two kinds of intelligent algorithms are implemented to obtain the approximately optimal solution of the model. They are the GA and SA algorithms. With two kinds of intelligent algorithms, we can distribute tasks based on considering the influence of heat recirculation and energy consumption by CRAC. Hence, they are more applicable to the practical operation and suitable for the model of node failure based on airflow distribution of data centers (Table 2).

Table 2. The meaning of symbols

Symbols	Meaning
$NIND$	Population size
T_0	Initial temperature
T_{end}	Final temperature
L	Chain length (iterations at each temperature)
$solution$	Task assignment scheme
k	Counter
q	Rate of cooling
$path$	The current optimal solution

Algorithm 1. GA algorithm

Input: $NIND$, T_0, T_{end}, L
Output: FinalSolution
1: Initial $population$; // all the solutions consist population
2: **for** $k \leftarrow 1$ to $NIND$ **do**
3:     Newsolution(); // crossover and mutation
4:     Apply the fitness function $fitness()$ on solution
5:     $population \leftarrow$ solutions with outstanding fitness
6: **end for**
7: $FinalSolution \leftarrow$ the solution with best fitness
8: **return** $FinalSolution$

5.1   GA Algorithm

GA algorithm can be used to get the approximately optimal solution (the optimal task scheduling for saving energy consumption) of the failure model. The task allocation matches chromosomes in the GA. In simple terms, the GA is an iterative algorithm, adopting the iterative optimization to obtain an approximately optimal solution. It uses a series of chromosomes (task allocation vector) to create new chromosomes by the crossover and mutation operations, and abandon the low fitness chromosomes until finding an approximately optimal solution. The pseudocode of GA algorithm is presented in Algorithm 1.

5.2   SA Algorithm

SA algorithm is one iterative and adaptive heuristic searching algorithm. It can be used to obtain the approximately optimal solution of optimal task scheduling in the proposed failure model. SA utilizes the Metropolis algorithm and properly controls the cooling process of temperature, getting the optimal solution via iteration. The pseudocode of SA algorithm is presented in Algorithm 2.

Algorithm 2. SA algorithm

Input: L, T_0, T_{end}, q
Output: Optimal path
1: Initial *path*; // *Using way of random arrangement to generate initial path*
2: $T = T_0$
3: **while** $T > T_{end}$ **do**
4:    **for** $k \leftarrow 1$ to L **do**
5:        Newpath(); // *generate new solution*
6:        Using Metropolis Criterion to decide whether accept new path
7:        Update path
8:    **end for**
9:    $T \leftarrow q \times T$ // *Cooling process*
10: **end while**
11: **return** *path*

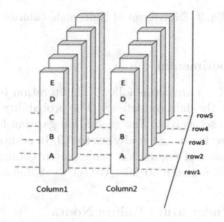

Fig. 2. The data center adapted in experiment.

6   Experiment Simulation

We simulate one data center to finish the experiment. This data center possesses two rows of racks meeting the 42U industry standards. It processes one typical cold (hot) aisle. The cold air flow is offered by $CRAC$ with the air speed as $8\,\mathrm{m}^3/\mathrm{s}$. The data center contains ten racks, each rack equipped with 5 nodes marked from low to high as: A, B, C, D and E (as shown in the Fig. 2). Each node has 10 servers and each server has two processors. Hence, this data center processes 1000 processors. That is, in this data center, the maximum permitted task load is 1000 ($maxC_{tot} = 1000$). We adopt the DELL PowerEdge 1855 server in this data center. The cross-interference coefficient matrix A and the heat distribution matrix D of this data center have worked out in [14]. We carry out the experiments on a computer with an Intel(R) Core Pentium(R) CPU G3220 @ 3.00 GHz, with 4 GB physical RAM. The algorithms are simulated by using Matlab 2012(a). We use three algorithms to execute task schedule within this experiment: the traditional UT algorithm, the intelligent GA and SA algorithms. In order to obtain the optimal solution, we set the iteration of two algorithms as 300.

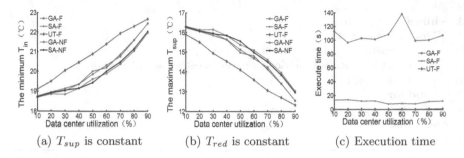

(a) T_{sup} is constant   (b) T_{red} is constant   (c) Execution time

Fig. 3. Experiment of multi node failure

6.1   Setting of Experimental

Parameters of GA and SA are set as follow. The iteration is set as 300 in each algorithm to guarantee the data consistency. The probability of mutation is usually extremely low and set as 0.05. The generation gap can be used to weed out the individuals with low fitness, generally set to 0.9. In addition, the experiment finds that a large number of population can't play a good optimization effect, and the general value is between 50–200. We set the value as 100.

6.2   Experiment Under Multi Failure Nodes

First, we conduct the experiment under different CPU utilization, and compare the minimum value of inlet air temperature with two failure nodes (the corresponding curves are GA-F,SA-F, and UT-F in Fig. 3(a) and GA-NF and SA-NF mean the situation of without failure nodes). It can be seen from curves that the minimum value of inlet air temperature of nodes increases with the CPU utilization, and compared to non-thermal-aware algorithms, intelligent algorithms can get one lower inlet air temperature.

Second, we set $T_{red} = 25\,^{\circ}\mathrm{C}$, to observe how low the air temperature (T_{sup}) offered by CRAC can meet the requirement (result has shown in Fig. 3(b)). It can be seen from the curve that the air temperature offered by CRAC get lower with increased CPU utilization. In other words, energy consumption of CRAC increases with CPU utilization. As the same as last experiment, intelligent algorithms effectively reduce the energy consumption of CRAC. Besides, the execute time of each algorithm under two failure nodes is shown in Fig. 3(c). From the curve, it can be obtained that SA has a lower time consumption than GA.

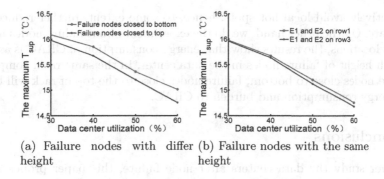

(a) Failure nodes with differ height

(b) Failure nodes with the same height

Fig. 4. Experiments of failure nodes in different positions

6.3   Failure Nodes in Different Positions

The simulated data center has five groups of racks, hence failure nodes may occur in different physical locations. First, we conduct the experiment with failure nodes in the same rack but different positions. We set the failure nodes as A2 and B2 in row1 ($A2_{row1}$ and $B2_{row1}$). These two nodes are close to the bottom of rack. And in another set of experiment, we set the failure nodes as D2 and E2 in row1 ($D2_{row1}$ and $E2_{row1}$), close to the top of rack. It can be obtained from the experiment above (Fig. 3(c)) that SA algorithm has a superior performance on time cost and optimize. Thus, experiments in this part manly uses SA algorithm to analyze between different environments. The threshold temperature of nodes is set as $T_{red} = 25\,^{\circ}C$, the highest temperature of airflow (T_{sup}) offered by CRAC is shown in Fig. 4(a). The trend shows that T_{sup} offered by CRAC with failure nodes $A2_{row1}$ and $B2_{row1}$ is higher than the other. Therefore, in the same rack, failure nodes close to the top will let CRAC consume more energy to provide a lower cold air for the need of data centers compared to failure nodes close to the bottom of rack.

Second, in the next experiment, we compare the airflow temperature T_{sup} offered by CRAC under the situation of failure nodes in different racks but in the same height. We set the failure nodes as E1 in row3 and E2 in row3 ($E1_{row3}$ and $E2_{row3}$) and set E1, E2 in row1 ($E1_{row1}$ and $E2_{row1}$) as compared. We set $T_{red} = 25\,^{\circ}C$, and this experiment is executed with SA algorithm. The result is shown in Fig. 4(b). Trend shows that T_{sup} offered by CRAC under different CPU use ratio has little difference under these two conditions. Thus, failure nodes in different racks but similar height hardly affect the energy consumption of CRAC compared to failure nodes in the same rack but different height.

Results of experiments in this section show that the failure model suits for different number nodes failure, and the intelligent task distribution algorithms based on model of failure nodes can solve the problem of task allocation after node failure. They can guarantee the reliability of data centers and effectively reduce the energy consumption of CRAC, so as to lower the whole power consumption of data centers. In addition, the intelligent task distribution algorithms can effectively avoid local hot spots, hence, to some extent, further reduce the failure rate. On the other hand, we do the experiment about failure nodes in the different locations, the results show that energy consumption of CRAC is associated with height of failure nodes in the data center. In the same rack, compared to failure nodes close to bottom, failure nodes close to the top of rack will bring more energy consumption and burden to CRAC.

7   Conclusions

To further study the data centers after node failure, this paper proposes the failure model based on the influence of heat recirculation. Experiments prove that the failure model suits for different number failure nodes, and the intelligent task scheduling algorithms can reduce the energy consumption of CRAC. The further experiments prove that failure nodes close to the top of racks will bring more energy consumption in data centers. Therefore, we propose to strengthen the top nodes when constructing the data center so that they are not easy to fail.

In the future work, we will focus on applying the failure model to I/O intensive data centers based on Hadoop framework, which is widely used in various data centers.

Acknowledgements. This work is supported by the NSFC (no.61572232), in part by the Science and Technology Planning Project of Guangzhou (no. 201802010028, and no. 201802010058), in part by the Science and Technology Planning Project of Nansha (no. 2017CX006), and in part by the Open Research Fund of Key Laboratory of Computer System and Architecture, Institute of Computing Technology, Chinese Academy of Sciences under Grant CARCH201705.

References

1. Bilal, K., Malik, S.U.R., Khan, S.U., Zomaya, A.Y.: Trends and challenges in cloud datacenters. IEEE Cloud Comput. **1**(1), 10–20 (2014)
2. Cheng, Y., Fiorani, M., Wosinska, L., Chen, J.: Reliable and cost efficient passive optical interconnects for data centers. IEEE Commun. Lett. **19**(11), 1913–1916 (2015)
3. Deng, Y.: What is the future of disk drives, death or rebirth? ACM Comput. Surv. **43**(3), 1–27 (2011)
4. Deng, Y., Hu, Y., Meng, X., Zhu, Y., Zhang, Z., Han, J.: Predictively booting nodes to minimize performance degradation of a power-aware web cluster. Cluster Comput. **17**, 1309–1322 (2014)
5. Deng, Y., Huang, X., Song, L., Zhou, Y., Wang, F.: Memory deduplication: an effective approach to improve the memory system. J. Inf. Sci. Eng. **33**, 1103–1120 (2017)
6. Elgelany, A.: Energy efficiency for data centers and cloud computing: a literature review. Energy **3** (2013)
7. Fan, X., Weber, W.D., Barroso, L.A.: Power provisioning for a warehouse-sized computer. ACM (2007)

8. Ferreira, A.M., Pernici, B.: Managing the complex data center environment: an integrated energy-aware framework. Compute **98**, 709–749 (2016)
9. Guitart, J.: Toward sustainable data centers: a comprehensive energy management strategy. Computing **99**(6), 597–615 (2017)
10. Hua, Y., Liu, X., Jiang, H.: Antelope: a semantic-aware data cube scheme for cloud data center networks. IEEE Trans. Comput. **63**(9), 2146–2159 (2014)
11. Lee, Y.C., Zomaya, A.Y.: Energy efficient utilization of resources in cloud computing systems. J. Supercomput. **60**(2), 268–280 (2012)
12. Li, H., Zhu, G., Cui, C., Tang, H., Dou, Y., He, C.: Energy-efficient migration and consolidation algorithm of virtual machines in data centers for cloud computing. Computing **98**(3), 303–317 (2016)
13. Li, L., Ho, D.W.C., Lu, J.: A consensus recovery approach to nonlinear multi-agent system under node failure (2016)
14. Lin, R., Deng, Y.: Allocating workload to minimize the power consumption of data centers. Front. Comput. Sci. **11**(1), 105–118 (2017)
15. Liu, Z., et al.: Renewable and cooling aware workload management for sustainable data centers. In: ACM Sigmetrics/Performance Joint International Conference on Measurement and Modeling of Computer Systems, pp. 175–186 (2012)
16. Moore, J., Chase, J., Ranganathan, P., Sharma, R.: Making scheduling "cool": temperature-aware workload placement in data centers. In: Usenix Technical Conference, Anaheim, CA, USA, 10–15 April 2005, pp. 61–75 (2008)
17. Polverini, M., Vasilakos, A.V., Ren, S., Cianfrani, A.: Thermal-aware scheduling of batch jobs in geographically distributed data centers. IEEE Trans. Cloud Comput. **2**(1), 71–84 (2014)
18. Popoola, O., Pranggono, B.: On energy consumption of switch-centric data center networks. J. Supercomput. 1–36 (2017)
19. Sahoo, R.K., Sivasubramaniam, A., Squillante, M.S., Zhang, Y.: Failure data analysis of a large-scale heterogeneous server environment, p. 772 (2004)
20. Sanjeevi, P., Viswanathan, P.: Nuts scheduling approach for cloud data centers to optimize energy consumption. Computing **11**, 1–27 (2017)
21. Schroeder, B., Gibson, G.A.: A large-scale study of failures in high-performance computing systems. IEEE Trans. Dependable Secure Comput. **7**(4), 337–350 (2010)
22. Tang, Q., Gupta, S.K.S., Stanzione, D., Cayton, P.: Thermal-aware task scheduling to minimize energy usage of blade server based datacenters. In: IEEE International Symposium on Dependable, Autonomic and Secure Computing, pp. 195–202 (2006)
23. Tang, Q., Gupta, S.K.S., Varsamopoulos, G.: Energy-efficient thermal-aware task scheduling for homogeneous high-performance computing data centers: a cyber-physical approach. IEEE Trans. Parallel Distrib. Syst. **19**(11), 1458–1472 (2008)
24. Wang, L., Khan, S.U.: Review of performance metrics for green data centers: a taxonomy study. J. Supercomput. **63**(3), 639–656 (2013)
25. Wang, L., Khan, S.U., Dayal, J.: Thermal aware workload placement with task-temperature profiles in a data center. J. Supercomput. **61**(3), 780–803 (2012)
26. Wei, J., Jiang, H., Zhou, K., Feng, D.: Efficiently representing membership for variable large data sets. IEEE Trans. Parallel Distrib. Syst. **25**(4), 960–970 (2014)
27. Wierman, A., Andrew, L.L.H., Thereska, E.: Dynamic right-sizing for power-proportional data centers. IEEE/ACM Trans. Networking **21**(5), 1378–1391 (2011)
28. Xie, J., Deng, Y., Min, G., Zhou, Y.: An incrementally scalable and cost-efficient interconnection structure for data centers. IEEE Trans. Parallel Distrib. Syst. **28**(6), 1578–1592 (2017)
29. Yang, L., Deng, Y., Yang, L.T., Lin, R.: Reducing the cooling power of data centers by intelligently assigning tasks. IEEE Internet Things J. **5**(3), 1667–1678 (2017)

30. Zhan, X., Reda, S.: Power budgeting techniques for data centers. IEEE Trans. Comput. **64**(8), 2267–2278 (2015)
31. Zhang, L., Deng, Y., Zhu, W., Zhou, J., Wang, F.: Skewly replicating hot data to construct a power-efficient storage cluster. J. Netw. Comput. Appl. **50**, 168–179 (2015)
32. Zhang, Y., Squillante, M.S., Sivasubramaniam, A., Sahoo, R.K.: Performance implications of failures in large-scale cluster scheduling. In: Feitelson, D.G., Rudolph, L., Schwiegelshohn, U. (eds.) JSSPP 2004. LNCS, vol. 3277, pp. 233–252. Springer, Heidelberg (2005). https://doi.org/10.1007/11407522_13
33. Zhou, K., Hu, S., Huang, P.H., Zhao, Y.: LX-SSD : enhancing the lifespan of NAND flash-based memory via recycling invalid pages. In: 33rd International Conference on Massive Storage Systems and Technology (MSST 2017) (2017)

Adaptive Load Balancing on Multi-core IPsec Gateway

Wei Li, Shengjie Hu, Guanchao Sun, and Yunchun Li[✉]

Beijing Key Lab of Network Technology,
School of Computer Science and Engineering, Beihang University,
Beijing, China
{liw,hushengjie,gcsun,lych}@buaa.edu.cn

Abstract. Cloud service providers usually offer IPsec VPN services to tenants by deploying the software IPsec gateway on the virtual machine. However, the current software IPsec gateway solutions cannot make full use of the allocated multi-core virtual machine resources and unable to meet the performance requirement of tenants. In order to optimize the IPsec gateway performance, the flow processing load must be properly allocated to multi-cores considering the multiple dimensions of load to improve the throughput of IPsec gateway. In this paper, we propose an optimizing scheme which separates the encryption and decryption computation from the packet forwarding process in the IPsec gateway, and implements fine-grained network flows scheduling in parallel processors. Furthermore, we present an adaptive load balancing algorithm based on quantifying the load of each processing core in real-time. Experimental results show that the performance of the IPsec gateway has significant improvement.

Keywords: IPsec gateway · Load balancing · Multi-core architecture

1 Introduction

With the development of hybrid cloud, tenants can extend their networks by deploying general applications, data and services in the public cloud, while deploying important services in their private cloud. The hybrid cloud bring great flexibility and scalability to tenants, which attracts more enterprise customers to deploy their network in the cloud environment.

IPsec is a typical point-to-point VPN protocol to establish a secure tunnel between public and private cloud gateways. Unlike the use of dedicated devices in traditional networks, software VPN (such as strongSwan [21]) is widely used in the cloud environment for resource constraints and flexibility. The IPsec gateway can be deployed on commercial-off-the-shelf (COTS) hardware platforms and virtual machines as well as other applications. However, due to the huge number of secure connections in the cloud environment, the processing capability of IPsec gateway face challenges. Limited by the traditional network packet processing architecture, existing software IPsec gateways cannot meet the requirement of the cloud computing environment. In the 10 Gbps network, these software IPsec gateways just reach a maximum of about 1 Gbps throughput [1].

© Springer Nature Switzerland AG 2018
J. Vaidya and J. Li (Eds.): ICA3PP 2018, LNCS 11334, pp. 215–228, 2018.
https://doi.org/10.1007/978-3-030-05051-1_15

In recent years, some IPsec gateways based on SDN architecture separate the control plane and data plane of IPsec gateway. Such a method can effectively improve the flexibility and resource utilization of IPsec gateway. However, the performance of IPsec gateway is still limited by its IPsec packet processing, because of the large amount of encryption and decryption operation [2]. To improve the performance of IPsec gateway, the IPsec packet processing must be optimized. In this paper, we implement the IPsec gateway for parallel processing based on the COTS multi-core platform. A multi-core load balancing algorithm is proposed for IPsec gateway in the cloud environment.

In summary, there are three aspects in our work. First, the IPsec gateway can be optimized on packet processing by separating the encryption and decryption from the forwarding process. Second, multi-core parallel scheduling and high-speed packet processing technique have been implemented to improve the performance of the gateway. Finally, we propose an adaptive load balancing algorithm for multi-core IPsec gateway. Experimental results show that our adaptive load balancing can achieve significant performance improvement and scalability in the multi-core IPsec gateway.

Specifically, we make the following contributions:

- We put forward the idea of separating the encryption and decryption process from the forwarding process in the IPsec gateway.
- We propose an adaptive load balancing algorithm to schedule the processes for multi-core IPsec gateway.
- We optimize the IPsec gateway by deploying DPDK to migrate the packets processing from kernel space to the user space for high performance.

The rest of this paper is organized as follows: Sect. 2 presents related work. Section 3 provides the detailed analysis of multi-core IPsec gateway based on DPDK. Section 4 presents the adaptive load balancing algorithm. Section 5 describes the experimental results of the load balancing. Section 6 concludes this paper.

2 Related Work

In recent years, with the development of SDN and NFV, the software defined network function become popular in the cloud computing network. Many software load balancers are designed and replacing traditional hardware ones. In earlier research, Duet [3] is a load balancer combined with hardware and software. Ananta [4] is a distributed software load balancer designed by Microsoft. It implements the separation of the control plane from the data plane. The design of Ananta well meets the scale, reliability and requirement of the multi-tenant cloud environment. Maglev [5] is the software load balancer of Google, which uses a forwarder thread to compute the 5-tuple hash of packets received by NICs, and then distributes packets to different receiving queues according to the results. With this separation thought, the processing performance of the single node is improved.

Although IPsec gateway has been studied for a long-term, there are still problems in performance and resources in the cloud environment. Protego [6] is a cloud-scale multi-tenant IPsec gateway. It separates the control layer from the data layer and adopts the distributed architecture to ensure high reliability. It realized the migration of the tunnel without the performance degradation. Protego's distributed method and control-forward separation idea are very enlightening for us. OpenStack [7] put forward the concept of VPN as a service, using SDN architecture to manage and configure VPN gateway efficiently and simply. SDIG [8] proposed a new IPsec gateway architecture. By using the SDN controller to manage the IPsec gateway centralized, this architecture not only facilitates the management of the gateway but also provides a good solution for the high reliability and load balancing on the IPsec gateway. It helps to combine IPsec VPN with cloud environment and makes better use of resources. Vajaranta et al. [9] use SDN to decompose the main functions of IPsec into multiple functional modules. They use IKE module to provide necessary information for the ESP processing module. Through this distributed method, the reliability and performance of IPsec are improved. The above related works have affected our design.

The granularity of load balancing is a primary problem in our design. Nelms et al. [10] analysis the multi-core DPI system. By comparing the flow-based and packet-based algorithms, they conclude that in the high-speed packet processing system, the improvement of the cache affinity can improve the performance of the system more than the balancing degree. Hanford et al. [11] suggest improving performance by dispatching the packet processing to multiple CPU cores. RouteBricks [12] points out using CPU multicore parallelism to enhance the processing performance of packets.

In recent years, the rapid development of kernel bypass technique has produced high-performance data packet processing schemes [13], such as DPDK [14], netmap [15], PF_RING [16], OpenOnload [17]. DPDK is a set of data plane development kits provided by Intel. DPDK send packets directly to the user space through bypassing Linux kernel protocol stack. This allows it to avoid all kinds of limitations of kernel protocol stack and achieve high-performance processing of data packets. At the same time, some high-performance IPsec gateway solutions based on other techniques and platforms have been put forward. PIPSEA [18] implements a high-performance IPsec gateway based on embedded APUs. Meng et al. [19] designed a high-performance IPsec gateway on Cavium OCTEON platform. In this paper, we build our gateway and load balancing based on DPDK.

3   Background

In this section, we first propose the multi-core IPsec gateway processing chain based on DPDK. Then, we analyze the suitable granularity of load balancing in multi-core IPsec gateway and summarize the common load allocation algorithm based on hash and its implementation.

3.1   Multi-core IPsec Gateway Based on DPDK

The assignment of the IPsec gateway is to encrypt and decrypt the inbound and outbound packets, and then forward the processed packets. In the traditional IPsec gateway architecture, the whole processing process is performed by parallel multi-thread. The processing of data packets depends on the kernel protocol stack, which greatly restricts its performance. During this process, computing resources are mainly consumed by the encryption and decryption process. In contrast, packets forwarding consumes fewer resources. Therefore, the concurrent scheduling of the whole process restricts the efficiency of resource utilization and further affects the performance of the gateway.

DPDK can help to migrate the processing of data packets from kernel space to user space. On the one hand, it avoids the inefficiency of kernel protocol stack in high-speed packets processing. On the other hand, user space means great flexibility for the parallel gateway. DPDK has excellent CPU affinity characteristics, which can help to improve the gateway performance by using multi-core architecture.

Therefore, we further optimize the multi-core gateway by separating the encryption and decryption from the forwarding process. A special class of cores is responsible for processing encryption and decryption called the processing core. The forwarding of the packets is placed on a forwarding core. At the same time, in order to allocate and balance the load for all the processing cores, a management core is needed. These three kinds of cores constitute the IPsec gateway processing chain, as shown in the Fig. 1.

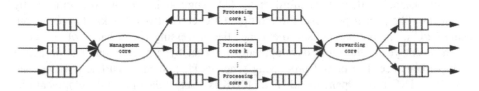

Fig. 1. Multi-core IPsec gateway processing chain

Management Core. The management core is responsible for distributing the flows, monitoring the load of each processing core in real-time, and implementing the load balancing algorithm.

Processing Core. The main task of processing core is to encrypt or decrypt the data packets in the processing queue, and then store the processed packets into the forwarding queue.

Forwarding Core. The forwarding core is responsible for collecting the processed packets of each processing core and forwarding them according to the forwarding flow table.

3.2   Multi-core Load Balancing Based on Toeplitz Hash

In the network packet processing system, load balancing granularity usually bases on packets or bases on flows. Load balancing based on packets has the advantage of better load balancing result. However, the overhead of synchronization between multi-cores is high. In high-speed packet processing systems, the frequent synchronization should be avoided, especially in multi-core architecture. Therefore, the flow-based load balancing is implemented in this paper.

In multi-core IPsec gateway, the static load allocation is used to distribute the load to each core. The conventional static load balancing uses the hash function to compute the index number of the target load node and then assigns the flow to it. For multi-core load balancing, Toeplitz hash [22] is most suitable, considering the distribution equilibrium and time consumption of many hash algorithms. Toeplitz hash uses the Toeplitz matrix to calculate the hash value, in which the element values are equal on the same diagonal. A Toeplitz matrix of n rows and m columns can be used to hash a sequence of length m to another sequence of length n. RSS (Receive Side Scaling) is a NIC driving technique that enables the received data packets to be distributed efficiently between multiple CPUs. The load balancing algorithm adopted by RSS is the Toeplitz hash. It can distribute the flows evenly to different worker nodes according to the index of flows.

Specifically, the Toeplitz hash can be deployed on the multi-core gateway based on DPDK. We can design a flow redirection information table (FRIT), which uses the form of hash table to store the corresponding relations between flows and processing cores. For the new inbound flows, we use the Toeplitz hash to gain a processing core to process this flow and then add this relationship to the FRIT. For the subsequent packets, the corresponding processing core information of this flow can be obtained by searching the FRIT, and then packets will be sent to that core for processing.

4 Adaptive Load Balancing Algorithm

In Sect. 3.2, we have presented the multi-core IPsec gateway processing chain and the common load allocation based on hash. However, the Toeplitz hash is not enough for the load imbalance in the multitenant environment. Therefore, we design an adaptive load balancing algorithm to improve the performance of multi-core IPsec gateway. Our adaptive load balancing algorithm complements the static load balancing based on Toeplitz hash and realizes load migration by quantifying the load of each processing core in real-time. This section introduces the adaptive load balancing algorithm in detail.

4.1 Multi-core Dynamic Adaptive Load Balancing

The static load allocation based on Toeplitz hash tries to ensure the relative balance of load on each processing core. However, it cannot guarantee the load skew caused by the change of traffic flow distribution in the subsequent process. Therefore, we need to monitor the load in real-time and dynamically adjust it through load migration.

There are three steps in the adaptive load balancing algorithm. First, we calculate the load value of each processing core. Then, we classify the processing cores by the load values. Finally, according to the classification results, load balancing source cores and destination cores are selected to perform load migration.

Load Quantification. First, we need to evaluate the load of each processing core. In the multi-core system, the dynamic load balancing algorithm is usually based on the real-time CPU utilization of the worker cores. However, its load balancing effect cannot be evaluated in real-time. In our algorithm, the load of each processing core is quantified by the load value of each flow processed on it. This can provide accurate load value calculation and help to accurately select the flow to be migrated. We use a processing core flows information table (PCFIT) to maintain the load value of each processing core's flows. PCFIT provides the basis for performing the calculation of the core load value as well as the load migration.

The packet receiving rate, packet length and the encryption algorithm of a flow in the period are combined to compute the load value of a flow. The load quantification formula proposed in this paper is concluded from a large number of previous experiments.

The load value of the flow F_i on the processing core is defined as V_i. The packet receiving rate of F_i within period t is R_i. The packet length is L_i. The encryption algorithm set is $A = \{a_1, a_2, \ldots a_z\}$, while p_i represents the influence factor of encryption algorithm a_i corresponding F_i. The ultimate forwarding rate of F_i is T_{max}^i. Then we can compute the load value V_i of F_i using formula (1):

$$V_i = \begin{cases} \frac{R_i}{T_{max}^i}, & R_i < T_{max}^i \\ 1, & R_i \geq T_{max}^i \end{cases} \tag{1}$$

In the formula (1), the value of T_{max}^i is estimated by our experiments. It satisfies the following formula (2):

$$T_{max} = \begin{cases} D - p_i & , & 64 \leq L \leq 500 \\ (k_1 \times L + b_1) - p_i & , & 500 \leq L \leq 900 \\ (k_2 \times L + b_2) - p_i & , & 900 \leq L \leq 1400 \end{cases} \tag{2}$$

In the formula (2), D, k_1, b_1, k_2, b_2 are constants related to processing capability, while L is the packet length. Among them, D represents the baseline value of the ultimate forwarding rate. k_1, b_1, k_2, b_2 describe the linear relationship between the ultimate forwarding rate and packet length. The final result needs to remove the influence of the encryption algorithm.

The set of processing cores in the system is represented as $AC = \{C_1, C_2, \ldots C_j\}$, where C_j represents any processing core. If this core is responsible to m flows represented as $AF = \{F_1, F_2, \ldots F_m\}$, then the load value ld_j of C_j can be calculated by the formula (3):

$$ld_j = \sum_{i=1}^{m} V_i \tag{3}$$

Processing Cores Classification. We classify the processing cores according to the load values, so as to provide the basis for load migration. First of all, we suppose all processing cores have the same processing capacity. We define the heavy load threshold of the processing core as ld_{max}. All processing cores are ordered in reverse order according to the load value ld_j. We classify the processing cores by traversing from the heaviest processing core of the load, using the following rules:

- If the core load value satisfies $ld_j < ld_{max}$, indicating that there are no heavy load processing cores in the current system. It can directly end the adaptive load balancing stage;
- If $ld_j \geq ld_{max}$, then the processing core is classified as a heavy load core and continues to traverse the other processing cores;
- In the subsequent cores, if $ld_j < ld_{max}$, then the processing core is classified as a light load core;
- If there are no light load cores after all the cores are traversed, then the current system is fully loaded. It cannot be optimized through adaptive load balancing, ending the adaptive load balancing stage.

Load Migration Based on BBFF Algorithm. The FF (First Fit) algorithm is a heuristic algorithm for the classical NP-complete problem bin packing problem. We make some hypotheses as flowing. The light load core is regarded as an empty box, while the heavy load threshold of the processing core is the volume of the box. The flow on the heavy load core is regarded as the object to be packed and the flow load value is the volume of the object. Then the load migration problem can be equated to the bin packing problem. However, unlike the bin packing problem, the capacity of light load cores are not the same. Hence, we propose the BBFF (Big Box First Fit) algorithm based on FF algorithm.

The BBFF algorithm carries out the load migration operation based on the result of processing cores classification. This load migration process has little influenced on the processing cores and reduces the balancing cost. It can maintain the stable operation of the system.

- *Selection of the flow to be migrated.* The management core maintains the PCFIT. Whenever a new flow is allocated to a processing core, the flow's identification information is added to the corresponding core's PCFIT. PCFITT also maintains flows' statistical information to facilitate the calculation of the flow load. The latest recorded flow is first selected, when we select the flow to be migrated from the heavy load core with the largest load value. This can help maintain the stability of the system and the integrity of the flow.
- *Selection of the target light load core based on BBFF algorithm.* We check each light load core in order of the load value from small to large and make sure the light load core's load value will not exceed the threshold if it accepts the migrated flow. Then we choose the first accessed core which satisfies the condition to be the destination of the migration. Each subsequently migrated flow loops through this process, finding the first light load core to accommodate the flow.
- *Updating the load value and rescheduling the heavy load core.* The load values of the corresponding cores are updated when a flow is migrated from one core to another. If the load value of the heavy load core is already lower than the heavy load threshold, the next heavy load core is selected as the source core of the load migration.
- *Completion of the load migration.* Repeat first three steps, until the system has no heavy load cores, or unable to find the target light load core. This is also the end of the adaptive load balancing.

The pseudo-code for the whole adaptive load balancing process is as follows:

Algorithm 1 Adaptive Load Balancing Algorithm
Input: *heavyNode[k], lightNode[n], ldmax*
Output: true or false
1: *ascendingSort(lightNode[n])*
2: *descendingSort(heavyNode[n])*
3: *j = 0*
4: *select F_m from heavyNode[j]*
5: *load value of F_m is V_m*
6: **while** *j < k* **do**
7:   **for** *i = 0* to *n* **do**
8:     **if** *lightNode[i] + V_m < ld_{max}* **then break**
9:     **end if**
10:   **end for**
11:   **if** *i == 0* **then return** false
12:   **end if**
13:   *F_m from heavyNode[j] to lightNode[i]*
14:   *lightNode[i] += V_m*
15:   *heavyNode[j] -= V_m*
16:   **if** *heavyNode[j] < ld_{max}* **then**
17:     *i ++*
18:   **end if**
19: **end while**
20: **return** true

4.2 Load Balance Degree

To evaluate the effect of load balancing, we propose load balance degree which estimates the difference between the distribution ratios of load among the processing cores. The smaller the load balance degree, the better the load balancing effect. We propose the formula of load balance degree as below:

$$\text{LBD(t)} = 1 - \frac{\left(\sum_{i=1}^{n} NL_i(t)\right)^2}{n \sum_{i=1}^{n} NL_i^2(t)} \tag{4}$$

In formula (4), $NL_i(t)$ represents any processing core's load value at time t, while n represents the total number of processing cores. Then we can get the load balance degree LBD(t).

We use speedup ratio to evaluate the multi-core parallel performance. Speedup ratio can also reflect the effect of load balancing. Suppose the forwarding rate of a single core is T_1, while T_n reflects the forwarding rate using n cores. Then the speedup radio can be calculated by formula (5).

$$S(n) = \frac{T_n}{T_1} \tag{5}$$

5   Experimental Results

In this section, we present experimental results about load balancing. Firstly, we evaluate the adaptive load balancing effect. Then we test the scalability of the algorithm in the multi-core gateway. Finally, we measure the performance through throughput and latency.

The experimental setup consists of two KNL platforms with 64 cores per node working at 1.3 GHz and Intel 82599 10 Gbps NIC. Each node has configured with DPDK 16.11.3 on CentOS 7. We deploy MoonGen [20] on the client node to generate load traffic at 10 Gbps line rate and capture the traffic processed.

Before the presentation of experiments, we show the parameter T^i_{max} in load quantitative formula (1) in our experimental setup. We evaluate the forwarding rate of a single processing core by changing the encryption algorithm. The result is recorded in Table 1. The following experiments involved load quantification are all based on this result.

Table 1. The capability of processing core with different encryption algorithm

Encryption algorithm	AEC_CBC_128	AEC_CBC_256	AEC_CTR_128	AEC_CTR_256
T^i_{max}(Mpps)	0.24	0.22	0.24	0.22

5.1   Load Balancing Effect

We design a set of experiments to evaluate the effect of load balancing. We send traffic at the 10 Gbps line rate with multiple unbalanced load flows to simulate the situation of the multitenant cloud environment. Then we test the load balance degree of the gateway before and after deploying adaptive load balancing. Further, we repeat the experiment in the case of changing the number of processing cores.

Figure 2 shows that the load balance degree changed with the number of processing cores. When the number of the core is less than 4, all the cores work at high load, so the load balance degree value approximates zero. While the number is more than 4, the

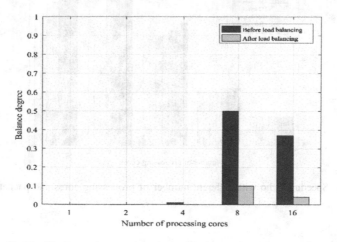

Fig. 2. Load balance degree changing with the number of processing cores

load balance degree is significantly decreased when adaptive load balancing is deployed. Therefore, the algorithm is effective to achieve load balance in the multi-core gateway.

5.2 Multi-core Scalability

To evaluate the scalability of the load balancing, we carried out the processing cores expansion experiments. We send packets with different packet size at the 10 Gbps line rate and deploy the load balancing at the gateway node. Then we change the number of processing cores deployed at the gateway and observe the speedup radio changes.

As shown in Fig. 3, the speedup radio is linearly correlated with the number of processing cores when the throughput doesn't reach line rate. This proves that the load balancing has expected scalability. In addition, when the number of processing cores is fixed, the decrease of speedup radio is mainly attributed to the additional processing overhead caused by the larger packet size.

5.3 Processing Performance

Multi-core Throughput. We first measure the throughput with different number of processing cores, while changing the packet size. The traffic transmission rate is 10 Gbps. Figure 4 shows the change of throughput caused by the variation of the number of processing cores and packet size. The throughput increases with the number of processing cores at any packet size. When more than 8 processing cores are deployed, the throughput can reach 10 Gbps. However, when the packet size smaller than 1024, the throughput can hardly reach the line rate, because of overhead of the excessively frequent packets processing.

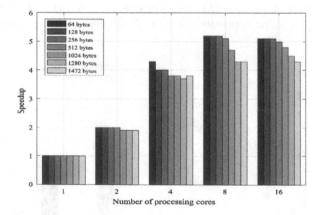

Fig. 3. Speedup radio with different number of processing cores and packet size

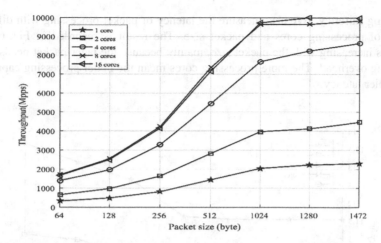

Fig. 4. Throughput with the packet size and number of processing cores

Then, we generate an imbalance load traffic to see the increase of throughput by deploying adaptive load balancing. We compare the throughput changing between RSS and our adaptive load balancing over a 20 s period. The two experiments are all configured with 8 processing cores, while imbalance traffic is sent at 10 Gbps. While measuring adaptive load balancing, we start the algorithm at 10 s. The result is shown in Fig. 5. While we deploy RSS, the throughput is half of receiving rate when the load is imbalanced. However, adaptive load balancing can effectively adjust imbalance load between different cores, and help gateway get the best performance. In addition, the throughput significantly reduced at 7 s and 16 s. The reason is that the packet generator must read the flow trace files from disk periodically.

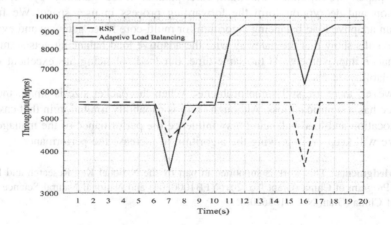

Fig. 5. Comparison throughput with the time of RSS and adaptive load balancing

Processing Latency. We also measure the latency of packet processing with different number of processing cores and packet size. The result is recorded in Fig. 6. The latency is increasing with the packet size, mainly because the lager packet needs more processing overhead. The more processing cores mean the better processing capability and smaller latency.

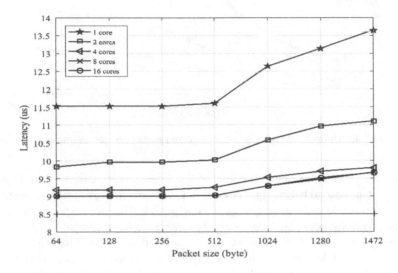

Fig. 6. Latency with the packet size and number of processing cores

6   Conclusion

In this paper, we optimize the multi-core parallel IPsec gateway by separating encryption and decryption form the forwarding process in user space. We further design an adaptive load balancing algorithm for multi-core IPsec gateway and evaluate it. The results show that the gateway with the adaptive load balancing gets significant performance improvement. At the same time, our load balancing has excellent multi-core scalability.

However, there are still some problems. When the packet size is small, the performance has a significant loss. Although there is capability limitation in that case, the load allocation and load balancing may influence the performance of the management core. We will keep on improving the algorithm to increase the performance.

Acknowledgments. This work is supported in part by the National Key Research and Development Program of China (Grant No. 2016YFB1000304) and National Natural Science Foundation of China (Grant No. U1636208).

References

1. Lacković, D., Tomić, M.: Performance analysis of virtualized VPN endpoints. In: 2017 40th International Convention on Information and Communication Technology, Electronics and Microelectronics (MIPRO), pp. 466–471 (2017)
2. Shue, C., Shin, Y., Gupta, M., Choi, J.Y.: Analysis of IPSec overheads for VPN servers. In: 1st IEEE ICNP Workshop on Secure Network Protocols, 2005 (NPSec), pp. 25–30 (2005)
3. Gandhi, R., et al.: Duet: cloud scale load balancing with hardware and software. ACM SIGCOMM Comput. Commun. Rev. **44**(4), 27–38 (2015)
4. Patel, P., et al.: Cloud scale load balancing. ACM SIGCOMM. Comput. Commun. Rev. **43** (4), 207–218 (2013)
5. Eisenbud, D.E., et al.: Maglev: a fast and reliable software network load balancer. In: NSDI, pp. 523–535 (2016)
6. Tan, K., Wang, P., Gan, Z., Moon, S.: Protego: cloud-scale multitenant IPsec gateway (2017)
7. Openstack Homepage. https://www.openstack.org/. Accessed 29 May 2018
8. Li, W., Lin, F., Sun, G.: SDIG: Toward software-defined IPsec gateway. In: 2016 IEEE 24th International Conference on Network Protocols (ICNP), pp. 1–8 (2016)
9. Vajaranta, M., Kannisto, J., Harju, J.: IPsec and IKE as functions in SDN controlled network. In: Yan, Z., Molva, R., Mazurczyk, W., Kantola, R. (eds.) NSS 2017. LNCS, vol. 10394, pp. 521–530. Springer, Cham (2017). https://doi.org/10.1007/978-3-319-64701-2_39
10. Nelms, T., Ahamad, M.: Packet scheduling for deep packet inspection on multi-core architectures. In: ACM/IEEE Symposium on Architectures for Networking and Communications Systems (ANCS) 2010, pp. 1–11 (2010)
11. Hanford, N., et al.: Characterizing the impact of end-system affinities on the end-to-end performance of high-speed flows. In: Proceedings of the Third International Workshop on Network-Aware Data Management, p. 1 (2013)
12. Dobrescu, M., et al.: RouteBricks: exploiting parallelism to scale software routers. In: Proceedings of the ACM SIGOPS 22nd Symposium on Operating Systems Principles, pp. 15–28 (2009)
13. Gallenmüller, S., Emmerich, P., Wohlfart, F., Raumer, D., Carle, G.: Comparison of frameworks for high-performance packet IO. In: Proceedings of the Eleventh ACM/IEEE Symposium on Architectures for Networking and Communications Systems, pp. 29–38 (2015)
14. Linux Foundation Project. DPDK. http://dpdk.org/. Accessed 29 May 2018
15. Rizzo, L.: Netmap: a novel framework for fast packet I/O. In: 21st USENIX Security Symposium (USENIX Security 12), pp. 101–112 (2012)
16. PF_RING. http://www.ntop.org/products/packet-capture/pf_ring/pf_ring-zc-zero-copy/. Accessed 29 May 2018
17. Jiang, H., Xie, G., Salamatian, K.: Load balancing by ruleset partition for parallel IDS on multi-core processors. In: International Conference on Computer Communications and Networks, ICCCN (2013)
18. Park, J., Jung, W., Jo, G., Lee, I., Lee, J.: PIPSEA: a practical IPsec gateway on embedded APUs. In: Proceedings of the 2016 ACM SIGSAC Conference on Computer and Communications Security, pp. 1255–1267 (2016)
19. Meng, J., Chen, X., Chen, Z., Lin, C., Mu, B., Ruan, L.: Towards high-performance IPsec on Cavium OCTEON platform. In: Chen, L., Yung, M. (eds.) INTRUST 2010. LNCS, vol. 6802, pp. 37–46. Springer, Heidelberg (2011). https://doi.org/10.1007/978-3-642-25283-9_3

20. Emmerich, P., Gallenmüller, S., Raumer, D., Wohlfart, F., Carle, G.: Moongen: a scriptable high-speed packet generator. In: Proceedings of the 2015 Internet Measurement Conference, pp. 275–287 (2015)
21. StrongSwan. https://www.strongswan.org/. Accessed 29 May 2018
22. Krawczyk, H.: New hash functions for message authentication. In: Guillou, Louis C., Quisquater, J.-J. (eds.) EUROCRYPT 1995. LNCS, vol. 921, pp. 301–310. Springer, Heidelberg (1995). https://doi.org/10.1007/3-540-49264-X_24

An Active Learning Based on Uncertainty and Density Method for Positive and Unlabeled Data

Jun Luo[✉], Wenan Zhou, and Yu Du

School of Computer Science,
Beijing University of Posts and Telecommunications, Beijing 100876,
People's Republic of China
jennyluo.com@qq.com, zhouwa@bupt.edu.cn

Abstract. Active learning can select most informative unlabeled samples to manually annotate to enlarge the training set. Many active learning methods have been proposed so far, most of them work for these data that have all classes of tagged data. A few methods work for positive and unlabeled data and the computational complexity of existing methods is particularly high and they can't work well for big data. In this paper, we proposed an active learning approach that works well when only small number positive data are available in big data. We utilize data preprocessing to remove most of the outliers, so the density calculation is simplified relative to KNN algorithm, and our proposed sample selection strategy Min-Uncertainty Density (MDD) can help select more uncertain and higher density unlabeled samples with less computation. A combined semi-supervised learning active learning technique (MDD-SSAL) automatically annotating some confident unlabeled samples in the each iteration is proposed to reduce the number of manually annotated samples. Experimental results indicate that our proposed method is competitive with other similar methods.

Keywords: Active learning · Positive and unlabeled data
Semi-supervised learning · Big data

1 Introduction

With the continuous development and evolution of digital media technology, we can get huge amounts of data. This requires that the computation and storage performance of computers should be continuously improved. In order to fully study and make use of these data, machine learning has been widely applied in many fields. But the traditional supervised learning algorithm needs a large number of labels to help learning the intrinsic link of data. Labeling data has to be done manually and is a time-consuming and expensive job. So the data set in reality has a large number of unlabeled data and a small number of annotation data. Exploiting unlabeled data to improve accuracy of classification and reduce the workload of manual annotation has attracted wide attention. Two of the representative methods are active learning and semi-supervised learning.

© Springer Nature Switzerland AG 2018
J. Vaidya and J. Li (Eds.): ICA3PP 2018, LNCS 11334, pp. 229–241, 2018.
https://doi.org/10.1007/978-3-030-05051-1_16

Active learning works by selecting the most informative samples from unlabeled data and then manually labeling it [1, 2]. Adding these samples to the training set will help promoting the accuracy of classification. Discovering the most informative sample is the core point of active learning. Semi-supervised learning effectively utilizes a small amount of labeled data along with a large amount of unlabeled data [3, 4]. Positive and unlabeled learning (PU Learning) deals with the situation where only positive samples and unlabeled samples are available, which is also a semi-supervised learning algorithm. Although there are many researches on active learning at present, the data set they studied has all the classification labels. In reality, there are a lot of data that are labeled with positive samples, such as information retrieval, text classification, anomaly monitoring, etc. Few efforts have been made to combine active learning with PU learning.

In this paper, we focus on researching active learning with positive unlabeled data. We have the following contributions. First, we propose a novel sample selection strategy Min-Distance-Density (MDD) based on uncertainty and density to find the most informative samples and we propose a based on MDD simple active learning method (MDD-SAL). Second, we present a based on MDD combining semi-supervised active learning method (MDD-SSAL) to improve the accuracy of classification and reduce the number of manually annotated samples for positive unlabeled data. Our Experimental results on our dataset (VoLTE users' bad quality record dataset) and two open dataset show that when we manually annotate the same proportion of samples, the performances of our proposed methods are more competitive than existing methods.

The reminder of this paper is organized as follows. In Sect. 2, we review recent related work in the fields of active learning and positive unlabeled learning. Then we introduce the proposed MDD, MDD-SAL and MDD-SSAL in Sect. 3. A comprehensive set of experiments on three datasets are conducted in Sect. 4. Finally, we conclude our work and present ideas for future work in Sect. 5.

2 Related Work

In practice, we encounter datasets with a small amount of annotated data and a large number of unlabeled data in most cases. PU learning applies to datasets with only positive samples and unlabeled samples. The key of PU learning is to identify reliable negative samples and potential positive samples. Liu et al. first proposed spy technique to mix partial positive samples and unlabeled samples as negative samples. Then according to the probability of spy samples, a threshold is set to find credible positive and negative samples [5]. In [6], Li and Liu regarded all unlabeled samples as negative set and used Rocchio with clustering to identify the reliable negative samples. Ren et al. firstly identified reliable negative and positive instances using spy technique and Rocchio technique based on Latent Dirichlet Allocation [7]. Zhang et al. firstly used the linear model proposed in [8] to find the most reliable negative instances in the first step. Then a classifier was applied on unlabeled data to add the most reliable negative and positive instances to update the training set [9]. However, when the ratio of positive samples to unlabeled samples is very small, the above methods could not get reliable samples. Active learning can be used to solve the highly imbalanced data, because it can iteratively query a user for the correct labels to some informative instances that help to build the correct classifier. So far many sample selection approaches have been proposed in [10–13]. These approaches can be mainly divided into the following categories.

Uncertainty Sampling [14]. Select the most uncertain data whose classes are most uncertain with the classifier. For instance, the margin sampling strategy selects the unlabeled samples which lie with the margin of the current SVM [15]. In [16], the authors proposed Best-versus-second best that selected the probability values of the two classes of the instances have the minimum difference. Another popular approach was query by committee strategy that selected unlabeled examples whose class is the most disagreement among the committee classifiers [17, 18]. Many ensemble methods have been adopted in QBC, such as boosting-QBC and bagging-QBC [19].

Density Sampling. Compute pair-wise Cosine distance between all examples in the unlabeled pool, and select ones with the lowest average distance to all the other examples [20]. Clustering-based approaches selected representative instances through clustering [21, 22]. In practice, the unlabeled corpus is very large so that it is unreasonable to exhaustively calculate all the corpus to obtain the density degree. If applying clustering-based technique, the size of resulting clustering is still large on a large dataset and it is difficult to determine how many clusters are appropriate.

Uncertainty-Density Sampling. Only selecting the examples by uncertainty sampling do not always improve the performance of classifier due to selecting some uncertain examples which are outliers. To avoid this situation, in [23], He et al. proposed a strategy to find unlabeled examples with high uncertainty and then the best one with highest utility was finally manually labeled. It could not consider uncertainty and utility at the same time. Li et al. proposed a reverse nearest neighbor based active semi-supervised learning method to combine uncertainty and density to evaluate comprehensively unlabeled samples [12], and similar work can be seen in [11, 13]. Although the existing literatures combine uncertainty and density to select informative unlabeled samples, they need use KNN algorithm to find the K nearest neighbors of each unlabeled instance, which has high computational complexity and is not suitable for large data sets because a distance is calculated for each pair of samples in all samples. Meanwhile, they use cosine similarity to measure the similarity between samples. Cosine similarity may ignore the distance between samples. In addition, it is difficult to determine how much the K value is appropriate.

In big data sets, outliers are only a few parts relative to normal data. In order to solve a small number of outliers, it is very wasteful to calculate distance between all samples pairs and the time complexity of calculating distance is N^2 when the size of the sample set is N. This paper first uses data preprocessing methods to remove most of the outliers, and then the average distance between each unlabeled sample and the labeled positive and negative sample set is calculated. The Each iteration reduces the size of the unlabeled sample set and the distance between an unlabeled sample and the labeled sample can be fast obtained based on last result. When the new manually annotated samples are added, the performance of the classifier is no longer enhanced and then we stop this process. Suppose that the size of the labeled sample is c times the size of all the samples when the process stops, where c is between 0 and 1 and according to the results of the experiment, it is usually about 0.3. And the time complexity of each iteration is N, and the number of iterations is approximately $c * N/b$, where b is the number of samples annotated at each iteration, so the time complexity of the calculating distances is approximately $c * N^2$. Therefore, this paper proposes MDD with less computational complexity and score is used to measure the combined effects of uncertainty and density. The unlabeled samples with highest score will be manually annotated. Then, based on MDD two active learning techniques are proposed. One is MDD-SAL iteratively and manually labeling the informative samples until satisfying stop criterion. Another is MDD-SSAL that in addition to manually annotating informative samples, the classifier automatically annotates some unlabeled samples with high confidence and adds them to the training set in the each iteration.

3 The Proposed Technique

In this section, we present two active learning techniques to enlarge training set. So we will discuss how to select informative samples to be manually labeled and then demonstrate the two active learning techniques how to obtain sufficient unlabeled samples as training set.

3.1 Min-Distance Density (MDD) Sample Selection Strategy

The more uncertain the sample is, the more difficult the classifier to determine its class. Because some outliers are also the most uncertain samples, which will mislead the classifier when we add them to the training set. Therefore, we have to simultaneously consider samples' density degree that helps to avoid outliers and supply how much information to update the learning model. In general, a more accurate classifier will be learned if we add some high uncertainty and density unlabeled data with accurate label. Next we will define the uncertainty and density of an unlabeled sample.

Definition 1 Score. For an unlabeled example $u \in U_i$, we can calculate the score of this unlabeled sample by

$$UCT(u) = abs\left(\frac{\sum_{j=1}^{n} distance(u, p_j)}{|P_i|} - \frac{\sum_{j=1}^{m} distance(u, n_j)}{|N_i|}\right) \tag{1}$$

$$Density(u) = min\left(\frac{\sum_{j=1}^{n} distance(u, p_j)}{|P_i|}, \frac{\sum_{j=1}^{m} distance(u, n_j)}{|N_i|}\right) \tag{2}$$

$$Score(u) = UCT(u) * Density(u) \tag{3}$$

where P_i, N_i and U_i is respectively a positive dataset, a negative dataset and an unlabeled dataset obtained by active learning in i^{th} iterations. $|P_i|$ and $|N_i|$ is respectively the size of positive and negative dataset. N and m is the maximum value of the size of a positive and negative sample set.

In this paper, we use Euclidean distance to calculate the distance between samples and we first have to find reliable negative samples. Because the most dissimilar examples far from original positive samples are uncertain to be reliable negative examples, we manually label the dissimilar examples until getting a certain number of confident negative samples. When the distance difference between an unlabeled sample and a positive sample set and a negative sample set is small, the unlabeled sample is ambiguous and likely at the boundary of classification. The smaller the distance between unlabeled samples from positive samples or negative samples, the closer it is to the center of the sample set, the less likely outliers are. In order to comprehensively consider the uncertainty and density of unlabeled samples, we define score to represent the value. In terms of the definition of score, all unlabeled examples are ordered and the most advanced part of the unlabeled samples with lower scores are selected for manual annotation iteratively.

3.2   Two Active Learning Techniques

In order to reduce the computational complexity, this paper first preprocesses the original data and removes most outliers. The value distribution of each attribute is drawn, and the sample frequency of each attribute value is counted. When the attribute values are too large or too small and the cumulative frequency exceeds the set threshold, these samples are set to candidate outliers. Similar operations are performed on all attributes, and the intersection of these samples is taken as a set of outliers to be removed. Based on MDD proposed in 3.1, we will discuss two active learning techniques to iteratively obtain reliable training set.

Based on Min-Distance Density Simple Active Learning (MDD-SAL)
The most straightforward and simplest way is iteratively adding manual annotation unlabeled samples to the training set until satisfying the stop criteria and the pseudo code is described in Table 1.

Table 1. Pseudo-code of MDD-SAL.

Algorithm:
Input:
a training dataset with a few positive samples P and large amount of unlabeled data U.
Output:
the labeled dataset.
1.   Initialize D=P.
2.   Calculating the similarity between each unlabeled sample and positive samples. Labeling a certain number of confident negative examples N in unlabeled data U.
3.   D=P+N; U=U-N.
4.   While(stopping criteria is not satisfied)
5.   Selecting unlabeled sample subset x with low score from the unlabeled samples.
6.   Labeling x manually.
7.   D=D + x, U=U-x.
8.   Return D.

Based on Min-Distance Density Semi-supervised Active Learning (MDD-SSAL)

As the simple active learning method is going on, newly labeled samples can offer more information for the classifier and it is convenient to combine semi-supervised methods to rapidly expand the size of labeled training set. The pseudo code is described in Table 2. This technique iterates faster than the previous method, because the classifier classifies the unlabeled samples and the samples with high classification confidence will be added to the corresponding positive and negative sets according to the classification results in each iteration. It can apparently reduce the amount of manual annotation.

Table 2. Pseudo-code of MDD-SSAL.

Algorithm:
Input:
a training dataset with a few positive samples P and large amount of unlabeled data U.
Output:
the labeled dataset.
1.   Initialize D=P.
2.   Calculating the similarity between each unlabeled sample and positive samples. Labeling a certain number of confident negative examples N in unlabeled data U.
3.   D=P+N; U=U-N.
4.   While(stopping criteria is not satisfied)
5.   Learning a classification model with labeled data D.
6.   Selecting unlabeled sample subset x with high score from the unlabeled samples.
7.   Labeling x manually.
8.   Classifying the unlabeled samples, and retaining the samples y with high confidence.
9.   D= D+ x+ y; U= U - x - y
10.   Return D.

4 Experiment Evaluation

4.1 Dataset

The experiments are carried out on several real-world datasets, that is, VoLTE users' bad quality record (VoLTE BQR) obtained from a carrier, QSAR biodegradation Data Set (QSAR) [24], Diabetic Retinopathy Debrecen Data Set (DRD) [25] and their detailed information is shown in Table 3. We use the F-measure to evaluate the performance of these approaches. The F-measure is defined by formula 4.The larger F-measure is better.

$$F - measure = \frac{2 * precision * recall}{(precision + recall)} \tag{4}$$

where precision and recall is respectively the precision and recall of the classifier.

Table 3. Datasets used in the experiments.

	VoLTE BQR	QSAR	DRD
Number of variables	7	41	20
Number of positive samples	575129	356	611
Number of negative samples	1752079	699	540
Number of class	2	2	2

4.2 Analysis of Sample Selection Strategy

Comparison Between Three Basic Methods and MDD-SAL Method with VoLTE BQR Dataset

The problem we encounter in VoLTE BQR data is based on complaints users to predict unsatisfied users in the whole network, so we have only 960 positive samples and 2,326,248 unlabeled samples, which is highly imbalanced. To solve this problem, we intuitively apply a cosine similarity sample expansion algorithm and a PU Learning spy algorithm, but the effect is poor. Then an active learning scheme is proposed and achieves good results. To illustrate the efficiency of our proposed MDD-SAL, we first compare a cosine similarity sample expansion algorithm, a PU Learning spy algorithm and a random sampling with the MDD-SAL proposed in this paper.

(1) Cosine similarity sample expansion algorithm: The average cosine similarity between each unlabeled sample and all the known positive samples is calculated, and the untagged samples are sorted according to the value, and some unlabeled samples with high similarity are added to the positive sample.

(2) PU Learning spy algorithm: Part of the positive samples S are added to the unlabeled U to form the original negative sample US, and a classifier is trained. The remaining positive samples and a probability threshold th is determined according to the subset S; the probability P (1|d) of the positive class is calculated by the Bias classifier for each of the samples in US, if the threshold is less than the threshold probability th, then add it to the reliable negative set.

(3) Random Sampling: selects examples from the unlabeled data randomly.

To show the changes in the performance of classification as the labeled examples gradually increasing, we do experiments on different percentage of labeled samples. Figure 1 shows different classifiers' results of the four methods with VoLTE BQR dataset. It is clear that our proposed MDD-SAL produces the best result. As the number of labeled samples increases, the classifier performance can be improved. As active learning continues iterating, we can constantly annotate the informative samples to inject new knowledge into the classifier.

Comparison Between Three Other Active Learning Methods and SAL Method Based On Two Other Data Sets

To illustrate the efficiency of our proposed sample selection method (MDD-SAL), in this section we compare with two classical sample selection methods as following. Because their computational complexity is particularly high, we utilize two open source datasets with smaller datasets to do experiments.

(1) SUD: A sampling method based on uncertainty and density in literature [13].

(2) IR: A sampling method considering uncertainty and local data density simultaneously in literature [11].

Here we use these sampling strategies to obtain the same number of labeled training data, which is utilized to learn different classifier. Then we compare the F-measure of these methods. Figure 2(a) and (b) are the results of the experiment using DRD dataset and Fig. 2(c) and (d) are the results of the experiment using QSAR dataset. The results reveal that when the number of manually labeled samples is smaller, the classification performance of our proposed sampling strategy MDD is more competitive. It indicates that MDD could select more informative unlabeled samples at the beginning of active learning. As the percentages of manually labeled samples become large, the performance of classifier become similar. This is because mostly informative samples have been manually annotated so that the training set is enough to train a more accurate classifier.

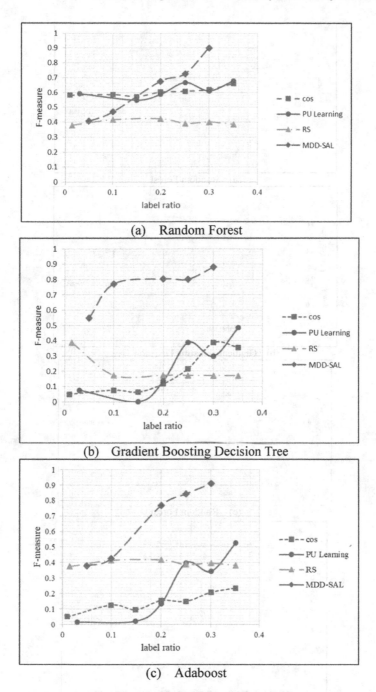

(a)   Random Forest

(b)   Gradient Boosting Decision Tree

(c)   Adaboost

Fig. 1. The experiment results of three classifiers on VoLTE BQR data, where the train data are coming from different ratios, which are manually labeled by our MDD-SAL or annotated by proposed algorithm.

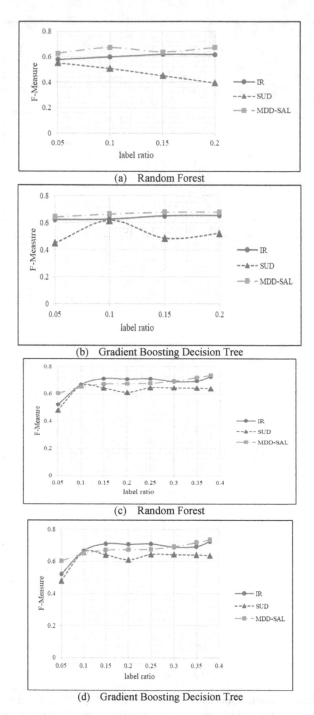

(a)   Random Forest

(b)   Gradient Boosting Decision Tree

(c)   Random Forest

(d)   Gradient Boosting Decision Tree

Fig. 2. The experiment results of two classifiers on two datasets, where the train data are coming from different ratios, which are manually labeled or annotated by 3 sampling methods.

4.3   Analysis of Two Active Learning Framework

In this section, we do some experiments to compare the two active learning techniques. The results are shown in Fig. 3. It is obvious that MDD-SAL need to label more unlabeled samples than MDD-SSAL. It is reasonable that many unlabeled samples could be automatically labeled using semi-supervised method in MDD-SSAL.

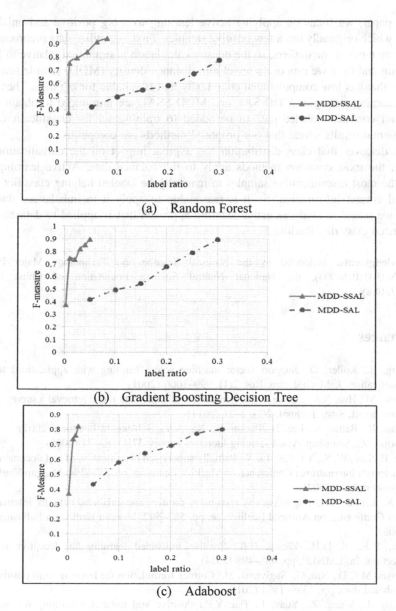

(a)   Random Forest

(b)   Gradient Boosting Decision Tree

(c)   Adaboost

Fig. 3. The comparison of the classification performance of two active learning methods on VoLTE BQR data. The label ratio is the proportion of manually labeled samples for unlabeled samples.

Therefore, we just need manually annotate a few informative unlabeled samples to get competitive classification performance. We note that the classification performance is ultimately similar due to most similar and informative samples found.

5 Conclusion and Future Work

In this paper, we focus on applying active learning to a big positive and unlabeled dataset which originally has a few positive samples. First, we utilize data preprocessing to remove most of the outliers, so the density calculation is simplified relative to KNN algorithm and then we propose a novel min-distance density (MDD) sample selection strategy that has low computational complexity and is suitable for big data. Then, two active learning strategies MDD-SAL and MDD-SSAL are introduced to obtain sufficient and confident labeled data to be added to training set for classification. The experimental results reveal that our proposed methods are competitive.

We discover that class distribution has a great impact on the classification. At present, the most common methods apply to the balance data. Active learning can select the most discriminative samples to manually be labeled helping classifier learn key and correct information. So it is reasonable to apply it to imbalanced data. In future, we intend to study an active learning approach that is applied to datasets with unbalanced class distribution.

Acknowledgments. Supported by the National Science and Technology Major Project (2018ZX03001019-003), the National Natural Science Foundation of China (Grant No.61372088).

References

1. Tong, S., Koller, D.: Support vector machine active learning with applications to text classification. J. Mach. Learn. Res. **2**(1), 999–1006 (2001)
2. Wang, M., Hua, X.S.: Active learning in multimedia annotation and retrieval a survey. ACM Trans. Intell. Syst. Technol. **2**(2), 1–21 (2011)
3. Raina, R., Battle, A., Lee, H., Packer, B., Ng, A.Y.: Self-taught Learning (2007)
4. Xiaojin, Z.: Semi-supervised learning literature survey **37**(1), 63–77 (2005)
5. Liu, B., Lee, W. S., Yu, P.S., Li, X.: Partially supervised classification of text documents. In: Nineteenth International Conference on Machine Learning, pp. 387–394. Morgan Kaufmann Publishers Inc. (2002)
6. Li, X., Liu, B.: Learning to classify texts using positive and unlabeled data. In: International Joint Conference on Artificial Intelligence, pp. 587–592. Morgan Kaufmann Publishers Inc. (2003)
7. Ren, Y.F., Ji, D.H., Zhang, H.B.: Positive unlabeled learning for deceptive reviews detection. In: EMNLP, pp. 488–498 (2014)
8. Plessis, M.C.D., Niu, G., Sugiyama, M.: Convex formulation for learning from positive and unlabeled data, pp. 1386–1394 (2015)
9. Zhang, J., Wang, Z., Yuan, J., Tan, Y.P.: Positive and unlabeled learning for anomaly detection with multi-features, pp. 854–862. ACM (2017)

10. Gu, Y., Jin, Z., Chiu, S.C.: Active learning combining uncertainty and diversity for multi-class image classification. IET Comput. Vis. **9**(3), 400–407 (2015)

11. He, G., Li, Y., Zhao, W.: An uncertainty and density based active semi-supervised learning scheme for positive unlabeled multivariate time series classification. Knowl.-Based Syst. **124,** 80–92 (2017)

12. Li, Y., He, G., Xia, X., Li, Y.: A reverse nearest neighbor based active semi-supervised learning method for multivariate time series classification. In: Hartmann, S., Ma, H. (eds.) DEXA 2016. LNCS, vol. 9827, pp. 272–286. Springer, Cham (2016). https://doi.org/10.1007/978-3-319-44403-1_17

13. Zhu, J., Wang, H., Ma, M., Ma, M.: Active learning with sampling by uncertainty and density for data annotations. IEEE Trans. Audio Speech Lang. Process. **18**(6), 1323–1331 (2010)

14. Huang, S.J., Jin, R., Zhou, Z.H.: Active learning by querying informative and representative examples. IEEE Trans. Pattern Anal. Mach. Intell. **36**(10), 1936–1949 (2014)

15. Guo, H., Wang, W.: An active learning-based SVM multi-class classification model. Pattern Recognit. **48**(5), 1577–1597 (2015)

16. Ghasemi, A., Rabiee, H.R., Fadaee, M., Manzuri, M.T., Rohban, M.H.: Active learning from positive and unlabeled data. In: IEEE, International Conference on Data Mining Workshops, pp. 244–250. IEEE (2012)

17. Seung, H.S., Opper, M., Sompolinsky.: Query by committee. In: Proceedings of the Fifth Workshop on Computational Learning Theory, vol. 284, pp. 287–294 (1992)

18. Hady, M.F.A., Schwenker, F.: Combining committee-based semi-supervised learning and active learning. J. Comput. Sci. Technol. **25**(4), 681–698 (2010)

19. Abe, N., Mamitsuka, H.: Query learning strategies using boosting and bagging. In: Fifteenth International Conference on Machine Learning, pp. 1–9. DBLP (1998)

20. Settles, B., Craven, M.: An analysis of active learning strategies for sequence labeling tasks. In: Conference on Empirical Methods in Natural Language Processing, pp. 1070–1079. Association for Computational Linguistics (2008)

21. Dasgupta, S., Hsu, D.: Hierarchical sampling for active learning. In: Proceedings of Icml, pp. 208–215 (2015)

22. Wang, M., Min, F., Zhang, Z.H., Wu, Y.X.: Active learning through density clustering. Expert Syst. Appl. **85**, 305–317 (2017)

23. He, G., Duan, Y., Li, Y., Qian, T., He, J., Jia, X.: Active learning for multivariate time series classification with positive unlabeled data. In: IEEE International Conference on TOOLS with Artificial Intelligence, pp. 178–185. IEEE (2016)

24. http://archive.ics.uci.edu/ml/datasets/QSAR+biodegradation

25. http://archive.ics.uci.edu/ml/datasets/Diabetic+Retinopathy+Debrecen+Data+Set

TAMM: A New Topology-Aware Mapping Method for Parallel Applications on the Tianhe-2A Supercomputer

Xinhai Chen[1] , Jie Liu[1(✉)], Shengguo Li[1], Peizhen Xie[1], Lihua Chi[2], and Qinglin Wang[1]

[1] Science and Technology on Parallel and Distributed Processing Laboratory, National University of Defense Technology, Changsha 410073, China
chenxinhai1995@aliyun.com, {liujie,nudtlsg,wangqinglin}@nudt.edu.cn
[2] Institute of Advanced Science and Technology, Hunan Institute of Traffic Engineering, Hengyang 421001, China

Abstract. With the increasing size of high performance computing systems, the expensive communication overhead between processors has become a key factor leading to the performance bottleneck. However, default process-to-processor mapping strategies do not take into account the topology of the interconnection network, and thus the distance spanned by communication messages may be particularly far. In order to enhance the communication locality, we propose a new topology-aware mapping method called TAMM. By generating an accurate description of the communication pattern and network topology, TAMM employs a two-step optimization strategy to obtain an efficient mapping solution for various parallel applications. This strategy first extracts an appropriate subset of all idle computing resources on the underlying system and then constructs an optimized one-to-one mapping with a refined iterative algorithm. Experimental results demonstrate that TAMM can effectively improve the communication performance on the Tianhe-2A supercomputer.

Keywords: High performance computing systems
Topology-aware mapping · Communication pattern · Network topology

1 Introduction

High performance computing (HPC) plays a vital role in the fields of scientific research and engineering technology, such as aerospace, astrophysics, biomedicine, weather, materials science, and nuclear engineering [6,20]. With the increasing demand for computing power, the performance of high performance computers forwards to exascale from petascale [10]. The huge scale of systems and the great complexity of applications have brought new challenges

© Springer Nature Switzerland AG 2018
J. Vaidya and J. Li (Eds.): ICA3PP 2018, LNCS 11334, pp. 242–256, 2018.
https://doi.org/10.1007/978-3-030-05051-1_17

to the efficient interprocess communication. However, default strategies of mapping application processes onto processors usually ignore the underlying network topology, and the distance spanned by communication messages may be particularly far. Since each traversal of a switch increases the message latency, the communication between processes could cause heavy congestion within the interconnection network.

In terms of the high communication overhead, topology-aware mapping has been validated as an effective solution for improving the communication performance of parallel applications on large-scale systems [1]. Especially, an optimized mapping of processes onto idle compute resources enables to improve the data locality. For instance, a suitable mapping allows communicating peers to be placed on the processors which are physically close to each other, such that the main communication takes place within the compute node or compute frame. Since these data accesses and exchanges are optimized to fully exploit the resources, the communication overhead and execution time can be reduced.

For topology-aware mapping, finding an optimal mapping is known to be a Quadratic Assignment Problem (QAP) which has been proven to be NP-hard [7]. Thus, the problem is often defined as finding a suitable mapping that minimizes an evaluation metric [34]. *HopByte* is the most common metric to guide the mapping process [13,14]. For a given mapping ϕ, *HopByte* metric is the total amount of communication (in bytes) weighted by the shortest path distance (in hops) between processors. Although the evaluation metric (like *HopByte*) do not directly measure the communication bottleneck caused by congestion, heuristics with lower metric values tend to have smaller communication overheads. It has been shown that minimizing the evaluation metric can reduce the application runtime on tree-based physical topologies [15].

In this paper, we contribute towards the goal of optimizing the communication performance on HPC systems. The main contributions are as follows:

- We provide an accurate model to characterize both the communication pattern of various parallel applications and the communication cost between noncontiguous processors on different network topologies. Based on this model, we apply a new cost metric to guide the mapping process.
- We propose a new topology-aware mapping method called TAMM. This method employs a two-step strategy to minimize the new cost metric. It first extracts an appropriate subset from all idle computing resources, then constructs a refined one-to-one mapping solution on the underlying system.
- We conduct a series of experiments on the Tianhe-2A supercomputer. Experimental evaluation of four NPB benchmarks and two scientific applications demonstrate that TAMM can achieve a better communication performance than that of default mapping strategies (up to 52.8%).
- We introduce modifications to optimize the runtime of the mapping, which further improves the practicality of TAMM.

The rest of the paper is organized as follows: Sect. 2 describes related works about topology-aware mapping. Section 3 presents the implementation of the proposed mapping method TAMM. Section 4 describes the experimental results on six benchmarks. Section 5 discusses the runtime of the mapping while Sect. 6 concludes the paper and discusses the direction for future works.

2   Related Works

The problem of topology-aware mapping has been studied extensively over the years. Jeannot and Mercier [16] introduced the TreeMatch algorithm to compute a solution by mapping the communication pattern graph onto the topology tree. Georgiou et al. [11] extended TreeMatch and implemented a new mapping strategy in the cons_res plugin of Simple Linux Utility for Resource Management (SLURM). Chen et al. [5] proposed a pair-exchange-based approach to find the optimized mapping for message passing applications. Brandfass et al. [3] proposed a local exchange algorithm. Its main intelligence relies on employing the neighborhood exchange to find a better mapping solution. Although exchange-based algorithms usually provide a good mapping quality, they take a long runtime to derive the mapping.

Graph partitioning has been proven to be an effective method to improve the mapping. Open source graph partitioning libraries like Scotch [25], METIS [17], Chaco [12] and Jostle [32] are available for the implementation. Mercier and Clet-Ortega [21] used the Scotch software to extract an embedding of the application's graph from the target machine's graph. Rodrigues et al. [26] also employed Scotch while changing the weight value in the physical topology graph. Tuncer et al. [31] used graph partition software METIS to partition the communication graph for multicore nodes. They iteratively mapped the vertex with the highest communication volume onto the node chosen by a greedy expansion algorithm. Galvez et al. [9] proposed a similar greedy mapping algorithm GreedyMap. This algorithm iterates over the set of processes and places the process in the best free processor, which is estimated using a cost function. Once every instance finishes or the time limit elapses, the leader processor chooses the best solution from multiple processors. However, these algorithms are greedy in nature and lack of backtracking mechanisms. The mapping results leading to a minimized evaluation metric based on greedy algorithms may not guarantee a visible runtime reduction in practice.

In order to reduce the practical load on links, Fujiwara et al. [8] presented a visual analytics system for identifying the bottleneck of massively parallel applications coupled with re-routing and re-mapping algorithms. PTRAM proposed by Mirsadeghi and Afsahi [22] also used the underlying routing information to derive a better evaluation of congestion. It updates the congestion information of the corresponding swapping and saves the swapping that leads to the highest reduction in maximum congestion. These methods require a detailed knowledge of the routing information in target systems. Moreover, users have to keep track of the load imposed over individual links across numerous runs. Wang et al. [33] proposed an aggregated quadratic assignment problem model and provided a process mapping optimization method based on clustering analysis. They used a spectral clustering algorithm to analyze the communication pattern and mapped the process clusters onto the compute node groups according to cluster-based mapping strategies. However, the cluster-based method relies heavily on the number of clusters and clustering procedures, which also require many efforts of users.

Above optimization methods address the mapping challenges for point-to-point message passing. On the other hand, many works have been done on providing a better mapping solution for specific collective operations. Mirsadeghi and Afsahi [23] presented four fine-tuned mapping heuristics for communication patterns commonly used in MPI *Allgather*, including recursive doubling communication, ring communication, binomial broadcast communication and binomial gather communication. Li et al. [18] designed three NUMA-aware algorithms (reduce-broadcast, dissemination, and tiled-reduce-broadcast) for thread-based HMPI *Allreduce* on clusters of NUMA nodes. Subramoni et al. [29] proposed a network topology-aware plugin for SLURM to allocate compute resources in a topology-aware fashion and reduce the amount of congestion for *Alltoall* FFT operations.

Topology-aware mapping on supercomputers has been studied intensively in recent years. Sreepathi et al. [28] developed several mapping methods such as spectral bisection and neighbor-join tree. They combined the node layout and application communication data for task placement on Titan supercomputer. Yu et al. [35] presented embedding and integration techniques for the embedding of three-dimensional grids and torus on Blue Gene/L supercomputer. Bhatele and Kale [1,2] proposed an HopByte-based automatic mapping framework which includes a suite of algorithms with capabilities to choose the best mapping for a problem with a given communication graph on ANL's Blue Gene/P and PSC's XT3. In this work, by generating an accurate description of the communication pattern and network topology, we present a two-step optimization strategy to obtain an efficient mapping solution for parallel applications with both collective communications and point-to-point communications on the Tianhe-2A supercomputer.

3   A New Topology-Aware Mapping Method

In order to get an accurate model of the topology mapping problem, the communication behavior of the parallel application (communication pattern) and the physical topology of the underlying system (topological distance) must be obtained first.

3.1   Modeling of Communication Pattern Matrix

The communication pattern matrix describes the communication information of a given parallel application. Generally, this matrix is extracted by collecting the volume of point-to-point communications between processes. However, it may not accurately describe distinct communication patterns. On the one hand, collective communications, which constitute many communications of parallel applications, are equally important to the topology mapping. On the other hand, the communication overhead between processes depends on not only the transmission distance but also the message size. Large messages are more sensitive to message volume while small messages are more susceptible to latency, especially when sending large amounts of short message data frequently. In this regard, we consider both the communication type and message size in TAMM.

By thinking over the implementation semantics of collective communications in MPI library (such as recursive doubling algorithm, ring algorithm, Rabenseifner's algorithm, binomial tree algorithm and so on), we acquire the accurate interprocess communication pattern in these algorithms. For example, the recursive doubling algorithm is one of the most commonly used algorithms for $MPI\_Allreduce$ and $MPI\_Allgather$. Figure 1 shows an example with eight processes. At each step i, processes communicate in pairs and exchange data with a distance of 2^{i-1}. Thus, we can easily transform the implementation into a series of point-to-point communication operations.

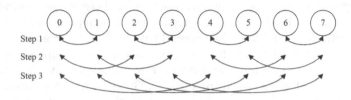

Fig. 1. The recursive doubling algorithm with eight processes.

Since it is difficult to find a proper weighting value to integrate point-to-point communications and collective communications, two communication types are designed to process separately in TAMM. For each parallel application, the steps of generating the communication pattern matrix are as follows: (1) select the communication type (point-to-point or collective communication) that occupies the dominant communication time to describe the communication pattern of a parallel application; (2) set the entry of the matrix to the appropriate value (message count or message volume) according to the message size of interprocess communications(for collective communication, we first transform it into a series of point-to-point communication). In this way, we obtain an accurate description of the communication behavior for various parallel applications.

3.2   Modeling of Topological Distance Matrix

The topological distance matrix is used to represent the cost of sending messages over the interconnect network. In TAMM, we set the entry of this matrix as the number of route hops traversed from one process to another. As only *node id* and the topology information are required, the topological distance matrix is easy to compute. Moreover, it is suitable for describing the communication cost of non-contiguous processors on different topologies like fat trees, torus, and hypercube. Once physical distances are extracted, this matrix can be saved and reused across numerous runs.

On the Tianhe-2A supercomputer, the interconnect network adopts a 3-level optic-electronic hybrid fat-tree topology to get the highest bisection bandwidth. The compute nodes at the leaves are packaged in compute frames which are connected by 20-port frame switches, 24-port leaf switches and 48-port root switches from bottom to top [4,19]. To represent the communication cost between non-contiguous idle processors, we extract the number of route hops between pairs of processors. Specifically, as the compute nodes are organized as a multi-CPU SMP system in the Tianhe-2A [24], we approximate the routing distance of processors within the same node to zero.

Based on these two matrices, the optimization mapping process is geared towards minimizing a new cost metric to find a suitable process-to-processor mapping. For an application with p processes, the *Costmetric* of a given one-to-one mapping ϕ is

$$Costmetric(\phi) = \sum_{i=0}^{p-1}\sum_{j=0}^{p-1} A_{ij} * B_{\phi(i)\phi(j)},\tag{1}$$

where A and B denote the communication pattern matrix and topological distance matrix respectively.

3.3 Two-Step Optimization Strategy

Since a high performance computer with tens of thousands of compute nodes is often shared by multiple applications concurrently, a large number of idle computing resources are usually non-contiguous. To find a suitable mapping of processes to processors, a two-step optimization strategy is proposed. We first select appropriate resources from all non-contiguous computing resources to schedule the uploaded task and construct an initial one-to-one mapping in a short time (the whole procedure is shown in Algorithm 1). Then, optimize this initial mapping with a refined iterative algorithm to further reduce the *Costmetric* and communication time (shown in Algorithm 2).

Initial Mapping Algorithm. Let P denote the set of processes in the uploaded task, and N denote the set of idle processors on the underlying system. The initial mapping algorithm builds an initial one-to-one mapping for each process in a short time.

First of all, all of the processes and processors are organized into two separate arrays: $P_{unselected}$ ($N_{unselected}$) and $P_{selected}$ ($N_{selected}$). Within each iteration, we calculate the communication load *comm* of each unselected process (line 8). The first summation represents the total communication value of the process p with its selected communicating peers while the second summation is the total communication value with its unselected peers. Note that the weight value ($|P_{selected}|$ or $|N_{selected}|$) is employed to give different weights to two summations.

We traverse all of the idle processors and map the process with the largest communication load (*comm*) onto the processor with the smallest total distance *dist*. After each mapping, we add the chosen process and processor to the *selected* array respectively ($P_{selected}$ and $N_{selected}$). The iteration terminates when an initial one-to-one mapping ϕ' is constructed.

Algorithm 1: Initial mapping algorithm

   Input: processes P, communication pattern matrix A, idle processors N, distance matrix B;

   Output: initial mapping result ϕ';

1   $P_{selected} \leftarrow \emptyset$;

2   $P_{unselected} \leftarrow P$;   //before mapping, all processes are unselected

3   $N_{selected} \leftarrow \emptyset$;

4   $N_{unselected} \leftarrow N$;   //before mapping, all processors are unselected

5   $k \leftarrow 0$;

6   **while** $k < |P|$ **do**

7   **for** *each process p in* $P_{unselected}$ **do**

8       $comm_p \leftarrow \sum_{i \in P_{selected}} A_{pi} + \frac{\sum_{j \in P_{unselected}} A_{pj}}{1 + |P_{selected}|}$

9   **end**

10   select the process p with the maximum value of *comm* ;

11   **for** *each processor n in* $N_{unselected}$ **do**

12      $dist_n \leftarrow \sum_{i \in N_{selected}} B_{ni} + \frac{\sum_{j \in N_{unselected}} B_{nj}}{1 + |N_{selected}|}$

13   **end**

14   select the processor n with minimum value of *dist* ;

15    $\phi'(p) \leftarrow n$;   //map p onto n

16   remove p from $P_{unselected}$ and add p to $P_{selected}$;

17   remove n from $N_{unselected}$ and add n to $N_{selected}$;

18    $k \leftarrow k + 1$;

19 **end**

20 return ϕ';

In the initial mapping algorithm, we update the weight value in each iteration aiming at improving the quality of the mapping result. At the beginning of the algorithm, unselected processes and processors are relatively more important since most of the processes and processors are unselected. As the mapping progresses, we give a relatively higher weight to the set of selected objects, which increases the impact of the selected objects on the next mapping. Overall, the initial mapping algorithm provides a method for extracting suitable resources from a large number of non-contiguous computing resources and constructs an initial one-to-one mapping. It is in line with the actual scenario of task mapping on large-scale systems with tens of thousands of compute nodes.

Refined Iterative Algorithm. The initial mapping algorithm finds an appropriate subset of all idle computing resources on the underlying system. The advantage of this algorithm is that the overall execution time is quite fast. However, this procedure is greedy, and it does not necessarily guarantee optimality at the end. In allusion to the problem mentioned above, we try to improve the quality of the initial mapping result through a refined pair-exchange-based method. To illustrate the simplicity of this algorithm, we provide the detailed description in Algorithm 2.

Algorithm 2: Refined iterative algorithm

Input: processes P, communication pattern matrix A, distance submatrix B,
        initial mapping result ϕ';
Output: final mapping result ϕ;

1   $Status[\|P\|] \leftarrow 0, \; k \leftarrow 0$ //Initialization;
2   //count is a user-defined number of iterations
    while $k < count$ **do**
3   **for** each $i, j \in P$ where $Status[i] \neq 1$ && $Status[j] \neq 1$ **do**
4   //exchange process i,j and calculate the change of the $Costmetric$
          $Cost_{ij} \leftarrow \sum_{l \in P}(A_{il}B_{\phi'(i)\phi'(l)} + A_{jl}B_{\phi'(j)\phi'(l)}) -$
                   $\sum_{r \in P}(A_{ir}B_{\phi'(j)\phi'(r)} + A_{jr}B_{\phi'(i)\phi'(r)})$;
5   **end**
6   //find the maximum value $Cost_{mn}$ in matrix $Cost$
        $Cost_{mn} \leftarrow findMaxElement(Cost)$;
7   add process m, n to array $Peer[]$;   //record the pair of processes
8   add $Cost_{mn}$ to array $Result[]$;   //record the change of the cost metric
9      $status[m] \leftarrow 1, \; status[n] \leftarrow 1$;
10   update the mapping result ϕ';
11     $k \leftarrow k + 1$;
12 **end**
13 //calculate t to maximize the sum of the first t elements in array $Result[]$
    $t \leftarrow MaxSum(Result[])$;
14 exchange the first t pairs of processes in $Peer[]$ and obtain final mapping ϕ;
15 return ϕ;

The main intelligence of the refined iterative algorithm relies on employing the pair-exchange method coupled with a backtracking mechanism to optimize the initial one-to-one mapping. At the beginning of the algorithm, the status of all processes is zero, which means these processes have not been exchanged. In each iteration, we calculate an exchange evaluation matrix $Cost$. The entry $Cost_{ij}$ of this matrix represents the changes of the $Costmetric$ after exchanging the mapping location of process i and process j (line 4). Then, we find the maximum value $Cost_{mn}$ in matrix $Cost$ and store the corresponding m, n and $Cost_{mn}$ in the exchange peers array $Peers[]$ and exchange result array $Result[]$ respectively. Meanwhile, change the status of process m and process n to one. Note that the number of iterations ($count$) is user-defined, which is used as a mechanism to control the iteration time. We find t to maximize the sum of the first t elements in array $Result[]$ (the total gain of pair-exchange is positive and maximum). At last, back to the result of the previous first t exchanges and obtain the final mapping result ϕ.

Compared with other local pair-exchange-based algorithms which lack backtracking mechanisms, the refined iterative algorithm we proposed is more efficient. The pair of processes with the maximal cost metric $Cost_{mn}$ is exchanged in each iteration. Finally, the mapping result falls back to the best exchange result. Moreover, the exchange process is expected to continue until every two processes have been exchanged once (both $status_i$ and $status_j$ are not equal to one), or it reaches $count$ iterations. For parallel applications with a long distance communication pattern, this criteria facilitates the exchanges between processes far apart, which helps to further enhance the communication locality. Meanwhile, it avoids repeatedly swapping the same pair of processes.

4   Experimental Results

To evaluate the performance of TAMM, we use four programs in NAS Parallel Benchmark Suite (version 3.3.1) [27] and two scientific applications as benchmarks. The NPB suite is a set of computation programs, which are developed for the performance evaluation of highly parallel supercomputers. Four programs with different communication patterns are selected (i.e. BT, SP, LU, and CG in class D). Two scientific applications are Sweep3D [30] and Snap [36]. Sweep3D is a simplified program which solves a neutron transport problem. It uses a pipelined wave-front method and a two-dimensional process mesh. Snap is a proxy application which mimics the 3D deterministic Sn transport equation.

We carry out experiments on the Tianhe-2A supercomputer and run 256, 512, 1024, 2048 and 4096 processes on five compute racks connected by the top-level 48-port switches. As the process number of BT and SP is required to be a square, only 256, 1024 and 4096 processes have been tested. For Snap, we set the number of uniformly-sized cells to 256 in the x-direction while 64 in the y-direction and 128 in the z-direction when the number of processes equals 256. As the number increases, we double the cells in the z-direction (e.g. the number of cells is $256 \times 64 \times 256$ when the number of processes equals 512). As for Sweep3D, the grid points in the x, y, z-direction are 1024, 1024 and 2048 respectively. We double the grid points in the y-direction with each increase in processes. The parameter $count$ in Algorithm 2 is set at half the number of uploaded processes.

We compare TAMM with two default mapping strategies in the Tianhe-2A (in-order and round-robin). $Costmetric$ values of these three strategies are shown in Fig. 2, and the detailed communication time is given in Fig. 3. The numbers in two figures are normalized by the results of the in-order strategy. To reduce the noise, we evaluate each mapping ten times and record the average under a "clean" network environment (without being prejudiced by other applications).

Figure 2(a) and (d) indicate that both BT and SP, with a nearest-neighbor communication pattern, show a significant reduction in the $Costmetric$. It achieves average improvements of 22.1% and 22.0% compared with in-order strategy while 41.3% and 41.4% compared with round-robin strategy respectively. The communication time also benefits a lot from TAMM (shown in

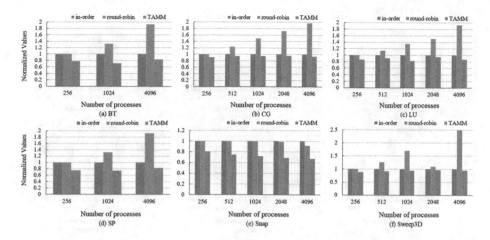

Fig. 2. Normalized cost metric for different mapping strategies on the Tianhe-2A super-computer.

Fig. 3(a) and (d)). These two benchmarks obtain improvements of 17.1% (up to 24.0%) and 18.6% (up to 20.5%) compared with in-order strategy respectively, 19.9% (up to 29.1%) and 22.3% (up to 38.5%) compared with round-robin strategy.

CG and LU show relatively low improvements in the *Costmetric* after the re-mapping (shown in Fig. 2(b) and (c)). The optimized mapping results of these two NPB programs are 6.1% and 11.7% better than in-order strategy while 33.1% and 33.0% better than round-robin strategy in the *Costmetric*. Accordingly, compared with two default mapping strategies, the communication time in Fig. 3(b) and (c) shows improvements of 6.9% (up to 11.9%) and 23.0% (up to 52.8%) for CG, 7.2% (up to 17.4%) and 9.4% (up to 17.4%) for LU respectively.

For the other two scientific applications (Sweep3D and Snap), the figures (Fig. 2(e) and (f), Fig. 3(e) and (f)) indicate that TAMM can also reduce the *Costmetric* and perform a lower practical communication time. The *Costmetric* of Sweep3D reduces by 6.7% and 31.3% while the communication time reduces by 19.8% (up to 29.5%) and 20.8% (up to 37.8%) compared with in-order and round-robin strategy. For Snap, we see average improvements of 27.4% over in-order and 25.8% over round-robin in the *Costmetric* while an improvement of 6.8% (up to 10.5%) and 6.4% (up to 10.1%) in the communication time.

We can see that the high-quality mapping provided by TAMM outperforms the default mapping strategies in the Tianhe-2A supercomputer. Notably, for applications with nearest-neighbor communication patterns (like BT, SP and Sweep3D), TAMM effectively maps the communicating peers on the processors which are physically close to each other. It helps to reduce the number of long-distance communications and enhance the communication locality. The effects on other applications are moderate (like CG, LU and Snap). This is mainly because

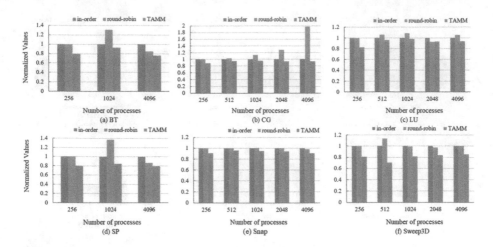

Fig. 3. Normalized communication time for different mapping strategies on the Tianhe-2A supercomputer.

these applications involve interprocess communications with variant distances, which are normally hard to be optimized in nature.

Overall, experimental results on the Tianhe-2A show that, by finding an appropriate subset of all idle computing resources and then optimizing the mapping with a refined iterative algorithm, the new topology-aware mapping method improves the evaluation metric and delivers high communication efficiency for various parallel applications.

5   Runtime of TAMM

For the initial mapping algorithm, the overall execution time is quite fast (for up to $p = 1024$ lower than 2.08 s). However, during the second algorithm, the complexity for each iteration in the refined pair-exchange-based method is $O(p^3)$, where p denotes the number of processes. Note that the execution time of the mapping optimization method is a one-time cost for a specific application or a class of problems with similar communication patterns. Although optimization results can be reused across numerous runs, it is still worthwhile to shorten the runtime of TAMM.

In the refined iterative algorithm, the main computation in each iteration is to update an exchange evaluation matrix $Cost$ which describes the pre-exchange gains. According to the architecture of the Tianhe-2A supercomputer, compute nodes directly connected by the same high-radix router chip are equivalent in the interconnection network. Thus, we can ignore the exchanges of those processes to reduce the calculation and improve mapping efficiency.

Besides, once the parallel application has a regular communication pattern, we can neglect the lower triangular elements of two input matrices because of the symmetry (the topological distance matrix we used is symmetric itself). In this regard, only less than half the elements of matrix $Cost$ need to be updated in each iteration. Other modifications, like limiting loop iterations as well as partition communication and distance matrices can also help reduce the runtime of the mapping process.

6 Conclusions

As the scale of supercomputers grows, topology-aware mapping has become a promising technique to improve the communication performance within the complex interconnection network. In this paper, we propose a new topology-aware mapping method called TAMM. The new method generates an accurate description of the communication pattern matrix and hop-based topological distance matrix. Based on these two matrices, TAMM employs a two-step optimization strategy to provide an efficient mapping solution for applications with both collective communications and point-to-point communications. The optimization strategy first selects appropriate resources from all non-contiguous computing resources to schedule the uploaded task and construct an initial one-to-one mapping in a short time. Then, optimizes this initial mapping with a refined iterative algorithm to further reduce the communication cost. Experimental results on four NPB benchmarks and two scientific applications have demonstrated that TAMM outperforms default mappings on the Tianhe-2A supercomputer. Besides, we introduce modifications to optimize the runtime of the mapping process, which further improves the practicality of TAMM. In the future works, we plan to derive a better evaluation of congestion by considering the routing algorithm of the Tianhe-2A. Moreover, it is also of great interest to conduct experiments at larger scales.

Acknowledgment. This research work was supported in part by the National Key Research and Development Program of China (2017YFB0202104), the National Natural Science Foundation of China under Grant No.: 91530324, No.: 91430218, China Postdoctoral Science Foundation (CPSF) Grant No.: 2014M562570, Special Financial Grant from CPSF Grant No.: 2015T81127.

References

1. Bhatele, A., Laxmikant, V.: An evaluative study on the effect of contention on message latencies in large supercomputers. In: 2009 IEEE International Symposium on Parallel and Distributed Processing (IPDPS), pp. 1–8 (2009). https://doi.org/10.1109/IPDPS.2009.5161094

2. Bhatele, A.: Automating topology aware mapping for supercomputers. Ph.D. thesis, University of Illinois at Urbana-Champaign, Champaign, IL, USA (2010)

3. Brandfass, B., Alrutz, T., Gerhold, T.: Rank reordering for mpi communication optimization. Comput. Fluids **80**, 372–380 (2013). https://doi.org/10.1016/j.compfluid.2012.01.019

4. Cao, J., Xiao, L., Pang, Z., Wang, K., Xu, J.: The efficient in-band management for interconnect network in Tianhe-2 system. In: 2016 24th Euromicro International Conference on Parallel, Distributed, and Network-Based Processing (PDP), pp. 18–26 (2016). https://doi.org/10.1109/PDP.2016.58

5. Chen, H., Chen, W., Huang, J., Robert, B., Kuhn, H.: MPIPP: an automatic profile-guided parallel process placement toolset for SMP clusters and multiclusters. In: Proceedings of the 20th Annual International Conference on Supercomputing, ICS 2006, pp. 353–360. ACM (2006). https://doi.org/10.1145/1183401. 1183451

6. Duff, I.S.: European exascale software initiative: numerical libraries, solvers and algorithms. In: Alexander, M., et al. (eds.) Euro-Par 2011. LNCS, vol. 7155, pp. 295–304. Springer, Heidelberg (2012). https://doi.org/10.1007/978-3-642-29737-3_34

7. Ercal, F., Ramanujam, J., Sadayappan, P.: Task allocation onto a hypercube by recursive mincut bipartitioning. In: Proceedings of the Third Conference on Hypercube Concurrent Computers and Applications: Architecture, Software, Computer Systems, and General Issues, C3P, vol. 1, pp. 210–221. ACM (1988). https://doi. org/10.1145/62297.62323

8. Fujiwara, T., Malakar, P., Reda, K., Vishwanath, V., Papka, M.E., Ma, K.L.: A visual analytics system for optimizing communications in massively parallel applications. In: IEEE Conference on Visual Analytics Science and Technology (2017)

9. Galvez, J.J., Jain, N., Kale, L.V.: Automatic topology mapping of diverse large-scale parallel applications. In: Proceedings of the International Conference on Supercomputing, ICS 2017, pp. 17:1–17:10. ACM (2017). https://doi.org/10.1145/3079079.3079104

10. Geist, A., Dosanjh, S.: IESP exascale challenge: co-design of architectures and algorithms. Int. J. High Perform. Comput. Appl. **23**(4), 401–402 (2009). https://doi.org/10.1177/1094342009347766

11. Georgiou, Y., Jeannot, E., Mercier, G., Villiermet, A.: Topology-aware job mapping. Int. J. High Perform. Comput. Appl. 63 (2017). https://doi.org/10.1109/SC.2006.63

12. Hendrickson, B., Leland, R.: The Chaco user's guide: version 2.0. Technical report, Sandia National Laboratory (1994)

13. Hoefler, T., Jeannot, E., Mercier, G.: An overview of topology mapping algorithms and techniques in high-performance computing, Chap. 5, pp. 73–94. Wiley-Blackwell (2014).https://doi.org/10.1002/9781118711897.ch5

14. Hoefler, T., Snir, M.: Generic topology mapping strategies for large-scale parallel architectures. In: Proceedings of the International Conference on Supercomputing, ICS 2011. pp. 75–84. ACM(2011). https://doi.org/10.1145/1995896.1995909

15. Jeannot, E., Mercier, G., Tessier, F.: Process placement in multicore clusters:algorithmic issues and practical techniques. IEEE Trans. Parallel Distrib. Syst. **25**(4), 993–1002 (2014). https://doi.org/10.1109/TPDS.2013.104

16. Jeannot, E., Mercier, G.: Near-optimal placement of MPI processes on hierarchical NUMA architectures. In: D'Ambra, P., Guarracino, M., Talia, D. (eds.) Euro-Par 2010. LNCS, vol. 6272, pp. 199–210. Springer, Heidelberg (2010). https://doi.org/10.1007/978-3-642-15291-7_20

17. Karypis, G., Kumar, V.: Metis: a software package for partitioning unstructured graphs. International Cryogenics Monograph, pp. 121–124 (1998)

18. Li, S., Hoefler, T., Snir, M.: NUMA-aware shared-memory collective communication for MPI. In: Proceedings of the 22nd International Symposium on High-Performance Parallel and Distributed Computing, HPDC 2013, pp. 85–96. ACM (2013). https://doi.org/10.1145/2462902.2462903

19. Liao, X.K., et al.: High performance interconnect network for Tianhe system. J. Comput. Sci. Technol. **30**(2), 259–272 (2015). https://doi.org/10.1007/s11390-015-1520-7

20. Liao, X., Xiao, L., Yang, C., Lu, Y.: Milkyway-2 supercomputer: system and application. Front. Comput. Sci. **8**(3), 345–356 (2014). https://doi.org/10.1007/s11704-014-3501-3

21. Mercier, G., Clet-Ortega, J.: Towards an efficient process placement policy for MPI applications in multicore environments. In: Ropo, M., Westerholm, J., Dongarra, J. (eds.) EuroPVM/MPI 2009. LNCS, vol. 5759, pp. 104–115. Springer, Heidelberg (2009). https://doi.org/10.1007/978-3-642-03770-2_17

22. Mirsadeghi, S.H., Afsahi, A.: PTRAM: a parallel topology-and routing-aware mapping framework for large-scale HPC systems. In: 2016 IEEE International Parallel and Distributed Processing Symposium Workshops (IPDPSW), pp. 386–396 (2016). https://doi.org/10.1109/IPDPSW.2016.146

23. Mirsadeghi, S.H., Afsahi, A.: Topology-aware rank reordering for MPI collectives. In: 2016 IEEE International Parallel and Distributed Processing Symposium Workshops (IPDPSW), pp. 1759–1768 (2016). https://doi.org/10.1109/IPDPSW.2016.139

24. Pang, Z., et al.: The TH express high performance interconnect networks. Front. Comput. Sci. **8**(3), 357–366 (2014). https://doi.org/10.1007/s11704-014-3500-9

25. Pellegrini, F., Roman, J.: Scotch: a software package for static mapping by dual recursive bipartitioning of process and architecture graphs. In: Liddell, H., Colbrook, A., Hertzberger, B., Sloot, P. (eds.) HPCN-Europe 1996. LNCS, vol. 1067, pp. 493–498. Springer, Heidelberg (1996). https://doi.org/10.1007/3-540-61142-8_588

26. Rodrigues, E.R., Madruga, F.L., Navaux, P.O.A., Panetta, J.: Multi-core aware process mapping and its impact on communication overhead of parallel applications. In: 2009 IEEE Symposium on Computers and Communications, pp. 811–817 (2009). https://doi.org/10.1109/ISCC.2009.5202271

27. Schreiber, R.S., et al.: The NAS parallel benchmarks. In: 1991 ACM/IEEE Conference on Supercomputing (Supercomputing 1991) (SC), pp. 158–165 (1991). https://doi.org/10.1145/125826.125925

28. Sreepathi, S., D'Azevedo, E., Philip, B., Worley, P.: Communication characterization and optimization of applications using topology-aware task mapping on large supercomputers. In: Proceedings of the 7th ACM/SPEC on International Conference on Performance Engineering, ICPE 2016, pp. 225–236. ACM (2016). https://doi.org/10.1145/2851553.2851575

29. Subramoni, H., et al.: Design of network topology aware scheduling services for large infiniband clusters. In: 2013 IEEE International Conference on Cluster Computing (CLUSTER), pp. 1–8 (2013). https://doi.org/10.1109/CLUSTER.2013.6702677

30. Sweep3D: The ASCI Sweep3D Benchmark Code (2014). http://www.llnl.gov/asci-benchmarks/scsi/limited/sweep3d/asci_sweep3d.html (2014)

31. Tuncer, O., Leung, V.J., Coskun, A.K.: PaCMap: topology mapping of unstructured communication patterns onto non-contiguous allocations. In: Proceedings of the 29th ACM on International Conference on Supercomputing, ICS 2015, pp. 37–46. ACM (2015). https://doi.org/10.1145/2751205.2751225

32. Walshaw, C., Cross, M.: Jostle: Parallel multilevel graph-partitioning software - an overview. Mesh Partitioning Techniques and Domain Decomposition Techniques (2007)
33. Wang, T., Qing, P., Wei, D., Qi, F.B.: Optimization of process-to-core mapping based on clustering analysis. Chin. J. Comput. **38**, 1044–1055 (2015)
34. Wu, J., Xiong, X., Berrocal, E., Wang, J., Lan, Z.: Topology mapping of irregular parallel applications on torus-connected supercomputers. J. Supercomput. **73**(4), 1691–1714 (2017). https://doi.org/10.1007/s11227-016-1876-7
35. Yu, H., Chung, I.H., Moreira, J.: Topology mapping for blue Gene/L supercomputer. In: Proceedings of the 2006 ACM/IEEE Conference on Supercomputing, SC 2006. ACM (2006). https://doi.org/10.1145/1188455.1188576
36. Zerr, R.J., Baker, R.S.: SNAP: SN (discrete ordinates) application proxy - proxy description. Technical report, Los Alamos National Laboratory (2013)

Adaptive Data Sampling Mechanism for Process Object

Yongzheng Lin[1,2,3], Hong Liu[1,2]([✉]), Zhenxiang Chen[3], Kun Zhang[3], and Kun Ma[3] [ID]

[1] School of Information Science and Engineering, Shandong Normal University, Jinan, China
lhsdcn@126.com
[2] Shandong Provincial Key Laboratory for Novel Distributed Computer Software Technology, Jinan, China
[3] School of Information Science and Engineering, University of Jinan, Jinan, China
{ise_linyz,czx,ise_zhangk,ise_mak}@ujn.edu.cn

Abstract. Process object is the abstraction of process. In process object, there are different type of entities and associations. The entities vary dependent on other entities. The performance and evolution of process object are affected by the association between entities. These changes could be reflected in the data collected from the process objects. These data from process object could be regard as big data stream. In the context of big data, how to find appropriate data for process object is a challenge. The data sampling should reflect the performance change of process object, and should be adaptive to the current underlying distribution of data in data stream. For finding appropriate data in big data stream to model process object, an adaptive data sampling mechanism is proposed in this paper. Experiments demonstrate the effectiveness of the proposed adaptive data sampling mechanism for process object.

Keywords: Process object · Data sampling · Big data · Data stream · Clustering · Stream processing

1 Introduction

Process object is an abstraction of process, where there is the dependency and constraint on the entity and association between them, such as learning process in school, delivery process in e-commerce, the industrial process in factory and so on. With the development of wireless sensor, smart phones, Internet of Things and other emerging technologies, data about process object could be collected, transferred, stored, and analyzed in a more convenient way. The evolution of process object could be modeled, which could be used to improve the performance of process object continuously. It is important to reduce waste and improve efficiency.

For finding appropriate data in big data stream to model process object, a adaptive data sampling mechanism is proposed in this paper. Firstly, life cycle of

J. Vaidya and J. Li (Eds.): ICA3PP 2018, LNCS 11334, pp. 257–266, 2018.
https://doi.org/10.1007/978-3-030-05051-1_18

process object is partitioned into different evolution stage based on the concept drift in data stream. Data from different evolution stage reflect the different state of process object. Then data from different stages should be sampled for modeling the evolution of process object. However, in the same evolution stage, association occurs between entities. There are different associations between entities in various stages. Then secondly, in a same evolution stage, the relevant entities are partitioned into community based on their behaviour similarity and associations. These communities are the sources of data sampling.

The organization of the paper is as follows: Sect. 2 makes a survey of related works. Section 3 introduces the architecture of adaptive sample mechanism for process object. Firstly, the partition of life cycle of process object based on concept drift is proposed. Secondly, the entities community detection in the same evolution stages is introduced. Section 4 makes experiments and analysis. Section 5 makes a conclusion.

2   Related Works

Process object is abstraction of process, which can be seen as a special case of workflow. It consists of entities and associations between them.

For mining latent association rule in process object, there has been a lot of related works [4,8,16,20]. In [16], process object is defined. It gives a scheme for mining state association rules of process object based on big data. For mining state association rules, it constructs a flow schema, including sampling, timing, clustering, association chain constructing and state association rule constructing. For mining state association rules, data are sampled through the life cycle of process object. The data segment with most information or variation is selected [16]. However, it does not consider the evolution stage where data segment lies. After sampling, timing is proposed to compute the delay time between different entities [20]. Afterwards, clustering [8] is used to find the similar state. However, existing work on process object modeling does not consider the evolution stage of process object. In fact, evolution stage exists. Using the stage modeling, the evolution pattern of process object could be modelled more accurately.

Considering the evolution stage of process object, concept drift in data stream [6] could be used for finding appropriate partition of life cycle of process object. Since the dynamic data streams are not independently and identically distributed, the concept drift will occur. The detection of concept changes tend to suffer from limitations with respect to one or more key performance factors such as high computational complexity, poor sensitivity to gradual change or drift, and the opposite problem of high false positive rate. There are some changes detection methods [13] for blocking input data in big data streams. However, it is very difficult to detect changes in high-dimensional data space. It introduces errors when detecting the concept drift in high-dimensional input space, so it is inefficient in the case of data stream mining. Reference [11] proposed a sequential change detection model which can offer statistically sound guarantees on false positive and false negative by using reservoir sampling. Just-In-Time (JIT) classifiers in [18] be used to detect concept drifts contains two ways based on Intersection of confidence intervals (ICI), one to detect concept drift and compare concepts using both the input data distribution and the supervised couples, the other is to detect changes in the capabilities of a particular classifier. The current big data stream has high capacity and high speed characteristics, which is very worth considering. Wang et al. [18] used a model combining method with a grouping attribute of constraint and penalty regression to track concept drift. There has been a lot of other research on concept drift detection [5,14,15,17]. All these approaches could be used in evolution stages partition.

After evolution stages partition, clustering approaches in data streams [2,7, 9,12] could be used to find similar entities in the same evolution stages. There are many research on data stream clustering [1,9,19], which could be used in entity community detection.

3 Adaptive Data Sampling

The adaptive data sampling architecture is proposed in this section. Firstly, the basic definition of process object is introduced. Then the adaptive data sampling process is introduced.

3.1 Basic Definition

The process object is an abstraction of process. Given the definition in [4,16], the process object consists of n links, and each link contains one or more sampling points. X_i ($i \in (1, n)$)is a link of the process object, and the system unified sampling period is T, and t_i ($i \in (1, m)$) is sampling time and $T = t_{i+1} - t_i$. The process object can be defined as

$$\chi = \left\{ \begin{array}{l} \chi_1(x_1(t_1), x_1(t_2), \ldots, x_1(t_m)) \\ \chi_2(x_2(t_1), x_2(t_2), \ldots, x_2(t_m)) \\ \ldots \\ \chi_n(x_n(t_1), x_n(t_2), \ldots, x_n(t_m)) \end{array} \right\} \tag{1}$$

Where $x_i(t_m)$ is sample value of i-th link when sampling time is t_m. However, there is delay time between links in process objects. For any two links X_i and X_j, a change in link X_i leads to corresponding change in link X_j when X_i is in upstream and is an ancestor of X_j. The delay in the propagation of the change is the delay time.

For generalization purpose, the link in process object is generalized to entity. It means that the link in process object has somewhat wisdom to be an entity. The entity could react according to the change of its neighbor entities, which reveal some underlying evolution rule of process object.

The process object is an abstraction of a group entities and its associations. There is association between entities. The association between entities could promote the evolution of the global process object. The association between entities could be explicit or implicit. The strength of association could change with time. The local change could influence the global evolution of process object. In other words, the local change could be detected by the global status change of process object, which is defined by the status combination of each entity. For a individual entity, its status could be defined by its observed value by IoT technology. The reaction between local entities could affect the evolution of global process object by the explicit or implicit association between them.

Definition 1 (Process Object). *The process object is an abstraction of a group entities and its associations, which could be modeled as a heterogeneous information network $G_{ProcessObject}(X_{entity}, E_{association})$. The association between entities may be implicit. The entities could be monitored through IoT technologies. At a given fixed time interval, the status of entities are monitored and collected. The local status of entity x_i could be represented as a vector $\chi_i = \{x_i(t_1), x_i(t_2), \ldots, x_i(t_m), \ldots\}$. The global status of process object at time t_i could be represented as a vector $\omega_{t_i} = \{x_1(t_i), x_2(t_i), \ldots, x_n(t_i)\}$, where n is the number of entities in process object. If there is association from entity χ_i to χ_j, there exists a corresponding dynamically changeable function $\chi_j = f(\chi_i)$, which is one attribute of the association.*

Due to the transitivity of association, the status of certain entity may be affected by a association chain of entities. On the other hand, change in one certain entity may affect other entities. The change and evolution of local entities cause the global process object evolve with time. When process object is running, it may evolve through different stages. When process object lies in different stages, the performance and association between entities may be different. In other words, the local association between entities may evolve, and influence the global evolution of process object. The association between entities may arise, disappear or change. The complexity of association between entities promote the evolution of process object.

For modeling the evolution of process object dynamically and precisely, the adaptive data sampling mechanism is proposed. The goal of the adaptive sampling mechanism is to find the appropriate samples representing the evolution of process object according to the dynamic feature of big data stream.

3.2   Data Sampling Process

The adaptive data sampling process is shown in Fig. 1. It consists of the following steps.

Life Cycle Recognition and Evolution Stages Partition. The life cycle of process object contains different continuous evolution stage. The performance and status of process object in different evolution stage is different. For modeling the process object accurately, data should be sampled from different evolution stages. So the first step is to recognize the life cycle of process object and partition the life cycle into different evolution stages according to the status of process object.

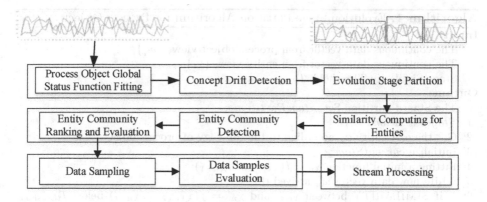

Fig. 1. Adaptive data sampling process.

Entity Community Detection and Ranking. In different evolution stages, the association between entities is different. The impact and role of entity in different evolution stage is different. Then in a certain evolution stage, the relevant entities are partitioned into community based on their behaviour similarity and associations. These communities are the sources of data sampling.

Data Sampling and Evaluation. After evolution stages partition and entity community detection, data sampling is processed to sample appropriate data for modeling process object.

Stream-Based Data Sampling and Evaluation. For big data stream environment of process object, a streaming processing architecture is proposed for sampling efficiently.

3.3 Evolution Stages Partition

The process object evolves along with time. There are many stages where the performance of process object is different. The underlying data representing the evolution stage is also different. For modeling the evolution of process object, the stages of evolution should be partitioned. Then data could be sampled through different evolution stages accordingly.

For data stream, concept drift could be detected and the evolution of data stream could be partitioned into different stages. For process object, the evolution life cycle could be partitioned into different stages. In a certain evolution stage, the process object lies in a steady state. When concept drift occurs, it means that process object move from one steady state to another new steady state. The data belonging to the same steady state could be collected and sampled for modeling the steady state of process object. Based on this idea, a evolution stage partition mechanism is proposed, as shown in Algorithm 1.

Algorithm 1. Evolution Stage Partition Algorithm for Process Object.

Input:
    The continuous data vector from process object view, $\{\omega_{t_i}\}$;
    The continuous data vector from entity view, $\{\chi_i\}$;
    Stage Similarity Threshold, $T_{StageThreshold}$;
Output:
    The Stages Partition Set, $StagePartitions$;
  1: $StagePartitions = \varnothing$;
  2: Get the exit entity x_n according to the topology of process object;
  3: Initialize $currentStage$;
  4: Fitting a initial function $\chi_n = f(\chi_1, \chi_2, ..., \chi_{n-1})$;
  5: **while** new data vector ω_{t_i} arrived **do**
  6:     **if** SIMILARITY between χ_{n,t_i} and $\chi_n' = f(\chi_1, \chi_2, ..., \chi_{n-1})$ below $T_{threshold}$ **then**
  7:         Process object is still in a steady state;
  8:         Prepare for next data vector $\omega_{t_{i+1}}$;
  9:     **else**
10:         Process object is moving to a new steady state;
11:         Prepare for fitting a new function for new steady state;
12:         Add the old steady state into set $StagePartitions$;
13:     **end if**
14: **end while**
15: **return** $StagePartitions$;

Using the topology of process object, the exit entity could be found. Based on concept drift in data stream, a fitting function could be used to detect change of underlying data distribution. When the fitting function is no longer available for the newly data vector of process object, it means that the process object is moving from one old steady state to another new state. A new evolution stage is found. Along with the time, the evolution stages is recorded into the set $StagePartitions$.

3.4   Entity Community Detection

Data could be sampled from the different evolution stage. However, in the same evolution stage, the importance and influence of entities are different. So the entities in the same evolution stage could be grouped into different clusters. Data could be sampled from these clusters to model in a certain steady stage.

For finding the similar entities in the same evolution stage, a entity community detection algorithm is proposed, as shown in Algorithm 2.

Consider the χ_i is a time-series data about entity X_i. In process object, association between entities are not in real-time fashion. There is time delay when change propagate [4,8,16,20]. So when compute the similarity between entities, it is important to take into account the time delay of associations. Based on previous work [4,8,16,20], the time delay between entities could be found. Then the similarity matrix based on Dynamic Time Warping (DTW) could be

---

Algorithm 2. Entity Community Detection for Process Object.

Input:

    Entity Vector Set in a certain Evolution Stage S_j, $\{\chi_i | \chi_i = (x_{i,t_m}, x_{i,t_{m+1}}, ..., x_{i,t_n}), [t_m, t_n] = TimeRange(S_j)\}$;

    The number of entity community, m;

Output:

    Entity Community Set, $EntityCommunity$;

1: Compute Similarity Matrix of $\{\chi_i\}$ using Dynamic Time Warping;
2: Adjust the Similarity Matrix by time delay influence;
3: Select m points in $\{\chi_i\}$;
4: Using k-means to finding cluster $EntityCommunity$ considering time delay;
5: Return $EntityCommunity$;

---

adjusted into a more appropriate state. Then k-means clustering methods could be used to find the entity communities in a certain evolution stage.

3.5 Data Sampling

After the evolution stages partition and entity community detection, the whole big data stream could be partitioned into different groups, which contain rich information about evolution of process object. Then the next step is to choose appropriate data for modeling.

For finding appropriate data for process object modeling, a adaptive sampling algorithm is proposed, as shown in Algorithm 3.

Algorithm 3. Adaptive Data Sampling for Process Object.

Input:

    The continuous data vector from process object view, $\{\omega_{t_i}\}$;

    The continuous data vector from entity view, $\{\chi_i\}$;

    Stage Similarity Threshold, $T_{StageThreshold}$;

    The number of entity community in each evolution stage, m;

Output:

    Sample Data Set, $SampleData$;

1: Call Algorithm 1 to get the stages partition set $StagePartition = \{Stage_i\}$;
2: Call Algorithm 2 to get the entity community set $EntityCommunity_i$ in evolution stage $Stage_i$;
3: **for** each community $c_{m,i}$ in $EntityCommunity_i$ in every stage $Stage_i$ **do**
4:     Initialize a sliding window;
5:     Get the average dispersion degree of communities in $EntityCommunity_i$;
6:     Slide the window to make the dispersion degree maximum;
7:     Get data from the max dispersion degree window as $sample_i$ for $Stage_i$;
8:     Add $sample_i$ to $SampleData$
9: **end for**
10: Return $SampleData$;

The proposed algorithm firstly use Algorithms 1 and 2 to get the evolution stage partition and the community set in each evolution stage. Then based on the average of dispersion degree of community set in certain evolution stage, the sliding window mechanism is proposed to get the appropriate window that contain the data varies greatly. It means that it contain much more rich information, which could be use for process modeling.

4   Experiments and Analysis

In this section, experiments and analysis are made to demonstrate the effectiveness of the proposed adaptive data sampling mechanism.

There has been a lot of public data set on the web, such as UCI machine learning repository [3]. The PM2.5 Data Set [10] in UCI machine learning repository is chose for experiments. The data time period is between Jan 1st, 2010 to Dec 31st, 2014. The attributes include row number, year, month, day, hour, PM2.5 concentration, dew point, temperature, pressure, combined wind direction, cumulated hours of snow and cumulated hours of rain.

Considering the PM2.5 data set, the PM2.5 concentration, dew point and temperature interact. In the proposed approach, these could be modeled as entities in process object. The association between entities could be modeled through process object. In our setting, the PM2.5 concentration is the focus, which could be the exit entity or dependent variable in process object. Other entities could be independent variables.

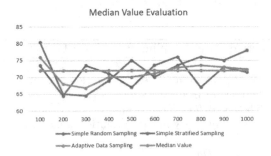

Fig. 2. Median value evaluation.

Given the simple random sampling, simple stratified sampling, and adaptive data sampling, the accuracy of sampling is compared. Data samples should preserve the synopsis of all data. Consider the mean value and median value, experiments are made to make a comparison between these three data samplings, as shown in Figs. 3 and 2.

The PM2.5 data set contains 41,757 data records. The three sampling mechanism is used to sample data at different scales, from 100 samples to 1000 samples. As we can see from the experiment result, the adaptive data sampling could get a more accurate synopsis of the PM2.5 data set.

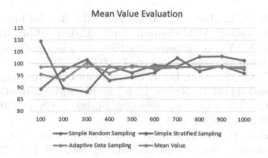

Fig. 3. Mean value evaluation.

5   Conclusion

For modeling the evolution of process object, data should be sampled from big data streams. For finding the appropriate data samples representing the evolution of process object, a adaptive data sampling mechanism is proposed in this paper. Experiments demonstrate the effectiveness of the proposed adaptive data sampling mechanism for process object. In future research, the role of entity played in evolution of process object should be considered. Based on data sampling from big data stream, association between entities could be modeled. Considering the local evolution between entities, the global evolution of process object could be modeled.

Acknowledgment. This work was supported by the National Natural Science Foundation of China (No. 61472232), Natural Science Foundation of Shandong Province of China (No. ZR2017BF016), and the Science and Technology Program of University of Jinan (No. XKY1623).

References

1. de Andrade Silva, J., Hruschka, E.R., Gama, J.: An evolutionary algorithm for clustering data streams with a variable number of clusters. Expert Syst. Appl. **67**, 228–238 (2017). https://doi.org/10.1016/j.eswa.2016.09.020
2. Bodyanskiy, Y.V., Tyshchenko, O.K., Kopaliani, D.S.: An evolving connectionist system for data stream fuzzy clustering and its online learning. Neurocomputing **262**, 41–56 (2017)
3. Dheeru, D., Karra Taniskidou, E.: UCI machine learning repository (2017). http://archive.ics.uci.edu/ml
4. Du, T., Qu, S., Hua, Z.: A novel timing series calculation algorithm based on statistical extremum for process object. In: 9th International Conference on Computer and Automation Engineering, ICCAE 2017, Sydney, Australia, 18–21 February 2017, pp. 94–98 (2017)
5. Duda, P., Jaworski, M., Rutkowski, L.: On ensemble components selection in data streams scenario with reoccurring concept-drift. In: 2017 IEEE Symposium Series on Computational Intelligence, SSCI, pp. 1–7. IEEE (2017)

6. Gama, J., Žliobaitė, I., Bifet, A., Pechenizkiy, M., Bouchachia, A.: A survey on concept drift adaptation. ACM Comput. Surv. (CSUR) **46**(4), 44 (2014)
7. Gong, S., Zhang, Y., Yu, G.: Clustering stream data by exploring the evolution of density mountain. arXiv preprint arXiv:1710.00867 (2017)
8. Hua, Z., Du, T., Qu, S., Mou, G.: A data stream clustering algorithm based on density and extended grid. In: Huang, D.-S., Jo, K.-H., Figueroa-García, J.C. (eds.) ICIC 2017. LNCS, vol. 10362, pp. 689–699. Springer, Cham (2017). https://doi.org/10.1007/978-3-319-63312-1_61
9. Hyde, R., Angelov, P., MacKenzie, A.: Fully online clustering of evolving data streams into arbitrarily shaped clusters. Inf. Sci. **382**, 96–114 (2017)
10. Liang, X., et al.: Assessing Beijing's PM2.5 pollution: severity, weather impact, APEC and winter heating. Proc. Roy. Soc. Lond. A: Math. Phys. Eng. Sci. **471**(2182) (2015). https://doi.org/10.1098/rspa.2015.0257
11. Pears, R., Sakthithasan, S., Koh, Y.S.: Detecting concept change in dynamic data streams. Mach. Learn. **97**(3), 259–293 (2014)
12. Puschmann, D., Barnaghi, P., Tafazolli, R.: Adaptive clustering for dynamic IoT data streams. IEEE Internet Things J. **4**(1), 64–74 (2017)
13. Ross, G.J., Tasoulis, D.K., Adams, N.M.: Nonparametric monitoring of data streams for changes in location and scale. Technometrics **53**(4), 379–389 (2011)
14. Sethi, T.S., Kantardzic, M.: Handling adversarial concept drift in streaming data. Expert Syst. Appl. **97**, 18–40 (2018)
15. Sidhu, P., Bhatia, M.: Online approach to handle concept drifting data streams using diversity. Int. Arab J. Inf. Technol. (IAJIT) **14**(3), 293–299 (2017)
16. Song, Q., Guo, Q., Wang, K., Du, T., Qu, S., Zhang, Y.: A scheme for mining state association rules of process object based on big data. J. Comput. Commun. **2**(14), 17–24 (2014)
17. Tennant, M., Stahl, F., Rana, O., Gomes, J.B.: Scalable real-time classification of data streams with concept drift. Future Gener. Comput. Syst. **75**, 187–199 (2017)
18. Wang, L.Y., Park, C., Yeon, K., Choi, H.: Tracking concept drift using a constrained penalized regression combiner. Comput. Stat. Data Anal. **108**, 52–69 (2017)
19. Yarlagadda, A., Jonnalagedda, M., Munaga, K.: Clustering based on correlation fractal dimension over an evolving data stream. Int. Arab J. Inf. Technol. **15**(1), 1–9 (2018)
20. Zhu, T., Du, T., Qu, S., Zhu, L.: A novel timing calculation algorithm based on statistical extremum for the time series of process object. Hans J. Data Min. **6**(4), 179–191 (2016)

MedusaVM: Decentralizing Virtual Memory System for Multithreaded Applications on Many-core

Miao Cai[1,2]([⊠]) [iD], Shenming Liu[1,2], Weiyong Yang[1,2], and Hao Huang[1,2]

[1] State Key Laboratory for Novel Software Technology, Nanjing University,
Nanjing, China
[2] Department of Computer Science and Technology, Nanjing University,
Nanjing, China
miaogecm@gmail.com, liushenming2@gmail.com,
yangweiyong@sgepri.sgcc.com.cn, hhuang@nju.edu.cn

Abstract. Virtual memory system multiplexes the single physical memory for multiple running processes with two centralized resources, i.e., virtual memory space and page table hierarchy. However, for multi-threaded applications running a single address space, current centralized VM system design encounters severe scalability bottlenecks and significantly impedes the application speedup increment on many-core systems. This paper proposes a novel VM system called MEDUSAVM to scale VM system to many cores. To this end, MEDUSAVM partitions the global virtual memory space and page table tree in a memory-efficient way, eliminating performance interference and lock contention between cores. Moreover, MEDUSAVM also provides a traditional shared memory interface for multithreaded applications.

Our prototype system is implemented based on Linux kernel 4.4.0 and glibc 2.23. Experimental results evaluated on a 32-core machine demonstrate that MEDUSAVM scales much better than Linux kernel and uses 22× less memory compared with the state-of-art approach. For microbenchmarks experiments, MEDUSAVM achieves nearly linear performance speedup. In multithreaded applications Metis and Psearchy, MEDUSAVM also significantly outperforms Linux kernel by up to a factor of 2.5×.

Keywords: Virtual memory system · Multithreaded application · Many-core system

1 Introduction

Multithreaded programming model sharing address space has been pervasively deployed due to its programming convenience and expected performance gains benefit from many-core systems [5,7]. However, current virtual memory systems in commodity operating systems exhibit poor scalability performance and under-utilize such hardware system parallelism [2,7,8,17].

© Springer Nature Switzerland AG 2018
J. Vaidya and J. Li (Eds.): ICA3PP 2018, LNCS 11334, pp. 267–283, 2018.
https://doi.org/10.1007/978-3-030-05051-1_19

OS kernels adopt several centralized design approaches to maintain a shared address space view for parallel executing threads. This paper focuses on the scalability problems introduced by such designs. First, commonly-used OS kernels (e.g., Linux kernel) provide a shared virtual memory space for applications which is split into a set of memory mapping regions. These regions are tracked with specific metadata (`vm_area_struct` in Linux kernel) which organized in a binary search tree (BST) data structure. However, concurrent tree operations like *insert*, *remove* and *lookup* are serialize by the global tree lock, e.g., `mm_sem` in Linux kernel. Coarse-grained locks not only serialize concurrent VM system operations but also induce severe lock contention [3,5,8,12]. Existing techniques such as refining current lock implementation or designing new lock scheme [12] only can mitigate the scalability bottlenecks. Other commodity OS kernels, such as FreeBSD and Solaris, follow the similar design approach and thus also face such scalability issues [7].

Further, threads share all memory mappings in a single page table tree. When they access these mappings, there would be multiple page faults manipulating centralized page table concurrently. So OS kernels protect the page table tree with a global lock (PGDIR lock) or a more fine-grained lock–separate lock per page table page (PTE lock). Since one page table page consists of 512 page table entries, even for fine-grained lock scheme, there would be hundreds of parallel executing threads accessing the page table pages under worst scenario, which results in heavy lock contention [5,8].

To deal with these problems, several approaches [7,8,12,17,18] have been proposed. Achieving the goals for VM system scalability, efficiency, and low memory consumption simultaneously are challenging. For example, BonsaiVM [7] applies rcu lock to the VM system, whereas it prohibits writers to proceed in parallel with readers. Cerberus [17] dispatches VM system requests into multiple guest kernels to mitigate shared data and lock contention. Unfortunately, there still exists contention inside same guest OS. SPECK [18] kernel utilizes scalable memory reclamation to reduce region tree lock contention, but they did not optimize the page table tree scalability. RadixVM [8] could achieve nearly linear performance speedup for applications, but it requires significant memory usage owing to its separate per-core page tables and radix tree data structure, as well as causes system inefficiency due to shared virtual memory space.

In this paper, we propose MEDUSAVM to address the above challenges. MEDUSAVM partitions the global virtual memory space into multiple disjoint, continuous per-core virtual memory spaces called *memory pool*. For each memory pool, MEDUSAVM applies a highly concurrent skiplist [11] with safe memory reclamation [13] as the backing store data structure. Independent index data structure per memory pool not only can improve the scalability within the same pool but also eliminate the operation interference between disjoint pools [8]. So threads can allocate, reclaim, modify memory mapping regions in their independent pools without any performance interference or lock contention. Then, through jointly combining separate per-core and shared page table approaches, we present a *hybrid page table* design aiming to achieve system scalability and memory-efficiency simultaneously. For private memory mapping regions, threads can access their page table entries in a *conflict-freedom* fashion. While for shared ones, MEDUSAVM allows multiple threads to handle page faults concurrently in a *wait-free* access manner.

We design and implement our prototype system in Linux kernel 4.4.0 and glibc 2.23. We also evaluate MEDUSAVM on an Intel 32-core machine with two microbenchmarks in THREADBENCH [5] and two VM-intensive multithreaded applications Metis & Psearchy in MOSBENCH [2]. Experimental results suggest that our scheme can eliminate VM system bottlenecks inside operating system kernel efficiently. For microbenchmark evaluation, MEDUSAVM exhibits nearly linear performance speedup and significantly reduces physical memory usage by up to 22× compared with previous work. Moreover, in application-level experiments, MEDUSAVM improves the performance by up to 2.5× relative to Linux kernel.

In summary, we make the following contributions in this paper:

- First, we explore and identify the existing scalability bottlenecks in commodity VM system;
- Second, through decentralizing VM system resources and leveraging other parallel programming techniques, we propose MEDUSAVM scaling VM systems to many cores;
- Finally, experiment results demonstrate that MEDUSAVM greatly improves the system scalability as well as shows efficient memory usage.

The rest of paper is organized as follows. In Sect. 2 we present background and motivation of this paper. Then design and implementation are provided in Sect. 3. In Sect. 4, we evaluate MEDUSAVM with a series of microbenchmarks and applications. Finally, related works and conclusion are given in Sects. 5 and 6.

2   Background and Motivation

2.1   Centralized Address Space

In this section, we take the Linux kernel as an example to introduce the conventional centralized VM system design and its scalability issues. We only investigate the user part of address space on x86_64 architecture, while the kernel part is isolated from users' and has different management mechanism. A VM system mainly consists of two components for virtualizing hardware memory system: a process-specific virtual memory space which multiplexes limited hardware memory resource, and a page table tree which translates the virtual address into physical address assisted with MMU unit. Virtual address space is divided into disjoint memory regions, and kernel assigns specific VMA structures to record the detailed information about these regions. Any operations (e.g., `page fault`, `mprotect`) regarding to a region must lookup or modify this metadata, until this region is recycled via `munmap` system calls or process exits.

In Linux kernel, all VMA structures are indexed by their region ending address and organized in a red-black tree protected by a global reader-writer semaphore mm_sem. Global lock not only serializes concurrent VM system operations but also induces significant lock contention overheads. The straightforward approach is to optimize current lock implementation to reduce lock contention. For example, Linux kernel adopts an optimistic spinning strategy in case of blocking cost when threads fail to acquire the lock. However, this solution only can mitigate lock contention and fail to address scalability problems fundamentally. Alternative technique like parallelizing BST data structures often requires sophisticated software technologies [4,10] or specific hardware mechanism [16] in the many-core environment.

Previous VM systems [8,18], which allow threads to manipulate the global address space concurrently, unfortunately, their centralized designs introduce extra performance interference among threads. In particular, when multiple threads compete for inserting the node into the global tree, failing threads have to retry the same process until succeeding. In the concurrent environment, such operation interferences happen frequently and bring system performance degradation. Currently, Linux kernel provides a size of 128 TB virtual memory space for applications. However, centralized address space design prevents threads from exploiting such huge memory resource efficiently.

2.2   Centralized Page Table Tree

Page table hierarchy records the address space mappings between virtual addresses and physical addresses. Threads query the same page table, perform a page table walk on page table hierarchy and check access permissions at each tree level. When a page fault occurs, faulting thread acquires the page table lock, constructs the page table hierarchy if necessary and fills the page table entries. Linux kernel provides two lock schemes with different granularity protecting the page table: i one global PGDIR lock protects the whole page table tree; ii independent spin lock PTE lock associating with last two page table levels (PMD and PTE). Differentiate from reader-writer semaphore mm_sem, page table locks are ticket spin lock. Lock handoff between threads is expensive, which mainly caused by cache coherence protocol. Modifying global ticket lock indicator with atomic instructions on x86_64 architecture is costly. To achieve atomic access, processor triggers a signal to lock the bus to prevent other CPUs from accessing the memory unit concurrently, which limits parallelism. Moreover, once the lock owner releases the lock, all waiting cores must re-fetch the latest value of lock indicator. Because the system must deliver amounts of messages to maintain cache coherence, this store operation is significantly costly. According to experimental observation [5], it delivers a latency of ~600 cycles on 32 cores, which is over 32× compared with one single core.

The state-of-art solution to remove page table locks is using per-core page table [8]. However, maintaining separate page tables may introduce additional performance cost and high memory usage, because per-core page table incurs n page faults per mapped page for n cores, while shared page table only has one. Moreover, to map the physical page, separate page table consumes n times page table pages than shared page table for n cores. For example, the size of the MapReduce application Metis used in our experiment in Sect. 4 is around 1.3 MB. It requires 16 KB for page table pages to map this ELF binary file. In contrast, for separate page tables, it is in proportion to the core number and costs (16×32) 512 KB memory. Multithreaded applications with hundreds of dynamic-link libraries and thousands of file or anonymous mappings, obviously, it put great pressure on kernel memory allocator and would exhaust physical memory finally.

3   Design and Implementation

3.1   System Architecture

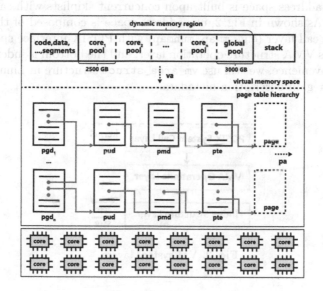

Fig. 1. System architecture

Figure 1 demonstrates our VM system architecture. Differentiating from other traditional VM systems, our architecture follows a decentralization strategy to avoid performance interference incurred by concurrent VM system operations. MEDUSAVM partitions the user virtual memory space into multiple *memory pools*. Notice that MEDUSAVM only partitions the memory space which is used for dynamic file or anonymous mappings. Regions which map code segment, data segment or stack remain intact. Every core has an individual memory pool, and all cores share a global memory pool. On current x86_64 48-bits virtual memory space, each memory pool is ~2500 GB, and all cores share a ~3000 GB global memory pool, which is sufficient for most applications' virtual memory requirement. MEDUSAVM assigns independent concurrent skiplist for organizing region metadata in each memory pool. It is important for system scalability because frequent accessing the same skiplist would cause unexpected cache line contention, which incurred by modifying interior nodes.

Further, MEDUSAVM decentralizes page table tree in a hybrid manner aiming to achieve system scalability and memory efficiency at the same time. When threads share the memory mapping regions with MAP_SHARED mapping flag, they also share the corresponding page table pages but perform concurrent page table entry access with *compare-and-swap* instructions. Otherwise, MEDUSAVM retains the conflict-freedom access for private memory mappings, which will not induce a single cache line bounce. We will discuss it in detail in Sect. 3.3.

3.2   Concurrent Address Space with SMR

Our scalable address space is built upon concurrent skiplists with safe memory reclamation. As shown in Fig. 2, our address space is composed of three layers: top is system call layer (e.g., mmap, munmap) with POSIX interface specification, middle level is VMA structure operation layer, and the bottom is index structure layer. For convenience, we still use vm_area_struct structure in Linux kernel as our memory region description metadata.

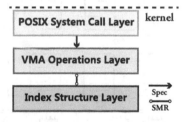

Fig. 2. VM system layers

Index structure layer leverages concurrent skiplist as the backing storing data structure for each core's memory pool. Every level in skiplist can be seen as a lock-free linked list, and the higher level list is the shortcut of the lower one. Thus our skiplist implementation provides lock-free *insert*, *remove* and *lookup* methods.

Garbage Collection. In case of *ABA hazard* or *access hazard* [11,13], an efficient GC algorithm based on hazard pointer [13] is integrated into index structure layer. Everytime each thread accesses current node curr and its predecessor pred while traversing each level in skiplist. These skiplist nodes could be freed by other concurrent threads, leading to memory access hazard. So we protect these memory nodes with hazard pointers. When a node is not linked in any levels of skiplist, it means the node can be freed. Thus the thread puts it on its local garbage list. Once accumulating some number of retired nodes, the thread will take a snapshot of all hazard pointers posted by others, and organize them in a hash table to guarantee $O(1)$ search time. After scanning all nodes protected by hazard pointers, it will free the node only after it confirms that the node is not used by others, or keep it until next scan. This method is *wait-free* since all threads share no data structure in GC system and it requires only one atomic operation (*read* or *write*) in core operations. Further, it is efficient because we use a hash table to keep constant search time for node retrieve. As it costs $O(M + N)$ excepted time in total, where M is the number of skiplist levels and N is the thread number.

The middle layer performs VMA structure operations, such as vma_insert, vma_remove. A vm_area_struct struct corresponds to a skiplist node in the bottom layer. When a thread invokes a mmap system call, MEDUSAVM allocates a VMA struct and a skiplist node. Then, it inserts this node into the skiplist. In contrast, the munmap system call would remove the corresponding VMA struct and skiplist node. Although skiplist nodes can be safely recycled by our GC system, unfortunately, directly freeing VMA structure may also cause *access hazard*. It is because other threads would access members of this VMA structure concurrently. To deal with this problem, we also reclaim these VMA structures based on the GC system. Specifically, any skiplist nodes store a pointer to the corresponding VMA structure. When thread performs vma_remove operation, it defers freeing VMA structure assisted with the GC system instead of freeing it directly. This defer-free scheme provides a safe memory grace period for other threads to access these VMA structures concurrently. They can access this VMA structure's members safely until free thread clears its hazard pointers and performs a reclamation operation on its garbage list.

The POSIX APIs specify the underlying system behaviors. Scalability commutativity rule [9] presents an insight into how to scale the system under APIs' constraint. If two address space operations commute, they can be implemented in a conflict-free way. However, pursuing such scalability sometimes is expensive, which sacrifices system efficiency and incurs huge memory usage.

For system calls like mmap and munmap, MEDUSAVM allocates, recycles and modifies the related memory regions in a decentralized way. MEDUSAVM prefers to manipulate the memory pool which thread belongs. For example, when the thread invokes mmap system call, MEDUSAVM first retrieves the local pool to find the memory region with enough size. If the thread has run out of its memory pool, the global pool will be retrieved. Fortunately, such situation is rare, and almost all requests can be serviced in thread's local pool. Then, the thread will create a VMA structure and insert it into the skiplist concurrently. Finally, MEDUSAVM calculates the region start address by aligning the region size according to different page table entry size (i.e., 512 GB, 1 GB, 2 MB, 4 KB). This policy can greatly reduce the number of shared page table entries and improves the page fault handling efficiency, as we will explain in Sect. 3.3.

3.3   Hybrid Page Table Design

Non-scalable page table locks prevent threads from accessing same page table entries concurrently. MEDUSAVM decentralizes hardware page table and coordinates differential page table entries to both reduce access contention and minimize page fault cost. Specifically, in MEDUSAVM, if multiple threads share the memory mapping regions with mapping flag MAP_SHARED, they use *compare-and-swap* (CAS) atomic instruction to fill the page table entries when page faults occur. Since CAS guarantees that *only one thread could be successful in updating the page table entry,* threads who fail just free their duplicated page back to the kernel. Such procedure is *wait-free*–any threads could finish this with finite steps (bounded by thread number). Otherwise, for private memory mapping regions (MAP_PRIVATE), Every thread constructs own core's page table hierarchy independently. Accesses to per-core page table pages are *conflict-free* and never cause a cache line contention.

However, existing memory mapping classification would face a dilemma with hybrid page table design. For instance, when thread substitutes its original address space via the exec system call, the kernel will load the ELF file and other necessary dynamic-link files into the memory. Currently, kernel maps those segments with MAP_PRIVATE mapping flag. It consumes much more memory to map these files than shared page tables, even access to these mappings are less contended. According to our observation, other private mappings may also meet this problem. The straightforward solution is to replace the mapping flag MAP_PRIVATE with MAP_SHARED. However, it may violate the semantics of current page fault handler, because kernel would handle the page faults as copy-on-write for private file mapping regions, while direct-write for shared file mapping regions.

To keep the semantics, MEDUSAVM divides all memory mapping regions into two categories: *core-shared* and *core-private*. Memory mapping region of *core-shared* means processors share this region so that they share the corresponding page table pages. Otherwise, this memory mapping region is private to the core, and it has separate page table subtree for this region. We treat threads' stack as private memory mapping region. On the contrary, some other segments are *core-shared*, such as code segment, data segment, bss segment, segments of dynamic-link files and program heap. Then, MEDUSAVM captures the application's mapping intention via MAP_FLAG in mmap system call. Any memory mapping region requests with MAP_SHARED are treat as *core-shared* or *core-private* otherwise. We also add a mapping flag MAP_CSHARED to instruct kernel to distinguish *core-shared* regions with others.

For x86_64 4-level hardware page table, MEDUSAVM supports sharing four different levels of page table entries, i.e., PGD entry (512 GB), PUD entry (1 GB), PMD entry (2 MB) and PT entry (4 KB). A memory mapping region may contain several kinds of page table entries. For instance, a shared memory mapping with a size of 266256 KB (1 GB × 1 + 2 MB × 8 + 4 KB × 16). It consumes at least one PUD entry, eight PMD entries and sixteen PT entries in page table tree. There could be substantial page table entries belonging to a memory map-

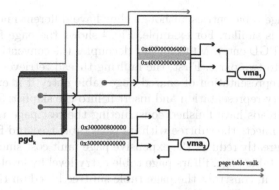

Fig. 3. Page fault execution flow of MEDUSAVM

ping region. So MEDUSAVM must retrieve these entries quickly during page fault procedure. For all page table entries associating with the *core-shared* VMA structure, MEDUSAVM use a *representation* structure to represent the page table entry and organizes these representations in a concurrent skiplist for progress guarantee which is same as the one in Sect. 3.1.

Figure 3 demonstrates the page fault execution flow of our hybrid page table design. During fault procedure, page fault handler has to distinguish whether current page table entry is shared or not. To this end, MEDUSAVM compares the two mapping ranges (page table entry at current page table level and memory mapping region). If the range of page table entry is inclusive within mapping range of VMA, it indicates that threads share this page table entry and its lower level entries. So threads have to fill this entry in shared mode, as we will explain later. Otherwise, this page table entry is private, and threads fill the entry on its own.

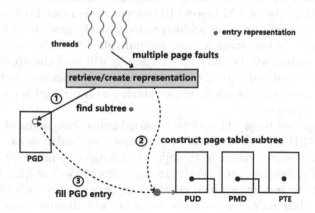

Fig. 4. Page fault flow of shared PGD entry

For shared page table entries, although they have different mapping size, the handling process is similar. For example, Fig. 4 shows the page fault execution flow for a shared PGD entry. MEDUSAVM decouples the conventional page fault execution flow into two parts. First, the faulting thread retrieves the skiplist to find the related representation of shared page table entry if it exists. If not, it will create an entry representation and insert it into the skiplist. Then, it checks whether other threads have finished constructing the rest page table hierarchy. If so, it simply connects the subtree with its page table tree and finishes in Step ①. This process greatly reduces the expensive page fault cost since threads need not allocate page table page, fill its page table entry level by level. Otherwise, in Step ②, threads will construct the page table subtree based on the entry representation concurrently. They allocate the specific page table page and performs a CAS operation to fill the corresponding page table entries (i.e., PUD, PMD, PT). If threads fail, they free the page back to the kernel memory allocator and continue this process until the last level of the page table. Finally, in Step ③, faulting threads connect the subtree to their page table hierarchy to complete the page fault.

3.4 Implementation and Bootstrap

We implement our prototype system in Linux kernel 4.4.0 and glibc 2.23. Currently, MEDUSAVM supports legacy virtual memory layout, i.e., dynamic mapping region starts from the heap and can grow up to stack. Complete replacing Linux VM system with ours is labor-intensive and complex [8], so we provide another solution to bootstrap our VM system flexibly. We add a new system call called `flex_vm_boot` which has one argument `vm_type` into Linux kernel. This approach offers much flexibility for multithreaded applications to choose which alternative VM system to run, either traditional lock-based VM system (i.e., `LINUX_VM`) or our scalable one (i.e., `MEDUSA_VM`). It also brings much convenience for debugging our VM system during system implementation. Once application determines which type of VM system to run via system call `flex_vm_boot`, we substitute application's previous address space with the new one. The bootstrap process is similar to executing a `exec` system call. First, the new VM system including GC system will be initialized. Then, it will load the application ELF binary from the hard disk into the memory, link with other necessary dynamic-link files, prepare application's new user stack and heap, and set up the entry point back to userspace, etc.

For dynamic-link binary files, default kernel maps these segments with mapping flag `MAP_PRIVATE` but MEDUSAVM requires they loaded as *core-shared*. We modify glibc's dynamic loader *ld* to support this memory mapping shared pattern. When *ld* parses the `.got` and `.plt` segments of loading ELF files, it asks kernel to load the segments which contains extern symbols with `MAP_CSHARED` mapping flag. MEDUSAVM maps these segments and allocates page table pages for all cores. After application finishes substituting the address space, it will start running on our scalable, efficient VM system. When application exits by invoking `exit` system call, it will destroy all its memory mappings, free the nodes in garbage lists of GC system, reclaim page table pages on each CPUs, leave the data structures (i.e., `mm_struct`) and PGD pages for other processes to recycle.

4   Evaluation

All experiments are performed on an Intel 32-core machine with four Xeon e5-2650 processors and 32 GB memory. Each processor has eight physical cores running at 2.0 GHZ. Our evaluation uses two microbenchmarks (*memalloc*, *hashtable*) in THREADBENCH [5] and two application benchmarks (Metis and Psearchy) from MOSBENCH [2]. We compare MEDUSAVM with several approaches, including default Linux kernel, prwlock [12] and RCUVM [7]. Below is a brief introduction of our benchmarks.

memalloc: This microbenchmark simulates a per-core memory allocator. Each thread pinning to its processor repeats the same working process. First, it allocates a private fix-size (256 KB) anonymous memory mapping via `mmap` system call with mapping flag `MAP_PRIVATE & MAP_ANON`. Then, it writes some random content into every physical page of this memory region to trigger page faults. Finally, it destroys the memory mapping via `munmap` system call. This benchmark pressures both the kernel virtual memory space and page table management. And such usage pattern is commonly used in real workloads.

hashtable: In this benchmark, we allocate a big size of memory region (200 MB) to map a file (`MAP_FILE & MAP_SHARED`). This region can be seen as a large database table or hash table. Then each thread performs read or write operations to every physical page in this memory region in a random order. Such operations result in substantial page faults (∼1,638,400 on 32 cores) and would cause heavy lock contention. In order to avoid disk I/O bottlenecks, all files are stored in `tmpfs`.

Metis: Metis is a MapReduce library on single multicore systems, which is widely used in benchmarking VM system scalability [2,7,8,18]. Metis uses Streamflow memory allocator [15] to mitigate Linux VM system scalability bottlenecks. While we aim to fully stress the VM system scalability, so we design and implement a simple, efficient, straightforward memory allocator *pcmalloc* for Metis and other applications benchmarked. In *pcmalloc*, we use per-core private free memory block list. When each thread requests small size of memory via `malloc`, *pcmalloc* preallocates a big size of memory from OS kernel, splits the memory into blocks with different sizes, organizes these memory blocks in buddy lists and returns a suitable size of block to the thread. When thread needs a big size memory allocation request beyond the prefix threshold (default is 16 KB), *pcmalloc* directly allocates it from OS kernel via `mmap` system call and `munmap` it after thread returns it to glibc via invoking `free`.

Psearchy: Psearchy contains a file indexer and a query. We only target at its index component because it is more VM system intensive. During its indexing process, each thread prepares a big hash table (32 MB) for storing the index results. Then, Psearchy thread opens each file with `fopen` function provided by glibc library. To accelerate file reading, glibc invokes `mmap` system call to load the file into memory. The thread reads each file's content and records each word's position in its local hash table. It closes the file via `munmap` system call. Finally, it writes the results in a BerkeleyDB file.

We distribute all worker threads on available cores evenly in experiments and group cores on as few sockets as possible to minimize access overhead due to cross-socket or cross-node. All evaluations run three times, and we report the average of three runs.

4.1 Microbenchmark Experiments

memalloc: We run this benchmark on the 32-core machine while varying the core number from 1 to 32. Figure 5a shows performance results of *memalloc* running on two different VM systems. *memalloc* scales poorly on Linux kernel VM system. Application total throughput on 32 cores even degrades as the single core. We use the profiling tool OProfile to collect the distribution of each function. Table 1 shows the top 5 hottest function in profiling report. There are several scalability bottlenecks in Linux VM system. Heavy lock contention is caused by memory region tree lock `mm_sem`, wait queue lock `wait_lock` and page table lock. *memalloc* spends almost 70% of executing time in acquiring these locks running on 32 cores. Although prwlock and RCUVM both utilize scalable lock schemes to mitigate heavy lock contention, threads still have to be serialized for servicing VM system requests which leads to their poor performance. In contrast, MEDUSAVM completely avoids these bottlenecks due to its decentralized virtual memory space and page table tree. Besides, MEDUSAVM services all these concurrent requests in each independent memory pool hence induces no performance interference. Together, all these factors contribute to *memalloc* nearly linear performance speedup on MEDUSAVM.

Table 1. Top 5 hottest functions

Function name	Percent
native_queued_spin_lock_slowpath	46.5%
osq_lock	13.2%
down_read_trylock	6.1%
rwsem_spin_on_owner	4.3%
smp_call_function_many	1.9%

hashtable: Benchmark *hashtable* stresses the scalability and performance of page table design. Figure 5b shows experimental results. When *hashtable* runs on few cores, total throughput for each scheme continues increasing. Linux kernel outperforms MEDUSAVM under 2-core configuration because MEDUSAVM spends extra time in managing the representation of page table entries in skiplist. However, as the number of cores increases, *hashtable* becomes bottlenecked by page table lock contention. Profiling results suggest that it spends 30% of execution time in contending the page table lock for Linux kernel VM system. While throughput of MEDUSAVM and RCUVM still increase because both of them have more scalable page fault than prwlock and Linux kernel.

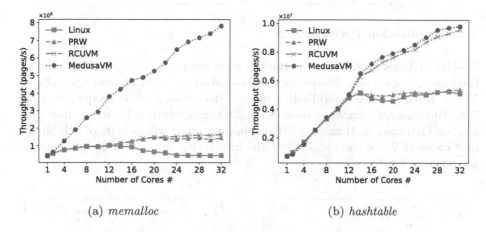

(a) *memalloc*

(b) *hashtable*

Fig. 5. Microbenchmark throughput on each VM system

Since *hashtable* is VM-intensive and requires substantial page table pages to map the big hash table. We take this microbenchmark as an example to study the physical memory consumption of our hybrid page table design. Table 2 summarizes the memory usage of three page table designs for different memory requirements on 32-core configuration. We vary the size of hash table mapped, because *hashtable* would write to every page of the hash table. It is the worst-case for three page table schemes. Linux consumes 53 page table pages to map a 100 MB hash table, and another 30 KB memory for mapping application image file, dynamic-link files, stack and other memory regions. While MEDUSAVM spends 584 KB memory for mapping the hash table, it also uses 128 KB per-thread stack and an additional 176 KB for shared or private mappings. Finally, Per-core page tables would incur 30.12× more memory than Linux and 5.76× over ours.

Moreover, it is noticeable that MEDUSAVM only costs 1.41× memory over shared page table for 1 GB hash table on 32 cores. It is due to our memory allocation strategy. The memory region size of the hash table is 1 GB, so MEDUSAVM aligns the start address to a PMD page. Therefore, all cores' page tables share the PUD entry (1 GB) and its lower-level page table pages, while per-core page table scheme has to use ~60 MB memory mapping 1 GB hash table in all cores' page tables.

Table 2. Memory usage with different page table schemes

RSS	Memory usage (rel. to Linux)		
	Shared	Hybrid	Per-core
100 MB	242 KB	1.24 MB (5.23×)	7.12 MB (30.12×)
500 MB	303 KB	2.12 MB (7.16×)	9.23 MB (31.19×)
1 GB	2.15 MB	3.02 MB (1.41×)	67.27 MB (31.29×)

4.2 Application Performance

Metis: In Metis experiment, we run the word inverse indexing application with the input file size 1 GB. The prefix threshold of our memory allocator *pcmalloc* is 32 KB. During the Map and Reduce phases, Metis would invoke `mmap` system call 788,310 times and `munmap` system call 3,520 times, which is far more than glibc `malloc` (100 `mmap` & 31 `munmap`). Therefore, *pcmalloc* will help us to exhibit the root cause of VM system scalability and investigate our system design schemes, as shown in Fig. 6a.

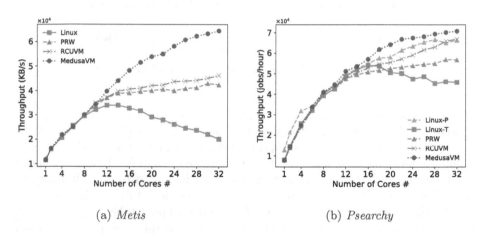

(a) *Metis*   (b) *Psearchy*

Fig. 6. Application throughput on each VM system

MEDUSAVM performs slightly worse than Linux kernel due to its performance overhead in page table management at a small number of cores (1–6). However, as the number of cores exceeds twelve, the application's total throughput on MEDUSAVM outperforms Linux kernel, which achieves a speedup of 2.36× over native Linux kernel on 32 cores. During merge and reduce phases, the system will reclaim memories for storing Map phase results which indirectly invokes `munmap` system calls. It results that Metis suffers from performance overhead caused by maintaining system TLB coherency on MEDUSAVM. Profiling results show that MEDUSAVM speeds 7% time in `smp_call_function_many` functions on 32 cores, which leads to the degraded speedup increment. RCUVM outperforms than prwlock in Metis experiment, because rcu lock allows one writer to execute in parallel with readers which contributes to more performance benefit, while prwlock prohibits such situation. However, both of them perform significantly worse than our approach since MEDUSAVM allows writers to proceed with each other concurrently.

Psearchy: Like Metis, we also use *pcmalloc* as the memory allocator in Psearchy experiment. Each thread in Psearchy uses `fopen` to read files, which internally invokes `mmap` & `munmap` system calls. In the default configuration, Psearchy uses `MAP_SHARED` flags to mmap files into the physical memory. For scalability optimization, we substitute it with `MAP_PRIVATE` to avoid cache line contention caused by atomic instructions on MEDUSAVM. In our experiment, we use Psearchy to index glibc-2.23 source files, which is a size of 359 MB and contains total 15,402 source files. Each thread processes own files independently. Psearchy will invoke `mmap` 46,928 times and `munmap` 44,349 times, both for reading files and memory allocator. We cache all files into the `tmpfs` to avoid I/O bottlenecks. Since threads of Psearchy never communicate with each other during its running first phase. So we also run the *multiprocess* version of Psearchy (**Linux-P**) in the experiment. Figure 6b shows the performance results on MEDUSAVM and two configurations of Psearchy on Linux kernel.

Both Linux-P and MEDUSAVM have isolated virtual memory spaces for processes/threads, so the performance speedup of these two configurations continue increasing. Multiprocess Psearchy has completely independent address space for every worker process, while threads on MEDUSAVM share the memory mappings. So processes of Psearchy have to establish the shared memory during the second phase. This accounts for the performance difference between MEDUSAVM and Linux-P. In contrast, *multithreaded* Psearchy (**Linux-T**) suffers from these scalability bottlenecks on Linux kernel. Application performance on Linux kernel starts to degrade on 16 cores, while MEDUSAVM outperforms 70% than Linux kernel on 32 cores. Similar to Metis experiment, there is a performance gap between RCUVM and prwlock because rcu lock is more scalable than the reader-writer lock. However, glibc sort function `msort_with_tmp` limits the speedup increment of multiprocess Psearchy and MEDUSAVM. Profiling results show that application spends 11% of execution time in sorting words on MEDUSAVM for 32 cores, which causes the decreased speedup.

5   Related Work

Recently, there are some research works aim at scaling the VM system. Clements et al. [7, 8] proposed two VM systems based on tree-like data structures (BONSAI & RadixTree) to address scalability problems. By leveraging RCU synchronization techniques, BONSAI VM system makes page fault scale to large numbers of cores. Readers (i.e., page fault) could proceed with either readers or writers concurrently. However, limiting by RCU, BONSAI VM system serializes multiple writers' execution. To overcome this limitation, Clements proposed a RadixVM system. By employing a scalable radix tree, per-core page tables, and other techniques, RadixVM could achieve linear scalability speedup when threads manipulate non-overlapping memory regions. However, there are a few drawbacks to RadixVM. First, when radix tree does not span out completely, it could cause thread blocked even they operate on non-overlapping regions because radix tree compresses low-level tree node into the high-level interior node, the thread has to compete with others to lock the specific interior node to span out the tree. Second, radix tree and per-core page tables incur significant memory overhead over the Linux kernel and ours.

PARSEC [18] used a scalable memory reclamation to scale system-level data structures. Through parallelizing a tree-like data structure used in their micro-kernel SPECK, PARSEC improves the VM system performance on multicore. However, they did not optimize page table scalability, which is quite vital for multithreaded applications.

Cerberus et al. [17] mitigated kernel shared data structures contention by clustering multiple commodity operating systems atop a VMM. In their work, multithreaded applications still run with the illusion of a single operating system kernel and traditional shared memory interface. When threads issue system call requests, Cerberus routes these requests to multiple VMs with different address space. Thus it could mitigate data or lock contention. However, in order to maintain the consistency of several OSes, Cerberus employed both message passing and shared memory mechanism which incurs communication overhead, and contention still happens in the single guest kernel.

Partitioning hardware resources into multiple running kernels is another solution to scale operating system. Hive [6] is structured as an internal distribute system, which organizes multiple independent kernels called *cell* and aims to improve system reliability and scalability. Barrelfish [1] and Helios [14] both use multikernel strategy to bridge the heterogeneity of different processing units in a platform. Our works are also inspired by multikernel approaches, as we partition the virtual memory system resources instead of hardware resources.

6   Conclusions

In this paper, we explore and identify scalability bottlenecks in centralized VM system design. Through decentralizing VM system resources and utilizing other parallel programming techniques, we present a novel VM system–MEDUSAVM. MEDUSAVM eliminates performance interference and lock contention between multiple disjoint memory pools, and thus significantly improves system scalability and efficiency. Moreover, our hybrid page table design in MEDUSAVM introduces much less physical memory consumption relative to the previous approach. Experimental results using microbenchmarks and multithreaded applications demonstrate that MEDUSAVM outperforms much better than native Linux kernel and show our decentralization strategy is promising.

Acknowledgment. This work was supported by the ministry of industry and information technology grants the project of key technology improvement of the industrial control system 2017.

References

1. Baumann, A., et al.: The multikernel: a new OS architecture for scalable multicore systems. In: Proceedings of the ACM SIGOPS 22nd Symposium on Operating Systems Principles, pp. 29–44. ACM (2009)
2. Boyd-Wickizer, S., et al.: An analysis of Linux scalability to many cores. In: OSDI, vol. 10, pp. 86–93 (2010)
3. Boyd-Wickizer, S., Kaashoek, M.F., Morris, R., Zeldovich, N.: Non-scalable locks are dangerous. In: Proceedings of the Linux Symposium, pp. 119–130 (2012)
4. Brown, T., Ellen, F., Ruppert, E.: A general technique for non-blocking trees. In: ACM SIGPLAN Notices, vol. 49, pp. 329–342. ACM (2014)
5. Cai, M., Liu, S., Huang, H.: tScale: a contention-aware multithreaded framework for multicore multiprocessor systems. In: 2017 IEEE 16th International Conference on Parallel and Distributed Systems, pp. 87–104. IEEE (2017)
6. Chapin, J., Rosenblum, M., Devine, S., Lahiri, T., Teodosiu, D., Gupta, A.: Hive: fault containment for shared-memory multiprocessors. In: ACM SIGOPS Operating Systems Review, vol. 29, pp. 12–25. ACM (1995)
7. Clements, A.T., Kaashoek, M.F., Zeldovich, N.: Scalable address spaces using RCU balanced trees. ACM SIGPLAN Not. **47**(4), 199–210 (2012)
8. Clements, A.T., Kaashoek, M.F., Zeldovich, N.: RadixVM: scalable address spaces for multithreaded applications. In: Proceedings of the 8th ACM European Conference on Computer Systems, pp. 211–224. ACM (2013)
9. Clements, A.T., Kaashoek, M.F., Zeldovich, N., Morris, R.T., Kohler, E.: The scalable commutativity rule: designing scalable software for multicore processors. ACM Trans. Comput. Syst. (TOCS) **32**(4), 10 (2015)
10. Drachsler, D., Vechev, M., Yahav, E.: Practical concurrent binary search trees via logical ordering. ACM SIGPLAN Not. **49**(8), 343–356 (2014)
11. Herlihy, M., Shavit, N.: The Art of Multiprocessor Programming. Morgan Kaufmann, Burlington (2011)
12. Liu, R., Zhang, H., Chen, H.: Scalable read-mostly synchronization using passive reader-writer locks. In: USENIX Annual Technical Conference, pp. 219–230 (2014)
13. Michael, M.M.: Hazard pointers: safe memory reclamation for lock-free objects. IEEE Trans. Parallel Distrib. Syst. **15**(6), 491–504 (2004)
14. Nightingale, E.B., Hodson, O., McIlroy, R., Hawblitzel, C., Hunt, G.: Helios: heterogeneous multiprocessing with satellite kernels. In: Proceedings of the ACM SIGOPS 22nd Symposium on Operating Systems Principles, pp. 221–234. ACM (2009)
15. Schneider, S., Antonopoulos, C.D., Nikolopoulos, D.S.: Scalable locality-conscious multithreaded memory allocation. In: Proceedings of the 5th International Symposium on Memory Management, pp. 84–94. ACM (2006)
16. Siakavaras, D., Nikas, K., Goumas, G., Koziris, N.: Combining HTM and RCU to implement highly efficient balanced binary search trees (2017)
17. Song, X., Chen, H., Chen, R., Wang, Y., Zang, B.: A case for scaling applications to many-core with OS clustering. In: Proceedings of the Sixth Conference on Computer Systems, pp. 61–76. ACM (2011)
18. Wang, Q., Stamler, T., Parmer, G.: Parallel sections: scaling system-level data-structures. In: Proceedings of the Eleventh European Conference on Computer Systems, p. 33. ACM (2016)

An Efficient Retrieval Method for Astronomical Catalog Time Series Data

Bingyao Li[1], Ce Yu[1(✉)], Xiaoteng Hu[1], Jian Xiao[1], Shanjiang Tang[1(✉)],
Lianmeng Li[1], and Bin Ma[2]

[1] College of Intelligence and Computing, Tianjin University,
Tianjin 300350, China
{libingyao,yuce,xiaotenghu,xiaojian,tashj,lilianmeng}@tju.edu.cn
[2] National Astronomical Observatories, Chinese Academy of Sciences,
Beijing 100101, China
mabin22@gmail.com

Abstract. Astronomical catalog time series data refer to the data collected at different time, which can provide a comprehensive understanding of the celestial objects' attributes and expose various astronomical phenomena. Its retrieval is indispensable to astronomy research. However, the existing time series data retrieval methods involve lots of manual work and extremely time-consuming. The complexity will also be augmented by the exponentially growth of observation data. In this paper, we propose an automatic and efficient retrieval method for astronomical catalog time series data. With the goal of identifying the same celestial objects time series data automatically, a cross-match scheme is designed, which labeled a unique MatchID for each record matched with the datum catalog. To accelerate the matching process, an in-memory index structure based on Redis is specially designed, which enables matching speed 1.67 times faster than that of MySQL in massive amounts of data. Moreover, Catalog-Mongo—an improved database of MongoDB—is presented, in which a Data Blocking Algorithm is proposed to improve the data partitioning of MongoDB and accelerate query performance. The experimental results show that the query speed is about 2 times faster than MongoDB and 7.6 to 8.7 times than MySQL.

Keywords: Astronomical catalog · Cross-match
Distributed retrieval method · MongoDB · Time series data

1 Introduction

In this Big Data era, the efficient storage and retrieval of massive data are becoming the critical problem for most applications, and especially in astronomy area. Projections indicate that by 2020, more than 60 PB of archived data will be accessible to astronomers [1]. The Large Synoptic Survey Telescope

© Springer Nature Switzerland AG 2018
J. Vaidya and J. Li (Eds.): ICA3PP 2018, LNCS 11334, pp. 284–298, 2018.
https://doi.org/10.1007/978-3-030-05051-1_20

(LSST) which will begin operations in 2022, will stream data at rates of 2 Terabytes per hour [11]. The Antarctic Schmidt Telescopes (AST3), an astronomical observation is completed every 2.4 min with generating an astronomical catalog which usually contains 10–30 million objects. Therefore, facing the continuously astronomical observation data generated, the retrieval system must consider the nice scalability of continuous incremental data, while ensuring the massive data retrieval in a timely manner persistently.

Additionally, to get a thorough understanding of the celestial objects, Time Series Data—a collection data of celestial objects generated over different time by one or more telescopes—is extremely needed. However, in the original catalog, each row of data records the observation data in a specific area at a time which has not corresponded to the particular celestial object. Users still need to manually cross-match the query results to identify which data belong to the same celestial object. Therefore, to take advantage of retrieving time series data automatically and efficiently, there are two challenges to be addressed. One is how to identify celestial object time series data automatically. The other is how to process astronomical catalogs to accelerate the retrieval of time series data.

In this paper, Time Series Data Retrieval Method (TSDRM), is proposed to retrieve the astronomical catalog time series data automatically and efficiently. A cross-match scheme is first designed to automatic identify the same celestial object by labeling a unique MatchID for each record in catalog comparing with datum catalog. In the query results, the items with the same MatchID are the time series data of a celestial object, so that users do not need to match desired items manually. The in-memory structure in cross-scheme can also accelerate the matching process. Additionally, Catalog-Mongo, the improvement of distributed MongoDB, is presented. A Data Blocking Algorithm is proposed to fit the characteristics of astronomical catalog retrieval. The query would be directly toward to a specific chunk, thus further improves the Time Series Data query performance and make it a breeze querying Astronomy Big Data.

The contributions of this paper can be summarized as follows:

(1) We propose an innovative retrieval method to obtain astronomical catalog time series data automatically;
(2) We design a cross-match scheme in TSDRM to identify and label the same objects automatically, and an improved the MongoDB, Catalog-Mongo, to accelerate the process of retrieving time series data;
(3) We evaluate the proposed cross-match scheme and Catalog-Mongo with the real data from the Antarctic Schmidt Telescopes. The results show that our method outperforms its alternatives in experiments.

The rest of this paper is organized as follows. Section 2 discusses the existing work related to the methods of cross-match and astronomical big data query. Section 3 describes the design of TSDRM, the evolution of the experiment is described in Sect. 4. The last section draws a conclusion from our work and discusses future work.

2   Related Work

2.1   Cross-Match of Celestial Objects

In many cases, astronomers need the observed data collected in different time periods to obtain a chronological view of what happened over time of the celestial objects. Cross-matching, which refers to finding the same objects from different catalogs by calculating their positions, is a fundamental procedure to accomplish the above analysis [16]. Due to the incredible growth of astronomical catalog volume, it is impractical to process every source of all catalogs by pair-wise comparing. A number of optimization methods have been proposed to accelerate the cross-match process.

Partitioning and parallelization functions are widely used to accelerate the cross-match. Gray et al. [9] proposed an early cross-match method, Zone, which divided the spherical space into equal height tripes and perform cross-match in related zones. On the basis of Zone, Wang et al. [27] divided celestial objects by their locations in zones and grid, and implemented index on the GPU. Later, Budavari [4], Lee et al. [15] adapt zone index on multiple GPUs. Similarly with Zone, the Hierarchical Triangular Mesh (HTM) [14] proposed by Kunszt et al. and the Hierarchical Equal Area isoLatitude Pixelization (HEALPix) [10] proposed by Gorski et al. are two widely used spatial indices for cross-matching, which partitioned the sphere into triangles and diamond-shaped cells, respectively. Based on these index methods, Soumagnac et al. [25] divide the celestial sphere using HTM and reformatted catalog into HDF5 files format. Jia et al. [13] speed up the cross-match by adopting HEALPix on a CPU-GPU clusters with seven nodes. And then Jia et al. [12] proposed a Multi-Assignment Single Join method and applied to the cross-match on clusters. However, these methods are mainly focused on cross-matching catalogs generated by different telescopes or wavebands. They cannot well fit the requirement of continuously generated astronomical catalogs. In recent years, the Bayesian model is also employed on cross-match [8,23], which is mainly used to solve the problem of uncertain position.

Moreover, there are several ready-made tools provide cross-match function, like CDS-Xmatch, ARCHES. The limitation of these web applications is that the user cannot implement a complete automatic procedure to deal with data. For example, the CDS-Xmatch has only 500 MB disk space available to store user's own data and all jobs are aborted if the computation time exceeds 100 min [2]. Other applications such as TOPCAT [26], SIMBAD [28], the Internet connection is also the limitation of the cross-match speed.

2.2   Querying Massive Astronomical Data

A number of methods have been proposed to store and retrieve tremendous amounts of astronomical catalogs. Relative Database Management System (RDBMS) is the most intuitive method [24]. Such as PostgreSQL [5], which imports the catalogs into database and then uses the existing retrieval function of the database. Unfortunately, the continuous high-volume of observation data makes the insertion and query of traditional database a bottleneck. According to the actual measurement, it will take 104 s to import an astronomical catalog containing 130,000 sources into an empty database. And a catalog containing 500,000 sources would take up to 10 min. The addition of a new catalog can require up to 4.6 million modifications or additions which perform dramatically slow [19]. These obviously are unable to satisfy real-time requirements.

Additionally, other popular NoSQL methods are also used to deal with such problem. For instance, SciDB [3,21], which is specially designed for multidimensional data. Hadoop [29], which supports the Map-Reduce model, is widely used in Big Data applications and Hive [22], a distributed query scheme based on Hadoop. MongoDB [6], the NoSQL database which is the closest to the traditional relational database, cannot only improve the reading and writing performance but also facilitate the index build. Moreover, the retrieval tool for astronomical catalog, VizieR [19], is widely utilized. VizieR is a database which the major part of the catalogs is managed by a relational database while the larger catalogs containing over 10 million rows are stored as compressed binary files. To reduce the response time, the CoCat (Co-processor Catalog) [20] is utilized to parallelize the VizieR large catalog treatments. Although the preceding methods have good performance in Big Data query, there is still room left for improvements in astronomical catalog retrieval. To meet our requirements, Catalog-Mongo, an improved NoSQL database is proposed.

3 Time Series Data Retrieval Method

3.1 Problem Definition

This work focuses on retrieving Time Series Data of the targets in a cone range automatically and efficiently. Given a set of astronomical catalog S, a pair of coordinates (T_{ra}, T_{dec}), radius R and a time frame (t_1, t_2), find all celestial objects (S_{ra}, S_{dec}) in S that satisfy the following formula and are created (observed) at or after t_1 but no later than t_2:

$$(S_{ra} - T_{ra})^2 + (S_{dec} - T_{dec})^2 \le R^2 \tag{1}$$

The architecture of TSDRM is shown in Fig. 1. The catalog would be first conducted cross-matching with the datum catalog to identify the same celestial object, and label the unique MatchID and time information for them. After, the matched astronomical catalog would be stored into Catalog-Mongo database, which is the improvement of MongoDB according to the characteristics of astronomical catalog retrieval. Ultimately, a command line-based query engine can take an area of the sky and a time period as inputs, and return all catalogs that (a) in that area and (b) was taken during that time period as the result. The query syntax is as follows.

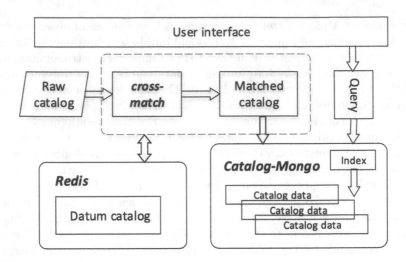

Fig. 1. Overview of TSDRM

QUERY
{ Center_RA, Center_DEC, Radius_R, Begin_Time, End_Time }
*SELECT * FROM { DataSourceList }*

From the discussion in Sect. 2, it is clear that both cross-matching and doing cone search among billions of records in a astronomical catalog is prohibitively time consuming. To accelerate this process, we create a new cross-match scheme, and an improved MongoDB structure to match and query time series data of targets efficiently.

3.2   Cross-Match Scheme

In the original catalog, each row of the records are a single observation data which have not corresponded to the particular celestial object. In order to obtain the corresponding observation data of celestial objects, each catalog generated at different time needs to perform cross-matching with each other. With the goal of retrieving Time Series Data of the target automatically, the first thing quite needed is an efficient mechanism to promptly identify and label the same celestial object time series data.

In the state of generating new catalogs continually in astronomical observations, we develop a Datum Catalog and each catalog will compare with it. The datum catalog is empty at the beginning, and the first record comes, we take it as the first celestial object. Then the new record comes, cross-matched with existing records. If it doesn't match successfully, add this new record into Datum Catalog. The matching formula will be demonstrated below. Considering that datum catalog will be queried frequently in cross-match process, put it in the main memory would work great for our needs. Moreover, each catalog takes up only one hundred to five hundred megabytes of space, it is projected that such size of several hundred megabytes is pretty manageable for in-memory database. Therefore, an efficient cross-match scheme based on Redis is created. A sample of key-value pairs and field mapping of datum catalog structure in Redis is shown in Table 1.

Table 1. Sample of the datum catalog structure

Key	Field	Value
Catalog_Name	Ra	338.666367
	Dec	0.69091709
	HealpixID	99069354
	MatchID	157894

We introduce the idea of HEALPix—a sky partition method—into astronomical catalog, assign each catalog with one or more HealpixIDs according to its covered area of the sky (Fig. 2). Due to the limitations of Redis Hash structure, it is not feasible to directly use the B-tree index on the HealpixID like other databases. Therefore, the core idea of our solution is to index the datum catalog by HealpixID with the help of the Sorted Set. Sorted set is a data structure that each member has an associated score, and members will be automatically kept sorted according to the score. Ordering and value uniqueness make sorted set a perfect fit for indices. Therefore, we regard "Key" in datum catalog as "member", "HealpixID" as "score". Table 2 is the healpixID table stored in Redis. In this way, it just like a skip list in memory offering to skip a number of elements when performing a designated range query.

Table 2. Sample of the HealpixID table structure

Key	Member	Score
Obj_Healpix1	Catalog_Name1	99069354
Obj_Healpix2	Catalog_Name2	99069678

The following demonstrates the whole process of cross-match scheme in detail. The overall architecture is illustrated in Fig. 3. First, extract the source position information (Ra and Dec) of the new generated catalog and calculate its HealpixID, ascertain the range of the error threshold and HealpixIDs that satisfy the following formula. Here, d is the error threshold, r_1 and r_2 are the error radius of the two astronomical catalogs.

$$d \leqslant 3 * \sqrt{r_1^2 + r_2^2} \tag{2}$$

Then select members that are within the range of HealpixIDs in the HealpixID table. Check the selected members in datum catalog, and label the unique matchID and time information to the corresponding object in the new generated catalog. If it does not exist in a matched member, then add this object data into datum catalog, HealpixID table and create a new matchID. Repeat the process above until all the objects in the new generated catalog are matched and have a MatchID. In this way, the Time Series Data of the same celestial object is matched automatically.

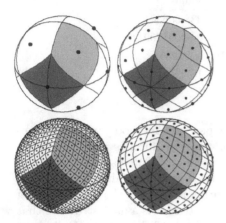

Fig. 2. HEALPix's partition of the celestial sphere [18]

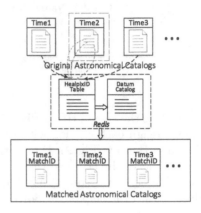

Fig. 3. The process of cross-match scheme

3.3   Distributed Catalog-Mongo

Considering the high performance and reliability requirements of the astronomical catalog database, the distributed Catalog-Mongo, an improvement of MongoDB, is proposed in TSDRM. MongoDB, as a kind of NoSQL which is closest to relational database, supporting distributed data storage, high performance of insertion and query, and reliable service of data backup. In Catalog-Mongo, the blocks of the sky based on Healpix are mapped to the chunk of distributed MongoDB and a Data Blocking Algorithm is designed to improve the auto data partitioning of MongoDB according to the requirement of astronomical catalog retrieval, which greatly accelerate the data query performance.

Database Indexing. Index is essential for large astronomical catalog databases, since retrieving the required record by sequential scan in large datasets is huge time-consuming. In Catalog-Mongo, we still choose HEALPix— a typical virtual spatial-indexing function—to map the RA and DEC (two-dimensional) to a single HEALPixID. After the cross-matching in Sect. 3.2, each celestial object in the astronomical catalog already has a HEALPixID according to its covered area of the sky, so we don't need repeated calculation. Then, the B-tree index will be built on the HEALPixID column.

Improved Data Blocking Algorithm. MongoDB provides sharding technology, which the data can be partitioned to different nodes. And a shard key is required for each collection to define how to partition the documents. In such distributed environment, each client connects to a master node called mongos process which can analyze and redirect the query to the corresponding nodes [7]. In our distributed Catalog-Mongo, HEALPixID is assigned as shard key.

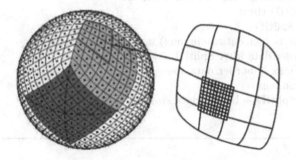

Fig. 4. Block-edge data resolution strategy

In actual query, if we want to find the objects in a certain sky block whose center is close to the block boundary, the target located in the adjoining block might be missed and caused incompleteness of query results. To deal with the block-edge data, we expand the scope of each block by adding 4 outer borders, the data on the four edges will also record the adjacent HEALPixID. In partitioning process, as shown in Fig. 4, each data block contains the data not only partitioned according to HEALPix, but also on the edge of the adjacent blocks. Therefore, the choice of HEALPix level is critical. If the partition level is too high, the comparison volume in cross-match is less but the proportion of redundancy data would increase. And if the level is too low, the missed objects will decrease but it also result in a long matching time. Thus, in the implementation, considering the proportion of redundancy data and according to the common radius of the cone search as far as we know, we partitioned the whole sky on the level 13 using HEALPix, the whole sky will divided into $12 * 4^{13}$ blocks. The breadth of outer border is partitioned on the level 8, the block-edge data stored in each block is $(2^{10} + 4)$. For each block, the ratio of the redundancy data to the original data is about 1.57%, which is pretty acceptable.

Then, these blocks will be mapped to the chunk of Catalog-MongoDB. The Data Blocking Algorithm, as shown in Algorithm 1, is proposed to improve the auto data partitioning of MongoDB. The specific process is as follows. Before partitioning, a special SplitID is first annotated for the partition point, then

(1) Continuous detection from the starting position of the partition, find the SplitID and identify the partition range (min,max);
(2) Compute the adjacent edge data of this partition range, add these data into the data block, and update the maximum value of partition range;
(3) Execute the partitioning command, and update the partition start position for the next partition.

Algorithm 1. Data Blocking Algorithm pseudo-code.

1: min = HEALPixID_min
2: max = HEALPixID_max
3: **for** HEALPixID_min : HEALPixID_max **do**
4:    **if** find SplitID **then**
5:       max = SplitID
6:       calculate_border_data (min,max) in HEALPix
7:       add border_data after SplitID
8:       max = max + border_data_size
9:       split (min,max)
10:      min = SplitID + border_data_size + 1
11:   **end if**
12: **end for**

When a query arrives, the corresponding HEALPixID(s) of the input target area is calculated first and identify the corresponding data block. Then all the records in this data block whose HEALPixID matched the target HEALPixID(s) got picked out. The records with same matchID are the time series data of a target celestial object. Ultimately, through the TSDRM, users will get all Time Series Data of the targets in a cone range.

4   Performance Evaluation

According to the parts of TSDRM, we conduct our experiments in two parts. First, we measure the time consumption of our cross-matching scheme in various catalogs size and compared with MySQL, which is widely used in practical cross-match function. Second, we evaluate the performance of Catalog-Mongo, including the time of data import, index build and the new data insertion. Additionally, we focused on evaluating the query performance by retrieving Time Series Data of the targets in a cone range in different sized datasets to showcase the splendid performance of TSDRM. All this series of experiments are compared with MySQL and distributed MongoDB.

4.1   Experimental Setup

All servers used in experiments are under the environment settings shown in Table 3. The series experiments of cross-match scheme and its comparison experiment are conducted on a same server. A cluster of three servers are used to build a distributed environment for Catalog-Mongo experiments. The bandwidth between each server is about 600 Mbps. The comparison experiments of distributed MongoDB is also implemented in this environment, which can demonstrate the performance of method fairly. The comparison experiment of MySQL is conducted on a single server.

Table 3. The parameters of experimental platform

Parameters name	Value
Operating system	ubuntu 14.04 LTS (64-bit)
CPU	Intel Core i7-3770 CPU 3.4 GHz
Memory	SAMSUNG DDR4 4 GB, 1600 MHz
HDD	Seagate ST3000DM002 1 TB

The datasets used in experiments are extracted from Antarctic Schmidt Telescopes (AST3) in Mohe, China.

4.2 Cross-Match Scheme Performance

In this series of experiments, cross-match is performed on a single server with six datasets, the sources number of datasets increase from ten thousand to twenty million. The execution time of initial data import, index build, and performing cross-match with datum catalog are recorded as the total time to measure the efficiency of cross-match scheme. We compared our scheme with MySQL in terms of total time consumption.

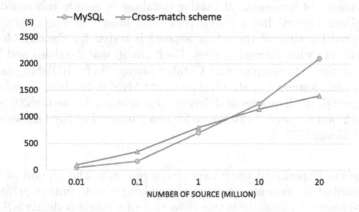

Fig. 5. Total execution time comparison between cross-match scheme and MySQL

The results are shown in Fig. 5. It can be seen that with the less number of records, the performance of MySQL is slightly outperformed than our scheme, while the performance of our scheme turns out to be 1.67 times faster than MySQL after the number of records scale up to ten million orders of magnitude.

We specially tested the performance of data import and index build time separately with no more than five million records, to find out why our scheme is slower than MySQL in smaller datasets. The performance comparison of redis and MySQL in Figs. 6 and 7 show that redis suffers a performance disadvantage in both these two parts. Therefore, in the initial stage, the slower import and update speed of datum catalog in redis lead to longer total cross-match time. And with the completeness of datum catalog, it hardly needs to update or insert, then our scheme proves the performance advantages.

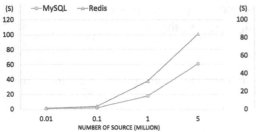

Fig. 6. Data import time comparison between Redis and MySQL

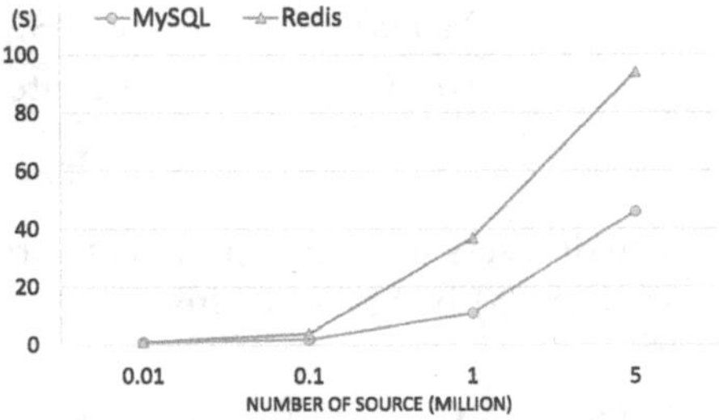

Fig. 7. Index build time comparison between Redis and MySQL

4.3   Catalog-Mongo Performance

The performance of astronomical catalog database is mainly concerned as the following: Data import, Index build, New data insertion, and Query. Therefore, the execution time of these four aspects is tested for Catalog-Mongo on multiple datasets with increasing sizes. Both traditional database and NoSQL database is deployed to compare with Catalog-Mongo. As for RDBMS, the experiment results in Mesmoudi et al. [17] shown that MySQL has better performance than PostgreSQL in all queries of different data volume. So, we directly selected MySQL with better query performance for comparison. For NoSQL, we selected distributed MongoDB.

Data Import. Experiment results are shown in Fig. 8. The support of concurrency in distributed environment obviously makes the data import performance of Catalog-Mongo significantly better than that of a single node MySQL. Compared with MongoDB, the time consumption of Catalog-Mongo is almost the same with the sources less than 70 million. However, because of the existing of data redundancy adding in each data block, the time consumption is 13% more than the distributed MongoDB when the number of sources up to 100 million.

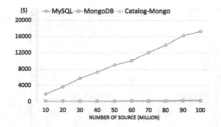

Fig. 8. Data import time of three methods under different sources number

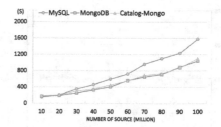

Fig. 9. Index build time of three methods under different sources number

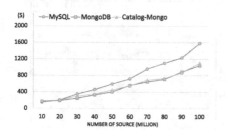

Fig. 10. New data insertion time of three methods under different sources number

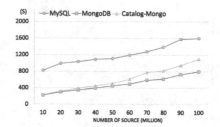

Fig. 11. Query time of three methods under different sources number

Index Build. In general, Catalog-mongo and distributed MongoDB have little differences in the performance of building index. As shown in Fig. 9, with the same number of sources, the index build time consumption of Catalog-Mongo is 1.8% to 4.7% more than MongoDB. This is also the result of the data redundancy in the Catalog-Mongo. Compared with MySQL, with the increasing of the sources, the performance advantage of Catalog-Mongo gradually increased, and used 8 min less than MySQL with 100 million sources.

New Data Insertion. The results are presented in Fig. 10. Also limited by the amount of redundant data and the process of adding redundant data, the time consumption of new data insertion of Catalog-Mongo is more than distributed MongoDB, and slightly larger as the data volume increases. However, compared with MySQL, Catalog-Mongo saves 39.8% to 71.9% of the insertion time, which means that we can flexibly add incremental file in updating phase.

Query. In this part, the retrieval performance of Catalog-Mongo is tested by executing the same query command (the syntax is shown in Sect. 3.1) on multiple data sets with increasing sizes. The results are shown in Fig. 11. Catalog-Mongo demonstrated excellent retrieval performance comparing to the MySQL and distributed MongoDB methods. The query time only took a fraction of the time

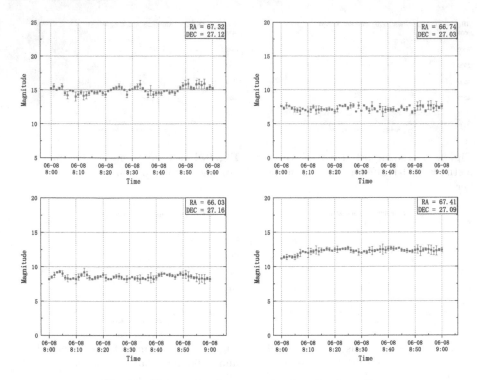

Fig. 12. Time series data sample of retrieval results

needed by the MySQL to complete the same task and query speed is twice times faster than MongoDB. Moreover, the advantage of our method becomes more and more obvious with the increase of data volume. Considering that users really needed is timely response to the query, although the performance of Catalog-Mongo is slightly worse than MongoDB in data import and new data insertion while significantly better than MySQL, which is quite acceptable in real life usage. Figure 12 is a visualization sample of the TSDRM retrieval results. We can see that a cone range of celestial objects' time series data can be retrieved successfully by TSDRM. It should be noted that the retrieval can only obtain the time series data, the astronomers still need data fitting to analyze the changing period of celestial objects.

5   Conclusion and Future Work

In this paper, TSDRM, a distributed retrieval method for astronomical catalog time series data is proposed. TSDRM helps user to obtain the target time series data automatically and efficiently. By introducing in-memory index structure into cross-match scheme, the same celestial object time series data can be identified and matched automatically and timely. Experimental results show that in ten million orders of magnitude, the response time of our cross-match scheme is

1.67 times faster than MySQL. Additionally, Catalog-Mongo, the improvement of MongoDB is presented to store and retrieve the matched catalogs, a Data Blocking Algorithm for accelerating query performance is proposed based on the characteristics of astronomical data retrieval. Evaluation results show that the retrieval speed of TSDRM can achieve 2 times of distributed MongoDB and 7.6 to 8.7 times of MySQL.

In addition, our methods can be applied to other applications aside from retrieving time series data in astronomy. Generally, any application that is required to cross-match and query massive data could benefit from it, such as remote sensing and digital map.

In future research, applying cross-match in distributed environment and optimizing the data layout for Catalog-Mongo is worth investigating. We will continue to make efforts to search for efficient retrieval method for astronomical catalog.

Acknowledgements. This work is supported by the Joint Research Fund in Astronomy (U1531111, U1731423, U1731125) under cooperative agreement between the National Natural Science Foundation of China (NSFC) and Chinese Academy of Sciences (CAS), the National Natural Science Foundation of China (11573019, 61602336).

References

1. Berriman, G.B., Groom, S.L.: How will astronomy archives survive the data tsunami? Commun. ACM **54**(12), 52–56 (2011)
2. Boch, T., Pineau, F.X., Derriere, S.: CDS xMatch service documentation (2016)
3. Brown, P.G.: Overview of SciDB: large scale array storage, processing and analysis. In: ACM SIGMOD International Conference on Management of Data, pp. 963–968 (2010)
4. Budavari, T., Lee, M.A.: Xmatch: GPU enhanced astronomic catalog cross-matching. Astrophysics Source Code Library, p. 03021 (2013)
5. Chilingarian, I., Bartunov, O., Richter, J., Sigaev, T.: PostgreSQL: the suitable DBMS solution for astronomy and astrophysics. Astron. Data Anal. Softw. Syst. (ADASS) **314**, 225 (2004)
6. Chodorow, K.: MongoDB: The Definitive Guide. O'Reilly Media, Inc., Sebastopol (2013)
7. Damodaran, B.D., Salim, S., Vargese, S.M.: Performance evaluation of MySQL and MongoDB databases. Int. J. Cybern. Inform. **5**, 387–394 (2016)
8. Fan, D., Budav, S.T.R., Norris, P.R., Hopkins, M.A.: Matching radio catalogues with realistic geometry: application to SWIRE and ATLAS. Mon. Not. R. Astron. Soc. **451**(2), 1299–1305 (2015)
9. Gray, J., Nieto-Santisteban, M.A., Szalay, A.S.: The zones algorithm for finding points-near-a-point or cross-matching spatial datasets. Microsoft Research (2007)
10. Górski, K.M.: HEALPix: a framework for high-resolution discretization and fast analysis of data distributed on the sphere. Astrophys. J. **622**(2), 759–771 (2004)
11. Huijse, P., Estevez, P.A., Protopapas, P., Principe, J.C., Zegers, P.: Computational intelligence challenges and applications on large-scale astronomical time series databases. IEEE Comput. Intell. Mag. **9**(3), 27–39 (2015)

12. Jia, X., Luo, Q.: Multi-assignment single joins for parallel cross-match of astronomic catalogs on heterogeneous clusters. In: Proceedings of the 28th International Conference on Scientific and Statistical Database Management, pp. 1–12 (2016)
13. Jia, X., Luo, Q., Fan, D.: Cross-matching large astronomical catalogs on heterogeneous clusters, pp. 617–624(2015)
14. Kunszt, P.Z., Szalay, A.S., Thakar, A.R.: The hierarchical triangular mesh. In: Banday, A.J., Zaroubi, S., Bartelmann, M. (eds.) Mining the Sky, pp. 631–637. Springer, Berlin (2001). https://doi.org/10.1007/10849171_83
15. Lee, M.A., Budavári, T.: Cross-identification of astronomical catalogs on multiple GPUs. Astron. Data Anal. Softw. Syst. **475**, 235 (2013)
16. Li, L., Tang, D., Liu, T., Liu, H., Li, W., Cui, C.: Optimizing the join operation on hive to accelerate cross-matching in astronomy. In: IEEE International Parallel and Distributed Processing Symposium Workshops, pp. 1735–1745 (2014)
17. Mesmoudi, A., Hacid, M.S.: A comparison of systems to large-scale data access. In: Han, W.S., Lee, M.L., Muliantara, A., Sanjaya, N.A., Thalheim, B., Zhou, S. (eds.) DASFAA 2014. LNCS, vol. 8505, pp. 161–175. Springer, Heidelberg (2014). https://doi.org/10.1007/978-3-662-43984-5_12
18. NASA: Jet propulsion laboratory HEALPix homepage. http://healpix.jpl.nasa.gov/
19. Ochsenbein, F., Bauer, P., Marcout, J.: The VizieR database of astronomical catalogues. Astron. Astrophys. Suppl. **143**(1), 23–32 (2000)
20. Ochsenbein, F., Derriere, S., Nicaisse, S., Schaaff, A.: Clustering the large VizieR catalogues, the CoCat experience. Astron. Data Anal. Softw. Syst. (ADASS) **314**(314), 58 (2004)
21. Planthaber, G., Stonebraker, M., Frew, J.: EarthDB: scalable analysis of MODIS data using SciDB. In: ACM SIGSPATIAL International Workshop on Analytics for Big Geospatial Data, pp. 11–19 (2012)
22. Richter, S., Quiané-Ruiz, J.A., Schuh, S., Dittrich, J.: Towards zero-overhead static and adaptive indexing in Hadoop. VLDB J. **23**(3), 469–494 (2014)
23. Salvato, M., et al.: Finding counterparts for all-sky X-ray surveys with NWAY: a Bayesian algorithm for cross-matching multiple catalogues. Mon. Not. R. Astron. Soc. **473**, 4937–4955 (2018)
24. Smareglia, R., Laurino, O., Knapic, C.: VODance: VO data access layer service creation made easy, vol. 442, p. 575 (2011)
25. Soumagnac, M.T., Ofek, E.O.: catsHTM - a tool for fast accessing and cross-matching large astronomical catalogs. ArXiv e-prints (2018)
26. Taylor, M.: TOPCAT - tool for operations on catalogues and tables. Starlink User Note **253** (2011)
27. Wang, S., Zhao, Y., Luo, Q., Wu, C., Yang, X.: Accelerating in-memory cross match of astronomical catalogs. In: IEEE International Conference on E-Science, pp. 326–333 (2013)
28. Wenger, M., Ochsenbein, F., Egret, D., et al.: The SIMBAD astronomical database. The CDS reference database for astronomical objects. Astron. Astrophys. Suppl. **143**(1), 9–22 (2000)
29. White, T., Cutting, D.: Hadoop: The Definitive Guide, vol. 215, no. 11, pp. 1–4. O'reilly Media Inc., sebastopol (2012)

Maintaining Root via Custom Android Kernel Across Over-The-Air Upgrade

Huang Zucheng[1], Liu Lu[1], Li Yuanzhang[1], Zhang Yu[2,3], and Zhang Qikun[4]($\boxtimes$)

[1] School of Computer Science and Technology, Beijing Institute of Technology, Beijing 100081, China

[2] School of Electrical and Information Engineering and Beijing Key Laboratory of Intelligent Processing for Building Big Data, Beijing University of Civil Engineering and Architecture, No.1 Zhanlanguan Road, Xicheng District, Beijing 100044, China

[3] State Key Laboratory in China for GeoMechanics and Deep Underground Engineering (Beijing), China University of Mining and Technology, Beijing 100083, China

[4] Department of Computer and Communication Engineering, Zhengzhou University of Light Industry, Zhengzhou 450001, Henan, China
zhangqikun04@163.com

Abstract. People can obtain the highest privileges and control devices by Android root. However, an Android phone has been rooted, it is difficult for the user to update the Android system. Aiming at these problems, this paper proposes a maintaining root via custom Android kernel across Over-The-Air (OTA) upgrade. By customizing the kernel in boot and recovery, the boot will be replaced with rooted boot after updating automatically, so that system not only can be updated successfully but also maintain root. Experiments show that there is no abnormal between rooted mobile with a customized kernel and normal mobile during a minor system update.

Keywords: Custom kernel · Root privilege · System update

1 Introduction

Android is the most popular smartphone operating system over the world [1]. The opening characteristic of the Android system enables major OEMs to create an operating system for their handsets based on Android [2], revamping the user interface, preinstalling software and system functions. However, consumers of Android phones do not have complete control over the purchased personal mobile devices. For example, users cannot delete music software pre-installed. To overcome these limitations, users must root their phones. Root allows users to bypass the restrictions set by operating systems to provide complete control of the device. Users can uninstall programs, enjoy the additional features of specialized applications that require root privileges.

© Springer Nature Switzerland AG 2018
J. Vaidya and J. Li (Eds.): ICA3PP 2018, LNCS 11334, pp. 299–309, 2018.
https://doi.org/10.1007/978-3-030-05051-1_21

However, there is a trouble with updating your android phone after it has been rooted. Usually, the firmware will be modified during the root process of Android. Because some operating system based on Android has the function of detecting the integrity of the system. So, there will be a great probability of failure when updating system [3]. The best scenario is that the system will be updated in the rooted Android phone while preserving root privileges.

In this paper, we analyzed the architecture of Android system, and the OTA update process, as well as the root principle of the Android. We found the system-less installation mode of root tool named SuperSU [4], so long as system update does not modify boot partition of Android, the Android device can still retain root privileges after the update. We decided to modify the kernel of the boot to prevent the boot partition update. In this paper, the kernel of recovery is also modified to meet the scheme.

The contributions of this paper are as follows:

- Analyzed the update procedure of Samsung Android device.
- Proposed a method of failing to detect when Samsung Android has been rooted. The update package can be downloaded through system update application.
- The update procedure of rooted Android mobile phone's update procedure is basically consistent with normal Android device's.

The rest of this paper is organized as follows: The related research associated with this area is described in Sect. 2. Section 3 analyzes the related procedures of updating Android system and rooting Android devices. The concrete realization of our scheme is presented in Sect. 4. After that, Sect. 5 introduces the experiment and evaluation. The limitations of our proposed scheme and the future works are in Sect. 6. We conclude our work in Sect. 7.

2 Related Works

FlashFire [5] can flash full firmware packages all while maintaining root. However, the AXXXX's OTA packet displays corrupt in FlashFire so that the packet cannot be applied to update the AXXXX's OS by FlashFire.

The kernel is the core part of Android OS. Therefore, some researchers have made efforts to find and repair security vulnerabilities. Reference [6] demonstrates how to penetrate into the Binder and control data exchange mechanism in Android OS by proposing a kernel level attack model based on the hooking method. JoKER [7] was presented to detect rootkits in the Android kernel by utilizing the hardware's Joint Test Action Group (JTAG) interface for trusted memory forensics.

By customizing the kernel, the system can be deeply optimized. The reference [8] compared current Android kernel-based modifications evaluating their impact on battery consumption. In the reference [9] a kernel module called MOS (Memory Orchestration System) is designed to address the problems caused by memory reclaiming in the Android platform. A mobile virtualization architecture, called Condroid [10], was developed for Android. Condroid enables a single device to run several virtual Android phones. The main approach used for Condroid is the Linux kernel technology of Containers.

3   Internals of Android Updating Process

3.1   Architecture and Partition of Android System

Android system architecture has adopted the idea of a hierarchical architecture. Generally, it is thought four layers from the top to the bottom, namely: the application layer, the application framework layer, the system library and the Android runtime, and the Linux kernel. The application framework, system libraries, and Android runtime are attributed to Android middleware.

We know eMMC memory chips of Android phones are usually used to store system and user data. Generally speaking, Android phones include the partitions shown in Fig. 1. The boot partition includes the Linux kernel and ramdisk as the root file system [11, 12]. The system partition contains the most code of the middleware layer and part of code of application layer. The cache partition serves as the system cache area, and the related data of the system update process can be saved here. The Recovery partition holds a relatively independent operating system. Just like the boot partition, it also includes a full Linux kernel and ramdisk as the root file system. The Linux kernel in recovery partition and boot partition is generally the same. Some vendors provide proprietary flash patterns and tools, such as Samsung's Odin [13].

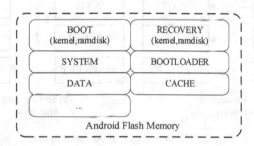

Fig. 1. Common partitions on flash memory in Android devices

3.2   Rooting Android Phone

Root access privileges of Android devices are generally divided into two ways [14], one is to use one-click root tools, such tools mainly use operating system vulnerabilities to mention the right; the other way is to flash third-party recovery TWRP [15], then flash the root package, SuperSU frequently. The old version of SuperSU program injects the program into the system partition. This will lead to undermines the integrity of the system partition. The new version provides a system-less mode. By modifying the ramdisk in the boot partition, and putting the related files in the data partition. Ultimately, the purpose of obtaining root privileges will be achieved.

3.3 Updating of Android Operating System

According to the different update packages, the update can be divided into the whole update and differential update. This section focuses on the related content of the differential update. Taking Samsung differential package as an example. The patch/directory includes patches for updating system partition. The recovery-from-boot.p in recovery/directory is a patch obtained by the difference between the new version of boot image and the new version of recovery image. The directory also contains the install-recovery.sh file, which is the script that updates the recovery partition.

As shown in Fig. 2, Android operating system update is divided into two stages: first stage, partitions that not include the recovery partition are updated; the second stage, the recovery partition is updated, which will be completed during the system first startup process after the end of the first stage. It is noteworthy that to update the recovery partition is not patched to the old recovery partition, but by patching the upgraded boot partition.

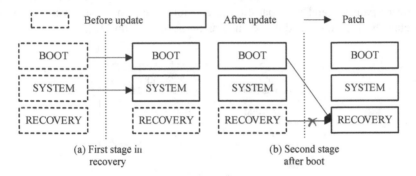

(a) First stage in   (b) Second stage
   recovery   after boot

Fig. 2. The two stages of Android update

4 Design and Implementation of Over-The-Air Upgrade

In order to retain rooted boot partition, it need customize the kernel, including the kernel in boot and recovery. The custom boot kernel allows the system update program to download update packages from the OTA server. Once the user chooses to install the system update package, the custom boot kernel can detect information about the upcoming update. At this time, custom boot kernel will save rooted boot partition, and restore the saved official boot image to the boot partition. Then, the Android phone reboots into recovery mode, the first stage of the system update will be completed soon. When the custom recovery kernel detects that, it will restore the saved rooted boot image to the boot partition. At this point, the device will restart again, and enter the Android main system update. The custom boot kernel will not allow update program to update the recovery partition.

4.1 Download Update Package Through OTA

Once Samsung operating system based on Android is rooted, the device status will be displayed as "custom", and you cannot download update package. It is found that the Samsung operating system detects its own integrity through the SysScope.odex program. Reverse engineering firmware is a popular method for identifying security weaknesses [16, 17]. By decompiling the program, it can see that it writes integrity flag by calling libcordon.so. In the process of calling, a parameter needs to be passed. If we modify the program's binary code to make it pass 1, even if the OS has been modified, so that the OS will not find that, and we can download update package through OTA. However, because the program is in the system partition, once the system partition is modified, the update process will get the wrong hash when the system partition is checked, resulting in an error in the update process.

Therefore, consider modifying the program's binary code in memory by the custom kernel when the program is loaded. Loading a program needs to access the contents of the corresponding file. There are two main ways to access the contents of the file: the read and mmap system call, as shown in Fig. 3. The experiment shows that the OS loads the SysScope.odex program through mapping file by mmap function. Therefore, after reading the SysScope.odex data in the kernel's page interrupt function, custom kernel searches and modifies the above-mentioned binary code. Up to this point, the device status of Samsung Android OS will be displayed as "official", so the update package can be downloaded via OTA.

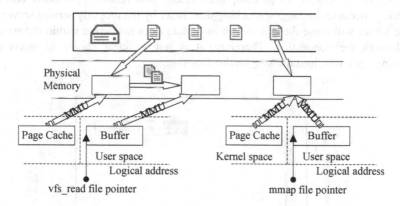

Fig. 3. Two system calls for accessing files

4.2 Update of Monitor OS

After the update package is downloaded, the user does not necessarily update the system immediately. Therefore, it is necessary to detect when system update will start. We know that the path of the update package and other information are passed to the recovery mainly through the cache partition. It is confirmed in system update of Samsung mobile phone, the update program writes the string "FOTA" to/cache/fota/fota.status, and write some contents into the /cache/recovery/command file. The "–update_org_package" is used to specify the storage path for the update package, and the default path of Samsung update package is /data/fota/update.zip.

In Android, there is an interface to restart or shut down the device provided to the developer, that is, the reboot function of the PowerManager class. Tracking the source code found that this function eventually turned off the phone by setting the Android system properties. The value of the key, "sys.powerctl", will be set to "reboot, recovery" when the phone restart to update OS. The set function will call the send_prop_msg function, which connects to the Android properties server via a temporarily created socket and then use a send function to send the desired property key-values to the server. It is found that the corresponding kernel function is sys_sendto. We filter the android system property by adding a piece of code in the kernel function sys_sendto, we can find that the Android phone is about to restart, and then enter into the recovery. At the same time, the contents of the above-mentioned files will be judged to confirm the OS is updated rather than restart.

4.3   Restore Official Boot Image to the Boot Partition

In the previous section, the code added to the sys_sendto kernel function is used to determine whether the OS will be updated. After it is detected, we also need to add code to back up the rooted boot partition and restore the official boot image to the boot partition. We use the vfs_read and vfs_write functions to test the time consumption of the backup and restore. As shown in Fig. 4, the time is related to the size of the buffer passed to the functions. In general, the backup and restore operations are time-consuming. Because the longest blocking time is set by the property service server only 2 s, the server will close the connection once data does not arrive within the specified time through the connection. Therefore, it is not an ideal choice to insert time-consuming operation into the sys_sendto function.

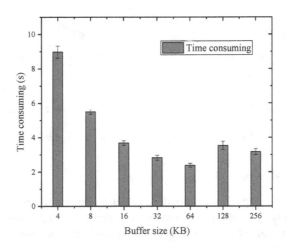

Fig. 4. The total time for backup and restore the boot partition using different buffer sizes

We find the "powerctl" command will be triggered, no matter how the "sys.pow-erctl" property is changed. The "powerctl" command eventually calls the __reboot system call to power off or reboot. We can find the kernel function corresponding to the __reboot system call is sys_reboot. Important functions in the restart process caused by OS update are shown in Fig. 5. When the parameter "cmd" passed to the sys_reboot function is LINUX_REBOOT_CMD_RESTART2 and another parameter "arg" is "recovery", it is possible to judge that the reboot is caused by OS update under normal circumstances. It can be assured that the phone is about to reboot to update OS through additionally comparing the contents of the files related to update in cache partition. Time-consuming operations can be inserted into this kernel function, so it is a suitable choice to backup and restores boot partition in this function.

4.4   Rewrite Rooted Custom Boot Image to the Boot Partition

In recovery, the first stage of the OS update will be completed. After this stage is completed and before the phone reboot itself, we should rewrite rooted custom boot image to boot partition. Adopting a similar approach to the previous section, we are prepared to add extra code snippets to the sys_reboot function in the kernel of recovery. When the parameter "cmd" is assigned as LINUX_REBOOT_CMD_RESTART2 and another parameter "arg" is assigned as "fota_bl", the first stage of OS update has been completed and the device is about to restart for the second stage of OS update. At this point, custom recovery kernel will save the boot partition, then rewrite the rooted custom boot image to the boot partition.

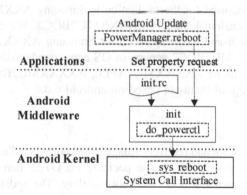

Fig. 5. The Android restart process caused by OS update

4.5   Prevent Updating the Recovery Partition

The extra operations described in the previous section require a custom recovery kernel to execute, so the recovery partition cannot be updated. Install-recovery.sh describes the procedure of updating recovery. The data of recovery partition can be generated by the applypatch program applying the differential package recovery-from-boot.p to the boot partition. However, due to the operations in the previous section, the data in the boot partition is the rooted custom boot image already. The applypatch program will exit abnormally and the recovery partition will not be updated. In this case, the script will write 454 to the fota.status file. When the OS update is successful, the value of fota.status is 200. We intercept the writing operation of the install-recovery process in the custom kernel of boot, the algorithm is as follows.

Algorithm 1 Change File Content During Write

1: Check vfs_write function to find the sign of update failed
2: filename ← name in d_name struct from f_dentry pointer of file struct
3: **if** filename is fota.status **then**
4:     Check current process name(PN)
5:     **if** PN == install-recovery **then**
6:         str1 ← buffer
7:         Converse str1 from 'const char' to 'char'
8:         **if** str1 == 454 **then**
9:             str1 ← 200

---

5 Evaluation

We evaluate the following two aspects mainly: Firstly, generality. We want to test whether the adjacent version of the operating system can update itself using the recovery and boot image with the custom kernel, and whether the OS can maintain root privilege after the update. Secondly, the stability of Android OS. We want to test whether the Android OS with custom boot can work normally.

The Android phone used for the evaluation is Samsung AXXXX, and the source code version for the custom kernel is AXXXXMU2BQC2. We compile it into two kernels for custom boot and recovery. We root Samsung AXXXX with TWRP and SuperSU. The AXXXXMU2BQC2 version of OS corresponds to the Android 6.0. The adjacent system versions are AXXXXMU2APL6, AXXXXMU2BQA2, and the latest AXXXXMU2BQI2. All of them are based on android 6.0.

5.1 Generality

We replace the custom boot and recovery image to the corresponding partition and then root the phone. We download the update package via OTA, then update the system, finally judge whether the updated OS has root privilege. The update results of various versions rooted OSs with custom kernel are shown in Table 1. The test results show that although there are only one custom boot and recovery image, it is capable of performing system update on a neighboring version of OS, and can maintain root privilege after the update.

Table 1. The update results of various version rooted OSs with the custom kernel

The version before update	Can update package be downloaded?	Size of an update package	The version after update	Whether Root privilege is lost after update?
AXXXXMU2APL6	yes	80.8 MB	AXXXXMU2BQI2	no
AXXXXMU2BQA2	yes	72.1 MB	AXXXXMU2BQI2	no
AXXXXMU2BQC2	yes	67.0 MB	AXXXXMU2BQI2	no

5.2 Stability

The system update in this paper only updates remain partitions except for boot and recovery partition, and the system updated still uses the rooted custom boot and custom recovery. The actual test needs to be performed to confirm whether the grafted system can run normally. We use Monkey for stress testing. Monkey will test all the apps if application is not specified. We use this feature to indirectly stress the grafted system to determine its stability. Table 2 shows the results of Monkey test on the various versions of the OSs which is grafted on rooted custom boot. The test results show that if we modify the kernel according to the proposed scheme in this paper, the system stability will not be affected; at the same time, this boot image can support the adjacent versions of OSs, the system stability is still guaranteed.

Table 2. Monkey test on the various version of AXXXX OSs grafted in the rooted custom boot

OS version	Seed	Count	Time-consuming (ms)	Exception?
AXXXXMU2APL6	2018	10000	141030	no
AXXXXMU2BQA2	2018	10000	134772	no
AXXXXMU2BQC2	2018	10000	121304	no
AXXXXMU2BQI2	2018	10000	113220	no

6 Discussion and Future Works

The update of Android major versions is usually accompanied by a larger change of Linux kernel version. In this case, we can cover boot partition with the official updated boot image, then update the system. Of course, the updated system will not retain root privilege, but the user data will not be affected. This scheme has two limitations, one is: the user should not modify the system partition after obtaining root privilege. The reason is mentioned in the previous section. Second is: each manufacturer uses different security mechanisms, if one wants to achieve the same function on its Android phones using the scheme of this paper, there will be some differences in implementation. We will try to modify recovery partition only to achieve the same function in the future, not by modifying kernel but inserting specific programs in the ramdisk.

7 Conclusions

In this paper, we customize the boot image and the recovery image by modifying the kernel, so the system thinks itself is official, and it can download the update package from the server. The customized boot image will restore the boot partition to the official image in the first stage of the system upgrade so that the upgrade process can be performed normally. The custom recovery image is able to re-use the customized boot image to overwrite the boot partition for root privileges in the second stage of the system upgrade. In this process, we detailed analyzed the Android OS upgrade process, as well as Samsung's custom integrity verification mechanism for Android OS. A series of experiments on the Samsung AXXXX shows that the custom kernel can run normally in adjacent small-version systems without affecting system functions. By customizing the kernel, there is no difference between a rooted phone and a phone without root, and root privileges can be preserved after the upgrade.

Acknowledgement. This work was supported by The Fundamental Research Funds for Beijing Universities of Civil Engineering and Architecture (Response by ZhangYu), and also Excellent Teachers Development Foundation of BUCEA (Response by ZhangYu), and also National Key R&D Program of China (No. 2016YFC060090).

References

1. Gasparis, I., Qian, Z., Song, C., Krishnamurthy, S.V.: Detecting android root exploits by learning from root providers. In: 26th USENIX Security Symposium (USENIX Security 17), pp. 1129–1144. USENIX Association (2017)
2. Kapoor, R., Agarwal, S.: Sustaining superior performance in business ecosystems: evidence from application software developers in the iOS and android smartphone ecosystems. Organ. Sci. **28**(3), 531–551 (2017)
3. Jo, H.J., Choi, W., Na, S.Y., Woo, S., Lee, D.H.: Vulnerabilities of android OS-based telematics system. Wirel. Pers. Commun. **92**(4), 1511–1530 (2017)
4. SuperSU. https://play.google.com/store/apps/details?id=eu.chainfire.supersu&hl=en_US. Accessed 30 May 2018
5. FlashFire. https://forum.xda-developers.com/general/paid-software/flashfire-t3075433. Accessed 30 May 2018
6. Salehi, M., Daryabar, F., Tadayon, M.H.: Welcome to binder: a kernel level attack model for the binder in android operating system. In: 2016 8th International Symposium on Telecommunications (IST), pp. 156–161. IEEE (2016)
7. Guri, M., Poliak, Y., Shapira, B., Elovici, Y.: JoKER: trusted detection of kernel rootkits in android devices via JTAG interface. In: 2015 IEEE Trustcom/BigDataSE/ISPA, vol. 1, pp. 65–73. IEEE (2015)
8. Zhu, R., Tan, Y.-A., Zhang, Q., Li, Y., Zheng, J.: Determining image base of firmware for ARM devices by matching literal pools. Digit. Invest. **16**, 19–28 (2016)
9. Ju, M., Kim, H., Kang, M., Kim, S.: Efficient memory reclaiming for mitigating sluggish response in mobile devices. In: 2015 IEEE 5th International Conference on Consumer Electronics-Berlin (ICCE-Berlin), pp. 232–236. IEEE (2015)
10. Chen, W., Xu, L., Li, G., Xiang, Y.: A lightweight virtualization solution for android devices. IEEE Trans. Comput. **64**(10), 2741–2751 (2015)

11. Zhang, X., Tan, Y.-A., Zhang, C., Xue, Y., Li, Y., Zheng, J.: A code protection scheme by process memory relocation for android devices. Multimedia Tools Appl. **77**(9), 11137–11157 (2018)
12. Xue, Y., Zhang, X., Yu, X., Zhang, Y., Tan, Y.-A., Li, Y.: Isolating host environment by booting android from OTG devices. Chin. J. Electron. **27**(3), 617–624 (2018)
13. Samsung Odin. https://samsungodin.com/. Accessed 30 May 2018
14. Tan, Y.-A., et al.: A root privilege management scheme with revocable authorization for android devices. J. Netw. Comput. Appl. **107**(4), 69–82 (2018)
15. TWRP. https://twrp.me/. Accessed 30 May 2018
16. Corral, L., Georgiev, A.B., Janes, A., Kofler, S.: Energy-aware performance evaluation of android custom kernels. In: 2015 IEEE/ACM 4th International Workshop on Green and Sustainable Software (GREENS), pp. 1–7. IEEE (2015)
17. Zhu, R., Zhang, B., Mao, J., Zhang, Q., Tan, Y.-A.: A methodology for determining the image base of ARM-based industrial control system firmware. Int. J. Crit. Infrastruct. Prot. **16**(3), 26–35 (2017)

Accelerating Pattern Matching
with CPU-GPU Collaborative Computing

Victoria Sanz[1,2]([✉]), Adrián Pousa[1], Marcelo Naiouf[1],
and Armando De Giusti[1,3]

[1] III-LIDI, School of Computer Sciences, National University of La Plata,
La Plata, Argentina
{vsanz,apousa,mnaiouf,degiusti}@lidi.info.unlp.edu.ar
[2] CIC, Buenos Aires, Argentina
[3] CONICET, Buenos Aires, Argentina

Abstract. Pattern matching algorithms are used in several areas such as network security, bioinformatics and text mining. In order to support large data and pattern sets, these algorithms have to be adapted to take advantage of the computing power of emerging parallel architectures. In this paper, we present a parallel algorithm for pattern matching on CPU-GPU heterogeneous systems, which is based on the Parallel Failureless Aho-Corasick algorithm (PFAC) for GPU. We evaluate the performance of the proposed algorithm on a machine with 36 CPU cores and 1 GPU, using data and pattern sets of different size, and compare it with that of PFAC for GPU and the multithreaded version of PFAC for shared-memory machines. The results reveal that our proposal achieves higher performance than the other two approaches for data sets of considerable size, since it uses both CPU and GPU cores.

Keywords: Pattern matching · CPU-GPU collaborative computing
CPU-GPU heterogeneous systems · Hybrid programming
Aho-Corasick

1 Introduction

Pattern matching algorithms are able to locate some or all occurrences of a finite number of patterns (pattern set or dictionary) in a text (data set). These algorithms are key components of DNA analysis applications [1], antivirus [2], intrusion detection systems [3,4], among others. In this regard, the Aho-Corasick (AC) algorithm [5] is widely used for multiple pattern matching since it efficiently processes the text in a single pass. The algorithm consists of two parts. In the first part, a finite state machine is constructed from the pattern set. In the second part, the text is applied as input to this machine, which signals whenever it has found a pattern.

The ever-increasing amount of data to be processed, sometimes in real time, led several authors to investigate the acceleration of AC on emerging parallel architectures. In particular, researchers have proposed different approaches

© Springer Nature Switzerland AG 2018
J. Vaidya and J. Li (Eds.): ICA3PP 2018, LNCS 11334, pp. 310–322, 2018.
https://doi.org/10.1007/978-3-030-05051-1_22

to parallelize AC on shared-memory architectures, distributed-memory architectures with homogeneous (conventional clusters) or heterogeneous processing elements (GPU clusters) and GPUs [6–10].

Today, most commercial computers include tens of CPU cores and at least one GPU. The use of both processing units or PUs (CPU cores and GPUs) can significantly improve the performance of the application, compared to using only CPU cores or GPUs. However, this is a challenge for programmers since the PUs differ in architecture, programming model and performance. The main challenges in CPU-GPU collaborative computing are to achieve load balancing and to minimize the data transfer between the PUs [11].

To our best knowledge, CPU-GPU collaborative computing has not been used to accelerate the matching phase of pattern matching algorithms. In this paper, we present a parallel algorithm for pattern matching on CPU-GPU heterogeneous systems, which is based on the Parallel Failureless Aho-Corasick algorithm (PFAC) for GPU [7]. We evaluate the performance of the proposed algorithm on a machine with 36 CPU cores and 1 GPU, using data and pattern sets of different size, and compare it with that of PFAC for GPU and the multithreaded version of PFAC for shared-memory machines. The results reveal that our proposal achieves higher performance than the other two approaches for data sets of considerable size, since it uses both CPU and GPU cores.

The rest of the paper is organized as follows. Section 2 discusses background and related work. Section 3 introduces a hybrid OpenMP-CUDA programming model and a workload distribution strategy, which are specific to CPU–GPU collaborative computing. Section 4 describes our parallel algorithm for pattern matching on CPU-GPU heterogeneous systems. Section 5 shows our experimental results. Finally, Sect. 6 presents the main conclusions and some ideas for future research.

2   Background and Related Work

The AC algorithm [5] has been widely used since it is able to locate all occurrences of user-specified patterns in a single pass of the text. The algorithm consists of two steps: the first is to construct a finite state pattern matching machine; the second is to process the text using the state machine constructed in the previous step. The pattern matching machine has valid and failure transitions. The former are used to detect all user-specified patterns. The latter are used to backtrack the state machine, specifically to the state that represents the longest proper suffix, in order to recognize patterns starting at any location of the text. Certain states are designated as "output states" which indicate that a set of patterns has been found. The AC machine works as follows: given a current state and an input character, it tries to follow a valid transition; if such a transition does not exist, it jumps to the state pointed by the failure transition and processes the same character until it causes a valid transition. The machine emits the corresponding patterns whenever an output state is found. Figure 1 shows the state machine for the pattern set {he, she, his, hers}. Solid lines represent valid transitions and dotted lines represent failure transitions.

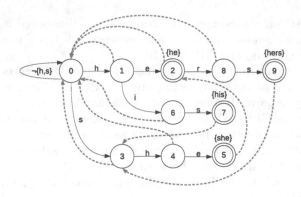

Fig. 1. Aho-Corasick state machine for the pattern set {he, she, his, hers}

Several researchers have proposed different approaches to parallelize AC on different architectures. In the following paragraphs, we summarize the most relevant studies on this topic.

One of these strategies is based on dividing the input text into segments and making each processor responsible for a particular segment (i.e., each processor performs AC on its segment). All processors use the same state machine. The disadvantage of this strategy is that patterns can cross the boundary of two adjacent segments. This problem is known as the "boundary detection" problem. In order to detect these patterns, each processor has to compute an additional chunk known as "overlapping area", whose size is equal to the length of the longest pattern in the dictionary minus 1. However, this additional computation is an overhead that increases as the text is divided into more segments of smaller size. Figure 2 illustrates this strategy.

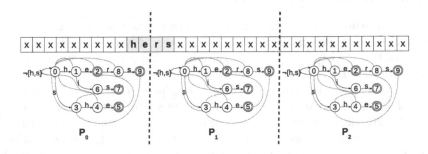

Fig. 2. Parallel AC

In [6] the authors parallelize AC using the aforementioned strategy on shared memory architectures, GPUs and distributed memory architectures (multicore cluster and GPU cluster). Then, they present a detailed comparison of the performance of such implementations, using test cases with different matching conditions, and conclude that software approaches for pattern matching on high-performance systems can reach high throughput with moderate programming efforts.

In [7] the authors present the Parallel Failureless Aho-Corasick algorithm (PFAC) that efficiently exploits the parallelism of AC and therefore is suitable for GPUs. PFAC assigns each character of the text to a particular thread. Each thread is responsible for identifying the pattern beginning at its assigned position and terminates immediately when it detects that such a pattern does not exist (i.e., when it cannot follow a valid transition). Note that PFAC does not use failure transitions and therefore they can be removed from the state machine. Figures 3 and 4 give an example of the PFAC state machine and the PFAC algorithm, respectively. Algorithm 1.1 shows the pseudocode of PFAC (code executed by each thread). The experimental results reveal that PFAC achieves good performance on GPUs and multicores.

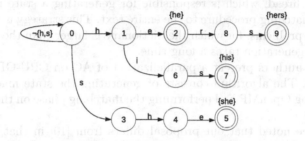

Fig. 3. PFAC state machine for the pattern set {he, she, his, hers}

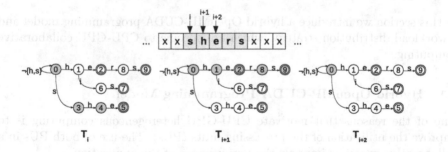

Fig. 4. Example of PFAC

Algorithm 1.1. Pseudocode of PFAC

```
pos = start
state = initial state
while ( pos < text size ){
    if (there is no transition for the current state and input character)
        break
    state = next state for the current state and input character
    if (state is an output state)
        register the pattern located at the position "start"
    pos = pos + 1
}
```

In [8,9] the authors explore a different strategy to parallelize AC on multicores, which is based on splitting the dictionary into chunks. Each chunk is assigned to a thread, which is responsible for generating a state machine and applying the matching procedure to the entire text. This strategy is used to solve bioinformatics problems, for which the dictionary is larger than the text and the state machine generation takes a long time.

In [10] the authors present a parallelization of AC on CPU-GPU heterogeneous systems. The algorithm consists of generating the state machine on the CPU cores using OpenMP and performing the matching phase on the GPU using CUDA.

It should be noted that our proposal differs from [10] in that we focus on improving the resource utilization of the CPU-GPU heterogeneous system by using both PUs to accelerate the matching phase of AC.

3   A CPU-GPU Collaborative Computing Model

In this section we introduce a hybrid OpenMP-CUDA programming model and a workload distribution strategy, which are specific to CPU-GPU collaborative computing.

3.1   Hybrid OpenMP-CUDA Programming Model

One of the reasons that motivate CPU-GPU heterogeneous computing is to improve the utilization of the processing units (PUs). The use of both PUs in a collaborative way may improve the performance of the application.

Assuming that the system is composed of N cores and 1 GPU, the proposed model firstly launches two OpenMP threads (T_0 and T_1). Each thread runs on a dedicated CPU core. T_0 is responsible for managing the computation on the GPU, which involves the following steps: allocating memory on the GPU to store input and output data, transferring the data from CPU to GPU, calling the kernel function, transferring the results from GPU to CPU and freeing memory on the GPU. On the other hand, T_1 is responsible for controlling the computation on the remaining N-1 CPU cores. Specifically, T_1 creates a team of threads and becomes the master thread, and then all these threads concurrently perform the corresponding calculations on the CPU cores. Figure 5 depicts this hybrid programming model.

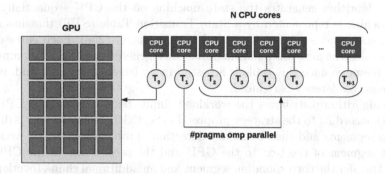

Fig. 5. Hybrid OpenMP-CUDA programming model

3.2 Workload Distribution Strategy

In order to perform CPU-GPU collaborative computing it is necessary to distribute the workload among the PUs. A workload distribution is optimal when both PUs complete their respective work within the same amount of time. We use a simple static workload distribution (i.e., the amount of work to be assigned to each PU is determined before program execution) based on the relative performance of PUs [12].

In order to distribute the work among the PUs, we estimate the CPU and GPU execution time in the collaborative implementation as $T'_{cpu} = T_{cpu} \cdot R$ and $T'_{gpu} = T_{gpu} \cdot (1 - R)$, respectively, where R is the proportion of work assigned to the CPU cores, T_{cpu} represents the execution time of the OpenMP algorithm on the available CPU cores and T_{gpu} is the execution time of the CUDA algorithm on the GPU. Clearly, the execution time of the collaborative implementation reaches its minimum when $T'_{cpu} = T'_{gpu}$, i.e. $T_{cpu} \cdot R = T_{gpu} \cdot (1 - R)$. From this equation we obtain $R = \frac{T_{gpu}}{T_{cpu} + T_{gpu}}$.

In our scenario, R has to be recalculated when the input data vary or the configuration of the system changes. According to R, the workload assigned to the CPU cores is $D_{cpu} = R \cdot D_{size}$ and the workload assigned to the GPU is $D_{gpu} = D_{size} - D_{cpu}$, where D_{size} is the length of the text string.

Although it is impractical to run both OpenMP and CUDA applications in order to obtain R, we plan to use this first approach as a baseline to derive an estimation model for R.

4 Pattern Matching on CPU-GPU Heterogeneous Systems

Our implementation is based on the PFAC algorithm and uses the hybrid programming model proposed in Sect. 3.1.

Our algorithm generates the state machine on the CPU sequentially. The state machine is represented by a State Transition Table (STT) that has a row for each state and a column for each ASCII character (256). Each entry of the STT contains the next state information. Once generated, the STT is copied to texture memory since this table is accessed in an irregular manner and, in this way, the access latency is reduced.

The algorithm distributes the workload (input text) between the CPU and the GPU according to the strategy proposed in Sect. 3.2. Thus, the text is divided into two segments and the "boundary detection" problem appears. If we assign the first segment of the text to the GPU and the second one to the CPU, we need to transfer the corresponding segment and an additional chunk (overlapping area) to the GPU. On the contrary, if we assign the first segment to the CPU and the second one to the GPU, we only need to transfer the corresponding segment to the GPU. We chose the second option since CPU-GPU memory transfers are time consuming and in this way we reduce the amount of data to be transferred. Figure 6 shows these two options.

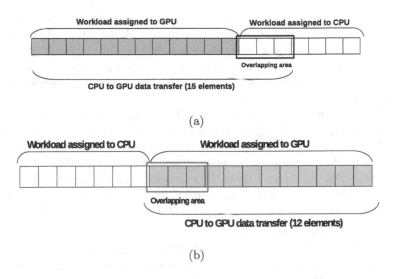

(a)

(b)

Fig. 6. Workload distribution between the CPU and the GPU

The thread in charge of managing the GPU (T_0) copies its segment into the global memory. Note that large segments may exceed the global memory capacity. In that case, T_0 subdivides the segment into smaller segments and then it transfers and processes them one by one. It should be noted that each sub-segment must be transferred with the corresponding overlapping area. The implementation details of the PFAC algorithm on GPU (PFAC kernel) can be found in [7]. In summary, the kernel is launched with 256 threads per block. Each thread block handles 1024 positions of the input segment (i.e., each thread processes 4 positions). Each thread block loads the corresponding data into shared memory. Then, threads read input bytes from the shared memory in order to perform their work.

The thread in charge of managing the CPU (T_1) creates as many threads as available cores. Then, the workload (segment) is distributed among threads via the 'for' work-sharing directive.

5 Experimental Results

Experimental tests were carried out on a machine composed of two Intel Xeon E5-2695 v4 processors and 128 GB RAM. Each processor has eighteen 2.10 Ghz cores, thus the machine has thirty-six cores in total (Hyper-Threading disabled). The machine is equipped with an Nvidia GeForce GTX 960 composed of 1024 cores and 2 GB GDDR5 memory. Each CUDA core operates at 1127 Mhz.

Test scenarios were generated by combining three English texts of different sizes with four English dictionaries with different number of patterns. All the texts were extracted from the British National Corpus [13]: text 1 is a 4-million-word sample (21 MB); text 2 is a 50-million-word sample (268 MB); text 3 is a 100-million-word sample (544 MB). The dictionaries include frequently used words: dictionary 1 with 3000 words; dictionary 2 with 100000 words; dictionary 3 with 178690 words; dictionary 4 with 263533 words.

To evaluate the effectiveness of our proposal, we generated the sequential version of the PFAC algorithm and the following parallel versions:

- PFAC_OMP36: implementation of PFAC on multicore using OpenMP and executed with 36 threads.
- PFAC_CUDA: implementation of PFAC on GPU using CUDA and executed with 256 threads per block.
- PFAC_Col36: CPU-GPU collaborative implementation of PFAC using CUDA and OpenMP. This version was executed with 36 OpenMP threads. One thread manages the computation on the GPU and the other threads compute on the remaining CPU cores.

For each test scenario, we ran each implementation 100 times and averaged the execution time.

The aforementioned versions of PFAC consist of two parts. The first part involves constructing the state machine. The second part involves performing the pattern matching. Our experiments focus on the second part since it is the most significant part of the algorithm.

The implementations of PFAC that use the GPU (PFAC_CUDA and PFAC_Col36) follow three steps to perform the pattern matching on this PU: (1) transferring the text from CPU to GPU - host-to-device (H2D) transfer; (2)

launching the kernel; (3) transferring the results from GPU to CPU - device-to-host (D2H) transfer. Our analysis considers the data transfer time (H2D and D2H) since it represents a significant portion of the total execution time (i.e. it is not negligible).

In order to demonstrate this, we compared PFAC_CUDA considering H2D/D2H transfers with PFAC_CUDA without considering such transfers. Figure 7 shows the normalized execution time of both versions, for each test scenario. The results reveal that H2D/D2H transfers considerably increase the execution time of PFAC_CUDA and represent a large percentage of the execution time. Figure 8 shows that the percentage of execution time spent in H2D/D2H transfers ranges between 26% and 42%.

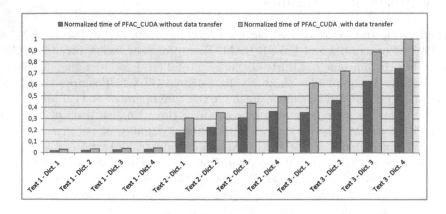

Fig. 7. Normalized time of PFAC_CUDA

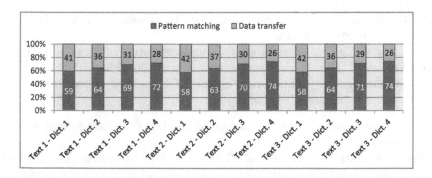

Fig. 8. PFAC_CUDA: percentage of execution time spent in H2D/D2H transfers

Then, we compared the performance (Speedup[1]) of PFAC_CUDA, PFAC_OMP36 and PFAC_Col36.

In the case of PFAC_Col36, we distributed the input text among the PUs according to the strategy proposed in Sect. 3.2. Table 1 shows the value of R for each test scenario and the current system configuration (36 cores and 1 GPU). We measured the load balance[2] between CPU and GPU in PFAC_Col36 when using this distribution strategy. Table 2 shows the load balance for each test scenario. A load balance value near 1 means a better distribution of load. The results reveal that this workload distribution strategy provides a good load-balance, which ranges between 0.71 and 0.98.

Table 1. Values of R used by PFAC_Col36, for each test scenario

Test scenario	R
Text 1 - Dict. 1	0.36
Text 1 - Dict. 2	0.39
Text 1 - Dict. 3	0.36
Text 1 - Dict. 4	0.39
Text 2 - Dict. 1	0.59
Text 2 - Dict. 2	0.61
Text 2 - Dict. 3	0.63
Text 2 - Dict. 4	0.65
Text 3 - Dict. 1	0.66
Text 3 - Dict. 2	0.67
Text 3 - Dict. 3	0.68
Text 3 - Dict. 4	0.71

Figure 9 illustrates the Speedup obtained by the parallel versions of PFAC, for different test scenarios.

In general, the results show that the speedup achieved by PFAC_OMP36 and PFAC_Col36 increases as the size of the text augments. These versions of PFAC have different sources of overhead such as thread creation and implicit synchronization. These overheads have less impact on the execution time as the size of the text augments.

On the other hand, the results show that the speedup of PFAC_CUDA does not increase significantly as the size of the text augments. This is mainly due to the fact that the data transfer time increases when the size of the text augments.

---

[1] Speedup is defined as $\frac{T_s}{T_p}$, where T_s is the execution time of the sequential algorithm and T_p is the execution time of the parallel algorithm.

[2] Load balance [14] can be defined as the ratio between the average time to finish all of the parallel tasks T_{avg} and the maximum time to finish any of the parallel tasks T_{max}.

Table 2. Load balance results (PFAC_Col36), for each test scenario

Test scenario	Load balance
Text 1 - Dict. 1	0.71
Text 1 - Dict. 2	0.74
Text 1 - Dict. 3	0.75
Text 1 - Dict. 4	0.79
Text 2 - Dict. 1	0.83
Text 2 - Dict. 2	0.98
Text 2 - Dict. 3	0.91
Text 2 - Dict. 4	0.94
Text 3 - Dict. 1	0.89
Text 3 - Dict. 2	0.98
Text 3 - Dict. 3	0.96
Text 3 - Dict. 4	0.94

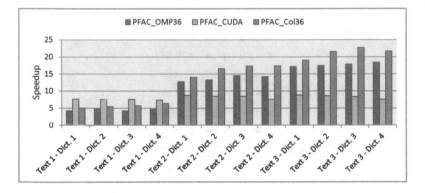

Fig. 9. Speedup obtained by PFAC_OMP36, PFAC_CUDA and PFAC_Col36

As it can be observed, PFAC_CUDA achieves the best performance for Text 1, followed by PFAC_Col36 and PFAC_OMP36. For this text, PFAC_CUDA, PFAC_Col36 and PFAC_OMP36 achieve an average speedup of 7.51, 5.63 and 4.44, respectively.

Furthermore, PFAC_Col36 achieves the best performance for Text 2 and Text 3, which in general increases as the size of the text and the size of the dictionary augment. Although PFAC_Col36 uses the GPU, its performance is less affected by data transfers. This is because PFAC_Col36 transfers only a portion of the data (text and results) between the CPU and the GPU, whereas PFAC_CUDA transfers the entire data.

In addition, for Text 2 and Text 3, PFAC_OMP36 outperforms PFAC_CUDA.

Finally, for a fixed text, the performance of PFAC_CUDA slightly decreases as the size of the dictionary augments. In PFAC_CUDA, the state machine (STT)

is stored in texture memory when it does not exceed the capacity of that memory (2^{27} elements), otherwise it is stored in global memory that has higher access latency. In particular, the size of the STT corresponding to Dictionary 4 exceeds the amount of texture memory, hence it is stored in global memory and this leads to a small loss of performance, for a particular input text.

In summary, for Text 2 PFAC_Col36 achieves an average speedup of 16.30, followed by PFAC_OMP36 (13.69) and PFAC_CUDA (8.31). For Text 3 PFAC_Col36 achieves an average speedup of 21.23, followed by PFAC_OMP36 (17.71) and PFAC_CUDA (8.33).

6   Conclusions and Future Work

In this paper, we presented a parallel algorithm for pattern matching on CPU-GPU heterogeneous systems, which is based on the Parallel Failureless Aho-Corasick algorithm (PFAC) for GPU.

To develop our algorithm, we introduced a hybrid OpenMP-CUDA programming model and a workload distribution strategy, which are specific to CPU-GPU collaborative computing.

We evaluated the performance of the proposed algorithm (PFAC_Col) on a machine with 36 CPU cores and 1 GPU, and compared it with that of PFAC for GPU (PFAC_CUDA) and the multithreaded version of PFAC for shared-memory machines (PFAC_OMP). The results reveal that our algorithm (PFAC_Col) outperforms both PFAC_CUDA and PFAC_OMP for texts of considerable size, since it uses both CPU and GPU cores. However, PFAC_CUDA achieves the best performance for small texts.

As for future work, we plan to extend the experimental work presented in this paper to evaluate the scalability of our algorithm as the number of CPU cores is increased. Also we plan to construct a model based load-balancing strategy.

References

1. Tumeo A., Villa O.: Accelerating DNA analysis applications on GPU clusters. In: IEEE 8th Symposium on Application Specific Processors (SASP), pp. 71–76. IEEE Computer Society, Washington D. C. (2010)
2. Clamav. http://www.clamav.net
3. Norton M.: Optimizing Pattern matching for intrusion detection. Sourcefire Inc., White Paper. https://www.snort.org/documents/optimization-of-pattern-matches-for-ids
4. Tumeo, A., et al.: Efficient pattern matching on GPUs for intrusion detection systems (2010)
5. Aho, A.V., Corasick, M.J.: Efficient string matching: an aid to bibliographic search. Commun. ACM. **18**(6), 333–340 (1975)
6. Tumeo, A., et al.: Aho-Corasick string matching on shared and distributed-memory parallel architectures. IEEE Trans. Parallel Distrib. Syst. **23**(3), 436–443 (2012)
7. Lin, C.H., et al.: Accelerating pattern matching using a novel parallel algorithm on GPUs. IEEE Trans. Comput. **62**(10), 1906–1916 (2013)

8. Arudchutha S., et al.: String matching with multicore CPUs: Performing better with the Aho-Corasick algorithm. In: 2013 IEEE 8th International Conference on Industrial and Information Systems, pp. 231–236. IEEE Computer Society, Washington D. C. (2013)
9. Herath, D., et al.: Accelerating string matching for bio-computing applications on multi-core CPUs. In: Proceedings of the IEEE 7th International Conference on Industrial and Information Systems (ICIIS), pp. 1–6. IEEE Computer Society, Washington D. C. (2012)
10. Soroushnia, S., et al.: Heterogeneous parallelization of Aho-Corasick algorithm. In: Proceedings of the IEEE 7th International Conference on Industrial and Information Systems (ICIIS), pp. 1–6. IEEE Computer Society, Washington D. C. (2012)
11. Mittal, S., Vetter, J.: A survey of CPU-GPU heterogeneous computing techniques. ACM Comput. Surv. **47**(4), 69:1–69:35 (2015)
12. Wan, L., et al.: Efficient CPU-GPU cooperative computing for solving the subset-sum problem. Concurr. Comput.: Pract. Exp. **28**(2), 185–186 (2016)
13. The British National Corpus, version 3 (BNC XML Edition). Distributed by Bodleian Libraries, University of Oxford, on behalf of the BNC Consortium (2007). http://www.natcorp.ox.ac.uk/
14. Rahman, R.: Intel Xeon Phi Coprocessor Architecture and Tools: The Guide for Application Developers. Apress, Berkeley (2013)

An Incremental Map Matching Algorithm
Based on Weighted Shortest Path

Jixiao Chen, Yongjian Yang, Liping Huang$^{(\boxtimes)}$, Zhuo Zhu,
and Funing Yang

Jilin University, Changchun, China
chen_jixiao@163.com, huangliping5727@163.com

Abstract. GPS (global position system) trajectories collected by urban cars
depict the citizens' daily trips and reflect the traffic situation in city areas. The
process called map matching is to match the GPS point sequence to the corresponding road which is the fundamental step for further travel pattern mining
and transport situation analysis. The existing research based on the incremental
map matching applies only to GPS trajectories of high-sampling-rate (0 to 30 s).
However most actually collected GPS trajectories are with a low-sampling-rate
(more than 2 min) for saving the collection and transmission costs. In this paper,
we proposed an incremental map matching algorithm based on weighted
shortest path, called WSI-matching. By matching single GPS point to its candidate road and filling the missing path between two GPS points, it improves the
overall matching accuracy with a relatively low time complexity compared to
the traditional global matching algorithm. Experiment results show that our
WSI-matching algorithm present obvious advantages over traditional incremental algorithms and global algorithms in terms of both matching accuracy and
running time, and it adapts to either high-sampling-rate trajectories or low-
sampling-rate trajectories.

Keywords: Map matching · GPS trajectory · Low-sampling-rate
Incremental algorithm · Shortest path

1 Introduction

With the popularity of GPS positioning devices equipped in urban floating vehicles, a
large number of urban travel trajectories can be collected every day. Those trajectories
play an important role in the fields of urban computing [8, 10], such as obtaining the urban
transport pattern [1], making urban construction planning [6], finding popular routes [5],
researching geographical social network [2], and mastering traffic condition [11].

However, the GPS equipment has certain positioning error and sampling error,
which will lead to the deviation between the trajectory of the GPS sampling point and
the real path of the floating car on the road, which is much obvious with a low sampling
rate. As shown in Fig. 1(a), if these trajectories are not matched to the road network, it
will be unconducive for further road based analysis and application.

In terms of the map matching problem, a GPS trajectory T is a sequence of GPS
points arranged in time order, each of which includes the location information of

J. Vaidya and J. Li (Eds.): ICA3PP 2018, LNCS 11334, pp. 323–336, 2018.
https://doi.org/10.1007/978-3-030-05051-1_23

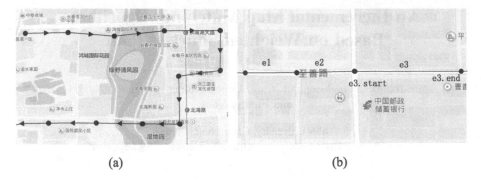

(a)   (b)

Fig. 1. Illustration of GPS positioning deviation and road segment

longitude and latitude. Meanwhile each location is attached with the point sampling time stamp and the moving direction. To match each GPS point to the corresponding road, a road segment e is depicted with the features of road ID, length, road level, starting point, ending point, direction and other attributes. Generally speaking, a road in a city contains several road segments, as shown in Fig. 1(b).

In the road network G, each road segment represents a node. If the two road segments are connected directly, there is an edge between the corresponding two nodes in the road network and each edge has a weight value of d. A travel path P is a continuous road segments sequence $<r_1, r_2, ..., r_n>$ in the road network G.

Thus the map matching problem for a coarse-grained GPS trajectory can be defined as: Given a GPS trajectory T and a road network G, find the path P from G that matches T with its real path.

The map matching problem can be divided into fine-grained map matching problem and coarse-grained map matching problem according to the sampling frequency of GPS points. Fine-grained sampling frequency takes about 10 s to 30 s to collect a GPS point, while coarse-grained sampling interval is usually 2 min or even longer. With the increase of GPS point sampling interval, more noise and interference are encountered in map matching, and the accuracy of matching results is greatly influenced. Therefore, the requirements of coarse-grained map matching are also higher. The map matching algorithm proposed in this paper is committed to get high accuracy matching results when coarse-grained map matching is applied.

The main contributions of this paper are as follows:

- In order to solve the problem of coarse-grained map matching, we propose a new incremental algorithm based on the weighted shortest path (WSI-matching).
- The proposed algorithm takes account of the spatial topology and the relationship between the two adjacent points and uses the weighted value when calculating the shortest path.
- The experimental results show that the WSI-matching algorithm can maintain high precision matching results when the sampling frequency of GPS points is lower than that of the traditional incremental matching algorithm and the global matching algorithm.

The rest of this paper is organized as follows: Sect. 2 discusses the related work. Section 3 details our WSI-matching algorithm and the algorithm complexity evaluation. Section 4 reports the experimental results, and Sect. 5 makes a summary of this paper.

2 Related Work

Map matching algorithm can be divided into incremental algorithm and global algorithm based on the range of GPS sampling points considered in map matching.

The incremental algorithm matches GPS points to the map based on the local features of the current GPS sampling points. The algorithm generally uses the greedy strategy to extend the final global solution from the results of the points that have been matched. A series of hidden Markov models are constructed in reference [9], and the incremental map matching is achieved by alternately expanding and shrinking of adjacent hidden Markov models. Reference [12] calculates the matching results based on the location and direction information of GPS collection points and the path accessibility of two adjacent time points. In references [13, 16], map matching is concerned with topological rules and traffic rules related to road connectivity. Incremental algorithm runs fast, and high matching accuracy can be achieved when the sampling interval is short. However, with the increase of sampling interval, the incremental algorithm will have an "edge skipping" phenomenon [12], the matching accuracy is significantly reduced, and ignoring the correlation of adjacent GPS points can also lead the matching result effected by the measurement error.

When the global algorithm matches, the whole GPS trajectory is considered. The algorithm finds the matching path closest to the trajectory from the road network. Many global map matching algorithms [3, 14] use the "frechet distance" or its variants to calculate the similarity between GPS trajectories and matching paths. The ST-matching algorithm in [15] considers the spatial and temporal features of the GPS trajectory and matching with the hidden Markov model, which is the most commonly used map matching algorithm at present. Based on ST-matching, papers [4, 7] applies conditional random field model to map matching problem. The accuracy of the global algorithm is high, as well as the time complexity. In addition, most of the global algorithm ignores the time or speed constraints of the trajectory. Therefore, these algorithms are also easily affected by the increase of sampling interval.

In contrast, our WSI-matching incremental algorithm considers the correlation between adjacent GPS points and the time/speed constraints of the trajectory, and obtains a higher matching accuracy at a smaller computation time and space cost.

3 The WSI-Matching Algorithm

3.1 System Overview

Figure 2 shows the framework of WSI-matching algorithm. The map matching algorithm takes the GPS trajectory and the road network as inputs. For each GPS point, the algorithm first finds out the candidate road segment of the current point in a certain range, and selects the best road segment as the matching road segment. As the GPS points are coarse-grained, the matching road segment of the two adjacent GPS points are not directly connected. Thus the algorithm predicts and fills the missing path between the matching road segment of the two adjacent GPS points to find a sub path P_i corresponding to the two adjacent GPS points. Finally, when all of the GPS points are processed, we combine the sub paths $P_1, P_2, \ldots, P_n$ calculated at the last step into the path P as the output of the algorithm.

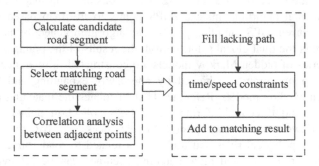

Fig. 2. Framework of WSI-matching algorithm

3.2   Candidate Road Segment Analysis

We take the point p as the center and r as the radius. All road segments covered by the circle in the road network G become candidates for p. As shown in Fig. 3(a), the road segments e_1, e_2, e_3 and e_4 are all candidate road segments of the point p. For selecting the value of radius r, the smallest possible value of r should be selected to reduce the running time of the algorithm while ensuring that the matching accuracy is not affected. In addition, in order to reduce the searching range, a grid spatial index is established for the road network G. After the candidate road segment of point p is determined, we combine the following three aspects to calculate the score of each candidate road segment: (1) The distance between point p and the candidate road segment; (2) The angle between the direction of p (the direction of the floating car on the road) and the direction of the candidate road segment; (3) Whether the candidate road segment is directly connected to the matching road segment of the last point in the GPS trajectory or they are the same road segment.

We use the Euclidean distance dist(p, e_i) to represent the distance metric from the point p to the candidate road segment e_i, as shown in Fig. 3(b), making vertical line from point p to e_1 and e_2, and the foot point f_1 is on e_1, dist(p, e_1) is the length of the vertical segment pf_1; the foot point f_2 is on the extended line of e_2, and dist(p,e_2) is the length of the line segment which is from p to the nearer endpoint of e_2.

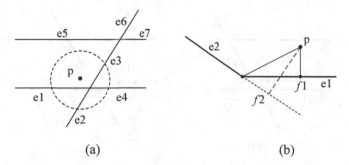

(a)   (b)

Fig. 3. Candidate roads and distance metric

The distance from the point p to the candidate segment e_i is in line with the Gaussian distribution $N(\mu, \sigma^2)$. If the map matching is only considered from the perspective of distance, its probability density function reflects the possibility of the point p matching to e_i. We define:

$$N_d(e_i) = \frac{1}{\sqrt{2\pi}\sigma_1} e^{-\frac{(x_1-\mu_1)^2}{2\sigma_1^2}} \qquad (1)$$

where $x_1 = \text{dist}(p, e_i)$. We define the angle between the direction of point p and the direction of the candidate road segment as $\text{incl}(p, e_i)$. Similarly, the $\text{incl}(p, e_i)$ is also in line with Gaussian distribution $N(\mu, \sigma^2)$. We define:

$$N_a(e_i) = \frac{1}{\sqrt{2\pi}\sigma_2} e^{-\frac{(x_2-\mu_2)^2}{2\sigma_2^2}} \qquad (2)$$

where $x_2 = \text{incl}(p, e_i)$. When the GPS sampling point appears at the intersection, taking into account the direction factor will eliminate the candidate road segment with a larger angle of the floating car, as shown in Fig. 4(a), the algorithm will select the segment e_1 with the similar direction of point p as the matching road segment.

Topological relationship between the candidate road segment of the current point and the matching road segment of the last point is further considered. If a candidate road segment of the current point is directly connected to the matching road segment of the last point or they are the same segment, then this candidate road segments have a higher probability of being taken as the final matching road segment.

When parallel road segments or multi-vehicle road segments occur, it is particularly important to consider this situation. As shown in Fig. 4(b), p_1 and p_2 are two adjacent points in the GPS trajectory, we know that the matching road segment of point p_1 is e_1, and the point p_2 has two candidate road segment e_2 and e_3. If only the distance and angle factors are considered, e_3 will be erroneously taken as the matching road segment. Therefore, the algorithm can effectively reduce the "edge skipping" problem by considering the relevance of two adjacent candidate road segments. We use $N_r(e_i)$ to describe this correlation:

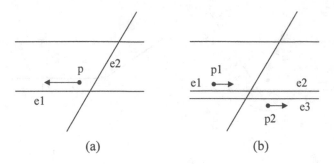

Fig. 4. Illustration of matching point to road

$$N_r(e_i) = \begin{cases} 1 & e_i \text{ is connected to last matching segment} \\ 1 & e_i \text{ and last matching segment are same} \\ 0 & \text{others} \end{cases} \tag{3}$$

Thus, we define the matching score of each candidate road segment $S(e_i)$:

$$S(e_i) = a \times N_d(e_i) + b \times N_a(e_i) + c \times N_r(e_i) \tag{4}$$

The parameters a, b, and c indicate the influence factors of N_d, N_a, and N_r on $S(e_i)$. For GPS sampling point p, the algorithm will select the candidate road segment with the largest $S(e_i)$ as the final matching road segment. Algorithm 1 describes the process of candidate road segment Analysis.

Algorithm 1 singlePointMatch
Input: GPS point p, road network G, search radius r, the matched road e_f of the last point.
Output: The matched road e_p of point p.
Initialize r, a, b, c, rSet;
s = getCandidates(p,G,r,e_f); //get a candidate roads set of point p
for each e_i **in** s, **do**
   $S(e_i) = a \times N_d(e_i) + b \times N_a(e_i) + c \times N_r(e_i)$;
   rSet.add($S(e_i)$);
e_p= argmax($S(e_i)$); //find e_p which has maximum score
return e_p;

3.3   Filling Missing Path Analysis

When the matching road segment e_p of the point p is found from the candidates, we compare the relationship between e_p and e_f (the matching road segment of the last point in the track T), if e_p and e_f are not directly connected, a missing path occurs between the two matching road segments, which needs to be predicted and filled. As shown in Fig. 5, the matching road segments of three consecutive points p_1, p_2, and p_3 are e_1, e_2, and e_3, and there is no need to fill the missing path due to e_1 and e_2 are directly connected, while there are other road segments between e_2 and e_3, which need to be filled with the missing path.

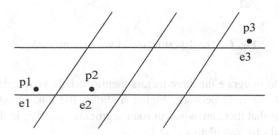

Fig. 5. Fill the missing path

With the increase of GPS sampling interval, the distance between the missing roads between e_f and e_p will become longer, and there will be many choices to fill these missing road segments. At this time, the shortest path from e_f to e_p in the road network is not necessarily the real path of the floating car passed. Therefore, our algorithm needs to find a "best" path between e_f and e_p rather than the shortest path based on distance simply. In order to obtain this "best" path, the algorithm considers the following three aspects:

1. The length of the path;
2. The grade of the road segments in the path;
3. The number of direction changes of the road segments in the path.

From the perspective of saving time and economic costs, people always choose a relatively short path when they go to a destination. In addition to the length of the path, the grade of the road segment is also an important factor affecting the matching accuracy. Besides the motor vehicle lanes, a large number of non-motorized lanes, sidewalks, residential roads, etc. are also distributed in the urban road network. These road may be selected to obtain a shorter path length when filling in missing path, but these roads are not allow or restrict the passage of motor vehicles. Therefore, we choose the road segment that is more suitable for motor vehicles to fill in the missing road segments according to the grade of the road segment.

The third factor that needs to be considered is the number of direction changes of the road segments in the path, this corresponds to the number of turns of the floating car in this path. Our algorithm is more inclined to the path with less turn times when filling the missing road segments. The basis for considering this factor comes from the driving habit that people prefer to go straight.

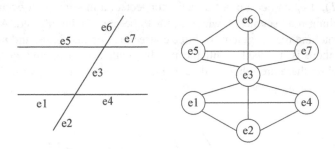

Fig. 6. The data structure of the road network

Now we need to integrate the three factors mentioned above to calculate the weight d of each edge of the road network. Figure 6 shows the data structure of the road network. Assuming that there are adjacent road segments e_a and e_b in the road network, we give the formula for calculating d_{ab}:

$$d_{ab} = (1+t) \times ((1+r_a) \times l_a + (1+r_b) \times l_b) \tag{5}$$

Where l_a and l_b represent the lengths of the road segments e_a and e_b, r_a and r_b represent the grade coefficients of the road segment, and the rules for their values are as follows:

$$r_i = \begin{cases} 0 & \text{If } e_i \text{ is a motorized lane} \\ 0.15 & \text{If } e_i \text{ is another kind of road} \end{cases} \tag{6}$$

$$t = \begin{cases} 0 & \text{If angle}(e_a, e_b) < 45° \\ 0.1 & \text{If angle}(e_a, e_b) \geq 45° \end{cases} \tag{7}$$

Thus it can be seen that we use the actual length of the road segment as the base for calculating the weight d. When a low-grade road or turn occurs, the algorithm will increase the base by a certain percentage and then use it as the final value of the weight d.

In order to avoid the catastrophic time consumption caused by executing the shortest path algorithm on the entire road network G, we cut the appropriately sized rectangular subgraph G' from G according to the positions of e_f and e_p, and perform the improved Dijkstra algorithm on G' to calculate the shortest path from e_f to e_p: The algorithm takes e_f as the starting point, when the shortest path P_{fp} from e_f to e_p is calculated, execution stops and there is no longer to calculate the shortest path from e_f to all of the other segments in G'. This can reduce the execution time of the algorithm. Finally, the algorithm obtains the average speed v of the path P_{fp} by the ratio of the mileage and the time. When v is less than the limit value of 80 km/h, we think that P_{fp}

is reasonable. Algorithm 2 describes the process of filling missing path Analysis.

Algorithm 2 fillMissingRoads
Input: Road network G, start road e_f, end road e_p.
Output: The best matched path P_{fp} from e_f to e_p.
Initialize t, r_a, r_b;
if linked(e_f, e_p) or e_f == e_p **then**
    return;
else then
    G' = getSubgraph(G, e_f, e_p);
    //calculate the weight for every edge in G'
    for each $edge_i$ in G', **do**
        a = startPoint($edge_i$);
        b = endpoint($edge_i$);
        $d_{ab} = (1 + t) \times \big((1 + r_a) \times l_a + (1 + r_b) \times l_b\big)$;
    P_{fp}= Dijkstra(G', e_f, e_p);
    if averageVelocity(P_{fp}) < maxVelocity **then**
        return P_{fp};

3.4 Complexity Analysis

Assume that n GPS points are collected in trajectory T, m road segments are in the road network G, k represents the number of road segments within a spatial index unit, and j represents the maximum number of road segments in subgraph G'.

For each GPS point, the matching road segment of this point in the road network G must be calculated at first. Since the spatial index is established for G, so that the time complexity of this part is $O(nk)$. Each time a missing path is filled, the subgraph G' needs to be established from G, this part takes $O(m)$, and the Dijkstra algorithm is executed in the subgraph G', requiring a time complexity of $O(j^2)$ at most. degree. Therefore, the time complexity of the WSI-matching algorithm in this paper is $O(nkm\ j^2)$.

4 Experiments

4.1 Data and the Measurement

We use a total of 20 trajectory data from 6:00 am to 10:00 pm of 20 taxis in the city of Changchun, which has the total length of 4122 km. The road network data of Changchun comes from the website of OpenStreetMap[1], which contains 22,693 urban roads. Some of the trajectory and road network data are shown in Fig. 7. Each point in the figure represents a sampling point. We use the software of ArcGIS as the experimental platform of our algorithm.

---

[1] http://www.openstreetmap.org/export.

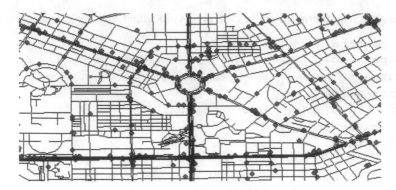

Fig. 7. GPS trajectory and road network of Chang Chun

The number of sampling points in the GPS trajectory corresponding to different sampling granularity and the average distance between adjacent points under the same length of the trajectory are shown in Table 1.

Table 1. Information of GPS trajectory with different sampling granularity

Sampling interval	Number of GPS points	Average distance
0.5 min	37859	92.35 m
1.0 min	18928	178.58 m
1.5 min	12619	260.07 m
2.0 min	9463	338.33 m
2.5 min	7570	412.37 m
3.0 min	6310	483.93 m
3.5 min	5409	553.61 m
4.0 min	4731	621.90 m
4.5 min	4206	688.13 m
5.0 min	3788	752.08 m

The parameter settings of the candidate road segment analysis: In the Gaussian distribution related to the factor about distance, we set $\mu_1 = 0$ and the standard deviation $\sigma_1 = 35$ m; In the Gaussian distribution related to the factor about direction, we set $\mu_2 = 0$ and the standard deviation $\sigma_2 = 45°$; For each factor about the score of candidate road segment, we set the parameter a = 0.35, b = 0.35, c = 0.3.

The parameter setting for filling the missing path analysis: We set the weight value r = 0.15 related to the road grade; set the weight value t = 0.1 related to the direction change; set the velocity constraint maxVelocity = 80 km/h.

Two accuracy metrics, Accuracy by Number (A_N) and Accuracy by Length (A_L), are defined as follows:

$$A_N = \frac{Number\ of\ correctly\ matched\ road\ segments}{Number\ of\ all\ road\ segments\ in\ trajectory}$$

$$A_L = \frac{Length\ of\ matched\ road\ segments}{Length\ of\ the\ trajectory}$$

We compare the experimental results with the global algorithm ST-matching and a traditional incremental algorithm SI-matching which does not consider direction factor and the relationship between the two adjacent candidate segments, and only uses the length of the road segment when calculating the edge weight of the road network, ignoring other weighting factors.

4.2 Experimental Results

The Influence of Different Search Radius on Algorithm Accuracy and Execution Time
We selected the trajectories with sampling intervals of 2 min and 4 min, and compared the accuracy and running time of the algorithm under different r values, as shown in Fig. 8(a) with sampling intervals of 2 min and Fig. 8(b) with sampling intervals of 4 min.

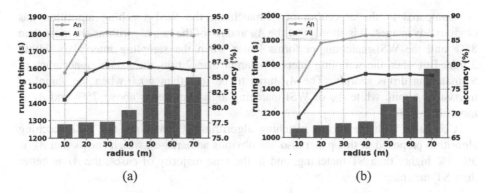

(a)   (b)

Fig. 8. Accuracy and running time w.r.t r

We observed the accuracy and running time of the algorithm when the r values are 10 m, 20 m, 70 m. As shown in figure, with the value of r increases, the running time of the algorithm also becomes longer whether in the sampling interval of 2 min or the sampling interval of 4 min. However, for the two accuracy metrics A_N and A_L, when the value of r is more than 40 m, it tends to be smooth or even slightly reduced. Therefore, we believe that when the value of r is 40 m in this algorithm, it can ensure the shortest running time without the loss of algorithm accuracy.

Accuracy Comparison Between WSI-Matching and SI-Matching and ST-Matching

The accuracy A_N of the WSI-matching algorithm and the SI-matching algorithm and the ST-matching algorithm with different granularity is compared in Fig. 9(a), and the accuracy A_L is compared in Fig. 9(b).

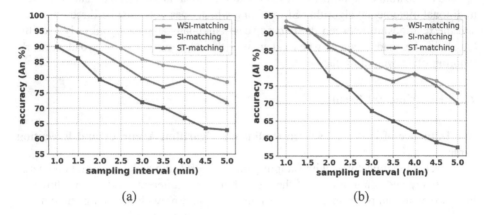

(a)   (b)

Fig. 9. A_N and A_L comparison w.r.t sampling interval

Compared to the algorithm of SI-matching, the WSI-matching algorithm has obvious advantages. It is shown that the A_N and A_L of the two algorithms are more than 85% and the WSI-matching performs better when the sampling interval is within 2 min. But when the sampling interval is larger than 2 min, the matching accuracy of SI-matching drops sharply. The A_L turns to be less than 60% when the sampling interval is 5 min, while A_N of WSI-matching algorithm keeps above 75% and A_L is more than 70%.

Compared with the global matching algorithm ST-matching, the WSI-matching algorithm proposed in this paper also has obvious advantages, which shows that A_N is 3%–5% higher than ST-matching, and in the vast majority of cases, the A_L is better than ST-matching.

Running Time Comparison of WSI-Matching and SI-Matching

The running time comparison of WSI-matching algorithm and SI-matching algorithm with different sampling interval is shown in Fig. 10. It can be found that WSI-matching runs less time than SI-matching, whether it is a fine-grained match with a sampling interval within 2 min or a coarse-grained matching with a sampling interval of more than 2 min. In addition, we find that when the sampling interval increases, the number of GPS points to be calculated is proportionally reduced, the running time of the algorithm is not reduced by the same proportion, but a state tends to be stable because of the bigger the sampling interval, the longer time to execute the shortest path algorithm will take. the WSI-matching algorithm can be optimized by optimizing the time efficiency of filling the missing path.

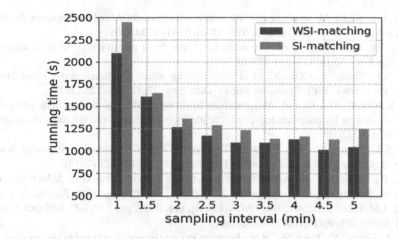

Fig. 10. Running time comparison w.r.t sampling interval

5   Conclusions

In this paper, we propose an incremental map matching algorithm based on weighted shortest path (WSI-matching) in order to achieve the map matching of low-sampling-rate GPS trajectories with lower time complexity. It solves the sparsity problem by filling the missing path between the candidate road segments of two GPS points. The experimental results show that compared to the traditional incremental algorithm and global algorithm, our WSI-matching algorithm has obvious advantages in terms of matching accuracy and running time both in fine-grained map matching and coarse-grained map matching.

In the follow-up research, we will add more constraints to improve the accuracy of filling missing path, and try to use the shortest path algorithm with lower time complexity (such as A* algorithm) to improve the time efficiency of the WSI-matching algorithm.

Acknowledgment. We thanks that this work was financially supported by National Natural Science Foundation of China (61772230, 61702215), Science & Technology Development Project of Jilin Province (20160204021GX) and Special Foundation Project for Industrial Innovation of Jilin Province (2017C032-1).

References

1. Gao, W.C., Li, G.L., Ta, N.: Map matching algorithm: a survey. J. Softw. **02**, 225–250 (2018)
2. Shim, C., Kim, W., Wan, H., et al.: Nearest close friend search in geo-social networks. Inf. Sci. **423**, 235–256 (2018). https://doi.org/10.1016/j.ins.2017.09.049
3. Sharma, K.P., Pooniaa, R.C., Sunda, S.: Map matching algorithm: curve simplification for Frechet distance computing and precise navigation on road network using RTKLIB. Cluster Comput. **2**, 1–9 (2018)

4. Liu, X., Liu, K., Li, M., et al.: A ST-CRF map-matching method for low-frequency floating car data. IEEE Trans. Intell. Transp. Syst. **18**(5), 1241–1254 (2017)
5. Gui, Z., Yu, H., Tang, Y.: Locating traffic hot routes from massive taxi tracks in clusters. J. Inf. Sci. Eng. **32**(1), 113–131 (2016)
6. Yuan, N.J., Zheng, Y., Xie, X., et al.: Discovering urban functional zones using latent activity trajectories. IEEE Trans. on Knowl. Data Eng. **27**(3), 712–725 (2015)
7. Ming, X., Du, Y., Wu, J., et al.: Map matching based on conditional random fields and route preference mining for uncertain trajectories. Math. Prob. Eng. **2015** (2015). http://dx.doi.org/10.1155/2015/717095
8. Yuan, N.J., Zheng, Y., Xie, X., et al.: Discovering urban functional zones using latent activity trajectories. IEEE Trans. Knowl. Data Eng. **27**(3), 712–725 (2015)
9. Szwed, P., Pekala, K.: An incremental map-matching algorithm based on hidden markov model. In: Rutkowski, L., Korytkowski, M., Scherer, R., Tadeusiewicz, R., Zadeh, L.A., Zurada, J.M. (eds.) ICAISC 2014. LNCS (LNAI), vol. 8468, pp. 579–590. Springer, Cham (2014). https://doi.org/10.1007/978-3-319-07176-3_51
10. Shang, J., Zheng, Y., Tong, W., et al.: Inferring gas consumption and pollution emission of vehicles throughout a city, pp. 1027–1036. ACM (2014)
11. Lint, H.V.: Network-wide traffic state estimation using loop detector and floating car data. J. Intell. Transp. Syst. **18**(1), 41–50 (2014)
12. Greenfeld, J.S.: Matching GPS observations to locations on a digital map. In: Transportation Research Board 81st Annual Meeting (2002)
13. Civilis, A., Jensen, C.S., Pakalnis, S.: Techniques for efficient road-network-based tracking of moving objects. IEEE Trans. Knowl. Data Eng. **17**(5), 698–712 (2005)
14. Chen, D., Driemel, A., Guibas, L.J., et al.: Approximate map matching with respect to the Fréchet distance. In: Meeting on Algorithm Engineering and Experiments, pp. 75–83. Society for Industrial and Applied Mathematics (2011)
15. Lou, Y., Zhang, C., Zheng, Y., et al.: Map-matching for low-sampling-rate GPS trajectories. In: Proceedings of ACM SIGSPATIAL International Symposium on Advances in Geographic Information Systems, ACM-GIS 2009, Seattle, Washington, USA, 4–6 November 2009, pp. 352–361. DBLP (2009)
16. Pink, O., Hummel, B.A.: statistical approach to map matching using road network geometry, topology and vehicular motion constraints. In: International IEEE Conference on Intelligent Transportation Systems, pp. 862–867. IEEE (2008)

Asynchronous Parallel Dijkstra's Algorithm on Intel Xeon Phi Processor

How to Accelerate Irregular Memory Access Algorithm

Weidong Zhang[1], Lei Zhang[2], and Yifeng Chen[1(✉)]

[1] EECS of Peking University, Beijing 100871, People's Republic of China
{zhangwd,cyf}@pku.edu.cn
[2] HuaWei Inc., Shenzhen, China
lei_z@pku.edu.cn

Abstract. As the instruction-level parallelism (ILP) on CPU develops to a rather advanced level, the exploration that whether many-core architecture is applicable for graph algorithms is generating more interests in researchers. However, due to the irregular memory access and the low ratio of computation to memory access, the performance of graph algorithms on many-core architectures has never worked good enough.

To obtain outstanding speedup on many-core architecture, first of all, we need to figure out three questions: (i) how to optimize the memory access, (ii) how to minimize the overhead of synchronization, (iii) how to exploit the parallelism in algorithm. Prior works hardly reach the goal if such questions are treated in separated way. Throughout this paper, we aim to settle these questions systematically, and try to provide a set of methods of optimizing graph algorithms on many-core architecture.

This paper mainly discusses how to accelerate the Single Source Shortest Path (SSSP) problem on Intel Many Integrated Core (MIC) architecture, on which we propose an asynchronous parallel Dijkstra's algorithm. It aims at maximizing parallelism and minimizing overhead of synchronization. Experimental result shows that the MIC architecture could efficiently solve the SSSP problem, and its performance could be sped up by 9.2x compared to the benchmark of DIMACS.

Keywords: Single source shortest path · Parallel algorithm
Intel MIC · Road network

1 Introduction

The single source shortest path (SSSP) is a classical problem in graph theory. It is not only considered as an independent problem, but also serves as a preprocessing step for many other graph algorithms, such as [1–4]. There have been a plethora of algorithms proposed to solve or improve this problem. Acknowledging the SSSP is a memory bounded problem, almost all the SSSP algorithms are based on the sequential Dijkstra's algorithm [5]. With optimization of binomial

© Springer Nature Switzerland AG 2018
J. Vaidya and J. Li (Eds.): ICA3PP 2018, LNCS 11334, pp. 337–357, 2018.
https://doi.org/10.1007/978-3-030-05051-1_24

heap [6] or Fibonacci heaps [7], etc., the sequential Dijkstra's algorithm can be implemented in $O(nlogn)$ time. However, as for many-core architecture, it is hard to improve the performance due to the irregular memory lookup and the overhead of consistency maintenance among cores.

This work concentrates on solving the SSSP problem on real-world road networks, which usually appear as sparse direct graph. On sparse graph, the implementations of graph algorithm based on Parallel Random-Access Machine Model (PRAM) are typically memory intensive, fine grained and highly irregular. On distributed cluster, due to the long memory latencies and high synchronization costs, the implementations usually hardly outperform the best sequential implementation [8,9]. On parallel shared memory platforms, they offer bigger on-chip cache, more global shared memory, higher bandwidth and lower latency. Nevertheless, the parallelism of most graph algorithms depends on their cache friendliness [10]. As far as we know, there is no general approach for cache optimization, because the pattern of memory access primarily depends on the graph structure and the memory organization of graph.

In our work, the latest Intel Many Integrated Core (MIC) device (Xeon Phi 5110/7210 Processor) [11] is adopted to accelerate the SSSP problem. Through simulating memory access pattern of SSSP, we find out the performance ceiling, which is boosting the performance of memory access to 70 GB/s. By benchmarking and profiling each component of SSSP, we explore and identify the performance bounds in each step.

On this basis, we test and evaluate various of simple optimization approaches, such as partitioning, renumbering, fixed outdegree and vertex padding. Using these simple optimization approaches or their combinations, the performance of memory access nearly approaches the simulation result. And the speedup outperforms benchmarks by 6.03–9.2 times.

The organization of the paper is as follows. Section 2 summarizes some related works, including Dijkstra's algorithm, Bellman-Ford algorithm and Delta-Stepping algorithm. Besides, we introduce the acceleration work on GPGPU, Cray supercomputer, etc. The main body of this paper consists of profiling, solving, optimizing and benchmarking which are presented in Sects. 3, 4, 5 and 6 respectively. Section 7 is the conclusion part.

The contribution of this work can be summarized as follows:

– **Asynchronous Parallel Algorithm.** We provide a asynchronous parallel algorithm to solve the SSSP problem on shared memory architecture.
– **Cache Optimization.** We introduce some general ways of cache optimization for graph parallel algorithm in this paper.
– **Performance.** Through benchmarking and profiling, we fully exploit the parallelism in SSSP problem, and provide a state-of-the-art fastest implementation of shortest path algorithm.

2   Related Work

Xeon Phi is a main/coprocessor designed to tackle High-Performance Computing (HPC) problems in computational physics, biology, finance, etc. Its architecture combines many processor cores into a single chip. Every Intel Xeon Phi processor mainly consists of processor cores, cache, memory controller, serial bus controller and a bidirectional ring bus with high bandwidth. Every processor core owns a private(or shared) L2 cache and the consistencies among cores are guaranteed by the global directory protocol. The latest Intel Xeon Phi 7210 processor is equipped with 16 GB of high-bandwidth on-chip memory and 64 1.3 GHz cores, each of which supports up to four hardware thread contexts.

The core of Xeon Phi processor is more similar to general purpose CPU than GPGPU's, which makes it more qualified in solving irregular problem like road network SSSP. According to our benchmarking and profiling, the relax operation in shortest path solution in the essence can be as fast as loading from GDDR to registers. That implies the MIC architecture could efficiently solve the real-world road network SSSP.

In mathematics, a directed simple graph G is an ordered pair G(V, A), where V is a finite vertex set, and A⊆V×V is a set of ordered pairs of vertices, called arrows or directed edges. Throughout this paper, the discussed graph is directed by default.

Given a graph G(V, A) which is a directed, degree-bounded graph, the shortest path problem requires finding a path of minimum length from a given source s∈V to a given target t∈V.

Dijkstra's algorithm [5] is a type of sequential greedy single source shortest path algorithm.

1. Initialize a shortest distances for each vertex, except that $D[v_0]$ is assigned 0, while others is set as $+\infty$;
2. Take v whose $D[v]$ is minimum from heap, and do Scan() operation on v;
3. Repeat step 2 until heap is empty.

In Step (2), many approaches can be used to optimize memory access, such as binomial heap, Fibonacci heap, Buckets [12,13], etc. Through experimental comparison, we select the binomial heap. Using the binomial heap, the complexity of Scan() is $O(log|V|)$, and the complexity of Dijkstra's algorithm is $O(|E|log|V|)$.

With the advent of sequential shortest path algorithm [5], a large amount of methods [7,12,14,15] have been proposed to improve it. Lots of works are based on the graph preprocessing, such as partitioning graph into neighboring subgraphs, pre-calculating shortest path on arterial network and so on. In literature [15], authors use kd-tree [16] and METIS [17] to preprocess graph and achieve dozens of times speedup. The graph partitioning, however, exists as a NP-hard problem. In the work of Zhu et al. [14], they could answer any distance query in $O(log(d_{max}/d_{min}))$ time and any shortest path query in $O(k + log(d_{max}/d_{min}))$ time, where d_{max}(resp. d_{min}) is the largest (resp. smallest) distance between any two vertices in the road network, and the k is the number of vertices on the shortest path. In these works, the work of Goldberg et al. [12] shows a significant improvement on the real-world road network. As a result, it has been considered as a benchmark during the 9th Center for Discrete Mathematics and Theoretical Computer Science (DIMACS) [18].

Bellman-Ford algorithm [19] is a dynamic programming algorithm that solves the shortest path problem. It runs as an iterative algorithm based on BSP model, and in each iteration, it executes Scan() operation on all vertices. Because the maximum length from source vertex to any other vertex is never greater than $|V|$, the maximum number of iteration is less than $|V|-1$. And the complexity of relaxation is $O(|E|)$, as a result, the overall complexity is $O(|V||E|)$. There are many improved implementations of Bellman-Ford algorithm, such as [11,20–24], etc.

Delta-Stepping algorithm is also an iterative algorithm [25]. Comparing Dijkstra with Bellman-Ford algorithm, the former only selects one vertex whose $D[v]$ is minimum while Bellman-Ford selects all the vertices to execute Scan() operation. As a compromise, Delta-Stepping algorithm selects Δ vertices. Therefore, Dijkstra and Bellman-Ford algorithm can be regarded as two special cases of Delta-Stepping algorithm.

Madduri et al. present a parallel shortest path implementation on the Cray MTA-2 [10]. The MTA-2 is a high-end shared memory system based on massively multithreaded parallel architecture. The processors of MTA-2 use the hardware multithreading to replace the data cache to tolerate the latency. However, the reported results show that the absolute running times on the MTA-2 and a 3.2 GHz Xeon processor are comparable for random, square grid and road network instances [10]. From the experimental study, the Cray MTA-2 does not boost the performance significantly in the real-world road network, in spite that the hardware used in them is very expensive. Contrast with supercomputer, the commodity shared memory device offers much higher cost performance (TFlops/Dollar), such as Intel MIC, GPGPU.

Commodity graphics hardware has been used to solve many general problems, such as linear algebra, computer vision, signal processing, etc. Although various graph algorithms have been implemented on GPGPU [26], they are severely constrained by the memory capability and architecture of the existing GPGPUs. Loops of non-uniform lengths are inefficient on SIMD architectures due to the restriction of memory on the CUDA device. As is shown in the experimental results of Harish's work [27], the implementations of Dijkstra's and Floyd Warshall's algorithm on GPU are orders of magnitude which are slower than the implementation on CPU if the scale of vertices is more than 1×10^6. Further, they have found that, owing to the vertex lookup cost in memory device, the time taken by SSSP increases almost linearly as the average degree of vertex does. What's more, they have found that graphs above 12 million vertices with $6°$ per vertex cannot be handled if using current GPUs.

In literature [28], the authors present a Delta-Stepping implementation on multi-core CPUs and Intel Xeon Phi. They tested and evaluated their implementations with the benchmark implemented in Boost Graph Library. The reported data show that their implementation outperforms the sequential algorithm implemented in benchmark on random graph and game graph with a small diameter. In their implementation, they used several approaches to improve the performance of memory access, such as data preprocessing, data padding, optimal buckets, etc. In our implementation, we also adopt corresponding manners to improve the performance of memory access, but the differences are that our approaches are selected after a more appropriate simulating, benchmarking and profiling process, and we achieve better speedup. Considering that there is no comparison with DIMACS Reference in their experiments, we compare their data with DIMACS Reference on the same vertices scale. Even though the DIMACS Reference owns much better speedup on all the out-degree graphs, our implementation still outperforms the DIMACS Reference.

A large family of algorithms [14,29,30] use preprocessing to explore locality and reachability in advance to accelerate the route planning. Generally, they could achieve several orders of magnitude speedup than Dijkstra's algorithm on CPU. For example, PHAST [29] gains three orders of magnitude faster than CPU through reordering vertices in advance to exploit locality; Arterial Hierarchy (AH) [14] yields the contemporary best speedup by organizing the nodes in the road network into a hierarchy. Whereas, these pretreatments usually require user to tolerate up to minutes to hours.

We select the real-world road networks dataset used in the 9th DIMACS. The challenge of the 9th DIMACS is to design and implement the shortest path algorithm on the real-world road network. It provides various scales of road networks. The basic statistics information of dataset is shown in Table 1. In the table, we can notice that these road networks share the properties of low outdegree and sparse adjacency.

Table 1. Basic statistics of dataset

	#vertex	#edge	averOutd	maxOutd	minOutd
USA	2,3947,347	58,333,344	2.4359	9	1
CTR	14,081,816	34,292,496	2.435232	9	1
W	6,262,104	15,248,146	2.434988	9	1
E	3,598,623	8,778,114	2.439298	9	1

3 Profiling: Exploring Acceleration Ceiling on Our Phi Processor

To saturate the pipelines and calculating units of Phi processor, the ratio of computation to memory access should be no less than 8:1, or even higher. However, in the SSSP problem, every Scan() operation consists of two additions, one comparison and multiple retrievals of two vertices, which show the SSSP problem in the essence is a memory bounded one. Therefore, the key of accelerating SSSP problem turns into accelerating memory access.

According to an official specification, the max memory bandwidth of Phi 7210 processor is 102 GB/s [31]. However, the access patterns of actual applications could hardly be as ideal as the official testing codes. In order to determinate the ceiling of memory access in the SSSP problem, we design three groups of progressive experiments:

(a) **Random jumping pointer chasing**: In this test, we first generate a sequence of pointers with a fixed size. The distance between any two pointers is multiples of 64 Bytes, which is the size of cache line in Phi processor. During the memory access, the given size memory area will be accessed.

(b) **Pure memory access in the order of the recorded SSSP accessing sequence**: In this test, we first record the accurate accessing sequence of SSSP algorithm, then retrieve those recorded vertices but without executing Relax().

(c) **Memory access with Relax() in the order of the recorded SSSP accessing sequence**: In this test, we first record the accurate accessing sequence of SSSP algorithm, then retrieve those vertices and execute Relax().

The result of test (a) is shown in Fig. 1, the average latency time rises dramatically from ∼70 to ∼340 ns when the size of accessing memory exceeds the size of L2 cache. If converting to bandwidth, the latency of 300 ns corresponds to a bandwidth of about 70 GB/s. The experiments of (b, c) also output the similar bandwidths. Accordingly, we infer that the latency time of memory access for this problem on Intel Xeon Phi processor is about 300 ns, which is also the shortest average time for processor to fetch data from GDDR in this problem.

The next two sections show our journey of shortening memory access delay step by step.

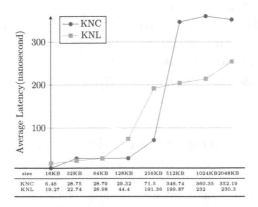

Fig. 1. Latency of random memory access on Intel Xeon Phi coprocessor. (KNC and KNL is the name codes of Intel MIC processors)

4   Solution: Asynchronous Parallel Dijkstra's Algorithm on MIC and Performance Evaluation

In order to minimize the synchronization overhead among cores, we propose the asynchronous parallel Dijkstra's algorithm and various variants on Intel Xeon Phi. In this section, we will describe and evaluate them in detail according to the order of the exploration journey.

4.1   Asynchronous Parallel Dijkstra's Algorithm Based on Lock

Algorithm Architecture. As is shown in Algorithm 1, the asynchronous parallel Dijkstra's algorithm is composed of rounds of iterations which mainly consists of:

(i) **LocalScan(G, pid):** as is shown in Algorithm 2, NUM_SCAN_PER_ITER active vertices will be selected to execute Scan(v) from a respective heap maintained by each thread. If there is a new updatable vertex v' found after executing Scan(v). v' will be inserted into local heap if it belongs to current thread, otherwise v' will be inserted into the corresponding pendingstack$_i$.

(ii) **LocalUpdate(G, pid):** LocalUpdate moves all the vertices from local pending stack into local heap.

(iii) **CheckForTermination(G, pid):** The termination condition is that all local heaps and pending stacks are empty.

As shown in Fig. 2, there is no global synchronization existing in the execution flow. Thus, the consumption of global synchronization and mutual wait are avoided.

Algorithm 1. Asynchronous Parallel Dijkstra's Algorithm

1: **procedure** PARALLELDIJKSTRA(G, v_0)
2:     InitializationForWorker
3:     **while** True **do**
4:         LocalScan(G, pid)
5:         LocalUpate(G, pid)
6:         **if** CheckForTermination(G, pid) **then**
7:             break

Design of Data Structure. In the asynchronous parallel Dijkstra's algorithm, every thread owns a local heap, which is designed as a binomial heap, as is shown in Fig. 3. In order to retrieve vertex by its serial number, we add an index for heaps.

As is shown in Algorithm 2, every thread owns a pending stack manipulated by all other threads. Because the pending stack can be modified by other threads simultaneously, the operation on stack is protected by lock. We also add an index to stack for vertex retrieve. The structure of pending stack and its index are similar to the heap shown in Fig. 3.

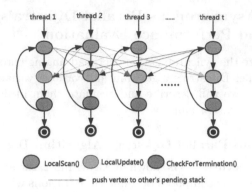

Fig. 2. Execution flow of asynchronous parallel Dijkstra's algorithm: (i) LocalScan() → (ii) LocalUpdate() → (iii) CheckForTermination(), which correspond to Sect. 4.1.

Algorithm 2. Local Scan Operation

1: **procedure** LOCALSCAN(G, pid)
2:     **for** i = 1 **to** NUM_SCAN_PER_ITER **and not** heap[pid].empty **do**
3:         $v_j \leftarrow heap[pid].pop()$
4:         $\mathbb{V} = \text{SCAN}(v_j)$
5:         **for** v' **in** $\mathbb{V}$ **do**
6:             **if** color[v'] == localColor[pid] **then**
7:                 heap[pid].pushAndUpdate(v')
8:             **else**
9:                 thread $\leftarrow color[v']$
10:                pendingStack[thread].pushAndUpdate(v')

Algorithm 3. Local Update Operation

1: **procedure** LOCALUPDATE(G, pid)
2:     **for** v' **in** pendingStack[pid] **do**
3:         heap[pid].pushAndUpdate(v')
4:     pendingStack[pid].clear()

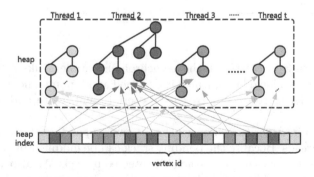

Fig. 3. The structure of heap and heap index.

Termination Checking Protocol Based on Lock. As is shown in Algorithm 1, the termination condition is that all the heaps and pending stacks become empty. Therefore, we use an array of booleans to indicate the execution states of threads, and the boolean array is shown in Fig. 4. Because S_i can be manipulated by all the threads simultaneously, thus all the operations on S_i are protected by locks.

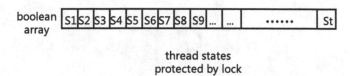

thread states
protected by lock

Fig. 4. Boolean array used to indicate the execution state of each thread.

4.2 Termination Checking Protocol with Version Controller Based on Atomic Operation

We also design and test the atomic operation to control the termination condition. As is shown in listing 1.35, the controller based on the atomic operation consists of a global *globalVersion* and a list of local *localVersions*. The globalVersion is applied to record the global overall execution state. Two events can cause *globalVersion's* value to increase: (i) Thread T_i updates some vertex owned by itself, and inserts the vertex into its heap; (ii) Thread T_i updates some vertex owned by others, and inserts the vertex into some other's pending stack.

The *localVersion$_i$* records the value of *globalVersion* when thread T_i latest operates *globalVersion*. Thus, we could infer that *localversion* $\leq$ *globalVersion*. The termination condition is that every *localVersion$_i$* equals *globalVersion*.

Listing 1.35. Version controller based on atomic operation.

```
1 struct SyncerBasedOnAtomic {
2   const int threadNum;
3   volatile int globalVersion;
4   volatile int *localVersion;
5   void incGlobalVersion() {
6 #pragma omp atomic
7     ++globalVersion;
8   }
9 };
```

4.3 Termination Checking Protocol with Version Controller Based on Lock-Free Atomic-Less Operation

As is shown in Fig. 5, Phi processor adopts bidirectional ring bus. All the synchronous messages need to be transferred in the ring bus. The transmission not only is constrained by the bandwidth of the ring bus, but also keeps the cores waiting. To evaluate the performances of lock and atomic operation, we conduct a simple test. As is shown in Fig. 6, the numbers present the time costs of 65,536 additions with different ways. The addition with lock and atomic operation costs several magnitude orders more time than the rest. Therefore, we design the lock-free and atomic-less termination checking protocol.

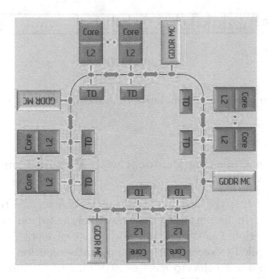

Fig. 5. Microarchitecture of Xeon Phi Processor [32], interleaved memory access is adopted to eliminate hotspots and provide a uniform access pattern.

As is shown in Listing 1.36, the version controller, WorkerInfo, consists of two parts: (i) the latest thread **state**, which indicates whether the local heap and pending queue are empty or not; (ii) the latest **version** of local heap update.

The function incVersion() is invoked when vertices of current thread are updated. incVersion() first obtains the maxVersion(=max{workInfo$_i$.version}), and then assigns (maxVersion + 1) to the current version. We should notice that, although the incVersion() function is neither protected by lock nor guaranteed by atomic operation and invoked by all threads simultaneously, it still ensures every workinfo$_i$.version monotonically increases.

The termination condition is that all the states of threads become STATE_READY_TO_STOP and all the workInfo$_i$.version $\leq$ max{workInfo$_i$.version}.

Listing 1.36. Version controller based on lock-free atomic-less operation.

```
1 enum State {
2    STATE_ACTIVE , STATE_READY_TO_STOP
3 };
4 struct WorkerInfo {
5    volatile State state;
```

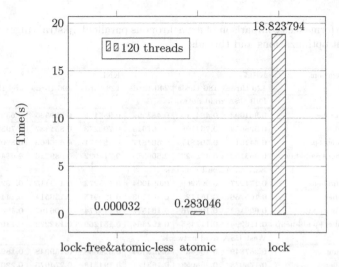

Fig. 6. Performance evaluation of lock and atomic operation on Xeon Phi KNL processor

```
 6   volatile unsigned int version;
 7 };
 8 volatile WorkerInfo *workerInfo;
 9 void incVersion(const int &pid) {
10    unsigned int maxVersion = 0;
11    for (int i = 0; i < THREAD_NUM; ++i)
12      if (maxVersion < workerInfo[i ]. version)
13        maxVersion = workerInfo[i].version;
14    workerInfo[pid].version = maxVersion + 1;
15 }
```

4.4 Performance Comparison Among Different Termination Checking Protocols

In order to evaluate the asynchronous parallel Dijkstra's algorithm and its variants, we implement various implementations. The implementation with lock-free atomic-less shows the best performance. Due to the space limitations, we aren't able to enumerate all the figures, but the ultimate result does achieve our expectation and the preliminary analysis.

Table 2. Performances comparison of asynchronous parallel Dijkstra's algorithm based with different optimizations and threads

Optimizations	KNC			KNL		
	120 thrds	180 thrds	240 thrds	128 thrds	196 thrds	256 thrds
Full USA road network						
No renumber	0.861093	0.484713	0.483094	0.985172	0.959535	0.635132
Renumber	0.526659	0.754198	0.461915	0.790273	0.851387	0.79861
Renumber+pad	0.44161	0.504817	0.504817	0.684171	0.660662	0.890518
renumber+pad+heap	0.463162	0.448823	0.506355	0.714022	0.689216	0.684432
East USA road network						
No renumber	0.171227	0.095269	0.094004	0.198272	0.158115	0.102461
Renumber	0.105266	0.16172	0.101503	0.119915	0.156514	0.144637
Renumber+pad	0.099184	0.109676	0.164527	0.118774	0.106492	0.193336
Renumber+pad+heap	0.116294	0.111485	0.122364	0.151269	0.132222	0.130046
West USA road network						
No renumber	0.287849	0.15883	0.158404	0.324668	0.259948	0.189357
Renumber	0.178078	0.265063	0.162121	0.194318	0.274075	0.220564
Renumber+pad	0.16162	0.181046	0.26399	0.195518	0.170387	0.291886
Renumber+pad+heap	0.176352	0.171667	0.193131	0.229628	0.217397	0.192037

5   Optimizing: Optimization Strategies on MIC and Performance Evaluation

5.1   Preprocessing by Graph Partitioning

To guarantee the load balance, a straightforward graph partitioning method is adopted to divide workload among processor cores on MIC. The partitioning algorithm first travels the given graph G from v_0 in the order of Breadth First Search (BFS). After obtaining the BFS tree T_{BFS}, it will be partitioned into numerous subtrees with the depth of deltaDepth, with the process shown in Fig. 7. Finally, depending on the thread number (THREAD_NUM), subtrees are allocated into different threads.

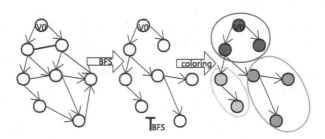

Fig. 7. Graph partitioning based on BFS

5.2   Preprocessing with Vertex Renumbering

The neighboring vertices are not always stored in consecutive memory areas is a crucial issue for SSSP problem on MIC. The discordance of continuities between graph topology and memory organization usually causes the vertices with consecutive serial numbers to bear topological long-distance in graph. For example, in Fig. 8, the vertices with number 5 and 117 are neighbors in the graph, when thread starts to execute Relax() operation on v_{117}, because v_5 likely does not exist in cache, v_5 is loaded in cache. And because v_4, v_6 and v_5 are stored consecutively in memory, they are loaded in cache with v_5 together, in spite that they will be hardly used. In this case, at least one cache line for each memory access is wasted. A considerable proportion of memory bandwidth is wasted on these useless access.

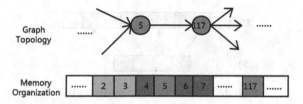

Fig. 8. The inconsistency of continuities of topology and memory organization

In addition to that problem, the inconsecutive memory organization of neighboring vertices is also possible to bring false sharing problem. The nonadjacent vertices are assigned to different threads, even if they own consecutive serial numbers, such as v_4 and v_5. However, in the essence they share the same cache line. In this case, the threads processing v_4 and v_5 will compete for the exclusive access of the cache line.

After renumbering, vertices owned by the same thread will be renumbered with consecutive serial numbers, which could greatly alleviate the false sharing problem. Additionally, if renumbering is based on the result of partitioning, the neighboring vertices will be approximately assigned to consecutive memory regions.

As is shown in Table 2, we carry out the tests on both KNC and KNL. The result shows that renumbering could significantly improve the performance of our algorithm when the number of threads is twice of the cores. However, the speedup of renumbering is poor when threads number is triple or quadruple of the cores. We infer that, as the threads number grows, two factors will counteract the effect: (i) the increased scheduling overhead within single core; (ii) the increased false sharing between cores.

5.3   Graph Storage with Fixed Outdegree

One property of real-world road networks is the low outdegree. Statistical numbers show that the average outdegree is no more than 3 which is shown in the fourth column of Table 1. Hence, the road network is usually represented as sparse adjacency matrix. The Compressed Row Storage (CRS) format is the most general format for sparse matrix storage. As is shown in Fig. 9, the starting vertices are stored in S[] and the ending vertices are stored in E[]. In order to get all the out edges of one vertex, thread needs multiple cache reading from memory.

With the help of the fixed outdegree, one vertex can be read in cache at one time. As is shown in Fig. 10, the vertex v is split into v_1 and v_2 which have a common outdegree. Between v_1 and v_2, a zero-weighted edge is inserted.

After fixing outdegree, all the vertices are stored in 64 bytes, which is the size of cache line. Because all the data of a vertex can be read in L1/L2 cache by one fetch, the false sharing is eliminated, and the role of graph partitioning is weakened too.

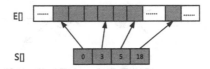

Fig. 9. The storage for sparse matrix

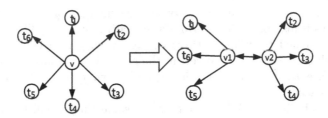

Fig. 10. Fixed outdegree of graph.

5.4   Vertex Padding and Prefetching

Vertex padding fills each cache line with a fixed outdegree vertex. This method could effectively prevent the false sharing problem. In addition, we further pack the index information into one cache line to accelerate the vertex retrieve.

Vertex prefetching utilizes prefetching instructions to prefetch the neighboring vertices of next vertex. It reduces the waiting time of memory access. Phi processor supports hardware prefetching and software prefetching. The hardware prefetcher predicts and prefetches the possible coming data into cache, while the software prefetcher performs fetching work by compiler-generated or programmer-coded directive codes.

As is shown in Table 2, the result shows that the performance of our algorithm could be further improved through vertex padding. Also, the best speedup is achieved when the number of threads is twice of the number of cores.

5.5   Graph Partitioning Based on Vertex Coordinate

The process of graph partitioning based on BFS can be equivalent to the way of solving the single source shortest path problem on a graph whose edges are all of the same weight. In response to the argument that the performance gain comes from graph partitioning based on BFS instead of the asynchronous parallel Dijkstra's algorithm, we select the coordinate based partitioning approach to verify the performance of our asynchronous parallel Dijkstra's algorithm.

The time complexity of KDTree-like algorithm is $O(nlogn)$. Compared with the BFS-based partitioning algorithm, although the coordinate based method bears higher complexity, it does not use the edge information, which contributes to explain that the performance gain come from BFS-based graph partitioning. The further experiments also come to the same conclusion, which is not enumerated due to the space limitation.

6   Benchmarking: Comparison with Benchmark

Some of the optimizations have been evaluated in Sect. 5, this section mainly focuses on evaluating the preprocessing methods and comparing our implementations with benchmarks.

The benchmark of 9th DIMACS is one of the most convincing benchmarks, and it is widely adopted in lots of latest works [33–35]. Through the representative benchmarks, readers could compare our results with more related work horizontally. The devices used in experiments are illustrated in Table 3, and the corresponding compilers.

Table 3. Devices and compilers used in our experiments

Processor	#Core	L2 Cache Size	Compiler
Xeon E5 2680v3	2(×12) @ 2.6 GHz	30 MB	icc 15.0.0
i7-4790	4 @ 3.6 GHz	8192 KB	gcc 4.4.7
Xeon Phi 5110p	60 @ 1.05 GHz	30 MB	icc 15.0.0
Xeon Phi 7120	64 @ 1.30 GHz	32 MB	icc 15.0.0

6.1   Analysis of Dataset

Influence of Fixed Outdegree. Table 4 shows the changes of graph after fixing vertex's outdegree to 4. The numbers of last column tell that the ratio of added vertices is no more than 5.1%.

By default, the following experiments related to fixed outdegree are all based on a fixed outdegree of 4.

Table 4. The graph after fixed outdegree

	#vertex	#vertex(fixed)	VertexIncrease(%)
USA	$23,947,347$	$24,048,152$	4.209
CTR	$14,081,816$	$14,153,067$	5.060
W	$6,262,104$	$6,281,414$	3.084
E	$3,598,623$	$3,608,831$	2.837

6.2   Performances of Preprocessing Methods

In this part, we adopt the profiling technology to explore the performance bounds of different optimizations working on Relax() operation. The default graph used in this section is the CTR.

As is shown in Fig. 11(a), the renumbering optimization improves the performance of Relax() operation dramatically. This improvement partly attributes to the fact that there are too much false sharing and useless cache before renumbering. Interestingly, we find that the fixed outdegree does not improve the performance. We conjecture that the overhead on the additional vertices and edges counteracts the effect of the fixed outdegree. But a great improvement is achieved by vertex packing, which fills each cache line with a fixed outdegree vertex. However, the improvement is less than renumbering's, because the former does not fully utilize the 64 bytes of cache line.

Comparing with the execution time, we pay much more attention to the time cost of Relax() on single vertex. As is shown in Fig. 11(b), after renumbering, the average time cost of Relax() is 450–500 ns, which is relatively close to the latency time of memory access (350 ns). Given the fact that the time cost of Relax() should be no less than the latency time of memory access, we still wonder whether there is another way to improve more.

We further evaluate the prefetching and batch processing technologies. Vertex prefetching utilizes prefetching instruction to prefetch the neighboring vertices of next vertex. Batch Relax() means executing Relax() operation on multiple vertices at the same time. As is shown in Fig. 12, the average time cost further reduces to 400 ns after using vertex prefetching. But, it costs more time as the number of threads increases.

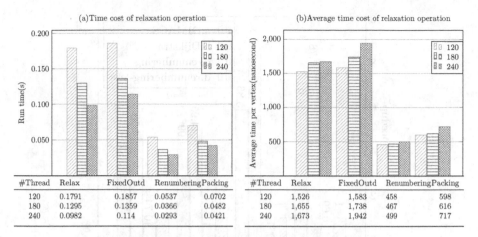

Fig. 11. Performances of preprocessing methods on KNC

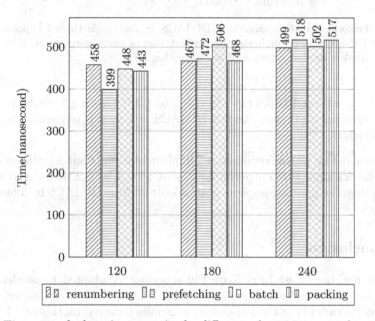

Fig. 12. Time cost of relaxation operation by different relaxation approaches on KNC.

The experiment results in this section confirm that our asynchronous parallel Dijkstra's algorithm and preprocessing approaches could efficiently exploit the potential of Intel Xeon Phi processor.

6.3 Asynchronous Parallel Dijkstra's Algorithm vs. DIMCAS

To demonstrate the overall speedup performance of asynchronous parallel Dijkstra's algorithm on MIC, we compare it with the following implementations:

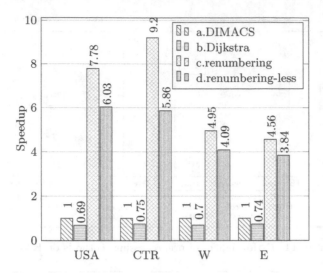

Fig. 13. Performances comparison: a. DIMACS; b. the single thread Dijkstra's algorithm on CPU; c. the renumbering implementation of our algorithm on KNC; d. the renumbering-less implementation of our algorithm on KNC.

(i) The single thread Dijkstra's algorithm on CPU (Xeon E5 2680v3).
(ii) The implementation of the 9th DIMACS, which is a sequential one based on Buckets.

As is shown in Fig. 13, the renumbering implementation of our asynchronous parallel Dijkstra's algorithm outperforms DIMACS by 4.56–9.2 times. And without renumbering, the padding implementation outperforms DIMACS by a maximum of 6 times.

7   Conclusion

In this paper, the latest Intel Xeon Phi processor is adopted to accelerate the SSSP problem on real-world road networks. Due to the low outdegree of real-world road network, the low parallelism is usually incurred on this problem. The traditional methods, like Delta-Stepping, maintain a global vertex set to monitor the vertices going to the next superstep. On MIC architecture, however, the cost of global structure is relatively high. As a result, most of prior works based on MIC architecture could not outperform the sequential implementations.

By the way of profiling, we find that improving SSSP on MIC architecture in the essence is an optimizing memory access problem, owing to the fact that the pattern of irregular memory access prevents the performance of SIMD instructions. In order to improve the performance of memory access, we evaluate many optimization approaches, such as renumbering, prefetching, padding and so on. Finally, we find that the time cost of Relax() on Intel Xeon Phi processor could get close to the latency time of loading data from GDDR to L2 cache.

Based on the evaluations above, we further evaluate a variety of their combinations. The experimental results show that the implementation with fixed outdegree + padding outperforms Goldberg's implementation [12] by 6.03 times. Combining with renumbering, the speedup could further increase to a maximum of 9.2 times than Goldberg's implementation.

Based on our knowledge, we have obtained the highest speedup on Intel Xeon Phi processor on real-world road network with simple preprocessing. Our work proves that the problems with irregular memory access could also be accelerated significantly on Intel MIC architecture processor, if the design could conform to the following standards:

- Design a appropriate synchronization way to avoid massive global sychronization.
- Exploit the potential parallelism in problem fully.
- Select a proper way to implement the algorithm.

Acknowledgments. This work is supported by National Key R&D Program of China (under Grant 2017YFB0202001) and National Natural Science Foundation of China (under Grants 61432018,61672208).

References

1. Brandes, U.: A faster algorithm for betweenness centrality. J. Math. Sociol. **25**(2), 163–177 (2010)
2. Freeman, L.C.: A set of measures of centrality based on betweenness. Sociometry **40**(1), 35–41 (1977)
3. Guimerá, R., Mossa, S., Turtschi, A., Amaral, L.A.N.: The worldwide air transportation network: anomalous centrality, community structure, and cities' global roles. Proc. Natl. Acad. Sci. U.S.A. **102**(22), 7794–7799 (2005)
4. Jeong, H., Mason, S.P., Barabási, A.L., Oltvai, Z.N.: Lethality and centrality in protein networks. Nature **411**(6833), 41–42 (2001)
5. Johnson, D.B.: A note on Dijkstra's shortest path algorithm. J. ACM **20**(3), 385–388 (1973)
6. Carlsson, S., Munro, J.I., Poblete, P.V.: An implicit binomial queue with constant insertion time. In: Karlsson, R., Lingas, A. (eds.) SWAT 1988. LNCS, vol. 318, pp. 1–13. Springer, Heidelberg (1988). https://doi.org/10.1007/3-540-19487-8_1
7. Fredman, M.L., Tarjan, R.E.: Fibonacci heaps and their uses in improved network optimization algorithms. J. ACM **34**(3), 338–346 (1984)
8. yuhc: Pregel and shortest path algorithm in graphx (2015). http://note.yuhc.me/2015/03/graphx-pregel-shortest-path/
9. Srinivasan, T., Balakrishnan, R., Gangadharan, S.A., Hayawardh, V.: A scalable parallelization of all-pairs shortest path algorithm for a high performance cluster environment. In: International Conference on Parallel and Distributed Systems, pp. 1–8 (2007)
10. Madduri, K., Bader, D.A., Berry, J.W., Crobak, J.R.: Parallel shortest path algorithms for solving large-scale instances. In: Dimacs Implementation Challenge - The Shortest Path Problem, vol. 74, pp. 249–290 (2011)
11. Intel xeon phi core micro-architecture (2016). https://software.intel.com/en-us/articles/intel-xeon-phi-core-micro-architecture

12. Goldberg, A.V.: A practical shortest path algorithm with linear expected time. Siam J. Comput. **37**(5), 1637–1655 (2008)
13. Denardo, E.V., Fox, B.L.: Shortest-route methods: 1. reaching, pruning, and buckets. Oper. Res. **27**(1), 161–186 (1979)
14. Zhu, A.D., Ma, H., Xiao, X., Luo, S., Tang, Y., Zhou, S.: Shortest path and distance queries on road networks: towards bridging theory and practice. In: Proceedings of the 2013 ACM SIGMOD International Conference on Management of Data, pp. 857–868 (2013)
15. Möhring, R.H., Schilling, H., Schütz, B., Wagner, D., Willhalm, T.: Partitioning graphs to speed up Dijkstra's algorithm. In: Nikoletseas, S.E. (ed.) WEA 2005. LNCS, vol. 3503, pp. 189–202. Springer, Heidelberg (2005). https://doi.org/10.1007/11427186_18
16. Miller, F.P., Vandome, A.F., Mcbrewster, J.: kd-tree. Alpha Press, Orlando (2009)
17. Karypis, G., Kumar, V.: METIS: a software package for partitioning unstructured graphs. In: International Cryogenics Monograph, pp. 121–124 (1998)
18. 9th DIMACS implementation challenge - shortest paths (2012). http://www.dis.uniroma1.it/challenge9/
19. Moore, E.F.: The shortest path through a maze. In: Proceedings of the International Symposium on the Theory of Switching, pp. 285–292 (1959)
20. Berteskas, D., Gallagre, R.: Distributed asynchronous Bellman-ford algorithm. In: Data Networks (1987)
21. Cheng, C., Riley, R., Kumar, S.P.R., Garcialunaaceves, J.J.: A loop-free extended bellman-ford routing protocol without bouncing effect. In: Symposium Proceedings on Communications Architectures and Protocols, pp. 224–236 (1989)
22. Chroboczek, J.: The Babel Routing Protocol. Heise Zeitschriften Verlag (2011)
23. Awerbuch, B., Bar-Noy, A., Gopal, M.: Approximate distributed bellman-ford algorithms. IEEE Trans. Commun. **42**(8), 2515–2517 (1994)
24. Pettie, S., Ramachandran, V.: Computing shortest paths with comparisons and additions. In: Thirteenth ACM-SIAM Symposium on Discrete Algorithms (2002)
25. Meyer, U., Sanders, P.: *delta*-stepping : a parallel single source shortest path algorithm. In: Bilardi, G., Italiano, G.F., Pietracaprina, A., Pucci, G. (eds.) ESA 1998. LNCS, vol. 1461, pp. 393–404. Springer, Heidelberg (1998). https://doi.org/10.1007/3-540-68530-8_33
26. Micikevicius, P.: General parallel computation on commodity graphics hardware: case study with the all-pairs shortest paths problem. In: International Conference on Parallel and Distributed Processing Techniques and Applications, PDPTA 2004 21–24 June 2004, Las Vegas, Nevada, USA, pp. 1359–1365 (2004)
27. Harish, P., Narayanan, P.J.: Accelerating Large graph algorithms on the GPU using CUDA. In: Aluru, S., Parashar, M., Badrinath, R., Prasanna, V.K. (eds.) HiPC 2007. LNCS, vol. 4873, pp. 197–208. Springer, Heidelberg (2007). https://doi.org/10.1007/978-3-540-77220-0_21
28. Kranjčević, M., Palossi, D., Pintarelli, S.: Parallel delta-stepping algorithm for shared memory architectures (2016)
29. Delling, D., Goldberg, A.V., Nowatzyk, A., Werneck, R.F.: PHAST: hardware-accelerated shortest path trees. J. Parallel Distrib. Comput. **73**(7), 940–952 (2013)
30. Geisberger, R., Sanders, P., Schultes, D., Delling, D.: Contraction hierarchies: faster and simpler hierarchical routing in road networks. In: McGeoch, C.C. (ed.) WEA 2008. LNCS, vol. 5038, pp. 319–333. Springer, Heidelberg (2008). https://doi.org/10.1007/978-3-540-68552-4_24
31. Intel xeon phi processor 7210 (2016). https://ark.intel.com/products/94033/Intel-Xeon-Phi-Processor-7210-16GB-1_30-GHz-64-core

32. Intel xeon phi x100 family coprocessor - the architecture, 12 November 2012. https://software.intel.com/en-us/articles/intel-xeon-phi-coprocessor-codename-knights-corner
33. Orlin, J.B., Madduri, K., Subramani, K., Williamson, M.: A faster algorithm for the single source shortest path problem with few distinct positive lengths. J. Discrete Algorithms **8**(2), 189–198 (2010)
34. Ortega-Arranz, H., Torres, Y., Gonzalez-Escribano, A., Llanos, D.R.: Comprehensive evaluation of a new GPU-based approach to the shortest path problem. Int. J. Parallel Prog. **43**(5), 918–938 (2015)
35. Sedeño-Noda, A., González-Barrera, J.D.: Fast and fine quickest path algorithm. Eur. J. Oper. Res. **238**(2), 596–606 (2014)

DA Placement: A Dual-Aware Data Placement in a Deduplicated and Erasure-Coded Storage System

Mingzhu Deng[1,2]([✉]), Ming Zhao[2], Fang Liu[3], Zhiguang Chen[1,3], and Nong Xiao[1,3]

[1] College of Computer, National University of Defense Technology, Changsha, China
dk_nudt@126.com
[2] Arizona State University, Tempe, USA
[3] School of Data and Computer Science, SUN YAT-SEN University, Guangzhou, China

Abstract. Simultaneously incorporating deduplication as well as erasure coding is preferred for modern storage systems for the enhanced storage efficiency and economical data reliability. However, simple incorporation suffers from the "read imbalance problem", in which parallel data accesses are curbed by throttled storage nodes. This problem is due to the uneven data placement in the system, which is unaware of the employment of both deduplication and erasure coding, each of whom alters the order of data if unattended. This paper proposes a systematic design and implementation of a Dual-Aware(DA) placement in a combined storage system to achieve both deduplication-awareness and erasure-coding-awareness at the same time. DA not only records the node number of each unique data to allow for quick references with ease, but also dynamically tracks used nodes for each writes request. In this way, deduplication awareness is formed to skip inconvenient placement locations. Besides, DA serializes the placement of parity blocks with a stripe and across stripes. Such realization of erasure coding awareness ensures the separation of data and parity, as well as maintains data sequentiality at bordering stripes. Additionally, DA manages to extend with further load-balancing through an innovative use of the deduplication level, which intuitively predicts future accesses of a piece of data. In short, DA manages to boost system performance with little memory or computation cost. Extensive experiments using both real-world traces and synthesized workloads, prove DA achieves a better read performance. For example, DA respectively leads an average latency margin of 30.86% and 29.63%, over the baseline rolling placement(BA) and random placement(RA) under CAFTL traces over a default cluster of 12 nodes with RS(8,4).

1 Introduction

In recent years, modern storage systems are transforming towards dual purposes of enhanced storage efficiency and economical fault tolerance, in light of growing

© Springer Nature Switzerland AG 2018
J. Vaidya and J. Li (Eds.): ICA3PP 2018, LNCS 11334, pp. 358–377, 2018.
https://doi.org/10.1007/978-3-030-05051-1_25

volume of data and various failure hazards [16]. *Deduplication*, a well-respected technique, plays a vital role in the goal of improving storage efficiency, due to its ability to eliminate repeated content under different application scenarios. In the meantime, regarding fault-tolerance, *erasure coding* has emerged as a more popular alternative to replication for its potential to provide higher reliability at a lower cost.

A system incorporated with both deduplication and erasure coding techniques, promises a more reliable and efficient means of storage. However, simply stacking of these two techniques inevitably suffers from the phenomenon of 'read imbalance,' in which read parallelism is severely straggled by throttled nodes. This is due to the uneven data placement in the system, which is unaware of the employment of both deduplication and erasure coding, each of whom alters the order of data if unattended. For example, deduplication disrupts original order by removing duplicates. In contrast, erasure coding interrupts sequentiality by injecting parities. In other words, in a combined system, the distortion of data order gets even worse with contribution and interaction from both deduplication and erasure coding, thus translating into degraded performance over an uneven data placement.

To this end, this paper proposes a systematic design and implementation of Dual Aware(DA) placement to be aware of both deduplication and erasure coding for better read balance. Firstly, this paper subdivides read requests based upon a comparison of the size of its first source write request. Such novel subdivision is supported by experimental observations and reveals the relationship between a read request and its first source write request. This provides better guidance to the placement design, which distributes written data in order to serve read requests. Before enabling awareness, this paper formulates a clear definition of both deduplication-awareness as well as erasure -coding-awareness. In terms of a systematic implementation, DA not only records the node number of each unique data to allow for quick references with ease, but also dynamically tracks used nodes for each writes request. In this way, deduplication awareness is formed to skip inconvenient placement locations. Besides, DA serializes the placement of parity blocks with a stripe and across stripes. Such realization of erasure coding awareness ensures the separation of data and parity, as well as maintains data sequentiality at bordering stripes. Additionally, DA manages to extend with further load-balancing through an innovative use of the deduplication level, which intuitively speculates future accesses of a piece of data. This exploitation stems from the assumption that each file shares an equal chance of being accessed, without prior-profiling of the workload. In short, DA manages to boost system performance with little memory or computation cost.

This paper considers two baseline approaches, with BA representing rolling placement, and RA as random placement. Experimental results with both real-world traces and synthesized workloads indicate DA achieves a more even placement, leading to better read performance in general, as compared to the BA and RA baselines. For example, DA has a respective average latency margin of 30.86% and 29.63% over BA and RA, under CAFTL traces. Under synthesized workloads of intra-request, whole-request, and random-sized sequential reads, DA gains an average advantage of 19.08% over BA, and 29.79% RA. Moreover, in the situation of degraded reads, DA outperforms BA and RA respectively by an average margin of 12.48% and 11.10%. All results are based on a defaulted cluster of 12 nodes with RS(8, 4).

The rest of this paper is organized as follows: Sect. 2 presents the basics, reviews related works, as well as discusses the motives for this paper. Section 3 details the design of DA placement. Section 4 experiments different workloads and analyzes results. Section 5 compares related work. Section VI concludes the paper.

2   Backgrounds and Motivations

2.1   Deduplication and Erasure Coding

Deduplication. Deduplication, as a technique to eliminate replicated contents [2], has attracted wide attention and been used in different storage systems, e.g. primary storage [2,4], backup and archival storage [11,12,14], and even in the cache [5]. In essence, a collision-resistant cryptographic hash function [17,18] lies in the core of deduplication to distinguish the replication of data contents. By removing duplicated data, deduplication instead stores a pointer to the first occurrence of the replica and thus manages to achieve significant storage saving. Additionally, the time in which deduplication takes place differentiates between in-line deduplication and out-of-line deduplication. This paper considers a system with in-line deduplication to remove replicas on the write path and focuses on the placement step of a conventional deduplication. In that sense, the work in this paper is perpendicular to existing deduplication studies and can be further integrated.

Erasure Coding. Instead of saving space, erasure coding [13] provides data protection at the cost of extra space. Essentially, by applying certain mathematical calculations in the encoding process, a reversible regenerate ability is produced between data and parity so that whenever a certain number of failure happens, data could be recovered in a reverse decoding manner [15,16]. Usually, input files are divided by a fixed size into blocks. Groups are formed with k data blocks encoded to produce m parity blocks. Such group containing $k + m$ blocks in total is called a stripe. Whenever no greater than m blocks are corrupted, a stripe is able to regenerate its whole content with at least k healthy blocks. Because erasure coding manages to provide satisfying fault tolerance at affordable space cost, it has gained increasing application in more and more production systems.

This paper considers a system with erasure coding for reasonable reliability concerns and studies how to distribute the data when encoding is finished.

2.2   Motivation

Although one can stack deduplication and erasure coding within one system to remove duplicated contents and provide data protection, such simple combination does not consider the read imbalance problem caused by both deduplication and erasure coding.

Figure 1 compares a distributed cluster *with* and *without* deduplication. In both systems, two write requests are inputted to the system and duplicate A and duplicate B are eliminated in the system with deduplication. Note that both systems assume the same rolling placement. When serving request 3, the system with deduplication suffers from read imbalance due to the throttled Node 0 and Node 1 (patterned nodes). In short, by removing replicas, which otherwise are stored, original data order is altered by deduplication, thus causing degraded read performance with throttled nodes.

Figure 2 compares a system *without* erasure coding and a system *with* a (3,1) MDS erasure codes (EC). Similarly, without EC, data is stored in a rotated manner across the nodes whereas two stripes are formed with an extra parity block each in the erasure-coded system. When reading file 1, the system with erasure coding can only exploit three independent nodes for four data chunks, throttled by the unbalanced Node 0(the patterned node), which needs to serve data A and data D. In other words, with the interjected parity contents, erasure coding results in the clustering of the otherwise separate data (e.g., data A and data D), leading to degraded read performance.

In summary, deduplication or erasure coding can result in the alteration of the original data layout. In a combined system with both deduplication and erasure coding, such alteration gets more severe with contribution and interaction from deduplication and erasure coding. Therefore, a comprehensive solution to this problem motivates this paper.

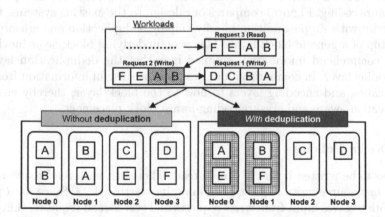

Fig. 1. Read imbalance caused by the simple addition of deduplication. Comparing to a system without duplication, a system with deduplication disrupts the original data order by removing duplicates (e.g. A and B), thus leading to throttled nodes, like Node 0 and Node 1.

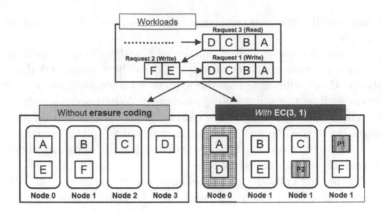

Fig. 2. Read imbalance caused by the simple addition of erasure coding. Comparing to a system without erasure coding, a system with a (3,1) MDS erasure codes (e.g. RS) interrupts data sequentiality across stripes (e.g. C and D) with produced parity, thus leading to throttled nodes, like Node 0.

3   DA Placement Design

3.1   Architecture

The motivating examples illustrate the uneven data layout, which plagues the simple combination of deduplication or erasure coding. This paper aims for an awareness-enabled block-level placement, in order to optimize for deduplication and erasure coding. Figure 3 compares our design to the existing systems. Existing systems with simple addition blindly employ deduplication and erasure coding on top of a generic block layer. This way, underlying block layer inevitably fails to comprehend information entailed by either the deduplication layer or the encoding layer. In comparison, our design allows useful information from the deduplication and encoding layers to flow to the block layer, thereby enabling deduplication-aware and erasure-coding-aware block placement.

3.2   Design Policies

Data has to be written before it can be read. Therefore, each read request must find its first source write request containing its starting data. Since data placement both receives input from write requests and serves read requests, this paper argues a good data placement design should consider the relationship between a read request and its first source write request. In that way, we manage to gain a clearer picture of what kind of read requests to serve with the placement of the written data.

Current classification normally divides data reads as either random or sequential, based upon the length of sequential data in an issued request. Although such

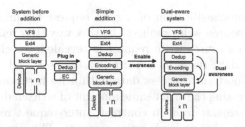

Fig. 3. The Design of DA placement. Compared to existing systems with simple addition, our design features a systematic dual awareness enabling, which conveys useful information respectively from deduplication and encoding layer downwards. In this way, the generic block is no longer loosely decoupled with upper layers. Instead, an informed block level with dual awareness is formed.

mainstream classification has shown its value in various studies, it lacks a concrete description for how a read request relates to its source write request and is, therefore, unable to guide our design of an awareness-enabled data placement.

This paper experiments with real-world traces (CAFTL traces) to profile both write and read requests. As a result, a new subdivision of read requests is proposed to reveal their relationship with its source written data and consequently guide a more practical design. Figure 4 plots the cumulative distribution of the size of a request from workloads h8. We can see over 87% of write requests access no greater than 12 pieces of data, as compared to approximately 42% for read requests of the same size. In other words, some read requests only access the same amount of data as its source write, while a portion access data greater than the size of the written data.

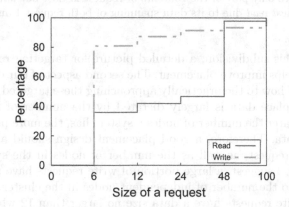

Fig. 4. The cumulative distribution of the size of a request from workloads (h8) of CAFTL traces. It is observed that data are written in smaller requests whereas more data is read in requests with bigger sizes. For example, over 87% of write requests access no greater than 12 pieces of data in comparison to only around 42% for read requests for the same number across a cluster of 12 nodes.

Therefore, our subclassification of a read request features a comparison of the size of its first source write request. In this way, the relationship between a read request and its source write request is revealed. Specifically, we divided common sequential data reads into: *intra-request read* and *inter-request read*. Intra-request reads pertain to access data within its first source write request. Note that, when accessing the exact same amount of written data, we specifically refer to it as *whole-request read*. In contrast, inter-request reads refer to those that contain data spanning multiple write requests. The size of an inter-request read can drastically vary. A pictorial example of proposed requests can be seen in Fig. 5. Request 3 is a *whole-request read* for reading the exact data written by Request 1. Request 4 is a *intra-request read* because it only partially accesses the contents of request 2. Lastly, Request 5 is an *inter-request read* as its data spans both request 1 and request 2. Real world examples of intra-request reads, include reading either a portion or the whole of a file, whereas a long sequential read is more often inter-request. Intra-request reads and inter-request read both exist in real-world applications, which makes our sub-classification practical.

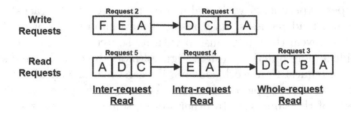

Fig. 5. Examples of two different sequential reads. Request 3 is a *whole-request read* for reading the exact data written by Request 1. Request 4 is an *intra-request read* because it accesses only part of the contents of request 2. Last but not least, Request 5 is an *inter-request read* due to its data spanning of both request 1 and request 2.

In light of this subdivision, a detailed picture for targeting read requests is drawn, which helps improve placement. The second aspect of our design requires consideration of how to the practically approaching these targeted read requests. The ability to place data is largely dictated by the number of nodes. Consequently, the greater the number of nodes a system has, the more possible choices to distribute data. Therefore, a good placement design should also regard the size of a write request, as well as the number of nodes in the system. As the statistics in Fig. 4 suggest, a large portion of write requests have a smaller data size compared to the number of independent nodes in the cluster. For example, over 87% of write requests have a data size no larger than 12 while the cluster has 12 nodes. Put simply, most write requests can fit into the cluster in an even manner.

Combining those two considerations forms the specific policies for our design: (1) In order to accommodate an intra-request read whose size is not greater than its first source write, it is both feasible and preferable to place data evenly within its source write request, over a cluster with a larger number of nodes. (2) In order to accommodate an inter-request read whose size is either potentially larger than the node number, it is important to keep data sequentially ordered across two adjacent write requests, to maximize data access.

3.3 Deduplication-Awareness and Erasure-Coding-Awareness

In systems without deduplication and erasure coding, data is distributed in a block-based manner. The simplest method of realizing the aforementioned design policies is a naive rolling placement, which serializes the placement of each block. However, in a combined system, deduplication and erasure coding respectively bring distinct changes to the system (e.g. the removal of duplicates, the introduction of parties, and stripe-based placement). Therefore, previous naive rolling placement fails to apply and a brand new approach with the awareness of the added techniques is needed to deliver our design policies. In order to enable deduplication and erasure coding awareness, we define both here.

Deduplication-Awareness. Deduplication removes duplicated content and collects repetition statistics. Accordingly, this paper defines deduplication awareness, which is useful for data placement, as:

(1) **Knowledge of the placement of duplicated content.** Original data chunks are identified as being either unique or duplicated through fingerprint matching. Unique chunks are placed, while only a pointer that refers to the first copy's location is stored for duplicates. Informed knowledge of the location of duplicates is necessary for the distribution of incoming chunks, as this avoids the throttled of nodes, caused by the removal of duplicates. For example in Fig. 1, if equipped with such knowledge of the location of duplicates(chunk A and chunk B) in the same request, chunk E and chunk F are able to avoid Node 0 and Node 1, thus leading to a balanced placement of Request 2.

(2) **Exploitation of the duplication level of a unique chunk.** Different unique chunks have different levels of duplication. This essentially represents how many times a chunk has been shared by multiple requests, assuming a chunk is not repeated twice within a request. In other words, the duplication level of a data indicates how many requests share it. In real-world applications, a workload's behavior is unknown until it finishes. Therefore, lacking any foreknowledge, it is reasonable to assume that each file would be accessed equally in the form of a whole-request read. Therefore, such deduplication hint manages to serve as a useful indicator to speculate future access. For example, unique chunk A with a deduplication level of 5 is located in Node 0, while chunk B, which is only repeated once, resides in Node 1. Suppose the incoming workloads access each written file once, by looking at the deduplication level of chunk A and B, we can easily speculate the future access time of Node 0 and Node 1 to be 5 and 2. In future practice, such useful indicator could be utilized to even out the future access across the nodes beforehand.

Erasure-Coding-Awarenss. Erasure coding provides data protection within the unit of formed stripes. Instead of a block-based placement without erasure coding, data placement now happens in a stripe-based manner. A stripe is of fixed size $k + m$, in which k data chunks are encoded to produce m parity chunks. For simplicity, we assume the number of nodes N equals $k + m$. As a result, with the introduction of erasure coding, requests are cut into different placement batches by the stripe size. Therefore, our two design policies based on a request-based approach need to be accordingly modified into a stripe-based manner with erasure coding awareness.

Although parity blocks do not support data access, they do take spots in the block placement. We define the erasure coding awareness useful for our block placement as follows:

(1) **Intra-stripe data sequentiality.** For the support of reads request whose sizes are less than a stripe, it is important to keep intra-stripe data sequentiality. This means placing data blocks and parity blocks into two separate sections. In this way, maximum data block sequentiality is reached within a stripe, without being interrupted by parity block(s).
(2) **Inter-stripe data sequentiality.** For the support of larger read requests that span more than one stripe, it is important to keep inter-stripe data sequentiality. In other words, this means maintaining data sections of adjacent stripes in an adjacent manner. In this way, requests that are cut off by a stripe do not suffer from a broken data order, thus preserving the ability to realize our design policies.

Additionally, to support more erasure codes, the erasure coding awareness in this paper aims to be applicable to general erasure coding, and as such are not code-specific. In other words, our erasure coding awareness supports various erasure codes, such as MDS [13] codes and LRC codes [3].

3.4   Putting Them Together

The read imbalance problem goes beyond just the mere addition of problems caused by deduplication and erasure coding respectively. This is because data placement in a combined system is influenced by both modules, thereby calling for an integrated approach to enable dual-awareness. This paper strives to enable seamless dual-awareness in a systematic way to implement our design policies.

In terms of deduplication awareness, we keep track of locations of the first occurrence of a data by adding bits to record its node number. The number of bits needed is $\lfloor \log_2 N \rfloor$. For example, 4 bits are enough to track up to $2^4 = 16$ nodes. Since the fingerprint is mostly stored in memory, the bits need to be used along with the fingerprint to avoid disk look-up. A *char* with 8 bits is enough for a cluster of up to 256 nodes. Additionally, we maintain N bits for each involved write request in the current placement batch, in order to record its used nodes. Bit operations are used to speed up such recording. An *int* is usually used as the container of bits. For example, if a prior chunk is already stored in Node 0, the first bit of the *int* of the same request will be set to 1. Note that a recorder is local to a write request. Whenever data placement of a request finishes, the *int* can be cleared for reuse. In this way, when a replica comes through deduplication, not only is it identified as a duplicate, but the recorder is also updated with the node number associated with its fingerprint. With such remembrance, incoming data can be skip used nodes to achieve better balance.

In terms of erasure coding awareness, we treated global parity and local parity blocks (if any) with no difference. In this way, MDS erasure codes and LRC erasure codes are equal in our placement. Moreover, we keep track of parity locations of the previous stripe through a sequential alignment of all parity blocks in each stripe and a rotation by a distance of m(the number of all parity blocks in a stripe) is employed per stripe. In this way, the data section and the parity section in each stripe are both sequential. As such, no data chunks are separated by parity chunks or vice versa. Meanwhile, data sequentiality across stripes is preserved as per the original goal.

Algorithm. Algorithm 1 shows the pseudo-code of the placement algorithm. The following inputs are: (1) N, the number of storage nodes; (2)k, the size of data chunks in a stripe; (3)s, the number of stripes to be placed per batch; (4)$t_j (1 \leq t_j \leq k)$, the number of requests included in the stripe j; (5)$I_i (1 \leq i \leq t_j)$, an *int* representing used nodes of request R_i in stripe j.

Result: Assign[]
while $j \leq s$ **do**
    Parity rotation(j);
    $Assign = SequentialInit()$;
    while $i \leq k$ **do**
        $node = \_1st\_sequential\_node\ available(I_i)$;
        if $node \neq -1$ and $node \neq Assign[i]$ **then**
        | Swap(Assign[i], node);
        end
        return Assign;
    end
end

Algorithm 1: DA placement

In comparison to the baseline approach, Fig. 6 illustrates how DA placement stores four separate requests across a cluster of 6 nodes with (4,2) erasure coding. Upon the placement of the first stripe, the initial value of data chunks are to be [A:0, B:1, C:2, D:3] and since A is the first chunk of Request 1, the set of used nodes **U1** represented by $intI_1$ is empty and Node 0 is the first available node for chunk A. After that $U1 = 0$. Likewise, by skipping used nodes in **U1**, B and C go respectively to Node 1 and Node 2. In terms of D, which belongs to request 2 and comes after a replicated chunk A, $U2 = 0$ and thus, Node 3 is found for chunk D to finish the assignment. Following stripes are processed in a similar manner. In terms of Swap, chunk J has an initial assignment of Node 3. Because $U4 = 1, 2, 3$, Node 4 is picked to swap with the original Node 3. In this way, incoming unique chunks are aware of the places of its preceding chunks from the same request, like chunk D to chunks A. Rotation is made to be aware of parity chunks of each stripe so that the sequentiality of different data components of the same request but across stripes is possible, like chunk D and chunk E. (Chunks in DA with different locations compared to the baseline are colored.)

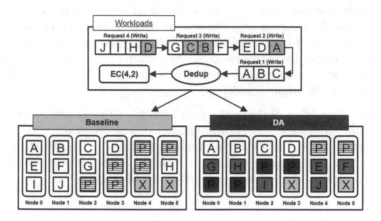

Fig. 6. How DA placement works with enabled dual awareness. Deduplication awareness enables DA to be aware of the location of removed duplicates and keeps tracking the used nodes of a write request, thus being able to distribute data more evenly for each request, e.g. I avoid the nodes used by D, H. Meanwhile erasure coding awareness manages to maintain inter-stripe sequentiality by serializing parity. (e.g. E is able to reside adjacent to D. (Color figure online)

As there is a potential for variances in the selection of available nodes, the flexibility of DA placement allows for additional extensions. One such extension is the ability to utilize the deduplication level for an access-speculation selection, which is explained in the definition of Deduplication awareness. Other extensions, designed to consider weighted factors such as transmission bandwidth, the least busy node, total access times, as well as different workload features are also possible.

4   Experiments

This paper considers two placement policies as the baseline: BA and RA. BA stands for a basic rolling placement, with neither deduplication awareness nor erasure coding awareness. RA represents a random placement policy, which is commonly adopted in distributed storage systems. In comparison, our proposed Dual-Aware placement is abbreviated as DA. Experiments are conducted with both real-world traces and synthesized workloads, to investigate the efficacy of enabled dual awareness in data placement.

4.1 Environments and Workloads

Simulator. This paper adopts a trace-driven simulation method for evaluation purposes. Our simulator simulates a distributed storage system with a cluster of storage nodes and bases on PFSsim [10], which is widely used in various research works [6–9].

Our simulator runs on node 19 of the computing cluster of VISA lab at ASU. The node has 2X Intel Xeon E5-2630 2.40 GHz processor and 62GiB of RAM with 2X 1TB disk of Seagate 7200 and the model number is ST1000NM0033-9ZM. The operating system of the machine is Ubuntu 14.04.1 with Linux version 3.16.0-30. By default, all simulations emulate a cluster of 12 storage nodes with an RS(8,4) code employed and 4KB fixed-size chunking for deduplication is used.

Datasets. This paper experiments with datasets from both real-world traces and synthesized traces. The chosen real-world traces come from ref [1] for deduplication use. The primary reason is that the CAFTL traces [1] contain the request field, which provides easy identification of a file and are widely used in academic studies and prototype implementations. Features of included workloads are provided in Table 1.

Table 1. Features of the CAFTL traces

Categories	Workloads	Dedup ratio	Read/Write
Desktop	d1	0.102512	1.078
	d2	0.222767	1.777
Transaction	t1	0.053642	1.157
	t2	0.182534	0.567
Hadoop	h1	0.124294	1.391
	h2	0.305313	1.829
	h3	0.126232	9.2
	h4	0.170053	1.418
	h5	0.229826	0.97
	h6	0.147617	2.583
	h7	0.106438	1.811479
	h8	0.161479	2.086

This paper generates three different workloads on the basis of the CAFTL traces to conduct more extensive tests. Specifically, the three synthesized workloads include: (1) Whole-request reads, which contain read requests of the exact same composition and order as the original write requests. (2) Intra-request reads, which randomize the composition and order of data within an original write request and forms a read request of a random size no larger than that of the original size. (3) Sequential reads of random size, which randomly select a starting point and issue sequential read requests of random sizes to at least cover all the data in storage once.

Metrics. Normally, read latency is used to characterize read performance. Complimentary to read latency, which fails to convey how parallel a read request is served, metrics to indicate load balancing make better candidates to measure and present the parallel essence of data access in distributed systems. This paper considers the *read balance gap* G_i for each read request, defined as follows:

$$G_i = 1 - \frac{E_i}{M_i}. \tag{1}$$

E_i is the *average read latency* of each chunk in Request i, and M_i is the *maximum read latency*, taken by the slowest chunk, assuming that its previous request has been finished before the current request arrives. Balanced Read of Request i is achieved by minimizing G_i, which attains minimum at *zero* (i.e., when all chunks of Request i are evenly placed). The closer G_i is to zero, the more balanced the placement policy is. On the other hand, when G_i gets closer to one, the degree of read imbalance becomes more severe. The same indicator is used in [19].

4.2 Effectiveness

In order to investigate the efficacy of our proposed dual awareness, two workloads of whole request reads are produced to respectively probe into deduplication awareness and erasure coding awareness. These workloads are divided into short and long requests, based on a comparison of the size of the cluster.

Deduplication Awareness. Since the size of any short request is no larger than the size of the cluster, each request possesses the potential for even placement in storage. Therefore, short requests are appropriate for testing the ability of a placement policy in even distribution. Figure 7 shows that DA achieves the best balance with an average G of 0.014 and RA the worst with a G of 0.053 per request. This is because random placement may lead to throttled nodes, while the inherent sequentiality of rolling placement benefits BA with an average G of 0.026. However, DA outperforms BA with informed avoidance of preceding data, thus achieving a smaller G. In other words, deduplication awareness does indeed help mitigate imbalanced placement.

Erasure Coding Awareness. Compared to short requests, long requests naturally have a larger G due to their request size. On average, DA also manages to achieve a better balance with a smaller G of 0.728 compared to 0.775 of BA, and 0.78 of RA. This is largely due to its awareness of erasure coding, which avoids the interruption of data sequentiality with the rotated parity. In contrast,

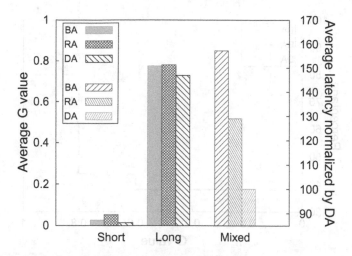

Fig. 7. Effectiveness of dual awareness. The two left clusters show the average G comparison of different policies under short requests and long requests. DA manages an evener data placement with a smaller G under short requests access. This benefits from deduplication awareness, which avoids used nodes by preceding duplicates with useful information. DA also outperforms other alternatives with regards to long requests. This proves the efficacy of the erasure coding awareness of DA, which better preserves data sequentiality across stripes. The right subplot presents the latency comparison under the mixed workload h8 of both short requests and long requests. Enabled dual awareness translates into the actual better performance of DA over other policies.

BA continuously suffers from broken sequentiality across stripes, resulting in reduced performance.

Combined Effects. Figure 8 provides the cumulative distribution of G of different placement policies, under the workload h8 of CAFTL traces. Initially, 38.00% and 34.60% of all requests have a G of zero under BA and RA respectively. In comparison, values increase to 41.10% under DA. In general, DA prevails over others, enabling more requests with smaller G values. Since real-world workload is a mixture of both short and long requests, the above results prove that through a combined contribution of deduplication awareness and erasure coding awareness, DA manages to truly provide more balanced placement as compared to the baseline policies.

The Read Latency. Although G closely relates to the read performance as a whole, it does not necessarily reflect practical read performance in time. The rightmost bars of Fig. 7 present the read latency comparison under the workload of h8. Specifically, we can observe that DA outperforms others with a margin of 57.21% over BA, 29.02% over RA respectively. Note that there is a significant difference between the results of the latency and by G. This is because the calculation of the latency includes waiting time, which is not considered in the calculation of G. Therefore, access congestion that leads to heavy waiting,

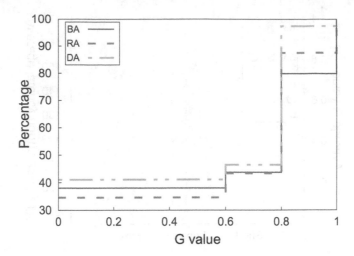

Fig. 8. The cumulative distribution of G of different placement policies, under the workload h8. With a bigger percentage of requests having a smaller G value, DA achieves a more balanced placement in comparison to other policies. For example, 41.10% requests achieve a *zero* G value while to 38.00% of BA and 34.60% of RA.

happens for unevenly placed data, and the effect is disproportionately magnified by a large number of requests.

Figure 9 provides more results by replaying all workloads of CAFTL traces. We can observe DA always ranks highest in performance regardless of the workload, while BA and RA alternate places depending on the workload. For example, BA outperforms RA under d1 by around 44%, whereas RA overtakes BA by approximately 28% under t1. DA's leading gap varies across workloads due to different deduplication ratios and workload patterns. On average, DA has a respective leading margin of 30.86% and 29.63%, over BA and RA.

4.3   Results on Synthesized Workloads

Three types of specialized workloads are synthesized on the basis of CAFTL datasets. Intra-request reads serve as a proper input to probe the balance of inner data placement within a request, whereas whole-request reads test inner data placement and sequentiality within a request as a whole. In comparison, random sequential reads are a more practical exhibition of sequential reads. Figures 10, 11 and 12 respectively compare the results of replaying whole-request reads, intra-request reads, and random sequential reads.

In general, DA exhibits the best results under all synthesized workloads. The range of the leading margin differs depending on workloads. For example, DA leads over BA by an average 18.57%, 31.05%, 14.05% separately under the whole-request reads, intra-request reads and random sequential reads. Additionally, results under whole-request reads and results under intra-request reads

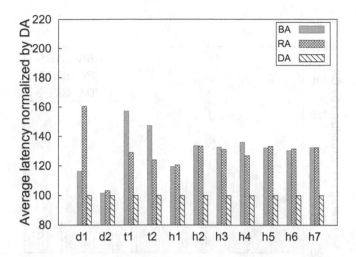

Fig. 9. Latency comparison under CAFTL traces. In general, DA outperforms the baseline policies under different CAFTL workloads. However, the leading gap varies depending upon the workload. On average, DA outruns BA and RA respectively by 30.86% and 29.63%

show a similar tendency. Note, DA performs slightly better under whole-request reads, as the workload of whole-request reads is a boundary case of the intra-request reads. Improvements of DA under random sequential reads show weaker momentum as compared to two other workloads. This is because this synthesis of workloads is a good mixture of the various sequential read requests of different sizes. On average, under all three synthesized workloads, DA gains an advantage of 19.08% over BA, 29.79% over RA, and 17.75% over DA-.

4.4   The Experiments on Degraded Read

System performance will be degraded by the data recovery process due to data unavailability. This paper also provides evaluations on degraded read performance of different placements. In order to create a reasonable degraded read situation, we bring down a random node during each run and make sure node failure is evenly distributed. Regarding the selection of participating nodes for each repair, a seeded random selection algorithm is used to ensure same repairs. The final results are averaged across 200 runs.

Figure 13 presents the degraded read performance in latency under CAFTL workloads. Generally, DA placement achieves the best-degraded read performance. Additionally, the runner-up and the leading gap of DA over any other placement actually vary depending upon different workloads. For instance, BA outperforms RA by around 26% under d1 while RA overtakes BA by over 6% under t1. On average, DA outperforms BA and RA respectively by an average margin of 12.48% and 11.10%. However, the average leading advantage of DA over others, in general, is smaller than the normal access scenarios. The reason

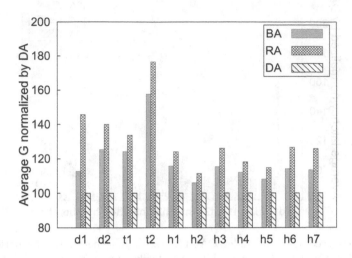

Fig. 10. Performance of different placements under whole-request reads, which correspond to "read exactly what you write". In general, DA shows the best performance while RA is the worst. Due to the collective effectiveness of deduplication awareness and erasure coding awareness, DA achieves an average leading margin of 30% over BA and 22% over RA.

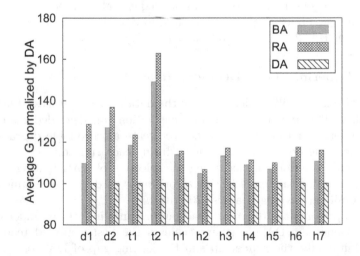

Fig. 11. Performance of different placements under whole-request reads. Similarly, DA achieves the best performance of all. However, the advantage of DA exhibits a slight weaker momentum than that of whole-request reads.

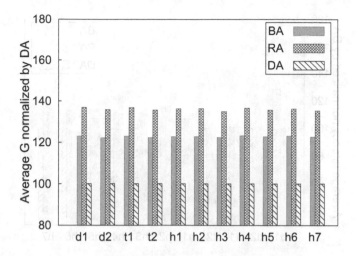

Fig. 12. Performance of different placements under sequential reads with random sizes. Likewise, DA performs the best among all the polices. However, the tendency exhibits a similar shape regardless of specific workloads.

for this is that a single failure unavoidably interrupts the system sequentially, regardless of data placement. However, as a whole, DA maintains better sequentiality than the others, in the face of various single failure cases. Meanwhile, workloads that do not necessarily conform to the same access pattern, contain different amounts of read requests, which thus impacts the advantageous margin of DA over other policies.

4.5 Summary

In summary, BA possesses naive sequentiality within a stripe along with interrupted across-stripe sequentiality whereas RA is random. In comparison, DA maintains even placement within a request and preserves the maximum across-stripe sequentiality with the full rotation of parties at the same time. Both real-world traces and synthesized workloads indicate that DA achieves better performance than other alternatives in both normal access scenarios and degraded access scenarios.

5 Conclusion

This paper proposes DA placement, a systematic study feathering integrated deduplication-aware and erasure-coding-aware data placement in a combined storage system. The novelties lie in a new systematic design that considers the interrelationship between write requests and read requests and enables clearly-defined dual awareness to realize an enlightened block layer for informed placement. Also, the suggestive use of the deduplication level for future access

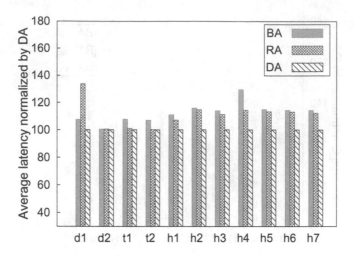

Fig. 13. Latency compasison under degraded reads. In general, DA performs better than others in degraded situations. The difference between DA and other policies varies. For example, DA outperforms BA by 7.54% under d1 whereas the number drops to 0.57% under d2. On average, DA outperforms BA and RA by 12.48% and 11.10% respectively.

speculation is both interesting and innovative. DA placement manages to provide better read balance compared to baseline approaches, which is proved by extensive experiments with both real-world traces and synthesized traces. Additionally, it bears little memory and computational overhead in system modification and has zero influence on deduplication and erasure coding. As its design is generic and not code-specific, it is able to support any mainstream erasure codes.

Acknowledgment. We would like to greatly appreciate the anonymous reviewers for their insightful comments. This work is supported by the National Natural Science Foundation of China under Grant Nos. 61433019, U1435217, and the National High Technology Research and Development Program of China under Grant No. 2016YFB1000302.

References

1. Chen, F., Luo, T., Zhang, X.: CAFTL: a content-aware flash translation layer enhancing the lifespan of flash memory based solid state drives. FAST **11**, 77–90 (2011)
2. Hong, B., Plantenberg, D., Long, D.D., Sivan-Zimet, M.: Duplicate data elimination in a SAN file system. In: MSST, pp. 301–314 (2004)
3. Huang, C., et al.: Erasure coding in windows azure storage. In: Usenix Annual Technical Conference, pp. 15–26. , Boston, MA (2012)

4. Jin, K., Miller, E.L.: The effectiveness of deduplication on virtual machine disk images. In: Proceedings of SYSTOR 2009: The Israeli Experimental Systems Conference, p. 7. ACM (2009)
5. Li, W., Jean-Baptise, G., Riveros, J., Narasimhan, G., Zhang, T., Zhao, M.: Cachededup: In-line deduplication for flash caching. In: FAST, pp. 301–314 (2016)
6. Li, X., Dong, B., Xiao, L., Ruan, L., Liu, D.: CEFLS: a cost-effective file lookup service in a distributed metadata file system. In: Proceedings of the 2012 12th IEEE/ACM International Symposium on Cluster, Cloud and Grid Computing (CCGrid 2012), pp. 25–32. IEEE Computer Society (2012)
7. Li, X., Dong, B., Xiao, L., Ruan, L., Liu, D.: HCCache: a hybrid client-side cache management scheme for i/o-intensive workloads in network-based file systems. In: 2012 13th International Conference on Parallel and Distributed Computing, Applications and Technologies (PDCAT), pp. 467–473. IEEE (2012)
8. Li, X., Xiao, L., Ke, X., Dong, B., Li, R., Liu, D.: Towards hybrid client-side cache management in network-based file systems. Comput. Sci. Inf. Syst. 11(1), 271–289 (2014)
9. Liu, N., et al.: On the role of burst buffers in leadership-class storage systems. In: 2012 IEEE 28th Symposium on Mass Storage Systems and Technologies (MSST), pp. 1–11. IEEE (2012)
10. Liu, Y., Figueiredo, R., Xu, Y., Zhao, M.: On the design and implementation of a simulator for parallel file system research. In: 2013 IEEE 29th Symposium on Mass Storage Systems and Technologies (MSST), pp. 1–5. IEEE (2013)
11. Meister, D., Brinkmann, A.: Multi-level comparison of data deduplication in a backup scenario. In: Proceedings of SYSTOR 2009: The Israeli Experimental Systems Conference, p. 8. ACM (2009)
12. Ng, C.H., Lee, P.P.: Revdedup: a reverse deduplication storage system optimized for reads to latest backups. In: Proceedings of the 4th Asia-Pacific Workshop on Systems, p. 15. ACM (2013)
13. Plank, J.S.: Erasure codes for storage systems: a brief primer. Usenix Mag. 38(6), 44–50 (2013)
14. Quinlan, S., Dorward, S.: Venti: a new approach to archival storage. FAST 2, 89–101 (2002)
15. Rashmi, K., Chowdhury, M., Kosaian, J., Stoica, I., Ramchandran, K.: EC-Cache: load-balanced, low-latency cluster caching with online erasure coding. In: OSDI, pp. 401–417 (2016)
16. Rashmi, K., Shah, N.B., Gu, D., Kuang, H., Borthakur, D., Ramchandran, K.: A Hitchhiker's guide to fast and efficient data reconstruction in erasure-coded data centers. ACM SIGCOMM Comput. Commun. Rev. 44(4), 331–342 (2015)
17. Rivest, R.: The MD5 message-digest algorithm (1992)
18. Secure Hash Standard: Federal information processing standards publication 180-1 (1995)
19. Xu, M., Zhu, Y., Lee, P.P., Xu, Y.: Even data placement for load balance in reliable distributed deduplication storage systems. In: 2015 IEEE 23rd International Symposium on Quality of Service (IWQoS), pp. 349–358. IEEE (2015)

Improving Restore Performance of Deduplication Systems by Leveraging the Chunk Sequence in Backup Stream

Ru Yang[1], Yuhui Deng[1,2(✉)], Cheng Hu[3], and Lei Si[1]

[1] Department of Computer Science, Jinan University,
Guangzhou 510632, People's Republic of China
yangru.ay@foxmail.com, tyhdeng@jnu.edu.cn, si_lei@foxmail.com
[2] State Key Laboratory of Computer Architecture, Institute of Computing,
Chinese Academy of Sciences, Beijing 100190, China
[3] School of Information Science and Technology,
Guangdong University of Foreign Studies, Guangzhou, China
huchengcs@gdufs.edu.cn

Abstract. Traditional deduplication based backup systems normally employ containers to reduce the chunk fragmentation, thus improving the restore performance. However, the shared chunks belonging to a single backup grows with the increase of the number of backups. Those shared chunks are normally distributed across multiple containers. This feature increases chunk fragmentation and significantly degrades the restore performance. In order to improve the restore performance, some schemes are proposed to optimize the replacement strategy of the restore cache, such as the ones using LRU and OPT. However, LRU is inefficient and OPT consumes additional computational overhead. By analyzing the backup and restore process, we observe that the sequence of the chunks in the backup stream is consistent to that in the restore stream. Based on this observation, this paper proposes an off-line optimal replacement strategy—OFL for the restore cache. The OFL records the chunk sequence of backup process, and then uses this sequence to calculate the exact information of the required chunks in advance for the restore process. Finally, accurate prefetch will be employed by leveraging the above information to reduce the impact of chunk fragmentation. Real data sets are employed to evaluate the proposed OFL. The experimental results demonstrate that OFL improves the restore performance over 8% in contrast to the traditional LRU and OPT.

1 Introduction

Data are continue growing at an explosive rate of over 52% per year [1,2]. Large data sets raise several challenges including huge disk overhead, sharp consumption of storage device lifespan [3], and so on [4]. For the reason that data deduplication can greatly reduce the disk overhead required for storing data, data deduplication becomes a key component of modern backup systems [5–9]. For

© Springer Nature Switzerland AG 2018
J. Vaidya and J. Li (Eds.): ICA3PP 2018, LNCS 11334, pp. 378–392, 2018.
https://doi.org/10.1007/978-3-030-05051-1_26

a traditional deduplication, the backup stream is first divided into fixed-size chunks or variable-sized chunks [10], and then each chunk is identified by SHA-1 digest [11,12]. Only when a chunk has no other identical copies in the store, it can be stored. Otherwise, the system only records the corresponding metadata of the chunk and clears the chunk immediately. Chunks, which are prepared to be written to disk, are aggregated in their arrival orders to a unit called a container. One container is an operating unit for the data reads and writes in a system, and it maintains the locality of backup stream. During a restoring process, containers serve as prefetching units.

When storing data in deduplication backup systems, the main concern is to achieve timely data recovery [13,14]. If an enterprise couldn't restore data in time when disks failed or database-related file corrupted, the losses would be immeasurable [15], and data backup would also become less significant. Therefore, the process of data recovery is very important, for the requirements of performing disastrous recovery and achieving quick access to historical backup data [16,17]. However, the shared chunks belonging to a single backup grows with the increase of the number of backups. Those shared chunks are normally distributed across multiple containers (e.g. distributed servers which are interconnected with some kind of high efficiency networks [18]). Those shared chunks are normally distributed across multiple containers. This feature increases chunk fragmentation and significantly degrades the restore performance [19]. The restore performance is important since it has became the main concern of users. In general, chunk fragmentation, which introduces data fragment, is unavoidable during the process of backup. Therefor, it is important to resist the degradation caused by the chunk fragmentation.

To this end, some schemes are proposed to optimize the replacement strategy of the restoring cache and improve the cache hit rate, such as in the studies of Lillibridge et al. [20] and Fu et al. [21]. In their studies, they improve the recovery performance of the system to a certain extent, but their schemes are deficiencies. Between them, Lillibridge et al. maintain the prefetched containers in the restore cache, and using a Least Recently Used (LRU) strategy for container eviction. The LRU strategy follows a First-In-First-Out (FIFO) way when allocating cache for containers. The LRU strategy, which is simple and easy to implement, is widely and effectively used for data recovery. However, under the environment where the data locality is not strong, the cache hit rate of LRU is not so good. Compared with LRU, an Optimal replacement (OPT) strategy, which is implemented in cache by Fu et al., obtains low cache misses. But OPT must calculate the optimal order for cache replacement online, thus introduces additional computational overhead. By the way, Primary and secondary deduplication systems can be subdivided onto inline ones and off-line ones [22]. An online deduplication system often leads to an increase in request latency. By contrast, because off-line systems [23,24] tend to dedulicate written data at the system idle time, they don't affect the write latency in general.

To address the problems exist in LRU and OPT, we propose an off-line optimal replacement strategy—OFL for the restore cache. The OFL records the chunk sequence of backup process, and then uses this sequence to calculate the exact information of the required chunks in advance for the restore process. Finally, accurate prefetch will be employed by leveraging the above information to reduce the impact of chunk fragmentation. Thereby, OFL can further improve the restoring performance. By the way, rather than performing backup operations in different time windows in traditional deduplication systems, the OFL is free in selecting time windows when analyzing off-line data and making backups.

The rest of this paper is organized as follows. Section 2 describes the related deduplication technology for backup and restoring. Section 3 describes the structure of a data restoring system where OFL is incorporated. Section 4 carries out the experimental evaluation. Finally, Sect. 5 draws conclusions.

2   Related Work

2.1   Container and Container ID

The container in deduplication systems are defined as a storage unit, so as to utilize the data locality to improve the backup performance. The size of each container, which contains many unique data chunks, is fixed. Different chunks can be identified according to their fingerprints, and different containers can be identified by the container IDs of them [5]. In fact, when a new container is created, a container ID number (abbreviate to container ID) is assigned to the container by the system. So, when a data chunk is needed for recovering data, the container which contains the chunk can located and prefetched to the cache. As a result, the hit rate in the cache can be improved when recovering data.

After the system completed a data backup, a metadata is generated for the backup. In the metadata, the ID number of the container which contains the unique chunk is recorded [25]. According to the ID number, the system can calculate the container address and do not have to save the full address, thus bringing a advantage of saving disk space. At the same time, if the reference count of the container is zero, the container data will be recovered and destroyed by the garbage collection mechanism. Due to this advantage, in our off-line cache strategy, different containers are identified by their ID numbers. Benefited from the ID numbers, can our strategy introduce off-line technology into the restoring process in online backup systems.

2.2   Least Recently Used

The LRU algorithm is a traditional cache replacement algorithm, which is efficient and easy to implement, due to its simplicity [20]. In the process of restoring data, LRU usually only needs to maintain a fixed-size cache queue. When a system receives the restoring request, it continually fills data into the containers in the cache. When using LRU, the data is added in a head or an end interpolation way. Figure 1 shows the replacement algorithm of LRU. As shown, when there is no space for inserting new data, the cache will first kick out the container at the head or the end of the queue, and then add the new data by the mean of the LRU. Because LRU only need to replace data in a straightforward way, it is a low-load cache replacement algorithm that does not require additional computational overhead.

The simplicity of the LRU algorithm is favored by many critics. However, a great lose of the cache hit rate might be caused due to its simplicity. The reason is that the main idea of LRU is taking the advantage of data locality, and assumes are implicated in LRU that the backup data are redundant and the current accessed chunk will be accessed again soon. Which means that when the cache is full, the data replaced by new data might be accessed soon, thus resulting in a cache miss. This can be worse, when the frequency of the deduplication for backup data is not high.

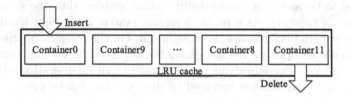

Fig. 1. The replacement algorithm of LRU

2.3 Optimal Cache Replacement

LRU may kick out wrong container which is called out-of-order container in the process of restoring data. In order to reduce the impact of out-of-order container on the recovery performance and promote the cache hit rate of LRU, Fu et al. achieves a Belady [26] optimal replacement cache (OPT) policy. Figure 2 shows the OPT replacement algorithm. To achieve the OPT algorithm, which data will be accessed in the future should first be known. Generally, this can found out from the metadata of data, and the reason is that the orders of data writing and reading are consistent.

With this deduplication characteristics, the system will generates a metadata which records ID number of the container have been accessed after backuping data. The OPT cache retrieves the container information that is accessed later from the metadata and figures out which container is not accessed for the longest time in the future in the online environment. When the cache is full and need to replace the data, the system will eliminate specific container from the restoring cache. Although Belady proves that the OPT algorithm can improve the hit rate of the cache, an additional computational overhead is introduced from finding out the data will be accessed in the future. This also has negative impact on the system recovery performance.

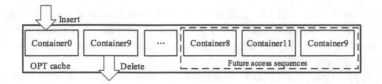

Fig. 2. The replacement algorithm OPT

2.4   Off-Line Deduplication Backup System

Traditional primary and secondary deduplication systems can be subdivided into online and off-line ones [22]. On one hand, the online deduplication systems require a write path before data are written to disk. A real-time demand is always need to be met in a online deduplication system, thus the system often manages lots of requests. As a result, a serious system delay, which will greatly degrade the system performance, is brought out. On the other hand, most of the off-line systems deduplicate the data have been written previously, during their idle periods [23,24]. Therefore, due to the few data writing operations during the idle periods, the system delay incurred by data writing can be greatly reduced. Inspired by this advantage of off-line systems, we apply an off-line mechanism for the cache strategy in restoring systems, with the purpose of optimizing the recovery performance.

3   System Architecture

3.1   Overview

In traditional backup systems, the sequence of the chunks in the backup stream is consistent to that in the restore stream. Therefore, our off-line cache replacement strategy—OFL can record the chunk sequence of backup process, and then uses this sequence to calculate the exact information of the required chunks in advance for the restore process. Finally, accurate prefetch will be employed by leveraging the above information to reduce the impact of chunk fragmentation and achieve optimal replacement. Besides, the replacement order of the restoring cache is also analyzed in advance. As a result, the extra overhead can be reduced, and the restoring performance can be further improved. By the way, rather than performing backup operations in different time windows as in traditional deduplication systems, the OFL is free in selecting time windows when making analyses and making backups.

In order to evaluate the effectiveness of OFL, we implement a real proto-type. Figure 3 shows the structure of a data restoring system which uses OFL. The figure contains the following modules: ① Access Sequences (AS), ② Off-line Cache Replacement (OCR), ③ Replaced Container ID (RCI), ④ Metadata (MD), ⑤ Data Recovery (DR), ⑥ Restoring Stream (RS). The OFL module mainly consists of the OCR and RM modules. The OCR simulate the procedure of data

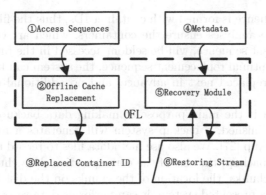

Fig. 3. The structure of a data restoring system which is based on the off-line replacement strategy

recovery in the idle periods of system, thus providing a reliable recovery cache replacement strategy for the later real data restoring processes. The main job of RM is complete data restoring by using the information provided by OCR. Figure 3 also shows the workflow of the system. The OFL mainly completes a data recovery operation through the following steps:

1. The system generates an access sequence file after completing a data backup. The access sequence file maintains the container ID for containers involved in the backup.
2. The OCR finds out the optimal replacement sequence of containers by performing a series of off-line simulation analyses, and then the sequence is recorded by RCI.
3. After the system received a restoring request, the DR starts a data recovery by referring to the MD. When a cache replacement happens, the corresponding container recorded in RCI for replacement is kicked out from the cache.
4. Finally, the RS serializes the restoring stream to the specified directory.

The access sequence file maintains the container ID for containers involved in the backup. In this way, the container information can be known in advance. Thus, the cache, which will be accessed in the future process of data recovery, can be predicted. According to the container information, the system can also know which containers are seldom accessed in the next period of time. These containers are the ones preferentially be replaced in the cache, so as to perform a optimal cache replacement. When the system makes data backup, it generates an access sequence file which stores a valid information for the later off-line analyses. By the way, generating an access sequence file has no negative impact on the system performance of data recovery.

Replaced container is the container need to be replaced in the restoring process, when the cache is full. By performing a series of off-line simulation analyses, OCR finds out the optimal replacement sequence of containers. Then this sequence is recorded in a cache replacement information file by RCI. By the way, in the file, the sequence is formed with container IDs, thus the file takes few disk space. The off-line analyses ensure the containers, which are contained in the optimal replacement sequence, will be seldom accessed in the future. Therefore, according to the optimal replacement sequence, the system can know which container should be replaced next in advance, and no additional calculations are needed.

Restoring data is the main purpose of making data backup. After a deduplication process finished, a backup system will generates a metadata file for corresponding backup [27]. We also use metadata files to record the logical order of the files in the backup, the size of the corresponding data chunks, the fingerprint of the data chunks, the location of the chunks on the disk and some other information. In the presented system, it can performs data recovery by referring to the MD module. As a result, according to a pre-specified recovery command, the system can restore the corresponding backup data to the specified directory. Finally, the backup data are in accordance with the original format plate.

3.2   Off-Line Cache Replacement

As Fig. 4 shows, the OFL module maintains the Access Record Table (ART), the Sorted Record Table (SRT) and the OFL simulation cache (often in memory). The SRT records the container IDs of the containers which are currently maintained in the cache. The art is a hash table, and it records the future access orders of containers. Based on the ART, the OCR sorts the containers in the cache, and finds out the container which is the least accessed one.

We implement an algorithm which can approximate to the optimal substitution. Unlike the traditional optimal replacement algorithm, when performing off-line simulation analyses, OFL use container IDs rather than real containers. The container ID is the basic operating unit for simulation. Through the analyses, the optimal replacement sequence of containers is obtained. Since the analyses are off-line, the real size of the containers in the replacement sequence must be known before performing data recovery, so as to prevent the cache overflowing.

OFL also simulate the process of data recovery in a simulated cache. In the simulation, it reads the previous access sequences, from the access sequence file generated by data backup. Then, in a LRU way, OFL inserts the container IDs of the required containers into the simulated cache. At the same time, by using a sliding window for the current cache, OFL periodically reads the access sequence file, and gets the container IDs of the containers which are accessed in a period of time. Then, these container IDs are organized into a sequence, and are maintained in the ART. When the cache size reaches the maximum value, the OFL sorts the container IDs in the SRT based on the current ART. Eventually, the last container ID is kicked out from the simulated cache. Meanwhile, the location of the corresponding real container in the real cache is written to a log automatically. When the simulation process is completed, all the containers, which need to be replaced, are recorded the log file. Thus when perform actually data recovery, no extra overhead are needed. Consequently, the system restoring performance can be improved.

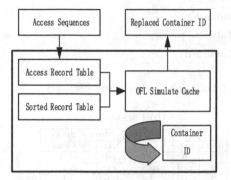
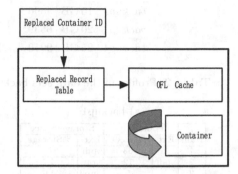

Fig. 4. The offline cache replacement module

Fig. 5. The data recovery module

3.3 Data Recovery Module

As shown in Fig. 5, the DR module roughly contains the Replaced Record Table (RRT) and the OFL cache. When OFL performs real data recovery, it completely prefetch the required containers into the memory, and records the container IDs of the replaced containers into RRT, so as to reduce the number of accesses disk. When the cache is not full, OFL inserts data into containers in the FIFO way. While, when the cache size reaches a predetermined threshold, the OFL cache will kick out the optimal container, by referring the RRT and SRT.

4   Performance Evaluation

4.1   Experimental Environment

We evaluate OFL along with the LRU and OPT in the procedure of data recovery, and LRU is used as the baseline. The experiments are conducted in a platform whose configuration is as follows: dual-core, four-thread Intel(R) Core(TM) i3-2100 CPU with the frequency of 3.10 GHz, 10 GB memory, 500G disks, and with the ubuntu (with the kernel version 3.16.0) operating system.

We employ four data sets backup1, backup2, backup3 and backup4 in the experiments. These four data sets are collected from our groups Linux servers and our personal cloud in DropBox. Expect the data set backup1, other three data sets are obtained by adding 5 GB data to the previous full backup. As shown in Table 1, the size of these data sets are 10 GB, 15 GB, 20 GB and 25 GB respectively, and the numbers of files contained in them are 3073, 4694, 6539 and 9910 respectively.

Table 1. Overview of the data sets

Data set	Size	Numbers	Profiles of the data sets
*backup*1	10 GB	3073	Table 2(a)
*backup*2	15 GB	4696	Table 2(b)
*backup*3	20 GB	6539	Table 2(c)
*backup*4	25 GB	9910	Table 2(d)

Table 2. Profiles of the data sets backup1, backup2, backup3 and backup4

(a) backup1

Rank	Popularity		Storage Space	
	Ext.	%Occur	Ext.	%Storage
1	.h	63	.pdf	82.4
2	.pdf	12	.rar	4.7
3	.c	5	.mp3	4.6
4	.mp3	3	.zip	2.7
5	.js	2.7	.txt	1.7
Total	–	85.7	–	96.1

(b) backup2

Rank	Popularity		Storage Space	
	Ext.	%Occur	Ext.	%Storage
1	.h	71.6	.pdf	87.5
2	.pdf	9.8	.rar	3.1
3	.c	3.4	.mp3	3.1
4	.mp3	2	.zip	1.8
5	.js	1.8	.txt	1.1
Total	–	88.6	–	96.6

(c) backup3

Rank	Popularity		Storage Space	
	Ext.	%Occur	Ext.	%Storage
1	.h	55.2	.pdf	88.3
2	.c	14.2	.mp3	3
3	.pdf	11.7	.rar	2.3
4	.jpg	7	.zip	1.4
5	NULL	2	.chm	1.3
Total	–	90.1	–	96.3

(d) backup4

Rank	Popularity		Storage Space	
	Ext.	%Occur	Ext.	%Storage
1	.h	45.6	.pdf	87
2	.cc	11.4	.rar	2.9
3	.c	9.4	.mp3	2.4
4	.pdf	7	.zip	1.9
5	.jpg	4.6	.chm	1.6
Total	–	78	–	95.8

For each data set, Table 2 shows the access popularity and the occupied storage space for five different types of files. The distribution shown in the table is representative, for it is consistent with the findings made by Agrawal et al. [28] and Meyer et al. [29]. Therefore, these data sets are representative ones. By the way, the classic variable content chunk algorithm [30] is adopted in the process of data backup, and the size of cache is measured by the maximum number of containers can be maintained in the cache.

4.2   Evaluating the Deduplication Ratio

In order to explore whether our strategy affect the deduplication, we successively deduplicate the four data sets with the average chunk sizes of 4K, 8K and 16K respectively. Figure 6 shows the deduplication ratio for these data sets under different chunk size, and each data set is incremental when making backups.

As the figure shows, the deduplication ratio of backup1 is relatively lower than other data sets, due to a small amount of redundant data in backup1. However, for other data sets, their deduplication ratios are much higher and reach more than 90%. This is because with the incremental backup, more chunks are

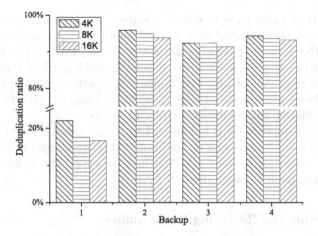

Fig. 6. The deduplication ratio of backup1, backup2, backup3 and backup4 with different chunk size

duplicate. In addition, the smaller the chunk size is, the more chunks are duplicate. Therefore, the deduplication ratios decrease as the chunk size increases. The results shown above are a normal appearance of the deduplication, thus revealing that our strategy does not affect the deduplication.

4.3 Determining the Cache Size

Since an off-line optimal cache replacement strategy involves the cache, we also test the corresponding recovery performance with different cache size. Here, the backup1 data set is used, due to its low deduplication ratio. As Fig. 7 shows, the restoring time of LRU, OPT and OFL change with different cache size. Specifically, with the increasing of cache size, the restoring time of LRU and OFL decrease. This is because the increase of cache size can not only improves the cache hit rate, but also reduces the number of disk accesses.

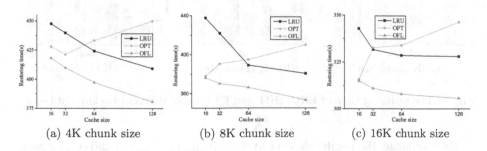

(a) 4K chunk size   (b) 8K chunk size   (c) 16K chunk size

Fig. 7. The restoring time of LRU, OPT and OFL with different cache size

OPT needs an extra time to online calculate the optimal replacement container, besides, it needs to deal with more element information as the cache size increases, so the restoring time of it increase with the cache size increasing. The restoring time of the OPT is 395.015 s when the cache size is 64, and the time is 5.831 s more than that of LRU. OPT achieves a better restoring performance than LRU when cache size is smaller than 32. In contrast with OPT, LRU is overall more efficient and relatively simpler to realize.

The restoring time of OFL is always lower than other two strategies, and this verifies that OFL can achieve the best system recovery performance. We did a further validation in Sect. 4.4. And in later experiments, we chose 32 as the default experimental cache size.

4.4   Evaluating the Restoring Performance

To evaluate the restoring performance of different strategies, we test the restoring time with the cache size equals 32. As Fig. 8 shows, for each backup data set, the corresponding restoring time of OFL is the least. This verifies the effectiveness of OFL in improving the system restoring performance. Compared with the single replacement rule of LRU, OFL are predictable thus can achieve a higher hit rate and reduce the overhead of disk accesses. Consequently, the restoring time of OFL is lower than that of LRU. Especially as shown in Fig. 8(a), for the case using backup2 with 4K chunk size, the restoring time of OFL is 409.902 s and the restoring time of OFL is 439.78 s. By comparison, OFL reduces about 7% the restoring time of LRU. In addition, OPT needs time to online calculate the optimal replacement sequence, while OFL is designed for saving this time and improving the restoring performance. As a result, OFL always achieves a lower restoring time than OPT. Especially as shown in Fig. 8(a), in contrast with OPT, OFL saves more than 8% restoring time.

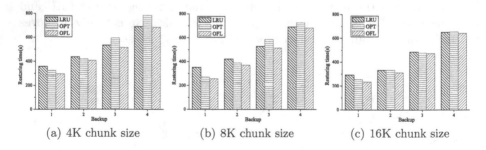

| (a) 4K chunk size | (b) 8K chunk size | (c) 16K chunk size |

Fig. 8. The restoring time of LRU, OPT and OFL under different backup data sets

By comparing the results shown respectively in Fig. 8(a), (b) and (c), for each backup data set, we can find that the restoring time is shortened in general as the cache size increased. This is because the system has a higher deduplication ratio under a smaller chunk size, thus introducing more fragments which have a negative effect on the recovery performance. In contrast, the number of fragments are less under a larger chunk size, thus the effectiveness of OFL is limited when the chunk size is large. That's why the restoring time of OFL is similar to other two strategies with the chunk size equals 16, as shown in Fig. 8(c). But on the whole, OFL achieves the best restoring performance in different cases.

4.5 Number of Misses

We also test the number of cache misses for restoring the four data sets respectively, and the results are shown in Fig. 9. Because both OFL and OPT strive to achieve an optimal replacement for the cache, the number of cache misses under OFL is nearly the same to that under OPT. This verifies that the optimal replacement made by OFL in an off-line way, is also as effective as that made by OPT in an online way. While, with the off-line way, OFL can cut down the additional computational overhead exist in the online way. Compared with LRU, OFL achieves a lower number of misses, which reflects that OFL significantly increases the cache hit rate.

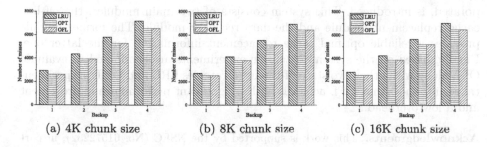

(a) 4K chunk size   (b) 8K chunk size   (c) 16K chunk size

Fig. 9. The number of cache misses for LRU, OPT and OFL

4.6 The Space Overhead for Storing the Container Sequence

The intention of using OFL to realize a replacement algorithm with a high hit rate and a small overhead. However, as described in Sect. 3.2, a certain space is needed for OFL to store the ART which maintains the container sequence. In order to explore the space overhead of OFL, the data sizes of the container sequences, which are generated during the previous experiment, are recorded. As shown in Table 3, the data size of the container sequence for OFL are at the KB level with different chunk sizes. In environments with data size with GB level, this space overhead is very small and negligible. All the experimental results show that OFL is a well-behaved optimal replacement strategy for the restore cache with a high hit rate and a small overhead.

Table 3. The data size of the container sequence

Chunk size	backup1	backup2	backup3	bakcup4
4K	10336 byte	15616 byte	21004 byte	26120 byte
8K	10200 byte	15432 byte	20764 byte	25864 byte
16K	10140 byte	15372 byte	20676 byte	25800 byte

5   Conclusion

The fragmentation problem significantly decreases the restore performance in chunk-based deduplication systems. Inspired by the off-line backup systems which deduplicates data in the idle time, we apply an off-line mechanism to the caching strategy for recovery systems and propose the OFL replacement strategy for the restore cache. OFL can off-line analyze the replacement sequence for the restoring cache in advance, thus cutting down the extra overhead required for on-line analysis, thereby further improving the restoring performance. To evaluate the effectiveness of OFL, a data restoring system, where OFL is incorporated, is introduced. This system consists of two main modules: the off-line cache replacement module and the data recovery module. The former module provides a reliable optimal cache replacement information for the latter one. Finally, based on the system, extensive experiments are conducted to evaluate OFL along with other two state-of-the-art strategies LRU and OPT. Experimental results show that OFL achieves both a significant performance improvement and a low overhead.

Acknowledgments. This work is supported by the NSFC (No. 61572232), in part by the Science and Technology Planning Project of Guangzhou (No. 201802010028, and No. 201802010060), in part by the Science and Technology Planning Project of Nansha (No. 2017CX006), and in part by the Open Research Fund of Key Laboratory of Computer System and Architecture, Institute of Computing Technology, Chinese Academy of Sciences under Grant CARCH201705.

References

1. Dubois, L., Amaldas, M., Sheppard, E.: Key considerations as deduplication evolves into primary storage. White Paper (2011)
2. Deng, Y.: What is the future of disk drives, death or rebirth? ACM Comput. Surv. **43**(3), 23:1–23:27 (2011)
3. Zhou, K., Hu, S., Huang, P., Zhao, Y.: LX-SSD: enhancing the lifespan of NAND flash-based memory via recycling invalid pages. In: Proceedings of the 33rd International Conference on Massive Storage Systems and Technology, MSST 2017 (2017)
4. Wei, J., Jiang, H., Zhou, K., Feng, D.: Efficiently representing membership for variable large data sets. IEEE Trans. Parallel Distrib. Syst. **25**(4), 960–970 (2014)

5. Benjamin, Z., Kai, L., Patterson, R.H.: Avoiding the disk bottleneck in the data domain deduplication file system. In: Proceedings of the 6th USENIX Conference on File and Storage Technologies, FAST 2008, vol. 8, pp. 269–282 (2008)
6. Bhagwat, D., Eshghi, K., Long, D.D.E., Lillibridge, M.: Extreme binning: scalable, parallel deduplication for chunk-based file backup. In: Proceedings of the 2009 IEEE International Symposium on Modeling, Analysis Simulation of Computer and Telecommunication Systems, pp. 1–9 (2009)
7. Mark, L., Kave, E., Deepavali, B., Vinay, D., Greg, T., Peter, C.: Sparse indexing: large scale, inline deduplication using sampling and locality. In: Proceedings of the 7th USENIX Conference on File and Storage Technologies, Fast 2009, vol. 9, pp. 111–123 (2009)
8. Wen, X., Hong, J., Dan, F., Yu, H.: SiLo: a similarity-locality based near-exact deduplication scheme with low ram overhead and high throughput. In: Proceedings of the 2011 USENIX Conference on USENIX Annual Technical Conference, USENIXATC 2011, pp. 26–28 (2011)
9. Zhou, Y., Deng, Y., Yang, L.T., Yang, R., Si, L.: LDFS: a low latency in-line data deduplication file system. IEEE Access 6, 15 743–15 753 (2018)
10. Erik, K., Cristian, U., Cezary, D.: Bimodal content defined chunking for backup streams. In: Proceedings of the 8th USENIX Conference on File and Storage Technologies, FAST 2010, pp. 239–252 (2010)
11. Quinlan, S., Dorward, S.: Venti: a new approach to archival storage. In: Proceedings of the Conference on File Storage Technologies, FAST 2002, vol. 2, pp. 89–101 (2002)
12. Athicha, M., Benjie, C., David, M.: A low-bandwidth network file system. In: Proceedings of the 18th ACM Symposium on Operating Systems Principles, vol. 35, no. 5, pp. 174–187. ACM (2001)
13. Nam, Y.J., Park, D., Du, D.H.: Assuring demanded read performance of data deduplication storage with backup datasets. In: Proceedings of the 2012 IEEE 20th International Symposium on Modeling, Analysis and Simulation of Computer and Telecommunication Systems, MASCOTS 2012, pp. 201–208. IEEE (2012)
14. Deng, Y., Huang, X., Song, L., Zhou, Y., Wang, F.: Memory deduplication: an effective approach to improve the memory system. J. Inf. Sci. Eng. 33(5), 1103–1120 (2017)
15. Deng, Y., Hu, Y., Meng, X., Zhu, Y., Zhang, Z., Han, J.: Predictively booting nodes to minimize performance degradation of a power-aware web cluster. Cluster Comput. 17(4), 1309–1322 (2014)
16. Qu, Z., Chen, Y.: Efficient data restoration for a disk-based network backup system. In: Proceedings of the IEEE International Conference, vol. 1, pp. 584–590 (2004)
17. Schulman, R.R.: Disaster recovery issues and solutions. Hitachi Data Systems White Paper, p. 23 (2004)
18. Xie, J., Deng, Y., Min, G., Zhou, Y.: An incrementally scalable and cost-efficient interconnection structure for datacenters. IEEE Trans. Parallel Distrib. Syst. 28(6), 1578–1592 (2017)
19. Kaczmarczyk, M., Barczynski, M., Kilian, W., Dubnicki, C.: Reducing impact of data fragmentation caused by in-line deduplication. In: Proceedings of the 5th Annual International Systems and Storage Conference, SYSTOR 2012, pp. 15:1–15:12 (2012)
20. Lillibridge, M., Eshghi, K., Bhagwat, D.: Improving restore speed for backup systems that use inline chunk-based deduplication. In: Proceedings of the 11th USENIX Conference on File and Storage Technologies, FAST 2013, pp. 183–198 (2013)

21. Fu, M., et al.: Accelerating restore and garbage collection in deduplication-based backup systems via exploiting historical information. In: Proceedings of the 2014 USENIX Conference on USENIX Annual Technical Conference, USENIX ATC 2014, pp. 181–192 (2014)
22. Srinivasan, K., Bisson, T., Goodson, G.R., Voruganti, K.: iDedup: latency-aware, inline data deduplication for primary storage. In: Proceedings of the 10th USENIX Conference on File and Storage Technologies, FAST 2012, vol. 12, pp. 1–14 (2012)
23. EMC: Achieving storage efficiency through EMC celerra data deduplication. White Paper (2010)
24. Adlercohen, C., Czarnowicki, T., Dreiher, J., Ruzicka, T., Ingber, A., Harari, M.: NetApp deduplication for FAS and V-series deployment and implementation guide. Technical report, vol. 2009, no. 1, pp. 141 753–141 753 (2011)
25. Min, F., et al.: Design tradeoffs for data deduplication performance in backup workloads. In: Proceedings of the 13th USENIX Conference on File and Storage Technologies, FAST 2015, pp. 331–344 (2015)
26. Belady, L.A.: A study of replacement algorithms for a virtual-storage computer. IBM Syst. J. 5(2), 78–101 (1966)
27. Meister, D., Brinkmann, A., Süß, T.: File recipe compression in data deduplication systems. In: Proceedings of the 11th USENIX Conference on File and Storage Technologies, FAST 2013, pp. 175–182 (2013)
28. Agrawal, N., Bolosky, W.J., Douceur, J.R., Lorch, J.R.: A five-year study of file-system metadata. Trans. Storage 3(3), 9 (2007)
29. Meyer, D.T., Bolosky, W.J.: A study of practical deduplication. Trans. Storage 7(4), 14:1–14:20 (2012)
30. Rabin, M.: Fingerprinting by random polynomials (1981)

Blockchain-Based Secure and Reliable Distributed Deduplication Scheme

Jingyi Li[1], Jigang Wu[1,2(✉)], Long Chen[1], and Jiaxing Li[1]

[1] Guangdong University of Technology, Guangzhou, China
ljyccgz@sina.com, asjgwucn@outlook.com, lonchen@mail.ustc.edu.cn,
jiaxing.li.cs@gmail.com
[2] Guangdong Key Laboratory of Big Data Analysis and Processing,
Guangzhou 510006, People's Republic of China

Abstract. Due to the explosive growth of data volume on the Internet, deduplication techniques have been wildly used in cloud storage to save both disk space and network bandwidth. However, conventional deduplication schemes lead to problems with data reliability that can be attributed to the algorithm implementation where there is only one copy for each file stored in the cloud. Furthermore, the participation of trusted third party in most of the previous work has brought about the security challenge as single point of failure. In this paper, we propose a blockchain based deduplication scheme with high reliability and confidentiality in which the files are distributed to multiple servers and the information of files is recorded on the time-stamped blockchain whose central authorities are replaced to automatically decentralized smart contracts. Based on the proposed scheme, we present relevant protocols to achieve secure cloud storage derived from the consensus and incentive mechanism. Security analysis demonstrates that our deduplication scheme can achieve the proposed security goals while it has limited overhead proved by simulation experiments.

Keywords: Deduplication · Blockchain · Distributed · Cloud storage
Security

1 Introduction

Cloud computing is a general term for anything that involves delivering hosted services over the Internet while the network connectivity in the cloud is represented without concern for how it is proposed to happen. As an important part of cloud computing, cloud storage provides users with a cross platform, high scalability, high availability and almost unlimited capacity of data outsource service.

Instead of maintaining large storage infrastructures, companies and individual users can store data in remote data centers which managed by third parties [9]. But according to the CISCO Global Cloud Index [3], global data center

© Springer Nature Switzerland AG 2018
J. Vaidya and J. Li (Eds.): ICA3PP 2018, LNCS 11334, pp. 393–405, 2018.
https://doi.org/10.1007/978-3-030-05051-1_27

traffic is expected to grow threefold and reach a total of 7.7 zettabytes annually by 2017, 10.4 zettabytes by 2019 while 83% of them will come from the cloud. In response to the explosive growth of data volume, data deduplication techniques are used to save both disk space and network bandwidth by storing only a single copy of redundant data [16]. It is reported that more than 90 percent disks and bandwidth are saved in a common business [8].

Although deduplication can effectively reduce the burden on users and cloud service providers, it also faces some challenges. The most important, it is difficult to achieve with guaranteed the confidentiality of data. Users are hard to protect their outsourced files from being used or tampered by malicious adversaries. But conventional encryption schemes, which are usually employed to solve the security problem, don't support deduplication because identical data copies of different users will lead to different ciphertexts when they encrypt them by their own keys. The first attempt to solve this problem is convergent encryption [19] which generate identifiable and coalescing supporting ciphertext through plaintext-based secret key. However, most of such secure deduplication schemes only consider the situation of a single server and only one copy for each different files will be stored on the cloud. Loss of a file or file block in this case will be expected to result in adverse effect on a large number of users who store the same file. Li et al. [12] proposed some distributed deduplication schemes to provide higher reliability with the utility of secret sharing technique. However, the trusted third parties in their systems are threatened by single point of failure.

In recent years, the blockchain has gained much more focus as a distributed computing paradigm for its high efficiency, high data security, high credibility and low cost. Its key technology derives from the consensus mechanism, which is an example of a distributed computing system with superior fault tolerance. With characteristic mentioned above, blockchain techniques can realize point-to-point transactions or collaboration in distributed systems with high traceability. Decentralized storage systems like Filecoin [7] and the architecture [10] takes advantages of blockchain which can achieve security file storage through an incentive mechanism and distributed construction. Some research like [11] use blockchain technology to solve the problem of excessive communication cost in cloud storage. But none of these systems attempt to achieve the storage efficiency that is possible through deduplication.

In this paper, three challenges on data storage including (1) confidentiality, (2) integrity and (3) reliability are considered and we will detail these later in Sect. 3. To address these challenges, we design a cloud storage deduplication system with high fault tolerance. To protect system confidentiality and data integrity, the blockchain technique is utilized, which is also compatible with the distributed storage systems. In more details, file fingerprints are showed in blockchain with transaction information about the storage payment of the file. Every data owner can make the duplicate check locally because of these unchangeable information. It reduces the communication frequency between data owner and storage servers which also reduce the risk of communications being monitored and information leakage. Different from existing work [12], our proposed system requires data owner encrypt their data by convergent encryption scheme to ensure file confidentiality in the case of displaying the information of files on blockchain. With these information, any participant can reconstruct the encrypted file though download a certain amount of file shards and only authenticated users can access to the plaintext. The deduplication system will gain greater reliability and fault tolerance by adding this incentive mechanism.

Specifically, the contributions of this paper are:

- A new blockchain based distributed deduplication system is proposed to provide efficient deduplication with high reliability. File tags are published on blockchain and used for locally duplicate check and data integrity check. Combining the convergent encryption algorithm and incentive mechanism, our construction can prevent outsource files from collusion attack by a specific number of adversaries.
- We demonstrates the proposed deduplication scheme has high confidentiality and reliability in security analysis. Threat and security models are defined to establish the security goals to demonstrate that the file remains secure under a collusion attack or malicious tampering in our scheme.
- Our evaluation results demonstrate that the proposed construction is efficient and the redundancies are optimized and comparable with the other storage system supporting the same level of reliability.

Organization. The rest of the paper is organized as follows. In Sect. 2, we give a brief overview of relate work. The system model and security model are proposed in Sect. 3. We present our contribution in Sect. 4 while the security analysis is given in Sect. 5. Finally, we show the performance analysis of simulation experiment in Sect. 6 and draw our conclusion in Sect. 7.

2 Related Work

Here we introduce a baseline of encryption which is wildly used in cross-user deduplication scheme. Furthermore, we introduce some emerging reliable cloud storage solutions in recent years. In addition, we give a short description of Blockchain and smart contract which is an important part to achieve decentralized storage and reliable verification.

2.1 Convergent Encryption

Convergent encryption schemes are used to enable deduplication over encrypted data [2,4]. A user derives a convergent key K through cryptographic hash algorithm and deterministically compute the same ciphertext from the same plaintext. There are several kinds of convergent encryption scheme for different security requirements and scenes [1,19,22]. Li [13] addressed the key-management issue in a distributed way after encrypting the files with private key and convergent key. The scheme mentioned above are adopted to enforce data confidentiality but these methods achieved confidentiality without considering reliability of the system which is a more realistic demand.

2.2 Decentralized Storage System

Most cloud storage systems like Dropbox [6], Google Drive [5], Mozy [14], are the construction that map distributed heterogeneous storage devices to a single continuous storage space and managed by a centralized platform. These systems use decentralized storage scheme to avoid single source download which will increase network burden and suffer from the risk of the attacking against server. In order to avoid being overly dependent on a single trusted entity which is threatened by a single point of failure, Storj [20] is proposed to provide a high privacy protected storage with confidentiality and reliability by means of using blockchain technology. Sia [18] is a decentralized storage platform which maintains the confidentiality of stored file by implementing an incentive mechanism to encourage servers provide long term storage service. Platform developer claims that Sia leverage underutilized hard drive capacity around the world to build a data storage marketplace that is more reliable and lower cost than traditional cloud storage providers. At the same time, these storage schemes guarantee the efficiency and security of the outsourced file based on revenue incentives. But all of the above systems keep their reliability with storing multiple copies of the same file across distributed servers. It brings about similar problems as traditional storage system that does not have deduplication scheme.

2.3 Blockchain

Blockchain is the underlying technique of Bitcoin, a distributed transaction ledger proposed in 2008 [15]. As the most important role, it provides a solution to deal with double spending in a distributed network by generating a chained time-stamped data structure. Without the administration from the central manager, all the participants follow the consensus that only the longest chain is extended and the others are deemed invalid. With such consensus, miners contribute their computational power to verify information correctness and integrity in blockchain network through proof of work protocol. The second generation of blockchain, such as Ethereum [23], uses the concept of smart contract to provide a general, programmable infrastructure. Smart contracts are deployed and running across the blockchain network which can express triggers, conditions, and even an entire business process automatically [21].

Separate from the above schemes, we proposed a novel scheme which can achieve both confidentiality and reliability. To reach this goal, blockchain-based distributed storage systems that are rarely involved in deduplication scheme have also been considered to enhance the security of our scheme in this paper. In the following sections, we will show more details about the presented scheme.

3 Problem Formulation

3.1 System and Security Models

Our proposed scheme mainly consists of two entities as shown in Fig. 1:

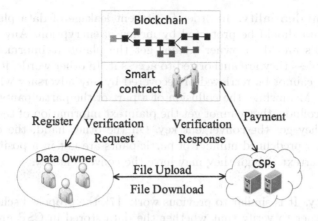

Fig. 1. System model

Cloud Service Provider (CSP) is an entity that in charge of data storage. In our deduplication scheme, the CSP only store a single copy of the same uploading files or file blocks. In order to provide confidentiality and fault tolerance, we consider a series of CSPs, they participate in a distributed storage system and the user data will be stored in multiple CSP servers.

Data owner outsources data storage to the CSP and accesses it whenever necessary. It makes deduplication check to avoid uploading deduplicate data to CSPs. Data owner also encrypts the original file through a fault-tolerant method for a higher level of reliability.

To access to the cloud storage service that supports data deduplication, Both CSP and data owner are ought to join the blockchain network as a node. Each node is free to join or leave the blockchain network and we assume that there are always enough active nodes to support it to run normally. They get unique private key and generate an address from the key to interact anonymously with other nodes. In our presented system model, the data owner do the duplicate check and only upload the unique data to multiple CSPs. All the duplication and transaction information are recorded on blockchain to ensure that the data are authentic. We deploy our deduplication mechanism on client-side to reduce the communication frequency and save the bandwidth.

3.2   Threat Model and Security Goals

We define CSPs are honest-but-curious which is a generic assumption. It means they are incentivized to follow designed protocols, while they desire to learn the user information other than the ciphertext they have already stored. Meanwhile, an adversary will act as a data owner to access unauthorized data out of the scope of their privileges. In addition, collusion attacks among the CSPs are concerned in our security goals. Specifically, we consider three kinds of security requirement in the proposed scheme.

Storage Confidentiality. In order to prevent leakage of data plaintext, the outsourced data should be protected by means of encryption. Any adversaries including CSPs and data owner cannot get the plaintext information of the stored data unless they are authorized to access it. In other words, it is required that the data cannot be retrieved or recovered by any adversary who does not own the data. Meanwhile, the collusion of a part of the participants is allowed. If only CSPs collude, they cannot get the plaintext information of the encrypted data unless they get the convergent key. On the other hand, the collusion of no more than a predefined number of participants are not in a position to gain complete ciphertext though they may have the convergent key.

File Integrity. It is similar to previous work [17], the proposed scheme should allow data owner to verify that whether the data stored in CSP are tempered or not. File integrity requires that the data downloaded from the cloud storage can be verified by data owner that it has not been altered. To achieve this, the credible tag is required to support verification mechanism and it is not allowed to be changed by authorized adversaries which may lead to a wrong verification. In addition, data owner can detect whether data is maliciously-generated with the correct tag.

System Reliability. Reliability means the storage system can prevent user data from the single point of failure and provide a predefined level of fault tolerance. In particular, files are distributed to multiple servers and data fault tolerance is achieved by redundancy. Specifically, the storage system is required to detect and repair missing data without the participant of the data owner. Follow the requirement of confidentiality mentioned above, the reconstruction will not reveal any plaintext information through encryption method.

3.3 Preliminary

Convergent Encryption. Convergent encryption is a cryptosystem that produces identical ciphertext files from identical plaintext files, irrespective of their encryption keys [4]. Specifically, a data owner generates convergent key from plaintext and encrypts the data with the convergent key. Hence encryption supports for deduplication and provides confidentiality. There are three primitive functions to define a convergent encryption scheme.

$KeyGen_{CE}(F) = K$: a key generation algorithm which maps data to a convergent key.

$Encrypt_{CE}(F, K) = C$: a symmetric encryption algorithm with convergent key K and file F as input then output ciphertext C.

$Decrypt_{CE}(C, K) = F$: using convergent key K to decrypt ciphertext C and return the plaintext which is file F.

Secret Sharing Scheme. In our implication, we will use a deterministic secret sharing schemes proposed in [12] to secretly split the data into shards and easily recover them to the original file. It is a protocol to distribute a secret into n shards in such a way that: (1) using k or more pieces of the shards can reconstruct the secret, (2) using t or less shards cannot gain any information on the secret. Two algorithms named *Share* and *Recover* are included in the (t, k, n) ramp scheme.

Share: divides a secret S into $(k - t)$ sub secret and generate t pieces with the same size. Then encodes the k pieces using a non-systematic k-of-n erasure code into n shares.

Recover: uses at least k out of n shares to reconstruct the secret S.

Secret sharing scheme maximizes the storage efficiency without sacrificing the ability to fault tolerate. For example, if a server is available $p = 50\%$ of the time and a file is stored by n - way replication, which stores n complete copies of the file. It provides $P = 1 - p^n$ available time to the file which can be more specifically when $n = 3$, $P = 87.5\%$. If the same file stored by k of m erasure code with triple redundancy, such as 20 of 60, it provides more than 99.6% available time according $P' = 1 - \sum_{k=0}^{m-1} C_m^k p^k \cdot (1 - p)^{m-k}$.

4 Blockchain Based Deduplication Scheme

4.1 Blockchain

We consider deduplication and distributed storage of the data across multiple storage servers that can make it possible. Furthermore, our construction utilizes the blockchain technique to implement a time-stamped recording, distributed duplicate check and a self-organized file reconstruction. Here we only describe the file level deduplication. Our proposed scheme can also be applied to block level deduplication it has the similar process except a file split operation before secret sharing.

Blockchain Initialization. Blockchain network is initialized by the Blockchain as a Service (BaaS) mode. This mode provides on-chain service through the Internet which means users do not need to consider the stability of the blockchain itself or participate in the generation of blocks. This makes the security of blockchain is depend on the whole network computational power of all participating nodes and we will discuss it in security analysis. It also allows every authorized participant joins the network and gains the blockchain service at any time. There are three steps in the process of initialization.

A. Each participants add in blockchain network where the smart contract for deduplication lives.
B. Each participant generate a public and private key pair, $\{PubK_D, PriK_D\}$ for data owner and $\{PubK_{CSPi}, PriK_{CSPi}\}$ for the i-th CSP, to sign transactions. As account to interact with smart contract or other nodes anonymously, $Addr_D$ and $Addr_{CSPi}$ are derived from key pairs.

C. Data owner prepares gas as storage payment to CSP or service fee to smart contract.

Algorithms with Smart Contract. Two kinds of smart contract are considered in our proposed scheme and both of them are implemented on blockchain network. The Business Smart Contract (BSC) should be initialized before the file is uploaded. BSC is mainly used to do the verification and manage the pointers of file shares. Additionally, an authorized participant can restore the missing file through information published on blockchain. Two algorithms are implemented by BSC.

Verify: In Verify algorithm, for simplicity, a typical proof of retrievability scheme is introduced as a sample of verification method. BSC send challenge $c = POR_F(C)$ to a prover and return $POR_v(c,r)$ when received $r = POR_F(c)$. Anyone can use this algorithm to prove all the files' retrievability at the cost of gas.

Register: Smart contract runs the POR to verify whether a data owner is actually has the file F. If the match between $Tag(C, Addr_{CSPi})$ and stored data is successfully, BSC create a TSC script with $Addr_{CSPi}$ and send it to the data owner.

The Transaction Smart Contract (TSC) is generated by BSC and published after file uploading. In our scheme, the storage service demander lock some of their gas on blockchain as a deposit to set up the TSC which is agreed by both data owner and CSP. To be more specific, a part of the gas is seen as prepaid storage fee which is paid to the CSP who provide long term storage service via an installment contract. If the contract is expired or no valid verification information is received within a long period of time, it terminates itself and return the remaining gas.

To download data, data owner and related CSP construct a TSC to make payment through piecewise payment channel. Which means each transaction is for a unit of data, such as 32bit, to pay for storage until the contract is completed or one of the parties has forcibly terminated the contract.

4.2 Data Deduplication Management

File Upload. To upload a file F as Fig. 2 shows, the data owner first encrypts the file with convergent encryption scheme. After using $K = KeyGen_{CE}(F)$ generate $C = Encrypt_{CE}(F, K)$, data owner computes the file tag $Tag(C)$ and performs a local duplicate check with the downloaded blockchain tag information $Tag(C')$ which is updated in real time.

If the file has been stored, data owner computes and sends $Tag(C, Addr_{CSPi})$ to BSC via a secure channel to authorize participants with *Register*. Then a TSC is signed by both data owner and CSP. CSP publish the TSC on blockchain and a pointer for the share $\{Tag(C), Tag(c_i), c_i\}$

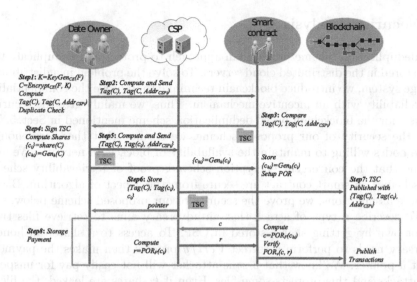

Fig. 2. File upload (no duplicate file)

stored at server $Addr_{CSPi}$ is offered to payer after the transaction created by TSC is conceded in blockchain network.

If no duplicate is found, the data owner performs the following procedure. Firstly, the secret sharing algorithm over C is executed and output $c_i = Share(C)$, where c_i is the i-th shard of C. And then, the data owner runs the tag generation algorithm to get $Tag(c_i)$ and $Tag(C, Addr_{CSPi})$ for each server with $Addr_{CSPi}$. After that, data owner uploads the set of values $\{Tag(C), Tag(C, Addr_{CSPi})\}$ and the signed TSC script with pre-agreed price to the i-th CSP. Finally, CSP stores these values then return a pointer to data owner while sign and broadcast the TSC to blockchain network.

File Download. To download a file F, data owner finds at least k shares c_i from CSP server then restores the file $C = Recover(c_i)$. After that, the data owner runs $F = Decrypt_{CE}(C, K)$ to retrieve the original file.

File Auditing. By periodically proving themselves to hold the file through offering the PoR_F, CSPs can get commercial benefits from the TSC through continuous provision of storage services using the $Verify$. Every transaction published by TSC contains $Tag(C)$, $Tag(c_i)$ and every participant can use this record to confirm whether a file C or c_i is stored or not. It is worth mentioning that the trading is completed through a micro-payment channel to avoid high transaction cost by making payment under the chain. Besides, files can be verified via blockchain information to prevent tampering through $Tag(C)$ and $Tag(c_i)$.

5   Security Analysis

Our deduplication scheme provides an approach to protect and deduplicate the data stored in the distributed cloud servers. To solve the problem in a distributed storage system, we introduce blockchain technique to improve the confidentiality and reliability with an incentive mechanism. Thus, we mainly give the security analysis for the blockchain based deduplication scheme mentioned in Sect. 5. To show the security of our proposed scheme, we assume that there are enough active nodes willing to maintain the availability of blockchain network. We also assume that the convergent encryption scheme, proof of retrievability scheme and schemes on smart contract are secure from the aspect of algorithm. Based on these assumptions, we prove the security of our proposed scheme below.

We describe a type of attack that an adversary aims to retrieve files they do not own by getting shares stored in CSP. To access to a share, an honest adversary needs to perform a correct $Verify$ process then makes the payment to get a pointer. We know that a sane attacker will not easily pay for unspecified attacks and this protects some files. Even if k shares are leaked, the file is encrypted by convergent key which is difficult to get plaintext without the secret key. Particularly, when we consider security against a colluding attack by CSPs, a secret key that only the data owners know is necessary.

When a file is outsourced to CSP, it is hard to check whether the file is tempered or not. The adversary is not possible to distort the shares secretly because of the periodic verification performed by smart contract during the storage. On the other hand, fewer than t CSPs make the shares collapse or loss does not affect file security. It is easy to reconstruct the missing file with the aid of blockchain data by incentive mechanism implemented by smart contract. When the adversary attempt to temper the published data, the blockchain makes it infeasible unless attacker controls over 51% of the whole network computational.

6   Performance Analysis

In this section, we implemented the proposed schemes and tested their performances to check with its feasibility.

6.1   Experiment Setup

The evaluations are performed on a laptop with AMD Ryzen 3 PRO 1200 Quad-Core Processor (3.10 GHz) and Ubuntu 16.04 LTS OS. We use the SHA-256 as hash function in our simulation which provides a 32 bytes output. And the RSSS is implemented on Jerasure Version 1.2 with Cauchy-Good generation matrix which is used to data encoding and decoding. We set the default block size as 4 KB which is used for the parameter of fixed-size chunking deduplication.

6.2 Experiment Analysis

The main tool of our deduplication scheme is the ramp secret sharing scheme, which is used to distribute the file among multiple server. Thus the computation cost of RSSS will be our primary consideration. Due to the increase in file size after encryption, computation cost of RSSS is affected and we use the method proposed in [12] as a baseline to make a comparison.

With different combination of parameter t, k and n in RSSS, we make simulation experiments to explore how they affect the computation cost. As showed in Figs. 3, 4 and 5, the encoding and decoding time of our proposed scheme are almost in the order of microseconds under the parameters we set. Meanwhile, the computation cost of our scheme is larger than baseline's because files become larger after being encrypted. Even so, the results of our scheme are still in the order of microseconds. We can also observe that the decoding time is less than the encoding time which is because the decoding algorithms use less computing resources. In addition, the change rate of decoding time is at a relatively stable level in each situation which is because the decoding operation only requires k shares of the file while the encoding operation involves all the n shares and has a opposite performance.

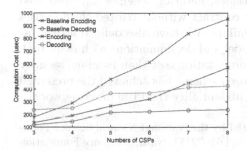

Fig. 3. $k = 2$, $t = 1$, $3 \leq n \leq 8$ **Fig. 4.** $k = 3$, $t = 1$, $4 \leq n \leq 8$

From the comparison between Figs. 4 and 5, we can find that with the increase of t, the computation cost becomes higher. It is because the size of each share will increase with the size of t. We design experiments to discover how encoding strategies influence the performance of our scheme. It is found that when k is the same, the increment of encoding time is inversely proportional to the ratio of k/t. Which means the computation cost of encoding decreases as when the k/t becomes smaller.

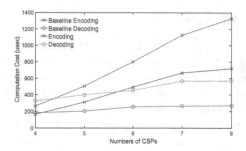

Fig. 5. $k = 3$, $t = 2$, $4 \leq n \leq 8$

7 Conclusion

In this paper, we have proposed a blockchain based distributed deduplication scheme to improve the reliability of data storage on the promise of ensuring the confidentiality. With the aid of blockchain, files are split and outsourced across multiple servers in a semi-trust decentralized storage system. Payment will be automatically assigned through blockchain smart contracts which contain a time-stamp based authentication protocol. Besides, auditing schemes have provided the security and integrity through smart contract without trusted third parties which are threatened by single point of failure. We have also defined attacks as the security goal to build our security model and do simulations with main tool. Although it has incurred a little higher computation cost than baseline, security analysis has demonstrated that our proposed scheme has achieved the presented goal and provided higher security and confidentiality than the previous work.

Acknowledgment. This work was supported by the National Natural Science Foundation of China under Grant Nos. 61702115 and 61672171, Natural Science Foundation of Guangdong, China under Grant No. 2018B030311007, and Major R&D Project of Educational Commission of Guangdong under Grant No. 2016KZDXM052, and China Postdoctoral Science Foundation Fund under Grant No. 2017M622632, and Opening Project of Guangdong Province Key Laboratory of Big Data Analysis and Processing No. 201805.

References

1. Anderson, P., Zhang, L.: Fast and secure laptop backups with encrypted deduplication. In: International Conference on Large Installation System Administration, pp. 1–8 (2010)
2. Bellare, M., Keelveedhi, S., Ristenpart, T.: Message-locked encryption and secure deduplication. In: Johansson, T., Nguyen, P.Q. (eds.) EUROCRYPT 2013. LNCS, vol. 7881, pp. 296–312. Springer, Heidelberg (2013). https://doi.org/10.1007/978-3-642-38348-9_18
3. CISCO: Cisco global cloud index (2012–2017). http://www.cisco.com/c/en/us/solutions/service-provider/global-cloud-index-gci/index.html/

4. Douceur, J.R., Adya, A., Bolosky, W.J., Simon, P.: Reclaiming space from duplicate files in a serverless distributed file system. In: Proceedings of International
   Conference on Distributed Computing Systems, pp. 617–624 (2002)
5. Google Drive. http://drive.google.com/
6. Dropbox: A file-storage and sharing service. https://www.dropbox.com/
7. Filecoin: A decentralized storage network. https://www.filecoin.io/
8. Harnik, D., Pinkas, B., Shulman-Peleg, A.: Side channels in cloud services: deduplication in cloud storage. IEEE Secur. Priv. 8(6), 40–47 (2010)
9. Kamara, S., Lauter, K.: Cryptographic cloud storage. In: Sion, R., et al. (eds.) FC
   2010. LNCS, vol. 6054, pp. 136–149. Springer, Heidelberg (2010). https://doi.org/
   10.1007/978-3-642-14992-4_13
10. Li, J., Liu, Z., Chen, L., Chen, P., Wu, J.: Blockchain-based security architecture
    for distributed cloud storage. In: 2017 IEEE International Conference on Ubiqui-
    tous Computing and Communications (ISPA/IUCC) and 2017 IEEE International
    Symposium on Parallel and Distributed Processing with Applications, pp. 408–411.
    IEEE (2017)
11. Li, J., Wu, J., Chen, L.: Block-secure: blockchain based scheme for secure P2P
    cloud storage. Inf. Sci. 465, 219–231 (2018). https://doi.org/10.1016/j.ins.2018.
    06.071, http://www.sciencedirect.com/science/article/pii/S0020025518305012
12. Li, J., et al.: Secure distributed deduplication systems with improved reliability.
    IEEE Trans. Comput. 64(12), 3569–3579 (2015)
13. Li, J., Chen, X., Li, M., Li, J., Lee, P.P.C., Lou, W.: Secure deduplication with
    efficient and reliable convergent key management. IEEE Trans. Parallel Distrib.
    Syst. 25(6), 1615–1625 (2014)
14. Mozy: A file-storage and sharing service. http://mozy.com/
15. Nakamoto, S.: Bitcoin: a peer-to-peer electronic cash system. https://bitcoin.org/
    bitcoin.pdf (2008)
16. Shin, Y., Koo, D., Hur, J.: A survey of secure data deduplication schemes for cloud
    storage systems. ACM (2017)
17. Shin, Y., Koo, D., Yun, J., Hur, J.: Decentralized server-aided encryption for secure
    deduplication in cloud storage. IEEE Trans. Serv. Comput. PP(99), 1 (1939)
18. Sia: Simple decentralized storage. http://www.sia.tech/
19. Storer, M.W., Greenan, K., Long, D.D.E., Miller, E.L.: Secure data deduplication.
    In: ACM International Workshop on Storage Security and Survivability, pp. 1–10
    (2008)
20. Storj: A peer-to-peer cloud storage network. https://storj.io/
21. Weber, I., Xu, X., Riveret, R., Governatori, G., Ponomarev, A., Mendling, J.:
    Untrusted business process monitoring and execution using blockchain. In: La
    Rosa, M., Loos, P., Pastor, O. (eds.) BPM 2016. LNCS, vol. 9850, pp. 329–347.
    Springer, Cham (2016). https://doi.org/10.1007/978-3-319-45348-4_19
22. Wilcox-O'Hearn, Z., Warner, B.: Tahoe: the least-authority filesystem. In: Proceed-
    ings of the 4th ACM International Workshop on Storage Security and Survivability,
    pp. 21–26. ACM (2008)
23. Wood, G.: Ethereum: a secure decentralised generalised transaction ledger (2014).
    http://gavwood.com/paper.pdf

Controlled Channel Attack Detection Based on Hardware Virtualization

Chenyi Qiang[1], Weijie Liu[1,2], Lina Wang[1], and Rongwei Yu[1(✉)]

[1] School of Cyber Science and Engineering, Wuhan University, Wuhan, China
roewe.yu@whu.edu.cn
[2] Tencent Technology Company Limited, Shenzhen, China

Abstract. Controlled-channel attack is a novel side-channel attack that uses page faults (#PF) to infer process-sensitive information of guest-VMs. Existing protection schemes focus on restricting malicious OS of virtual machine access to page number information. They need to copy memory page content frequently or manually mark and recompile sensitive programs, which takes a lot of time and labor overhead. This paper introduces a hardware-based detection method against it in a different way. The Hypervisor monitors the modification of the guest page table entry (PTE) and the Interrupt Descriptor Table (IDT) entries to find the trace of adversary's operations. As there is a semantic gap between VMs and Hypervisor, we take advantage of VMI (Virtual Machine Introspection) to convert important data. To overcome the challenge of changeable page tables, we grasp the feature of the target attack and filter out required records. Experiments show that this method can effectively detect controlled-channel attacks. In general, the performance overhead of the operations related to context switching will increase but within an acceptable range.

Keywords: Virtualization security · Side channel attack
Extended page table

1 Introduction

The operating system (OS) was once considered to be the Achilles heel of the system security architecture. In a traditional system, the OS is considered as the root of trust and has the highest privilege at *ring 0*. Successful attacks towards the OS will gain the highest level of control, and the problem is also acute in virtualized systems [12].

The past work only focused on how to extract the protected code or data in the OS [19]. Checkoway and Shacham [7] proposed the Iago attack that uses OS authority to modify the return address of the system calls so as to get application's access rights and steal user data in memory. In order to defend it, some security systems have been proposed. For example, *Inktag* [11] successfully restricts the OS access to user space by modifying the Hypervisor, and *Haven* [5]

J. Vaidya and J. Li (Eds.): ICA3PP 2018, LNCS 11334, pp. 406–420, 2018.
https://doi.org/10.1007/978-3-030-05051-1_28

uses the hardware feature SGX to run the program in a closed environment (enclave) securely. Both of them are applied by leveraging the presence of higher privilege levels i.e. Hypervisor and hardware.

However, in 2015, controlled-channel attack proposed by Xu [4] successfully bypassed the above-mentioned state-of-the-art security system. The adversary exploits the limited information that leaks in page fault (#PF) handler and infers sensitive data in the protected process. Specifically, Xu et al. restored fine-grained data from three applications (FreeType, Hunspell, Libjpeg); the Pigeonhole [18] attack took the channel to steal the encryption key from the procedure in the OpenSSL and Libgcrypt libraries.

There are two types of defenses against controlled-channel attack. Among them, the methods based on modifying process space layout [14,16,18] are all implemented in pure software, and the page content is re-arranged through memory copying or encrypted when accessed, which confuses the information leaked by the channel. They always introduces huge inevitable time overheads. Another type of scheme implements the redistribution of system routines [17]. After adding new hardware feature support (TSX), the OS no longer handles some interrupt events such as #PF separately, but distributes them to the hardware for further processing. It will block the attacker's access to information, but at the same time it requires manual analysis and recompilation of existing legacy program sources.

In view of the shortcomings of the above existing solutions, this paper proposes a detection method based on hardware virtualization. It no longer prevents the OS from acquiring leaked information, but positively identifies the adversary's attack behavior and performs alarm blocking. The scheme will locks the memory by directly modifying the read and write permission bits of the EPT entry (page table level of the 4-layer structure) to limit the modification of the guest page table. At the same time, the VMM reads the IDT address in the Virtual-Machine Control Structure (VMCS) to obtain its complete content, and ensures that the IDT will not be modified. Changes to IDT routines and writes to page table structures leave relevant records at the VMM layer. According to the attack model we can distinguish the special behavior of the malicious OS to the system structure (the guest PTE changes alternately) and figure out the guest process suffers from the attack.

The technical solution of this paper solves the following challenges. (1) There is a semantic gap between the VM and the Hypervisor. Geting and dealing with information from the VM is a major problem. We use VMI technology to break this limit. (2) As the PT is process-dependent, the VMM needs to filter useless recorded items. The system has to add a new interface for the user to pass target protected process. This paper modifies Qemu sources to reach the goal.

The contribution of this paper is as follows:

1. Construct a prototype of a typical controlled-channel attack scenario and test it with our defense method.
2. A detection framework against controlled-channel attack based on hardware virtualization is proposed. Attack behavior can be successfully detected

by locking memory, monitoring IDT contents and further analyzing page sequence patterns.
3. By adding new commands in Qemu, we are able to pass important parameters to the VMM and intelligently switch the detection function.

The remainder of the paper is organized as follows. In Sect. 2 we explain the threat model. In Sect. 3, we outline our design and provide in-depth details about our prototype implementations. Section 4 describes the result of experiments as well as the performance evaluation of the prototype. Section 5 describes related work and finally Sect. 6 provides brief concluding remarks and future works.

2   Threat Model

Although some security systems (e.g. *Haven*) usually mask the visited page offset so that the OS can only get the address granularity to size of page and ordinary attacks cannot know which function the process has executed, controlled-channel attack infers from the page frame numbers instead of a simple address during #PF. That is to say, currently, the mainstream security system and security hardware cannot defend against this kind of attack. As in Fig. 1, we cannot identify which function is called from the page number 0x402 alone. However, it is easy to infer from the sequence 0x401-0x402-0x403 and 0x401-0x402. The answer is that the former one is F2's sequence and the latter one is related to F1.

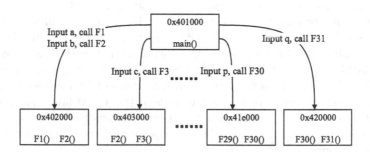

Fig. 1. Control transfer; the adversary can infer function calls from the correlation sequence (F1:0x401-0x402 F2:0x401-0x402-0x403).

Threat Model. We assumes that the adversary controls the OS and has the following characteristics when stealing sensitive information.

At first, the OS has the ability to manage system resources (such as set_pte or load_idtr function). Normally, when a process tries to access an unmapped page, the OS will receive a #PF event and handle it. During the routines, the OS attempts to remap the page and resume the program to continue execution or generate an access violation and terminate the related process.

Secondly, the adversary needs to understand the specific logical jumps inside the process, especially the different memory access patterns based on the user's inputs. To realize it, he must first search the application's source code or binary files in the preparation phase. Additionally, processes that have confused memory access patterns (such as Oblivious RAM [14,16]) are out of consideration. Here we also assume the adversary has all those above-mentioned abilities.

Thirdly, in a secure OS, the adversary manipulates the OS to actively trigger #PF and obtains the current access pattern and compares with the former to infer the user input.

Finally, as the context info obtained is noiseless, unlike other noisy measurement channels such as cache and memory bus, the adversary can get accurate information from it. In this paper, the sample attack which is launched according to the work of Xu [20] is relatively simple but still accomplish its goal, and we have a faith in that it can demonstrate our defense adequately.

Attack Sample. In order to demonstrate the attack, we simulate the kernel rootkit in guest OS. The victim is a simple process whose execution flow will jump to different pages caused by different inputs. In the preparation phase, we run the application outside the protected environment and record page fault traces by restricting access to all pages. Then, we need find out the unique accessd page trace due to the certain input by the reference algorithm [20]. The subset of the pages is used as the tracking pages during the attack phase.

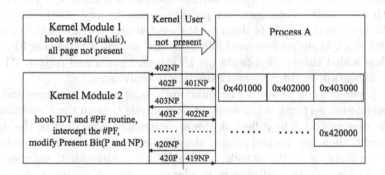

Fig. 2. Framework of the attack case

After the preparation, we make relevant hooks in a kernel module where it overrides the original IDT and #PF handler. Besides this, we hook a system call to restrict access to the set of tracking pages trained from the offline analysis through setting the reserved bit or clearing the present bit in PTE. Figure 2 is just the framework of our attack case. During the execution of the trampoline in our new handler, the information available is limited due to the security mechanism. We just record the page numbers, enable access to the current page and remove access to the previous one. Combined with the tracking pages and recorded page numbers, the input content is eventually able to be inferred.

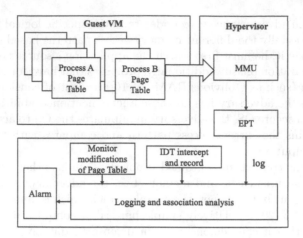

Fig. 3. Controlled-channel attack detection architecture

3   Design and Implementation

The key point we have found in this paper is that the data leakage behavior caused by controlled channel attack has typical characteristics: proactive trigger of interrupts, change of guest PTs, and hooks on page fault handler routines. In this regard, according to logs about the modified page content and the changed IDT with its associated routines, our prototype can detect the attack and alert users. We base on the KVM to describe the overall architecture of the detection scheme when a VM suffers from controlled channel attack. As shown in Fig. 3, our system has added three components i.e. IDT interception and record, PT(Page Table)modification monitoring and association analysis.

This paper intends to study the interruptions of system routines and EPT access permission settings, using association analysis to scan the abnormality in a specific time period. The collected files are extracted according to the defined event format, then our method cleans, standardizes, and forms event metadata, so that the features of the attack are highlighted. After that, we merge the events that meet certain conditions from a large number of logs into one stream of events. We can extract the main behavior, eliminate the interference of irrelevant events, and improve the system's processing capabilities by merging. Finally, according to the sequence of these events, the characteristics of the side-channel attack are correspondingly identified, so as to determine the threat point and achieve the purpose of detection. During the entire inspection, our monitoring and attack component do not interfere with each other, and the monitor in VMM is completely transparent to the VMs.

3.1   Virtual-to-Physical Mapping Monitoring

In KVM, the guest OS runs in the non-root mode. A guest virtual address (GVA) can be translated by the MMU to a guest physical address (GPA). In fact, each

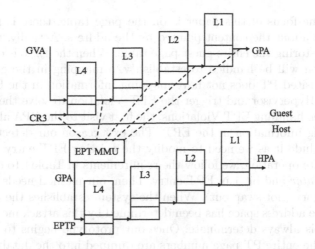

Fig. 4. Two-level PT address mapping; The addresses in PT structure are all gpas which need to be further translated by MMU to get the host physical addr (HPA).

GPA is also truly stored in physical memory. The address space where the VM is located is not the real physical address space. Therefore, the GPA needs to walk the EPT to further translate to the host physical address (HPA). Finally, the real content read from the HPA is obtained. The walking is shown in Fig. 4.

In Intel x86 micro-architecture, when Paging mode is enabled, the base address of the entire page table structure is stored in the CR3 register. The address space of each process can also be determined by CR3. The user-space linear address is translated to a physical address by the translation unit in traditional OS. The entire procedure involves address mapping (v2p mapping). Kernel-level malicious programs often change the contents of the PT structure to affect the mapping result.

The v2p mapping uses a multi-level PT structure. The number of levels depends on the mode of the processor, such as PAE mode (3 levels) or long mode (4 levels). Leaving aside the impact of EPT, if given a GVA and CR3 value, the easiest way to modify the result of the mapping is to modify the data in the PTE, which is also the method adopted in our target. In order to capture these behaviors, our method takes advantage of the EPT structure. First, the corresponding page of guest PT in the EPT is set to read-only(lock). When an adversary writes on these pages, the system will trap into the Hypervisor due to EPT Violation. Once the Hypervisor takes control, the system records the contents along with its address and set the page permission to writable. Unlike previous work [9,10,15] which enables single-stepping by setting the TF (trap flag) in the guest EFLAGS register, we set the *Monitor Trap Flag* (MTF) to temporarily resume the guest into single step mode. After the write operation completes, the single-step execution will again trap into the Hypervisor automatically. When dealing with the MTF, read the new contents of above address and set the EPT entry read-only again to monitor the next write operation.

Because the focus of this paper is on the page table, there is no need for excessive care about the content pointed by the address. Actually, the real difficulty lies in storing the entire guest page table. When the EPT is enabled, the #PF exception will be handled to establish v2p mapping in the guest. When the GPA in visited PT does not have mapping information in the EPT, it will trap into the Hypervisor and trigger the EPT Violation to solve the problem.

Thus, when handling EPT Violations, the first visit to the GPA always establishes mapping information in the EPT. The exit reason our detection focuses on should exclude it as we need to modify the existing EPT entry. To capture the target write operation, we follow the requirements in Table 1 to clear the bit 6 in *EPT Pointer* and bit 1 in EPT entry. Then, our method needs to keep the pages in memory (not swap out). When the system establishes the database to record PT, the address space has been determined by this attack method, so the PT mapping is always determinate. Once our prototype begins to scan in the Hypervisor, the entire PT page numbers are dumped into the database.

Table 1. EPT Violation triggering conditions

EPTP	Access	EPT entry	Exit_qualification
Set EPTP bit6 when access guest page table	Read	Clear bit1	WRITE_MASK
	Write	Clear bit1	WRITE_MASK
Clear EPTP bit6	Read	Clear bit0	READ_MASK
	Write	Clear bit1	WRITE_MASK
No effect	Execute	Clear bit2	FETCH_MASK

We have implemented the prototype system based on Qemu [6] + Kvm [13]. In Qemu, our prototype has added two new commands i.e. *start_monitor pid* and *stop_monitor*. The pid needs to be further converted to the information available in KVM(i.e. CR3). The system takes advantage of *virsh+libvmi* to read the name, pid and pgd in the struct *task_struct* of certain process using the unified virsh interface. Then the CR3 value can be generated by the pgd and offset value. In KVM, we have added two new ioctl handlers (*KVM_START_MONITOR* and *KVM_STOP_MONITOR*) to turn on and off the procedure. Once the KVM receives the start command, it walks the PT to create the hash-link database and begins to catch the target VM-EXIT. The data in database has a new structure named *mmu_guest_page_hash* containing guest frame numbers(gfns) which is one of the most important elements to screen out the useful logs. Beside of this, we have modified the EPT Violation handler to take notes on the traps with the following features: (1) The exit qualification is *WRITE_MASK*. (2) The current *GUEST_CR3* must belong to the protected process. (3)The current *GUEST_PHYSICAL_ADDRESS* exists in the database which we have established before. If the conditions are all satisfied, the EPT will be set "unlock" or "lock" state mentioned above. After that, the MTF handler needs to be added.

Its operation is relatively simple, mainly consisting of (1) setting the page to be read-only; (2) restoring the MTF; (3) comparing the changed value after writing with the previous one. After completing the interception and recording work, we need to further analyze the logs in Sect. 3.3.

3.2 IDT Monitoring

Since the guest OS is untrusted, guest IDT contents may be overwritten by the adversary. We cannot test the integrity of the system in the guest kernel, which means it is hard to tell if the OS has been hooked. Therefore, we decide to monitor the integrity in the VMM layer instead as a necessary condition for judgement.

When the system starts up, the IDT's address (base) and size (limit) have been determined. In other words, unless the kernel is recompiled, the IDT will be determined by the *system.map* file. The adversary generally uses the LKM (Loadable Kernel Modules) to hook the system routines. In order to observe the hooked function, the VMM records the address of critical structure like IDT and #PF handler. As our focus is on the PT modification and the frequency of it is far greater than the IDT change frequency, we just need to monitor IDT in each EPT Violation.

The basic steps are as follows: First, we get the IDT address through the *system.map* file, and use the address of *do_page_fault()* in file as a reference of #PF handler. Then, during the handler, the system reads the *IDTR_BASE* field in *VMCS* which is a gate descriptor pointer that we name idtr_base. The pointer can be used to compute the detailed #PF handler(pf_addr) and other system routine address. More concretely, we first get the 14th value from the pointer idtr_base [1] called pf_sel, then calculate the pf_addr by pf_sel:

$$pf\_addr = ((u64)pf\_sel.offset\_high \ll 32) \mid (pf\_sel.offset\_middle \ll 16) \mid (pf\_sel.offset\_low)$$

As soon as the pf_addr or the idtr_base changes, our system will fill in the log files as an important indicator of system integrity. If the address changes twice, the related routine or the IDT is proved to have been hooked, which means the kernel is no longer safe.

3.3 Association Recognition

Since the task of logging has been completed, we need to further deal with the records and analyze attack signatures. Figure 5 (actions on the present bit) is a possible execution flow. The present bit of the neighbouring PTE in tracking pages are modified in pairs. In the figure, 0x401000 and 0x402000 are significant page addresses. When the instruction at 0x402000 is accessed, it walks the PT and the bit 0 of PTE will be set at 0x1010. immediately, the PTE of 0x401000 is cleared at 0x1008. Then we repeat the operation when it runs to 0x402000 again to facilitate the next triggering. From the analysis of records, the chain at 0x0x1010 is 0x4024→0x4025→0x4024, and the corresponding actions inferred from it is the transition from the setting to the clearing on present bit.

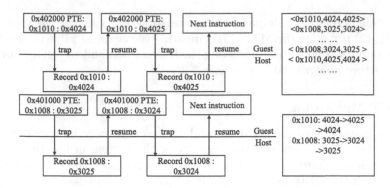

Fig. 5. Execution flow when following page sequence 0x401-0x402; the values in target address are gathered to form a chain to infer the OS behaviors.

Algorithm 1. Filter and standardize the log

    Input: Record set R_n
    Output: Standardized set E_n
1 $r1 = r2 = R_0, index = 0, n = 0;$
2 **while** $R_n \neq NULL$ **do**
3   **if** $r1.gpa \neq r2.gpa$ *or* $r1.val == r2.val$ *or*
       $r1.val \oplus r2.val \neq BIT\_PRESENT | BIT\_RESERVED$ **then**
4       $n + +; r3 = R_n;$
5       $r1 = r2, r2 = r3;$
6   continue;
7     $E = (r1.gpa, index + +, action[clear/set]);$
8   add E to $E_n;$
9 **return** $E_n;$

Our method divides the whole analysis procedure into two steps: filtering and identifying. As shown in Algorithm 1, our system filters useless modifications first. If the gpas of two adjacent items are equal and only the bit that would trigger #PF is different, an associated item will be formed. Otherwise, they are noisy information and we just ignore them. In next step, we use the formatted items to index the order of appearance and decide the behavior (set or clear).

After all logs are processed, we would further detect whether it has been attacked according to the Algorithm 2. We can know that during a controlled channel attack, the length of the page sequence is usually 2 or 3 [20]. As for this feature, taking 10 items for a comparative interval is sufficient. Records that are too far from the current item must be formed at the second visit. Since pages in sequence will appear adjacent to each other, their PTEs will change in certain bits when accessed. So if there is a continuous alternating clear and set behavior, it can be judged that the gpa is suspicious, and the total number increases. Finally, if the num is not smaller than 3, it can be judged that It exists a suspicious sequence.

Algorithm 2. identify the presence of a page sequence

   Input: Standardized set E_n
   Output: Bool to Judge the existence of a page sequence T
1   $E = E_0, S_n = null, tmp[BUF\_NUM], num = 0, T = false, n = 0$;
2   **while** $E_n \neq NULL$ **do**
3   **if** $E.gpa$ *is in* S_n **then**
4         $goto$ label;
5   **while** $i \leq 10$ **do**
6   **if** $E.gpa == E[i].gpa$ **then**
7   add $E[i]$ to $tmp[]$;
8   **while** $j \leq tmp.size()$ **do**
9   **if** $tmp[j].action \oplus tmp[j+1].action \neq 1$ **then**
10           $goto$ label;
11   add $E.gpa$ to S_n; $num + +$;
12   **if** $num \geq 3$ **then**
13         $T = true$;
14   label: $n + +$; $E = E_n$;
15   **return** T;

---

4 Evaluation

In order to verify the effectiveness of this method and evaluate the performance overhead of this solution, our prototype deployed the KVM 4.4.1 virtualization environment on an Intel i5-7400 3G processor with 8 GB of memory. Without loss of generality, the VM is allocated a single vCPU and 2 GB memory. The guest OS is 64-bit Ubuntu 14.04, and the kernel version is 3.16.36. The host OS is 64-bit Ubuntu 14.04 and the kernel version is 4.4.1. To adapt to a stable libvmi version, the Qemu version is 1.2.

4.1 Effectiveness

As mentioned above, we have implemented two main monitor components. In this section, we will show their effectiveness separately.

IDT Monitoring. When the new module is loaded, the address of the IDT and the #PF handler are automatically recorded during the startup of the VM and can be monitored in the Hypervisor at any time. Figure 6(a) is the case before and after the OS being attacked. The First highlighted part is the normal address of IDT and #PF handler. In our experiment, we overwrote both of IDT and #PF routines (may be #PF only). At last, their addresses became the second highlighted value in the figure. As the IDT and those system routines are system-wide, they will not alter unless we take the initiative to change it. From the figure, we can tell the guest OS is no longer integrate.

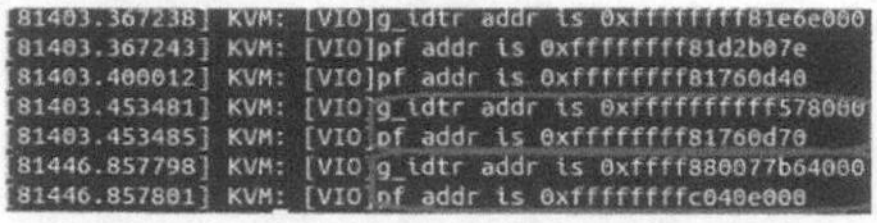

(a) IDT and #PF handler address after being hooked

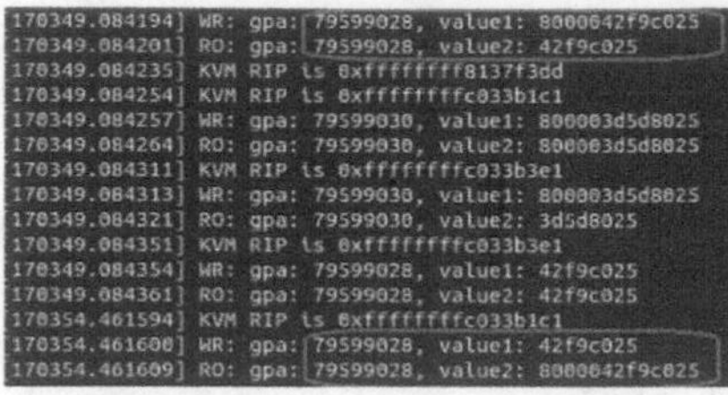

(b) Changes in guest Page Table

Fig. 6. Modified IDT and PT

PT Monitoring. As mentioned before, this paper traversed the target PT, dumped out the page numbers, and finally stored these contents in the hash table to facilitate the search. There were many modification on PTE reflected in the VMM (Fig. 6(b)). When the user entered a letter like 'm', the control flow jumped to the instruction in a certain page. As the page was found not present when walk through the page table, it would modify the PTE value at the guest physical address 0x79599028 during the execution of new #PF handler. when the adversary was ready to clear the reserved bit in the routine, it trapped into Hypervisor and left the first record in the Figure. Then, in the next VM-EXIT caused by MTF, we got the new value in the second record after write operation. The two data before and after the write operation appeared in pairs and finally the values at 0x79599028 form the chain 0x8000042f9c025→0x42f9c025→0x8000042f9c025. In addition to the phenomenon at address 0x79599028, we also found other suspicious gpa like 0x79599030. Eventually, we can tell that the guest OS suffered from the controlled channel attack.

4.2 Performance

In order to test the method's overhead to the VM, this paper uses UnixBench 5.1.3 [4] as the benchmark test suite. We performed 25 performance tests in total. After the provided cases are run in the guest, the overheads of arithmetic operations and system calls do not change much.

The result of our experiments is shown in Fig. 7. When the detection is enabled, it can be found that the effect of execl call, the process creation, the context switch and the shell execution is even more significant. For example, the performance overhead of the shell test is twice that of the original, and the performance of the process creation degrades the most. This is because when the system writes on the page table, it will trap into the Hypervisor. Any cases related to context switch especially containing operations involving PT will introduce additional VM-EXIT. As is known to us all, The more VM-EXIT occurs, the greater the performance overhead introduced. To some extent, it is the main reason for the increase in overhead. In the perspective of CPU load, our system also imposes some overhead on the execution of the target victim process. In

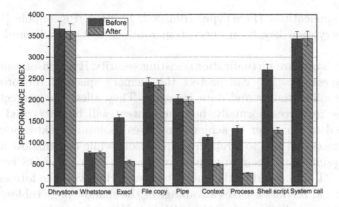

Fig. 7. Unixbench performance test results before and after the function is enabled

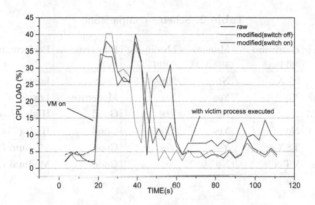

Fig. 8. CPU load when the victim executed

our experiments, we try to ensure that the target process is not interfered by other processes. As shown in Fig. 8, after the high load at the beginning of the VM startup, when the function is turned on, the total CPU load is increased by 5%–6% during the execution of victim. This experimental phenomenon shows the switching between VM and VMM brings additional burdens to the CPU.

5 Related Work

Side channel attacks become a major threat recently. In fact, some existing security systems are no longer safe due to various side channels. For example, there have been two side-channel attacks, based on cache [21] and page fault [20] correspondly, against SGX programs. The cache-based side channels are relatively passive and the available information is also limited. Compared with the former, the latter, namely the controlled side channels, is more effective and almost noiseless. Specifically, Wu [20] successfully presented fine-grained data from three applications (FreeType, Hunspell, libjpeg). Pigeonhole [18] attack stole the encryption key from encryption routines in OpenSSL and libgcrypt libraries.

Based on hardware virtualization, existing security Hypervisor (such as Inktag [11], Overshadow [8]) can protect the memory space of the process, and ensure the confidentiality and data integrity. They allow the protected application to use resources normally, but the content will be encrypted when OS viewing the data. In order to achieve processes' isolation, Inktag uses a high-assurance process (HAP) to wrap the application, while overshadow uses *cloaking* to encapsulate it. Their principles are similar. When the OS accesses the process, the PT is mapped to the encrypted page. However, the former uses different EPTs and the latter takes advantage of the shadow page tables. However, neither of them can fight against the #PF side-channel attacks.

Table 2. Scheme comparison

Methods	Hardware support	Manual analysis	Modifying compiler	Effectiveness	Performance
SSA	SGX	No	No	Poor	Low
Static analysis	No	Yes	No	Moderate	Low
Obvious RAM	No	No	Yes	Good	High $((log_2 t)^3)$
Shinde	No	Yes	Yes	Good	High (75x–4000x)
T-SGX	TSX+SGX	Yes	Yes	Good	Medium (1.0x–2.2x)
Our methods	VT-x	No	No	Good	Medium (1.0x–3.1x)

Although protective measures against controlled-channel attack have been proposed, It seems that they are not widely used or have insufficient security. Among them, Intel has modified the SGX feature to support the recording of #PF and #GP events in the State Save Area (SSA) [2]. However, the malicious OS can still cover the contents of the SSA. In addition, Intel [3] also proposed to remove the input-related code and data flow through static and dynamic analysis methods, which added more burden to the developers. Afterwards, Shinde et al. [18] proposed a software deterministic multiplexer. Before executing, the sensitive code and data were copied in the same pages by the compiler, so the adversary could not get the real page numbers any more. Shih et al. [17] developed the T-SGX system. In T-SGX, The TSX feature prevents the #PF event from being submitted to the OS. Instead, it is submitted to the TSX abort code in the enclave so that the adversary cannot obtain the #PF information. However, in order to realize it, it is necessary to modify a specific compiler to recompile the enclave program. Finally, Shinde et al. proposed an ideal execution mode called self-paging that it allows the enclave program to manage a certain number of memory pages by itself. However, doing so requires modifying the processor hardware, which hardware technology cannot support currently. We have comprehensively compared the above solutions in Table 2.

6   Conclusion

Virtualization technology and hardware features have gradually become a powerful tool for researchers to defend and detect attacks. Virtualization is powerful, but pure software costs a lot, hardware technology runs fast, but its function is simple and it requires huge costs to implement complex features. The use of hardware virtualization can effectively synthesize the advantages of both, which is also a major mainstream today. However, for the needs of system security, how to produce hardware with more features in virtualization, such as the storage of some key data, the correspondence between the guest PT and the EPT, and the system integrity of the guest are issues that need to be solved urgently.

This paper proposes a method to use virtualization to detect controlled channel attacks, adding about 2,000 lines of code to the KVM module and Qemu source code. The method uses the permission setting function of the EPT to lock the content of the related page to realize the monitoring of the PT modification. Since the PT and IDT are critical structure in each VM, we can detect more kind of attacks based on our prototype. As we only monitor the write action to the guest PT, it has no side effect on those system calls or arithmetic operations. But once it comes to PT operations like context switching or process creation, our method would cause a certain loss of performance. The system implemented in this paper is easy to deploy, completely transparent to the VM, and can intelligently switch and pass parameters through Qemu. The experiment proves that our prototype can effectively detect the #PF side channel attacks and the performance overhead is relatively small. To improve the method, our future work will focus on finding solutions to reduce the high performance overhead because of the frequent VM-EXIT.

Acknowledgment. This work was supported by National Natural Science Foundation of China (No. U1536204); Foundation of Science and Technology on Information Assurance Laboratory (No. 614211203011621120009).

References

1. Intel 64 and IA-32 Architectures Software Developer's Manual. http://www.intel.com/content/www/us/en/processors/architectures-software-developer-manuals.html
2. Intel software guard extensions programming reference (rev2). https://software.intel.com/sites/default/files/managed/48/88/329298-002.pdf
3. SGX Tutorial. http://sgxisca.weebly.com/
4. UnixBench Benchmark. https://github.com/kdlucas/byte-unixbench
5. Baumann, A., Peinado, M., Hunt, G.: Shielding applications from an untrusted cloud with haven. ACM Trans. Comput. Syst. (TOCS) **33**(3), 8 (2015)
6. Bellard, F.: QEMU, a fast and portable dynamic translator. In: USENIX Annual Technical Conference, FREENIX Track, vol. 41, p. 46 (2005)
7. Checkoway, S., Shacham, H.: Iago attacks: Why the system call API is a bad untrusted RPC interface. In: Eighteenth International Conference on Architectural Support for Programming Languages & Operating Systems, pp. 253–264 (2013)

8. Chen, X., et al.: Overshadow: a virtualization-based approach to retrofitting protection in commodity operating systems. ACM SIGOPS Oper. Syst. Rev. **42**(2), 2–13 (2008)
9. Dinaburg, A., Royal, P., Sharif, M., Lee, W.: Ether: malware analysis via hardware virtualization extensions. In: Proceedings of the 15th ACM Conference on Computer and Communications Security, pp. 51–62. ACM (2008)
10. Grace, M., et al.: Transparent protection of commodity OS kernels using hardware virtualization. In: Jajodia, S., Zhou, J. (eds.) SecureComm 2010. LNICST, vol. 50, pp. 162–180. Springer, Heidelberg (2010). https://doi.org/10.1007/978-3-642-16161-2_10
11. Hofmann, O.S., Kim, S., Dunn, A.M., Lee, M.Z., Witchel, E.: InkTag: secure applications on an untrusted operating system. In: ACM SIGARCH Computer Architecture News, vol. 41, pp. 265–278. ACM (2013)
12. King, S.T., Chen, P.M.: SubVirt: implementing malware with virtual machines. In: IEEE Symposium on Security and Privacy, pp. 14–pp. IEEE (2006)
13. Kivity, A., Kamay, Y., Laor, D., Lublin, U., Liguori, A.: KVM: the Linux virtual machine monitor. In: Proceedings of the Linux symposium, vol. 1, pp. 225–230 (2007)
14. Maas, M., et al.: Phantom: practical oblivious computation in a secure processor. In: Proceedings of the 2013 ACM SIGSAC Conference on Computer & Communications Security, pp. 311–324. ACM (2013)
15. Nguyen, A.M., Schear, N., Jung, H., Godiyal, A., King, S.T., Nguyen, H.D.: MAVMM: lightweight and purpose built VMM for malware analysis. In: Annual Computer Security Applications Conference, ACSAC 2009, pp. 441–450. IEEE (2009)
16. Rane, A., Lin, C., Tiwari, M.: Raccoon: closing digital side-channels through obfuscated execution. In: USENIX Security Symposium, pp. 431–446 (2015)
17. Shih, M.W., Lee, S., Kim, T., Peinado, M.: T-SGX: eradicating controlled-channel attacks against enclave programs. In: Proceedings of the 2017 Annual Network and Distributed System Security Symposium (NDSS), San Diego, CA (2017)
18. Shinde, S., Chua, Z.L., Narayanan, V., Saxena, P.: Preventing page faults from telling your secrets. In: Proceedings of the 11th ACM on Asia Conference on Computer and Communications Security, pp. 317–328. ACM (2016)
19. Wu, R., Chen, P., Liu, P., Mao, B.: System call redirection: a practical approach to meeting real-world virtual machine introspection needs. In: 2014 44th Annual IEEE/IFIP International Conference on Dependable Systems and Networks (DSN), pp. 574–585. IEEE (2014)
20. Xu, Y., Cui, W., Peinado, M.: Controlled-channel attacks: deterministic side channels for untrusted operating systems. In: 2015 IEEE Symposium on Security and Privacy (SP), pp. 640–656. IEEE (2015)
21. Zhou, Z., Reiter, M.K., Zhang, Y.: A software approach to defeating side channels in last-level caches. In: Proceedings of the 2016 ACM SIGSAC Conference on Computer and Communications Security, pp. 871–882. ACM (2016)

CuAPSS: A Hybrid CUDA Solution
for AllPairs Similarity Search

Yilin Feng, Jie Tang, Chongjun Wang[✉], and Junyuan Xie

State Key Laboratory for Novel Software Technology,
Department of Computer Science and Technology, Nanjing University,
Nanjing 210046, China
jspz_linxiaer@hotmail.com, {tangjie,chjwang,jyxie}@nju.edu.cn

Abstract. Given a set of high dimensional sparse vectors, a similarity function and a threshold, AllPairs Similarity Search finds out all pairs of vectors whose similarity values are higher than or equal to the threshold. AllPairs Similarity Search (APSS) has been studied in many different fields of computer science, including information retrieval, data mining, database and so on. It is a crucial part of lots of applications, such as near-duplicate document detection, collaborative filtering, query refinement and clustering. For cosine similarity, many serial algorithms have been proposed to solve the problem by decreasing the possible similarity candidates for each query object. However, the efficiency of those serial algorithms degrade badly as the threshold decreases. Other parallel implementations of APSS based on OpenMP or MapReduce also adopt the pruning policy and do not solve the problem thoroughly. In this context, we introduce CuAPSS, which solves the All Pairs cosine similarity search problem in CUDA environment on GPUs. Our method adopts a hybrid method to utilize both forward list and inverted list in APSS which compromises between the memory visiting and dot-product computing. The experimental results show that our method could solve the problem much faster than existing methods on several benchmark datasets with hundreds of millions of non-zero values, achieving the speedup of 1.5x–23x against the state-of-the-art parallel algorithm, while keep a relatively stable running time with different values of the threshold.

Keywords: Similarity search · Load balancing · CUDA

1 Introduction

Given a set of objects, a similarity function and a similarity threshold, Similarity Search finds out all objects, whose similarity values with a query object are higher than or equal to the threshold. AllPairs Similarity Search (APSS) is a specific version of Similarity Search, which finds all similar pairs of objects in a dataset. Similarity Search has been studied in many different fields of computer science, including information retrieval, data mining, database and so on. It is

© Springer Nature Switzerland AG 2018
J. Vaidya and J. Li (Eds.): ICA3PP 2018, LNCS 11334, pp. 421–436, 2018.
https://doi.org/10.1007/978-3-030-05051-1_29

a crucial part of lots of applications, such as near-duplicate document detection [12], collaborative filtering [20] and clustering [13].

In general, APSS can be solved by a naive approach, enumerating all pairs of objects, computing their similarity values, and verifying whether these values reach the threshold, which executes $O(n^2)$ object comparisons. However, the basic method is a computation-intensive algorithm and consumes a large amount of time, especially over a massive dataset. Thus, some researches have been done to speed up the process of APSS. At present, there are mainly two ways, filtering strategy [4,6,9] and parallelization [2,8] to expedite the process.

Taking each object as the query object, serial algorithms solve APSS in three steps: inverted list construction, candidate generation and candidate verification. The inverted list (inverted index) is an important data structure in the domain of information retrieval, which ensures that only the similarities of pairs with common features are computed. Previous serial algorithms use effective filtering strategies to prune as many false positive candidates for each query object as possible. Existing filtering strategies include size filtering, prefix filtering, residual filtering and so on. However, the efficiencies of those methods are affected by the distribution of the data and the threshold values.

Parallel algorithms were introduced on multi-core system [5,7] and MapReduce [1,2,19] framework. Like serial algorithms, these approaches also use an inverted index and some more radical filtering strategies to reduce unnecessary computations. While achieving some improvements in performance, MapReduce approaches suffer from high communication costs due to shuffle processes as well as the scheduling overhead, not to mention the cost of the system and the power consumption. Implementations on multi-core systems use index sharing technique and multi-threads to execute APSS method independently, trying to optimize the utilization of the memory hierarchy and suffer from the limitation of computing resources.

In this paper, we provide a CUDA-based parallel implementation to the APSS problem over a set of high-dimensional sparse vectors using cosine similarity function. Compared with distributed system and multi-core CPU, GPU has higher ratios of performance to price and energy consumption. Moreover, GPU is a very appropriate computing platform for the APSS problem, due to massively parallel operations on objects and features. However, parallelization of such methods is not straightforward, given the existing serial algorithms' characteristics, including frequent and irregular memory access, complex logic with many branches and loops, and the use of data structures in C++, such as hash map. Thus, we firstly propose parallel data structures for forward and inverted list on CUDA. Then we fulfill the APSS problem in two steps, i.e. the similarity computations on the inverted list and the similarity computations on the forward list, which trades off between the memory accessing and dot product computing. Our method outperforms the state-of-the-art serial and parallel algorithms and scales better than previous methods as the similarity threshold decreases, showing its usefulness in real-world applications, such as disease surveillance, face recognition in Ministry of Public Security and literature search for extensive results.

The main contributions of this paper are as follows:

- We propose two data structures on CUDA, i.e. SFL (Segmented-based Forward List) and CU-IL (CUDA-based Inverted List) for high dimensional sparse vectors.
- Based on the above two data structures, we develop a new parallel cosine similarity search algorithm named CuAPSS, which combines a feature-parallel scan and a pair-parallel scan executed on different parts of vectors.
- Taking into account the statistical characteristics of high-dimensional sparse datasets, we propose a parameter tuning method for the user-defined p parameter in CuAPSS.

2 Related Work

The APSS problem stems from the similarity join problem [10] in database field. While there was a lot of work on the extended problems, such as similarity search for euclidean distance [16], top-k similarity search [3] and approximate similarity search [18], little work focused on APSS for high-dimensional sparse vectors and cosine similarity. Thus, Bayardo et al. [9] firstly introduced a solution to this problem using filtering strategies, namely the AllPairs algorithm.

Previous work on APSS has made much efforts to expedite the time-consuming process. There have been two ways for speeding up the cosine-based APSS. The first one prunes a number of dissimilar vectors in advance to avoid unnecessary computations by leveraging effective filtering strategies, just as All-Pairs. Most of the subsequent serial approaches [4,6,14] followed this way and based on the filtering framework of AllPairs, put forward more effective filtering strategies to prune dissimilar candidates as many as possible.

According to the filtering framework, each vector as the query vector, one searches similar vectors for each query vector d in the dataset. The filtering framework consists of three steps: (1) Inverted index construction. A inverted index of the dataset is constructed for avoiding computing d's similarities with vectors that have no common non-zero feature with d. (2) Candidate generation. By traversing the inverted index for non-zero features in d, one can find d's possible candidate vectors. (3) Candidate Verification. Compute d's similarity value with each candidate fully and verify whether they are similar.

To further expedite the process, various filtering strategies were proposed. In AllPairs, Bayardo et al. first proposed size-filtering, which prunes candidates of size less than a pre-defined minimum size. Bayardo et al. also introduced residual-filtering, which uses an upper bound on the query vector's similarities with other vectors to stop generating new candidates for the query vector in advance. Then, both APT [7] and MMJoin [14] provide tighter bounds on the candidate minimum size. In MMJoin, based on the non-negativity of the square of a real number, Lee et al. also proposed a tighter bound for residual-filtering. L2AP algorithm [4], the state-of-the-art serial algorithm, based on the Cauchy-Schwarz inequality, introduces new residual filtering to improve its performance.

The other way solves the APSS problem in parallel, including MapReduce and multi-core solutions. Most of the parallel methods are based on the MapReduce framework and they take advantage of the framework's characteristics to design algorithms. Some MapReduce methods [8,11] firstly use mappers to compute partial similarity values of vector pairs. After the shuffle phase, partial similarity values of the same pairs are transmitted to a reducer to be accumulated. However, these MapReduce methods suffer from high communication costs among nodes and scale poorly as the dataset size increases. Thus, partition-based MapReduce methods [1,2,19] address the problem by only using map tasks, which first partition the dataset into some blocks and execute serial APSS algorithm in each block in parallel. Some filtering strategies are also used to prune dissimilar vectors. Besides, only two work focus on multi-core solutions, namely pAPT [7] and PL2AP [5]. The pAPT was introduced by Awekar and Samatova based on APT and it uses the indexing sharing technique such that threads can execute searches independently. Taking advantage of the features of memory hierarchy, PL2AP improves its performance using cache-tiling optimizations.

3   Background

In this section, we review some preliminary knowledge, including the cosine-based APSS problem and the inverted list representation, i.e. inverted index.

Firstly, some notations used in this paper are listed. Let $D = \{d_1, d_2, \ldots, d_n\}$ be a set of n objects, where each d_i is a real-valued, non-negative, sparse vector in an m dimensional feature space, $d_i = \{w_{i,1}, w_{i,2}, \ldots, w_{i,m}\}$, where $w_{i,k}$ is the k-th feature value of d_i, such as TF-IDF weight of a document [17]. In addition, f_k is the k-th feature's frequency, namely the number of $w_{i,k}$ s.t. $i = 1, 2\ldots n$ and $w_{i,k} \neq 0$. In this paper, features have been sorted in decreasing frequency order. For lots of problems, especially those involving text-based dataset, objects are represented as high-dimensional sparse vectors, where a vast majority of feature values are zero. Thus, a sparse vector d_i could be represented as a set of all pairs $(k, w_{i,k})$, such that $w_{i,k} \neq 0$ over $k = 1, \ldots, m$. we refer to a list of vectors in D represented as such pairs as the forward list, denoted by F, $F = \{F_1, F_2, \ldots, F_n\}$. F_i is a set of $(k, w_{i,k})$ s.t. $w_{i,k} \neq 0$.

Following the definition in [4], we denote the L_2-norm of d_i by $\| d_i \| = \sqrt{\sum_{k=1}^{m} w_{i,k}^2}$. For simplicity, all the vectors in D have been normalized, namely $\| d_i \| = 1, i = 1, 2, \ldots, n$. The prefix of a vector d_i is denoted as $d_i^{<p} = \{w_{i,1}, w_{i,2}, \ldots, w_{i,p-1}, 0, \ldots, 0\}$. Similarly, the suffix of d_i is denoted as $d_i^{\geq p} = \{0, \ldots, 0, w_{i,p}, w_{i,p+1}, \ldots, w_{i,m}\}$.

$sim(d_i, d_j)$ is a similarity function, indicating the similarity between vectors d_i and d_j. σ is a similarity threshold.

3.1 APSS

Each vector has been normalized and the cosine similarity $sim(d_i, d_j)$ is computed as:

$$sim(d_i, d_j) = dot(d_i, d_j) = \sum_{k=1}^{m} w_{i,k} \times w_{j,k} \tag{1}$$

d_i, d_j are similar if their similarity exceeds the threshold σ, i.e. $sim(d_i, d_j) \geq \sigma$. According to Formula 1, we only need to compute the product of $w_{i,k} \times w_{j,k}$ s.t. $w_{i,k} \neq 0$ and $w_{j,k} \neq 0$, which we call the common non-zero features between d_i and d_j.

Following the definition in [9], APSS seeks all pairs (d_i, d_j) such that d_i, $d_j \in D$, $d_i \neq d_j$, and $sim(d_i, d_j) \geq \sigma$. Due to $sim(d_i, d_j) = sim(d_j, d_i)$, the result only includes pairs (d_i, d_j), $i > j$.

3.2 Inverted List

The inverted list, namely inverted index, is a common data structure in the domain of information retrieval. The inverted list of D contains m lists, $I = \{I_1, I_2, \ldots, I_m\}$, one for each dimension. List I_k contains all pairs $(i, w_{i,k})$ such that vector $d_i \in D$ and $w_{i,k} \neq 0$. To avoid many time-consuming atomic operations, this paper only constructs the inverted list for the suffix $d_i^{\geq p}$ of each vector, i.e. $I' = \{I_p, I_{p+1}, \ldots, I_m\}$, called the inverted sub-list.

4 CUDA Based APSS

Parallelization of APSS on large sparse dataset is by no means straightforward because of the frequent and irregular memory access, complex logic with many branches and loops, and the use of data structures such as hash map. Implementation on CUDA is even plaguy due to its memory allocation and thread scheduling. Thus, we firstly propose two parallel data structures for forward and inverted list representation on CUDA. Then we perform the APSS in two steps, i.e. computing partial similarity values on inverted list (feature-parallel scan) and computing the rest similarity values on the forward list (pair-parallel scan), which trades off between the memory accessing and dot product computing. Finally, according to the statistical characteristics of datasets, we introduce a parameter tuning method for the best performance.

The overall framework of CuAPSS is depicted in Fig. 1. Firstly, due to the limited storage space, global memory does not have enough storage space to store all pairs' similarity values. CuAPSS solves the problem by computing pairs' similarities in batches. The input vectors are divided into a set of partitions, and pairs of partitions (P_b, P_a) s.t. $b \geq a$, are possessed one by one. Then, partitioned vectors are transmitted to GPU. To ensure that all pairs' similarities are computed, CuAPSS computes similarities of all pairs (d_i, d_j) s.t. $d_i \in P_b$ and $d_j \in P_a$. In the case of $a = b$, CuAPSS only needs to compute the similarity

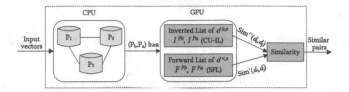

Fig. 1. The framework of CuAPSS

of (d_i, d_j) s.t. $j < i$, because $sim(d_i, d_j) = sim(d_j, d_i)$. On GPU, CuAPSS uses a hybrid data structure, i.e. vectors' suffixes $d^{\geq p}$ are represented as inverted list, and prefixes $d^{<p}$ are represented as forward list. Therefore, when (P_b, P_a) is possessed, we construct forward lists F^{Pb}, F^{Pa} and inverted lists I^{Pb}, I^{Pa} for P_b and P_a respectively. Then, CuAPSS computes $sim(d_i, d_j)' = \sum_{k=1}^{p-1} w_{i,k} \times w_{j,k}$ on F^{Pb} and F^{Pa}, and computes $sim(d_i, d_j)'' = \sum_{k=p}^{m} w_{i,k} \times w_{j,k}$ on I^{Pb} and I^{Pa}. Adding them up, CuAPSS calculates all pairs' full similarities and outputs similar pairs.

4.1 The SFL Structure

We first propose a data structure named SFL (Segmented-based Forward List) for high-dimensional sparse vectors, which is used to represent forward lists with coalesced memory access and achieves thread load balance during computing.

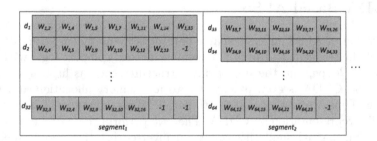

Fig. 2. Segmented-based forward list

In SFL, the input vectors are divided into segments each of which has ω vectors. ω is usually set to be equal to the size of a warp, which is the SIMD execution unit for GPU. We set $\omega = 32$ for the NVIDIA GPUs. So, each thread in a warp deals with a vector in a segment. If the last vectors cannot make up a complete segment, i.e. $n\%32 \neq 0$, zeros are padded in it to complete the segment. Assuming there are v segments in all, the s-th segment is denoted by $segment_s$. Because vectors have been sorted in decreasing order of the number of non-zero features, vectors in a segment have almost the same number of non-zero features, which achieves thread load balance within a warp. Then, $segment_s$ is transformed into a matrix M_s. Due to the pre-defined sort order of vectors, the first vector in $segment_s$ has the most number of non-zero features, denoted by nnz_s. As illustrated in Fig. 2, M_s is a matrix of size $32 \times nnz_s$ and $M_s[m][n]$ stores the n-th non-zero feature of the m-th vector in $segment_s$. In the case of vectors' number of non-zero features less than nnz_s, every remaining location in M_s is padded with -1. For coalesced memory access, M_s is stored in column-major order in global memory.

As shown in the left part of Fig. 3, we implement the SFL structure using CUDA with three arrays, including dim, val and $tile\_start$: (1) dim array stores the dimensionality of features in matrixes from M_1 to M_v in column-major order, namely the subscript k of $w_{i,k}$ (there are v segments in all). (2) val array stores the values of features in matrixes, which means that $val[i]$ stores the feature value corresponding to $dim[i]$. (3) $tile\_start$ array stores the starting pointers of all matries. Its size is v, so $tile\_start[s]$ stores the starting pointer of M_{s+1} in the dim and val array.

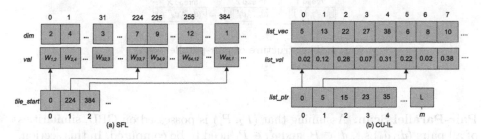

Fig. 3. The implementation of SFL and CU-IL on CUDA

4.2 CU-IL

Inverted list is a significant data structure for APSS algorithms, which helps avoid unnecessary computations between pairs with no common non-zero feature. We provide an CUDA-based implementation of the inverted list, named CU-IL.

The right part of Fig. 3 shows that CU-IL consists of three arrays, namely $list\_vec$, $list\_val$ and $list\_ptr$. $list\_vec$ and $list\_val$ save pairs $(i, w_{i,k})$ in the inverted list I in turn, so $list\_vec[ptr]$ saves the vector id i and $list\_val[ptr]$ saves the feature value $w_{i,k}$ of list I_k at the pointer ptr. $list\_ptr$ saves the pointer for each list and $list\_ptr[k]$ is the starting pointer for I_{k+1} in $list\_vec$ and $list\_ptr$.

4.3 Algorithm

Based on the data structures SFL and CU-IL for sparse vectors, we develop two parallel methods. Firstly, because the computations on pairs' similarity are independent, we propose a pair-parallel scan, which assigns a thread to each pair. Secondly, as APSS computes the product of common non-zero features of pairs independently too, we propose a feature-parallel scan, in which a thread calculates the product of values at a common non-zero feature for each pair of vectors. However, when the two parallel methods are executed independently on the whole dataset, frequent memory access and atomic operations waste much time. By combining the two parallel methods, we solve these tricky problems and get better performance. we also use shared memory to store re-used data.

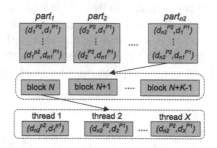

Fig. 4. The structure of pair-parallel scan.

Pair-Parallel Scan. Assuming that (P_2, P_1) is possessed on GPU, similarities of all pairs (d_i, d_j) s.t. $d_i \in P_2$ and $d_j \in P_1$ need to be computed. In this section, we denote the i-th vector in P_a as $d_i^{P_a}$. The number of vectors in P_a is denoted by na, such as $n1$ for P_1. As shown in Fig. 4, pair-parallel scan divides all pairs into $n2$ parts and $part_i$ has $n1$ pairs $(d_i^{P_2}, d_j^{P_1}), j = 1, 2...n1$. Then, the pair-parallel scan allocates each part to blocks to compute pairs' similarities. In Fig. 4, K blocks are assigned for $part_{n2}$ from block N to block $N + K - 1$, and each thread computes $d_{n2}^{P_2}$'s similarity with a vector of P_1. So, if the block size is X, one of the K blocks computes similarities of $d_{n2}^{P_2}$ with X vectors in P_1. In this case, we set $K = \lfloor \frac{n1}{X} \rfloor + 1$ s.t. $n1\%X \neq 0$ or $K = \frac{n1}{X}$ s.t. $n1\%X = 0$.

The process of calculating $sim(d_i^{P_2}, d_j^{P_1})$ is shown in Algorithm 1. We store $d_i^{P_2}$'s features in shared memory (line 5–8) because they are used by all threads of a block. Then, accumulate $w_{i,k} \times w_{j,k}$ s.t. $w_{j,k} \neq 0$ to sim to get $sim(d_i^{P_2}, d_j^{P_1})$ (line 10). Due to the limited size of shared memory, we only store L features of $d_i^{P_2}$ each time, and repeat line 5–10 until all non-zero features are scanned.

Feature-Parallel Scan. On CU-IL, we propose a feature-parallel scan. Assuming that (P_2, P_1) is possessed too, on I^{P_2} and I^{P_1}, the feature-parallel scan only computes similarities of pairs (d_i, d_j) s.t. $d_i \in P_2, d_j \in P_1$ with common non-zero features. Figure 5 shows the structure of the feature-parallel scan. Vectors in $I_k^{P_2}$ and vectors in $I_k^{P_1}$ have the common non-zero feature, i.e. the k-th feature. We compute the products of the k-th feature values for all pairs (d_i, d_j) s.t. $d_i \in I_k^{P_2}$

Algorithm 1. pair-parallel scan

Require: F^{P2}, F^{P1}

Ensure: sim

1: __shared__ $vector\_i[L+1]$
2: $sim \leftarrow 0$
3: $i \leftarrow getVectorIdinP_2(threadIdx.x, blockIdx.x)$
4: $j \leftarrow getVectorIdinP_1(threadIdx.x, blockIdx.x)$
5: $vector\_i[k] \leftarrow 0$ **for** $k = 1, 2..., L$
6: __syncthreads();
7: $vector\_i[k] \leftarrow w_{i,k}$ **for** $k = 1, 2..., L$ $s.t.$ $w_{i,k} \neq 0$
8: __syncthreads();
9: **for** $k = 1$ **to** L $s.t.$ $w_{j,k} \neq 0$ **do**
10:     $sim+ = vector\_i[k] * w_{j,k}$
11: **end for**

---

and $d_j \in I_k^{P1}$. On CUDA, we calculate products of features by matrix-matrix multiplication, i.e. features in I_k^{P2} form a row matrix B and features in I_k^{P1} form a row matrix A, so by computing $B^T \times A$, we get all products $w_{i,k} \times w_{j,k}$ s.t. $w_{i,k} \neq 0, w_{j,k} \neq 0$. To utilize thousands of computing cores in GPU, we divide B and A into segments of fixed size ω and allocate many blocks to compute $B^T \times A$. Assuming that B and A are divided into s and t segments respectively, we denote the s-th segment of B and A as B_s and A_s. Thus, $s \times t$ blocks are allocated for $B^T \times A$, and each block computes $B_u^T \times A_v$, $1 \leq u \leq s$ and $1 \leq v \leq t$. In terms of each block, a 2-dimensional block is used, whose $blockDim.x$ and $blockDim.y$ are set to ω ($\omega = 4$ in Fig. 5). Each thread computes the product of features $B_u[threadId.y] \times A_v[threadId.x]$. Finally, the product $w_{i,k} \times w_{j,k}$ is accumulated into a location in the global memory by an atomic operation. The location is decided by id i and j, so it stores the accumulated dot-product of d_i and d_j.

Hybrid Solution. However, the two parallel methods have their own drawbacks. Firstly, the pair-parallel scan has to read the non-zero features of a vector repetitively for so many times. As the input dataset size increases, a large amount of time for accessing memory degrades the performance. Secondly, the feature-parallel scan involves lots of atomic operations, which also cost a large amount of time.

To deal with these problems, we propose CuAPSS, combining the two parallel method on an hybrid representation for vectors. CuPASS applies pair-parallel scan and feature-parallel scan on different parts of vectors, overcoming the above problems. Features have been sorted in decreasing frequency order, thus, feature-parallel scan executed on features with high frequency involves most of the atomic operations. In order to reduce atomic operations, we divide a vector d_i into its prefix $d_i^{<p}$ and suffix $d_i^{\geq p}$, such that $d_i = d_i^{<p} + d_i^{\geq p}$. In CuAPSS, $d_i^{<p}$ is represented as forward list (SFL on CUDA), while $d_i^{\geq p}$ is represented as inverted list (CU-IL on CUDA). In this case, a inverted sub-list $I' = \{I_p, I_{p+1}, \ldots, I_m\}$ is

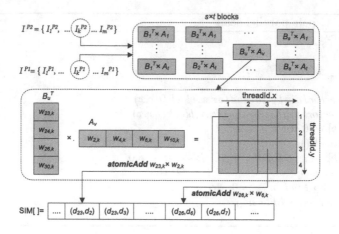

Fig. 5. The structure of feature-parallel method.

constructed. CuAPSS solves the APSS problem by combining the pair-parallel scan executed on $d_i^{<p}$ for $sim'(d_i, d_j) = \sum_{k=1}^{k=p-1} w_{i,k} \times w_{j,k}$, and the feature-parallel scan executed on $d_i^{\geq p}$ for $sim''(d_i, d_j) = \sum_{k=p}^{k=m} w_{i,k} \times w_{j,k}$. CuAPSS executes the two parallel method successively and $sim(d_i, d_j) = sim'(d_i, d_j) + sim''(d_i, d_j)$.

Tunning Method for the Value of p. In the hybrid solution, the p is a user-defined parameter and CuAPSS is controlled by it. According to the statistical characteristics of high-dimensional sparse vectors, we propose a method to tune the p parameter for the best performance.

In the feature-parallel scan, the number of atomic operations is controlled by the frequencies of features, i.e. the more frequent features need more atomic operations. By analyzing the statistical information of datasets, we find that only a small part of features account for 90% non-zero values in the whole dataset, i.e. features ranking top account for 90% of the non-zero values, as features have been sorted in decreasing frequency order. Thus, we do not construct the inverted list for these more frequent features, otherwise it would take a large amount of time for atomic operations.

Based on the analysis, we propose a tuning method for p parameter. According to Formula 2, we set the value of p. In Formula 2, f_k is the k-th feature's frequency and nnz is the number of non-zero values in the dataset. So features in $d^{<p}$ account for more than 90% of all non-zero values. Moreover, due to a positive correlation between the pair-parallel scan's execution time and the value of p, Formula 2 makes sure a large amount of atomic operations have been avoided and p is set to the minimum value for the fastest execution of the pair-parallel scan.

$$p = \min p \ \ s.t. \ \ \frac{\sum_{k=1}^{p-1} f_k}{nnz} \geq 0.9 \ (2 \leq p \leq m+1) \tag{2}$$

5   Experiment Evaluation

This section describes the performance evaluation of CuAPSS. We first describe the executing environment and datasets used in the experiments. Then, we verify the accuracy of CuAPSS and compare it with the state-of-the-art algorithms and the NIVIDA CUDA library cuSPARSE. In addition, we assess the effectiveness of the hybrid data structure, and verify the tuning method for the parameter p. Finally, we evaluate its scalability.

5.1   Setup

We implement CuAPSS on three GPUs: NVIDIA GeForce GTX 1080Ti with 11 GB VRAM, NVIDIA Tesla P100 with 16 GB VRAM and NVIDIA Tesla M40 with 12 GB VRAM. We use CUDA 9.0 and Nsight Eclipse Edition 9.0 running on Ubuntu 16.10.

We use 4 datasets to evaluate all algorithms. we give their details below.

- **WW500** is a set of documents extracted from the October 2014 article dump of the English Wiki. Each document contains over 500 different features.
- **WW200** contains documents with over 200 different features from the article dump of the English Wiki.
- **RCV1** is a standard benchmark corpus [15].
- **Twitter** contains the directed graph of users' follow relationships. Each user follows over 1000 other users.

In the pre-processing phase, we sort features in decreasing frequency order. All textual datasets are represented as TF-IDF weighted vectors [17]. Their statistical information are listed in Table 1, including number of vectors (n), features (m), and non-zeros (nnz), mean vector size (mvl) and mean feature frequency (mff).

Table 1. Dataset statistical information

Dataset	n	m	nnz	mvl	mff
RCV1	804414	50000	62E6	76	1347
WW500	240211	660000	202E6	830	306
WW200	1020035	660000	437E6	430	659
Twitter	146170	143469	200E6	1370	1395

In this section, the results of CuAPSS are an average of 10 runs, and results of serial and multi-core algorithms are from [5], where each algorithm was executed on a server with two twelve-core 2.5 GHz Intel Xeon E5-2680v3 processors and 64 GB RAM. Like the experimental setup in [5], we measure CuAPSS execution time in seconds for the similarity search phase and I/O time for loading data into the memory and writing results to the disk are ignored because they are the same for all algorithms.

5.2   Comparison

Firstly, We implement AllPairs algorithm [9] in C++, which is an exact serial APSS algorithm. Then, we compare the output of CuAPSS with that of AllPairs, both of which are executed on WW500. Similar pairs in CuAPSS' output are the same as those in AllPairs' completely, which verifies the accuracy of CuAPSS.

We compare CuAPSS with the following algorithms in terms of execution time:

- **IdxJoin**, **APT** and **L2AP** are baseline serial algorithms.
- **pIdxJoin** is a multi-core parallel algorithm based on IdxJoin, using cache-tiling optimizations.
- **pAPT** is a parallel APSS algorithm based on APT, which is the first multi-core solution.
- **PL2AP** is the state-of-the-art parallel algorithm in a multi-core environment, using a number of cache-tiling optimizations.
- **cuSPARSE** is the NIVIDA CUDA library to accelerate sparse matrix operations. we use it to solve the APSS problem by a naive method of sparse matrix multiplication.

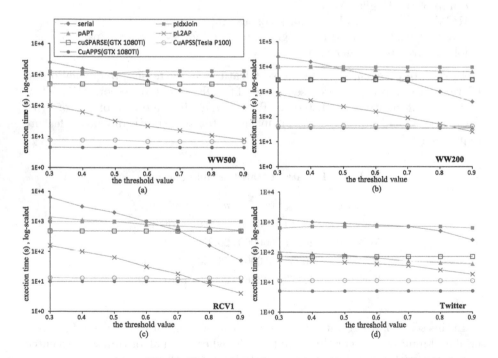

Fig. 6. Comparison of execution time

We get the experimental results of serial and multi-core algorithms from [5]. In [5], all multi-core parallel methods are executed with 24 threads, and the best serial execution time is achieved by any serial algorithm that runs fastest. For comparison, we use the same datasets as those in [5]. we use cuSPARSE to solve APSS on NVIDIA GTX 1080Ti and CuAPSS is implemented on GTX 1080Ti and Tesla P100. Figure 6 shows the execution time of all methods at similarity thresholds between 0.3 and 0.9. In most cases, CuAPSS outperforms all other algorithms, while keeps a relatively stable running time with different values of the threshold. On GTX 1080Ti, CuAPSS achieves the speedup of 5-718x over the best serial execution, and 2-23x against the state-of-the-art parallel algorithm PL2AP at the threshold $\sigma \leq 0.7$. On Tesla P100, CuAPSS achieves the speedup of 4-598x against the best serial execution, and 1.5-19x against PL2AP at the threshold $\sigma \leq 0.7$. Thus, both GPUs deliver higher performance. It is noteworthy that CPU algorithms achieve the best performance in the case of the maximum threshold, because they use threshold-based filtering strategies to prune candidates to avoid a number of computations, nevertheless filtering methods are not so effective when the threshold is lower. While CuAPSS relies on thousands of computing cores on GPU to improve the performance instead of filtering strategies. So CuAPSS keeps a stable execution time and has a significant advantage over PL2AP in the case of $\sigma \leq 0.6$, showing its usefulness in search tasks with lower thresholds, such as disease surveillance, face recognition in Ministry of Public Security, literature search for extensive results and so on. Moreover, CuAPSS is very appropriate for the network dataset, in which non-zero values are evenly distributed among vectors, achieving the speedup of 3.6-18.6x against PL2AP on GTX 1080Ti.

Due to limited memory, vectors are possessed on GPU in batches (CuAPSS and cuSPARSE). For only a pair (P_2, P_1) in WW500, the running time of CuAPSS is 0.8 s while that of cuSPARSE is 10 s, so CuAPSS still runs much faster than cuSPARSE.

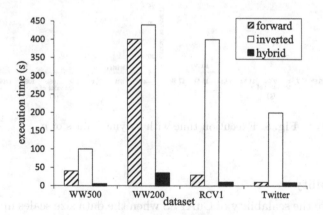

Fig. 7. Execution time of different data structures

5.3 Effectiveness of Hybrid Structure

For assessing the effectiveness of the hybrid structure, we conduct three distinct experiments on each dataset, namely the pair-parallel scan on the forward list, the feature-parallel scan on the inverted list, and CuAPSS on the hybrid representation in which p is tuned as Formula 2. The execution time of the three algorithms ran on GTX 1080Ti are shown in Fig. 7. We can see that compared with the other two structures, the hybrid structure helps improve the performance drastically.

In CuAPSS, a tuning method for the value of p is proposed. According to Formula 2, we get $p = 33197$ for WW500, $p = 30551$ for WW200, $p = 4605$ for RCV1 and $p = 133113$ for Twitter. To verify its effectiveness, we vary the value of p in CuAPSS executed on Tesla M40, Tesla P100 and GTX 1080Ti respectively. Figure 8 show the results of varying values of p. we can see the performance is sensitive to the value of p and when p is set according to our method, CuAPSS can reach the best performance nearly on all GPUs, which concludes that our tuning method for the value p can be applied to different GPUs

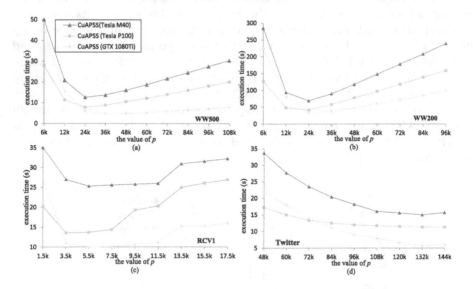

Fig. 8. Execution time with varying values of p

5.4 Scalability

We investigate the scalability of CuAPSS when the data size scales up. When the number of vectors increases, we evaluate the performance of CuAPSS which is executed on GTX 1080Ti and Tesla P100. Figure 9 show the execution time with increasing number of vectors, on the four datasets. The results show CuAPSS scales well as the data size increases in any dataset, achieving nearly linear scalability on both GPUs.

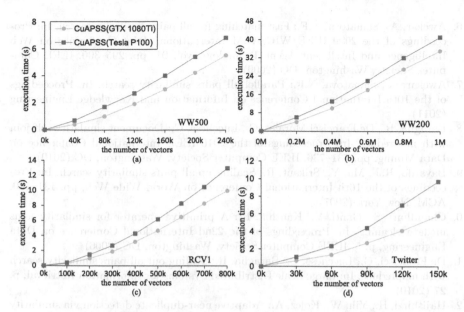

Fig. 9. Execution time with varying number of vectors

6   Conclusions

We have proposed and implemented a new parallel cosine similarity search algorithm CuAPSS in CUDA environment on GPUs, which achieves good performance based on a hybrid method. Experimental results show the effectiveness and efficiency of CuAPSS.

References

1. Alabduljalil, M., Tang, X., Yang, T.: Cache-conscious performance optimization for similarity search. In: Proceedings of the 36th International ACM SIGIR Conference on Research and Development in Information Retrieval, pp. 713–722. ACM, New York (2013)
2. Alabduljalil, M.A., Tang, X., Yang, T.: Optimizing parallel algorithms for all pairs similarity search. In: Proceedings of the Sixth ACM International Conference on Web Search and Data Mining, pp. 203–212. ACM, New York (2013)
3. Alewiwi, M., Orencik, C., Savaş, E.: Efficient top-k similarity document search utilizing distributed file systems and cosine similarity. Cluster Comput. **19**(1), 109–126 (2016)
4. Anastasiu, D.C., Karypis, G.: L2AP: fast cosine similarity search with prefix L-2 norm bounds. In: IEEE 30th International Conference on Data Engineering, ICDE 2014, 31 March–4 April 2014, Chicago, IL, USA, pp. 784–795 (2014)
5. Anastasiu, D.C., Karypis, G.: PL2AP: fast parallel cosine similarity search. In: Proceedings of the 5th Workshop on Irregular Applications: Architectures and Algorithms, pp. 8:1–8:8. ACM, New York (2015)

6. Awekar, A., Samatova, N.F.: Fast matching for all pairs similarity search. In: Proceedings of the 2009 IEEE/WIC/ACM International Joint Conference on Web Intelligence and Intelligent Agent Technology, vol. 01, pp. 295–300. IEEE Computer Society, Washington, DC (2009)
7. Awekar, A., Samatova, N.F.: Parallel all pairs similarity search. In: Proceedings of the 10th International Conference on Information and Knowledge Engineering (2011)
8. Baraglia, R., De Francisci Morales, G., Lucchese, C.: Document similarity self-join with mapreduce. In: Proceedings of the 2010 IEEE International Conference on Data Mining, pp. 731–736. IEEE Computer Society, Washington, DC (2010)
9. Bayardo, R.J., Ma, Y., Srikant, R.: Scaling up all pairs similarity search. In: Proceedings of the 16th International Conference on World Wide Web, pp. 131–140. ACM, New York (2007)
10. Chaudhuri, S., Ganti, V., Kaushik, R.: A primitive operator for similarity joins in data cleaning. In: Proceedings of the 22nd International Conference on Data Engineering, p. 5. IEEE Computer Society, Washington, DC (2006)
11. De Francisci, G., Lucchese, C., Baraglia, R.: Scaling out all pairs similarity search with mapreduce. In: Large-Scale Distributed Systems for Information Retrieval, p. 27 (2010)
12. Hajishirzi, H., Yih, W., Kolcz, A.: Adaptive near-duplicate detection via similarity learning. In: Proceedings of the 33rd International ACM SIGIR Conference on Research and Development in Information Retrieval, pp. 419–426. ACM, New York (2010)
13. Haveliwala, T.H., Gionis, A., Indyk, P.: Scalable techniques for clustering the web. In: Suciu, D., Vossen, G. (eds.) WebDB (Informal Proceedings), pp. 129–134 (2000)
14. Lee, D., Park, J., Shim, J., Lee, S.: An efficient similarity join algorithm with cosine similarity predicate. In: Bringas, P.G., Hameurlain, A., Quirchmayr, G. (eds.) DEXA 2010. LNCS, vol. 6262, pp. 422–436. Springer, Heidelberg (2010). https://doi.org/10.1007/978-3-642-15251-1_33
15. Lewis, D.D., Yang, Y., Rose, T.G., Li, F.: Rcv1: a new benchmark collection for text categorization research. J. Mach. Learn. Res. 5, 361–397 (2004)
16. Matsumoto, T., Yiu, M.L.: Accelerating exact similarity search on CPU-GPU systems. In: 2015 IEEE International Conference on Data Mining, pp. 320–329, November 2015
17. Salton, G.: Term-weighting approach in automatic text retrieval. In: Readings in Information Retrieval (1998)
18. Satuluri, V., Parthasarathy, S.: Bayesian locality sensitive hashing for fast similarity search. Proc. VLDB Endow. 5(5), 430–441 (2012)
19. Tang, X., Alabduljalil, M., Jin, X., Yang, T.: Load balancing for partition-based similarity search. In: Proceedings of the 37th International ACM SIGIR Conference on Research & Development in Information Retrieval, pp. 193–202. ACM, New York (2014)
20. Zeng, C., Xing, C.X., Zhou, L.Z.: Similarity measure and instance selection for collaborative filtering. In: Proceedings of the 12th International Conference on World Wide Web, pp. 652–658. ACM, New York (2003)

A Parallel Branch and Bound Algorithm for the Probabilistic TSP

Mohamed Abdellahi Amar[1]($\boxtimes$)(iD), Walid Khaznaji[2], and Monia Bellalouna[1]

[1] CRISTAL Laboratory POLE GRIFT, University of Manouba, National School of
Computer Sciences, Manouba, Tunis, Tunisia
medabdellahiamar@yahoo.fr, monia.bellalouna@gmail.com
[2] Tunisia SESAME University, Ariana, Tunisia
walid.khaznaji@sesame.com.tn

Abstract. The paper presents parallelization of exact algorithm of resolution for the Probabilistic Traveling Salesman Problem (PTSP). This
algorithm allows us, first, to verify the stability of well-solvable special
cases and also to optimally solve useful instances of PTSP. It again allows
to perform our version of Karp partitioning algorithm, where real problems are very large-sized. The implementation of the algorithm of Karp
consists in subdividing the square plan, into sub-plans. So we transform
the resolution of a large size problem to the resolution of many small size
sub-problems which can be exactly solved. This application can be grid-
ified and these different sub-problems would be processed in parallel by
different nodes since they are totally independent. In each sub-plan the
Branch and Bound algorithm is used. In this paper we propose two parallelizations of the Branch and Bound algorithm for the resolution of the
PTSP. On the one hand, the parallelization of the branches used in the
exploration of the tree, on the other hand the parallelization of the algorithm associated with the notion of partitioning introduced by Karp. We
perform an experimental study conducted in a multi-core environment
to evaluate the performance of the proposed approach.

Keywords: PTSP · Parallel algorithm · Open MP · Simulations

1 Introduction

Today, parallel processing is being incorporated into several data processing
domains in the form of shared data in order to provide real-time responses and
also makes applications more reliable. Parallel processing is a form of information processing that allows the exploitation of competing events in the course of
execution. These events are on several levels, we can mention: at the level of the
program, the procedure, the instruction. At the highest level, parallel processing allows the simultaneous execution of several independent programs. In fact,
inside of program, this process requires the decomposition of the program into
tasks, the search for dependency relationships between these tasks, and then, at
the end, to program the independent tasks according to the number of available

© Springer Nature Switzerland AG 2018
J. Vaidya and J. Li (Eds.): ICA3PP 2018, LNCS 11334, pp. 437–448, 2018.
https://doi.org/10.1007/978-3-030-05051-1_30

processors. It can be done at the level of the operating system (automatic paral-lelization of programs, intelligent compilers) or at the algorithmic level [10–12].

Our goal is to propose parallel strategies for the exact algorithm for the solution of the PTSP that proposed in [1]. The development of methods for res-olution of the PTSP is a very active research field, the reason is that it can be used to model many real-world applications [3,9,13]. The Probabilistic Traveling Salesman Problem (PTSP) is a type of NP-complete problem. It is a variation of the well-known Traveling Salesman Problem (TSP). This probabilistic ver-sion was initially introduced by Jaillet [13], it can be formulated as follows: we consider here a complete connected graph $G = (V, E)$, where its arcs are valued, V is the set of vertices, E the set of edges. Let P be a probability distribution defined on the sub-set of V: $\mathbb{P}(V)$, T be a given an a priori tour through V. For each sub-set $S \subseteq V$, we consider $\mathcal{U}$ a modification method, it consists in erasing from an a priori tour the absent vertices by remaining in the same order. Let L_T be a real random variable defined on $\mathbb{P}(V)$, which in an a priori tour T and for each S of $\mathbb{P}(V)$, associates the length of the tour through S. The solution of problem consists in finding an a priori tour visiting all points that minimizes the expected length of a tour T [13]. For each sub-set $S \in \mathbb{P}(V)$.

$$E(L_{(T,\mathcal{U})}) = \sum_{S \subseteq V} P(S) L_{(T,\mathcal{U})}(S)$$

It was explicitly exhibited by Jaillet [13] for the heterogeneous and homogeneous version. As regards the last, it is shown as follows: let $d(i, j)$ be a distance between the nodes i, j, and $p = P(k)\ \forall k \in T$, $q = 1 - p$, the expected length of a tour T is

$$E(L_T) = p^2 \sum_{r=0}^{n-2} q^r \sum_{i=1}^{n} d(i, T^r(i)) \tag{1}$$

where $T^r(i)$ is the successor number r of i in the tour T.

Bertsimas et al. [5] showed that the PTSP is a NP-Complete problem, and it's harder than its deterministic version TSP [2,5]. Therefore many approximate methods were proposed to solve the PTSP. On the one hand we cite the more effective heuristics considered in the literature: we find the heuristic of nearest neighbor and clarke-wright [23], space filling curve experimentally analyzed in [5], local search heuristics 2-opt and 1-shift [5,6], and other variations of local search heuristics were proposed in [17]. On the other hand a wide variety of meta-heuristics were proposed for the PTSP, we cite for example, simulated annealing [2,8], different type of ant colony system [6], genetic algorithm [18,19]. Very few papers of exact algorithms were proposed to solve the PTSP as an integer nonlinear programming formulation and a Branch and Cut [4,15].

Compared to the literature on the PTSP, there is very little work, which is interested in the parallelization of the PTSP. In this paper, we propose paral-lelization strategies for the PTSP in a multi-core environment. In the context of NP-Complete problems, computation time is an important factor as the sequen-tial versions show. The development of powerful machines in general with several processors directs us to study a parallel version for this method of exact resolution that we have already developed.

Technological evolution has reduced the production costs of the various components of a processor. The technological level achieved is such that it is now possible to build multiprocessor architectures and use them efficiently while increasing their performance in terms of computation time, volume and reliability. Among the main motivations for parallelization of the algorithms, we can mention the performance gain, the adequacy to real-time processing. In this paper, we adapt two parallelizations of this exact method which are, on the one hand, the parallelization of the evaluations "node of tree". On the other hand the parallelization of the algorithm Branch and Bound associated with Karp partitioning algorithm.

The paper is organized as follows: Sect. 2 presents a sequential Branch and Bound algorithm. Section 3 offers background on process of parallelization. Section 4 elaborates on parallelization of exact resolution Branch and Bound algorithm. Section 5 elaborates on parallelization of Karp combined with Branch and Bound. Section 6 reports on the experimental evaluation of the proposed strategies and conclusions are given in Sect. 7.

2   Sequential Branch and Bound Algorithm

We present here the exact Branch and Bound algorithm [1], in order to solve the instances of PTSP. The global idea is to perform a depth-first traversal of a binary tree by assigning to each branch a probabilistic evaluation. We consider C the distance matrix between the cities (Table 1).

Table 1. Example of distance matrix

$$C=\begin{array}{c|c|c|c|c|}
 & A & B & C & D \\
\hline
A & \infty & d_{AB} & d_{AC} & d_{AD} \\
\hline
B & d_{BA} & \infty & d_{BC} & d_{BD} \\
\hline
C & d_{CA} & d_{CB} & \infty & d_{CD} \\
\hline
D & d_{DA} & d_{DB} & d_{DC} & \infty \\
\hline
\end{array}$$

This exact algorithm for solution of the PTSP proposed by Amar et al. [1], is based on the expected length of a tour that introduced by Jaillet [13]. Let $d(i,j)$ be a distance between the nodes $i =' 123.. = ABCD..'$, $j =' 123.. = ABCD.'$, and $p = P(k)\ \forall k \in T$, $q = 1 - p$ is the probability of presence, the expected length of a tour $T = 1,...n$ is shown by the Eq. 1.

$$E(L_T) = p^2 \sum_{r=0}^{n-2} q^r \sum_{i=1}^{n} d(i, T^r(i))$$

Where $T^r(i)$ is the successor number r of i in the tour T.

This design takes the form of "Branch and Bound of Little et al. [16]" but in the probabilistic framework, by deriving the equations of the evaluations, in order to direct the search space towards the promising sub-spaces (i.e., the possibility of finding the optimal solution is very feasible). In the same manner of Littel's algorithm for the TSP, we reduce the matrix. The lower bound for the TSP equals Ev_{TSP}, which will help us to calculate the initial evaluation for the PTSP.

$$Ev_{TSP}(n) = \sum_{i=1}^{n} \min R_i + \sum_{j=1}^{n} \min C_j \qquad (2)$$

where R_i is the ith row and C_i is the jth column.

Let $G = (V, E, C)$ be a graph such as $|V| = n$, V is the set of vertices, E the set of edges and C is distance matrix. The probabilistic evaluation $P.E_{PTSP}$: which is defined as follows is considered as a lower evaluation for the PTSP

$$P.E_{\mathbb{R}} = P.Ev_{PTSP}(n) = Ev_{TSP}(n)(p^2 \sum_{r=0}^{n-2} q^r)$$

$$= Ev_{TSP}(n)p(1 - q^{n-1}) \qquad (3)$$

This first evaluation associated with the root $\mathbb{R}$ of the tree shown in Fig. 1. Then, for the next two nodes of the tree Amar et al. [1] give the next two transitional probabilistic evaluations due to choice of an arc, according to its effect on the construction of the optimal tour. For the arc AB(the same for other arcs):

1. Choose AB: increase the expected length of the tour at least by

$$P.Ev_{AB} = P.Ev_{\mathbb{R}} + p^2 \sum_{r=1}^{n-2} q^r [\min_{X \neq A}^{(r)} d(A, X)]$$

$$+ p^2 Ev_{TSP_{Next}} \qquad (4)$$

Where $Ev_{TSP_{Next}}$ is the evaluation of resulting matrix for the TSP where row A and column B are removed.

2. Not choose AB: increase the expected length of the tour at least by

$$P.Ev_{\overline{AB}} = P.Ev_{\mathbb{R}} + p^2 [\min_{K \neq B}^{(1)} d(A, K)$$

$$+ \min_{K \neq A}^{(1)} (d(K, B))] + p^2 \sum_{r=2}^{n-2} q^r [\min_{X \neq K}^{(r)} d(A, X)$$

$$+ \min_{X \neq B}^{(r)} d(K, X)] \qquad (5)$$

$P.Ev_{\overline{AB}}$ represents the probabilistic penalty cost for the arc $\overline{AB}$, $min^{(i)} d(A, X)$ is the ith minimum of row A, n is the size of the initial matrix, these formulas are valid for all iterations.

The construction starts from the root of the tree, which equals $P.E_{\mathbb{R}}$. The problem is divided into two sub-problems with the approach(depth-first, breadth-first) according to the probabilistic penalties cost. After the penalty calculation, it is easily to get the biggest probabilistic penalty cost. So, we separate according to this arc. First remove the row, column and replace the chosen *arc* by ∞ to prohibiting the parasitic circuits (Table 2).

Table 2. Probabilistic penalty cost

$$
C_{reduced}=
\begin{array}{c|ccccc}
 & A & B & C & D \\
\hline
A & \infty & 0^{(P.Ev_{\overline{AB}})} & - & - \\
B & - & \infty & - & 0^{(P.Ev_{\overline{BD}})} \\
C & 0^{(P.Ev_{\overline{CA}})} & - & \infty & - \\
D & - & - & 0^{(P.Ev_{\overline{DC}})} & \infty \\
\end{array}
$$

According to this probabilistic penalty calculation we construct the first branching of the tree, which is shown in Fig. 1.

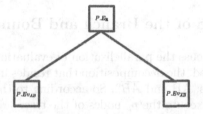

Fig. 1. Branching of the tree

The search continues until all branches have been visited either eliminated or the end of the process is reached. That is, the present evaluation is less than the all evaluations, which are defined by the expected length of each final branch by profiting that the expected length can be calculated in $O(n^2)$ time Jaillet [13].

3 Process of Parallelization

The process of parallelization of an algorithm goes through three essential steps. The first is to split the sequential algorithm into tasks (instruction or group of instructions). The size of these tasks defines "granularity". The parallelization of programs could be achieved at several levels of granularity. The granularity reflects the number of operations performed by each processor compared to the total number of parallel program operations. In general, there are three basic types of granularity that we can specify as follows. Fine granularity: the decomposition of the program can be done at the level of the instructions or operations.

Medium granularity: it is a medium granularity, it is between the fine granularity and the coarse granularity, where the parallelization can be done at the level of a block or a set of instructions. Coarse granularity: this time the decomposition is done at the level of procedures or modules in a program.

The performance of a parallel algorithm is evaluated through the following two factors: acceleration "speed-up" and efficiency [10].

The speed-up is defined by the ratio $s_p = \frac{t_s}{t_p}$. It evaluates the gain in time between the sequential and parallel versions, i.e., the time deviation between the two versions.

The efficiency of a parallel algorithm is defined by the ratio $e_p = \frac{s_p}{p_p}$. The e_p efficiency is in fact, the average rate of processor usage. We proceed to the elaboration of a graph of temporal precedence called task graph, in order to represent, in fact, the relations of precedence and independence of the tasks. In the next sections, we discuss two strategies for parallelization the Branch and Bound algorithm for the PTSP. This parallelization represents our originality. In the first place, we adapt an approach in which the calculation of the evaluations is parallelized. In second, the parallelization of the algorithm Branch and Bound associated with the notion of partitioning introduced by Karp.

4   Parallelization of the Branch and Bound Algorithm

In this part, we will discuss the parallelization of evaluations for the Branch and Bound algorithm. Indeed, the decomposition that resides in the creation of nodes of the tree "evaluations: AB and $\overline{AB}$". So according to the available processors p_p we simultaneously execute the p_p nodes of the tree.

Here we solve an example to illustrate the process. For each node of tree each processor calculates the penalty and the evaluations that is described through the following equations:

$$P.Ev_{AB} = P.Ev_{\mathbb{R}} + p^2 \sum_{r=1}^{n-2} q^r [\min_{X \neq A}^{(r)} d(A, X)] + p^2 Ev_{TSP_{Next}} \tag{6}$$

$$P.Ev_{\overline{AB}} = P.Ev_{\mathbb{R}} + p^2 [\min_{K \neq B}^{(1)} d(A, K) + \min_{K \neq A}^{(1)} (d(K, B))]$$
$$+ p^2 \sum_{r=2}^{n-2} q^r [\min_{X \neq K}^{(r)} d(A, X) + \min_{X \neq B}^{(r)} d(K, X)] \tag{7}$$

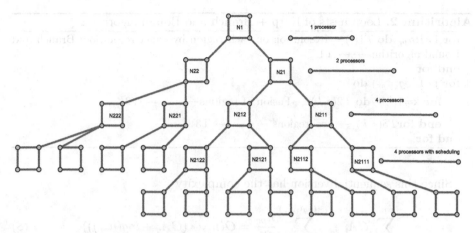

Fig. 2. Precedence graph for the parallelization of the nodes of the tree. Ni represents the node number i in each level

---

Algorithm 1. Parallel version

> **while** Conditions are not verified **do** In each level we create a number of nodes equal to a number of available processors.
> Each processor must do
>   – penalties cost
>   – evaluations
> **end while**

The nodes are independent, so it is easy to parallelize them as shown in Fig. 2. Finally, the last step is to assign the previously described tasks to the processors of the machine on which the processing is taking place. This step, better known as the scheduling problem, greatly affects the performance (speed-up and efficiency) of parallel algorithm.

5 Parallelization of Karp Combined with Branch and Bound Algorithm

The Karp partitioning algorithm was initially introduced by Karp [14] in 1977 For the TSP. It consists in partitioning the space of the points into much smaller spaces and to apply any search method on each of these sub-spaces. It is then sufficient to construct the overall solution from the obtained solutions. This method consists of subdividing the plane (in our case) into a number of 2^k under generally square planes. Each one would be separately treated using the Branch and Bound algorithm.

The Karp partitioning algorithm combined with Branch and Bound Algorithm is nests of loops, as shown in the Algorithm 2.

Algorithm 2. Loop nests of Karp + Branch and Bound algorithm

for i=1:n_{pr} do $T1(i)$ —Resolution on each region by exact resolution: Branch and Bound algorithm——↦ T1
end for
for j=1:$log(n_{pr})$ do
    for k=1:$\frac{n_{pr}}{2^j}$ do $T2(j,k)$ —Fusion of regions————↦ T2
    end for$T3(j,k)$ —new regions ————↦ T3
end for

Since this sequential version has the complexity

$$\sum_{i=1}^{i=n_{pr}} CA_i + \sum_{i=1}^{i=log(n_{pr})} \frac{n_{pr}}{2^i} = O(n_{pr} * (CA_g + log(n_{pr}))) \tag{8}$$

where n_{pr} is the number of partitions and CA_g the complexity of algorithm A to complete the largest region.

This complexity in practice represents the execution time, hence the interest of the parallelization of the algorithm. First, we transform the Karp partitioning algorithm into a perfect nests of loops by using the fusion in the same level as shown in the version LMN in the Algorithm 3. Then we will apply program automatic parallelization [7,20,21]. By choosing coarse granularity for reasons of practical efficiency. Indeed, since n_{pr} can be large, it is more interesting to assign all the available processors to the process iterations of the (first) parallel loop L in Algorithm 3. The parallel Karp + Branch and Bound algorithm can be written as follows:

Algorithm 3. Parallel loops

    for L=1:n_{pr} do $T1(L)$ —parallel loop
    end for
    for M=1:$log(n_{pr})$ do
        for N=1:$\frac{n_{pr}}{2^M}$ do $T2(M,N)$—1th sequential loop and 2th parallel loop
        end for
    end for

First, if the number of available processors equals n_{pr}, each processor will be associated with a specific partition of the nest's iteration space. So Karp + Branch and Bound algorithm has parallel complexity

$$CA_g + log(n_{pr})CF = O(CA_g)$$

where CF the complexity of merging the two major regions.

Second, if the number of partitions is greater than the number of processors, then we must play on the scheduling, that is the assignment of tasks to the different processors. This method consists in assigning a task not yet processed to the first free processor. So there is a p_p number of available processors, let $n_{pr} = p_p \times q_q + r_r$ be the Euclidean division of n_{pr} by p_p. We then assign each of the first r_r processors to the processing of $q_q + 1$ partitions, and each of the remaining $p_p - r_r$ processors to the processing of q_q partitions. We will then have a parallel complexity:

$$\begin{cases} (q_q + 1) \times CA_g, & \text{if } r_r \neq 0, \\ q_q \times CA_g, & \text{if } r_r = 0. \end{cases}$$

6   Numerical Results

In this numerical part, we want to validate our contribution and evaluate its practical interest, through a realization of a series of experiments on a set of input of different sizes. For these parallel experiments, we used OpenMP library [22], of shared memory to ensure the communication between the processors through the programming language C. We chose 4 values for the number of cores p_p, namely 2, 4, 6 and 8 on a multicore architecture. The implementation was made through a machine whose characteristics are: Intel(R) Xeon(R) E5-2630 v3(2.40 GHz) processor, number of cores is 8, with operating system Windows 7. For the first experiment, we perform the first strategy that resides in the parallelization of nodes of tree which used in the Branch and Bound algorithm. We found the results shown in Fig. 3.

On problems of size n, number of points equals 10, 20 and 30 with $p = \{0.1, 0.5, 0.7, 0.9\}$ (we have a 10-run average for each experience). The Fig. 3, presents the speed-up obtained for different values of the number of points n and also for Branch and Bound algorithm. The analysis of this figure shows that the speed-ups improve when n increases (for a fixed number of processors p_p), and also with the number of processors p_p (for a fixed number of points n), and that the execution time is well diminished. More precisely, the Fig. 3 clearly shows that we have good speed-up and that speed-up is an increasing function as a function of the number of processors. These experiments were made with several probabilities and several sizes of points. So this allows us to conclude that the gain in execution time is considerable, in fact, compared to a sequential implementation this gain is imposing.

The second is the parallelization strategy of the partitioning of Karp algorithm on a parallel machine. First case where the number of processors is equal to the number of partitions, the size of the PTSP n ranging from 20 to 100. The experiment results found were shown in the Fig. 4.

For the second experiment, the number of partitions is greater than the number of processors. As we have already mentioned, we must then play on the scheduling, that is the assignment of tasks to the different processors. In this case, for Karp + Branch and Bound algorithm, the size of the PTSP n ranging from 50 to 200 with a 50 interval. We notice that for most instances, the speed-up uniformly increases with n_{pr}. According to the Figs. 4 and 5 this parallelization of the partitioning algorithm of Karp is efficient if one wants to obtain a considerable gain in time.

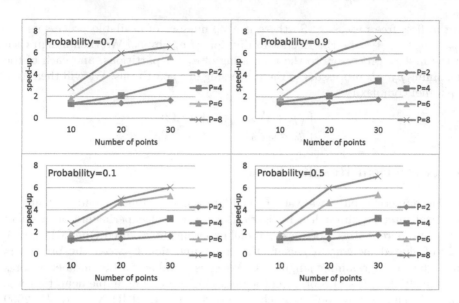

Fig. 3. Average speed-up with $p_p = 2$, 4, 6 and 8 for Branch and Bound algorithm

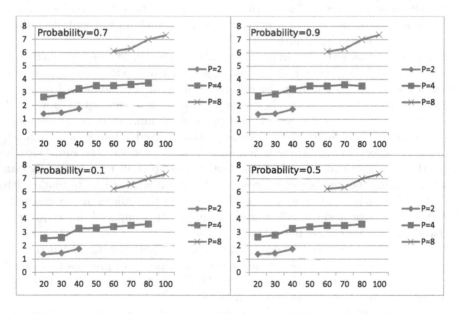

Fig. 4. Average speed-up if $n_{pr} = p_p$ Karp+ Branch and Bound algorithm

After this series of experiments and the measurements carried out as shows the in Figs. 4 and 5, we can conclude that the parallelization strategies gave satisfactory results. It is clear that these parallelization strategies considerably speed up the execution by distributing the calculations on the different processors.

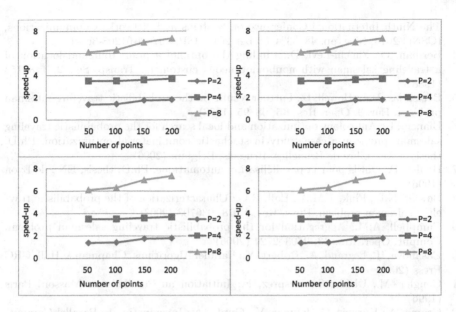

Fig. 5. Average speed-up if $n_{pr} > p_p$ for Karp+ Branch and Bound algorithm

7   Conclusion and Future Work

In this paper, a parallel exact Branch and Bound algorithm was proposed for solution of the PTSP, where, this probabilistic problem can be used to model many real-world applications. It is a NP-Complete problem, hence the interest of the parallelization of Branch and Bound algorithm. Two parallelization strategies were subsequently developed. The performances evaluated through a series of experiments carried out in a multicore machine. The proposed parallel strategies have been well adapted for the Branch and Bound algorithm. Indeed, satisfactory results have been obtained in terms of speed-up, through multiple tests with different sizes and various probabilities. For the future, we plan to investigate a parallel implementation with massive grids. Also, the use of services and resources in cloud computing assuming that a large number of computers with different characteristics is available.

References

1. Amar, M.A., Khaznaji, W., Bellalouna, M.: An exact resolution for the probabilistic traveling salesman problem under the a priori strategy. In: International Conference on Computational Science, Zurich, Switzerland, vol. 108C, pp. 1414–1423 (2017)
2. Bellalouna, M.: Problèmes d'optimisation combinatoire probabilistes. Ph.D. thesis, Ecole Nationale des Ponts et Chaussées, Paris, France (1993)
3. Bellalouna, M., Gharbi, A., Khaznaji, W.: The k-means and TSP based mobility protocol modeling as a probabilistic combinatorial optimization problem. In:

The Ninth International Conference on Systems and Networks Communications, ICSNC 2014, Nice, pp. 48–53, October 2014. ISBN 978-1-61208-368-1

4. Berman, O., Simchi-Levi, D.: Finding the optimal a priori tour and location of a traveling salesman with nonhomogeneous customers. Transp. Sci. **2**, 148–154 (1988)

5. Bertsimas, D.J., Howell, L.: Further results on the probabilistic traveling salesman problem. Eur. J. Oper. Res. **65**, 68–95 (1993)

6. Bianchi, L.: Ant colony optimization and local search for the probabilistic traveling salesman problem: a case study in stochastic combinatorial optimization. Ph.D. thesis, Univ. Libre de Bruxelles, Brussels, Belgium (2006)

7. Boulet, P.: Outils pour la parallélisation automatique. Ph.D. thesis, ENS de Lyon (1996)

8. Bowler, N.E., Fink, T.M.A., Ball, R.C.: Characterization of the probabilistic traveling salesman problem. Phys. Rev. E **68**, 036703 (2003)

9. Campbell, A.M.: Aggregation for the probabilistic traveling salesman problem. Comput. Oper. Res. **33**, 2703–2724 (2006)

10. Casanova, H., Legrand, A., Robert, Y.: Parallel Algorithms. Chapman & Hall/CRC Press (2008)

11. Gengler, M., Ubéda, S., Desprez, F.: Initiation au Parallélisme. Masson, Paris (1996)

12. Grama, A., Karypis, G., Kumar, V., Gupta, A.: Introduction to Parallel Computing. Addison Wesley, Boston (2003)

13. Jaillet, P.: The probabilistic traveling salesman problems. Technical report 185, operations research, Ph.D. thesis, MIT, Cambridge (1985)

14. Karp, R.M.: The probabilistic analysis of partitioning algorithms for the traveling salesman problem in the plane. Math. Oper. Res. **2**, 209–224 (1977)

15. Laporte, G., Louveaux, F., Mercure, H.: An exact solution for the a priori optimization of the probabilistic traveling salesman problem. Oper. Res. **42**, 543–549 (1994)

16. Little, J.D.C., Murat, K.G., Sweeney, D., Karel, M.: An algorithm for traveling salesman problem. Oper. Res. **11**, 972–989 (1963)

17. Liu, Y.H.: Diversified local search strategy under scatter search framework for the probabilistic traveling salesman problem. Eur. J. Oper. Res. **191**, 332–346 (2008)

18. Liu, Y.H.: Different initial solution generators in genetic algorithms for solving the probabilistic traveling salesman problem. Appl. Math. Comput. **216**, 125–137 (2010)

19. Liu, Y.H., Jou, R.C., Wang, C.-J.: Genetic algorithms for the probabilistic traveling salesman problem. In: Proceedings of the Conference on E-logistics, pp. 77–82. Taoyuan, Taiwan (2004)

20. Mabrouk, B.B., Hasni, H., Mahjoub, Z.: On a parallel algorithm for the determination of multiple optimal solutions for the LCSS problem. In: Carretero, J., Garcia-Blas, J., Ko, R.K.L., Mueller, P., Nakano, K. (eds.) ICA3PP 2016. LNCS, vol. 10048, pp. 440–448. Springer, Cham (2016). https://doi.org/10.1007/978-3-319-49583-5_33

21. Megson, G.M., Chen, X.: Automatic Parallelization for a Class of Regular Computations. World Scientific Publishing Co., River Edge (1997)

22. Quin, M.J.: Parallel programming in C with MPI and OpenMP. International edn. McGraw-Hill Higher Education, Pennsylvania (2003)

23. Rossi, F.A., Gavioli, I.: Aspects of heuristic methods in the probabilistic traveling salesman problem. In: Advanced School on Statistics in Combinatorial Optimization, pp. 214–227 (1987)

Accelerating Artificial Bee Colony Algorithm with Elite Neighborhood Learning

Xinyu Zhou[✉], Yunan Liu, Yong Ma, Mingwen Wang,
and Jianyi Wan

School of Computer and Information Engineering, Jiangxi Normal University,
Nanchang 330022, China
xyzhou@whu.edu.cn

Abstract. Artificial bee colony (ABC) algorithm has been shown good performance over many optimization problems. For some complex optimization problems, however, ABC often suffers from a slow convergence speed, because it is good at exploration but poor at exploitation. To achieve a better tradeoff between the exploration and exploitation capabilities, we introduce the breadth-first search (BFS) framework and depth-first search (DFS) framework into different phases of ABC respectively. The BFS framework is combined with the employed bee phase to focus on the exploration, while the DFS framework is integrated into the onlooker bee phase to concentrate on exploitation. After that, an elite neighborhood learning (ENL) strategy is proposed to enhance the information exchange between the employed bee phase and the onlooker bee phase, because in ABC the employed bees cannot well communicate with the onlooker bees which may also cause slow convergence speed. Extensive experiments are conducted on 22 well-known test functions, and six well-established ABC variants are included in the comparison. The results showed that our approach can effectively accelerate the convergence speed and significantly perform better on the majority of test functions.

Keywords: Artificial bee colony · Breadth-first search framework
Depth-first search framework · Elite neighborhood learning

1 Introduction

Artificial bee colony (ABC) algorithm was developed by Karaboga in 2005 [1], which simulates the intelligent foraging behavior of honey bee swarm. However, similar to other evolutionary algorithms (EAs), ABC also tends to suffer from the problem of poor convergence. The possible reason is that the solution search equation, which is used to generate new candidate solutions, has good exploration capability but poor exploitation capability, and thereby it causes the problem of slow convergence speed. Therefore, how to accelerate the convergence of the ABC algorithm is crucial for improving the performance of ABC.

To improve the performance of ABC, many ABC variants have been developed in the last few years. Zhu *et al.* [2] modified the solution search equation based on particle swarm optimization (PSO) and proposed Gbest-guided ABC (GABC) algorithm.

© Springer Nature Switzerland AG 2018
J. Vaidya and J. Li (Eds.): ICA3PP 2018, LNCS 11334, pp. 449–464, 2018.
https://doi.org/10.1007/978-3-030-05051-1_31

Inspired by the mutation strategies of differential evolution (DE), Gao *et al.* [3] proposed a modified ABC (MABC) algorithm based on their new proposed search equation, i.e., ABC/best/1. Yu *et al.* [4] designed an adaptive greedy position update strategy in their proposed AABC algorithm. Zhou *et al.* [5] proposed a new ABC variant (GBABC) by replacing the original solution search equation with a Gaussian bare-bones search equation. Based on the elite group, Cui *et al.* [6] designed a novel ABC algorithm with depth-first search framework and elite-guided search equation (DFSABC-elite), in which the global best individual is used as well. Very recently, draw inspiration from the DFSABC-elite algorithm, Kong *et al.* [7] proposed a novel ABC algorithm (ECABC) based on elite group guidance and the combined breadth-depth search strategy, in which a modified neighborhood search equation is designed by utilizing the center of the elite group. Xiang *et al.* [8] proposed an attractive force model based on the gravity and combined it with multiple solution search equations in their proposed ABC variant (ABCG).

Although the aforementioned improved ABC variants have achieved good results, there still exist some insufficiencies for ABC, such as slow convergence speed and easily be trapped into local minima on complex optimization problems. To solve some of these insufficiencies, we propose a modified ABC with elite neighborhood learning strategy, named ENLABC, to effectively accelerate the convergence speed of ABC. In the ENLABC, the breadth-depth search (BFS) framework and depth-first search (DFS) framework are integrated into the employed bee phase and the onlooker bee phase, respectively. The BFS framework aims to focus on the exploration, while the DFS framework is utilized to concentrate on exploitation. After that, an elite neighborhood learning (ENL) strategy is designed based on the global neighborhood search (GNS) operator which has shown effectiveness in previous works. The ENL strategy is helpful to enhance the information exchange between the employed bee phase and the onlooker bee phase. To validate the performance of ENLABC, 22 well-known test functions are used in the experiments, and the experimental results are compared with other six well-established ABC variants, such as AABC [4], GBABC [5], DFSABC-elite [6], ABCG [8], and ENCABC [7]. The comparison results show that ENLABC outperforms or at least comparable to the competitors on most of test functions.

2   Related Work

2.1   The Original ABC

ABC is a swarm intelligence-based algorithm that mimics the intelligent foraging behavior of honeybee swarms. In ABC, honeybees can be divided into three groups: employed bees, onlooker bees, and scout bees. Therefore, the entire search process is accordingly divided into three phases. It is worth noting that, similar to other EAs, ABC also starts with SN randomly generated food sources as initialization. Each food source $X_i = (x_{i,1}, x_{i,2}, ..., x_{i,D})$ corresponds to a candidate solution to the optimization problem, and D indicates the size of the problem. The three stages of ABC are described below.

Initialization. In this phase, an initial population containing SN food source positions (solutions) is generated according to Eq. (1).

$$x_{i,j} = x_j^{min} + rand(0,1) \cdot (x_j^{max} - x_j^{min}) \tag{1}$$

where $i = 1, 2, \cdots, SN$ and $j = 1, 2, \cdots, D$. The two variable x_j^{min} and x_j^{max} denote the lower and upper bounds of the jth dimension, respectively. $rand(0,1)$ is a random number in the range [0, 1]. Without loss of generality, we assume that the objective optimization problem is a minimization problem. After that, the fitness of each solution X_i represented by fit_i is calculated according to Eq. (2).

$$fit_i = \begin{cases} \frac{1}{1+f(x_i)} & \text{if} (f(x_i) \geq 0) \\ 1 + abs(f(x_i)) & \text{otherwise} \end{cases} \tag{2}$$

where fit_i is the fitness value of the ith food source X_i, and $f(X_i)$ is the objective function value of food source X_i for the optimization problem.

Employed Bee Phase. The employed bees are responsible for exploring the sources of food near the hive. After all of the employed bees have completed the search, they will share information on the number of nectars with the onlooker bees on the dance area. Each employed bee generates a candidate solution $V_i = (v_{i,1}, v_{i,2}, ..., v_{i,D})$ according to Eq. (3).

$$v_{i,j} = x_{i,j} + \emptyset_{i,j} \cdot (x_{i,j} - x_{k,j}) \tag{3}$$

where $i = 1, 2, ..., SN$ and $j = 1, 2, \cdots, D$. $k \in \{1, 2, ..., SN\}$ and it has to be different from i. $\emptyset_{i,j}$ is a random number in the range [- 1, 1]. If $v_{i,j}$ beyond the bound, it will be randomly generated according Eq. (1).

Onlooker Bee Phase. After all employed bees complete the search process, the onlooker bees start to perform search on a chosen food source, and the used solution search equation is the same as Eq. (3). It's worth to note that whether a food source can be chosen is related to the selection probability, and the selection probability value can be calculated by the following Eq. (4).

$$p_i = \frac{fit_i}{\sum_{j=1}^{SN} fit_j} \tag{4}$$

where fit_i is the fitness value of solution X_i, which is proportional to the nectar amount of the ith food source. If a new food source beyond the bound, it will be randomly generated according Eq. (1).

Scout Bee Phase. In this phase, when a food source is exhausted by a honey bee through several consecutive iterations, then this scout bee will seek a new food source randomly according to Eq. (1) on all dimensions.

2.2   DFSABC-Elite Algorithm

Breadth-first search (BFS) framework and depth-first search (DFS) framework are two typical search models in the EAs. Generally speaking, from the perspective of designing EAs, BFS emphasizes on exploration, while DFS focuses on exploitation. Very recently, Cui et al. [6] proposed a modified ABC variant, called DFSABC-elite, based on the DFS framework and a novel elite-guided search equation. In DFSABC-elite, for each generation, only some randomly selected solutions are searched in the employed bee phase, which is different from that all solutions are exploited in the original ABC. In the onlooker bee phase, only the top T elite solutions are selected by onlooker bees to search, where $T = p \cdot SN$ and p is a real number in the range [0, 1]. What's more, the number of onlooker bees in DFSABC-elite is not SN but $r \cdot T$, $r \in \{1, 2, 3, \cdots, \text{ceil}(1/p)\}$, and parameter r can control the computing resource allocation. For the parameter p, Cui et al. provided an empirical value 0.1 [6].

In DFSABC-elite, in order to further improve the performance of ABC, the useful information of some good solutions is utilized in two novel designed solution search equations which are introduced into employed bee phase and onlooker bee phase respectively. The two solution search equations are described as follows:

$$v_{i,j} = x_{e,j} + \emptyset_{i,j} \cdot \left(x_{e,j} - x_{k,j} \right) \tag{5}$$

$$v_{e,j} = \frac{1}{2} \left(x_{e,j} + x_{best,j} \right) + \emptyset_{e,j} \cdot \left(x_{best,j} - x_{k,j} \right) \tag{6}$$

where X_e is randomly chosen from the elite solutions (the top T solutions), X_k is randomly selected from the population, and X_e and X_k are distinct and both of them are different from X_i. X_{best} is the current best solution in the population, $\emptyset_{i,j}$ and $\emptyset_{e,j}$ are two random real numbers within $[-1, 1]$. The pseudo-code of the complete DFSABC-elite can be referred to the literature [6].

3   Our Approach

3.1   Elite Neighborhood Learning Strategy

When solving complex optimization problems, ABC often suffers from the problem of premature convergence that its individuals easily be trapped into local optima. A possible reason behind this is that the search step size is too large, so that the true solution may be skipped with a high probability. However it is worth to note that some of the local optima are very close to the global optimum, if an individual is unfortunately trapped by one of them, searching the neighborhoods of this individual would be helpful to find better solutions or even the global optimum.

After observing this, different neighborhood search operators have been designed, and they also have been shown effectiveness in some EAs [9–12]. Especially, Wang et al. [9] presented an efficient global neighborhood search (GNS) operator to improve particle swarm optimization (PSO) algorithm. During searching the neighborhood of a food source X_i in the GNS operator, a trial solution TX_i can be generated using the following equation:

$$TX_i = r_1 \cdot X_i + r_2 \cdot gbest + r_3 \cdot (X_a - X_b) \tag{7}$$

where r_1, r_2, and r_3 are three mutually exclusive numbers distributed randomly in [0, 1], and they have to accord with the condition: $r_1 + r_2 + r_3 = 1$. $gbest$ is the global best solution of the entire population, a and b are two indexes of the randomly selected food sources and they have to different from i. Note that, in the GNS operator, $gbest$ is employed as a component in the equation. Although the utilization of $gbest$ is indeed beneficial to enhance the exploitation, it may also run the risk of causing the algorithm too greedy. Therefore, in order to retain the exploitation but without losing exploration, we propose a modified GNS operator, i.e., the ENL strategy.

In general, $gbest$ plays an important role during the search process, it may gradually approach the global optimum solution to an optimization problem. However, for some complex problems, there exist many local optima solutions which raise huge challenges for EAs. In such circumstances, the fitness landscape would be very rugged, and $gbest$ may be near to one of the local optima solutions rather than the global optimum solution. At this time, the utilization of $gbest$ is no more a good choice, and it may causes the problem of premature convergence. To alleviate the problem to some extent, we attempt to utilize the elite solutions instead of $gbest$ in the ENL strategy. Based on the search equation in the GNS operator, we propose a modified version by utilizing elite solutions, which is listed as the following equation:

$$TX_i = r_1 \cdot X_i + r_2 \cdot X_e + r_3 \cdot (X_a - X_b) \tag{8}$$

where r_1, r_2, and r_3 are three mutually exclusive numbers distributed randomly in [0, 1], and they have to accord with the condition: $r_1 + r_2 + r_3 = 1$. X_e is an elite solution randomly selected from the top T elite solutions ($T = p \cdot SN$ and $p = 0.1$). a and b are two indexes of the randomly selected food sources from non-elite solutions and they have to be different from i.

3.2   ENLABC Algorithm

In this subsection, we propose a modified ABC variant, called ENLABC, by combining three components: the BFS framework, the DFS framework, and the ENL strategy. From internal mechanism of the original ABC, it can be observed that the employed bees play the role of exploring while the onlooker bees exploiting. Similarly, as mentioned, the BFS framework emphasizes on exploration, but the DFS framework focuses on exploitation. Therefore, we use BFS in the employed bee phase and DFS in the onlooker bee phase. By doing this, the modified employed bee phase and onlooker bee phase can complement each other. The pseudo-code of the complete ENLABC is demonstrated in the Algorithm 1.

In the employed bee phase, each bee will participate in search process one by one. And they generate candidate solutions learning from a randomly selected elite solution at one dimension by Eq. (5). These solutions will be close to the elite solution and be better than its parent solution with a high probability. In the onlooker bee phase, a control parameter *flag* is set to 1. The parameter can control whether the updated food source is replaced. If *flag* == 1, a solution X_e is chosen randomly from the elite solutions to generate a candidate solution V_e by using Eq. (6) [6]. Only when the candidate solution V_e worse than X_e, the *flag* is set to 0 and X_e will be renew at the next search. Otherwise, X_e will be updated continuously.

Although the employed bees utilized new search equation Eq. (5) to generate candidate solutions, they explore only one direction (dimension) at a time, which like search model of the original ABC. What is more, the directions employed bees searched for are not necessarily what onlooker bees will be searching for, because both the two directions are generated randomly. This makes the two phases of the work not closely linked. Especially in the onlooker bee phase using the DFS framework, if one direction dose not suffers from failed search, it will continue searching until it does not find a better solution and reduce the chances of performing searches in other directions. This makes the algorithm have a slower convergence speed.

In order to enhance the relationship between the two phases and accelerate the convergence of the algorithm, we introduce the ENL strategy to the employed bee phase with. When every search for solutions is completed, the ENL strategy will be executed with a probability P_{enl}, $P_{enl} \in (0,1)$. The solution executing the ENL strategy will conduct an omni-directional search, and then this search is beneficial to the convergence of the population. Therefore, the probability P_{enl} may significantly affect the performance of the proposed algorithm. The influence of the probability P_{enl} will be analyzed in Sect. 4.2.

4   Experimental Results and Parameter Analysis

4.1   Benchmark Functions and Parameters Setting

There are 22 well-known benchmark functions with dimension $D = 30$ used in the following experiments, which are also widely used in other work [3, 9, 11].Among these problems, the first 11 functions are unimodal problems, while these unimodal functions can be used to test the convergence speed of the algorithms. The global optimums of all of these problems are zero. F05 is the Rosenbrock function which is unimodal for $D = 2$ and 3 but is multimodal in high dimension cases. F06 is a discontinuous step function, and F07 is a noisy quartic function. The remaining ones are more complex multimodal functions. All functions are summarized briefly in Table 1.

All experiments are conducted with dimension $D = 30, 50, 100$ for all the functions. Each algorithm is run 25 times independently for each function, and the mean results are used in comparison. Moreover, we make use of the Wilcoxon's rank sum test at $\alpha = 0.05$ to evaluate the statistical significance of the results in Sect. 4.4.

For each algorithm, we have set the population size $SN = 75$ uniformly, the terminal condition $MaxFEs = 5000 \times D$, and other parameters are set empirical values according to the experiments of their original papers. In this paper, the probability P_{enl} will be determined in next subsection.

Algorithm 1: The procedure of ENLABC
1   Generate *SN* solutions by Eq. (1) $\{X_i \mid i = 1, 2, \ldots, SN\}$ as the initial population;
2     $FEs = SN$;
3   **WHILE** $FEs < MaxFEs$
4   /* Employed bee phase*/
5   **FOR** $i = 1$ to SN
6   Generate a new candidate solution V_i according to Eq. (5);
7         $FEs = FEs + 1$;
8   **IF** V_i is better than its parent X_i **THEN**
9   Replace X_i with V_i;
10          $trial_e = 0$;
11   **ELSE**
12          $trial_e = trial_e + 1$;
13   **END IF**
14   /* The elite neighborhood learning strategy*/
15   **IF** $rand(0,1) < P_{enl}$ **THEN**
16   Generate a trial solution TX_i according to Eq. (8)
17           $FEs = FEs + 1$
18   **IF** TX_i is better than its parent X_i **THEN**
19   Replace X_i with TX_i;
20   **END IF**
21   **END IF**
22   **END FOR**
23   /* Onlooker bee phase*/
24       $flag = 1$;
25   **FOR** $i=1$ to rT /* $r \in \{X_i \mid i = 1, 2, \ldots, ceil(1/p)\}$ */
26   **IF** $flag == 1$
27   Randomly choose an elite individual from elite group for using Eq. (6);
28   **END IF**
29   Generate a new solution V_e according to Eq. (6);
30         $FEs = FEs + 1$;
31   **IF** V_e is better than its parent X_e **THEN**
32   Replace X_e with V_e;
33           $trial_e = 0, flag = 0$;
34   **ELSE**
35           $trial_e = trial_e + 1, \; flag = 1$;
36   **END IF**
37   **END FOR**
38   /* Scout bee phase*/
39   Choose the solution X_{max} with $trial_{max}$
40   **IF** $trial_{max} > limit$ **THEN**
41   Replace X_{max} with a new solution generated according to Eq. (1)
42         $FEs = FEs + 1$;
43   **END IF**
44   **END WHILE**

Table 1. The 22 benchmark functions used in the experiments

Func.	Name	Search range	Func.	Name	Search range
F01	Sphere	[− 100, 100]	F12	Schwefel 2.26	[− 500, 500]
F02	Schwefel 2.22	[− 10, 10]	F13	Rastrigin	[− 5.12, 5.12]
F03	Schwefel 1.2	[− 100, 100]	F14	Ackley	[− 32, 32]
F04	Schwefel 2.21	[− 100, 100]	F15	Griewank	[− 600, 600]
F05	Rosenbrock	[− 30, 30]	F16	penalized 1	[− 50, 50]
F06	Step	[− 100, 100]	F17	penalized 2	[− 50, 50]
F07	Quartic with noise	[− 1.28, 1.28]	F18	NCRastrigin	[− 5.12, 5.12]
F08	Elliptic	[− 100, 100]	F19	Alpine	[− 10, 10]
F09	SumSquare	[− 10, 10]	F20	Levy	[− 10, 10]
F10	SumPower	[− 1, 1]	F21	Bohachevsky_2	[− 100, 100]
F11	Exponential	[− 1.28, 1.28]	F22	Weierstrass	[− 0.5, 0.5]

Table 2. Testing results of probability P_{enl} at $D = 30$

Func.	$P_{enl} = 0.1$	$P_{enl} = 0.3$	$P_{enl} = 0.5$	$P_{enl} = 0.7$	$P_{enl} = 0.9$
F01	4.06E−52	1.54E−100	3.11E−148	3.43E−191	1.71E−230
F02	1.25E−27	6.23E−52	3.97E−75	3.04E−96	3.17E−116
F03	1.11E−29	1.42E−87	1.98E−137	3.84E−182	8.13E−225
F04	2.22E−16	1.21E−44	9.73E−69	4.65E−91	2.24E−111
F05	2.63E+01	2.48E+01	2.52E+01	2.59E+01	2.66E+01
F06	0.000+00	0.00E+00	0.00E+00	0.00E+00	0.00E+00
F07	2.53E−04	9.96E−05	5.99E−05	4.35E−05	4.51E−05
F08	9.01E−49	1.92E−97	1.51E−144	4.62E−187	7.81E−227
F09	4.95E−53	9.25E−102	5.50E−149	4.23E−191	1.05E−231
F10	4.08E−51	4.96E−84	6.21E−115	1.78E−143	8.71E−170
F11	0.00E+00	0.00E+00	0.00E+00	0.00E+00	0.00E+00
F12	3.82E−04	3.82E−04	3.82E−04	3.82E−04	9.48E+00
F13	0.00E+00	0.00E+00	0.00E+00	0.00E+00	0.00E+00
F14	4.44E−16	4.44E−16	4.44E−16	4.44E−16	4.44E−16
F15	0.00E+00	0.00E+00	0.00E+00	0.00E+00	0.00E+00
F16	1.57E−32	1.57E−32	1.57E−32	1.57E−32	1.57E−32
F17	1.35E−32	1.35E−32	1.35E−32	2.20E−03	3.97E−03
F18	0.00E+00	0.00E+00	0.00E+00	0.00E+00	0.00E+00
F19	1.64E−27	5.87E−28	7.57E−76	2.42E−97	5.63E−117
F20	1.35E−31	1.35E−31	1.35E−31	1.35E−31	8.79E−03
F21	0.00E+00	0.00E+00	0.00E+00	0.00E+00	0.00E+00
F22	0.00E+00	0.00E+00	0.00E+00	0.00E+00	0.00E+00

4.2   Influence Analysis of Probability P_{enl}

In this experiment, the probability P_{enl} will be determined on dimension $D = 30, 50, 100$, respectively. It is obvious that the value of P_{enl} determines the frequency of ENL operation in the proposed algorithm. But in the past study, we discovered that the efficiency of the GNS operator have a great relationship with dimension size D of the solutions [10]. Therefore, it is necessary to analyze the influence of probability P_{enl} on different dimension sizes, respectively.

Table 3. Testing results of probability P_{enl} at $D = 50$

Func.	$P_{enl} = 0.1$	$P_{enl} = 0.2$	$P_{enl} = 0.3$	$P_{enl} = 0.4$	$P_{enl} = 0.5$
F01	1.42E−69	1.58E−114	3.61E−158	2.70E−200	6.41E−239
F02	1.01E−35	2.20E−58	2.98E−80	5.65E−101	2.34E−120
F03	6.65E−51	8.42E−102	5.76E−146	7.98E−191	4.29E−230
F04	1.35E−26	8.82E−51	5.63E−74	6.71E−95	1.37E−114
F05	4.57E+01	4.47E+01	4.48E+01	4.54E+01	4.61E+01
F06	0.00E+00	0.00E+00	0.00E+00	0.00E+00	0.00E+00
F07	1.28E−04	7.29E−05	6.15E−05	5.10E−05	3.72E−05
F08	1.33E−65	5.74E−111	1.02E−153	1.22E−195	8.96E−235
F09	1.09E−69	1.99E−115	1.62E−159	1.46E−200	3.87E−239
F10	3.53E−64	2.09E−94	3.14E−124	1.20E−151	9.30E−177
F11	0.00E+00	0.00E+00	0.00E+00	0.00E+00	0.00E+00
F12	6.36E−04	4.74E+00	6.36E−04	4.74E+00	9.48E+00
F13	0.00E+00	0.00E+00	0.00E+00	0.00E+00	0.00E+00
F14	4.44E−16	4.44E−16	4.44E−16	4.44E−16	4.44E−16
F15	0.00E+00	0.00E+00	0.00E+00	0.00E+00	0.00E+00
F16	9.42E−33	9.42E−33	9.42E−33	9.42E−33	9.42E−33
F17	1.35E−32	1.35E−32	1.35E−32	1.32E−03	5.71E−03
F18	0.00E+00	0.00E+00	0.00E+00	0.00E+00	0.00E+00
F19	1.03E−26	1.52E−58	6.42E−81	1.78E−101	8.11E−121
F20	1.35E−31	1.35E−31	1.35E−31	1.35E−31	9.64E−04
F21	0.00E+00	0.00E+00	0.00E+00	0.00E+00	0.00E+00
F22	0.00E+00	0.00E+00	0.00E+00	0.00E+00	0.00E+00

Firstly, we test the possible values of the P_{enl}, and P_{enl} are selected from {0.1, 0.3, 0.5, 0.7, 0.9}. The results are given in Table 2. Table 2 shows that as increasing the value of P_{enl}, the results are better for unimodal functions, but unstable for some multimodal functions, such as F12, F17 and F20. For balancing performance on different problems, $P_{enl} = 0.5$ is best choices at $D = 30$.

Secondly, test of the probability P_{enl} is started at $D = 50$. According analysis of Table 2 and considering the increasing of the dimension size, P_{ns} are selected from {0.1, 0.2, 0.3, 0.4, 0.5} in this test. The test results are listed Table 3. Due to the dimension size becoming larger, the results at $D = 50$ are better than at $D = 30$ for unimodal functions, but more unstable for some multimodal functions. Therefore, $P_{enl} = 0.3$ is a moderate set at $D = 50$.

Furthermore, test results of the probability P_{enl} at $D = 100$ are listed Table 4. In the end, we chosen $P_{enl} = 0.1$ as an algorithm parameter setting for the following experiments at $D = 100$.

According to the above three tests, the value of the probability P_{enl} is proportional to the performance of the ENL operation on unimodal functions, but is inversely proportional to the stability of the algorithm on some multimodal functions. For the phenomenon, we suggest that if the scale (dimension) of the problem is larger, the probability P_{enl} should be a smaller value; otherwise, the probability P_{enl} can be properly enlarged.

Table 4. Testing results of probability P_{enl} at $D = 100$

Func.	$P_{enl} = 0.1$	$P_{enl} = 0.2$	$P_{enl} = 0.3$	$P_{enl} = 0.4$	$P_{enl} = 0.5$
F01	5.28E−119	3.01E−213	5.32E−304	0.00E+00	0.00E+00
F02	4.49E−60	4.44E−108	1.69E−152	3.55E−195	9.82E−235
F03	1.53E−103	4.58E−205	2.61E−297	0.00E+00	0.00E+00
F04	8.73E−53	2.16E−102	7.93E−148	1.75E−189	2.61E−231
F05	9.45E+01	9.49E+01	9.60E+01	9.66E+01	9.70E+01
F06	0.00E+00	0.00E+00	0.00E+00	0.00E+00	0.00E+00
F07	5.69E−05	3.43E−05	2.32E−05	2.13E−05	2.06E−05
F08	1.41E−114	9.38E−210	1.22E−299	0.00E+00	0.00E+00
F09	9.10E−119	8.91E−214	2.70E−304	0.00E+00	0.00E+00
F10	4.97E−99	1.83E−164	3.24E−225	1.79E−282	0.00E+00
F11	0.00E+00	0.00E+00	0.00E+00	0.00E+00	0.00E+00
F12	4.74E+00	1.82E−02	9.48E+00	3.32E+01	4.74E+01
F13	0.00E+00	0.00E+00	0.00E+00	0.00E+00	0.00E+00
F14	4.44E−16	4.44E−16	4.44E−16	4.44E−16	4.44E−16
F15	0.00E+00	0.00E+00	0.00E+00	0.00E+00	0.00E+00
F16	4.71E−33	4.71E−33	4.71E−33	4.71E−33	4.71E−33
F17	1.35E−32	8.79E−04	1.67E−02	1.67E−02	3.77E−02
F18	0.00E+00	0.00E+00	0.00E+00	0.00E+00	0.00E+00
F19	1.32E−29	4.04E−109	9.27E−154	3.86E−196	2.86E−235
F20	1.35E−31	2.45E−15	8.03E−02	3.28E+00	2.29E+01
F21	0.00E+00	0.00E+00	0.00E+00	0.00E+00	0.00E+00
F22	0.00E+00	0.00E+00	0.00E+00	0.00E+00	0.00E+00

4.3   Validity of ENL Strategy

In this experiment, the original ABC and following three variants (i.e. ABC-ENL, DFSABC-elite and ENLABC) are used to analyze the effectiveness of the ENL strategy. These three compared ABC variants are listed as follows:

Table 5. Experimental results of validity of ENL at $D = 30$

Func.	ABC	ABC-ENL	DFSABC-elite	ENLABC
F01	2.57E−10	3.20E−138	2.20E−57	**3.11E−148**
F02	9.86E−07	1.40E−69	6.33E−30	**3.97E−75**
F03	7.15E+03	1.62E−134	4.98E+03	**1.98E−137**
F04	3.09E+01	1.75E−66	4.01E−01	**9.73E−69**
F05	**5.64E−01**	2.88E+01	1.58E+00	2.52E+01
F06	**0.00E+00**	**0.00E+00**	**0.00E+00**	**0.00E+00**
F07	1.77E−01	1.77E−04	1.34E−02	**5.99E−05**
F08	1.05E−04	7.67E−134	3.11E−54	**1.51E−144**
F09	1.10E−11	2.11E−138	2.13E−58	**5.50E−149**
F10	2.52E−11	5.72E−99	1.46E−38	**6.21E−115**
F11	6.00E−07	**0.00E+00**	2.70E−06	**0.00E+00**
F12	**3.82E−04**	**3.82E−04**	**3.82E−04**	3.82E−04
F13	6.96E−06	**0.00E+00**	**0.00E+00**	**0.00E+00**
F14	3.20E−06	**4.44E−16**	2.76E−14	**4.44E−16**
F15	6.24E−08	**0.00E+00**	**0.00E+00**	**0.00E+00**
F16	7.51E−12	2.37E−11	**1.57E−32**	**1.57E−32**
F17	4.19E−10	5.47E−07	**1.35E−32**	**1.35E−32**
F18	**0.00E+00**	**0.00E+00**	**0.00E+00**	**0.00E+00**
F19	8.02E−05	2.71E−70	1.14E−27	**7.57E−76**
F20	3.17E−08	8.09E−08	**1.35E−31**	**1.35E−31**
F21	5.70E−08	**0.00E+00**	**0.00E+00**	**0.00E+00**
F22	3.98E−04	**0.00E+00**	**0.00E+00**	**0.00E+00**

- ABC: basic ABC
- ABC-ENL: ABC introduce ENL strategy into employed bee phase
- DFSABC-elite: Using DFS framework and two novel solution search equations, Eqs. (5) and 6).

Similarly, ABC and three ABC variants algorithms run on different sizes of dimension, which are 30, 50 and 100 corresponding P_{enl} which are 0.5, 0.3 and 0.1. The results listed Tables 5 and 6 respectively.

As shown in Tables 5 and 6, the ENL strategy can effectively speed up the convergence rate of ABC. To be specific, ABC-ENL and ENLABC outperform respectively ABC and DFSABC-elite on most test functions in terms of solution accuracy and convergence speed. Simultaneously, the experimental results also proved the effectiveness of the ENL strategy on different sizes of dimension.

4.4 Comparison of ENLABC with Several ABC Variants

In final experiment, ENLABC is compared with some state-of-the-art ABC variants, i.e. AABC [4], GBABC [5], ABCG [8] and ECABC [7] on all 22 test functions with $D = 30, 50, 100$. Brief introductions of these ABC variants are listed as follows:

Table 6. Experimental results of validity of ENL at $D = 50$ and $D = 100$

Func.	$D = 50$		$D = 100$	
	DFSABC-elite	ENLABC	DFSABC-elite	ENABC
F01	6.42E−57	**3.61E−158**	3.09E−56	**5.28E−119**
F02	1.38E−29	**2.98E−80**	4.55E−29	**4.49E−60**
F03	1.63E+04	**5.76E−146**	6.65E+04	**1.53E−103**
F04	1.83E+00	**5.63E−74**	8.09E+00	**8.73E−53**
F05	**1.38E+00**	4.48E+01	8.46E+00	9.45E+01
F06	**0.00E+00**	**0.00E+00**	**0.00E+00**	**0.00E+00**
F07	2.46E−02	**6.15E−05**	6.03E−02	**5.69E−05**
F08	2.36E−53	**1.02E−153**	2.96E−52	**1.41E−114**
F09	2.02E−57	**1.62E−159**	1.90E−56	**9.10E−119**
F10	5.35E−39	**3.14E−124**	9.41E−40	**4.97E−99**
F11	1.50E−06	**0.00E+00**	7.50E−07	**0.00E+00**
F12	**6.36E−04**	**6.36E−04**	1.27E−03	4.74E+00
F13	**0.00E+00**	**0.00E+00**	**0.00E+00**	**0.00E+00**
F14	5.02E−14	**4.44E−16**	1.17E−13	**4.44E−16**
F15	**0.00E+00**	**0.00E+00**	**0.00E+00**	**0.00E+00**
F16	**9.42E−33**	**9.42E−33**	**4.71E−33**	**4.71E−33**
F17	**1.35E−32**	**1.35E−32**	**1.35E−32**	**1.35E−32**
F18	**0.00E+00**	**0.00E+00**	**0.00E+00**	**0.00E+00**
F19	8.88E−18	**6.42E−81**	6.00E−17	**1.32E−29**
F20	**1.35E−31**	**1.35E−31**	**1.35E−31**	**1.35E−31**
F21	**0.00E+00**	**0.00E+00**	**0.00E+00**	**0.00E+00**
F22	**0.00E+00**	**0.00E+00**	4.09E−14	**0.00E+00**

- AABC: ABC with An adaptive greedy position update strategy (2016);
- GBABC: Gaussian bare-bones artificial bee colony algorithm (2016);
- ABCG: Artificial bee colony algorithm base d on the gravity model (2018);
- ECABC: DFSABC-elite combined breadth-depth search strategy (2018);

To make a fair comparison, for all the compared algorithms, the initial population is generated randomly according to Eq. (1); *SN* and *limit* are set to 75 and $SN \times D$ respectively; *MaxFEs* is used as the termination condition, which is set to $5000 \times D$; the detailed parameter settings of all the algorithms are set as suggested in their original papers. Each algorithm is run 25 times independently per function. The source codes of these four algorithms are implemented in Java language.

The final results are given in Tables 7, 8 and 9, respectively. To compare the significance between ABC variant and the proposed algorithms, the paired Wilcoxon signed-rank test is used. This non-parametric statistical hypothesis test can be used as an alternative to the paired t test when the results cannot be assumed to be normally distributed. In Tabless 2 and 3, the signs "†", "‡" and "≈" indicate our approach is, respectively, better than, worse than, and similar to its competitor according to the Wilcoxon signed-ranked test at $\alpha = 0.05$. In the last row, the overall performance is summarized as $w/l/t$, which denotes that our approach wins on w functions, loses on l functions, and ties on t functions.

As seen from Tables 7, 8 and 9, ENLABC wins in 16, 16 and 18 functions, when compared with AABC in terms of mean value at $D = 30$, 50, 100, respectively, and only loses 1 function F05. In comparing with GBABC, ENLABC has better or least comparable performance than the competitors on all functions. And ENLABC surpassed ABCG and ECABC on the most of the test functions. Especially on high-dimensional problems, ENLABC showed outstanding performance and faster convergence speed.

Table 7. Comparisons of ENLABC and ABC variants on 22 test functions at $D = 30$

Func.	AABC	GBABC	ABCG	ECABC	ENLABC
F01	$1.93\text{E}{-}24^\dagger$	$2.05\text{E}{-}26^\dagger$	$1.55\text{E}{-}26^\dagger$	$1.25\text{E}{-}63^\dagger$	$\mathbf{3.11E{-}148}$
F02	$4.13\text{E}{-}13^\dagger$	$3.48\text{E}{-}16^\dagger$	$1.11\text{E}{-}15^\dagger$	$4.10\text{E}{-}33^\dagger$	$\mathbf{3.97E{-}75}$
F03	$9.87\text{E}{+}03^\dagger$	$2.84\text{E}{+}03^\dagger$	$3.02\text{E}{+}03^\dagger$	$7.25\text{E}{+}03^\dagger$	$\mathbf{1.98E{-}137}$
F04	$2.16\text{E}{+}01^\dagger$	$6.70\text{E}{-}01^\dagger$	$1.32\text{E}{-}01^\dagger$	$1.40\text{E}{-}01^\dagger$	$\mathbf{9.73E{-}69}$
F05	$\mathbf{9.48E{-}01}^\ddagger$	$2.34\text{E}{+}01^\dagger$	$4.20\text{E}{+}01^\dagger$	$3.00\text{E}{+}00^\ddagger$	$2.52\text{E}{+}01$
F06	$\mathbf{0.00E{+}00}^\approx$	$\mathbf{0.00E{+}00}^\approx$	$\mathbf{0.00E{+}00}^\approx$	$\mathbf{0.00E{+}00}^\approx$	$\mathbf{0.00E{+}00}$
F07	$9.76\text{E}{-}02^\dagger$	$2.32\text{E}{-}02^\dagger$	$1.21\text{E}{-}02^\dagger$	$6.71\text{E}{-}03^\dagger$	$\mathbf{5.99E{-}05}$
F08	$3.91\text{E}{-}20^\dagger$	$1.64\text{E}{-}18^\dagger$	$5.93\text{E}{-}18^\dagger$	$3.03\text{E}{-}60^\dagger$	$\mathbf{1.51E{-}144}$
F09	$3.34\text{E}{-}25^\dagger$	$3.90\text{E}{-}25^\dagger$	$2.81\text{E}{-}14^\dagger$	$1.27\text{E}{-}64^\dagger$	$\mathbf{5.50E{-}149}$
F10	$1.38\text{E}{-}19^\dagger$	$3.76\text{E}{-}50^\dagger$	$2.80\text{E}{-}56^\dagger$	$6.76\text{E}{-}45^\dagger$	$\mathbf{6.21E{-}115}$
F11	$1.51\text{E}{-}06^\dagger$	$1.52\text{E}{-}06^\dagger$	$7.91\text{E}{-}06^\dagger$	$3.31\text{E}{-}06^\dagger$	$\mathbf{0.00E{+}00}$
F12	$\mathbf{3.82E{-}04}^\approx$	$\mathbf{3.82E{-}04}^\approx$	$\mathbf{3.82E{-}04}^\approx$	$\mathbf{3.82E{-}04}^\approx$	$3.82\text{E}{-}04$
F13	$\mathbf{0.00E{+}00}^\approx$	$2.50\text{E}{-}03^\dagger$	$\mathbf{0.00E{+}00}^\approx$	$\mathbf{0.00E{+}00}^\approx$	$\mathbf{0.00E{+}00}$
F14	$1.40\text{E}{-}12^\dagger$	$1.03\text{E}{-}10^\dagger$	$3.87\text{E}{-}14^\dagger$	$1.72\text{E}{-}14^\dagger$	$\mathbf{4.44E{-}16}$
F15	$4.91\text{E}{-}14^\dagger$	$8.81\text{E}{-}07^\dagger$	$\mathbf{0.00E{+}00}^\approx$	$4.81\text{E}{-}05^\dagger$	$\mathbf{0.00E{+}00}$
F16	$1.32\text{E}{-}26^\dagger$	$9.03\text{E}{-}26^\dagger$	$2.99\text{E}{-}26^\dagger$	$\mathbf{1.57E{-}32}^\approx$	$\mathbf{1.57E{-}32}$
F17	$2.68\text{E}{-}25^\dagger$	$3.33\text{E}{-}24^\dagger$	$2.09\text{E}{-}25^\dagger$	$\mathbf{1.35E{-}32}^\approx$	$\mathbf{1.35E{-}32}$
F18	$\mathbf{0.00E{+}00}^\approx$	$\mathbf{0.00E{+}00}^\approx$	$\mathbf{0.00E{+}00}^\approx$	$\mathbf{0.00E{+}00}^\approx$	$\mathbf{0.00E{+}00}$
F19	$2.06\text{E}{-}10^\dagger$	$1.43\text{E}{-}07^\dagger$	$1.98\text{E}{-}03^\dagger$	$3.61\text{E}{-}04^\dagger$	$\mathbf{7.57E{-}76}$
F20	$2.66\text{E}{-}16^\dagger$	$7.04\text{E}{-}23^\dagger$	$4.10\text{E}{-}24^\dagger$	$\mathbf{1.35E{-}31}^\approx$	$\mathbf{1.35E{-}31}$
F21	$\mathbf{0.00E{+}00}^\approx$	$\mathbf{0.00E{+}00}^\approx$	$\mathbf{0.00E{+}00}^\approx$	$\mathbf{0.00E{+}00}^\approx$	$\mathbf{0.00E{+}00}$
F22	$2.19\text{E}{-}14^\dagger$	$2.15\text{E}{-}13^\dagger$	$\mathbf{0.00E{+}00}^\approx$	$\mathbf{0.00E{+}00}^\approx$	$\mathbf{0.00E{+}00}$
$w/l/t$	16/1/5	17/1/4	15/0/7	12/1/9	–

Table 8. Comparisons of ENLABC and ABC variants on 22 test functions at $D = 50$

Func.	AABC	GBABC	ABCG	ECABC	ENLABC
F01	$1.60E{-}23^\dagger$	$9.96E{-}19^\dagger$	$3.83E{-}26^\dagger$	$3.63E{-}63^\dagger$	**3.61E−158**
F02	$9.04E{-}13^\dagger$	$7.68E{-}15^\dagger$	$7.41E{-}16^\dagger$	$5.23E{-}33^\dagger$	**2.98E−80**
F03	$3.21E{+}04^\dagger$	$2.11E{+}04^\dagger$	$1.68E{+}04^\dagger$	$2.35E{+}04^\dagger$	**5.76E−146**
F04	$5.19E{+}01^\dagger$	$6.93E{+}00^\dagger$	$6.88E{-}01^\dagger$	$8.96E{-}01^\dagger$	**5.63E−74**
F05	**1.31E+00‡**	$7.66E{+}01^\dagger$	$5.80E{+}01^\dagger$	$1.31E{+}01^\ddagger$	4.48E+01
F06	**0.00E+00$^\approx$**	**0.00E+00$^\approx$**	**0.00E+00$^\approx$**	**0.00E+00$^\approx$**	**0.00E+00**
F07	$2.69E{-}01^\dagger$	$5.94E{-}02^\dagger$	$2.51E{-}02^\dagger$	$1.52E{-}02^\dagger$	**6.15E−05**
F08	$3.79E{-}20^\dagger$	$5.89E{-}43^\dagger$	$1.43E{-}16^\dagger$	$5.43E{-}58^\dagger$	**1.02E−153**
F09	$1.55E{-}24^\dagger$	$5.84E{-}19^\dagger$	$1.61E{-}13^\dagger$	$7.64E{-}64^\dagger$	**1.62E−159**
F10	$4.99E{-}15^\dagger$	$1.14E{-}51^\dagger$	$1.87E{-}71^\dagger$	$7.27E{-}44^\dagger$	**3.14E−124**
F11	$7.85E{-}07^\dagger$	$7.31E{-}07^\dagger$	$5.06E{-}06^\dagger$	$2.02E{-}06^\dagger$	**0.00E+00**
F12	**6.36E−04$^\approx$**	**6.36E−04$^\approx$**	**6.36E−04$^\approx$**	$9.48E{+}00^\dagger$	**6.36E−04**
F13	**0.00E+00$^\approx$**	$1.10E{+}01^\dagger$	**0.00E+00$^\approx$**	**0.00E+00$^\approx$**	**0.00E+00**
F14	$2.86E{-}12^\dagger$	$5.45E{-}09^\dagger$	$5.44E{-}14^\dagger$	$3.53E{-}14^\dagger$	**4.44E−16**
F15	$3.71E{-}14^\dagger$	$1.51E{-}12^\dagger$	**0.00E+00$^\approx$**	$3.31E{-}05^\dagger$	**0.00E+00**
F16	$3.48E{-}26^\dagger$	$9.75E{-}23^\dagger$	$4.86E{-}25^\dagger$	**9.42E−33$^\approx$**	**9.42E−33**
F17	$1.54E{-}24^\dagger$	$9.17E{-}23^\dagger$	$6.54E{-}24^\dagger$	**1.35E−32$^\approx$**	**1.35E−32**
F18	**0.00E+00$^\approx$**	**0.00E+00$^\approx$**	**0.00E+00$^\approx$**	**0.00E+00$^\approx$**	**0.00E+00**
F19	$9.62E{-}10^\dagger$	$1.79E{-}05^\dagger$	$1.05E{-}02^\dagger$	$8.16E{-}04^\dagger$	**6.42E−81**
F20	$2.37E{-}16^\dagger$	$4.38E{-}17^\dagger$	$4.14E{-}23^\dagger$	**1.35E−31$^\approx$**	**1.35E−31**
F21	**0.00E+00$^\approx$**	$2.09E{-}16^\dagger$	**0.00E+00$^\approx$**	**0.00E+00$^\approx$**	**0.00E+00**
F22	$2.27E{-}13^\dagger$	$3.80E{-}10^\dagger$	**0.00E+00$^\approx$**	**0.00E+00$^\approx$**	**0.00E+00**
w/l/t	16/1/5	19/0/3	15/0/7	13/1/8	–

Table 9. Comparisons of ENLABC and ABC variants on 22 test functions at $D = 100$

Func.	AABC	GBABC	ABCG	ECABC	ENLABC
F01	$5.30E{-}23^\dagger$	$8.43E{-}10^\dagger$	$1.01E{-}23^\dagger$	$1.39E{-}62^\dagger$	**5.28E−119**
F02	$2.73E{-}12^\dagger$	$2.35E{-}11^\dagger$	$6.02E{-}15^\dagger$	$1.98E{-}32^\dagger$	**4.49E−60**
F03	$1.25E{+}05^\dagger$	$9.78E{+}04^\dagger$	$9.15E{+}04^\dagger$	$9.13E{+}04^\dagger$	**1.53E−103**
F04	$8.14E{+}01^\dagger$	$3.43E{+}01^\dagger$	$4.62E{+}00^\dagger$	$4.55E{+}00^\dagger$	**8.73E−53**
F05	**4.62E+00‡**	$1.91E{+}02^\dagger$	$1.01E{+}02^\dagger$	$3.63E{+}01^\ddagger$	9.45E+01
F06	**0.00E+00$^\approx$**	**0.00E+00$^\approx$**	**0.00E+00$^\approx$**	**0.00E+00$^\approx$**	**0.00E+00**
F07	$8.83E{-}01^\dagger$	$3.68E{-}01^\dagger$	$6.73E{-}02^\dagger$	$3.71E{-}02^\dagger$	**5.69E−05**
F08	$4.89E{-}19^\dagger$	$1.12E{-}11^\dagger$	$8.53E{-}16^\dagger$	$1.64E{-}58^\dagger$	**1.41E−114**
F09	$2.22E{-}23^\dagger$	$2.03E{-}10^\dagger$	$9.25E{-}11^\dagger$	$1.80E{-}62^\dagger$	**9.10E−119**
F10	$3.98E{-}08^\dagger$	$1.52E{-}43^\dagger$	$2.07E{-}76^\dagger$	$3.42E{-}44^\dagger$	**4.97E−99**
F11	$4.61E{-}07^\dagger$	$3.38E{-}07^\dagger$	$2.52E{-}06^\dagger$	$1.40E{-}06^\dagger$	**0.00E+00**
F12	**1.27E−03‡**	$1.60E{+}03^\dagger$	**1.27E−03‡**	**1.27E−03‡**	4.74E+00

(*continued*)

Table 9. (*continued*)

Func.	AABC	GBABC	ABCG	ECABC	ENLABC
F13	$1.42E{-}16^{\dagger}$	$3.06E{+}01^{\dagger}$	$2.69E{-}12^{\dagger}$	$\mathbf{0.00E{+}00}^{\approx}$	$\mathbf{0.00E{+}00}$
F14	$5.43E{-}12^{\dagger}$	$1.02E{-}05^{\dagger}$	$3.54E{-}13^{\dagger}$	$8.64E{-}14^{\dagger}$	$\mathbf{4.44E{-}16}$
F15	$1.95E{-}14^{\dagger}$	$2.07E{-}09^{\dagger}$	$0.00E{+}00^{\approx}$	$5.44E{-}06^{\dagger}$	$\mathbf{0.00E{+}00}$
F16	$9.86E{-}26^{\dagger}$	$8.00E{-}17^{\dagger}$	$1.73E{-}21^{\dagger}$	$\mathbf{4.71E{-}33}^{\approx}$	$\mathbf{4.71E{-}33}$
F17	$9.16E{-}24^{\dagger}$	$3.09E{-}17^{\dagger}$	$6.38E{-}20^{\dagger}$	$\mathbf{1.35E{-}32}^{\approx}$	$\mathbf{1.35E{-}32}$
F18	$0.00E{+}00^{\approx}$	$8.00E{-}02^{\dagger}$	$\mathbf{0.00E{+}00}^{\approx}$	$\mathbf{0.00E{+}00}^{\approx}$	$\mathbf{0.00E{+}00}$
F19	$3.70E{-}09^{\dagger}$	$7.50E{-}02^{\dagger}$	$6.16E{-}02^{\dagger}$	$2.43E{-}03^{\dagger}$	$\mathbf{1.32E{-}29}$
F20	$8.88E{-}18^{\dagger}$	$2.17E{-}08^{\dagger}$	$2.11E{-}19^{\dagger}$	$\mathbf{1.35E{-}31}^{\approx}$	$\mathbf{1.35E{-}31}$
F21	$2.00E{-}17^{\dagger}$	$4.95E{-}08^{\dagger}$	$\mathbf{0.00E{+}00}^{\approx}$	$\mathbf{0.00E{+}00}^{\approx}$	$\mathbf{0.00E{+}00}$
F22	$1.17E{-}12^{\dagger}$	$1.61E{-}04^{\dagger}$	$4.09E{-}14^{\dagger}$	$\mathbf{0.00E{+}00}^{\approx}$	$\mathbf{0.00E{+}00}$
w/l/t	18/2/2	21/0/1	17/1/4	12/2/8	–

5 Conclusion

In this work, breadth-depth search (BFS) framework and depth-first search (DFS) framework are integrated into the employed bee phase and the onlooker bee phase, respectively. To speed up the convergence rate, the elite neighborhood learning (ENL) strategy is used in employed bee phase for enhancing the relationship between the two phases. Combining the above ideas, we propose the accelerating ABC algorithm, named ENLABC. The experimental results show that our approach achieves significant performance in term of solution accuracy and accelerates evidently the convergence of the ABC algorithm.

Acknowledgments. This work is supported by the National Natural Science Foundation of China (Nos. 61603163, 61462045 and 61562042) and the Science and Technology Foundation of Jiangxi Province (No. 20151BAB217007).

References

1. Karaboga D.: An Idea Based on Honey Bee Swarm for Numerical Optimization (2005)
2. Zhu, G., Kwong, S.: Gbest-guided artificial bee colony algorithm for numerical function optimization. Appl. Math. Comput. **217**(7), 3166–3173 (2010)
3. Gao, W., Liu, S.: A modified artificial bee colony algorithm. Comput. Oper. Res. **39**(3), 687–697 (2012)
4. Yu, W., Zhan, Z., Zhang, J.: Artificial bee colony algorithm with an adaptive greedy position update strategy. Soft. Comput. **22**(17), 1–15 (2016)
5. Zhou, X., Wu, Z., Wang, H., Rahnamayan, S.: Gaussian bare-bones artificial bee colony algorithm. Soft. Comput. **20**(3), 907–924 (2016)
6. Cui, L., Li, G., Lin, Q., Du, Z., Gao, W., Chen, J., Lu, N.: A novel artificial bee colony algorithm with depth-first search framework and elite-guided search equation. Inf. Sci. **367–368**, 1012–1044 (2016)

7. Kong, D., Chang, T., Dai, W., Wang, Q., Sun, H.: An improved artificial bee colony algorithm based on elite group guidance and combined breadth-depth search strategy. Inf. Sci. **54**, 442–443 (2018)
8. Xiang, W.L., Meng, X.L., Li, Y.Z., He, R.C., An, M.Q.: An improved artificial bee colony algorithm based on the gravity model. Inf. Sci. **429**, 49–71 (2018)
9. Wang, H., Sun, H., Li, C., Rahnamayan, S., Pan, J.: Diversity enhanced particle swarm optimization with neighborhood search. Inf. Sci. **223**(2), 119–135 (2013)
10. Zhou, X., Wang, H., Wang, M., Wan, J.: Enhancing the modified artificial bee colony algorithm with neighborhood search. Soft. Comput. **21**(10), 1–11 (2017)
11. Das, S., Abraham, A., Chakraborty, U.K., Konar, A.: Differential evolution using a neighborhood-based mutation operator. IEEE Trans. Evol. Comput. **13**(3), 526–553 (2009)
12. Gao, W., Chan, F.T.S., Huang, L., Liu, S.: Bare bones artificial bee colony algorithm with parameter adaptation and fitness-based neighborhood. Inf. Sci. **316**(C), 180–200 (2015)

Distributed Parallel Simulation
of Primary Sample Space Metropolis
Light Transport

Changmao Wu, Changyou Zhang$^{(\boxtimes)}$, and Qiao Sun$^{(\boxtimes)}$

Laboratory of Parallel Software and Computational Science, Institute of Software,
Chinese Academy of Sciences, Beijing, China
{changmao,changyou,sunqiao}@iscas.ac.cn

Abstract. Monte-Carlo rendering algorithms are known for producing highly realistic images, but at a significant computational cost, because they rely on tracing up to trillions of light paths through a scene to simulate physically based light transport. For this reason, a large body of research exists on various techniques for accelerating these costly algorithms. As one of the Monte-Carlo rendering algorithms, PSSMLT (Primary Sample Space Metropolis Light Transport) is widely used nowadays for photorealistic rendering. Unfortunately, the computational cost of PSSMLT is still very high since the space of light paths in high-dimension and up to trillions of paths are typically required in such path space. Recent research on PSSMLT has proposed a variety of optimized methods for single node rendering, however, multi-node rendering for PSSMLT is rarely mentioned due in large part to the complicated mathematical model, complicated physical processes and the irregular memory access patterns, and the imbalanced workload of light-carrying paths.

In this paper, we present a highly scalable distributed parallel simulation framework for PSSMLT. Firstly, based on light transport equation, we propose the notion of sub-image with certain property for multi-node rendering and theoretically prove that the whole set of sub-images can be combined to produce the final image; Then we further propose a sub-image based assignment partitioning algorithm for multi-node rendering since the traditional demand-driven assignment partitioning algorithm doesn't work well. Secondly, we propose a physically based parallel simulation for the PSSMLT algorithm, which is revealed on a parallel computer system in master-worker paradigm. Finally, we discuss the issue of granularity of the assignment partitioning and some optimization strategies for improving overall performance, and then a static/dynamic hybrid scheduling strategy is described. Experiments show that framework has a nearly linear speedup along with the CPU core count up to 9,600 on the Tianhe-2 supercomputer, which suggests that the proposed framework has a high scalability and efficiency.

Keywords: Primary sample space metropolis light transport
Physically based ray tracing · Assignment partitioning
Hybrid scheduling · Distributed computing · Performance optimization

© Springer Nature Switzerland AG 2018
J. Vaidya and J. Li (Eds.): ICA3PP 2018, LNCS 11334, pp. 465–482, 2018.
https://doi.org/10.1007/978-3-030-05051-1_32

1   Introduction

Monte Carlo rendering algorithms simulate the propagation of light by sampling random paths connecting the light source and a virtual sensor, and are attractive techniques for rendering photorealistic image because it can produce high quality images that faithfully represent the physically based phenomena [1–4]. It attempts to simulate reality, i.e. it uses principles of physics to model the interaction of light and matter, accurately simulates the light transport in a scene and renders a large variety of natural phenomena. In contrast to Monte Carlo rendering algorithms, interactive ray tracing sacrifices realism for frame rate, and nonphotorealistic rendering strives for artistic freedom and expressiveness [4–6].

Studies on highly scalable algorithms for Monte Carlo rendering algorithms tend to be an urgent demand as the request for photorealistic images becomes a common trend [1–3,7]. Since the path tracing algorithm [8] appeared, the discipline of Monte Carlo rendering algorithms has seen significant advances, such as the bidirectional path tracing [9], the MLT (Metropolis light transport) algorithm [10], and the PSSMLT (Primary Sample Space Metropolis light transport) algorithm [11] as well. Veach and Guibas [10] firstly applied the Metropolis sampling algorithm [12] to solving the light transport equation. Since then, many researchers have attempted to improve the performance of the MLT algorithm. Kelemen et al. [11] developed a formulation for Metropolis rendering, which was easier to implement than Guibas's approach and we will refer to it as PSSMLT for reasons that will become clear shortly. Fan et al. [13] developed a method which permitted the user explicitly provide a number of important paths that could be used in Metropolis sample generation. Pharr et al. developed a multi-threading algorithm for PSSMLT rendering in their famous book [1], abbreviating for PBRT. However, their multi-threading algorithms are still too slow for PSSMLT rendering.

Nowadays, most work on simulation of PSSMLT algorithm are still running on single processor machines, which usually require many hours or days to render an image. Therefore, how to accelerate the PSSMLT algorithm on a cluster becomes important and urgent. However, developing a simulation framework for the PSSMLT algorithm on a cluster can be notoriously hard due to imbalanced calculation time, irregular memory access patterns and domain knowledge.

In this paper, we have developed an efficient and scalable parallel ray tracer for the PSSMLT algorithm based on [1,14]. The remainder of the paper is organized as follows. We will start by introducing the most important theoretical concepts for PSSMLT in Sect. 2. Section 3 presents parallelization strategies for the PSSMLT algorithm in a cluster. The framework of implementation and the methodologies for load balancing are discussed in Sects. 4 and 5. Large-scale results on the Tianhe-2 supercomputer are given in Sect. 6. We conclude the paper in Sect. 7.

2   Primary Sample Space Metropolis Light Transport

PSSMLT is often considered to be the most sophisticated of the unbiased light transport simulation algorithms, with a reputation to be able to render scenes efficiently where other methods fail. Photorealistic image synthesis of Monte Carlo rendering image synthesis usually are divided into two parts: computing the radiance function throughout the scene and then projecting that function onto the grid of pixels. The value I_j of a pixel j with a single integral over the space of light transporting paths:

$$I_j = \int_\Omega h_j(\overline{X})f^*(\overline{X})d\mu(\overline{X}) = \int_\Omega f_j(\overline{X})d\mu(\overline{X}) \tag{1}$$

The integration domain Ω is called the path space and denotes the union of all paths of finite length along which light can potentially travel through a scene, h_j denotes the pixel filter function of j indicating how much the path measurement $\overline{X} = (X_0, X_1, X_2, ...)$ (with X_0 on the camera and the last vertex on the light) contributes to the pixel j, and f^* is the spectral image contribution function which defines the amount of light that reaches the image through the path. The product of the filter and image contribution function is called the path contribution function f_j and gives the contribution of a path specifically to the pixel j (see [15] for more details).

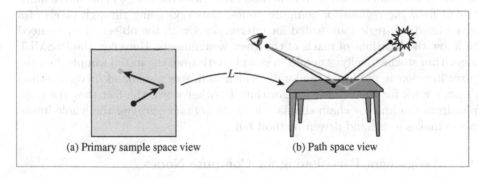

(a) Primary sample space view   (b) Path space view

Fig. 1. PSSMLT turns points in the primary sample space (i.e. random numbers) into paths, instead of exploring light paths directly. By performing small jumps in primary sample space, it can explore the neighborhood of a path. A deterministic mapping L constructs corresponding light paths on path space and estimates their radiance. (Figure from Pharr et al. [1]).

Path tracing is the first general-purpose unbiased Monte Carlo light transport algorithm used in graphics, which generates samples by simulating a random walk through the scene. A path, starting at the camera, is traced backward into the scene, and ends at the light source. Although path tracing works well for many outdoor scenes, it often exhibits high variance in indoor scenes that contain significant amounts of indirect light and caustics. Indoor scenes can be handled more effectively by constructing paths that start from the camera on one end and from the light source on the other end and are connected in the middle with a visibility ray. This method is called bidirectional path tracing. Importance sampling is a variance reduction technique in a Monte Carlo estimator by sampling approximately proportional to the measurement contribution function; the more probability distribution function is similar to the measurement contribution function, the lower the variance. The PSSMLT algorithm generates such a sequence of light-carrying samples through the scene by using a Markov chain in which the next sample X_{i+1} is generated from X_i by mutating the previous path in some manner [16]. These mutations ensure that the overall distribution of sampled paths is proportional to the contribution paths made to the image being rendered. The PSSMLT algorithm is not only able to render outdoor scenes as most path tracing or bidirectional path tracing methods do, but also able to process indoor scenes effectively.

3   Parallelization of PSSMLT

The first issue of making an PSSMLT algorithm run in parallel over a cluster is how to allocate assignments across compute nodes and inside each one of them. Unfortunately, currently available demand-driven assignment partitioning algorithm such as those in [17–19] doesn't work for the PSSMLT algorithm, largely because a demand-driven method subdivides the image plane into a number of *fixed sub-regions* for compute nodes, thus rays going through pixels of a given fixed sub-region are tested for intersections with the objects, i.e., we need to know the locations of pixels of the given assignments. However, the PSSMLT algorithm stochastically generates a sample path from the initial sample, i.e., the pixel location is produced randomly, which indicates a demand-driven method doesn't work for the PSSMLT algorithm. In other word, the fact that the samples from the Markov chain simulation *randomly move around* the whole image plane makes a demand-driven method fail.

3.1   Assignment Partitioning for Compute Nodes

Due to the fact that path samples in the PSSMLT algorithm are generated independently from the initial seed path sample through large steps and small steps [1,20] for the PSSMLT algorithm, the radiance I_j of a pixel j is randomly accumulated by the light-carrying paths of different length on the whole image plane instead of computing integrals pixel by pixel. Taking a pixel j as an example, when we compute the contribution of light paths with six vertices to I_j, the total contribution of all such path of length six (i.e., a vertex X_0 at the camera, four vertices at points on surfaces in the scene, and the last vertex at the light source), just as the fifth term of the Eq. 1 in Sect. 2 shows. Therefore, the computational process of each pixel's radiance can be considered as the process of exploring all of the surfaces in the scene for light-carry paths through tens of thousands of large step mutations and small step perturbations.

Let us define some notations for further discussion.

1. *lsp:* the large step probability for the PSSMLT algorithm to explore the entire surfaces in the scene.
2. *spp:* the number of samples per pixel in the image.

A sub-image is responsible for performing exactly *one large step mutation* for each pixel on the whole image plane as well as the *appropriate number of small step perturbations*. The number of large steps and small steps depend on the large step probability (lsp) and samples per pixel (spp) given by the scene. Given the concept of the sub-image, we can further define two variables as follows:

1. *LargeStepCycle:* the number of a large step and the small steps per pixel in a sub-image.
2. *numSubimages:* the number of sub-images to render an image using the PSSMLT algorithm.

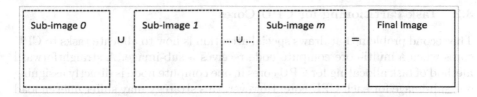

Fig. 2. Decomposing the rendering process of the PSSMLT algorithm into *m + 1 sub-images*, where *m* relies on *lsp* and *spp*. A subimage can be the basic compute unit for the compute node.

Based on the idea of sub-image, the PSSMLT algorithm regularly alternates the large step mutation and the small step perturbations in a sub-image: one large step mutation, LargeStepCycle-1 small step perturbations, another large step, and so forth. All the sub-images are mutually independent, since they only rely on the same initial sample (also called *seed path*) and the seeds for the pseudo-random number generator which are sufficiently independent. Based on the idea of sub-image, the process of rendering an image using the PSSMLT algorithm can be treated as the process of rendering all the sub-images independently and synthesizing all the intermediate results of sub-images as the final image by splatting style. Therefor, we can theoretically formalize the rendering process of PSSMLT as Eq. 2:

$$PSSMLT\ Imaging \equiv \overbrace{\bigcirc \rightarrow (scycle - 1)\odot}^{Subimage\ Rendering} + \cdots + \overbrace{\bigcirc \rightarrow (scycle - 1)\odot}^{Subimage\ Rendering}.$$

$$\underbrace{\qquad\qquad\qquad\qquad\qquad\qquad\qquad\qquad\qquad\qquad}_{The\ number\ of\ total\ Subimages\ is\ numSubimages}$$

(2)

In contrast to a fixed sub-region partitioned by a demand-driven method, a sub-image owns the entire region of the image plane. Therefore, the sub-image can be the basic assignment unit of the compute node when parallelizing the PSSMLT algorithm over a cluster. For example, if the image size is 4096 by 2160 pixels and the user set the large step probability $lsp=0.25$, and the average number of pixel samples $spp=8192$, then the corresponding variables are listed as follows.

1. $lsp = 0.25$,
2. $spp = 8192$,
3. $numSubimages = spp \times 0.25 = 2048$,
4. $LargeStepCycle = 8192 \div NumSubimages = 4$.

From the above analysis, we can see that the rendering process for the given image of 4096 by 2160 pixels is decomposed into 2048 independent sub-images (assignments) on compute nodes, each assignment has a total of $(4096 \times 2160) \times 4$ samples, with 0.25 of them large steps and 0.75 of them small steps.

3.2   Task Partitioning for CPU Cores

The second problem that draws special attention is how to allocate tasks to CPU cores when a multi-core compute node receives a sub-image. A straightforward method of task allocating for CPU cores in one compute node is directly assigning one sub-image for each CPU core. However, this strategy may suffer uneven load balancing problem due to the fact that the computational time of each sub-image may vary dramatically as the essence of randomly generated samples. In such case, some CPU cores would finish before others and keep idle while waiting for the slowest ones. Therefore, one sub-image as a computing unit for one CPU core is not suitable for load-balance. We need to decompose one sub-image into smaller ones called sub-sub-images.

The compute nodes in a cluster are classified into two types, one master node and m worker nodes, where m is the number of rendering compute nodes. When a worker node receives a new sub-image from the master node, it immediately decomposes the sub-image into smaller ones called *sub-sub-images* or *tasks* and puts the tasks into a sharing pool. The size of tasks, however, needs to be carefully taken into account, because task granularity may affect load balancing on multi-core platform. There are two factors to trade off in deciding how many tasks to be created: load-balancing and per-task overhead. On one hand, we would like to have significantly more tasks than the number of CPU cores in the system. On the other hand, having too many tasks may introduce overhead that degrades the efficiency. From our practical experience, we set the number of tasks equal to $8 * nc$, where nc is the number of CPU cores in the compute node. The number of these tasks here attempts to trade off the two factors mentioned above. The basic idea of the task partitioning algorithm for CPU cores is that the shuffled pixels of a sub-image is simply segmented in similar size by the number of $8 * nc$.

Algorithm 1: Task partitioning algorithm for CPU cores

Data: int numTasks, int xResolution, int yResolution
Result: Task jobs[numTasks]
float crop[2];
for *int i ← 0; i < numTasks; i++* **do**
　　crop[0] ← (float)i/((float)numTasks);
　　crop[1] ← (float)(i+1)/((float)numTasks);
　　cpucoresTasks[i].TaskId ← i;
　　cpucoresTasks[i].xSampleStart ← 0;
　　cpucoresTasks[i].xSampleCount ← xResolution;
　　cpucoresTasks[i].ySampleStart ← ⌈yResolution*crop[0]⌉;
　　cpucoresTasks[i].ySampleCount ← max(1,⌈yResolution*crop[1] -
　　cpucoresTasks[i].ySampleStart⌉);
　　cpucoresTasks[i].numSamples ←
　　cpucoresTasks[i].xSampleCount*cpucoresTasks[i].ySampleCount;
　　cpucoresTasks[i].offset ← xResolution*cpucoresTasks[i].ySampleStart;

Algorithm 2: Algorithm on the master node

Parse scene data;
Assignments partition;
assignmentID ← -1;
for *node ← 1; node < numberOfNodes; node++* **do**
　　assignmentID++;
　　Send assignment *assignmentID* to Worker node;
assignmentCompleted ← 0;
receivedResultsNodes ← 0;
sumSplatResults[nPixels] ← 0;
while *assignmentCompleted + receivedResultsNodes < numberOfAssignments +
numMPIProcesses -1* **do**
　　wait and receive for a message msg;
　　if *msg.tag ≡ DONE* **then**
　　　　assignmentCompleted++;

　　if *msg.tag ≡ RESULTS* **then**
　　　　Splat msg.results on *sumSplatResults*; *receivedResultsNodes*++;

　　if *assignmentID < numAssignments -1* **then**
　　　　allocate a new assignment to the sending Worker node;
　　　　assignmentID++;
　　else
　　　　Send EXIT message to Worker node;
Save final image;
Finalize;

Each pixel in the image plane should receive a single large step mutation for each sub-image, and the order for each pixel in each sub-image should be visited stochastically by the large step mutation so as to meet the prerequisite that the transition densities between samples for large step mutations is uniform. Therefore, each pixel in the sub-image is assigned an index and an array of the pixel indices of the image is randomly shuffled. The task partitioning algorithm for CPU cores is shown as Algorithm 1, which partitions the array of the shuffled pixel indices into similar segmentation by the number of $8*nc$.

Algorithm 3: Algorithm on the worker nodes

Parse scene data;
Compute Initial Seed Sample;
sumSplatResults[nPixels] ← 0;
Wait for initial assignment msg;
while *msg.TAG* ≠ *EXIT* **do**
> Decompose assignment *msg* into tasks;
> Place tasks into a share pool;
> Render the tasks in parallel;
> Splat current assignment results on *sumSplatResults*; Request a new assignment *msg* from *Master*;

Send *sumSplatResults* to master node;
Finalize;

At the first look, the task partitioning algorithm for CPU cores in Algorithm 1 resembles the demand-driven algorithm, such those in [1,2,18,19]. The demand-driven algorithm subdivides the image into *fixed sub-regions*. Nevertheless, the Algorithm 1 is distinct from the demand-driven algorithm due to the following aspects. First, tasks partitioned by the Algorithm 1 store shuffled pixel indices, and randomly visit the pixels of the sub-image, while, the demand-driven algorithm directly visits the locations of the pixels of the image. Moreover, the Algorithm 1 subdivides all the shuffled pixel indices of the total image into similarly equal size of tasks (also called sub-sub-images); however, the demand-driven algorithm partitions a fixed sub-region of the image into more smaller ones.

4   Framework and Algorithm

The master node and the worker nodes in a cluster are responsible for different functionality during the rendering process of the PSSMLT algorithm. The master node is connected to all worker nodes and responsible for allocating assignments, collecting assignment results and assembling the final image. The worker nodes are in charge of dynamically rendering allocated assignments. The worker nodes render assignments repeatedly until the assignment queue is empty.

First, from Sect. 3, the rendering process using the PSSMLT algorithm can be decomposed into tens of thousands of *sub-images* called *assignments*. The MPI process on the master node knows the number of worker nodes at the beginning. Therefore, after distributing the initial *assignments*, the master node waits for querying messages from the worker nodes. As soon as a worker node completes rendering, the assignment results is not sent to the master node for composing but synthesized by splatting style on the worker node. Then, a new requesting assignment message is sent to the master node at once. When the master node finds that a new message arrives, it immediately checks whether the message is a request for a new assignment. In this manner, the corresponding worker node will be assigned a new assignment as long as the assignment queue is not empty. When all the assignments are rendered and synthesized by the worker nodes, the worker nodes send their corresponding results to the master node for final image assembling. Our distribution strategies are outlined in the Algorithms 2 and 3. In Algorithm 3, we employ the method proposed in [1] to eliminate the start-up bias.

5 Load Balancing

Load balancing is particularly challenging in the context of a ray tracing application, especially for the PSSMLT algorithm due to its nature of generating path samples stochastically. Each ray takes a different amount of processor time to compute, depending on the complexity of the intersections that occur: ray can travel long distances as it is reflected by mirrorlike surfaces, or can be rapidly attenuated by collisions with nonreflective surfaces. Even though all of the lights could travel the same distance due to reflection and refraction over surfaces of objects in the scene, the lights will still lead to uneven workload and incoherent execution between light samples since light samples will be terminated randomly by Russia roulette. Since it is hard to predict the complexity of the bounces for a given part of the scene and light termination, one reasonable solution is to distribute the ray tracing work dynamically among the worker nodes.

Communication Overhead Optimization. In a typical master-worker scenario, the workers communicate only with their master. Thus, the master can soon become a performance bottleneck [18, 21, 22] when it has to deal with lots of MPI messages and assignment results. Under such circumstances, a worker node w sends the results of a sub-image to the master node and the master node receives the corresponding results to synthesize and then sends a new sub-image to the worker node w. If we set the time for splatting the results of a sub-image as T, then in the T interval, the worker node w is idle. In addition, the master node needs a duration of $numsub\text{-}images \times T$ to splat all the results of sub-images, in other words, the total idle time of all the worker nodes is $numsub\text{-}images \times T$, this situation often leads to poor CPU usage. Through further study, we find that the results of a sub-image can be accumulated by splatting style on the worker node and just send one accumulated results to the master node when the *assignment queue* is empty. In this manner, we overlap the process of synthesizing the results of sub-images and the process of communication between the master node and worker nodes. In addition, the number of results of sub-images accumulated by the master node decreases by *numsub-images* to *numWorkerNodes*, the amount of data transferred from the worker nodes to the master node reduces by $numsub\text{-}images \times MegaBytesPerSub\text{-}image$ to $numWorkerNodes \times MegaBytesPerSub - image$, as shown in Table 1. As we know $numsub\text{-}images \gg numWorkerNodes$, the optimization method can decrease the number of messages transferred between the master node and the worker nodes as well as can reduce the amount of data between the master node and the worker nodes. It may be a better design to enhance the overall performance to a certain extent. In Table 1, *nWorkers* is the number of worker nodes, $nMsg_{ori}$ is the number of messages that master node receives from worker nodes before optimization, $nMsg_{opt}$ is the number of messages that the master node receives from the worker nodes after optimization, $data_{ori}$ in MB is the total amount of data that the worker nodes send to the master node before optimization, and $data_{opt}$ in MB is the total amount of data that the worker nodes send to the master node after optimization.

Table 1. Communication overhead optimization results, *Image Size: 2560 × 1440 pixels, lsp = 0.25, spp = 16384, numsub-images = 4096.*

$nWorkers$	$nMsg_{ori}$	$nMsg_{opt}$	$data_{ori}$	$data_{opt}$
50	4096	50	4096 * 84.375	50 * 84.375
100	4096	100	4096 * 84.375	100 * 84.375
200	4096	200	4096 * 84.375	200 * 84.375
300	4096	300	4096 * 84.375	300 * 84.375
400	4096	400	4096 * 84.375	400 * 84.375
450	4096	450	4096 * 84.375	450 * 84.375

Load Balance Between CPU Cores. In order to gain load balancing on a single worker node, the number of tasks we divide a sub-image should be carefully taken into account. Firstly, we may want to divide the sub-image into more tasks for multi-core worker node, but, more tasks means higher synchronization overhead. Secondly, if we partition one sub-image into fewer tasks (e.g., just equal the number of CPU cores), the synchronization overhead may decrease, while this may result in severe imbalance. So, we should make a tradeoff between synchronization overhead and load balance. From our practical experience, we set the number of tasks equal to 8 times of the CPU cores in the system.

Hybrid Scheduling Strategies. Strategies to solve the load balancing problem are usually categorized as either static or dynamic. Our distributed load

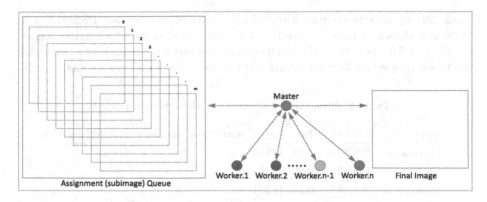

Fig. 3. Hybrid scheduling strategies, it has three features. One *static* feature, assignments for worker nodes are statically partitioned before rendering. Two *dynamic* features, one is that master node dynamically sends assignments to idle worker nodes, the other is that each worker nodes subdivides the assignments into small tasks that are put into a *sharing pool* and multi-threads (CPU cores) dynamically render tasks concurrently.

balancer uses a combination of static and dynamic scheduling scheme in an attempt to achieve good load balancing. 'Static' means that the number of sub-images is partitioned before rendering, 'dynamic' means the master node allocates assignments to the worker nodes dynamically and the tasks of each assignment are dynamically assigned to each CPU core. In our implementation, each worker node is initially assigned a single assignment to work on at the beginning. After receiving a new assignment, each worker node firstly divides the sub-image into similar tasks by the Algorithm 1, and then the rest of assignments are put into an *assignment queue* by the master node. Other assignments are assigned one-at-a-time by the master node to the worker nodes that finish processing an assignment whose results are accumulated in their memory and then request more work. Assignments are allocated to the worker nodes until the worker nodes indicate to the master node that they are free to render a new assignment. In this way, slower worker nodes will tend to be assigned fewer assignments over time, and no more than one assignment which takes a long time to render will be assigned to any one worker node at a time. Once a worker node successfully attains an assignment, it further subdivides the assignments into finer granularity called tasks and puts tasks into a *sharing pool*. Each CPU core (thread) of the worker node concurrently requests a task from the *sharing pool* and renders the task independently, see Fig. 3.

6   Evalution

The hardware platform used for our experiments is the Tianhe-2 supercomputer [23], located in the National Supercomputer Center in Guangzhou, China. For all of our experiments to be discussed below, we select three well-known test scenes [24] of various complexities, which are rendered by our PSSMLT ray tracer and shown in Figs. 5, 7 and 9. The three typical yet challenging scenes are selected for their high illuminating and geometrical complexity, material reflectance properties, further information about selected scenes see [24].

Table 2. Detail information of the three test scenes.

Scene	Triangles	lsp	spp	maxDepth	Russian roulette length
Classroom	103,832	0.25	16384	∞	8
Kitchen	1443,513	0.25	16384	∞	8
Diningroom	269,537	0.25	16384	∞	8

Fig. 4. Intermediate image of Scene *Classroom*. Rendered by our *physically based parallel ray tracer for the PSSMLT algorithm*, synthesized by 4 subimages with resolution 2560 by 1440 pixels.

To evaluate the performance achieved by our PSSMLT algorithm, we test the scenes mentioned above on the Tianhe-2 supercomputer using 1,200 to 9,600 cores, and we set related parameters of the PSSMLT algorithm as Table 2 depicts. What needs illustration in Table 2 is that the parameter *maxDepth*, which specifies the longest path depth in the generated output image, its value ∞ represents the light path is as long as possible if the light path really bounces in the scene. Because rendering an image by the PSSMLT algorithm often needs a great amount of time, we choose the results on 1,200 CPU cores as our baseline. Figure 10a shows the rendering time (in seconds) with CPU cores increasing

Fig. 5. Final image of Scene *Classroom*. Rendered by our *physically based parallel ray tracer for the PSSMLT algorithm* with the following configuration: $lsp = 0.25$, $spp = 16384$, image resolution 2560 by 1440 pixels.

Fig. 6. Intermediate image of Scene *Kitchen*. Rendered by our *physically based parallel ray tracer for the PSSMLT algorithm*, synthesized by 4 subimages with resolution 2560 by 1440 pixels.

Fig. 7. Final image of Scene *Kitchen*. Rendered by our *physically based parallel ray tracer for the PSSMLT algorithm* with the following configuration: $lsp = 0.25$, $spp = 16384$, image resolution 2560 by 1440 pixels.

Fig. 8. Intermediate image of Scene *Diningroom*. Rendered by our *physically based parallel ray tracer for the PSSMLT algorithm*, synthesized by 4 subimages with resolution 2560 by 1440 pixels.

Fig. 9. Final image of Scene *Diningroom*. Rendered by our *physically based parallel ray tracer for the PSSMLT algorithm* with the following configuration: $lsp = 0.25$, $spp = 16384$, image resolution 2560 by 1440 pixels.

from 1,200 to 9,600. The corresponding speedup graph is presented in Fig. 10b. The above three scenes have been traced at a resolution of 2560 by 1440 pixels, and the final rendered images are shown in Figs. 5, 7 and 9. We also provide the intermediate images synthesized by 4 subimages, illustrate as Figs. 4, 6 and 8.

From Figs. 5, 7 and 9, we can see clearly that our physically based PSSMLT ray tracer creates photorealistic images from the three scenes. In the *Classroom* scene, our algorithms correctly rendered it though almost no direct lighting is inside the classroom. For the *Kitchen* scene, our framework correctly models the physics of light reflection and light energy propagation. The *Diningroom* scene is full of strong indirect illumination just as the *Kitchen* scene.

As for the intermediate images Fig. 4, variance is higher and the image is noisier than that of Fig. 5, this is because the PSSMLT algorithm doesn't reach convergence. Figures 6 and 8 have the same trend.

Figure 10a shows the rendering time of the three scenes using CPU cores from 1,200 up to 9,600. From Fig. 10a, we can see that when the number of CPU cores increases from 1,200 to 9,600, the rendering time of the three scenes steadily decrease.

Figure 10b illustrates the corresponding speedup of the four scenes. We set the rendering time of 1,200 CPU cores as the baseline, the speedup is the ratio of the runtime against the baseline using 1,200 cores. As is seen from Fig. 10b, it is clear that with the increase of CPU cores from 1,200 to 9,600, the speedup increases linearly along with the core count, which suggests that our algorithms have good scalability.

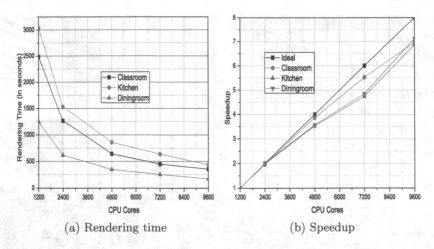

(a) Rendering time   (b) Speedup

Fig. 10. Configuration for *physically based parallel ray tracer for the PSSMLT algorithm* with $lsp = 0.25$ and $spp = 16384$.

7   Conclusion

In this paper, we have developed an efficient and scalable parallel ray tracer for the PSSMLT algorithm based on [1,14]. To the best of our knowledge, no one has previously implemented such a parallel ray tracer in a cluster. Our physically based framework for the PSSMLT algorithm can efficiently create high-quality photorealistic images in the areas such as film, television production, virtual reality and product exhibition etc.

Acknowledgment. The work is supported by the National Natural Science Foundation of China under Grant No. 61672508, No. 61379048. and the National Key Research and Development Program of China under Grant No. 2017YFB1400902. We thank Benedikt Bitterli [24] for providing the test scenes used in our evaluation. Further, special acknowledgement goes to Dong Wang, Yuanyuan Wan and Huizhong Lu for answering our technical questions on how to using Tianhe-2 supercomputer. We are particularly grateful to Matt Pharr and Wenzel Jakob et al. for the making the PBRT and Mitsuba renderers publicly available [1,14].

References

1. Pharr, M., Jakob, W., Humphreys, G.: Physically Based Rendering: From Theory to Implementation, 3rd edn. Morgan Kaufmann Publishers Inc., San Francisco (2016)
2. Pharr, M., Humphreys, G.: Physically Based Rendering: From Theory To Implementation, 2nd edn. Morgan Kaufmann Publishers Inc., San Francisco (2010)
3. Pharr, M., Humphreys, G.: Physically Based Rendering: From Theory To Implementation, 1st edn. Morgan Kaufmann Publishers Inc., San Francisco (2004)

4. Keller, A.: Quasi-Monte: Carlo image synthesis in a nutshell. In: Dick, J., Kuo, F., Peters, G., Sloan, I. (eds.) Monte Carlo and Quasi-Monte Carlo Methods 2012, pp. 213–249. Springer, Heidelberg (2013). https://doi.org/10.1007/978-3-642-41095-6_8

5. Davidovič, T., Křivánek, J., Hašan, M., Slusallek, P.: Progressive light transport simulation on the GPU: survey and improvements. ACM Trans. Graph. **33**(3), 29:1–29:19 (2014)

6. Ritschel, T., Dachsbacher, C., Grosch, T., Kautz, J.: The state of the art in interactive global illumination. Comput. Graph. Forum **31**(1), 160–188 (2012)

7. Dutré, P., et al.: State of the art in Monte Carlo global illumination. In: ACM SIGGRAPH 2004 Course Notes, SIGGRAPH 2004. ACM, New York (2004)

8. Kajiya, J.T.: The rendering equation. SIGGRAPH Comput. Graph. **20**(4), 143–150 (1986)

9. Veach, E., Guibas, L.: Bidirectional estimators for light transport. In: Sakas, G., Müller, S., Shirley, P. (eds.) Photorealistic Rendering Techniques, pp. 145–167. Springer, Heidelberg (1995). https://doi.org/10.1007/978-3-642-87825-1_11

10. Veach, E., Guibas, L.J.: Metropolis light transport. In: Proceedings of the 24th Annual Conference on Computer Graphics and Interactive Techniques, SIGGRAPH 1997, pp. 65–76. ACM Press/Addison-Wesley Publishing Co., New York (1997)

11. Kelemen, C., Szirmay-Kalos, L., Antal, G., Csonka, F.: A simple and robust mutation strategy for the metropolis light transport algorithm. Comput. Graph. Forum **21**(3), 531–540 (2002)

12. Metropolis, N., Rosenbluth, A.W., Rosenbluth, M.N., Teller, A.H., Teller, E.: Equations of state calculations by fast computing machines. J. Chem. Phys. **21**, 1087–1091 (1953)

13. Fan, S., Chenney, S., Lai, Y.C.: Metropolis photon sampling with optional user guidance. In: Proceedings of the 16th Eurographics Symposium on Rendering, pp. 127–138. Eurographics Association (2005)

14. Jakob, W.: Mitsuba renderer (2018). http://www.mitsuba-renderer.org

15. Veach, E.: Robust Monte Carlo methods for light transport simulation. Ph.D. thesis, Stanford University, Stanford (1998). AAI9837162

16. Keller, A., Premoze, S., Raab, M.: Advanced (quasi) Monte Carlo methods for image synthesis. In ACM SIGGRAPH 2012 Courses, SIGGRAPH 2012, pp. 21:1–21:46. ACM, New York (2012)

17. Wu, C., Zhang, Y., Yang, C.: Large scale satellite imagery simulations with physically based ray tracing on Tianhe-1A supercomputer. In Proceedings of the 15th IEEE International Conference on High Performance Computing and Communications (HPCC), HPCC 2013, Zhangjiajie, China, pp. 549–556. IEEE (2013)

18. Freisleben, B., Hartmann, D., Kielmann, T.: Parallel raytracing: a case study on partitioning and scheduling on workstation clusters. In: Proceedings of the Thirtieth Hawaii International Conference on System Sciences, vol. 1, pp. 596–605, January 1997

19. Reinhard, E.: Scheduling and data management for parallel ray tracing. Technical report, Bristol, UK (1999)

20. Kelemen, C., Szirmay-Kalos, L.: Simple and robust mutation strategy for metropolis light transport algorithm. Technical report TR-186-2-01-18, Institute of Computer Graphics and Algorithms, Vienna University of Technology, Favoritenstrasse 9–11/186, A-1040 Vienna, Austria, July 2001. Human contact: technical-report@cg.tuwien.ac.at

21. Plachetka, T.: POV Ray: persistence of vision parallel raytracer. In: Proceedings of Spring Conference on Computer Graphics, Budmerice, Slovakia, pp. 123–129 (1998)
22. Tanenbaum, A.S., Van Steen, M.: Distributed Systems: Principles and Paradigms, 2nd edn. Prentice-Hall, Upper Saddle River (2006)
23. Tianhe-2 (milkyway-2) (2013). http://www.top500.org/system/177999
24. Bitterli, B.: Rendering resources (2016). https://benedikt-bitterli.me/resources/

Parallel Statistical and Machine Learning Methods for Estimation of Physical Load

Sergii Stirenko[1], Peng Gang[2], Wei Zeng[2], Yuri Gordienko[1(✉)],
Oleg Alienin[1], Oleksandr Rokovyi[1], Nikita Gordienko[1],
Ivan Pavliuchenko[1], and Anis Rojbi[3]

[1] National Technical University of Ukraine "Igor Sikorsky Kyiv Polytechnic
Institute", Kyiv, Ukraine
yuri.gordienko@gmail.com
[2] Huizhou University, Huizhou, China
[3] CHArt Laboratory (Human and Artificial Cognitions),
University of Paris 8, Paris, France

Abstract. Several statistical and machine learning methods are proposed to estimate the type and intensity of physical load and accumulated fatigue. They are based on the statistical analysis of accumulated and moving window data subsets with construction of a kurtosis-skewness diagram. This approach was applied to the data gathered by the wearable heart monitor for various types and levels of physical activities, and for people with various physical conditions. The different levels of physical activities, loads, and fitness can be distinguished from the kurtosis-skewness diagram, and their evolution can be monitored. Several metrics for estimation of the instant effect and accumulated effect (physical fatigue) of physical loads were proposed. The data and results presented allow to extend application of these methods for modeling and characterization of complex human activity patterns, for example, to estimate the actual and accumulated physical load and fatigue, model the potential dangerous development, and give cautions and advice in real time.

Keywords: Statistical analysis · Physiological signals · Heart beat
Classification · Machine learning · HCI and human behaviour

1 Introduction

Recently due to development of wearable electronics and Internet of Things, complex physiological signals can be registered including cerebral (electroencephalography, functional magnetic resonance imaging, etc.) and peripheral (heart rate, biological activity, temperature, etc.) ones [1, 2]. They can be recorded and processed during various multimodal human-machine interactions. Quantitative characterization and interpretation of the mentioned physiological signals is non-trivial task which attracts attention of experts from various fields of science including medicine, biology, chemistry, electrical engineering, computer science, etc [3, 4]. The main aim of this paper is to present the new approach to monitor and predict the type and level of current physical load by heart rate/beat analysis only (without accelerometry used in all

© Springer Nature Switzerland AG 2018
J. Vaidya and J. Li (Eds.): ICA3PP 2018, LNCS 11334, pp. 483–497, 2018.
https://doi.org/10.1007/978-3-030-05051-1_33

other works). The Sect. 2, Background and Related Work gives the brief outline of the state of the art. The Sect. 3, Experimental contains the description of the experimental part related with main terms, parameters and metrics. The Sect. 4, Results reports about the results obtained and processed by some statistical and machine learning methods. The Sect. 5, Discussion is dedicated to discussion of the results obtained and Sect. 6, Conclusions summarizes the lessons learned.

2   Background and Related Work

Estimation of the actual physical load and fatigue is of great importance nowadays in the context of human-machine interactions, especially for health care and elderly care applications [3–6]. Evolution of information and communication technologies allows everyone to apply the range of the wearable sensors and actuators, which are already become de facto standard devices in the ordinary gadgets [1, 7–9]. Recently several approaches of fatigue estimation were proposed on the basis of multimodal human-machine interaction and machine learning methods [4, 10–14]. The valuable output can be obtained by usage of machine learning and, especially deep learning techniques, which are recently used for analysis of human physical activity [11–14]. During the last years various techniques were applied to measure physical load, stress, and fatigue by analysis of heart-rate, especially by measuring the RR interval or heart period variability [4, 15–20]. Unfortunately, the type (walking, running, skiing, biking, etc.) and intensity (distance, time, pace, power, etc.) of the actual physical load hardly can be recognized by heart rate analysis only. Usually, to recognize them the heart monitors are used along with other wearable sensors like accelerometers, power meters, etc. [21, 22]. Moreover, any estimation of 'stress' and 'fatigue' should take into account the complex physiochemical and psychological state of humans under investigation, especially by heart rate analysis only. The more complicated wearable devices like EEG-monitors and brain-computer interfaces are applied for this purpose [1, 23]. The data obtained often can be explained by various complex models including numerous parameters. Here the progress of the work is reported as to the new statistical method for characterization of the actual physical load by heart rate/beat analysis only with incentives for creation of some models describing the observed behaviors.

3   Experimental

The proposed statistical method is based on monitoring the human heart behavior, which can be estimated by heart beat/heart rate (HB/HR) monitors in the modern smartphones, smartwatches, fitness-trackers, or other fitness-related gadgets (like FitBit heart rate monitor, Armour39 heart rate monitor by Under Armour, etc.).

The typical example of the recorded HB/HR values is shown in Fig. 1, where the previous rest phase is shown before the green vertical line with letter S for 'Start', the exercise itself (walking upstairs) is between the green and red vertical lines, and the following rest phase is located after the red vertical line with letter E for 'End'. The evident tendency is to have the high (very fluctuating part of the time series) HB/HR variability in the both rest states, and the much lower (the smoother part of the time series) HB/HR variability during exercise itself. This phenomenon is actively investigated to track and estimate stress states [4, 15–20]. The main idea of the approach proposed here is to consider the time series of HB/HR values as statistical ensembles of values: (a) accumulated from the beginning of the physical activity; (b) contained inside a sliding timeslot window (for example, one hundred neighboring HB/HR measurements obtained by a sliding window). These ensembles are processed by calculation of mean, standard deviation, skewness, and kurtosis. Finally, these statistical parameters are plotted on the Pearson (kurtosis-skewness) diagram (see below in Fig. 2), where kurtosis values are plotted versus square of skewness [24–27]. The similar approach in different ways was widely used for analysis of distributions and was successfully applied in various fields of science, including computer science, physics, materials science, finance, geoscience, etc. [28–32].

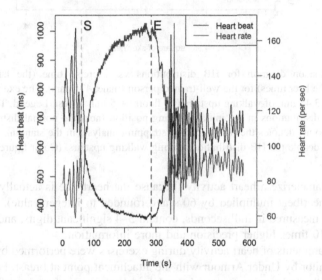

Fig. 1. Time series of heart beat and heart rate values vs. exercise time for walking upstairs for the well-trained person (male, 47 years). The exercise was like: 1 min of rest (before the green vertical line with letter S for 'Start') + 3.45 min of walking upstairs (between the green and red vertical lines) + 5 min of rest (after the red vertical line with letter E for 'End'). (Color figure online)

The following important aspects of this approach should be emphasized. The absolute HB/HR values are volatile and sensitive to its instant state (mood, stress, tremor, etc.) including momentary external disturbances and sources of noise. But the distributions of HB/HR values (cumulative or inside sliding timeslot window) and the statistical parameters of these distributions (mean, std, skewness, kurtosis) are not so volatile and can be more characteristic for the person itself (age, gender, physical maturity, fitness, accumulated fatigue, etc.) than for its instant state. In addition to this, the heart rate values are actually the integer values with 2–3 significant digits and not

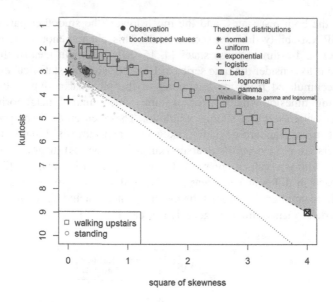

Fig. 2. The Pearson diagram for HB distributions vs. exercise time (the larger symbols correspond to the later times) for the well-trained person (male, 47 years). The exercise was like: 1 min of rest + 3.45 min of walking upstairs (13 floors) + 5 min of rest. Legend: The red circles denote the HB distributions in the initial standing position (near the normal distribution). The rose cloud of points denotes the results of bootstrapping analysis in the standing position. The blue rectangles denote the HB distributions during walking upstairs. (Color figure online)

adequately characterize a heart activity (because the heart rate is actually the reverse value of the heartbeat multiplied by 60 s and rounded to integer value). In contrary, heartbeats are measured in milliseconds, contain 3–4 significant digits, and their usage gives at least10 times higher precision and more information.

The measurements of heart activity during exercises were performed by Armour39 heart rate monitor by Under Armour with the attachment point at breast. For the initial tests (feasibility study only) four male and female persons of various fitness (from beginners to marathoners) with age from 18 to 47 (mean weight 65 ± 4 kg, mean height 1.71 ± 0.05 m) were included in the study. All of them were volunteers and had not any known cardiac abnormalities. The next stages of this research will include the wider range of volunteers and these results will be reported separately elsewhere. The raw data were obtained for various physical activities in two experiments. The first experiment included analysis of HB distributions for walking upstairs, squats, dumb-bells, push-ups (Sect. 4.1). The second experiment included analysis of influence of HR data on the models predicting the types of physical activities (Sect. 4.2).

4 Results

4.1 Heart Beat Distributions

The time series of HB values were obtained during various physical exercises and then they were considered as statistical samplings. Then the distributions of HB values in these samplings were analyzed (by calculation of mean, standard deviation, skewness, and kurtosis values) and plotted on the Pearson diagram (Fig. 2).

The example of raw data obtained for one of exercises (namely, for walking upstairs) is shown on the time series plot (Fig. 1), and the example of the processed accumulated data is shown on the Pearson diagram (Fig. 2). For the better visualization the size of symbol grows with the time of experiment and the bigger symbols corresponds to the later time moments. It allows us to observe the following tendency. Initially, in the preliminary rest state the distribution of HB values is close to the normal distribution. Then with the start of the physical exercise (walking upstairs) the distribution of HB values moves away from the location of normal distribution (black asterisk in Fig. 2), but confines itself in the region of beta-distributions (gray zone in Fig. 2).

After the end of exercises the HB distribution returns to the location of normal (black asterisk in Fig. 2) and uniform (black triangle in Fig. 2) distributions.

The dataset included numerous long time sequences ($>10^3$) and the statistical processing required numerous sub-samplings ($\sim 10^3$) with many bootstrapping trials ($>10^3$ for each sub-sampling). That is why the several parallel processing techniques were implemented in R language designed for statistical analysis on various levels of granularity among different: (a) time sequences, (b) sub-samplings, and (c) random subsets of sub-samplings for bootstrapping analysis.

The following metrics were proposed to characterize the accommodation and recovery levels during these exercises: on the Pearson diagram the distance from the normal distribution (Metric1) that corresponds to the rest state (where heart beats are not correlated) and the distance from the uniform distribution (Metric2) that corresponds to the increasing load on the heart (where heart beats grow with time). The plots in Fig. 3 show evolution of the two metrics of the HB distributions in the experiment described above and shown in Figs. 1 and 2. For accumulated HB distribution (Fig. 3a) the monotonous steady increase of Metric1 corresponds to the growing physical load, and the similar monotonous steady decrease does to the recovering during the rest after the end of the exercise (after the red vertical line with letter E) with some delay. For HB distribution in the sliding timeslot window (Fig. 3b) the changes of the regime (start of exercise. end of exercise, recover) are followed by the sharp peaks of statistical parameters and the proposed Metric1. The slopes of Metric1 increase and decrease can be used also to characterize the accommodation and recovery levels during the exercises.

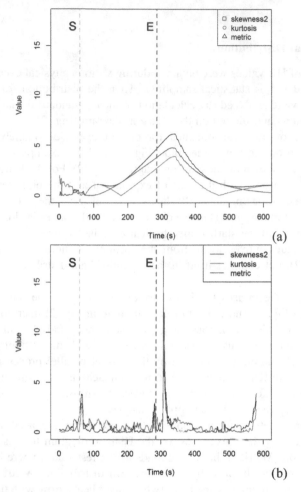

Fig. 3. Plots of statistical parameters (kurtosis and square of skewness) and Metric1 (the distance from the normal distribution on the Pearson diagram) of the HB distribution vs. exercise time: (a) accumulated from the beginning of the physical activity; (b) contained inside the sliding timeslot window.

The similar results were obtained for other types of exercises with various workloads: squats, dumbbells, push-ups (Fig. 4). This method allows us to determine the level of workload even (compare location of HB distributions for dumbbells of various weight in Fig. 4) and recovery rate after workloads.

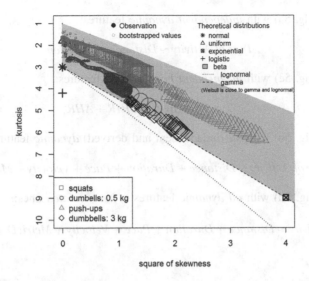

Fig. 4. The Pearson diagram for HB distributions vs. exercise time (the larger symbols correspond to the later times) for the well-trained person (male, 47 years). The exercises were like: squats, dumbbells of various weights (0.5 and 3 kg), push-ups. The active phases of the exercises without the rest and recovery stages are shown here.

4.2   Influence of HR Data on Models Predicting the Type of Physical Activities

At the moment the empirical results as to the change of distribution type for the accumulated HB values during physical exercise hardly have any simple explanations. But due to the recent success of various machine learning methods for analysis of the complex processes the incentive to apply some of them naturally appeared. The direct application of machine learning methods for the analysis of HB distributions is under work right now, but the preliminary similar tests on the simpler experiment are reported below.

The same focus group performed several physical activities of similar, but different types (actually running, skiing, and walking) with various intensities (distances and durations). The aim of experiment was to investigate feasibility to predict the type of physical activity from some dynamic features (distance, time, pace, velocity, etc.) and improve this prediction by adding heart activity features (average heart rate, maximal heart rate, etc.) by heart rate/beat analysis (not by accelerometry like in all other works) with some well-known methods including linear regression, neural network, and deep neural network. The features were divided in independent and derived. For example, distance and time are independent ones among the dynamic features, but pace (time/distance in minute/kilometer units), velocity (distance/time in meter/minute units), and MetricD (pace in square) are derived ones. Similarly, HR in rest (HRrest), maximal HR (MHR), minimal HR (minHR), average HR (AHR) are independent among the heart-related features, but working range HR (MHR-minHR), HR reserve (MHR - HRrest), and HR recovery (MHR - HRrest after exercise) are derived ones. To the moment the results are reported here on the following models:

Model 1 (Fig. 5a) with *independent dynamic* features:

$$Type\ of\ Activity \sim Distance + Duration \tag{1}$$

Model 2 (Fig. 5c) with *independent heart-related* features:

$$Type\ of\ Activity \sim MHR + AHR \tag{2}$$

Model 3 (Fig. 5b) with *all* (independent and derived) *dynamic* features:

$$Type\ of\ Activity \sim Distance + Duration + Pace + Velocity + MetricD \tag{3}$$

Model 4 (Fig. 5d) with *all dynamic* features + *heart-related* ones:

$$Type\ of\ Activity \sim Distance + Duration + Pace + Velocity + MetricD + MHR + AHR \tag{4}$$

The idea behind inclusion of derived features (like pace, velocity, MetricD) consists in inclusion of non-linear relations among independent parameters. On this stage of research, inclusion of heart-related features is limited to MHR and AHR, but usage of the more complex statistical parameters of HB/HR distributions (which are described in the previous Subsect. 4.1, Heart Beat Distributions) is under work now and will be reported elsewhere.

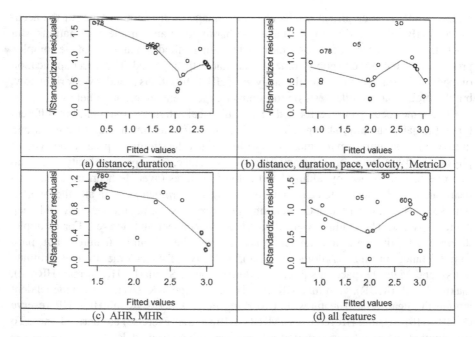

Fig. 5. Linear regression results: square root of standardized residuals vs. some fitted values.

Linear Regression. The multiple linear regression model contains only one predictor variable (type of the physical activity), several explanatory variables (see above), and the relationship between the predictor variable and explanatory variables is assumed to be linear in this model. The results of application of the linear regression for various models are shown in Fig. 5 for the standardized residuals (response minus fitted values) versus the fitted values (numbers near circles denote the numeration of exercises – only several of them are shown here). Some predicted types of the physical activities are demonstrated in Fig. 8 and are discussed below in Sect. 5, Discussion.

Neural Network. The simple neural network (Fig. 6) was used with various (depending on the model) input nodes (I), one output node (O) for the predicted value of the type of physical activity, 6 neurons (H1–H6) and biases (B). The dark lines mean positive values of weights, and light lines—negative ones. The widths of lines demonstrate the relative values of the weights, for example, contribution of the velocity

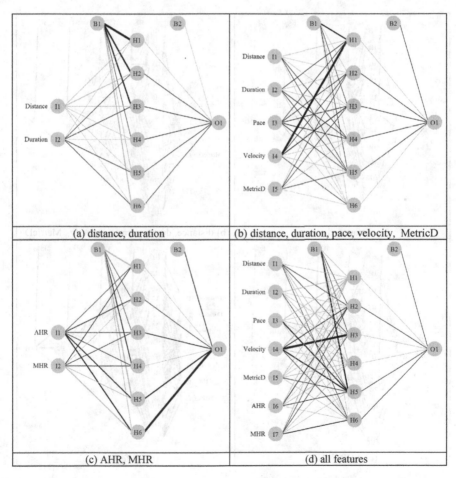

Fig. 6. Neural network with the contribution of some neurons graphically shown by the width of the lines (dark - positive weights, light - negative weights).

is significant in models 1 (Fig. 5a) and 3 (Fig. 5b), that is graphically shown by the thicker lines. Again the examples of the predicted types of the physical activities are demonstrated in Fig. 8 and are discussed below in Sect. 5, Discussion.

Deep Neural Network. The deep neural network (Fig. 7) was used with various (depending on the model) input nodes (I), one output node (O) for the predicted value of the type of physical activity, 4 layers with (12, 8, 6, 3) neurons (H) and biases (B). Here the dark lines also mean positive values of weights, and light lines—negative ones after training the deep neural network with the tuned learning rate (0.001), the thresholds (0.001) for the partial derivatives of the error function as stopping criteria, logistic activation functions, and globally convergent algorithm based on the resilient backpropagation [33–35]. Here contribution of some features is not so evident like in the case of the shallow neural network from the previous subsection. The widths of

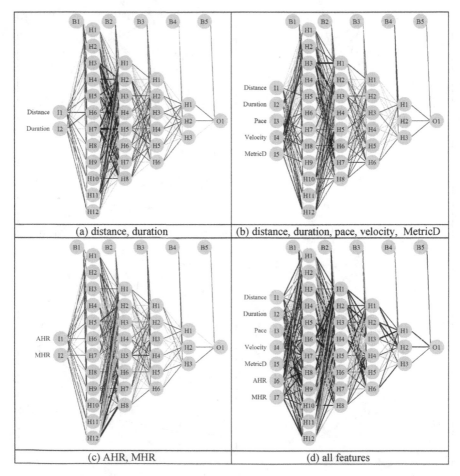

Fig. 7. Neural network with the contribution of some neurons graphically shown by the width of the lines (dark - positive weights, light - negative weights).

lines demonstrate the relative values of the weights, and the contributions from neurons have the very complex patterns on all layers. For example in model 1 (with *independent dynamic* features) some intermediate hidden values propagated from the 1st layer to the 2nd layer contribute the most (Fig. 7a) while for model 4 (with *all dynamic* features + *heart-related* ones) most of the connections are almost equally important (Fig. 7d). At the moment these results are given for comparison with other machine learning methods (linear regression and neural network in previous subsections) and should be investigated thoroughly, especially in the view of hyper-parameter tuning that is planned to be performed, explained and discussed in the future work.

5 Discussion

Some types of the physical activities predicted by the above mentioned models are shown in Fig. 8, where the codes for types of the physical activities are as follows: 1—running, 2—skiing, 3—walking. The linear regression demonstrate the worst prediction abilities for all models, but addition of heart-related features in model 4 (Fig. 8d) slightly decrease the error and improve predictions for skiing and walking. In general,

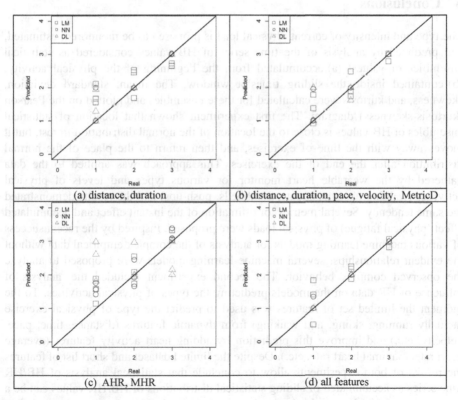

Fig. 8. Examples of the types of physical activities (1—running, 2—skiing, 3—walking) predicted by linear regression (LM), shallow (NN) and deep learning (DL) neural network.

the larger models (with more input features) like model 3 (Fig. 8b) and model 4 (Fig. 8d) gives the better predictions than the smaller models like model 1 (Fig. 8a) and model 2 (Fig. 8c). But the most significant improvement of prediction was obtained for the shallow (1-layer) and deep (4-layer) neural networks in model 4 due to inclusion of the additional independent heart-related features.

In fact, the increase of the number of independent input features should theoretically enlarge the information processed by neural networks (shallow and deep) and improve predictions. In this sense, inclusion of the heart-related features (even in such a limited way like addition of AHR and MHR) contribute the additional information about the physical exercise. But this contribution can be very sensitive to other aspects of the humans under tests, for example, typical for some focus groups (like age, gender, weight, physical maturity, etc.), and personal peculiarities (like fitness, mood, accumulated fatigue, etc.). On the one hand it does not allow to apply the models trained on some limited focus group for the wider range of users without understanding the influence of personal peculiarities. But on the other hand this influence of personal peculiarities can allow to create the personal models previously trained on the typical group and later tuned to the personal peculiarities of the concrete persons.

6   Conclusions

The type and intensity of current physical load is proposed to be monitored, estimated, and predicted by analysis of the time series of HB values considered as statistical ensembles of values: (a) accumulated from the beginning of the physical activity; (b) contained inside the sliding timeslot window. The mean, standard deviation, skewness, and kurtosis were calculated for these ensembles and plotted on the Pearson (kurtosis-skewness) diagram. The first experiment shown that location of statistical ensembles of HB values is close to the location of the normal distribution in rest, but it moves away with the time of exercises, and then return to the place of the normal distribution after the end of the exercises. This approach was applied to the data gathered by the wearable heart monitor for various types and levels of physical activities (walking upstairs, squats, dumbbells, push-ups) and the results demonstrated the same tendency. Several metrics for estimation of the instant effect and accumulated effect (physical fatigue) of physical loads were proposed. Inspired by the recent success of various machine learning models for analysis of the complex empirical data without the evident relationships, several machine learning models were proposed to analyze the observed complex behavior. The second experiment included the analysis of influence of HR data on the models predicting the types of physical activities. To the moment the limited set of features was used to predict the type of physical exercise (actually running, skiing, and walking) from dynamic features (distance, time, pace, velocity, etc.) and improve this prediction by adding heart activity features (average heart rate, maximal heart rate, etc.). Despite the limited dataset and short list of features the results of both experiments allow to conclude that statistical analysis of HB/HR time series as accumulated or sliding statistical distributions of HB/HR values can be a promising way for characterization of the actual physical load. Moreover the statistical parameters for distributions of HB/HR values (like maximum, minimum, normalized mean, standard deviation, skewness, and kurtosis) can be used as additional independent features in shallow and deep neural networks.

The obtained predictions can be very sensitive to many additional collective (like age, gender, weight, physical maturity, etc.), and individual (like personal fitness, mood, accumulated fatigue, etc.) aspects of the humans under tests. That is why the much larger datasets and additional research will be necessary for the more collectively and personally tailored models. In this context, the further progress can be reached by sharing the similar datasets around the world in the spirit of open science, volunteer data collection, processing and computing [36–38]. The data and results presented allow us to extend application of these methods for modeling and characterization of complex human activity patterns. For example, under condition of the further improvement the models presented here can be used to estimate the actual and accumulated physical load and related fatigue, model the potential dangerous development, and give cautions and advice in real time, that is very important for many health and elderly care applications.

Acknowledgment. The work was partially supported by Ukraine-France Collaboration Project (Programme PHC DNIPRO) (http://www.campusfrance.org/fr/dnipro) and by Huizhou Science and Technology Bureau and Huizhou University (Huizhou, P.R.China) in the framework of Platform Construction for China-Ukraine Hi-Tech Park Project # 2014C050012001.

References

1. Kumari, P., Mathew, L., Syal, P.: Increasing trend of wearables and multimodal interface for human activity monitoring: A review. Biosens. Bioelectron. **90**, 298–307 (2017)
2. Koydemir, H.C., Ozcan, A.: Wearable and implantable sensors for biomedical applications. Ann. Rev. Anal. Chem. **11** (2018) https://doi.org/10.1146/annurev-anchem-061417-125956
3. Faust, O., Hagiwara, Y., Hong, T.J., Lih, O.S., Acharya, U.R.: Deep learning for healthcare applications based on physiological signals: a review. Comput. Methods Programs Biomed. **161**, 1–13 (2018)
4. Mohanavelu, K., Lamshe, R., Poonguzhali, S., Adalarasu, K., Jagannath, M.: Assessment of human fatigue during physical performance using physiological signals: a review. Biomed. Pharmacol. J. **10**(4), 1887–1896 (2017)
5. Edward, C.W., Nemeroff, C.B. (eds.): The Concise Corsini Encyclopedia of Psychology and Behavioral Science. Wiley, Hoboken (2004)
6. Gordienko, Y., et al.: Augmented coaching ecosystem for non-obtrusive adaptive personalized elderly care on the basis of Cloud-Fog-Dew computing paradigm. In: 2017 40th International Convention on Information and Communication Technology, Electronics and Microelectronics (MIPRO), pp. 359–364. IEEE, Opatija (2017)
7. Banaee, H., Ahmed, M.U., Loutfi, A.: Data mining for wearable sensors in health monitoring systems: a review of recent trends and challenges. Sensors **13**(12), 17472–17500 (2013)
8. Bunn, J.A., Navalta, J.W., Fountaine, C.J., Reece, J.D.: Current state of commercial wearable technology in physical activity monitoring 2015–2017. Int. J. Exerc. Sci. **11**(7), 503 (2018)
9. Amft, O., Van Laerhoven, K.: What will we wear after smartphones? IEEE Pervasive Comput. **16**(4), 80–85 (2017)

10. Gang, P., et al.: User-driven intelligent interface on the basis of multimodal augmented reality and brain-computer interaction for people with functional disabilities. Future of Information and Communications Conference (FICC), Singapore. arXiv preprint arXiv: 1704.05915 (2017)

11. Du, L.H., Liu, W., Zheng, W.L., Lu, B.L.: Detecting driving fatigue with multimodal deep learning. In: 2017 8th International IEEE/EMBS Conference on Neural Engineering (NER), pp. 74–77. IEEE (2017)

12. Lopez, M.B., del-Blanco, C.R., Garcia, N.: Detecting exercise-induced fatigue using thermal imaging and deep learning. In: 2017 Seventh International Conference on Image Processing Theory, Tools and Applications (IPTA), pp. 1–6. IEEE (2017)

13. Gordienko, Y., et al.: Deep learning for fatigue estimation on the basis of multimodal human-machine interactions. XXIX IUPAP Conference in Computational Physics (CCP2017), Paris, France. arXiv preprint arXiv:1801.06048 (2017)

14. Hajinoroozi, M., Zhang, J. M., Huang, Y.: Driver's fatigue prediction by deep covariance learning from EEG. In: 2017 International Conference on Systems, Man, and Cybernetics (SMC), pp. 240–245. IEEE (2017)

15. Togo, F., Takahashi, M.: Heart rate variability in occupational health-a systematic review. Ind. Health 47(6), 589–602 (2009)

16. Aubert, A.E., Seps, B., Beckers, F.: Heart rate variability in athletes. Sports Med. 33(12), 889–919 (2003)

17. Schmitt, L., et al.: Fatigue shifts and scatters heart rate variability in elite endurance athletes. PLoS ONE 8(8), e71588 (2013)

18. Pichot, V., et al.: Relation between heart rate variability and training load in middle-distance runners. Med. Sci. Sports Exerc. 32(10), 1729–1736 (2000)

19. Gonzalez, K., Sasangohar, F., Mehta, R.K., Lawley, M., Erraguntla, M.: Measuring fatigue through heart rate variability and activity recognition: a scoping literature review of machine learning techniques. In: Proceedings of the Human Factors and Ergonomics Society Annual Meeting, vol. 61, no. 1, pp. 1748–1752. SAGE Publications, Los Angeles (2017)

20. Morgan, S.J., Mora, J.A.M.: Effect of heart rate variability biofeedback on sport performance, a systematic review. Appl. Psychophysiol. Biofeedback 42(3), 235–245 (2017)

21. Yang, C.C., Hsu, Y.L.: A review of accelerometry-based wearable motion detectors for physical activity monitoring. Sensors 10(8), 7772–7788 (2010)

22. Evenson, K.R., Goto, M.M., Furberg, R.D.: Systematic review of the validity and reliability of consumer-wearable activity trackers. Int. J. Behav. Nutr. Phys. Act. 12(1), 159 (2015)

23. Lin, C.T., et al.: Review of wireless and wearable electroencephalogram systems and brain-computer interfaces–a mini-review. Gerontology 56(1), 112–119 (2010)

24. Cramer, H.: Mathematical Methods of Statistics, vol. 9. Princeton University Press, Princeton (1999)

25. Delignette-Muller, M.L., Pouillot, R., Denis, J.-B., Dutang, C.: fitdistrplus package for R (2012)

26. Cullen, A., Frey, H.: Probabilistic Techniques in Exposure Assessment: A Handbook for Dealing with Variability and Uncertainty in Models and Inputs. Springer, Heidelberg (1999)

27. Gordienko, Y.G.: Generalized model of migration-driven aggregate growth–asymptotic distributions, power laws and apparent fractality. Int. J. Mod. Phys. B 26(01), 1250010 (2012)

28. Ma, X., Xu, F.: Peak factor estimation of non-Gaussian wind pressure on high-rise buildings. Struct. Des. Tall Spec. Build. 26(17), e1386 (2017)

29. Gordienko, Y.G.: Molecular dynamics simulation of defect substructure evolution and mechanisms of plastic deformation in aluminium nanocrystals. Metallofiz. Noveishie Tekhnol. 33(9), 1217–1247 (2011)

30. Ketchantang, W., Derrode, S., Martin, L., Bourennane, S.: Pearson-based mixture model for color object tracking. Mach. Vis. Appl. **19**(5–6), 457–466 (2008)
31. Tison, C., Nicolas, J.M., Tupin, F., Maître, H.: A new statistical model for Markovian classification of urban areas in high-resolution SAR images. IEEE Trans. Geosci. Remote Sens. **42**(10), 2046–2057 (2004)
32. Sornette, D., Zhou, W.X.: Predictability of large future changes in major financial indices. Int. J. Forecast. **22**(1), 153–168 (2006)
33. Anastasiadis, A.D., Magoulas, G.D., Vrahatis, M.N.: New globally convergent training scheme based on the resilient propagation algorithm. Neurocomputing **64**, 253–270 (2005)
34. Intrator O., Intrator N.: Using neural nets for interpretation of nonlinear models. In: Proceedings of the Statistical Computing Section, pp. 244–249. American Statistical Society (eds.), San Francisco (1993)
35. Beck, M.W.: Visualizing neural networks. https://github.com/fawda123. Accessed 03 May 2018
36. Goldberger, A.L., et al.: Physiobank, physiotoolkit, and physionet. Circulation **101**(23), e215–e220 (2000)
37. Gordienko, N., Lodygensky, O., Fedak, G., Gordienko, Yu.: Synergy of volunteer measurements and volunteer computing for effective data collecting, processing, simulating and analyzing on a worldwide scale, In: Proceedings of the 38th International Convention on Inf. and Communication Technology, Electronics and Microelectronics (MIPRO), pp. 193–198. IEEE, Opatija (2015)
38. Chen, Y., Wang, Z.Y., Yuan, G., Huang, L.: An overview of online based platforms for sharing and analyzing electrophysiology data from big data perspective. WIREs Data Min. Knowl. Discov. **7**(4), e1206 (2017)

Parallel Communication Mechanisms in Solving Integral Equations for Electromagnetic Scattering Based on the Method of Moments

Lan Song[1,2,3(✉)], Dennis K. Peters[3], Weimin Huang[3], Zhiwei Liu[2], Lixia Lei[2], and Tangliu Wen[1]

[1] School of Computer, State Key Laboratory of Software Engineering, Wuhan University, Wuhan, Hubei 430072, China
`sll30com@163.com, wqtlglk@163.com`
[2] School of Information Engineering, East China Jiaotong University, Nanchang, Jiangxi 330013, China
`zwliul982@hotmail.com, llx77@163.com`
[3] Electrical and Computer Engineering, Faculty of Engineering and Applied Science, Memorial University, St. John's, NL, Canada
`{dpeters,weimin}@mun.ca`

Abstract. In this paper, a parallel solution of impedance filling was studied to improve the efficiency for the method of moments (MOM) in solving the integral equation for electromagnetic scattering. Based on the formalization method, the correctness verification method of the parallel communication protocol was proposed to avoid the abnormal situation such as deadlock caused by unsynchronized MPI message delivery. Finally, a numerical example is given to verify the accuracy of the parallel algorithm in a multi-core cluster environment, and the parallel efficiency and computational capability are also tested. From the experiment data, it can be seen that the results of the parallel-based integral equation match well with the results of the Mie analytical solution. The parallel algorithm proposed in this paper is evaluated in terms of the acceleration ratio and parallel efficiency. The experimental results demonstrate the reliability and effectiveness of the method.

Keywords: Formal verification · Parallel communication
Electromagnetic scattering · Petri net

1 Introduction

Based on Maxwell's theory, the numerical method (instead of the mathematical analytical method), is used to analyze the electromagnetic field, so as to liberate the human brain from a large number of complex operations. The common algorithms used for the

© Springer Nature Switzerland AG 2018
J. Vaidya and J. Li (Eds.): ICA3PP 2018, LNCS 11334, pp. 498–507, 2018.
https://doi.org/10.1007/978-3-030-05051-1_34

electromagnetic computing include the method of moments (MOM) [1], finite-difference time domain (FDTD) [2, 3], and finite element method (FEM) [4]. All these methods require the objects to be divided into small elements for further analysis. FDTD, which is based on the differential form of Maxwell's equations, is mainly used to analyze the shielding problem and the bio-electromagnetic effect. FEM, which is based on the differential form of the Maxwell equation, is usually employed to analyze the cavity and the waveguide filter. MOM, which is based on the integral form of Maxwell equations, is mainly used to analyze problems such as long wire simulation and super large electrical size. Among them, MOM has a high accuracy of calculation. With the conductor being divided into small elements, by calculating the current on all the conductor units, the overall electromagnetic field generated by the conductor can be determined. MOM can improve the accuracy of complex media scattering calculation. However, the disadvantage is that it needs higher computational complexity to generate the impedance matrix. The impedance matrix is a dense matrix with a computational complexity of $O(n^2)$ The calculation is time consuming and the matrix occupies a significant amount of memory, so it is a bottleneck for its application [5].

Parallel techniques for numerical solution of electromagnetic field can effectively overcome the bottleneck of computational speed. In [6], the performance of various computational electromagnetic techniques and the application of parallel technology in computational electromagnetics were investigated. The solution of electromagnetic field based on Message Passing Interface (MPI) technology mainly focused on the number of iterations for accelerating the convergence. In [7], a hybrid parallel strategy for solving electromagnetic integral equations involving different electric sizes and geometrical-complex targets was proposed, and MPI message passing is employed for the distributed computation among all the nodes. In [8], a parallel algorithm for the construction and application of a preconditioner was proposed, and the MPI techniques were applied to the conjugate gradient method to accelerate convergence.

Our proposed method aims to address the time-consuming double loop that is $O(n^2)$. The parallel implementation mechanism of MPI for solving impedance matrix is studied to improve the efficiency of numerical calculation. To address the problem of significant matrix-filling computations using the MOM and improve the safety and reliability of numerical calculation, this paper presents a parallel communication method to solve the integral equation of electromagnetic scattering. The parallel efficiency can be enhanced with a good parallel communication model between the multiprocessors. A formalization method is used to verify its reliability. A parallel algorithm for solving electromagnetic scattering is proposed, and the accuracy, parallel efficiency, and computational power are evaluated.

The remainder of this paper is organized as follows: Sect. 2 introduces the parallel communication mechanism and the modeling based on the formal method. Section 3 contains experimental analysis, and Sect. 4 concludes the paper.

2 Research on Parallel Communication Mechanism

2.1 Parallel Matrix Filling Method

To increase the speed of matrix filling, the MPI message passing method is adopted to parallelize the matrix-filling algorithm. The process is described in the flow diagram in Fig. 1, in which the parallel interaction and parallel computing modules are considered mainly for the four pairs of positive and negative triangles in impedance matrix filling. In this paper, the mechanism of message sending and receiving, data broadcasting and reduction is used. When data is broadcast on the inner edge, the root process sends the message to all other processors in the communicator which represents a one-to-many pattern. The flow chart is illustrated in Fig. 2.

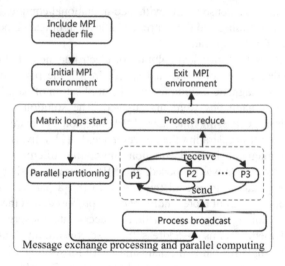

Fig. 1. The flow chart of parallel matrix filling

After each process completes the numerical calculation, the respective results are returned to the root process. The reduction operation with the many-to-one model is adopted to realize addition of complex quantities. The data flow is illustrated in Fig. 3.

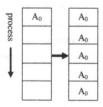

Fig. 2. The broadcast of the inner edges

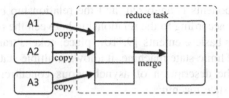

Fig. 3. The data reduction of the minus and the plus triangles

2.2 Method of Message Communication

With the number of processors being increased, the parallel computing time is reduced, and the communication time increases. This affects the scalability of the parallel algorithm. The proposed method addresses the tradeoff between speed and performance and adopts the message communication method described below.

Each process can be divided into five states (ready, waiting, send, receive, halt), which represent the prepared state, waiting state, sending state, receiving state, and idle state, respectively.

The communication step (using the interactive communication between process 1 and process 2 as an example):

(1) The initial state of process 1 and process 2 is set to the waiting state, and each process calculates the inner, outer, and singular integrals.
(2) After calculating the integrals, the process state will be changed to the ready state, and the process then sends an inquiry to the other process for required data.
(3) Process 2 receives the inquiry from process 1, converts the state to the sending state, and compares the triangles number passed by process 1 with the requested number. If it is within this range, then the results of the singular integral will be passed to process 1.
(4) Process 1 receives the value from process 2 and converts the state to the receiving state.
(5) Process 1 takes the inner and outer integrals calculated in the first step, stores the result, and changes the state to ready.
(6) If process 1 is in the ready state, then set a counter with an initial value of 0. The counter is incremented by 1 until the value of the counter is equal to the number of processes. The state is then changed to idle.

2.3 Formalized Modeling of the Communication Mechanism

In the case of obstructive process communication, when the MPI blocking-standard, mode-messaging function is used, the program is deadlocked due to the mismatch of sending and receiving operations caused by asynchronous operation. Such errors are often not easily noticeable. Verification of the communication protocol based on for-malized methods will effectively avoid the deadlock.

The MPI messaging scheme in Sect. 2.2 is represented as a Petri-net. The process in the system is symbolized into a series of states and modeling the interaction process between the two components is analyzed, and the relationship between the state and input event is obtained according to the relationship between the process and the event. The Petri-net has four basic elements [9, 10]: place, token, transition, and arc with arrows. As one type of finite-state machine, it allows multiple state transitions to occur simultaneously, and the description of asynchronous concurrent processes is more convenient than finite state machines.

According to the above description, the Petri-net model of inter-process information interaction is shown in Fig. 4, where the rectangle indicates the triggered event, the circle represents the state of the reader or tag, and the arrow means state transition.

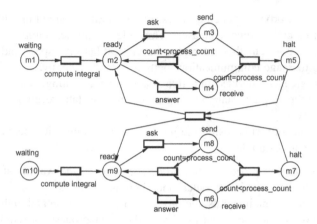

Fig. 4. The Petri-net model $\sum_1$ between process interaction

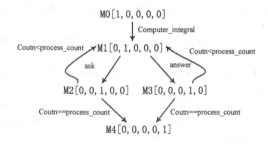

Fig. 5. Reachable marking graph RG $\left(\sum_1\right)$

Through a Petri-net's reachable graph, we analyze the state changes and sequence of transition in the network, and the boundedness and liveness of the model. We can obtain the reachable marking graph as shown in Fig. 5.

3 Experiment

We present our results from three aspects: formal verification of communication mechanisms, and the verification of computational accuracy and parallel efficiency.

3.1 Formal Verification of Communication Mechanisms

In this paper, we design the linear temporal logic (LTL) to verify the correctness of the proposed parallelism algorithm. For related literature of LTL, please refer to [11]. The communication protocol proposed in the previous section is described in the Promela language and is analyzed and simulated using the spin tool. We then determine whether our defined LTL formula is satisfied or not by setting assertions. The two transition rules for state transitions are described by LTL as follows:

$$G((waiting \rightarrow X(ready)) \wedge (ready \rightarrow X(send)) \vee (ready \rightarrow X(receive))) \quad (1)$$

This requirement indicates that a process can send or receive the data from other processes, and its status changes with time sequences.

$$G((send \rightarrow F(halt)) \wedge (receive \rightarrow F(halt))) \quad (2)$$

This rule indicates that the process will complete the dot product of the triangle inner and outer integral after the process sends or receives data.

Figure 6(a) shows that LTL formulation p->\<>q describes how each process can obtain data from all other processes and finally complete the numerical calculation of the inner and outer integrals allocated to each process. Defining #define p t7 > 0, #define q t3 > 0,means that p and q obtain the token in different time sequences. The test validates the communication mechanisms.

Figure 6(b) shows the transmission and reception of all messages in the simulated process. The evaluation of the model found no errors.

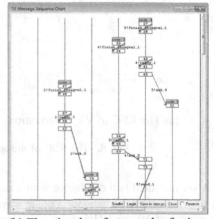

(a) LTL verify result graph   (b) The visual surface graph of spin

Fig. 6. Verification using spin tool

3.2   Verification of Computational Accuracy

Mie series method [12] is an analytic method to provide an exactly accurate solution. This paper selects the Mie series method to verify the correctness of the proposed method. Experiments are conducted on the Intel® Core ™ i3-3217U CPU @ 1.80 GHz and Inter® Core ™ i5-6300U CPU@2.40 GHZ, 4-core processor, and 64-bit operating system. An ideal ball conductor with a radius of 1 m is divided into 426 nodes, 848 triangles, and 1272 inner edges, with a plane wave of 300 MHz and an incidence angle of 0. Figure 7(a) and (b) show the comparison of the MOM and Mie results of VV and HH polarization, respectively. It is clearly seen from the figure that both results agree well with each other.

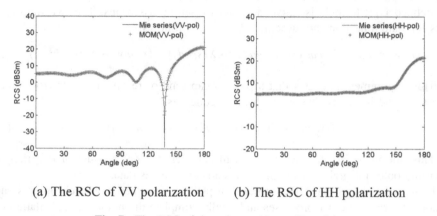

(a) The RSC of VV polarization   (b) The RSC of HH polarization

Fig. 7. The RSC of the sphere with a radius of 1 m

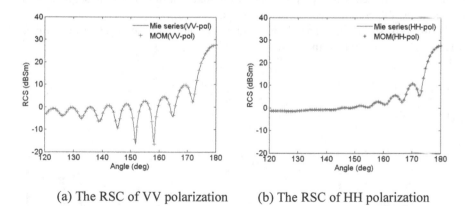

(a) The RSC of VV polarization   (b) The RSC of HH polarization

Fig. 8. The RSC of the sphere with a radius 0.46 m

A second ideal ball conductor with a radius of 0.46 m is divided into 738 triangles, 371 nodes, and 1107 edges, for a plane wave with same frequency and incidence angle. The results of VV and HH polarization are shown in Fig. 8(a) and (b), respectively. The results of two methods are consistent.

Some subtle deviations were observed in the experiment. One of the reasons is that errors are caused by geometric modeling that generates errors in the network. The other reason is that the errors are caused by iterative calculations when solving the linear equations. However, this error is very small and does not affect the overall experimental results.

3.3   Parallel Efficiency

The program was implemented in C++ on the MPICH2-1.4, where the number of processes is 8. Two PCs were connected to the network. The first CPU (i5 2.4 GHZ) is configured as the master, and the other CPU (i3 1.8 GHZ) is configured as the slave. Figure 9 shows the run time of the parallel program.

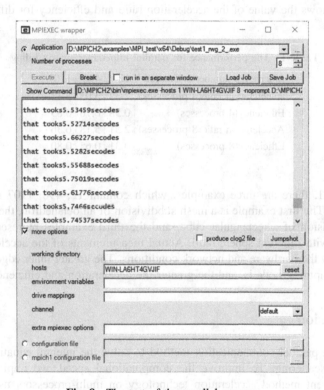

Fig. 9. The test of the parallel program

To test the efficiency of parallel processing, the parallel acceleration ratio and efficiency are used.

The acceleration ratio is defined as:

$$S_p = \frac{T_s}{T_p} \tag{3}$$

and the efficiency is defined as:

$$E_p = \frac{S_p}{p} \tag{4}$$

where T_s represent the run time of a single processor. T_p represents the time required for p processes to execute in parallel after the program parallelization. The number of single-parallel processes p is set to 4, and the number of two-parallel processes is set to 8. Table 1 shows the value of the acceleration ratio and efficiency for different input.

Table 1. The performance for parallel impedance matrix filling

Inner edge number\evaluation	12	498	1107
Acceleration ratio(4 processes)	2.32	3.03	3.38
Efficiency(4 processes)	0.58	0.76	0.85
Acceleration ratio(8 processes)	2.51	5.18	6.36
Efficiency(8 processes)	0.31	0.65	0.80

In Table 1, there are three examples, which contain 12, 498, 1107 inner edges, respectively. The first example is a mesh subdivision of an octahedron, the second is a mesh subdivision of a rectangular cube, and the third examples represent the mesh subdivision with different sphere radii. Actual measurements of the acceleration ratio are limited by the hardware and network conditions. The greater inner edge number is, the more computing node is, and the greater the acceleration and efficiency ratio are.

4   Conclusion

We present a parallel communication method to solve the integral equation for electromagnetic scattering. To improve the computational speed, we implemented the parallel moment method acceleration technology on multi-processors using MPI to communicate between processes. To address the deadlock caused by the synchronization of the MPI message, the verification mechanism of the parallel communication protocol was proposed based on the formal method. Finally, the accuracy of the parallel algorithm was verified, and the parallel efficiency and computational ability were tested. The experimental results prove the reliability and effectiveness of the method.

Acknowledgments. This work is supported in part by the project of science and technology department of Jiangxi province (No. 20161BBH80039, 20171BAB202013), the National Natural Science Foundation (No. 61462041, 61763014, 61762049),Jiangxi University humanities and social science (No. JC1507).

References

1. Harrington, R.: Origin and development of the method of moments for field computation. IEEE Antennas Propag. Mag. **32**(3), 31–36 (1990)
2. Mur, G.: Absorbing boundary conditions for the finite-difference approximation of the time-domain electromagnetic-field equations. IEEE Trans. Electromagn. Compat. **EMC-23**(4), 377–382 (1981)
3. Oskooi, A.F., Roundy, D., Ibanescu, M., Bermel, P., Joannopoulos, J.D., Johnson, S.G.: MEEP: a flexible free-software package for electromagnetic simulations by the FDTD method. Comput. Phys. Commun. **181**(3), 687–702 (2010)
4. Surana, K.S., Reddy, J.N.: The Finite Element Method for Boundary Value Problems: Mathematics and Computations. CRC Press, USA (2016)
5. Zhan, Y.: CAD modeling method in numerical simulation of electromagnetic fields. Master thesis. Xian: Xidian University (2008)
6. Sumithra, P., Thiripurasundari, D.: Review on computational electromagnetics. Adavanced Electromagn. **6**(1), 42–55 (2017)
7. Guo, H., Hu, J., Nie, Z.P.: An MPI-OpenMP hybrid parallel H-LU direct solver for electromagnetic integral equations. Int. J. Antennas Propag. **2015**, 1–10 (2015)
8. Kaporin, I., Milyukova, O.: MPI + OpenMP parallel implementation of explicitly preconditioned conjugate gradient method, pp. 1–27. Preprints of the Keldysh Institute of Applied Mathematics (2018)
9. Wu, Z.: Introduction to Petri net, pp. 10–30. China Machine Press, Beijing (2006)
10. Yuan, J.: Petri Net Modeling and Intelligent Analysis, pp. 39–122. National Defence Industry Press, Beijing (2011)
11. Holzmann, G.J.: The spin model checker: primer and reference manual, pp. 95–123. Addison-Wesley, New Jersey (2003)
12. Wiscombe, W.J.: Improved Mie scattering algorithms. Appl. Opt. **19**(9), 1505–1509 (1980)

POWER: A Parallel-Optimization-Based Framework Towards Edge Intelligent Image Recognition and a Case Study

Yingyi Yang[✉]📷, Xiaoming Mai, Hao Wu, Ming Nie, and Hui Wu

Electric Power Research Institute of Guangdong Power Grid Co., Ltd.,
GuangZhou, China
yangyingyi10@126.com

Abstract. To improve the intelligent image recognition abilities of edge devices, a parallel-optimization-based framework called POWER is introduced in this paper. With FPGA (Field-Programmable Gate Array) as its hardware module, POWER provides well extensibility and flexible customization capability for developing intelligent firmware suitable for different types of edge devices in various scenarios. Through an actual case study, we design and implement a firmware prototype following the specification of POWER and explore its performance improvement using parallel optimization. Our experimental results show that the firmware prototype we implement exhibits good performance and is applicable to substation inspection robots, which also validate the effectiveness of our POWER framework in designing edge intelligent firmware modules indirectly.

Keywords: Edge intelligence · Image recognition · Framework
Parallel optimization · Substation inspection robot

1 Introduction

With the massive accumulation of data and the rapid improvement of computing power in recent years, artificial intelligence technology based on deep learning [5] has developed greatly. Deep convolutional neural networks (CNN) [3] have attracted extensive attentions in academia and industry due to its excellent performance in certain application areas, especially in computer vision. Nowadays, computer vision based on CNN has been widely studied and applied in many fields, such as intelligent security and e-Commerce. The amount of images in such fields is huge and the training of CNN models still depends on powerful cloud or data centers.

With the development of Internet of Everything (IoE) and the growing popularity of edge applications, edge devices are changing their roles to act as both

Supported by Guangdong Power Grid Co., Ltd. Science and Technology Program under Grant No. GDKJXM20161136.

J. Vaidya and J. Li (Eds.): ICA3PP 2018, LNCS 11334, pp. 508–523, 2018.
https://doi.org/10.1007/978-3-030-05051-1_35

data producers and consumers. They are required to apply predictive analysis to data collected on site and recognize its pattern in real time [13], for consideration of bandwidth saving, data safety and efficiency promotion. Edge intelligence, a promising technique that garners much attention recently [6], provides the ability to process data intelligently in real time. Using this technique, the intelligent image recognition based on deep learning can realize inference on edge hardware modules or devices by migrating learned models, though models still rely on large-scale training running in the cloud or data centers.

However, it is tricky to design and implement firmware modules end-to-end for intelligent image recognition, for a couple or reasons. (a) Since there are various types of edge devices (e.g. access control system, surveillance camera) that can use embedded intelligent firmware, it is a difficult but meaningful task to specify the procedure of firmware implementation to accelerate edge intelligence in different application areas. (b) Due to the diversity in image scene, the intelligent firmware modules should be able to be updated or upgraded dynamically as their application scenarios change. It would not be appropriate for such scenarios using those methods without good customization capability. (c) The inference based on deep learning still involves lots of convolutional operations in a feedforward network. To design intelligent firmware modules with their performance and power consumption optimized for edge devices is an issue worthy of concern.

The contributions of this paper are as follows: (a) we propose a *Parallel − Optimization − based frameWork towards Edge Intelligent Image Recog − nition* (called POWER), which specifies the whole procedure from network design to model solidification, in order to provide well extensibility for implementing intelligent firmware modules. (b) our framework adopts FPGA (Field-Programmable Gate Array) of semi-customization as its hardware module [16], providing flexible customization capability for different application scenarios through supporting the design of different firmware modules specific to different scenarios. (c) we provide a real-world case that implements intelligent firmware for substation inspection robots based on the hardware module, following the specification provided by our framework. We also explore the way that can improve the performance and power consumption of the firmware prototype based on parallel-optimization. The firmware prototype for intelligently recognizing images based on our framework is analyzed experimentally and the framework itself is also validated indirectly.

The rest of paper is organized as follows. Section 2 presents related work. Section 3 proposes our intelligent image recognition framework in detail, describes the design process of image recognition firmware based on deep learning, and introduces the hardware scheme. Section 4 concretely explains how to apply our framework to a real-world case, and validates its effectiveness indirectly through analyzing the performance of the firmware prototype implemented. Finally, Sect. 5 concludes the paper.

2   Related Work

In recent years, the flexibility and scalability of FPGAs for addressing the hardware needs of deep learning have been increasingly recognized [4].

In [2], an efficient and customizable hardware architecture for implementation of feed-forward DNN accelerator on FPGA was proposed. A VHDL code generator for customizable and synthesizable DNN architectures on FPGA was also developed. However, no further details about this generator were revealed. Zeng et al. [19] developed a Python design automation tool to generate FPGA-based CNN accelerators. This tool takes a high-level description of the CNN model and the target FGPA device as its input, and generates fully synthesizable Verilog. The effectiveness of this tool has been illustrated on a variety of CNNs and target FPGA devices.

Yu et al. [18] designed a FPGA-based accelerator for the deep learning prediction process, using data access optimization and high throughput pipeline structure. Compared with core2 CPU, the performance of the accelerator was significantly improved. Nevertheless, the accelerator didn't fully reflect its scalability. By using pipelined processing units and tile techniques, deep learning accelerator unit (DLAU) [17] is a scalable accelerator architecture for large-scale deep learning networks, which uses FPGA as its hardware prototype. The performance of the DLAU accelerator was also evaluated experimentally.

For the critical problem that the computation throughput may not well match the memory bandwidth provided, Zhang et al. [20] firstly quantitatively analyzed the computing throughput and required memory bandwidth for any solution of a CNN design using various optimization techniques, then identified the solution with the best performance and lowest resource requirement using the roofline model. By taking advantage of data reuse, the implementation of a CNN accelerator on FPGA board balanced limitations of bandwidth and FPGA computation power. [8] aimed to accelerate the residual network (ResNet) in the inference application on FPGA by using OpenCL. This work claimed that FPGA accelerator, data parallel, data pipeline, and model parameters convertor were employed for optimizing the ResNet. However, details on these methods were not revealed in the paper.

We propose a FPGA-based framework using parallel optimization, partly inspired by the above methods. Unlike those methods, our framework provides a complete process specification for end-to-end design and implement intelligent image recognition firmware. Through parallel optimization, the framework based on FPGA can better bring advantages of extensibility and customization capability for developing different types of edge devices in various scenarios.

3   POWER: A Parallel-Optimization-Based FrameWork Towards Edge Intelligent Image Recognition

3.1   Framework Overview

The overall framework of POWER is shown in Fig. 1. The framework is designed based on a hybrid platform including deep learning framework and server clusters in the cloud, embedded control module and hardware module on the edge.

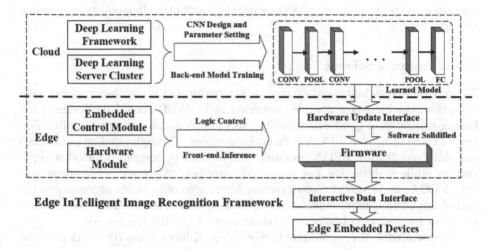

Fig. 1. The overall framework of POWER.

The function of each part in POWER is illustrated as follows.

The deep learning framework and server clusters are used for obtaining deep learning models trained for specific application scenarios. The deep learning framework running on a cluster is used for constructing neural networks, tuning structural parameters for specification image recognition applications. The trained models will be finally migrated to the hardware module.

The hardware module is used for instantiating trained models and supporting inference on the edge. It supports the model solidification and works as the physical carrier of edge intelligent firmware, providing interactive data interfaces for edge devices (e.g. robots, drones and cameras) and hardware resources for inference on the edge.

The firmware generated based on the hardware module is the concrete digital logic for implementing models trained, which provides inferential capability for edge devices. The firmware is updated via hardware update interface. The embedded control module in our framework controls the whole operating logic of the firmware generated.

The implementation procedure of edge intelligent firmware based on POWER is as follows:

STEP 1 - Model training: deep neural networks are constructed for specific applications. Based on networks, models are trained in deep learning server clusters using labeled image samples.

STEP 2 - Firmware and embedded software design: the firmware logic for network layers is designed according to network architecture and parameters, supporting the embedded software to control the whole process of model inference.

STEP 3 - Hardware instantiation: both the firmware and embedded software are solidified into the hardware module, supporting the edge inference on incoming images from interactive data interface and providing real-time response to edge devices.

3.2 Hardware Scheme

To provide extensibility and ensure better performance and lower power consumption, the hardware module contained in POWER should be designed following principles of good extendibility, easy maintenance and fine stability. Following these principles, FPGA is an optimal choice. Through pipeline parallelism and data parallelism, FPGA provides high enough performance for edge applications while maintaining low power consumption. As a semi-customized circuit, FPGA can be used for constructing hardware components according to the actual application requirements. All these advantages make FPGA an effective platform for designing hardware module in our POWER framework.

For main control programmable SOC chip, Xilinxs Zynq-7000 series can be adopted as the core of hardware module, considering the number of I/O, cache size, logic gates, the highest frequency, etc. This series of chips employs a dual-core 800 MHz ARM Cortex A9 MPCore processor as its embedded processor. Compared with competitive products, Zynq-7000 provides performance gains of approximately 20% while reducing power consumption.

Zynq-7000 includes processing system (PS) and programmable logic (PL). The PS adopts a dual-core 800 MHz ARM Cortex A9 MPCore processor, with NEON and double-precision floating point engine. In addition to fully integrate caches, memory controller and common peripherals, it can configure programmable logic as required. The PL provides powerful parallel processing ability for application development, and supports petabyte data transmission with high bandwidth and very low power dissipation, which solve the bottleneck problem of control, I/O, etc.

The overall design scheme of the hardware module is based on Zynq-7000. The peripheral image-collecting module delivers images to the PS of Zynq chip via RJ45 interface. The PS provides DDR3 ESRAM, QSPI FLASH and SD card storage. It also provides SRAM cache. The final hardware module employs three power supply chips to provide power to the main control unit, memory and interface chip. The types of components and their specifications are listed in Table 1.

Table 1. Component specifications.

Component	Type	Quantity	Specifications
Processor	XC7Z030-FF676	1	27 mm × 27 mm
DDR3	MT41J256M16RH-15E	2	1 GByte, 32 bit, 9 × 10.5 mm
Flash	N25Q128A13E1241F	1	128 Mb, 4 bit, 6 × 8 mm
SRAM	CY7C1061G30-10BVXI	2	4 MByte, 32 bit, 10 ns
Micro SD	1041681620	1	1 GByte, 13 × 17.8 mm
Gigabit Ethernet	88E1512	1	RJ45, 8 × 8 mm
	RJ45:L829-1J1T-43	1	17.58 × 24 mm
UART Interface	GPIO	1	TTL voltage; 4 × 4 mm
Power	LTC3374	1	1.8 V@2 A, 5 × 7 mm + 4 × 4 mm/ch
	TPS54618	1	1 V@6 A, 3 mm × 3 mm
	TPS51200	1	0.75 V, 3 mm × 3 mm
	TYPE C: 105450-0101	1	5 V@2 A, 8 mm × 9 mm

4   A Case Study: Substation Inspection Robots' On-Board Intelligent Object Recognition in Smart Grid

In this section, we take substation intelligent inspection as an example, illustrating how to design and implement an intelligent hardware module which can promote the on-board intelligent object recognition for substation inspection robots and satisfy robots requirements of performance and power dissipation.

4.1   Background

One important function of substation inspection robots is to accurately detect and recognize objects (e.g. meters installed on key equipment) in substation, supporting subsequent state analysis on them. A substation inspection robot can detect objects (e.g. gas-pressure meters and switch states) with its Pan-Tile-Zoom (PTZ) camera and then read their readings or identify their states. Traditional feature-based methods are usually adopted by robots to detect and identify meters, but they usually don't work very well, with low recognition accuracy, limited network bandwidth and poor real-time performance. Therefore, intelligent perception capabilities of robots on the edge should be enhanced to address all the above challenges.

Based on our POWER framework, edge intelligent firmware can be instantiated on the hardware module and be embedded in substation inspection robots (i.e. the edge device in this case) to detect and identify meters (i.e. intelligent image recognition capability in this case) in time, reducing bandwidth demands and improving real-time performance.

For improving accuracy, object detection algorithms based on deep learning can be used. They can provide high precision of meters detection directly, further improving the recognition success rate with key points matching only on meter areas. That means the critical step to improve the recognition success rate is to detect meters in advance and this step can be finished using deep CNN. Therefore, meters detection is taken as an example to demonstrate the effectiveness of our POWER framework without loss of generality.

4.2   Structure Design and Training of Deep Neural Networks Towards Meter Detection

Object detection is one of subjects in computer vision, whose aim is to accurately detect target objects and show their boundaries [7]. Unlike traditional algorithms (e.g. SIFT [10]), object detection algorithms based on CNN [21] can extract features and detect objects with the same framework, which can greatly improve the performance of object detection through automated features extraction with their loss functions been optimized.

There are two popular approaches based on deep CNN, i.e. two-shot approach and single-shot approach. A two-shot approach proceeds in two stages, the first stage aims to find out potential regions with target objects using region proposal network (RPN), while the second stage accurately detects and classifies objects. As for one-shot approach, it is usually considered as an enhanced approach optimizing away the first step in two-shot approach for accelerating the speed of algorithms. R-CNN and its variants (e.g. Fast-RCNN and Faster-RCNN [12]) are algorithms based on the two-shot approach, while SSD [9] and YOLO [11] are algorithms based on the single-shot approach.

In order to choose a basic network for meter detection, we compare experimentally the performance of two most representative algorithms based on two-shot and single-shot approaches respectively, i.e. Faster-RCNN and SSD. The results are shown in Table 2.

Table 2. Experimental comparison between Faster-RCNN and SSD.

Method	Precision	Recall	Time cost	Frame per second
Faster-RCNN(two-shot)	93%	85%	850 ms	1.17
SSD(one-shot)	90%	90%	100 ms	10

As we can see in Table 2, the precision of Faster-RCNN is slightly higher than that of SSD, since Faster-RCNN uses specialized branches in its second stage for object classification. As for Recall, SDD gains a better improvement due to multi-scale branches employed. With similar feed-forward network, SSD is about 8 times faster than Faster-RCNN, since SSD directly learns to regress the object shape and classify object categories instead of using two decoupled stages.

Generally speaking, two-shot approach is the primary reason why Faster-RCNN is slower than SSD, indicating that it is not suitable for real-time object detection. Besides, it is difficult to optimize Faster-RCNN based on parallel-optimization, since the two stages dramatically limit the performance on FPGA platform. As a consequence, the standard SSD network structure is adjusted to construct our neural network for detecting meters in this scenario. The standard SDD network structure is built based on VGG16 [14], using max pooling as its basic layer and only 3 × 3 convolution kernel. By replacing fully connected layers with convolutional layers, the original SSD network is changed as a full convolutional network (FCN), which supports for images with arbitrary size and scale. In our case, two methods are considered for optimizing SSD network structure, i.e. adjusting the feed-forward network structure and adjusting the number of network branches.

Since many feed-forward networks (e.g. GoogLeNet [15]) are not suitable for running in robots with limited computing resources, a new network with a simpler structure is needed in this case. To simplify network design and ensure efficient implementation on our hardware module, a network similar to VGG is adopted and adjusted. More precisely, we adopt a 24-layer full convolutional network, which is composed of multiple 3 × 3 convolutional layers and max pooling layers.

Theoretically, more objects can be detected with more branches, indicating higher recall and lower precision. The opposite is true when fewer branches are designed. More importantly, computing quantity increases with more branches and more layers involved. The performance of SSD with different branches can also be compared experimentally, as shown in Table 3.

Table 3. Performance of SSD with different branches.

Method	Precision	Recall	Time cost
3 branches	91%	81%	92 ms
5 branches	90%	90%	100 ms
6 branches	86%	92%	115 ms

As we can see in Table 3, precision and recall of five-branches SSD always remain at a high level and has moderate time consumption compared with the other two. Consequently, we adopt 5-branches SSD to train our model.

By tuning the model, parameters of each layer in our SSD network structure optimized are listed in Table 4, where *_loc and *_cls both represent convolutional branches.

Table 4. Parameters of each layer in SSD with five branches.

Layer name	Width	Height	Input channels	Output channels	Conv kernel
conv1_1	256	256	3	16	3×3
conv1_2	256	256	16	32	3×3
conv2_1	128	128	32	32	3×3
conv2_2	128	128	32	32	3×3
conv3_1	64	64	32	48	3×3
conv3_2	64	64	48	48	3×3
conv3_3	64	64	48	48	3×3
conv4_1	32	32	48	64	3×3
conv4_2	32	32	64	64	3×3
conv4_3	32	32	64	96	3×3
conv4_loc	32	32	96	16	3×3
conv4_cls	32	32	96	8	3×3
conv6	32	32	96	128	3×3
conv7_loc	16	16	128	24	3×3
conv7_cls	16	16	128	12	3×3
b8/cov3 × 3	16	16	128	128	3×3
b8_loc	8	8	128	24	3×3
b8_cls	8	8	128	12	3×3
b9/cov3 × 3	8	8	128	128	3×3
b9_loc	4	4	128	24	3×3
b9_cls	4	4	128	12	3×3
b10/conv1 × 1	4	4	128	128	3×3
b10_loc	2	2	128	16	3×3
b10_cls	2	2	128	8	3×3

4.3   Firmware Design and Performance Optimization

To provide efficient meter detection on the edge, the model trained on our 5-branches SSD should be instantiated on the hardware module as a firmware (i.e. model solidification), which can then be embedded into the substation inspection robots.

For improving performance, two optimizations are considered during model solidification: (a) parallel-optimization method. By optimizing the parallelism degree of convolutional kernels, the performance of firmware can be improved to satisfy the real-time computing requirements on the edge. (b) data flow computing framework. Additional chip resources are needed when optimizing the hardware module with limited resources using parallel-optimization. Data flow computing framework is adopted to achieve a breakthrough on the performance bottleneck.

To ensure the reliability and reusability, the firmware is designed in a modular manner based on characteristics of network layers. That is to say, for convolutional layers and fully connected layers, we design corresponding calculation modules respectively. Based on these calculation modules, the whole firmware architecture can be implemented by adding other functional units, such as caches and registers, as shown in Fig. 2.

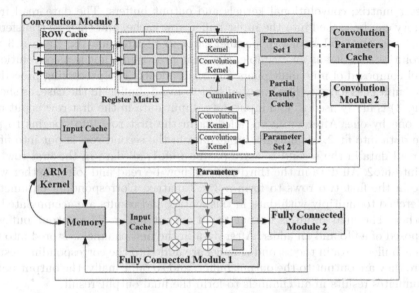

Fig. 2. The firmware architecture of deep convolutional neural networks.

The whole firmware architecture is composed of an ARM processor, a memory controller, multiple convolutional layers and fully connected layers. Fully connected layers are also discussed here, since the full convolutional SSD network discussed in Subsect. 4.2 can be considered as a special case. The operation of this architecture is controlled by the ARM controller. The input/output data of convolutional layers and fully connected layers is transferred from/to off-chip DDR3 SDRAM by the memory control via DMA.

As shown in Fig. 2, multiple convolutional modules are connected through on-chip connection resources. The output of the convolutional module is used as the input of convolutional module 2 through on-chip connection resources. For network structures including multiple convolutional layers, the firmware architecture supports the serial connection of multiple convolutional modules. The fully connected modules can be connected in a similar way. The convolutional modules connect to DDR, read input data and convolution parameters from off-chip memory, and then write the convolution results back to off-chip memory. The fully connected modules work in a similar way. The off-chip memory is controlled by ARM kernel. As for convolutional modules, fully connected modules and ARM kernel, they can connect with each other based on the shared memory space.

Convolutional modules take feature maps as their input and obtain new feature maps as their temporary output by convolving their input with convolutional kernels. The final output is all temporary output adding offsets. In general, the non-linear activation function acts on output will be appended to the convolutional layer. For example, AlexNet [3] takes ReLU (Rectified Linear Unit) as its activation function.

A single convolutional module is composed of input buffers, row caches, a register matrix, convolutional kernels and output buffers. The data read from memory can be cached into the input buffer, row cache, and then be transferred to the convolutional kernel in parallel through register matrix. Take a 3×3 convolutional kernel as an example, the basic processing unit is a convolutional kernel composed of nine multipliers and eight adders. The processing procedure of this unit is as follows. The 'line_buffer' ('Conv_in _buffer' in the case, as shown in Fig. 3) is firstly used to join input data. Input data in the first row is put into fifo1 one by one. After receiving all data in the first row, fifo1 begins to put these data into fifo2. Meanwhile, input data in the second row is put into fifo1. After all data in the second row are put into fifo1, all data in the first row are put into fifo2. All data in the third row can now be read and join together with those in the first two rows to form a 3×3 matrix. Corresponding parameters are fetched to multiply with data in this matrix and results are accumulated all together. The final result is output to an output buffer. The output buffer is composed of a fifo and an adder. After data in the first channel is stored into the output buffer, data in the second channel are added to the corresponding results before they are output to the output buffer, and so on. Finally, the output buffer accumulates results in all channels to form the final output result.

For our hardware architecture, we can tune its performance based on the parallelism degree. The basic idea is to instantiate multiple convolutional kernels on the FPGA platform so as to maximize the utilization of resources. In a clock cycle, multiple convolutional kernels can accumulate multiple vectors in parallel, saving calculation time. This optimization supports large-scale parallel computation in terms of data parallelism degree P_v and output channel parallelism degree P_f, improving the overall performance effectively. Therefore, we get the total parallelism degree P_t:

$$P_t = P_v \times P_f \qquad (1)$$

With this optimization, the architecture shown in Fig. 2 can support 32-bit wide parallel computation with four convolutional kernels and four fully connected modules. The parallelism degree of convolutional modules depends on how many convolutional kernel modules can run in parallel with hardware resources provided, and the parallelism degree of fully connected modules depends on how many matrix-vector multipliers are supported with hardware resources provided.

When designing the convolution neural network accelerator based on FPGA, fixed-point type is usually used to achieve efficient design for high performance and low-power optimization. On FPGA platform, low-precision computation leads to higher frequencies and lower computing resources, which can support

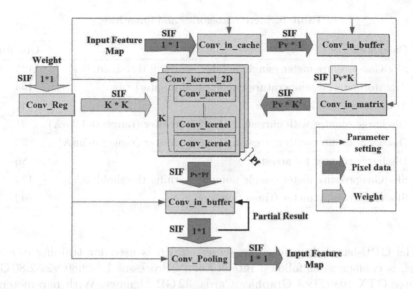

Fig. 3. The hardware architecture of convolution module.

higher parallelism degree for deep CNN and reducing chip power consumption. For this reason, this optimization is also adopted when we design the convolutional module for our SSD network.

With these optimizations, the peak performance P_p of the firmware is given in Eq. 2.

$$P_p = clk \times P_t \times (K_r \times K_c) \tag{2}$$

Here clk stands for clock frequency, P_t stands for the maximum parallelism degree, K_r and K_c stand for the number of rows and columns of the convolutional kernels, respectively.

4.4 Experimental Results and Analysis

In this subsection, we experimentally evaluate the performance of firmware prototype designed based on our POWER framework, validating the effectiveness of the framework on edge intelligent image recognition indirectly.

There are 2,678 images of 1080p taken by the PTZ camera of a substation inspection robot. According to the quantity and quality, images in some categories (the number of each category is less than 200) are eliminated in order to reduce the noise. The remaining images are pre-processed, such as denoising and transformation, and then form the final sample set used for model training and testing, as shown in Table 5. Training samples and testing samples are selected randomly from the sample set with the ratio of 9:1, ensuring to form disjoint sets.

Table 5. Meter categories and quantities.

No.	Categories	Quantity
1	SF_6 Gas-pressure meter (single pointer, warning threshold: 0.4)	1123
2	Transformer's oil temperature gauge (dual-pointer)	194
3	Transformer's oil level gauge	41
4	Discharge counter with current meter for arrester (range: 0-3.0mA)	91
5	Discharge counter with current meter for arrester (range: 0-5mA)	95
6	Discharge counter for arrester	86
7	SF_6 Gas-pressure meter (single pointer, warning threshold: 0.55)	174
8	SF_6 Gas-pressure meter (three pointers)	392

The GPU-based deep learning server, which is used for training our SSD model, is configured as follows: Intel®Xeon®Processor E5-2680 v2@2.80 GHz, GeForce GTX 1080Ti×4 Graphics Cards, 32 GB Memory. With parameters in Table 4, the SSD model is trained for several rounds on this server with TensorFlow [1] deployed. The model learned is finally solidified into the hardware module.

The performance optimization of firmware for deep learning depends on the parallelism degree and clock frequency. The evaluation of parallelism degree on our firmware is shown in Fig. 4. Subject to DSP resources, the parallelism degree of fully connected modules is 4 with 16-bit width, while the parallelism degree of convolutional modules reaches 128 in this case. According to Eq. 1, the total parallelism degree P_t is equal to $8 \times 16 = 128$, which is not shown in Fig. 4, where the data parallelism degree P_v is 8 and the channel parallelism degree P_f is 16. When maximizing the clock frequency by pipeline operation, the firmware can run efficiently at 200 MHz. According to Eq. 2, the firmware reaches its peak performance $0.2 \times 128 \times 9 = 230.4$ Gflops, using a 3×3 convolutional kernel.

Under above configuration, the firmware prototype for meter detection on our testing set achieves the following performance: (a) the detection speed reaches 10 pfs (frames per second); (b) the maximum number of objects (i.e. meters) that can be detected in a single image is 3; (c) the precision reaches over 90% in the case of 90% recall. (d) the average power consumption is less than 5 watts. These all meet practical demands for substation inspection robots.

To illustrate the effectiveness of our meter detection on improving the success rate of meters recognition, we also compare the performance of our SSD-based method with that of traditional feature-based methods. Experimental results show that the SSD-based method provides around 80% success rate, which is 30% higher than that of the traditional feature-based methods. Meanwhile, the latency of meters detection on robots is kept no longer than 200 ms.

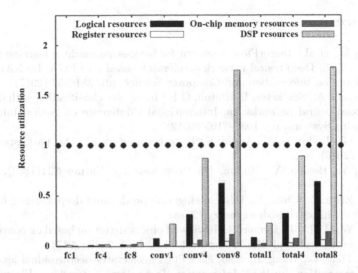

Fig. 4. The resource utilization of hardware modules (conv1, conv 4 and conv8 stand for convolution modules with parallelism degree of 1, 4 and 8, respectively. fc1, fc4 and fc8 stands for fully connected modules with parallelism degree of 1, 4 and 8, respectively. Total1, total4 and total8 stands for hardware architectures containing (conv1, fc1), (conv4, fc4) and (conv8, fc8), respectively).

5 Conclusions

Through training models on powerful cloud or data centers with massive image samples, intelligent image recognition methods based on deep learning have accomplished great advances in certain applications. However, along with the uprising requirements on intelligent edge devices, it is a great challenge to design embeddable hardware modules and implement model solidification on them for intelligent image recognition. To address this challenge, a parallel-optimization-based framework towards edge intelligent image recognition (i.e. POWER) is proposed. Taking FPGA cards as its hardware module, POWER supports the design and implementation of firmware modules for various edge devices in different scenarios, which provides well extensibility and flexible customization capability. By designing the firmware with pertinence and improving it with parallel-optimization, the performance of our firmware prototype is validated experimentally, which also shows the effectiveness of POWER framework in designing edge intelligent firmware indirectly. Our future work includes exploring the many possible improvements: better and more accurate models with regards to other parameters (e.g. energy consumption) and further optimum design of firmware based on these models.

Acknowledgement. This work is funded by the Guangdong Power Grid Co., Ltd. Science and Technology Program under Grant No. GDKJXM20161136.

References

1. Abadi, M., et al.: TensorFlow: a system for large-scale machine learning (2016)
2. Huynh, T.V.: Deep neural network accelerator based on FPGA. In: NAFOSTED Conference on Information and Computer Science, pp. 254–257 (2017)
3. Krizhevsky, A., Sutskever, I., Hinton, G.E.: ImageNet classification with deep convolutional neural networks. In: International Conference on Neural Information Processing Systems, pp. 1097–1105 (2012)
4. Lacey, G., Taylor, G.W., Areibi, S.: Deep learning on FPGAs: past, present, and future (2016)
5. Lecun, Y., Bengio, Y., Hinton, G.: Deep learning. Nature **521**(7553), 436–444 (2015)
6. Li, E., Zhou, Z., Chen, X.: Edge intelligence: on-demand deep learning model co-inference with device-edge synergy (2018)
7. Li, X., Ye, M., Li, T., Center, R.: Review of object detection based on convolutional neural networks. Appl. Res. Comput. **34**(10), 2881–2886 (2017)
8. Li, X., Ding, L., Wang, L., Cao, F.: FPGA accelerates deep residual learning for image recognition. In: IEEE Information Technology, Networking, Electronic and Automation Control Conference, pp. 837–840 (2017)
9. Liu, W., et al.: SSD: single shot multibox detector. In: Leibe, B., Matas, J., Sebe, N., Welling, M. (eds.) ECCV 2016. LNCS, vol. 9905, pp. 21–37. Springer, Cham (2016). https://doi.org/10.1007/978-3-319-46448-0_2
10. Lowe, D.G.: Object recognition from local scale-invariant features. In: IEEE International Conference on Computer Vision, p. 1150 (2002)
11. Redmon, J., Divvala, S., Girshick, R., Farhadi, A.: You only look once: unified, real-time object detection. In: IEEE Conference on Computer Vision and Pattern Recognition, pp. 779–788 (2016)
12. Ren, S., He, K., Girshick, R., Sun, J.: Faster R-CNN: towards real-time object detection with region proposal networks. IEEE Trans. Pattern Anal. Mach. Intell. **39**(6), 1137–1149 (2015)
13. Shi, W., Sun, H., Cao, J., Zhang, Q., Liu, W.: Edge computingan emerging computing model for the internet of everything era. J. Comput. Res. Dev. **54**, 907–924 (2017)
14. Simonyan, K., Zisserman, A.: Very deep convolutional networks for large-scale image recognition. Comput. Sci. arXiv preprint arXiv:1409-1556 (2014)
15. Szegedy, C., et al.: Going deeper with convolutions, pp. 1–9 (2014)
16. Venieris, S.I., Kouris, A., Bouganis, C.S.: Toolflows for mapping convolutional neural networks on FPGAs: a survey and future directions. ACM Comput. Surv. **51**(3), 56 (2018)
17. Wang, C., Gong, L., Yu, Q., Li, X., Xie, Y., Zhou, X.: DLAU: a scalable deep learning accelerator unit on FPGA. IEEE Trans. Comput.-Aided Des. Integr. Circuits Syst. **36**(3), 513–517 (2017)
18. Yu, Q., Wang, C., Ma, Xiang, L.X., Zhou, X.: A deep learning prediction process accelerator based FPGA. In: Proceedings of the Annual ACM Symposium on Theory of Computing, pp. 585–594 (2015)
19. Zeng, H., Zhang, C., Prasanna, V.: Fast generation of high throughput customized deep learning accelerators on FPGAs. In: International Conference on Reconfigurable Computing and FPGAs, pp. 1–8 (2017)

20. Zhang, C., Li, P., Sun, G., Guan, Y., Xiao, B., Cong, J.: Optimizing FPGA-based accelerator design for deep convolutional neural networks. In: ACM/SIGDA International Symposium on Field-Programmable Gate Arrays, pp. 161–170 (2015)
21. Zhang, H., Wang, K.F., Wang, F.Y.: Advances and perspectives on applications of deep learning in visual object detection. Acta Autom. Sin. **43**(8), 1289–1305 (2017)

SP-TSRM: A Data Grouping Strategy
in Distributed Storage System

Dongjie Zhu[1], Haiwen Du[1], Ning Cao[2(⊠)], Xueming Qiao[3],
and Yanyan Liu[3]

[1] School of Computer Science and Technology,
Harbin Institute of Technology at Weihai, Weihai, China
[2] College of Information Engineering,
Qingdao Binhai University, Qingdao, China
ning.cao2008@hotmail.com
[3] WeiHai Power Supply Company, No. 23, Kunming Road, Weihai, China

Abstract. With the development of smart devices and social media, massive
unstructured data is uploaded to distributed storage systems. Since the characteristics of multi-users and high concurrency the unstructured data accesses
have, it brings new challenges to traditional distributed storage systems designed
for large files. We propose a grouping strategy to analyze relevant data in access
according to disk access logs in the real distributed storage systems environment. When any data in the group is accessed, the whole group is prefetched
from disk to the cache. Firstly, we conduct statistical analysis on the access logs
and propose a preliminary classification method to classify files in spatiotemporal locality. Secondly, a strength-priority tree structure relation model (SP-
TSRM) is proposed to mine file group efficiently. Finally, experiments show that
the proposed model can improve the cache hit rate significantly, thereby
improving the read efficiency of distributed storage systems.

Keywords: Prefetching model · Storage optimization · Unstructured data
Distributed storage systems

1 Introduction

Massive amounts of unstructured data such as pictures, audio, documents, etc. are
being generated by users during the daily usage of social applications [1]. These data
have the access characteristics of heavy reading and writing but seldom updating and
deletion, which has higher requirements on the reading and writing efficiency of the
data server. In order to not affect the number of concurrent and real-time services
servers, the vast majority of Internet companies store such unstructured data to a
distributed storage platform to reduce its impact on business server performance.
According to the report of International Data Center, the world has entered the era of
ZB, and the quantity of global data doubles itself in two years [2]. However, since the
distributed storage system architecture is mainly designed for large files, it may rise
performance issues in access task scheduling and metadata data management when
faced with massive unstructured data [3].

© Springer Nature Switzerland AG 2018
J. Vaidya and J. Li (Eds.): ICA3PP 2018, LNCS 11334, pp. 524–531, 2018.
https://doi.org/10.1007/978-3-030-05051-1_36

To solve this problem, researchers proposed a series of methods to improve the access speed of the storage system by reducing the number of disk I/O accesses. Dong et al. starts with the file writing process [4]. By combining smaller unstructured data into larger files for storage, the multiple I/O operations are combined into single I/O operation to increase the disk write speed. However, optimization of writing generally adopts a sequential merging strategy due to the high real-time requirements of file writing [5]. On the other hand, researchers mines the relevance of data in data reading process, the data that have high probability of being accessed are taken to the memory or cache in advance, and the disk I/O is reduced by increasing the cache hit rate [6, 7]. Since this type of solution have slight effect on the availability of the storage system, it has a large research space.

The traditional data prefetching model uses the method of analyzing user behavior or application logs to mine their data access rules for data to predict the next data access behavior [8]. However, for a distributed storage system, the upper application is transparent to it. Therefore, we analyze the disks access records of the distributed storage system and propose a data grouping strategy to group the access-related files. When accessing any file in the group, the entire group of files is prefetched to the cache. In addition, we propose a tree-structured file relation analysis model, which can ensure that the relationship with strong correlation is fully mined and the efficiency of relation mining is improved.

The paper is organized as follows. In Sect. 2, we analysis background and limitations of existing file associations mining algorithms. The design are detailed in Sect. 3. Section 4 we give a brief introduction of the dataset and the cache architecture to evaluate SP-TSRM and Sect. 5 concludes our contributions.

2 Related Work

The mining of file associations has been a hot topic of research. Kroger et al. [9] proposed that the relationships between files can be mined by the user's access to files. However, in a distributed storage environment, the number of transactions and items is excessive. In this case, the mining result of frequent items contains a collection of all files that meet the degree of support, causing the combinatory explosion. Furthermore, we want to prefetch the most relevant file with the current file, which is the most likely to be accessed at the next moment. The calculation result of the frequent item mining algorithm contains a lot of redundant data.

Wildani et al. [10] proposed a graph structure to represent the degree of association between files. The edge weight is calculated by disk offset and access time interval between files. By setting a threshold value, the edge whose weight is larger than the threshold is discard and the edge whose weight is below the threshold is retained. Then, the complete subgraph is searched on the map, and the searched result is taken as the grouping result. This approach solves the problem of combinatory explosion. However, when a certain point (file) belongs to multiple complete subgraphs at the same time, the grouping relationship is hard to determine.

In addition, in the case of a large number of files and frequent file reading, any two files may need to calculate a distance and generate an edge (relationship). With tens of millions of files and accesses of a distributed storage system, mining associations in file directly units can cause serious performance problems.

The access time and offset in the disk I/O access log are important attributes for user access pattern analysis. Therefore, the statistical analysis of the temporal and spatial distribution characteristics of data access is conducted. It is found that some disk locations in close proximity are always accessed together within a short period of time like red circled areas in Fig. 1, also for some files that far away in offset like green circled areas. Which provides theoretical support for the study of the feasibility of association relationship mining for spatiotemporal locality.

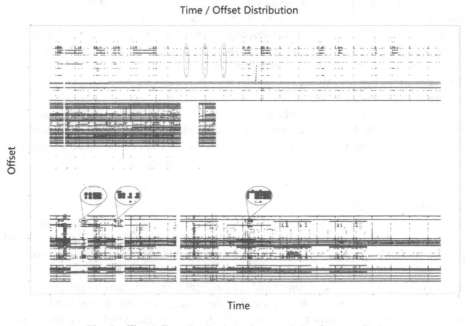

Fig. 1. Time/offset distribution of trace (Color figure online)

3 Proposed Architecture

In this chapter, we propose SP-TSRM to solve the file association mining problem we mentioned above. By making a great amount of research on the characteristics of files spatiotemporal locality in distributed storage systems, the model can support a larger number of files and file accesses. What's more, the strength-priority tree structure relation model we proposed can clearly divide files that may belong to multiple file sets. We will introduce the following three aspects:

3.1 File Spatial Locality Relation Mining

Since files with spatial locality are accessed in similar patterns, files that are closer in position and accessed-times are more likely to belong to the same category. Therefore, we define two-dimensional vectors (X, Y), where X represents the storage location of the file (disk offset) and Y represents the number of times file X was accessed. These vectors are classified using the clustering method.

However, due to the division of transactions and the errors caused by random fluctuations, we cannot guarantee that files with spatial locality is accessed in exactly the same times, and this error will tend to be amplified as the number of file access increases. Therefore, most of the files with lower Y-coordinates will be clustered into one class if these vectors are directly clustered based on the original coordinates, making the clustering result unsatisfactory. Therefore, we performed a statistical analysis on the file's access times, and found that it conformed to the normal distribution feature. To solve this problem, a coordinate scaling method is proposed to uses the exponential function to scale the Y-coordinate values. As shown in Fig. 2.

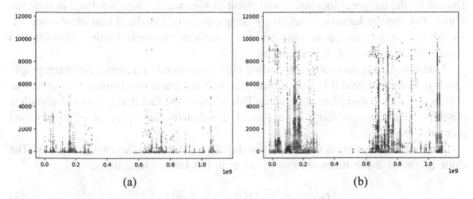

| | (a) | (b) |

Fig. 2. (a) Is the distribution and clustering result before coordinate scaling, and (b) is the distribution and clustering result after coordinate scaling. We can clearly see that using (a) clustering will cause the clustering result to skew toward the point where the Y value is low, and the clustering result in (b) can effectively avoid this problem.

3.2 File Access Relationship Classification

Obviously, clustering by spatial locality alone cannot accurately reflect the category relationships between files. Files that are close in disk storage location and have a close number of access times are not necessarily in the same file category. Therefore, we need to perform a second classification of the file categories obtained in Sect. 3.1.

We define a vector T to represent the occurrence of a file in transactions.

$$T_F = (x_1, x_2, \ldots, x_n). \tag{1}$$

For a file F_a, $T_{F_a}(i) = 1$ if F_a occurs in the ith transaction, otherwise $T_{F_a}(i) = 0$. We calculate the vector T for the same category of files after the first classification and define the distance D between files

$$D_{i,j} = |T_i - T_j| * \omega. \tag{2}$$

An Improved hierarchical clustering method is proposed to classify the vector T for the second time. Firstly, since the range of values in each dimension of the vector T is 0 or 1, bit-operations is adopted here to speed up the calculation. In addition, due to the errors caused by random fluctuations, files with a large number of access times should be less sensitive to transaction differences. Therefore, we dynamically adjust the clustering stop condition t according to the dimension of T.

3.3   Strength-Priority Tree Structure Relation Model

After the classification of the first two steps, we get the initial category of each file. Since the preliminary category is divided according to the spatial locality before being divided by the temporal locality, it will result in files whose time is related in time but whose disk storage location is relatively large cannot be classified into same category. Therefore, we propose a strength-priority complete subgraph finding algorithm to classify the relevance of file categories.

Traditional complete subgraph finding algorithms need to traverse the entire graph, which is inefficient, and it is hard to make explicit subgraph partitioning for points that belong to multiple complete subgraphs. This leads to the fact that traditional complete subgraph finding algorithms have certain deficiencies in terms of efficiency and accuracy.

We define the strength of the relationship $D(i,j)$ between the two categories. The value of $D(i,j)$ is the times set i and j occur in the same transactions.

$$D(i,j) = \sum \left(1 | F_i \in C_k, F_j \in C_k\right). \tag{3}$$

If the calculation is performed under all transactions, it will generate a huge number of relationships. Therefore, a threshold parameter $\sigma(\sigma < 1)$ is set to delete the relationships that have less contribution to the grouping result. We define the relationships is useless when $S(i) * \sigma > D(i,j)$ or $S(j) * \sigma > D(i,j)$. Where $S(i)$ denotes the times that set i shows in total transactions.

At this point, we got all the relations that meet the rules. We use the categories as points, the strength of the relations as the weight of edges to perform a complete subgraph search. To avoid the problem in Fig. 2, we propose a complete subgraph search algorithm with a high degree of association preference so that the point will be merged when the first time it is able to form a complete subgraph, as shown in Fig. 3.

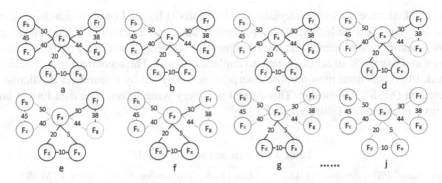

Fig. 3. Points represent a set of files, edges represent relationships that meet the requirements of the set, and numbers on the sides indicate the strength of the relationship. The gray dots represent the files that have been calculated but do not identify the collection to which they belong, and the colored dots represent the different file sets to which the files belong. Since point Fa already forms a complete. (Color figure online)

4 Experiment

In the experiment, we adopt the architecture in Fig. 4 to implement the entire cache model, in which the Storage Server obtains the disk I/O access logs and uses the model training method in 3 to train the prefetching model. When a new I/O request arrives, the cache model determines if the file is already in the cache. If it is, the file is returned. If the file is not in the cache, all the files contained in the file group are prefetched into the cache for subsequent requests for access.

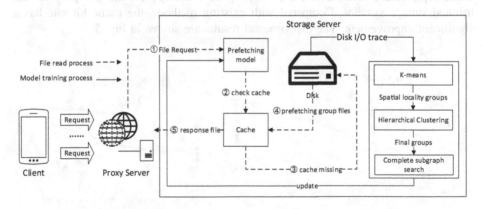

Fig. 4. The architecture we implement the entire cache model

In order to prove that our proposed model can be applied to various scenarios, we use the trace that are currently published on the Internet and have been tested in similar studies to evaluate the effectiveness of our model.

The first trace is Florida International University (FIU) and traces researchers' local storage. This is a multiuser, multi-application trace, with activities including developing, testing, experiments, technical writing, and plotting. There are 17836701 access times and over 33% of accesses were to duplicate blocks. The second trace is 1 week of block I/O traces from multipurpose enterprise servers used by researchers at Microsoft Research (MSR), Cambridge. This dataset was very write heavy. The data format and sample is shown in Tables 1 and 2.

Table 1. Format and sample of FIU

Timestamp	PID	Process	LBA	Size	R/W	Maj. device #	Min. device #	MD5
0	4892	syslogd	904265560	8	W	6	0	531e779...
39064	2559	kjournald	926858672	8	W	6	0	4fd0c43...
467651	2522	kjournald	644661632	8	W	6	0	98b9cb7...

Table 2. Format and sample of MSR

Timestamp	Type	Block offset	Size	Response time
128166372003061629	Read	7014609920	24576	41286
128166372016382155	Write	1317441536	8192	1963
128166372026382245	Write	2436440064	4096	1835

In order to reflect the superiority of method we proposed, we compare the two data sets with the ordinary LRU cache replacement method and the existing file grouping cache replacement method. Overall, we propose a strategy for file grouping in distributed storage systems. Compared with existing methods, the cache hit rate has a significant improvement. The experimental results are shown in Fig. 5:

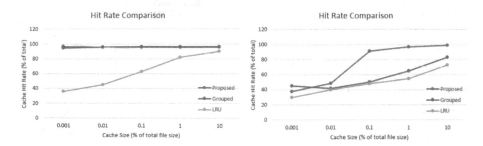

Fig. 5. The left side is the cache prefetch effect of the FIU data set and the right side is the cache prefetch effect of the MSR data set. It can be seen that the proposed method is far better than the LRU cache strategy in terms of overall effect. Except for the very small cache size (0.001 percent of file size), the overall cache hit rate is better than the existing grouping method.

5 Conclusion

In this paper, we propose a strength-priority tree structure relation model (SP-TSRM) to mine file group efficiently. For the distributed storage system, the cache can be implemented using memory, so we only need 1 MB of memory to provide more than 90% cache hit rate for 1 GB disk files. This is a memory saving solution for improving the read efficiency of distributed storage systems.

However, clustering operations are performed during the calculation of the model, which will consume a large amount of memory. We have tried 16 million file accesses and 640,000 files. The peak memory usage during the model training process will reach 3 GB.

Acknowledgements. Thanks to the students of HIT at Weihai. This work is supported by project under Grant no. 520613170002, SGSDWH00YXJS1700522, SGSDWH00YXJS 1700270, the Fundamental Research Funds for the Central Universities (Grant No. HIT. NSRIF.201714), Weihai Science and Technology Development Program (2016DXGJMS15) and Key Research and Development Program in Shandong Provincial (2017GGX90103).

References

1. Dong, B., Zheng, Q., Tian, F.: An optimized approach for storing and accessing small files on cloud storage. J. Netw. Comput. Appl. **35**(6), 1847–1862 (2012)
2. Zhu, Y., Zhang, X., Zhao, R., Dong, X.: Data De-duplication on similar file detection. In: Innovative Mobile and Internet Services in Ubiquitous Computing, pp. 66–73. IEEE Press (2014)
3. Cui, Y., Lai, Z., Wang, X., Dai, N.: QuickSync: improving synchronization efficiency for mobile cloud storage services. IEEE Trans. Mob. Comput. **16**, 3513–3526 (2017)
4. Dong, B., Qiu, J., Zheng, Q., Zhong, X., Li, J., Li, Y.: A novel approach to improving the efficiency of storing and accessing small files on hadoop: a case study by powerpoint files. In: Services Computing (SCC), pp. 65–72. IEEE Press (2010)
5. Bok, K., Lim, J., Oh, H., Yoo, J.: An efficient cache management scheme for accessing small files in distributed file systems. In: Big Data and Smart Computing (BigComp), pp. 151–155. IEEE Press (2017)
6. Lin, L., Li, X., Jiang, H., Zhu, Y., Tian, L., AMP: an affinity-based metadata prefetching scheme in large-scale distributed storage systems. In: Cluster Computing and the Grid, pp. 459–466. IEEE Press (2008)
7. Zhu, D., et al.: An access prefetching strategy for accessing small files based on swift. Procedia Comput. Sci. **131**, 816–824 (2018)
8. Cherubini, G., Kim, Y., Lantz, M., Venkatesan, V.: Data prefetching for large tiered storage systems. In: Data Mining (ICDM), pp. 823–828. IEEE Press (2017)
9. Kroeger, T.M., Long, D.D., Mogul, J.C.: Exploring the bounds of web latency reduction from caching and prefetching. In: USENIX Symposium on Internet Technologies and Systems, pp. 13–22 (1997)
10. Wildani, A., Miller, E.L.: Can we group storage? Statistical techniques to identify predictive groupings in storage system accesses. ACM Trans. Storage (TOS) **12**(2), 7–40 (2016)

Abstract Parallel Array Types and Ghost Cell Update Implementation

Shuang Zhang$^{(\boxtimes)}$, Bei Wang, and Yifeng Chen

EECS, Peking University, Beijing 100871, China
{10948882,wangbei.sei,cyf}@pku.edu.cn

Abstract. Stencil patterns are widely used in scientific simulations and image processing. To parallelize these problems, we have to divide data into chunks that are processed by different processors. One challenge with this approach is the update of ghost cells, which are the neighbor values that calculated on remote processes. This paper focus on the update communication. We provide an abstract array types to describe distribution patterns, such as ghost cells, from global and intuitive view. Based on this description, a general *copyto* function is provided to perform communication automatically. Furthermore, our work makes it possible to design a distribution-independent algorithm. This results in better productivity on tuning performance.

Keywords: MPI · Stencil · Ghost cell

1 Stencil Problem

Many problems can be modeled as a set of points in a structured grid that are updated in successive iterations based on the values of their neighbors from the previous iteration. Stencil is the shape of neighborhood used during the updates. The most common stencils are the 2D or 3D versions of the von Neumann neighborhood and Moore neighborhood, also briefly called 5-point and 9-point stencil in 2D version (see Fig. 1). For example, the edge detection in image processing is a 5-point stencil. And the Conway's Game of Life is a 9-point stencil.

These problems can be divided geometrically into chunks that are computed on different processors. However, since updating a point requires the values of its neighbors, each chunk needs values from neighboring chunks to update the points at its borders. This results in communication between processes before each iteration. How can we communicate these values in an efficient and intuitive manner?

Supported by National Key R&D Program of China under Grants No. 2016YFB0200502; and National Natural Science Foundation of China Grants No. 61672208, 61432018.

J. Vaidya and J. Li (Eds.): ICA3PP 2018, LNCS 11334, pp. 532–541, 2018.
https://doi.org/10.1007/978-3-030-05051-1_37

2   Related Work

Message Passing Interface is the most popular and ubiquitous choice for communication between processes. The stencil problems are discussed based on variety MPI advanced features considering the performance [2]. The interfaces in MPI should be used carefully to avoid message blocking, deadlock and redundant synchronization. However, the non-blocking operations are recommended, like MPI_Isend and MPI_Irecv. Furthermore, for the left and right edges of ghost cells, the data is not contiguous in memory. It looks like a perfect place to use MPI datatypes to construct a datatype for columns. In practice, unfortunately, many MPI implementations do not provide high performance when using derived datatype for communication [2,3]. A better approach is to move the column data into a buffer that in contiguous memory location. This is still requiring instantiation by programmers.

Considering the performance, some structured ghost cell patterns are provided based on MPI [1]. This work designs different communication procedures for 5-point-stencil, 9-point-stencil with corner cells and thicker edges called deep halo. It also chose non-blocking operations to avoid bottlenecks and to launch multiple messages in parallel if it is supported. This work discusses many factors that may affect performance, such as the difference between machines, the size and shape of chunk, and the trade-offs between computation and communication. Therefore, it is usually to tune the performance based on experimental results with configurable parameters.

Considering the productivity, some languages or toolkits chose the Partitioned Global Address Space (PGAS) model to simplify communications [5,6]. This model assumes a global memory address space that is logically partitioned and a portion of it is local to each process. The runtime performs one-sided communication operations automatically according to the data requirement on each process. Therefore, the communication in PGAS model is implicit.

Another solution is Domain Specific Language (DSL) [9,11], Snowflake is designed for GPU-acceleration system. It provides several data structures to describe stencil problems, such as *WeightArray*, *Component*, *RectDomain*, *DomainUnion* and *StencilGroup*. The construction is not in an intuitive manner.

3   Solution

We conclude two kernel principles, considering both the performance and productivity, to solve communications in stencil. First, explicit communication and configurable parameters. Programmers should be aware of the data locality and performance related parameters. Second, implicit MPI detail and buffering process for noncontiguous data. Non-blocking MPI operations and buffering are common choices for stencil communication that should be simplified.

Lightweight Toolkit. For these two reasons, we designed a lightweight toolkit called Parallel Dimension (PADM). PADM is implemented by using classes in C++. Instead of compiling another domain specific language, user can include our library file to the MPI program when needed. Therefore, user is able to use MPI and PADM together.

Abstract Description. The distributed array is described as a abstract dimension in PADM. Our dimension has several features. Firstly, dimension is constructed from global view, which means it will expose the data locality. Secondly, although the rules behind the dimension are algebraic expressions, the construction of dimensions is intuitive. Thirdly, each dimension is constructed into a binomial tree, which contains enough information to calculate the process number and local offset of each element.

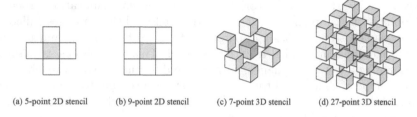

(a) 5-point 2D stencil   (b) 9-point 2D stencil   (c) 7-point 3D stencil   (d) 27-point 3D stencil

Fig. 1. Common 2d and 3D stencils. White ones are the neighbor values.

General Data Transfer. In PADM, we use a pair of dimensions to describe one communication. PADM provides a general *copyto* sentence to perform data transfer automatically by using MPI non-blocking operations. The core idea is calculating the process numbers and offsets for each element at both source and target ends, which is called scanning in PADM. Therefore, we can launch an non-blocking operation for this element. Furthermore, we calculate a regular contiguous length for each dimension before scanning. The source and target dimensions may have different values of contiguous length. The greatest common divisor of these two values is the *continuity* of this communication. We use *cnt* to represent this value. It means that every *cnt* indexes refer to the same source and target process number, and their offsets are contiguous in memory at both ends. Therefore, only the first element in each contiguous segment is need to be scanned. The calculation is reduced, while the message size is more reasonable.

Configurable Parameters and Buffering. It seems that the message length is limited by continuity. Actually, PADM provides configurable *granularity* for user to assign it. Furthermore, *continuity* and *granularity* are the two factors to decide whether to buffer. The noncontiguous elements with same target process will be packed into buffer to reach the granularity, and then sent together. On the target process, the received data will be unpacked later.

4 Neighbor Processes

Before the ghost cells description, we want to discuss the neighbors first to introduce PADM. Processes are organized into some topologies, like line, grid and cube. Take the line topology for example, the index sequence of n processes should be $0, 1, 2, ..., n - 1$. Right neighbor of i-th process can be calculated as $(i + 1)\%n$. The modulo operations ensure the last process can get a valid neighbor number in the original sequence. Therefore, the right neighbors sequence is $1, 2, ..., n - 1, 0$. And the left one can be calculated as $(i + n - 1)\%n$.

4.1 Description

In PADM, the original processes can be described as:

```
1  dim P = proc(n)
```

Type keyword *proc* means process, while *data* means local memory, which is used later. Keyword *dim*, an abbreviation for dimension, is the super class of both process and data. Dimension is our abstract description of distributed data. The basic components of each dimension is:

$$type(size, step) + disp \tag{1}$$

Here *type* and *size* are necessary. The *step*, which is also called stride in other languages, can be omitted with default value 1. And the *disp*, an abbreviation of displacement, can be omitted with default value 0. For index i, the offset (process number in this case) is calculated as follow:

$$(i\%size + disp) * step. \tag{2}$$

Therefore, the offset of dimension P is calculated as $(i\%n + 0) * 1$.

Obviously, these basic components are not able to describe the neighbors, because of the different order of modulo operation. To enrich the descriptive ability, we introduced *reference mechanism*, which results in nested computation of index. By using this, the left and right neighbors can be described as follow:

```
1  dim Right = array(dim(n)+1,   P);
2  dim Left  = array(dim(n)+n−1, P);
```

This mechanism is associated with keyword *array*. It takes two dimensions to construct *Right*. Dimension $dim(n)+1$ that before the comma is a rearrangement that based on P. When calculating the offset of i-th index, it will calculate a middle result i_m by using the rearrangement dimension first. And then it take i_m as input to calculate the final offset by using dimension P.

Furthermore, we use multiplication operator "*" to construct multi-dimensional description. The corresponding binominal tree may be different according to the multiplication order (see Fig. 2). The two children of the root/-parent node represent the *column* and *row* dimension, respectively. This structure is used in designing a distribution-independent algorithm in the following section.

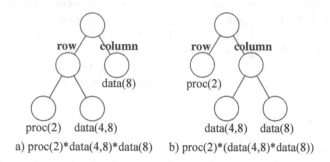

a) proc(2)*data(4,8)*data(8)   b) proc(2)*(data(4,8)*data(8))

Fig. 2. Binominal trees for different order of multiplication.

4.2   Transformation Functions

When constructing the *Left* dimension, the displaced value of rearrangement should be set to $n - 1$. However, we provided a more intuitive way to replace it. Since we "+1" distance for right neighbors, we should also "−1" distance for the left ones. Therefore, we designed some transformation functions to help the programmers constructing dimensions in a more intuitive and effective way. By using the transformation function *cyclic*, the neighbors can be described as follow:

```
1 dim Right = cyclic(P,  1);
2 dim Left  = cyclic(P, -1);
```

The most useful transformation functions are shown in Table 1. Transformation will return new dimension without changing the input. By using these functions, it is easy to describe the neighbor processes in 2D stencil as follow:

```
1 dim P = proc(p,p)*proc(p);
2 dim EastNb  = cyclicRow(P, 1);
3 dim WestNb  = cyclicRow(P,-1);
4 dim NorthNb = cyclicCol(P, 1);
5 dim SouthNb = cyclicCol(P,-1);
```

Table 1. Transformation functions.

Functions	Usage
dim get_low(dim D, int k)	Get k units from D that near the origin
dim get_high(dim D, int k)	Get k units from D that far from the origin
dim cut_low(dim D, int k)	Remove k units from D that near the origin
dim cut_high(dim D, int k)	Remove k units from D that far from the origin
dim cyclic(dim D, int k)	Cyclic D with k units
dim row(dim D)	Return the row dimension
dim col(dim D)	Return the column dimension
dim cyclicRow(dim D, int k)	Cyclic row dimension of D
dim cyclicCol(dim D, int k)	Cyclic column dimension of D
dim block_major(dim D, int k)	Block-major order with k*k block size

5 Ghost Cells Updating

The ghost cells in 5-point stencil are allocated around the chunk, and form a *halo* that contains replicates of the borders of all immediate neighbors. We assumes the chunk with halo is in size of $n * n$. The east edge and its destination west cells (see Fig. 3) can be described as:

```
1 dim H = data(n*n); //chunk with halo
2 dim chunkCol = dim(n-2, n); //column of chunk
3 dim EastEdge = array(chunkCol, H+(2*n-2));
4 dim WestCell = array(chunkCol, H+n);
5 //prt is the local memmory pointer
6 copyto(P*EastEdge, ptr, EastNb*WestCell, ptr, elem_size);
```

The strategy is to find the column of chunk with different shift distance in $n * n$ scope.

In this case, the last line calls *copyto* function to perform the communication. The parameters list is shown as follow:

```
1 copyto(dim Source, void *s, dim Target, void *t, int elem_size)
```

where *Source* is the source distribution, and *Target* is the target one of the same size. The void pointers are the source and target data addresses. If there is no read-write conflict, we can use the same address for both pointers. The last one requires the size of data element, such as $sizeof(float)$.

5.1 Distribution-independent Updating

The shape and size of chunk may be changed when tuning. It is efficient to design a distribution-independent updating algorithm. The reference mechanism is able to get the scope we need without caring about the specific original distribution. Therefore, we use transform functions to proceed updating in a more intuitive way as follow:

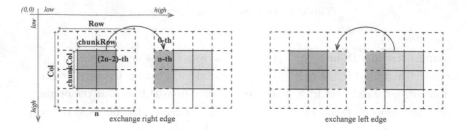

Fig. 3. Right and left edge exchange in 5-point stencil.

```
1  void five_point_stencil(dim P, dim H, float *a){
2      dim Row = row(H);
3      dim Col = col(H):
4      dim chunkRow = cut_high(cut_low(Row,1), 1);
5      dim chunkCol = cut_high(cut_low(Col,1), 1);
6      dim EastEdge = P                  * chunkCol * get_high(chunkRow, 1);
7      dim WestCell = cyclicRow(P, 1) * chunkCol * get_low(Row, 1);
8      copyto(EastEdge, a, WestCell, a, sizeof(float));
9      dim WestEdge = P                  * chunkCol * get_low(chunkRow, 1);
10     dim EastCell = cyclicRow(P,-1) * chunkCol * get_high(Row, 1);
11     copyto(WestEdge, a, EastCell, a, sizeof(float));
12     //then, similar vertical updating
13 }
```

There is no specific chunk width or height, and no calculated shift distance. The only problem-specific number "1" is the depth of edge, which will be modified in the next section for more general situation. When calling this updating function, programmers should be aware of that P and H are two-dimensional, and their top level children in tree structure represent *column* and *row*, respectively. This rule is like an agreement between caller and callee to ensure that the distribution-independent program is working properly.

5.2   Deep Halo and Corner Cells

The previous section discussed solution about halo updating. That algorithm uses a border with a depth of one since that is sufficient to correctly implement the 5-point stencil. However, there are some situations that either require or benefit from a deeper halo [1]. For the correctness, the corner cells are required in updating. Therefore, we extend the previous code to a more general situation with deep halo and corner cells as follow:

```
1  void update(dim P, dim H, float *a, int e){
2      dim Row = row(H);
3      dim Col = col(H):
4      dim chunkRow = cut_high(cut_low(Row,e), e);
5      dim chunkCol = cut_high(cut_low(Col,e), e);
6      //first wave: horizontal
7      dim EastEdge = P                  * chunkCol * get_high(chunkRow, e);
```

```
 8|    dim WestCell = cyclicRow(P, 1) * chunkCol * get_low(Row, e);
 9|    copyto(EastEdge, a, WestCell, a, sizeof(float));
10|    dim WestEdge = P                * chunkCol * get_low(chunkRow, e);
11|    dim EastCell = cyclicRow(P,-1) * chunkCol * get_high(Row, e);
12|    copyto(WestEdge, a, EastCell, a, sizeof(float));
13|    //second wave: vertical
14|    dim SouthEdge = P                * get_high(chunkCol, e) * Row;
15|    dim NorthCell = cyclicCol(P, 1)* get_low(Col, e)         * Row;
16|    copyto(SouthEdge, a, NorthCell, a, sizeof(float));
17|    dim NorthEdge = P                * get_low(chunkCol, e)   * Row;
18|    dim SouthCell = cyclicCol(P,-1)* get_high(Col, e)        * Row;
19|    copyto(NorthEdge, a, SouthCell, a, sizeof(float));
20| }
```

We used a common updating algorithm that each wave updates the halo in one direction along each dimensional axis. Considering the two-dimensional updating shown in Fig. 4. In the first wave the processes update cells along horizontal axis, and if the chunks are of size $m * m$ and halo are of depth e, then they exchange $m * e$ cells with their left and right neighbors. Therefore, when the second wave starts, the processes have already received the borders from their horizontal neighbors and can include corner cells from these in the vertical border exchanges. This effectively folds the corner cells exchange into the second wave. This wave will therefore exchange rows that contains $n * e$ cells. For two-dimensional updating this saves us from having to perform 4 extra communications per chunk to exchange corners with diagonal neighbors.

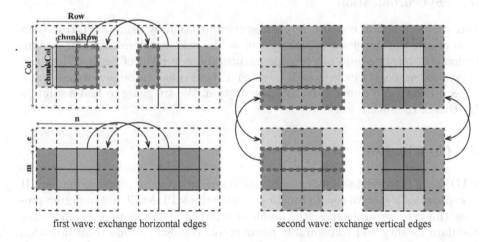

first wave: exchange horizontal edges   second wave: exchange vertical edges

Fig. 4. Two wave updating for corner cells.

5.3   27-Point 3D Stencil

The previous code discussed ghost cells updating in 2D stencil problem. Here we want to discuss a 3D case, molecular dynamics simulation of crystalline silicon

[4]. In this case each process computes elements in a cube by using the values from 26 neighboring cubes. Elements in each cube are contiguous. Therefore, we can treat the cube as a huge point. If we numbered the cube along x, y and z axes from 0, then the center one is the 13-th cube. The wave algorithm in the previous section is applied in this case. In first wave, we copy the 13-th cube to the neighbors along x axis. And then, 3 successive cubes from No. 12 is copied to the neighbors along y axis. In the last wave, the whole 9 cubes of middle layer should be copied to the neighbors along z axis. Similar to the first version code of 5-point stencil, the updating in 3D case is shown as follow:

```
1  //there are N elements in a cube, the size of element is elem_size
2  dim D = data(27,1);
3  dim Px = proc(p,1);
4  dim Py = proc(p,p);
5  dim Pz = proc(p,p*p);
6  dim P = Pz * Py * Px;
7  dim Point = P * get_low(cyclic(D,13),1);
8  dim Left  = Pz * Py * cyclic(Px, 1) * get_low(cyclic(D,12),1);
9  dim Right = Pz * Py * cyclic(Px,-1) * get_low(cyclic(D,14),1);
10 copyto(Point, ptr, Left, ptr, elem_size*N);
11 //other direction...
```

Although the cubes represent three-dimensional elements, we can still manipulate it in a one-dimensional way to simplify our description.

5.4 Synchronization

Our *copyto* function contains implicit synchronization by using MPI_Test. This is to ensure that *copyto* is completed before the next communication or computation. Currently we do not provide asynchronous version of *copyto*. However, there are two *copyto* calls in each wave, and these calls can be performed simultaneously to avoid unnecessary synchronization. We are going to find a solution for this in the future work.

6 Conclusion

PADM is a lightweight toolkit to describe distribution in an intuitive manner. It also provides a general *copyto* function to hide the MPI detail and buffering process. However, we still expose the performance-related factors to users, including the data locality and configurable parameters. We also provide transformation functions to simplify the description.

Since our work PADM is based on non-blocking MPI operations, programmers can use both PADM and MPI at the same time. Actually, the regular collective operations in MPI can be described by using our tool. Such as MPI_Alltoall:

```
1  dim A = proc(p)*data(p,n)*data(n);
2  dim B = data(p,n)*proc(p)*data(n);
3  copyto(A, ptr_a, B, ptr_b, elem_size);
```

Yet we can not describe non-regular collective communication (like MPI_Alltoallv) and reduction operations.

Our work is open source on GitHub, https://github.com/zs192001/padmV0. It contains both the source code and study cases, such as matrix multiplication and molecular dynamics simulation.

References

1. Kjolstad, F.B., Snir, M.: Ghost cell pattern. In: Proceedings of the 2010 Workshop on Parallel Programming Patterns. ACM (2010)
2. Gropp, W., Thakur, R., Lusk, E.: Using MPI- 2: Advanced Features of the Message Passing Interface. MIT Press, Cambridge (1999)
3. Gropp, W., Lusk, E., Swider, D.: Improving the performance of MPI derived datatypes. In: Third MPI Developer's and User's Conference (MPIDC 1999) (1999)
4. Hou, C., Xu, J., Wang, P., et al.: Petascale molecular dynamics simulation of crystalline silicon on Tianhe-1A. Int. J. High Perform. Comput. Appl. **27**(3), 307–317 (2013)
5. Draper, J.M., Culler, D.E., Yelick, K.: Introduction to UPC and Language Specification. Center for Computing Sciences, Institute for Defense Analyses (1999)
6. Numrich, R.W., Reid, J.K.: Co-arrays in the next fortran standard. ACM SIG-PLAN Fortran Forum **24**(2), 4–17 (2005)
7. Chen, Y., Cui, X., Mei, H.: PARRAY: a unifying array representation for heterogeneous parallelism. ACM SIGPLAN Symp. Princ. Pract. Parallel Program. **47**(8), 171–180 (2012)
8. Thakur, R., Rabenseifner, R., Gropp, W.: Optimization of collective communication operations in MPICH. Int. J. High Perform. Comput. Appl. **19**(1), 49–66 (2005)
9. Zhang, N., Driscoll, M., Markley, C.: Snowflake: a lightweight portable stencil DSL. Lawrence Berkeley National Laboratory (2017). https://escholarship.org/uc/item/45w9j3z0
10. Zhu, X., Zhang, J., Yoshii, K.: Analyzing MPI-3.0 process-level shared memory: a case study with stencil computations. In: 2015 15th IEEE/ACM International Symposium on Cluster, Cloud and Grid Computing (CCGrid), pp. 1099–1106 (2015)
11. Rawat, P., Kong, M., Henretty, T.: SDSLc: a multi-target domain-specific compiler for stencil computations. In: Proceedings of the 5th International Workshop on Domain-Specific Languages and High-Level Frameworks for High Performance Computing. ACM (2015)

High Performance Computing

Accelerating Low-End Edge Computing with Cross-Kernel Functionality Abstraction

Chao Wu, Yaoxue Zhang, Yuezhi Zhou(✉), and Qiushi Li

Department of Computer Science and Technology, TNList, Tsinghua University,
Beijing, China
{chaowu,zyx,zhouyz}@tsinghua.edu.cn, lqs17@mails.tsinghua.edu.cn

Abstract. This paper envisions a future in which high performance and energy-modest parallel computing on low-end edge devices were achieved through cross-device functionality abstraction to make them interactive to cloud machines. Rather, there has been little exploration of the overall optimization into kernel processing can deliver for increasingly popular but heavy burden on low-end edge devices. Our idea here is to extend the capability of functionality abstraction across edge clients and cloud servers to identify the computation-intensive code regions automatically and execute the instantiation on the server at runtime. This paper is an attempt to explore this vision, ponder on the principle, and take the first steps towards addressing some of the challenges with edgeBoost. As a kernel-level solution, edgeBoost enables edge devices to abstract not only application layer but also system layer functionalities, as if they were to instantiate the abstracted function inside the same C kernel programming. Experimental results demonstrate that edgeBoost makes cross-kernel functionality abstraction efficient for low-end edge devices and benefits them significant performance optimization than the default scheme unless in a constraint of low transmission bandwidth.

Keywords: Edge computing · Remote procedure call
Functionality abstraction · Performance optimization

1 Introduction

The engineering principles of today's edge computing were first raised in the past two decades, when data is increasingly produced at the edge of the network [18]. By promoting the "*edge*" as any computing and network resources along the path between data sources and cloud data centers, this principle now refers to the enabling technologies allowing computation to be performed at the edge of the network, on downstream data on behalf of cloud services and upstream data on behalf of mobile and fog services, and thus to offer better efficiency for existing networked systems. In practice, edge computing has the potential to

© Springer Nature Switzerland AG 2018
J. Vaidya and J. Li (Eds.): ICA3PP 2018, LNCS 11334, pp. 545–561, 2018.
https://doi.org/10.1007/978-3-030-05051-1_38

address the concerns of response latency requirement, battery life constraint, as well as bandwidth usage saving.

Since the popularity of data parallelism methodology, computation-intensive and emerging applications including artificial intelligence and their attachments such as machine learning, deep learning and control theory, have become cheap, ubiquitous commodities. Their ever-shifting demands on quicker service response time and easier big data access have been resulted in a great opportunity of implementing data parallelism techniques in edge computing and accelerating the procedure through parallel programing languages and general-purpose Graphics Processing Units (GPUs) on any edge devices.

However, there still sees a number of issues that constrain the overall system performance of data-parallel computing on low-end edge devices, e.g., Arduino and Raspberry Pi hardware, which arising from three important points:

1. *Power-hungry:* Energy (battery life) is the biggest limiting factor in low-end edge devices, it is not immediately obvious if those computation-intensive workloads will result in energy-justified performance.
2. *Resource-constraint:* Devices with low-end (or even no) GPU would limit the feasibility of data-parallel computing immensely in the "edge" landscape.
3. *Runtime-incompatible:* Parallelism execution, e.g., CUDA on non-NVIDIA GPU runtime, is easily misplaced, turning to rely on serial CPU execution.

Toward such three limits, offloading the general-purpose computation to cloud has been proved as the right solution to improve the system performance of low-end hardwares. Rather, existing studies often focus on thread or process migration [13,22]. The most key problem lies here is that all of the referred data are demanded to be offloaded to the cloud at the same time, whereas the intention of edge computing makes no sense. Thus, it raises a challenge how to address all the above issues while keeping the benefits of edge computing.

In this paper, we present **edgeBoost** to specify this challenge. **edgeBoost** keeps an eye on C kernel functionality abstraction, instantiation and execution. By cross-device binder internet process connection (IPC), it enables cross-kernel parallel programming and execute computation-intensive code regions within the C kernel functionalities on remote GPUs at runtime, thus to improve the time efficiency, memory usage and energy overheads. **edgeBoost**'s optimization strategy is a little similar to cloud offloading but makes fewer demands on data delivery and extra engineering efforts, giving it many more attractive properties.

edgeBoost is designed as an extension of dynamic functional connectivity. As a C-kernel-level optimization solution, **edgeBoost** now allows Linux clients to abstract not only application functionalities but also system functionalities across devices to instantiate and execute them on the server, as if they were to utilize them inside the same OpenCL or CUDA C libraries. For security, **edgeBoost** also allows performing of permission checks (over SSL connection) for remote applications in the same way as for local. Additionally, **edgeBoost** brings significant performance optimization, e.g., achieving 76% time and 78% energy overhead decreases on average, than the default scheme unless in a constraint of low transmission bandwidth.

We describe the primitives, system design and operations of **edgeBoost** in Sects. 2 through 4. Then, Sect. 5 gives an example case to use **edgeBoost**. In Sect. 6 we evaluate and discuss performance using **edgeBoost** platform. Finally, in Sects. 7, we reveal related work and conclude.

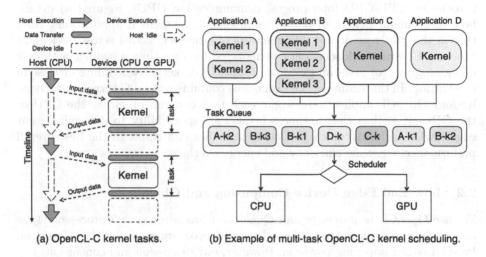

(a) OpenCL-C kernel tasks.   (b) Example of multi-task OpenCL-C kernel scheduling.

Fig. 1. OpenCL-C kernel scheduling on CPU/GPU heterogeneous systems.

2 Low-End Edge Device Meets the Parallel Computing

This section details the operation and issues of C kernel programming language in *data-parallel* computing, elaborates on OpenCL programming model as a study case, and highlight some of the challenges it presents for high performance C kernel computing on low-end edge devices to justify the motivation of edgeBoost.

2.1 C-Kernel in Parallel Computing

There are great efforts in the past decades have made plenty of developer-friendly parallel programming languages available. Yet, C kernel programming offers the most benefit of being an open widely adopted standard [11]. Today, C kernel programming has been a statically compiled language in contrast to many other parallel programming languages which is a important point in CPU-GPU system co-design [14]. To accelerate the computing performance in parallel, for instance, OpenCL is made as an extension of the C language. Programmers write an application with two portions of code, i.e., functions to be executed on the CPU host and functions to be executed on the GPU device. The entry functions of the device code are tagged with a CL_ keyword, and are referred to as *C kernels*. A C kernel executes in parallel across a set of parallel threads in a Single

Instruction Multiple Thread (SIMT) model [20]. As the host and device codes execute in two different memory spaces, the host code must include special calls for host-to-device and device-to-host data transfers. Figure 1 shows the sequence of steps involved in a typical OpenCL invocation whereas C kernel example task is referred to as an OpenCL kernel at runtime consisting of computation and associating CPU-GPU inter-process communication (IPC). Figure 1(a) details how tasks might belong to one or more than one OpenCL applications. Note that in this paper we do not split the work of a single C kernel across devices. In practice, C kernel task scheduling is managed by a runtime scheduler with task queue. Figure 1(b) gives an example of OpenCL-C kernel scheduling for ease of illustration. In this example, the task queue contains several C kernels submitted by four OpenCL applications, where each task can run on either the CPU or the GPU. It is thus the runtime scheduler's responsibility to determine what edge device performs which particular task that can result in the best overall performance, e.g. time efficiency and energy overheads.

2.2   Low-End Edge Device Computing and Challenges

We use OpenCL terminology and Qualcomm Snapdragon 805 processor [4] as an example to explore how C kernel parallel programming model performs on low-end edge computing platform. However, our discussion and conclusions can apply equally to other C kernel programming language, such as, NVIDIA with CUDA [15]. To an edge OpenCL application, a computing system-on-chip (SoC) consists of a host that is traditionally a CPU, e.g., the Snapdragon 805 Krait CPU, and one or more devices (e.g., Adreno GPU [1]) that communicate with the host to execute parallel computation. Applications written in OpenCL consist of host code (C API extensions) and device code (OpenCL C kernel language). Thus, the IPC between the two is performed by issuing commands to a command queue through the host program space. Example commands are transferring data from host to device memory, or launching a kernel for execution on the device. Kernels specify the data-parallel steps of the application that would be executed by the device threads. Once a kernel is launched, all the threads execute the same code but on different parts of the data.

Emerging edge execution like machine learning or deep inference revolves around the process of tasks [13], and a natural candidate for data parallelization is to make each C kernel thread analyze a task. However, the number of tasks in an inference window is on the order of tens to even thousands, whereas the SoC typically GPU requires myriad of threads for any significant speedups to begin to appear, and thus brings computation-intensive workloads to perform. In practice, one of the challenges of high-performance OpenCL applications on low-end, i.e., resource-constrained and power-hungry, edge device is to matchup the right level (priority) of kernel task granularity. Namely, if the C kernel tasks are too computation-intensive, the SoC will struggle with hiding memory access or IPC latency due to not being able to switch between compute-ready threads while others are stalled on a memory transaction.

Another challenge lies in low-end edge computing is that advanced parallel programming languages including CUDA are not yet fully support by neither the software nor the hardware environment. Today, user have only a limited set of tools to optimize the overall performance of low-end edge computing. Tools for improving the heavy burden on resource-constrained SoC from already deployed techniques (e.g., [7–9]) demand people to use stiff schemes for whatever kernel tasks or even just none. Thus, users are first unified and constrained before the performance can be enhanced. Through limited-scale field tests (e.g., small group evaluation or internal dogfooding) log analytics can be applied prior to public adaption but these tests lack broad (particularly global) coverage of application.

Together, the above challenges figure out the improving space of today's edge computing on low-end side, and motivate us to dig deeper in the kernel layer for a better solution, whereas demanding the performance optimization to be obtained while incurring few or none extra engineering efforts on both software and hardware layers.

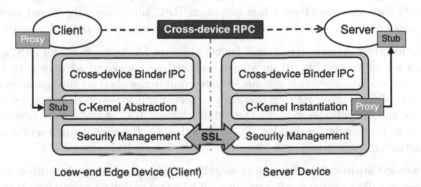

Fig. 2. edgeBoost design overview whereas the cross-kernel RPC is achieved by cross-device binder IPC, kernel abstraction and SSL connection.

3   edgeBoost Platform Overview

edgeBoost is designed to mitigate the disconnection between *high performance parallel computing* and *low-end edge devices*. Indeed, edgeBoost overrides part of C kernel programming libraries to allow auto-tunable functional abstraction (on the client side) and remote instantiation and execution of both application and system functionalities (on the server side) across edge to cloud infrastructure. Figure 2 shows the overview of edgeBoost platform, whereas computation-intensive OpenCL-C and CUDA-C kernel tasks are processed at runtime by cross-device remote procedure call (RPC) execution. Namely, edgeBoost is oblivious to the type of kernel programming models without incurring great extra engineering efforts. By now, edge application can be programmed the same as using default OpenCL or CUDA C APIs, and **edgeBoost** transparently extends their IPC calls within C kernel language to cross-device binder IPC. As Fig. 2 indicates, **edgeBoost** consists of three main components, i.e., cross-kernel RPC execution, C kernel functionality abstraction and instantiation, and network security.

Cross-Kernel RPC Execution: edgeBoost aims to build an environment in which kernel functionalities referred in low-end edge devices can be executed correctly on remote server machines. However, most of such RPC operations might not execute properly across different devices as compilers, e.g., OpenCL or CUDA compiler, are currently designed to support RPC execution within a single device [6,12]. Such a gap evolves another different set of challenges that are not yet fully addressed to support cross-kernel RPC consisting of cross-kernel binder IPC and cross-device RPC execution. For example, **edgeBoost** needs to maintain execution semantics properly across edge client and cloud server if the RPC executions were done among devices, while the C programming compiler does it only within the device boundary. Besides, the server may request IPC semantics about edge client while executing RPC functions. **edgeBoost** should also make such information available on server devices in a bilateral manner.

Functionality Abstraction and Instantiation: In the cross-kernel RPC execution workflow, one important step **edgeBoost** also seeks to address is to find computation-intensive code regions so as to employ the abstraction-instantiation model to deliver those RPC kernel calls to server processes on different devices. To this end, **edgeBoost** extends the default binder IPC of the kernel functions to create a cross-device binder IPC connection by functional abstraction and instantiation respectively, yet offers the illusion of a within-device IPC.

Network Connection Security: edgeBoost allows server and multiple edge devices to collaborative work over network whereas various security issues arise. For example, **edgeBoost** needs to distinguish multiple kernel task instances in multi-device scenarios so as to execute permission checks effectively. In addition, the existence of various kinds of attacks, e.g., DDoS, constantly threaten the quality of service. To protect **edgeBoost** from potential attacks, there establishes a secure connection between the clients and the server with SSL protocol.

In current implementation, **edgeBoost** provides an extensible support that does not require large-scale code rewriting for any OpenCL or CUDA C kernel applications. Meanwhile, it provides easily optimization access by overriding C API of kernel functionalities. Programmer can simply specify any code regions, particularly that are computation-intensive, to the server through the offered APIs. We describe this in detail in Sect. 4.

4   Details of Cross-Kernel RPC Optimization

As mentioned earlier, there are two main phases of RPC execution on the client, i.e., target kernel code selection and cross-device binder IPC. The first phase uses a heuristic target selection algorithm. The cross-device binder IPC in the second phase is to seek the right place to intercept binder IPC parcels. The server is responsible to receive, instantiate and execute the abstracted functions from the client. During the edgeBoost operations, data transfer may be required between the server and the client. Thus, I/O operations and some system calls during the transmission need to be protected from potential attacks. The following sections discuss these design issues in more details.

4.1 Target Kernel Code Selection for Abstraction

edgeBoost avoids the target kernel code selection issue by programmer-specific or sending the abstraction of (1) hot (computation-intensive) functions that include C kernel characteristic and (2) its referred application or system libraries to the server, thus ask the server to instantiate these functional abstraction and execute the entire C kernel functionality from the start. Since the manual specification method requires no automation, this section details the design space of the latter, which utilizes profiling to identify hot code regions as abstracting targets.

Input : (1) a ranked linked list $\mathcal{F}$ of hot functions based on hotness, i.e. execution time;
(2) a DCG graph $G = (V, E)$
Output: a final target set S of selected abstracting code regions

```
1  S ← φ
2  f ← HEAD(F)
3  while f ≠ NULL do
4      // Step 1
5      if f ∉ S and f is not called within the execution of any functions in S then
6          // Step 2
7          T_f ← total execution time of f
8          I_f ← total data size of I/O in f
9          if I_f/T_f < M then
10             S ← S + {f}
11             // Step 3
12             foreach v ∈ V do
13                 if e : v →^P f ∈ E or e : f →^P v ∈ E then
14                     if p > P and v ∉ S and v is not called within the execution of any
                          functions in S then
15                         T_v ← total execution time of v
16                         I_v ← total data size of I/O in v
17                         if I_v/T_v < M then
18                             S ← S + {v}
19     f ← f → next
20 return S
```

Algorithm 1: Target hot codes selection for abstraction.

To simplify the target code selection process, given a function is selected as an abstracting target, all of its callee functions would also be selected for abstraction. Similar to [21], edgeBoost constructs a directed data communication graph (DCG), i.e., $G = (V, E)$, to facilitate the selection. Each node $v \in V$ indicates every C kernel function, and an edge $e : v_1 \xrightarrow{n} v_2 \in E$ connects the functions v_1 and v_2 when there are p memory pages produced in v_1 and accessed in v_2 at runtime. Thus, if v_2 is abstracted and sent to the server and v_1 stays on the client, these memory pages p also need to be transferred from the client to the server over the network. The initial target set is picked up by the hotness of each function, i.e., the total execution time including its callee functions. Algorithm 1 shows the target selection process in a heuristic manner. The input $\mathcal{F}$ is the ranked list of hot functions in the initial target set based on the hotness. The output $\mathcal{S}$ is the final selected target set. For each target $f \in \mathcal{F}$, there are three steps in the algorithm.

In the first step, edgeBoost checks if f_1 has been included in $\mathcal{S}$, or called during the execution of any function in $\mathcal{S}$. If yes, edgeBoost skips f_1 and goes to next target f_2 in $\mathcal{F}$. Otherwise, it moves to the second step.

In the second step, edgeBoost examines the I/O operations in f (including its callee functions) to seek if they are excessive in f with a pre-set threshold M. If they are not excessive, f is included into $\mathcal{S}$ and moves to the third step.

In the third step, edgeBoost traverses each node $v \in V$ in G which is also connected with f, namely, $e : v \xrightarrow{p} f \in E$ or $e : f \xrightarrow{p} v \in E$. If the value of p is large than available memory space P (which results in overflow), it indicates that function v should be abstracted together with f to reduce potential overfitting. Indeed, edgeBoost also examines the I/O operations in v to further check if it works for abstraction. If yes, v would be included into $\mathcal{S}$. The selection process iterates until all of the functions are examined.

For every single target in $\mathcal{S}$, edgeBoost now locates all of its call sites in the collected calling context and their referred return location, which are referred to as the beginning and the ending logistical memory address of this abstraction target. As seen in Fig. 2, the edgeBoost on the client replaces the beginning address by a branch address to a jump stub that enables the abstraction of this target. Similarly, the edgeBoost on the server uses the ending address to terminate the process of the abstracted target. In practice, such decision of beginning and ending memory address can be extended easily to other kernel types of byte-compiled parallel programming language, e.g., Java, with different granularities, such as hot loops or traces, only with engineering work required.

4.2   Cross-Device Binder IPC

A cross-kernel RPC is executed by a client using a binder IPC proxy object for a server's binder IPC stub, as earlier shown in Fig. 2. In fact, edgeBoost demands to intercept parcels from applications to create a cross-device IPC channel instead of within-device IPC calls transparently. Thus, a key challenge in seeking such IPC channel is how to determine the right interface to intercept parcels, and thus supports a broad range of kernel function abstracting without many engineering efforts, e.g., rewriting C language programs. As Fig. 3 demonstrates, edgeBoost uses a parcel goes through a number of binder layers. The first layer, which is the interface layer, is designed to override the same function interfaces and provide the C abstraction APIs. In most cases, the abstraction interfaces are then instantiated and invoked in C kernel programming codes. They next call underlayer interfaces of C language compiler (for application functionalities), such as gcc [19]; or OS libraries (for system functionalities), e.g., GPU drivers. Note that if the parcels is designed to be intercepted in the interface layer, function interfaces in C kernel applications must be modified by re-compilation, which does not what edgeBoost aims to in this paper.

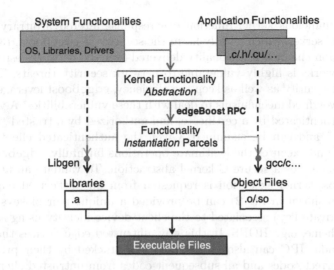

Fig. 3. Operating principle in edgeBoost functionality abstracting. Black dashed arrows indicate the default C kernel compilation and execution, and red arrows show the workflow of cross-kernel RPC execution.

All the layers below the interface layer belong to the OS runtime, whereas kernel applications are compiled into object files and then dynamically linked with system libraries. Hence, intercepting the parcels here brings an opportunity to support existing C programming models without engineering modifications. In current implementation, similar to [16], edgeBoost leverages BpBinder (in Android environment) as the parcel intercept point and a third-party binder, i.e., the binder-for-linux [2], for a binder Linux object at the native IPC layer. This is because a binder object is located at the native IPC layer, all kernel layer functionalities would be passed through this object for binder IPC. Thus, edgeBoost is able to intercept any parcels at this layer to create cross-device binder IPC channels for any functionalities no matter whether they are generated by OpenCL or CUDA compilers. Another key challenge here is to seek the parcels to intercept. As wrong parcel point or a large amount of parcel intercept might impose significant overheads. To intercept the smallest set of parcels, edgeBoost now initiates interactions with other kernel applications. We give examples of this in detail in Sect. 5.

4.3 Network Security Protection

Running the cross-kernel RPC execution with direct binder IPC over network connection can raise concerns about security. To offer adequate protection as well as keeping the efficiency, edgeBoost considers all potential vulnerabilities for the network security module design, including: (1) untrusted clients: since each client sends IPC parcels directly to the server, an untrusted client could take arbitrary action (e.g. altering and replacing) on the parcels; (2) malicious function: a malicious kernel function can response altered/arbitrary inference results to the server, which greatly harm the security of **edgeBoost**. (3) insecure communication channel: functionality delivered over the networks especially the wireless networks is highly vulnerable to network security threats. To provide assurance of security as well as keep the efficiency, **edgeBoost** leverages a whole set of light-weighted mechanisms to deal with these vulnerabilities. A valid client device is authenticated by a certificate, and authorized by a trusted "certificate of authority" and can be examined. Given the authenticated client device is trustworthy and executes the legitimate operations faithfully. **edgeBoost** makes sure client generates a secure C kernel abstraction. To validate an abstraction, when an cross-kernel execution is requested from an authorized edge device, its proxy (as shown in Fig. 2) can be provided a unique pair of keys (a public key and a private key) associated to the client device identity using an efficient signature scheme, e.g., HORS. In this way, untrusted edge devices that request incorrect binder IPC can also be detected and tracked by their private keys, and the incorrect codes and all subsequent codes from untrusted clients will be abandoned. In addition, **edgeBoost** adopts the SSL transport protocol to ensure the integrity and confidentiality of all the network traffic, which is resistant to eavesdropping, man-in-the-middle and tampering attacks.

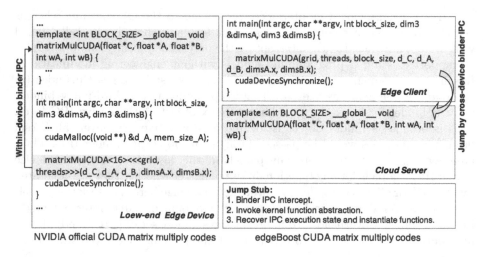

NVIDIA official CUDA matrix multiply codes   edgeBoost CUDA matrix multiply codes

Fig. 4. A real-world example from NVIDIA matrixMul demo, with its CUDA code before and after edgeBoost code, and the jump stub.

5   Example Case of Using edgeBoost

This section shows a real-world application, i.e., NVIDIA matrixMul [3], as an example case. It is a sample implements matrix multiplication with CUDA C kernel to illustrate parallel benefits for matrix multiply. As Fig. 4 shows, the edgeBoost first identifies that over 90% of the execution time is spent in the kernel function `matrixMulCUDA<16><<<grid, threads>>>()`, which is called by the `main()` function through within-device binder IPC. This particular function evaluates all potential moves and picks the best move among them. Thus, the function `matrixMulCUDA()` is selected as an abstracting target.

The edgeBoost then overrides the target as an functional abstraction, i.e., `matrixMulCUDA(grid, threads, ...)`, uses arguments of `grid` and `threads` as the input to carry out the cross-device binder IPC across client and server with a RPC call and directs its execution to a jump stub as shown in the figure. Note that the `main()` function would be transiently suspended at this moment. When the execution reaches the tail of `matrixMulCUDA()`, the jump stub is executed and a return request is sent from the server. Once received, edgeBoost on the client side fetches the results to the `main()` function and finally ends the whole procedure. By that analogy, all C kernel functions like `matrixMulCUDA()` can be cross-kernel executed on the server seamlessly through RPC calls.

6 Evaluation

This section evaluates edgeBoost principle by comparing it to state-of-the-art work with a focus on the following points: (1) how much time efficiency can edgeBoost accelerate; (2) how many energy are saved after using edgeBoost; (3) how much the techniques within edgeBoost affect system overhead; and (4) what is the potential limitation of edgeBoost.

6.1 Experiment Setup and Function Coverage

As a study case, most of the experiments are carried out on small single-board computers, i.e., Raspberry Pi 3 (Model B), as the low-end edge client. It owns a Broadcom BCM2837 SoC and 1 GB memory. In this paper, the edge client runs Raspbian Linux OS. Besides, the built-in GPU is Broadcom VideoCore 4 which **cannot naturally support** CUDA applications, thus all computing are *defaulted in serial* manner. The server has a GTX 1080 Ti GPU with 8 GB RAM and runs Ubuntu 14.04 LTS. All devices are in the same local area network (LAN) and connected to a LinkSys AC1900 access point via 802.11n Wi-Fi. Note that the results we measured are also applicable to any OpenCL-C kernel programming or low-end edge devices that use the same setup as building blocks.

To precisely measure the client's energy cost, we attach a hardware power meter, i.e., the UT658 USB Tester [5] to the Raspberry Pi 3's USB interface (as Fig. 5 shows) to record voltage (in V) and electricity (in mA) to evaluate performance of edgeBoost. This power meter provides precise measurements as it samples the current drawn from the power overhead with a frequency of 5 KHz and a mean error of around ±1%.

We use CUDA programming to explore what edgeBoost benefits low-end edge device at large. To this end, we employ 10 most representative CUDA

Fig. 5. USB power tick.

applications used in data-parallel computing and resulted in GPU-intensive. All the study cases can be obtain from NVIDIA official site [3]. Table 1 shows a list of these applications referring to machine learning and deep inference, whereas **edgeBoost** utilizes hot code abstraction from client to server as example in Sect. 5. In practice, those C kernels within the use cases will apply multiple independent binder IPC channels while cross-device execution a single RPC call. Those two binder connections should be made between the same client and server pair for correct operation on each's GPU.

6.2   Optimization in Low-End Edge Computing

We first evaluate the benefits of overall system performance, i.e., time efficiency, memory consumption and energy overheads, obtained by applying **edgeBoost** to different CUDA applications. As Sect. 5 introduced, by auto-selecting the hot codes (which uses over 90% time consumption of the whole) in these test cases, **edgeBoost** is able to leverage the C kernel abstraction and instantiation techniques to provide the performance optimization of **edgeBoost** prototype on Raspberry Pi. In addition to distinguish the improvements of different test cases that are affected by diverse hot code regions, we normalize the optimized (saving) results comparing to default computing scheme in percentages. Table 1 shows our obtained results to different baselines. Within the 10 test cases, on average, **edgeBoost** can reduce the time consumed to functionality execution by **76.5%**, ranging from 32.8% (in Vector Addition) to 91.3% (in Monte Carlo Estimation). In the aspect of memory usage, **edgeBoost** on average achieves **52.8%** space reduction, varying from 3.9% (in DCT8x8) to 92.7% (in Vector Addition). In addition, **edgeBoost** benefits low-end edge device with **78.3%** energy saving on average, which ranges from 32.1% (in Vector Addition) to 90.4% (in Monte Carlo Estimation of Pi). It demonstrates that **edgeBoost** provides promised and significant overall system performance optimization.

Table 1. Normalized performance optimization (the savings) arising from edgeBoost comparing to default execution (the baselines) on local device.

NVIDIA CUDA	Baselines (default scheme)			edgeBoost Saving (in %)		
Application Examples	Latency	Memory	Energy	Latency	Memory	Energy
FFT-based 2D convolution	11620 ms	31.6 MB	38.8 J	78.3%	39.2%	86.1%
Recursive gaussian filter	8714 ms	187.0 MB	30.0 J	82.1%	84.7%	85.1%
Sobel Filter	4842 ms	24.5 MB	15.9 J	67.0%	29.0%	74.9%
Matrix multiplication	85377 ms	93.7 MB	243.6 J	88.5%	70.4%	87.6%
Vector addition	5275 ms	384.4 MB	17.8 J	32.8%	92.7%	32.1%
Monte Carlo estimation of Pi	10507 ms	21.5 MB	29.1 J	91.3%	66.3%	90.4%
DCT8x8	9727 ms	14.3 MB	30.6 J	83.5%	3.9%	82.2%
Merge sort	4241 ms	32.9 MB	13.3 J	68.2%	50.1%	69.3%
Bilateral filter	1007 ms	1.1 MB	3.3 J	86.3%	4.9%	85.5%
Haar wavelet decomposition	1699 ms	7.6 MB	5.7 J	86.9%	87.0%	89.3%
Benefits on average	-	-	-	**76.5%**	**52.8%**	**78.3%**

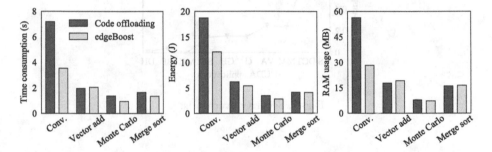

Fig. 6. Overall performance among time consumption, memory usage and energy overheads in edgeBoost and thread-level code offloading.

6.3 edgeBoost vs Cloud Offloading

edgeBoost is something similar to code offloading. However, code offloading is based on a thread- or process- level workload migration, while edgeBoost uses functionality abstraction scheme. This section evaluates the general performance enhancing benefits from edgeBoost against with existing cloud code offloading (thread-level) method. For comprehensive benchmark coverage, we also note types of system performance in the evaluations as: (1) time efficiency, i.e., time used to execute a CUDA application via the two methods; (2) memory usage, i.e., RAM capacity on the client side during the whole workload processing; and (3) energy overheads, i.e., the battery decrease after using the two methods for the same CUDA applications. Due to space limits, Fig. 6 compares the optimized performance with four representative types of C kernel functionalities obtained from edgeBoost and code offloading. We observe that, in most cases, edgeBoost can provide a better time efficiency, memory usage and energy saving benefits comparing to today's thread-level code offloading. For the four test cases, to execute data-parallel and intensive computation, the system energy overhead reaches to an average value of 8.1 J. By using edgeBoost with automatically hot code region selecting for all the four types of C kernels, we see that there brings an 25.1% energy saving benefit on average. When we turn the hot code selection to manual mode, i.e., manually set up functions to use **edgeBoost**, on average for the four test cases, **edgeBoost** can reduce the time consumption by 35.2% than the code offloading scheme, ranging from 4.1% (in 2D Convolution) to 50.3% (in Vector Addition). There brings similar benefits in energy (25.0% saving on average) and memory usage (11.8% decrease on average) performance. Taken together, the evaluations demonstrate that **edgeBoost** can provide better optimization than existing cloud offloading. Moreover, the effectiveness of target selection mechanism within **edgeBoost** is as efficient as programmer-specific.

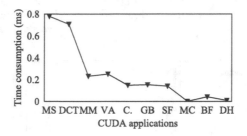

Fig. 7. Security overheads.

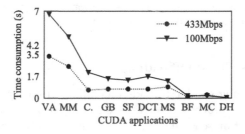

Fig. 8. Limits of network bandwidth.

6.4 Security Overheads

edgeBoost is able to establish a secure network connection in the transport layer with SSL protocol. Thus, communication between client and server can be protected from malicious attacks. Here, we evaluate the overheads of using the SSL protocol in terms of time consumption. Figure 7 evaluates the specific time consumed to build SSL connections in each use case test. Specifically, using the SSL connections incurs overheads in encrypting and decrypting data to transfer.

During our experiments, an SSL connection increases time consumption range from 1 ms (in Monte Carlo) to 778 ms (in Merge Sort). This also comforts to the memory usage performance of each case. On average, the client uses 246 ms more time consumption when using SSL connections, compared to the case of using edgeBoost without SSL.

6.5 Limitation

In very a few case, edgeBoost might be *first* limited by a low transmission bandwidth. For example, as Fig. 8 shows, edgeBoost would have 2.1X latency increase in a 100 Mbps environment comparing to 433 Mbps environment. It is not sure whether edgeBoost can achieve the same or negligible performance loss with more bandwidth constraint scenarios. Our implementation of edgeBoost *then* limited that it is mostly only developed, tested and tried out on Raspberry Pi single-board computers. We are not confident if it works perfectly for other types of commercial edge devices. Also, despite our kernel functionality abstraction scheme is general used in Android and Linux OS, more efforts are needed to study how to implement the design and test it on more OS and programming languages. *Last*, edgeBoost benefits overall system performance for cross-kernel RPC executions in low-end edge environments, however, we can conduct this execution with functional abstracting/instantiating and cross-device binder IPC, we are motivated to study an easier way to relief unnecessary engineering efforts.

7 Related Work

This section reviews previous studies of edge computing and cloud offloading.

What is Edge Computing. Edge computing is referred as an promising technology to allow computation to be performed at the edge of the network, on downstream data on behalf of cloud services and upstream data on behalf of edge/IoT services. Today, the "edge" is defined by [18] as any computing and network resources along the path between data sources and cloud data centers. Such as, a smartphone is the edge between body things and cloud, a gateway in a smart home is the edge between home things and cloud, a micro data center and a cloudlet [17] is the edge between a mobile device and cloud. This rationale of edge computing is that computing could happen at the proximity of data sources.

How Cloud Offloading Works. How to overcome the resource constraints of edge devices by partitioning programs between a device and more powerful server infrastructure is challenging. By offloading, MAUI [9] uses features of managed-language runtimes to automatically partition a program depending on runtime prediction of the partition's energy and performance benefits. Rather, all of these systems are made for CPU workloads and are inappropriate for tasks like fast-action games that heavily rely on a GPU. With the proliferation of general purpose GPU computing on mobile platforms, researchers proposed different solutions, e.g., [10], to alleviate the burden of the mobiles by offloading the heavy workloads from low-powered devices to more powerful machines.

8   Conclusion

This paper proposes edgeBoost platform to address performance optimization issues lie in low-end edge device. edgeBoost uses a cross-kernel RPC technique within it to identify and abstract computation-intensive code regions. By binder IPC channel across client and server, edgeBoost instantiates and executes the abstracted C kernel functions on the server at runtime. Experimental results with CUDA data-parallel applications demonstrate the significant optimization and effectiveness arising from edgeBoost in achieving fast parallel computing response time with modest system overheads. As a future work, we will consider extending edgeBoost platform with a comprehensive implementation to support more kernel types of byte-compiled parallel programming language, e.g., Java.

Acknowledgement. We thank the anonymous reviewers for their valuable and insightful comments. This work is supported by Tsinghua University Initiative Scientific Research Program under Grants No. 20161080066.

References

1. Adreno GPU. https://developer.qualcomm.com/software/adreno-gpu-sdk/gpu
2. Binder-for-linux. https://github.com/hungys/binder-for-linux
3. CUDA Samples. https://docs.nvidia.com/cuda/cuda-samples/
4. Qualcomm Snapdragon Processor. https://www.qualcomm.com/snapdragon
5. UNI-T UT658 USB Tester. http://www.uni-trend.com
6. Aoki, R., et al.: Hybrid OpenCL: enhancing OpenCL for distributed processing. In: ISPA, pp. 149–154. IEEE (2011)
7. Bui, D.H., et al.: Rethinking energy-performance trade-off in mobile web page loading. In: MobiCom, pp. 14–26. ACM (2015)
8. Chun, B.G., et al.: Clonecloud: elastic execution between mobile device and cloud. In: EuroSys, pp. 301–314. ACM (2011)
9. Cuervo, E., et al.: Maui: making smartphones last longer with code offload. In: MobiSys, pp. 49–62. ACM (2010)
10. Cuervo, E., et al.: Kahawai: high-quality mobile gaming using GPU offload. In: MobiSys, pp. 121–135. ACM (2015)
11. Culler, D.E., et al.: Parallel programming in split-C. In: Proceedings of the Super-computing 1993, pp. 262–273. IEEE (1993)
12. Fung, W.W., Aamodt, T.M.: Thread block compaction for efficient SIMT control flow. In: HPCA, pp. 25–36. IEEE (2011)
13. Georgiev, P., et al.: Accelerating mobile audio sensing algorithms through on-chip GPU offloading. In: MobiSys, pp. 306–318. ACM (2017)
14. Jäskeläinen, P.O., et al.: OpenCL-based design methodology for application-specific processors. In: SAMOS, pp. 223–230. IEEE (2010)
15. Nvidia, C.: Programming guide (2010)
16. Oh, S., et al.: Mobile plus: multi-device mobile platform for cross-device functionality sharing. In: MobiSys, pp. 332–344. ACM (2017)
17. Satyanarayanan, M., et al.: The case for VM-based cloudlets in mobile computing. IEEE Pervasive Comput. **8**(4) (2009)

18. Shi, W., et al.: Edge computing: vision and challenges. IEEE Internet Things J. **3**(5), 637–646 (2016)
19. Stallman, R.: Using and porting the GNU compiler collection. In: MIT Artificial Intelligence Laboratory. Citeseer (2001)
20. Stone, J.E., et al.: OpenCL: a parallel programming standard for heterogeneous computing systems. CiSE **12**(3), 66–73 (2010)
21. Wang, W., et al.: Enabling cross-ISA offloading for COTS binaries. In: MobiSys, pp. 319–331. ACM (2017)
22. Wu, C., et al.: Butterfly: mobile collaborative rendering over GPU workload migration. In: INFOCOM 2017, pp. 1–9. IEEE (2017)

A High-Performance and High-Reliability RAIS5 Storage Architecture with Adaptive Stripe

Linjun Mei[✉], Dan Feng, Lingfang Zeng, Jianxi Chen, and Jingning Liu

School of Computer Science and Technology, Wuhan National Laboratory for Optoelectronics, Key Laboratory of Information Storage System Ministry of Education of China,
Huazhong University of Science and Technology, Wuhan 430074, China
{ljmei,dfeng,lfzeng,chenjx,jnliu}@hust.edu.cn

Abstract. In the era of big data, the traditional RAID storage system has been incapable of meeting the requirements of performance and reliability for the large amount of data storage and computing. In view of the situation, Solid State Disks (SSDs), which can provide better performance than Hard Disk Drives (HDDs), are widely used to construct storage arrays in enterprise environments. Today many studies on Redundant Array of Independent SSDs (RAIS) storage systems concentrate more on improving write performance, and show less attention on the reconstruction performance of RAIS storage systems. In this paper, we proposed RAIS5AS, a novel RAIS5 storage architecture with adaptive stripe for improving the performance and reliability of RAIS5. RAIS5AS distinguishes between logical stripe and physical stripe. Logical stripe is a traditional RAID stripe. Physical stripe consists of the blocks (in a logical stripe) which have been written data. When handling write requests, RAIS5AS uses physical stripe as the basic processing unit to choose which blocks are read to compute the new parity block. When recovering data, RAIS5AS skips the unused failed blocks. In addition, RAIS5AS simplifies the synchronization process of RAIS5 storage system. We have implemented the proposed scheme and carried out a series of experiments. RAIS5AS on average improves write performance and reconstruction performance of the basic RAIS5 by up to 7.92% and 95.65% respectively, and those of JOR by 9.16% and 14.57% respectively.

Keywords: Physical stripe · Performance · Reconstruction time RAIS5

1 Introduction

With the explosive growth in data volume, the I/O bottleneck has become an increasingly daunting challenge for big data analytics [1]. The emergence of SSD, which is a new semiconductor storage device, alleviates this performance problem

© Springer Nature Switzerland AG 2018
J. Vaidya and J. Li (Eds.): ICA3PP 2018, LNCS 11334, pp. 562–577, 2018.
https://doi.org/10.1007/978-3-030-05051-1_39

[2]. SSD does not require head seeks and plate rotations to read and write data, and has many advantages over HDD, such as low energy consumption, high performance, high robustness to vibrations and temperature, and so on. Due to the high cost, SSD is originally used as a cache in the storage systems [3,4]. With the development of technology and price decline, SSDs are widely used in data center and enterprise storage systems. However, it is difficult to meet the requirements of high performance, large capacity and high reliability for a single SSD. Thus, many studies use RAID technology to construct array systems for meeting these requirements [5].

Considering the high cost/GB of SSD and the reliability requirements of SSD-based disk arrays, RAIS5 is a good choice for SSD-based disk arrays [6]. In the paper, RAIS stands for Redundant Array of Independent SSDs. The different levels of RAIS are short for RAIS0, RAIS5 and so on. The small write problem in RAIS5 storage system may result in degraded performance and shortened SSD lifetime. Therefore, many studies focus on the user requests processing, and pay no attention to the parity synchronization and the data reconstruction in RAIS5.

In the paper, we proposed RAIS5AS, a novel RAIS5 storage architecture with adaptive stripe for improving write performance and reconstruction performance of RAIS5. The traditional n-disk RAID5 stripe is composed of $n - 1$ data blocks and 1 parity block. The adaptive stripe consists of the blocks (in a traditional stripe) which have been written data. When handling write requests, RAIS5AS uses adaptive stripe instead of the traditional stripe as the basic processing unit. When recovering data, RAIS5AS skips the failed blocks that are not in adaptive stripes. Moreover, RAIS5AS simplifies the synchronization process of RAIS5 storage system. The contributions of this article are described as follows:

(1) We proposed a novel RAIS5 storage architecture with adaptive stripe, called RAIS5AS. To the best of our knowledge, RAIS5AS is the first study to optimize the synchronization performance, write performance and reconstruction performance simultaneously.
(2) RAIS5AS used a new algorithm to generate parity blocks. This algorithm reduces the pre-read operations so that write performance is improved.
(3) RAIS5AS only recovers the used failed blocks to speed up the reconstruction process.
(4) We have implemented a RAIS5AS prototype in the Linux Software RAID framework and carried out extensive performance measurements using RAID-meter [7].

The rest of the paper is organized as follows. We present the background and the motivation in Sect. 2. Section 3 describes the design and implementation of RAIS5AS. The experimental results are presented in Sect. 4. In Sect. 5, related works are introduced. We conclude our paper in Sect. 6.

2   Background and Motivation

2.1   Characteristics of Flash-Based SSD

Flash-based SSDs are made of silicon memory chips and store information in cells which are called floating-gate transistor. They have many characteristics, such as high performance, low energy consumption, and so on. In addition, flash-based SSDs have the following two main characteristics different from HDDs.

First, SSDs update data out-of-place. The reason is that each block in the SSD must be erased in advance before any page in it can be rewritten, which is known as "erase-before-write" [6]. The unit of write operation is a single page, whereas the unit of erase operation is a single block which is composed of 64 to 256 pages. Thus, the time that an erase operation takes is one order of magnitude higher than the completion time of a write operation.

Second, the erase time of the flash memory cell is limited. Generally, NAND flash memory can be divided into two categories: Single-Level Cell (SLC) which can stores one bit, and Multi-Level Cell (MLC) which can store two bits or more. A SLC flash memory has around 100,000 erase cycles. However, a MLC flash memory has only around 10,000 erase cycles or less.

Because of these two limitations, previous studies pay more attention to the user requests processing and ignore the synchronization and reconstruction performance.

2.2   Reconstruction Algorithm

There are many studies focus on how to shorten the RAID reconstruction time. Most of the reconstruction algorithms rebuilt all stripes in RAID. Sivathanu et al. [8] proposed a live-block recovery method which only recovers the live data to reduce the reconstruction time. However, the live-block recovery method must rely on file system's semantic knowledge to know which blocks are live and should be recovered. More importantly, the live-block recovery method may cause the data loss in RAID5 or RAID6 storage systems [9].

Inspired by live-block recovery, Wu et al. [9] proposed a journal-guided reconstruction algorithm (JOR) to improve RAID reconstruction performance. JOR uses a journal bitmap table to store the storage space utilization status at the block level. JOR can know which stripes are used by the journal bitmap table so that only the failed data on used stripes is reconstructed. JOR is not only suitable for replication-based disk arrays, but also for parity-based disk arrays.

2.3   Motivation

Each block and stripe in RAID storage system has three states: allocated, released and unallocated. Journal-guided reconstruction algorithm(JOR) refers to the first two states as used and the unallocated state as unused. JOR recovers the used stripe and skips the unused stripe. However, the failed data blocks in the used stripe may be invalid, which also can be skipped. The reason is that all blocks in JOR storage system are initialized to zero. If the failed data block has never been written after synchronization, the value of its corresponding data block in the spare disk is the same as its value. Figure 1 gives an example to illustrate the scenario in detail.

(1) The data blocks of one stripe are written with value zero during synchronization, as shown in Fig. 1(a). D_0, D_1, D_2 and D_3 denote the data blocks, P_0 denotes the parity block, while Sp denotes the corresponding block in the spare disk. "1" indicates that the data in the block is all "1" while "0" indicates that the data in the block is all "0".

(2) When a small write arrives at the D_0, The value in the D_0 and P_0 are "1", as shown in Fig. 1(b).

(3) The third disk fails. The failed block in this stripe is D_2. The value in the D_2 is the same as that in the spare disk. Thus, it does not need to be reconstructed. While this stripe is regarded as an used stripe in JOR, the data block D_2 must be reconstructed. *Note: D_2 is recovered by D_0 xor D_1 xor D_3 xor P_0 in JOR.*

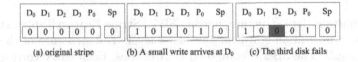

D_0	D_1	D_2	D_3	P_0	Sp		D_0	D_1	D_2	D_3	P_0	Sp		D_0	D_1	D_2	D_3	P_0	Sp
0	0	0	0	0	0		1	0	0	0	1	0		1	0	0	0	1	0

    (a) original stripe   (b) A small write arrives at D_0 (c) The third disk fails

Fig. 1. An example of unnecessary data recovery in JOR.

Our proposed RAIS5AS only recovers the used data blocks in stead of used stripes. The operation of initializing all blocks to zero in RAIS5 will result in serious performance degradation. Thus, RAIS5AS does not write all blocks with value zero during synchronization. To ensure data consistency, RAIS5AS uses a new algorithm to choose which blocks are read for computing new parity block. This new algorithm reduces the pre-read operations so that write performance is improved.

3 Design and Implementation

3.1 Definition of Logical Stripe and Physical Stripe

Generally, an n-disk RAID5 stripe is composed of n-1 data blocks and 1 parity block. In the paper, we refer to the traditional RAID stripe as logical stripe. A logical stripe has a corresponding physical stripe. A physical stripe is composed of the blocks (in the corresponding logical stripe) which have been written data. For example, in Fig. 1(b), the logical stripe is $(D_0, D_1, D_2, D_3, P_0)$, while the corresponding physical stripe is (D_0, P_0).

RAIS5AS uses a vector $(t_1, t_2, ..., t_k)$ to represent the relationship between a logical stripe and its corresponding physical stripe, where k is the number of

SSDs in RAIS5. For example, in Fig. 1(b), the relationship vector is (1, 0, 0, 0, 1). "1" indicates that a block has been written data, while "0" indicates that a block has not been written data after synchronization.

If a block has been written data, we regard it as a used block. Otherwise, it is an unused block. On block device layer, we can know whether a block has been written data by bio. When the RAIS5 is created, all blocks are unused blocks. If a bio write or read a block, we regard the block as a used block by setting the corresponding bit in SBT (Stripe Bitmap Table) to "1".

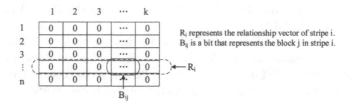

Fig. 2. SBT of a k-disk RAIS5AS which has n stripes.

An important data structure, namely SBT (Stripe Bitmap Table), stores the RAIS5 space utilization status at the block level. The structure of the SBT is shown in Fig. 2. The SBT is composed of N entries. Each entry corresponds to a stripe in the RAIS5 array. Actually, SBT is the set of relationship vectors for each stripe. In Fig. 2, R_i represents the relationship vector of stripe i. B_{ij} is a bit that represents the block j in stripe i. RAIS5AS uses B_{ij} to indicate whether the corresponding block has been written or not. When RAIS5 is created, all bits of SBT are initialized to "0", indicating that all blocks in the RAIS5 have not been written. When a block is written, RAIS5AS finds the corresponding relationship vector R_i, then finds the corresponding B_{ij}, and B_{ij} is set to be "1" at last, which indicates that the block is now written.

SBT cannot be lost when a RAIS5AS system is created. Otherwise the data in the RAIS5AS will become inconsistent. To prevent the loss of the SBT due to sudden power outage or a system crash, RAIS5AS stores the SBT in a nonvolatile RAM (NVRAM). If a RAIS5AS is composed of 8 SSDs and each SSD capacity is 100 GB, it total needs 25MB (i.e. 100 GB/4 KB * 8bits) NVRAM to store the SBT. Since the size of NVRAM is small, it will not incur significant hardware cost. NVRAM, which is usually buildup of DRAM backed with a battery, is generally deployed in the RAID controller to improve the write performance. Besides, in the high-end RAID storage systems, the NVRAM is commonly mirrored to prevent a single point of failure.

3.2 Parity Block Generation Algorithm

To compute new parity blocks, there are two alternative methods, namely *read-modify-write* and *reconstruction-write* respectively. The main difference between the two methods lies in the data blocks that must be pre-read for the computation of the new parity blocks [10]. The *read-modify-write* method reads the data blocks to be updated and the old parity block to compute new parity block. The *reconstruction-write* method reads the data blocks not to be updated to compute new parity block. We use rcw and rmw to represent the number of pre-read operations when the controller chooses the *reconstruction-write* and the *read-modify-write* method. In the traditional RAID5, rcw is the total number of the data blocks that are not to be updated in the stripe, and rmw is the total number of the parity block and data blocks that are to be updated in the stripe. However, in the RAIS5AS, rcw is the total number of the data blocks that are not to be updated in the **physical stripe**, and rmw is the total number of the parity block and data blocks that are to be updated in the **physical stripe**. To minimize the number of pre-read operations, the RAID5 controller dynamically chooses one of the two methods according to rcw and rmw.

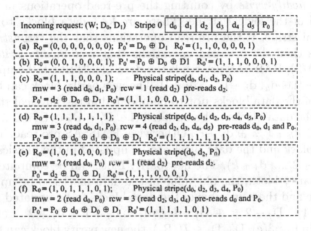

Fig. 3. Illustration of parity block generation in the RAIS5AS. *Note: (W; D0, D1) represents a write request updates d_0 and d_1 to D_0 and D_1. R_0 is the relationship vector of Stripe 0.*

In RAIS5AS parity block generation algorithm, R_i is the corresponding relationship vector, P_i is the parity block, D_j, $D_j + 1$, $D_j + 2$, ..., $D_j + k$ are the data blocks that are to be updated in the **logical stripe**, d_h, $d_h + 1$, $d_h + 2$, ..., $d_h + l$ are the data blocks that are not to be updated in the **physical stripe**, $D_j \in \Pi(R_i)$ represents that D_j is in physical stripe i (i.e. $B_{ij} = 1$), $D_j \notin \Pi(R_i)$ represents that D_j is not in physical stripe i (i.e. $B_{ij} = 0$), $C(R_i)$ is the total number of the blocks that are in physical stripe i. The parity block generation strategy is divided into three cases as follows.

Case 1: The data blocks to be updated are all **not** in the physical stripe (i.e. D_j, $D_j + 1$, ..., $D_j + k \notin \Pi(R_i)$).

In this case, RAIS5AS needs to know whether the logical stripe has been used or not. If the logical stripe is unused (i.e. $P_i \notin \Pi(R_i)$), the new parity block can be computed by the new value of the data blocks to be updated (i.e. $P'_i = D_j \oplus D_j + 1 \oplus D_j + 2 \ldots \oplus D_j + k$). Otherwise, the new parity block can be computed by the old value of the parity block and the new value of the data blocks to be updated in the physical stripe (i.e. $P'_i = P_i \oplus D_j \oplus D_j + 1 \oplus D_j + 2 \ldots \oplus D_j + k$).

Figure 3 shows an illustration of parity block generation in the RAIS5AS, where $(W; D_0, D_1)$ represents a write request updates d_0 and d_1 to D_0 and D_1. As shown in Fig. 3(a), $D_0, D_1 \notin \Pi(R_i) \,\&\&\, P_0 \notin \Pi(R_i)$, the new parity block can be computed by D_0 and D_1 (i.e. $P'_0 = D_0 \oplus D_1$). As shown in Fig. 3(b), $D_0, D_1 \notin \Pi(R_i) \,\&\&\, P_0 \in \Pi(R_i)$, the new parity block can be computed by P_0, D_0 and D_1 (i.e. $P'_0 = P_0 \oplus D_0 \oplus D_1$).

Case 2: The data blocks to be updated are all in the physical stripe (i.e. D_j, $D_j + 1, \ldots, D_j + k \in \Pi(R_i)$).

In this case, RAIS5AS dynamically chooses one of the *reconstruction-write* and the *read-modify-write* by counting the pre-read operations in the physical stripe instead of the logical stripe. There are k+1 data blocks to be updated in the physical stripe. If the pre-read operations that the *reconstruction-write* needs are less than the pre-read operations that *read-modify-write* needs (i.e. $k+1 \geq C(R_i)/2$), RAIS5AS pre-reads the data blocks **not** to be updated in the physical stripe (i.e. $d_h, d_h + 1, \ldots, d_h + l$). The new parity block can be computed by the value of the data blocks **not** to be updated in the physical stripe and the new value of the data blocks to be updated (i.e. $P'_i = D_j \oplus D_j + 1 \oplus D_j + 2 \ldots \oplus D_j + k \oplus d_h \oplus d_h + 1 \ldots \oplus d_h + l$). Otherwise, RAIS5AS pre-reads the old value of the parity block and the data blocks to be updated in the physical stripe (i.e. $d_j, d_j + 1, d_j + 2, \ldots, d_j + k$). The new parity block can be computed by the old value of the parity block, the old value of the data blocks to be updated in the physical stripe and the new value of the data blocks to be updated (i.e. $P'_i = P_i \oplus D_j \oplus D_j + 1 \oplus D_j + 2 \ldots \oplus D_j + k \oplus d_j \oplus d_j + 1 \oplus d_j + 2 \ldots \oplus d_j + k$).

As shown in Fig. 3(c), $D_0, D_1 \in \Pi(R_i)$, the new parity block can be computed by P_0, d_0, d_1, D_0 and D_1 (i.e. $P'_0 = P_0 \oplus d_0 \oplus d_1 \oplus D_0 \oplus D_1$). Meanwhile, the new parity block also can be computed by d_2, D_0 and D_1 (i.e. $P'_0 = d_2 \oplus D_0 \oplus D_1$). To minimize the number of pre-read operations, RAIS5AS chooses the latter.

As shown in Fig. 3(d), $D_0, D_1 \in \Pi(R_i)$, the new parity block can be computed by P_0, d_0, d_1, D_0 and D_1 (i.e. $P'_0 = P_0 \oplus d_0 \oplus d_1 \oplus D_0 \oplus D_1$). Meanwhile, the new parity block also can be computed by d_2, d_3, d_4, d_5, D_0 and D_1 (i.e. $P'_0 = d_2 \oplus d_3 \oplus d_4 \oplus d_5 \oplus D_0 \oplus D_1$). To minimize the number of pre-read operations, RAIS5AS chooses the former.

Case 3: Some data blocks to be updated are in the physical stripe (i.e. D_j, $D_j + 1, \ldots, D_j + m \in \Pi(R_i) \,\&\&\, D_j + m + 1, D_j + m + 2, \ldots, D_j + k \notin \Pi(R_i)$, *Note: $m < k$*).

In this case, there are m+1 data blocks to be updated in the physical stripe, and other k-m data blocks to be updated are not in the physical stripe. If $m+1 \geq C(R_i)/2$, RAIS5AS pre-reads the data blocks **not** to be updated in the physical stripe (i.e. $d_h, d_h + 1, \ldots, d_h + l$). The new parity block can be computed by the value of the data blocks **not** to be updated in the physical stripe and the new value of the data blocks to be updated (i.e. $P'_i = D_j \oplus D_j + 1 \oplus D_j + 2 \dots \oplus D_j + k \oplus d_h \oplus d_h + 1 \dots \oplus d_h + l$). Otherwise, RAIS5AS pre-reads the parity block and the data blocks to be updated in the physical stripe(i.e. d_j, $d_j + 1$, $d_j + 2$, ..., $d_j + m$). The new parity block can be computed by the old value of the parity block, the old value of the data blocks to be updated in the physical stripe and the new value of the data blocks to be updated (i.e. $P'_i = P_i \oplus D_j \oplus D_j + 1 \oplus D_j + 2 \dots \oplus D_j + k \oplus d_j \oplus d_j + 1 \oplus d_j + 2 \dots \oplus d_j + m$).

As shown in Fig. 3(e), $D_0 \in \Pi(R_i) \,\&\&\, D_1 \notin \Pi(R_i)$, the new parity block can be computed by P_0, d_0, D_0 and D_1 (i.e. $P'_0 = P_0 \oplus d_0 \oplus D_0 \oplus D_1$). Meanwhile, the new parity block also can be computed by d_2, D_0 and D_1 (i.e. $P'_0 = d_2 \oplus D_0 \oplus D_1$). To minimize the number of pre-read operations, RAIS5AS chooses the latter.

As shown in Fig. 3(f), $D_0 \in \Pi(R_i) \,\&\&\, D_1 \notin \Pi(R_i)$, the new parity block can be computed by P_0, d_0, D_0 and D_1 (i.e. $P'_0 = P_0 \oplus d_0 \oplus D_0 \oplus D_1$). Meanwhile, the new parity block also can be computed by d_2, d_3, d_4, D_0 and D_1 (i.e. $P'_0 = d_2 \oplus d_3 \oplus d_4 \oplus D_0 \oplus D_1$). To minimize the number of pre-read operations, RAIS5AS chooses the former.

3.3 Data Recovery Algorithm

To ensure data consistency, the traditional RAID5 needs to do parity synchronization when it is created. For each stripe, RAID5 controller reads the data blocks, computes the parity block, and writes it to the corresponding location. However, RAIS5AS modifies the synchronization process. When RAIS5 is created or initialized, RAIS5AS only needs to set all bits in SBT to zero. RAIS5AS changes the value of the bits in SBT when handling write requests. When a block is written, the corresponding B_{ij} is set to "1".

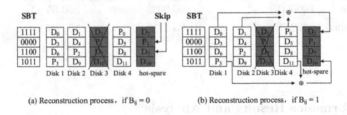

(a) Reconstruction process, if $B_{ij} = 0$ (b) Reconstruction process, if $B_{ij} = 1$

Fig. 4. Data recovery process in the RAIS5AS.

The data recovery algorithm in the RAIS5AS depends on the corresponding B_{ij} of the failed block. Figure 4 shows the reconstruction process in the RAIS5AS. When recovering a failed block, RAIS5AS first checks its corresponding B_{ij}. If the failed block is unused (i.e. $B_{ij} = 0$), RAIS5AS skips the stripe, as shown in Fig. 4(a). Otherwise (i.e. $B_{ij} = 1$), all surviving blocks in the physical stripe are read to recover the failed block. As shown in Fig. 4(b), D_2 and D_{10}

are needed to be rebuilt. For D_2, the corresponding physical stripe is (D_0, D_1, D_2, P_0), thus, RAIS5AS reads D_0, D_1 and P_0 to recover D_2 (i.e. $D_2 = D_0 \oplus D_1 \oplus P_0$). For D_{10}, the corresponding physical stripe is (P_3, D_{10}, D_{11}), thus, RAIS5AS reads P_3 and D_{11} to recover D_{10} (i.e. $D_{10} = P_3 \oplus D_{11}$).

4 Performance Evaluations

4.1 Experimental Setup

The performance evaluations are conducted on a platform of server-class hardware with an Intel Xeon 3.0 GHz processor and 8 GB DDR memory. A SATA disk is used to house the operating system (Linux kernel 2.6.32) and other software (MD, mdadm, and RAIDmeter [7]). We use eight workload traces to evaluate the performance. Fin1 and fin2 were collected from online transaction processing applications [11]. Mds0, prn0, proj0, and usr0 were collected from Microsoft Cambridge Research [12]. IOzone and postmark are the standard file system benchmarks run on a workstation class PC with a 750 GB SATA disk [13]. The traces characteristics are shown in Table 1.

Table 1. Trace information

Trace file	Total request number	Write request ratio	Average size (KB)
fin1	249496	67.18%	7.24
fin2	450453	17.61%	2.22
mds0	91021	90.49%	7.27
prn0	80147	78.10%	9.09
proj0	164971	64.41%	16.37
usr0	168422	60.41%	18.66
iozone	100000	100.00%	280.05
postmark	62257	83.17%	152.07

4.2 Performance Results and Analysis

We first conducted an experiment on RAIS5AS, RAIS5, and JOR in the normal mode driven by the 8 traces as shown in Table 1. In our experiments, the RAIS5AS, RAIS5 and JOR storage systems are all configured with 4 SSDs. Each SSD capacity is set to be 10 GB. The stripe chunk sizes are all 512 KB. We use the RAIDmeter to replay each of the traces on the three systems for an hour, respectively. The performance results are shown in Fig. 5 where Record_RAIS5 represents the RAIS5 system that uses the same method as RAIS5AS to record the used status of the blocks. In other words, Record_RAIS5 estimates the extra computation costs. Recording the stripes used status in the JOR system leads to around 1.38% performance loss in terms of average user response time. Recording the blocks used status in the RAIS5AS system leads to around 2.10% performance loss in terms of average user response time. In terms of the average response time, RAIS5AS on average outperforms RAIS5 and JOR by 7.92% and 9.16%, respectively. The reason is that RAIS5AS uses a new parity block generation algorithm to reduce the pre-read blocks number when handling write requests. Writing a block that is not in the physical stripe, RAIS5AS does not need to read the old value of this block. Thus, RAIS5AS can alleviate the small write problem in the basic RAIS5 storage system.

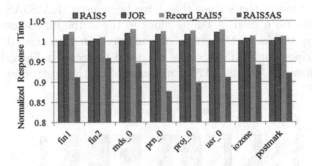

Fig. 5. Response time comparison among the RAIS5, JOR, Record_RAIS5 and RAIS5AS schemes.

Table 2. Reconstruction performance comparison among the different schemes

Trace file	Reconstruction time (s)				Reconstructed stripes number		
	RAIS5	JOR	RAIS5AS	RAIS5AS improved by	RAIS5	JOR	RAIS5AS
fin1	231.45	8.51	7.90	96.6%\7.2%	2620544	36746	36567
fin2	238.73	5.41	5.19	97.8%\4.2%	2620544	16461	11961
mds0	235.00	4.57	3.82	98.4%\16.3%	2620544	39269	23759
prn0	238.14	15.90	11.97	95.0%\24.7%	2620544	223578	139242
proj0	235.75	4.93	4.04	98.3%\18.1%	2620544	45602	26238
usr0	236.33	5.52	4.20	98.2%\23.9%	2620544	54924	30381
iozone	236.37	11.71	10.81	95.4%\7.7%	2620544	90591	90230
postmark	232.68	39.42	33.70	85.5%\14.5%	2620544	425805	358873

To evaluate the off-line reconstruction performance, we then conducted experiments on the recovery process of the RAIS5, JOR, and RAIS5AS systems. Since the reconstruction time of the JOR and RAIS5AS are affected by the used blocks, we first run the eight traces on the three systems for an hour as initialization before evaluating reconstruction time. Then we make an SSD fail to measure the reconstruction time. Table 2 shows the measured data recovery time for the three systems. From Table 2, we can see that the basic RAIS5 reconstruction time of different traces is nearly the same. The reason is that the original off-line data recovery process has nothing to do with the I/O requests that have been serviced in normal mode. In terms of the reconstruction time, RAIS5AS on average outperforms RAIS5 by 95.65%, and JOR on average outperforms RAIS5 by 94.89%. The reconstruction time of JOR and RAIS5AS is two orders of magnitude less than that of RAIS5. This is because RAIS5 needs to recover all stripes in the system, whereas JOR and RAIS5AS recover partial stripes. JOR recovers the stripes that have been used. RAIS5AS recovers the blocks that have been used. A failure block in the stripe maybe not used, while other surviving blocks in the stripe maybe used. In this case, JOR needs to recover the stripe, but RAIS5AS does not need to recover. Thus, RAIS5AS on average outperforms JOR by 14.57% in terms of the reconstruction time.

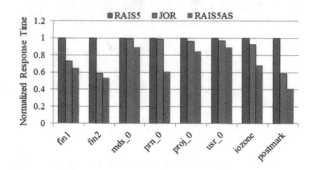

Fig. 6. Response time comparison in degraded mode.

As shown in Table 2, besides the evaluation on reconstruction time, we also counted the number of reconstructed stripes during the reconstruction. In RAIS5, the total reconstructed stripes number of different traces are all 2620544. Compared with RAIS5 and JOR, RAIS5AS on average decreases the number of reconstructed by 96.58% and 26.04%, respectively.

To see RAIS5AS on-line data recovery efficiency, we next conducted on-line reconstruction experiments on the RAIS5, JOR and RAIS5AS systems. Similarly, we first run the eight traces on the three systems for an hour as initialization. And then, when making an SSD of the RAIS5 fail, we run the eight traces for an hour once again. Figure 6 shows the average user response time comparison driven by the traces in degraded mode and Table 3 shows the corresponding on-line reconstruction time for three systems. The experimental results prove that RAIS5AS performs the best in terms of the average user response time and data recovery time. RAIS5AS on average outperforms RAIS5 and JOR by 31.03% and 18.04%, respectively, in terms of the average user response time. RAIS5AS

Table 3. Reconstruction time

Trace file	On-line reconstruction time (s)			
	RAIS5	JOR	RAIS5AS	RAIS5AS improved by
fin1	345.580	13.300	9.705	97.19%\27.03%
fin2	533.218	17.875	14.180	97.34%\20.67%
mds0	236.806	5.678	4.930	97.92%\13.17%
prn0	260.353	25.465	16.749	93.57%\34.23%
proj0	236.286	5.320	4.598	98.05%\13.57%
usr0	248.674	5.832	4.301	98.27%\26.25%
iozone	293.216	13.695	12.662	95.68%\7.54%
postmark	563.192	180.828	168.163	70.14%\7.00%

on average outperforms RAIS5 and JOR by 93.52% and 18.68%, respectively, in terms of the reconstruction time. When RAIS5 recovers data in degraded mode, the user I/Os and reconstruction I/Os compete for disk resources. Thus, the average user response time in degraded mode is higher than that in normal mode, and the on-line reconstruction time is higher than the off-line reconstruction time. RAIS5AS only recovers the used blocks so that the contentions between the user I/O and reconstruction I/O can be significantly alleviated. Therefore, compared with RAIS5, RAIS5AS reduces the average user response time and reconstruction time simultaneously.

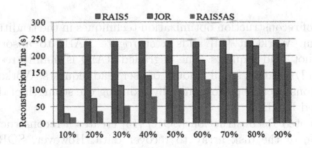

Fig. 7. Comparison of the reconstruction time for the RAIS5, JOR, and RAIS5AS with different percentage of used storage space.

In addition, to examine the impact of RAIS5AS to the percentage of used storage space, we also conducted experiments on the three systems with different percentage of used storage space. Figure 7 shows the comparison of the reconstruction time for the RAIS5, JOR, and RAIS5AS with different percentage of used storage space. Figure 8 shows the comparison of the corresponding total number of the reconstructed stripes in the RAIS5, JOR, and RAIS5AS systems. As shown in Fig. 7, we can see that the reconstruction time for JOR and

RAIS5AS increases with the increasing percentage of used storage space. Furthermore, RAIS5AS performs the best in terms of reconstruction time. When the SSDs have high space utilization (90% used space), JOR only outperforms the RAIS5 by 4.09%. However, RAIS5AS outperforms the RAIS5 and JOR by 26.31% and 23.17%, respectively. The reason is that the number of the reconstructed stripes in the RAIS5AS system is the least for each percentage of used storage space, as shown in Fig. 8. Compared with RAIS5 and JOR, RAIS5AS reduces the reconstruction time and the number of reconstructed stripes.

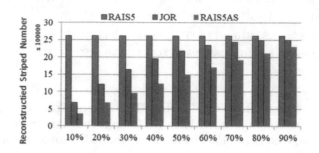

Fig. 8. Comparison of the number of reconstructed stripes in the RAIS5, JOR, and RAIS5AS with different percentage of used storage space.

5   Related Work

There is a lot of reconstruction optimization techniques in the traditional RAID5 storage system. WorkOut [14] adds a surrogate RAID to absorb the write requests and hot read requests. The degraded RAID is mainly responsible for reconstruction I/Os and a small amount of user read requests. Workout improves the on-line reconstruction performance by reducing the strength of the user I/Os in the degraded RAID.

Stripe-Oriented Reconstruction (SOR) [15] creates a reconstruction process for each stripe of the disk array to recover data. However, SOR can't take advantage of all the free disks bandwidth. Holland et al. [16] proposed Disk-Oriented Reconstruction (DOR). DOR creates a reconstruction process for each disk instead of each stripe. Lee et al. [17] proposed a Pipelined Reconstruction (PR) algorithm, which makes use of the sequential characteristic of track access to pipeline the reconstruction read and write processes, thus solving the reliability problem of continuous-media servers. To reduce the movement of the disk head, popularity-based multi-threaded reconstruction optimization (PRO) [7] allows the reconstruction process rebuild the frequently accessed areas prior to infrequently accessed areas.

Since SSDs have a lot of advantages over HDDs, many studies use SSDs to construct RAID-based storage systems. HPDA [18] and HRAID6ML [19], where data disks are SSDs and the parity disks are HDDs, make full use of the advantages of HDDs and SSDs to improve the performance of the storage systems and extend the SSDs lifetime. In addition, they all use the free space of HDDs to absorb the small random write requests with the log technology. Wu et al. [6] proposed a log disk mirroring (LDM) scheme, which consists of a HDD-based RAID1 and a SSD-based RAIS5, to improve the performance and reliability of RAIS5. LDM uses the RAID1 as a write buffer to absorb the small write requests. In degraded mode, the RAID1 can be used to improve the reconstruction performance of the RAIS5 by acting as a surrogate RAID.

6   Conclusion

Recently, SSD is widely used in RAID-based storage systems. However, previous studies concentrate more on improving write performance, and show less attention on the reconstruction performance of RAIS storage systems. In the paper, we proposed RAIS5AS, a novel RAIS5 storage architecture to improve write performance and reconstruction performance simultaneously. RAIS5AS distinguishes between logical stripe and physical stripe. Logical stripe is a traditional RAID stripe. RAIS5AS uses SBT to record whether the blocks in a logical stripe have been written or not. Physical stripe consists of the blocks (in a logical stripe) which have been written data. RAIS5AS uses a new parity block generation algorithm, in which parity block equals to the XOR result of the data blocks in the corresponding physical stripe. The new algorithm reduces the pre-read operations to improve the write performance. Since SBT records the status of each block in the system, RAIS5AS only recovers the used failed blocks and skips the unused failed blocks when there is an SSD failure. RAIS5AS improves the reconstruction performance by reducing the number of the stripes that needs to be reconstructed. RAIS5AS on average improves the write performance and the reconstruction performance of the basic RAIS5 by up to 7.92% and 95.65% respectively, and those of JOR by 9.16% and 14.57% respectively. Even when 90% space is used, RAIS5AS outperforms the RAIS5 and JOR by 26.31% and 23.17%, respectively.

Acknowledgements. This work was supported by the National High Technology Research and Development Program (863 Program) No. 2015AA016701, No. 2015AA015301; NSFC No. 61772222, No. U1705261, No. 61472153, No. 61402189, No. 61303046; State Key Laboratory of Computer Architecture, No. CARCH201505; Wuhan Applied Basic Research Project (No. 2015010101010004).

References

1. Mei, L., Feng, D., Zeng, L., Chen, J., Liu, J.: A write-through cache method to improve small write performance of SSD-based RAID. In: Proceedings of the 12th International Conference on Networking, Architecture, and Storage, Shenzhen, China, pp. 1–6, August 2017

2. Kim, T., Lee, S., Park, J., Kim, J.: Efficient lifetime management of SSD-based RAIDs using dedup-assisted partial stripe writes. In: Proceedings of the 5th Non Volatile Memory Systems and Applications Symposium, Daegu, South Korea, pp. 1–6, August 2016

3. Wan, J., Wu, W., Zhan, L., Yang, Q., Qu, X., Xie, C.: DEFT-cache: a cost effective and highly reliable SSD cache for RAID storage. In: Proceedings of the 2017 IEEE International Parallel and Distributed Processing Symposium, Orlando, FL, pp. 102–111, May 2017

4. Lee, E., Oh, Y., Lee, D.: SSD caching to overcome small write problem of disk-based RAID in enterprise environments. In: Proceedings of the 30th Annual ACM Symposium on Applied Computing Software Verification and Testing Track, Salamanca, Spain, pp. 2047–2053, April 2015

5. Pan, Y., Li, Y., Xu, Y., Shen, B.: DCS: diagonal coding scheme for enhancing the endurance of SSD-based RAID arrays. IEEE Trans. Comput.-Aided Des. Integr. Circ. Syst. **35**(8), 1372–1385 (2016)

6. Wu, S., Mao, B., Chen, X., Jiang, H.: LDM: log disk mirroring with improved performance and reliability for SSD-based disk arrays. ACM Trans. Storage (TOS) **12**(4), 22 (2016)

7. Tian, L., et al.: PRO: a popularity-based multi-threaded reconstruction optimization for RAID-structured storage systems. In: Proceedings of the 2007 USENIX Conference on File and Storage Technologies, San Jose, CA, pp. 277–290, February 2007

8. Sivathanu, M., Prabhakaran, V., Arpaci-Dusseau, A., Arpaci-Dusseau, R.: Improving storage system availability with D-GRAID. ACM Trans. Storage (TOS) **1**(2), 133–170 (2005)

9. Wu, S., Feng, D., Jiang, H., Mao, B., Zeng, L., Chen, J.: JOR: a journal-guided reconstruction optimization for RAID-structured storage systems. In: Proceedings of the 15th IEEE International Conference on Parallel and Distributed Systems, Shenzhen, China, , pp. 609–616, December 2009

10. Jin, C., Feng, D., Jiang, H., Tian, L.: RAID6L: a log-assisted RAID6 storage architecture with improved write performance. In: Proceedings of the IEEE 27th Symposium on Mass Storage Systems and Technologies, Denver, Colorado, pp. 1-6, May 2011

11. UMass Trace Repository: Two I/O traces from OLTP applications running at two large financial institutions (2007). http://traces.cs.umass.edu/index.php/Storage/Storage

12. Microsoft Enterprise Traces (2009). http://iotta.snia.org/traces/list/BlockIO

13. Agrawal, N., Prabhakaran, V., Wobber, T., Davis, J., Manasse, M., Panigrahy, R.: Design tradeoffs for SSD performance. In: Proceedings of the 2008 USENIX Annual Technical Conference, Boston, MA, pp. 57–70, June 2008

14. Wu, S., Jiang, H., Feng, D., Tian, L., Mao, B.: WorkOut: I/O workload outsourcing for boosting RAID reconstruction performance. In: Proceedings of the USENIX Conference on File and Storage Technologies, San Francisco, CA, pp. 239–252, February 2009

15. Holland, M., Gibson, G., Siewiorek, D.: Architectures and algorithms for on-line failure recovery in redundant disk arrays. J. Distrib. Parallel Databases **2**(3), 295–335 (1994)

16. Holland, M., Gibson, G., Siewiorek, D.: Fast, on-line failure recovery in redundant disk arrays. In: Proceedings of the 23 Annual International Symposium on Fault-Tolerant Computing, Toulouse, France, pp. 422–431, June 1993

17. Lee, J., Lui, J.: Automatic recovery from disk failure in continuous-media servers. IEEE Trans. Parallel Distrib. Syst. **13**(5), 499–515 (2002)
18. Mao, B., et al.: a hybrid parity-based disk array for enhanced perfromance and reliability. ACM Trans. Storage **8**(1), 1C20 (2012)
19. Zeng, L., Feng, D., Chen, J., Wei, Q.: HRAID6ML: a hybrid RAID6 storage architecture with mirrored logging. In: Proceedings of the IEEE 28th Symposium on Mass Storage Systems and Technologies, Pacific Grove, CA, pp. 1–6, April 2012

ADAM: An Adaptive Directory Accelerating Mechanism for NVM-Based File Systems

Xin Cui, Linpeng Huang$^{(\boxtimes)}$, and Shengan Zheng

Shanghai Jiao Tong University, Shanghai, China
{cuixindd,lphuang,venero1209}@sjtu.edu.cn

Abstract. Byte-addressable non-volatile memory (NVM) offers fast, fine-grained random access to persistent storage, which revolutionizes the architecture design of file systems. Existing NVM-based file systems seldom optimize the directory-access performance despite that directory operations significantly impact application performance. These file systems still follow the traditional design of multi-level directory namespace which is inadequate for byte-addressable NVM and involves redundant access overhead.

In this paper, we propose an adaptive directory accelerating mechanism (ADAM) for NVM-based file systems. ADAM analyzes different directory states including read/write frequency and size and then builds adaptive full-name directory namespace (AFDN) areas as well as an evolving strategy. Compared with multi-level directory namespace, AFDN areas offer fast read access and low write latency. Besides, the evolving strategy helps AFDN areas maintain a stable performance during system runtime. We implement ADAM on NOn-Volatile memory Accelerated (NOVA) log-structured file system and build an efficient hybrid index for DRAM/NVMM architecture. Experiments show that NOVA with ADAM achieves up to 43% latency reduction and 76% throughput improvement, compared with original NOVA. Moreover, ADAM generally outperforms other state-of-the-art NVM-based file systems in various tests.

Keywords: Non-volatile memory · File system
Adaptive directory mechanism

1 Introduction

Emerging non-volatile memory (NVM) techniques promise to offer both byte-addressability and persistent memory storage, e.g., spin-torque transfer, phase change [13], resistive memories [19], and Intel and Micron's 3D-XPoint [11] technology, which revolutionize the architecture design of file systems. As a result, many file systems are proposed to exploit the performance benefit of NVM, such as NOVA [16], PMFS [6], SCMFS [14] and HMVFS [20]. These NVM-based file

© Springer Nature Switzerland AG 2018
J. Vaidya and J. Li (Eds.): ICA3PP 2018, LNCS 11334, pp. 578–592, 2018.
https://doi.org/10.1007/978-3-030-05051-1_40

systems significantly improve the performance through redesigning structures which are considered to be inefficient or unsuitable for NVM characteristics.

Directory operations have a large impact on application performance [9, 10, 12]. There are two main traditional designs of directory namespace: multi-level directory namespace and full-name directory namespace. Multi-level directory namespace supports fast renames but increases read latency because of recursive scans [18]. This kind of mechanism tightly couples directory metadata and inode since the directory index and update involve both directory names and inode numbers, thus it brings a large overhead in consistency guarantee. On the contrary, full-name directory namespace offers fast direct access but brings heavy write overhead in renames, because changes of the path name may cause a large amount of small random writes which are amplified [8] in traditional disk-based file systems.

It is a trade-off to choose one of the above mechanisms for a disk-based file system, however, both of which are not suitable for NVM-based file systems. For multi-level directory namespace, it is unnecessary to sacrifice directory read performance because the write amplification problem no longer exists in byte-addressable NVM. Besides, the tight coupling of directory metadata and inodes causes redundant access to inodes and large NVM writes which have a negative impact on access performance. For these reasons, full-name directory namespace is more appropriate for NVM. However, problems arise when implementing full-name directory namespace on NVM-based file systems since it naturally brings a large number of random writes when renaming directories. Current NVM-based file systems seldom consider these issues and implement their directory mechanisms following the improper traditional design of multi-level directory namespace.

In this paper, we propose ADAM, an adaptive directory accelerating mechanism, which provides fast read access as well as low write overhead. ADAM introduces a new design of directory layout called adaptive full-name directory namespace (AFDN). Each AFDN area defines a root directory with a full path name and sub-directories with adaptive path names relative to the root directory name. The adaptive path names not only avoid the rename overhead when the root directory name changes, but also improve both read and write performance of directories by decoupling directory metadata and inodes.

Moreover, ADAM classifies directory states based on read frequency, write frequency and directory size. We introduce an evolving strategy which defines three evolvements for AFDN areas: *splitting, merging* and *inheriting*. The evolving strategy ensures that each AFDN area is selected reasonably and keeps the division of AFDN areas always be adaptive to the directory changing states during system runtime.

We implement ADAM on NOVA, a hybrid DRAM/NVMM file system, and build an efficient hybrid index includes hash tables and radix trees.

We conclude our contributions as follows:

- We analyze the previous, unsuitable directory designs in NVM-based file systems and propose ADAM, an adaptive directory accelerating mechanism, which offers fast directory access as well as low write overhead.
- We introduce AFDN, adaptive full-name directory namespace which labels different directory states in the state-map and reduces directory access overhead by decoupling directories/files and inodes.
- We propose an evolving strategy to keep the most beneficial namespace division and a stable performance of AFDN areas during system runtime by involving three evolvements for AFDN areas.
- We implement an efficient index including radix trees in DRAM and multi-level hash tables in NVM. The hybrid index ensures the best utilization of both larger, persistent NVM and faster, volatile DRAM.
- We implement ADAM on NOVA [16] and evaluate the performance on several benchmarks. The results show that NOVA with ADAM achieves up to 43% latency reduction and 76% throughput improvement compared with original NOVA and generally outperforms other state-of-the-art NVM-based file systems.

The rest of this paper is organized as follows. We introduce the ADAM design in Sect. 3 and implementation details in Sect. 4. We discuss the evaluation results in Sect. 5. Finally, we provide related works in Sect. 6 and conclude our paper in Sect. 7.

2   Background and Motivation

2.1   Non-volatile Memory

Table 1 summarizes the characteristics of different memory technologies. NVM provides slightly shorted read latency to DRAM, while its write latency is apparently longer than DRAM. Similar to NAND Flash, the write endurance of NVM is limited especially for PCM. But unlike flash that is block-addressable, NVM is byte-addressable. Besides, NVM has high performance of random access like DRAM, which is better than traditional Flash.

Table 1. Comparison of different memory characteristics [7,17]

Category	Read latency	Write latency	Write endurance	Byte- addressable
DRAM	60 ns	60 ns	10^{16}	Yes
PCM	50–70 ns	150–1000 ns	10^{9}	Yes
ReRAM	25 ns	500 ns	10^{12}	Yes
NAND Flash	35µs	350µs	10^{5}	No

In hybrid DRAM/NVMM architecture, the drawback of NVM is the long write latency while the advantage of NVM is byte-addressability [1]. Thus, our work aims to accelerate the directory access by designing a new directory mechanism, which suits NVM byte-addressability and reduces the number of writes.

2.2 High Directory Access Overhead

The directory mechanism significantly impacts file system performance since directory operations are commonly involved in many applications such as *tar*, *git-clone*, and *git-diff*. However, there are three problems in current NVM-based file systems directory mecahnisms: (i) Current NVM-based file systems mainly follow the traditional directory design, which is suitable for the block-addressable disk but not byte-addressable NVM. Though NVM solves the write-amplification problem, known as the bottleneck of full-name directory namespace, the write overhead remains heavy when renaming the full path names, and slows down directory operations. (ii) The directory name is not unique and can not be considered as an independent index in current multilevel directory namespace. Therefore, directory metadata and inodes are tightly coupled, which increases the write overhead to keep consistency for inode and directory metadata. (iii) The states of directories, e.g., read/write-frequency and directory size, always change in system lifetime and have a different impact on system performance while it is not well utilized in current file systems.

To overcome the above problems, it is necessary for us to design an NVM-friendly directory mechanism which accelerates directory access. The new directory design needs to weaken the coupling between directories and inodes so not only do we reduce the write overhead of consistency guarantee but also we reduce the access latency to directories and files. Besides, it is beneficial to utilize different directory states and design an adaptive mechanism to make the system maintain the best performance during runtime.

3 Design

3.1 ADAM Layout

Figure 1 shows the design of ADAM layout which contains four parts: AFDN areas, Multi-level hashtables, AMT areas and DRAM cache trees.

AFDN Areas. ADAM initializes each AFDN area in a 2 MB block array. Each directory and file entry is initially aligned on a 128-Byte boundary. ADAM assigns new directory/file entries to the AFDN area in a round-robin order, so that directories/files are evenly distributed among AFDN areas.

Each AFDN area has a root directory with a full path name and plenty of sub-directories which stores an adaptive path name relative to the root directory name. Therefore, AFDN decouples directory metadata and inodes by using this kind of unique path names. Moreover, renaming a directory that is the root of an AFDN area causes no write overhead to the sub-directories. Every AFDN area has an area_ID which is the hash value of the root name. As shown in Fig. 2, an AFDN area contains two parts: directory/file entries and a state-map.

State-Map. A state-map is a two-bit bitmap, in which each slot labels the state of an entry in the AFDN area. As shown in Fig. 2, the state-map is in the head of an AFDN area. A 2-bit slot in a state-map can represent four different states:

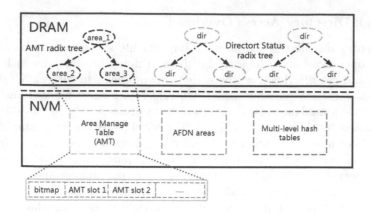

Fig. 1. ADAM layout

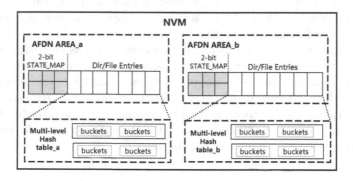

Fig. 2. AFDN areas and hash tables

00 represents an invalid entry in AFDN area, *01* represents a valid file or a *cold* directory, *10* and *11* represent *warm* directories and *hot* directories respectively. Hot labels represent higher access overhead. ADAM gains the best performance when *hot* directories are selected as root directories in order to reduce rename overhead and read latency. The computation and design details of the state labels are introduced in Sect. 3.3.

Multi-level Hash Tables. We build multi-level hash tables for each AFDN area to support fast directory/file locating as shown in Fig. 2. A hash entry contains a hash value of an adaptive path name and the position of an AFDN entry as a hash pair. To reduce the hash table size, each hash entry contains a valid bit, thus we can reuse invalid hash entries for new files and directories.

Area Manage Table (AMT). The AMT records the addresses of both AFDN areas and corresponding hash tables, and it is allocated and initialized as a 4 KB block as shown in Fig. 1. An AMT has two parts: a bitmap and 54-Byte slots. The bitmap manages the allocations and releases of the slots and each slot is cached in DRAM in order to reduce index latency.

DRAM Cache Trees. ADAM keeps two kinds of radix tree in DRAM: an AMT radix tree and status radix trees. The status radix tree is used to calculate the directory states and it records the read frequency, write frequency and the directory size for each accessed directory.c The leaves of the AMT radix tree store the same information as NVM AMT slots. The AMT radix tree is an important part of the hybrid index which is introduced in Sect. 3.2.

3.2 Hybrid Index

Since the index structure has a great influence on hybrid DRAM/NVMM storage systems [3], we pay close attention to the directory searching and design an efficient hybrid index.

The hybrid index contains three parts: AFDN hash tables, AMT and DRAM radix trees. The multi-level hash tables provide a good solution to hash conflicts and offer a fast access at the same time. We use a radix tree because there is a mature, well-tested, widely-used implementation in the Linux kernel. Throughout DRAM radix tree searching, we can easily and quickly find the right AFDN area and corresponding hash tables. According to Table 1, DRAM owns the fastest access speed which is suitable to store the most frequently accessed index structures. It is easy to see that the AMT has a high-frequency access with small space requirement for DRAM space.

Applications can quickly locate the directory and file with our hybrid index through the following step: (i) calculate the AFDN area_ID with the path name; (ii) searching the right leaf in the AMT radix tree; (iii) find the address of AFDN area and the corresponding hash table; (iv) locate the directory by the hash key-value pair.

Table 2. Directory states and state-map labels

States			Label	Bit-value
Size	Write	Read		
small	frequent	frequent	warm	10
		rare		
	rare	frequent	cold	01
		rare		
large	frequent	frequent	hot	11
		rare		
	rare	frequent		
		rare	warm	10
invalid			invalid	00

3.3   States of Directories

We consider read frequency, write frequency and size as three important states to label different directories. The state of a directory changes among different applications and is categorized into 5 groups: {*small size, large size, frequently read, rarely read, frequently write, rarely write*}. The write overhead is caused mainly by directory renames and creates. And we define 3 labels to classify different directories, they are {*hot, warm, cold*}. Different labels represent different access overhead, which means a *hot* directory brings the largest access overhead. Table 2 lists the mapping from directory states to labels.

Three Important States: Read frequency is an important state because selecting a large, *frequently read* directory to be a root directory of a new AFDN area will greatly reduce the access latency to this new root and its sub-directories. Root directories or children of root directories only need one calculation to find which AFDN area the target file belongs to, while others need more recursive calculations for the correct AFDN area. The worst case involves the same number of calculations as the number of recursive scans in traditional multi-level directory namespace.

Since write overhead affects most to the performance of NVM, we consider write frequency as the prime factor in calculating directory labels.

Size is also an important factor because larger directories are more likely to generate a large amount of write overhead.

Calculation: To calculate the read frequency, ADAM first counts access times for each accessed directory and records the value in DRAM status tree. And then ADAM calculates the average read time of the AFDN area. Third, ADAM marks *frequently read* if the directory access time is more than the average value or marks *rarely read* if less than the average value.

Since rename brings the largest write overhead, ADAM marks a directory *frequently write* once it is renamed. A *rarely write* directory is the one which is never renamed during the runtime.

In size calculation, ADAM introduces $Size\_Max$ and $Size\_Min$ to determine the size state of a directory. Each directory that is not the root of its AFDN area has the size at most $Size\_Max$. Each area has size at least $Size\_Min$. In our implementation, $Size\_Max = Size\_Min = 512\,\mathrm{KB}$ [18]. ADAM marks a directory *large* when its size is larger than $Size\_Max$, and *small* when it is smaller than $Size\_Min$.

According to the above calculating rules and the mapping ralation shown in Table 2, we update the values stored in NVM state-map every 5 s before executing our evolving strategy which is introduced in Sect. 3.4.

3.4   Evolving Strategy

For purpose of adapting to changing states during system runtime, we define three evolvements among AFDN areas: *splitting*, *merging* and *inheriting*, shown

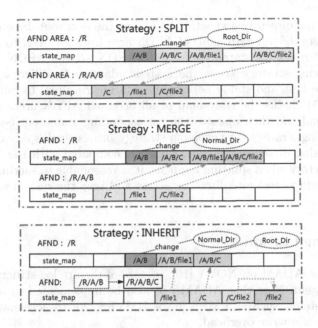

Fig. 3. Adaptive evolving strategy

in Fig. 3. ADAM executes these evolvements on the base of labels recorded in the state-map.

Splitting is the way to create new AFDN areas as well as to select corresponding root directories. When splitting happens, ADAM copies all the sub-files and sub-directories to the new allocated AFDN area and then changes their adaptive names. The root directory still stays in the original AFDN area. ADAM executes splitting when the system periodically checks labels in a state-map and finds a *hot* directory which brings a large access overhead.

Merging happens when an old AFDN area is small and seldom accessed. This kind of AFDN area wastes nearly a 2MB block array because the invalid entries take up the most space and the rest sub-directories and sub-files are seldom visited or renamed. Once we find a root directory satisfies the conditions we will merge the directories and files back to their parent AFDN area and then free this area to make it reusable.

Inheriting defines an AFDN evolvement that a strong sub-directory replaces its parent root directory. The strong sub-directory represents a kind of the directory which owns large size and contributes to the vast majority access to the AFDN area.

For an inheriting evolvement, the operations follow the steps shown in Fig. 3. First, ADAM detects the directory /C, which is a strong sub-directory in AFDN /R/A/B and meets the inheriting conditions. Second, ADAM merges /C and its brother-directories/files back to the parent AFDN area /R and sets their new adaptive path names. Third, ADAM changes the type of the old root directory

/A/B to normal directory and sets /A/B/C as the new root directory. Fourth, ADAM changes the full path name of AFDN area from /R/A/B to /R/A/B/C. Fifth, ADAM resets the state-map for both AFDN /R and AFDN /R/A/B/C.

The evolving strategy keeps the system adaptive to different states and maintains the best and stable performance during runtime. In our implementation, ADAM checks the state-map of all accessed AFDN areas every 5 s at the background and then updates the corresponding state-map before executing the evolving strategy. The evolving strategy brings small space overhead for copying splitting directories entries. However, compared with the total size of files and directory when splitting happens, it is reasonable to sacrifice the small space overhead to accelerate directory access and keep the system stable during runtime.

4   Implementation

We implement ADAM on NOVA [16], a state-of-the-art log-structured NVM-based file system. Note that ADAM can also be implemented in other NVM-based file systems, such as PMFS [6] or HMVFS [20] to accelerate directory access and reduce write overhead.

Optimized Index. Considering that DRAM and NVM show different characteristics, the index in hybrid DRAM/NVMM file system should utilize the strength of both faster DRAM and larger NVM. It is not yet well-balanced in NOVA as it caches all directories and files in DRAM [16], which take too much space of DRAM. Inspired by HiKV [15], we implement an optimized hybrid directory index with large hash tables in NVM and frequently accessed radix trees in DRAM which only caches the index of AFDN areas to save DRAM space overhead. Moreover, compared with the linear linked list for directory log-entries in NOVA, hash tables can greatly accelerate name searching for directories and files.

Efficient Logging. NOVA involves large overhead for keeping the consistency between DRAM radix trees and NVM structures since it copies all the directories and files into DRAM. The consistency overhead includes checking the large radix tree and journalling for logs. ADAM reduces the scale needed to write logs. In our mechanism, we atomically update 2-bit slots of the NVM state-map by writing to a log buffer first. The log buffer size is fixed to the same size of a state-map, which is much smaller than keeping a large number of log entries for each cached directory and file in NOVA. Under this consideration, ADAM greatly reduced the consistency overhead compared with NOVA. Besides, we enforce write ordering by using instructions of *mfence* and *clflush* in ADAM which are widely implemented in NVM-based storage systems [5,16] to ensure consistency.

Lightweight Update. Since multi-level directory namespace tightly couples directories and inodes, the file systems which follows this traditional mechanism brings heavy write overhead in frequent directory/inode logging and updating. However, directories in ADAM with adaptive path names are able to be found and updated independently, which avoids the redundant updates to and caused by inode updates. Therefore, ADAM greatly reduces the frequency of updating and minimized the directory update overhead.

5   Evaluation

5.1   Experimental Setup

We evaluate the performance of ADAM with NOVA against PMFS, original NOVA, and EXT4-DAX. We conduct experiments on a commodity server with 64 Intel Xeon 2 GHz processors and 128G DRAM, running Linux 4.3.0 kernel, and we change the kernel to 3.11.0 for PMFS. For EXT4-DAX, we use ramdisk carved from DRAM and configure 64 GB as ramdisk to simulate NVM. For PMFS and NOVA, we reserve 64 GB of memory using the grub option memmap. User processes and buffer cache use the rest of the free DRAM space. Since NVM has similar read performance but apparently slower write performance compared with DRAM, we introduce extra latencies for NVM write to emulate the longer write latency of NVM. We consider the write latency as 500ns which is the average value of different NVMs shown in Table 1.

Table 3. Micro-benchmark characteristics

Name	Workload
filetest	(i) create (10^4) (ii) unlink (10^4)
dirtest	(i) mkdir (10^4) (ii) rmdir (10^4)

5.2   Write Performance Improvement

Micro-benchmarks. We use two single-threaded micro-benchmarks to evaluate the write performance of ADAM-NOVA, as shown in Table 3. The *filetest* create 10^4 files in one directory and then deletes all of them. The *dirtest* is similar to the *filetest* but the operated objects are directories instead of files. Our micro-benchmarks are write-sensitive since both of the create and delete operations for directories and files involve large write overhead. All the results are averaged over five runs.

Figure 4 shows the experimental results of *filetest* and *dirtest*, with throughput and latency in (a) and (b) respectively. Among the assessed operations *create*, *mkdir*, *unlink*, and *rmdir*, ADAM-NOVA consistently achieves the best performance. In *create* and *mkdir* tests, compared with NOVA, ADAM-NOVA increases throughput by 8.6% and 24% and reduces latency by 7.7% and 19%. In *unlink* and *rmdir* tests, ADAM-NOVA outperforms NOVA by 76% and 37% in throughput and outperforms NOVA by 43% and 29% in latency.

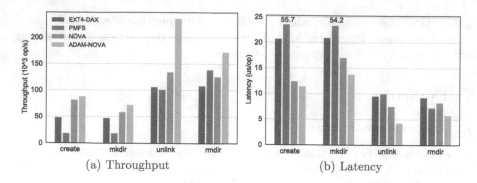

(a) Throughput   (b) Latency

Fig. 4. Throughput and latency of file system operations

We attribute the write performance improvement to the reduction of NVM writes. ADAM offers each directory and each file an adaptive path name which makes them independent of their inodes. Thus, system calls is excuted without redundant access to inodes which increases the total access latency. On the contrary, directories/files are tightly coupled with inodes in original NOVA. In order to quickly update the directory entry, NOVA maintains two pointers in inodes which point to the coupling directory entries. Such pointers produce large write overhead once the old directory is changed or a new directory is appended.

Except for excessive write operations, PMFS has high latency and low throughput because the cost of write overhead grows linearly with the number of directory entries. This is notable for *create* and *mkdir* since one insertion to directory needs to scan all existing dentries to find an available slot. ADAM reduces the latency by 74% to 79% for *create* and *mkdir* compared with PMFS. EXT4-DAX leverages hashed B-tree to speed up directory access, thus it achieves better performance than PMFS for *create* and *mkdir*, and in these cases, ADAM outperforms EXT4-DAX by 34% to 44%.

5.3   Read Performance Improvement

Filebench. We evaluate the read performance of ADAM-NOVA with a real-world application by running a *Listdir* workload in Filebench. We choose the *Listdir* workload of 10000 directories and run it with 1 to 10 threads. We run these experiments multiple times and report the average results.

As shown in Fig. 5, the performance of *ListDirs* increases rapidly when thread $\leq$ 4. ADAM-NOVA performs better than original NOVA and EXT4-DAX. ADAM improves up to 9.7% throughput compared with original NOVA and outperforms EXT4-DAX by up to 41%.

ADAM shows faster read than original NOVA because (i) each directory in indexed by multilevel hash tables; (ii) each directory in NVM is read directly by adaptive path name without recursive scans. NOVA also performs well when thread increases, since it leverages in-DRAM radix trees to manage directories. However, these radix trees consume much more DRAM space which is optimized

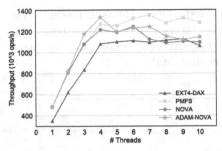

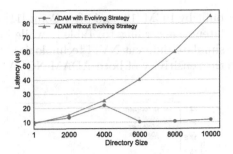

Fig. 5. Throughput of Filebench   **Fig. 6.** Rename latency comparison

in ADAM by a hybrid index. EXT4-DAX performs the worst because the hashed B-tree is not suitable for the in-memory file system which is mainly used to optimize the disk I/O.

5.4   Benifits of Strategy

We evaluate the directory *rename* performance for ADAM with evolving strategy and ADAM without evolving strategy. Then we choose one directory named Dir-A in dirtest microbenchmark and create 1–10000 subfiles. Then we increasing the access time of Dir-A by accessing this directory multiple times to make it a read frequently directory. Note there is no difference to make a *large* directory *hot* by increasing the read frequency or changing the write frequency.

As shown in Fig. 6, the *rename* latency is similar for ADAM with evolving strategy and ADAM without evolving strategy when the number of subfiles is ≤ 4000. It is decreased in ADAM with evolving strategy when the number of subfiles is > 4000. Because in our implementation, the size of a directory is considered *large* when the size of it takes more than 512 KB. ADAM with evolving strategy performs a low and stable rename latency compared with ADAM with evolving strategy. For ADAM without evolving strategy, the rename latency keeps increasing when the number of subfiles increases.

ADAM with evolving strategy performs lower rename latency because the Dir-A is split to be a root directory of a new AFDN when it is *large* and its label becomes *hot*. The rename of root directory involves no overhead to sub-files and sub-directories. For ADAM without evolving strategy, the rename of directory cause a large rename overhead for its sub-files and sub-directories. Therefore the evolving strategy shows great benefits to reduce the rename latency and keeps system stable during runtime.

5.5   Sensitivity to Different NVMs

Although NVM has similar read latency compared with DRAM, different NVM technologies have different write latencies which are all longer than DRAM. NVM built by PCM [13] and 3DX-Point [11] is expected to have 150ns to 1000ns write latency according to Table 1, while the write latency of DRAM is 60ns. We simulate different NVM technologies by inserting different delays [5] to evaluate the sensitivity of both ADAM-NOVA and original NOVA.

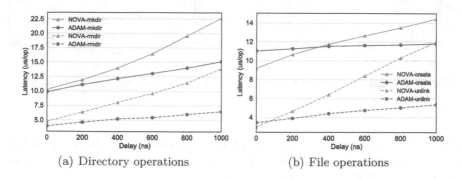

(a) Directory operations   (b) File operations

Fig. 7. Latency with different delays

Figure 7 shows the latency of directory operations and file operations in our micro-benchmarks with different delays. In different cases of *mkdir, rmdir, create, unlink*, original NOVA shows drastically increasing latency, while ADAM-NOVA performs more stable because of the reduction of writes. Increasing the delay from 0 to 1000ns, the latency of original NOVA increases 1.

21% for *mkdir*, 193% for *rmdir*, 57% for *create*, 291% for *unlink* compared with its original values, while the corresponding increases of ADAM-NOVA are 54% for *mkdir*, 65% for *rmdir*, 7% for *create*, 56% for *unlink*.

ADAM performs better on involving fewer NVM writes. Because ADAM provides adaptive path names for each directory and file, which decouples directories/files and inodes. In contrast, the design of multi-level directory namespace in original NOVA tightly couples directories/files and inodes which involves a large number of redundant write for consistency guarantees during system calls. Therefore, ADAM performs better scalability to different NVMs.

To summarize, ADAM achieves a significant improvement for both read and write performance compared with original NOVA, PMFS, and EXT4-DAX. Besides, ADAM successfully reduces the rename overhead by executing the evolving strategy which keeps the systems adaptive to different states during system runtime. Moreover, ADAM is more suitable for NVM characteristics which are decided by different write latencies.

6   Related Work

NOVA is a state-of-the-art log-structured NVM-based file system, which performs well in file/directory access and atomic updates. However, NOVA implements their directory mechanism following the traditional multi-level directory namespace which is not suitable for NVM characteristics and involves long access latency. We implement ADAM in NOVA to optimize the problems and experiments show that we greatly reduce the access latency.

BetrFS 0.2 [18] uses write-optimized dictionaries [2] and proposes zones to optimize file system performance. However, BetrFS 0.2 is designed for disk-based storage and uses write-optimized dictionaries to combine the small random writes into large sequential writes which are not necessary for NVM with byte-addressable random access. Besides, the detection of zones is only based on the size of directories and files, which is not accurate in zone-root selection.

HiKV [15] introduces an efficient hybrid index for DRAM/NVMM KV-store [4] mixture systems. Our mechanism optimizes it in NVM-besed file systems by implementing radix trees in DRAM which suits well in Linux kernel and using multi-level hash tables to avoid hash conflicting.

7   Conclusion

In this paper, we propose ADAM, an adaptive directory accelerating mechanism, which suits byte-addressable NVM and offers fast read performance as well as low write latency for NVM-based file systems. ADAM is adaptive to different states of directories and keeps good, stable performance during system runtime. We also implement an efficient hybrid index to combine the best characteristics of DRAM and NVM. Our experiments show that NOVA with ADAM achieves up to 43% latency reduction and 76% throughput improvement compared with original NOVA and generally performs better than other state-of-the-art NVM-based file systems.

Acknowledgments. We thank anonymous reviewers for their insightful and helpful comments, which improve the paper. This work is supported by the National Key Research and Development Program of China (No. 2018YFB10033002) and the National Natural Science Foundation of China (No. 61472241).

References

1. Condit, J., et al.: Better I/O through byte-addressable, persistent memory. In: Proceedings of the 22nd ACM Symposium on Operating Systems Principles 2009, SOSP 2009, Big Sky, Montana, USA, 11–14 October 2009, pp. 133–146 (2009). https://doi.org/10.1145/1629575.1629589
2. Conway, A., et al.: File systems fated for senescence? Nonsense, says science! In: FAST, pp. 45–58 (2017)
3. Debnath, B., Haghdoost, A., Kadav, A., Khatib, M.G., Ungureanu, C.: Revisiting hash table design for phase change memory. In: Proceedings of the 3rd Workshop on Interactions of NVM/FLASH with Operating Systems and Workloads, INFLOW 2015, Monterey, California, USA, 4 October 2015, pp. 1:1–1:9 (2015). https://doi.org/10.1145/2819001.2819002
4. Decandia, G., et al.: Dynamo: Amazon's highly available key-value store. In: ACM SIGOPS Symposium on Operating Systems Principles, pp. 205–220 (2007)

5. Dong, M., Chen, H.: Soft updates made simple and fast on non-volatile memory. In: 2017 USENIX Annual Technical Conference, USENIX ATC 2017, Santa Clara, CA, USA, 12–14 July 2017, pp. 719–731 (2017). https://www.usenix.org/conference/atc17/technical-sessions/presentation/dong

6. Dulloor, S.R., et al.: System software for persistent memory. In: Proceedings of the Ninth European Conference on Computer Systems, p. 15. ACM (2014)

7. Lee, B.C., Ipek, E., Mutlu, O., Burger, D.: Architecting phase change memory as a scalable dram alternative. In: ACM SIGARCH Computer Architecture News, vol. 37, pp. 1–13 (2009)

8. Lee, E., Kim, J., Bahn, H., Lee, S., Noh, S.H.: Reducing write amplification of flash storage through cooperative data management with nvm. ACM Trans. Storage (TOS) **13**(2), 12 (2017)

9. Lensing, P.H., Cortes, T., Brinkmann, A.: Direct lookup and hash-based metadata placement for local file systems. In: Proceedings of the 6th International Systems and Storage Conference, p. 5. ACM (2013)

10. Lu, Y., Shu, J., Wang, W.: ReconFS: a reconstructable file system on flash storage. In: FAST, vol. 14, pp. 75–88 (2014)

11. Newsroom, I.: Intel and micron produce breakthrough memory technology (2015)

12. Tsai, C.C., Zhan, Y., Reddy, J., Jiao, Y., Zhang, T., Porter, D.E.: How to get more value from your file system directory cache. In: Proceedings of the 25th Symposium on Operating Systems Principles, pp. 441–456. ACM (2015)

13. Wong, H.S.P., et al.: Phase change memory. Proc. IEEE **98**(12), 2201–2227 (2010)

14. Wu, X., Reddy, A.: SCMFS: a file system for storage class memory. In: Proceedings of 2011 International Conference for High Performance Computing, Networking, Storage and Analysis, p. 39. ACM (2011)

15. Xia, F., Jiang, D., Xiong, J., Sun, N.: HiKV: a hybrid index key-value store for DRAM-NVM memory systems. In: 2017 USENIX Annual Technical Conference, USENIX ATC 2017, Santa Clara, CA, USA, 12–14 July 2017, pp. 349–362 (2017). https://www.usenix.org/conference/atc17/technical-sessions/presentation/xia

16. Xu, J., Swanson, S.: NOVA: a log-structured file system for hybrid volatile/non-volatile main memories. In: FAST, pp. 323–338 (2016)

17. Yang, J., Wei, Q., Chen, C., Wang, C., Yong, K.L., He, B.: NV-tree: reducing consistency cost for NVM-based single level systems. FAST, vol. 15, pp. 167–181 (2015)

18. Yuan, J., et al.: Optimizing every operation in a write-optimized file system. In: FAST, pp. 1–14 (2016)

19. Zangeneh, M., Joshi, A.: Design and optimization of nonvolatile multibit 1T1R resistive RAM. IEEE Trans. Very Large Scale Integr. Syst. **22**(8), 1815–1828 (2014)

20. Zheng, S., Huang, L., Liu, H., Wu, L., Zha, J.: HMVFS: a hybrid memory versioning file system. In: 2016 32nd Symposium on Mass Storage Systems and Technologies (MSST), pp. 1–14. IEEE (2016)

A Parallel Method for All-Pair SimRank Similarity Computation

Xuan Huang[1,2], Xingkun Gao[1,2], Jie Tang[1,2(✉)], and Gangshan Wu[1,2]

[1] Department of Computer Science and Technology, Nanjing University,
Nanjing 210023, China
tangjie@nju.edu.cn
[2] State Key Laboratory for Novel Software Technology, Nanjing University,
Nanjing 210023, China

Abstract. How to measure SimRank similarity of all-pair vertices in a graph is a very important research topic which has a wide range of applications in many fields. However, computation of SimRank is costly in both time and space, making traditional computing methods failing to handle graph data of ever-growing size.

This paper proposes a parallel multi-level solution for all-pair Sim-Rank similarity computing on large graphs. We partition the objective graph first with the idea of modularity maximization and get a collapsed graph based on the blocks. Then we compute the similarities between verteices inside a block as well as the similarities between the blocks. In the end, we integrate these two types of similarities and calculate the approximate SimRank simlarities between all vertex pairs. The method is implemented on Spark platform and it makes an improvement on time efficiency while maintaining the effectiveness compared to SimRank.

Keywords: SimRank similarity · Spark · Parallel computing

1 Introduction

As an abstract structure that can describe the relationships between entities, graph has important applications in many fields. Similarity measure, which compares the similarity between different objects, is a classic problem and widely used in recommendation system [10], information retrieval [7], network parsing [3], etc. In order to accurately measure the similarity, scholars have proposed a variety of similarity indicators. Among them, SimRank [14], which is similar to the PageRank [27], becomes more and more popular in recent years. Different from the traditional methods, it considers the topological structure of the graph, that is, if the neighbour vertices of two vertices are very similar, then the two vertices are similar. Since SimRank tries to make full use of the topological information of graph, its time complexity and space complexity are very high. With the development of Internet technology, social network has entered the era of big data. The traditional SimRank similarity calculation method can no longer

© Springer Nature Switzerland AG 2018
J. Vaidya and J. Li (Eds.): ICA3PP 2018, LNCS 11334, pp. 593–607, 2018.
https://doi.org/10.1007/978-3-030-05051-1_41

be applied to the current large-scale graph data. Therefore, it is very necessary to design a new distributed SimRank similarity calculation method to meet the increasing demand for large-scale graph data processing.

Apache Spark [31], which is developed by UC Berkeley AMP Lab, is a fast and general-purpose distributed computing system. It provides high level APIs in Java, Scala and Python, and an optimized engine that supports general execution graphs. Spark is a MapReduce-like cluster computing framework. Compared with Hadoop [6], Spark enables memory distributed data sets, provides interactive query and optimized iterative workloads. Most importantly, Spark introduces the concept of memory computing and resilient distributed dataset (RDD), i.e., data sets can be cached in the memory to shorten the access latency, which is very efficient for some applications. Thus, users can focus on their own computing tasks and quickly deploy their own solutions without having to worry about the underlying complex network communication, resource allocation, and resource scheduling issues of the distributed platform.

In this paper, we propose a distributed parallel algorithm for SimRank similarity computing on large-scale graph data and implement it on Spark. The algorithm uses a divide-and-conquer method to solve the problem. For large-scale graph data, a distributed graph partitioning method is proposed. The graph is firstly partitioned into several sub-graphs based on modularity maximization. The local dense subgraphs are well preserved within blocks and the edge cut weights between blocks are minimized. The algorithm then computes the similarities between vertex pairs inside a block as well as the similarities between sub-graphs. The global similarities for all vertex pairs is computed based on these two similarities. The method is implemented on Spark platform and the experiments show that the effectiveness of our algorithm is comparable to SimRank, while the computing efficiency is increased by several to tens of times (3–16×).

2   Related Work

SimRank Similarity. How to measure the similarity between entities has always been a research hotspot in various fields. Many studies have proposed various similarity metrics in specific application fields. For example Jaccard similarity [13], cosine similarity [2], Dice similarity [8] and so on. Among them, SimRank [14] becomes more and more popular for measuring similarity of vertices in graphs because it takes into more consideration on the topological structure of a graph. Its basic idea is, if the neighbors of two vertices are similar, then the two vertices are similar. SimRank's time and space complexity are high. In order to be able to handle the ever-increasing scale of graph data, many methods which are dedicated to improving SimRank's computational efficiency have been put forward in recent years. Typical acceleration techniques include fast matrix multiplication [30], Monte Carlo sampling methods to reduce the number of random walks [20], linearized algebraic methods to eliminate computational recursion [25], algorithms based on distributed computing [5] and so on. These algorithms are oriented to specific scenarios and increase the computational efficiency more or less. However, these single-node algorithms are incapable of processing super-large-scale graph data. On the other hand, some new similarity metrics aiming at improving the effectiveness of SimRank have also been proposed. Typical examples are coSimRank [28], SimRank++ [1], P-Rank [32] and so on. In addition, some work has studied how to extend SimRank to special graph data, such as how to measure the similarity of vertex pair on an uncertain graph [33].

Graph Partition. Graph partitioning is a classic NP complete problem. The main optimization objectives of the typical graph partitioning problem include: the partitioning results strive for equalization, i.e., the number of vertices in each block is approximately equal, and the number of edges across different blocks is minimized. Figure 1 shows two partitions of the same graph. From the figure we can get a very intuitive distinction on the quality of partition. At present, extensive and in-depth researches have been conducted on the issue of graph partitioning. The traditional partitioning method can be divided into the following categories: spectrum method, heuristic algorithm, intelligent optimization algorithm, multi-level partitioning algorithm and so on. Spectral method [12] was first applied to the bipartition of graph. Its basic idea is to use the second largest eigenvalue and eigenvector of the Laplacian matrix of the graph to realize the partition of graph. Its computational cost is very large. Heuristic method solves the problem based on the local heuristic information in graph. Representative examples are the KL [19] algorithm and the FM [9] algorithm. However, the graph scales they can handle are very limited. Typical intelligent methods are genetic algorithm [4], simulated annealing algorithm [15] etc. They optimize the partitioning problem by performing bionic simulations on some behaviors in the natural world, and their partitioning results have a certain probability of falling into the local optimal solution. The typical representative of the multi-level graph partitioning algorithm is METIS [17]. Through the iterative process of collapse, preliminary partitioning and recovery, it first reduces the scale of the graph to an acceptable extent and then based on some certain optimization idea, the partition of the small-scale graph is given. Finally, the partition is projected back into the partition of the original graph. The multi-level approach can handle larger-scale graph data, and its ideas are referenced by many other methods.

However, in general, compared with the huge data size in the era of big data, the scale of the graph data that these methods can handle is still small. With the continuous expansion of users in the network, some network graphs have billions of vertices and trillions of edges, and ordinary computers cannot handle them due to memory constraints. This poses a huge challenge to common graph computing tasks. In this context, the design and development of efficient distributed graph data partitioning methods are the main directions in the future.

All-Pair SimRank Similarity. If further consideration is given to the problem of calculating the similarities of all vertex pairs in the graph G, either using the method of iterative matrix calculation directly according to the definition of SimRank or considering the problem simply as computing the similarity of $|V|$

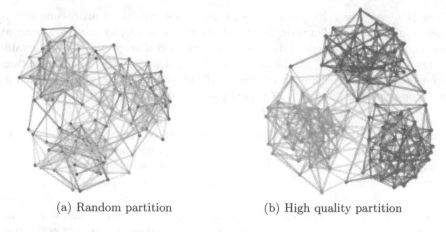

(a) Random partition   (b) High quality partition

Fig. 1. Two partitions of the same graph.

single source vertices, the entire computational cost is undoubtedly unbearable. Jeh and Widom [14] proposed the first SimRank iterative calculation method based on matrix multiplication, which can calculate the similarity of all-pair with complexity of $O(kn^2d^2)$. In [24], the time complexity of the algorithm is reduced to $O(kn^2d)$ at the level of matrix multiplication by techniques such as pruning and local access. Reference [30] uses fast matrix multiplication to speed up the calculation process. Reference [29] further reduces the time complexity of the algorithm to $O(kn^2d')$, where $d' < d$. Reference [21] proposed a non-iterative algorithm based on Kronecker product and matrix singular value decomposition (SVD). The algorithm first calculates some auxiliary matrices in $O(r^4N^2)$ time, where r is the rank of the adjacency matrix of the input graph, and then get the similarity between vertices in $O(r^4N^2)$ time. Reference [11] uses GPU to speed up the calculation of the matrices. [23] proposed a distributed Monte Carlo sampling distributed computing method. [22] proposed a MapReduce-based distributed matrix multiplication method. This algorithm stores one of the matrices in the memory of all compute nodes, reads another row-by-row split matrix from the disk, and multiplies the matrix in memory with each row, thereby realizing the distributed computation of the matrix. [29] proposed a delta-based DeltaSimRank algorithm. The algorithm finds that SimRank can be rewritten as an iterative incremental calculation method. That is, in the iterative process, the similarity between vertex pair is not directly calculated but the increment relative to the previous iteration is calculated. This method makes full use of the fact that the similarity increments between many vertex pairs in the iterative calculation process are zero, and reduces the amount of data transmission in the calculation process, thereby accelerating the computational efficiency.

3 Method

In this paper, we use $G = (V, E)$ to represent a directed graph, in which V is the set of vertices and $E \subseteq V \times V$ is the set of edges. The similarity between two vertices u, v is

$$s(u, v) = \begin{cases} 1 & u = v \\ \dfrac{c}{|I(u)||I(v)|} \displaystyle\sum_{u' \in I(u), v' \in I(v)} s(u', v') & u \neq v \end{cases} \tag{1}$$

here c is the attenuation coefficient used to increase the weight contributed by the neighborhood structure to the final similarity, and $I(u) = \{v : (v, u) \in E\}$ represents the set of vertices connect to u. Reference [14] proves that the above equation always has a unique solution, and with the definition of SimRank, an iterative algorithm based on matrix multiplication is proposed. Let S_k be the similarity matrix S in the k-th iteration and S_0 be the initial matrix. Then when $u = v$, we have $S_{uv}^0 = 1$, otherwise $S_{uv}^0 = 0$. We can obtain S^{k+1} by

$$S_{uv}^{k+1} = \begin{cases} 1 & u = v \\ \dfrac{c}{|I(u)||I(v)|} \displaystyle\sum_{u' \in I(u), v' \in I(v)} S_{u'v'}^{k+1} & u \neq v \end{cases} \tag{2}$$

Reference [14] had proved that $\lim_{k \to \infty} S_{uv}^k = s(u, v)$. It can be seen that the time complexity of the calculation is $O(n^2)$ and the space complexity is $O(kn^2 d^2)$. In order to reduce the complexity of all-pair SimRank similarity calculation, we present an algorithm for calculating SimRank similarity between vertex pairs based on a partition of graph in advance. For hyperscale graphs, the task of partitioning faces two main challenges:

1. The algorithm needs to have excellent scalability, which requires that the algorithm itself can fully exploit the computational parallelism of the partitioning process, and can obtain greater processing power by stacking computing nodes.
2. The results of partition require better preservation of the original graph's semantics. The graphs in real life are not randomly generated, and their topological structure often implies some information at semantic level.

We use an effective distributed algorithm for graph partitioning, the details will be described in Sect. 3.1.

Reference [16] describes a method to speed up the calculation of PageRank based on several properties of the Block Structure in the diagram structure, our method to calculate SimRank similarity is directly inspired by this algorithm. The real-life graph dataset can be naturally divided into several dense blocks. Semantically speaking, these dense blocks often contain the most information that people are interested in. We make full use of this property and divide the computation of similarity into two different levels: the similarity between blocks and the similarity of internal pairs of blocks, and thus propose an algorithm to calculate the approximate similarity between full-pairs. Compared with the original SimRank calculation method, our algorithm performs well both on effectiveness and computational efficiency.

Assuming the graph has been partitioned into several blocks, the similarity between vertex pairs can be divided into two types:

1. Vertex pairs in the same dense block. In the last section, we have explained the method of dividing graph G into several dense blocks which are stored in some computing node of cluster. In this case, the similarity of the vertex pair can be calculated by using the serial calculation method according to Formula 2.
2. Vertex pairs in the different blocks. If the size of the block is sufficiently large, then the two vertices are respectively in different dense blocks meaning that the distance between the two vertices will be relatively large with a high probability. In reviewing the random walk model, two random walkers separated by a large distance are often unable to meet at a certain point by walking in a short distance (<10). This shows that the similarity of the two vertices will be numerically very small, so we directly calculate their approximate similarity.

3.1   Modularity-Based Graph Partition

Our distributed algorithm for graph partitioning is inspired by the idea of Multi-Level Partitioning. There are mainly three steps, which are shown in Fig. 2:

1. First of all, the scale of the original image is gradually reduced through the collapse. Each time the collapse occurs, a simple partitioning of the graph is done first, and then each partition of the partitioned result is treated as a new vertex. The edges between the partitions act as new edges, forming a smaller scale graph.
2. After several iterations of collapse, the scale of the graph is small enough to reach an acceptable threshold, and then some traditional high-quality single-node algorithms such as KL or FM can be used to directly partition the small graphs to obtain the preliminary results.
3. Finally, we project these partitioning results back to the original graph to obtain the final partition.

Our collapse process draws on the idea of Community Detection. The community, intuitively speaking, refers to some dense groups in the network. The connections between the vertices inside each community are relatively close, but the connections between various communities are relatively sparse. The difference between the task of community detection and graph partitioning is that the former does not fix the number of communities, because the number of specific communities is determined by the internal structure of the input graph, but the latter often sets the number of blocks to be divided. The similarity between the two is that the partially-closed substructures in the community detection process often share the same community ID, which is consistent with the intrinsic

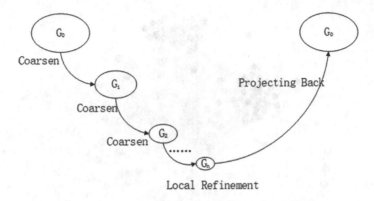

Fig. 2. Steps of multi-level partitioning

requirements of the graph partitioning task. Figure 3 shows a typical community detection result, from which it can be seen intuitively that the algorithm detected a total of 4 communities. If we directly consider it a 4-partition of the graph $P = (C_1, C_2, C_3, C_4)$, the quality of this partition is also good. We use the idea of modularity maximization [26] to better retain the dense substructures in the original graph, also the semantic information.

3.2   Block Similarity

Assuming that each block in the graph is a vertex, the partition of the graph forms a collapsed graph. Based on this collapsed map, we first define the weights of the edges in the graph.

Definition 1. *The weights of the edges in the collapsed graph. Assume that the graph G has a partition $P = (C_1, C_2, \ldots, C_n)$, let $L(C_i)$ denote the number of all edges in the partition C_i, including the edges inside the partition and the edges connected to other partitions, let $L(C_i, C_j)$ denote the number of edges connected to the block C_i and the block C_j. Set graph G' as the collapsed graph formed by partitioning P, $v_i, v_j \in G'$, v_i is the vertex corresponding to the block C_i and v_j is the vertex corresponding to the block C_j. Then we define the weight of edge (v_i, v_j) as*

$$w(v_i, v_j) = \frac{L(C_i, C_j)}{L(C_i)} \tag{3}$$

the weight of v_i to itself as

$$w(v_i, v_i) = 1 - \sum_{v_j \in O(v_i)} w(v_i, v_j) \tag{4}$$

Obviously, $w(v_i, v_j)$ and $w(v_j, v_i)$ are different in common condition.

So the collapsed graph G' is a weighted directed graph, and the weight of the edge (v_i, v_j) can be roughly understood as the probability that a random

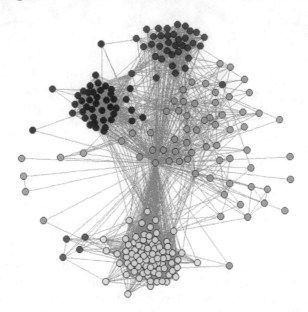

Fig. 3. Result of community detection, each color represents one ID (Color figure online)

walker "escaped" from point v_i to point v_j. The larger $w(v_i, v_j)$ is, the more intersecting edges of the block C_i and C_j in the original graph G are and the closer the correlation between them is. Based on these definition, we give the definition of similarity between each block in graph G.

Definition 2. *With regard to the partition $P = (C_1, C_2, \ldots, C_n)$ of the original graph G, we define the similarity between blocks C_i, C_j as the similarity between vertices v_i, v_j in the collapsed graph G'.*

In order to introduce edge weights into the SimRank model, [1] proposes the SimRank++ algorithm. The algorithm uses the following formula to calculate similarity

$$s_{k+1}(u, v) = c \cdot evidence(u, v) \sum_{u' \in I(u), v' \in I(v)} s_k(u', v') W(u', u) W(v', v) \qquad (5)$$

with c as the attenuation coefficient and

$$evidence(u, v) = \sum_{i=1}^{|I(u) \cap I(v)|} 2^{-i} \qquad (6)$$

$$W(u', u) = w(u', u) \cdot \exp(-Var(\{w(u', u) \mid u \in O(u')\})) \qquad (7)$$

If written in matrix form, let V be the evidence matrix and satisfy $V(i, j) = evidence(i, j)$, then the SimRank similarity calculation process of the whole weighted directed graph is shown in Algorithm 1.

Algorithm 1. Weighted All-pair SimRank:wapSimRank

1: **procedure** WEIGHTEDSIMRANK(G', u, c, k)
2:     $N \leftarrow |V|$;
3:     $S \leftarrow$ identity matrix I_N;
4:     **for** $i = 1$ to k **do**
5:         $T \leftarrow c \cdot W^T \cdot S \cdot W$;
6:         $S \leftarrow T + I_N - D(diag(T))$;   ▷ D is the diagonal matrix.
7:     **end for**
8:     $S \leftarrow$ element-wise multiplication of V and S;
9:     **return** S.
10: **end procedure**

3.3   Global Vertex Pair Similarity Estimation

Definition 3. *Similarity between vertex pairs in different blocks. If the two vertices of the pair (u, v) belong to different blocks C_i and C_j of the graph respectively, and the similarity of the blocks C_i and C_j is $s_{block}(C_i, C_j)$, we use the following formula to calculate the similarity of (u, v)*

$$s(u, v) = s(C_i, u) \cdot s_{block}(C_i, C_j) \cdot s(C_j, v) \tag{8}$$

in this equation, we can regard $s(C_i, u)$ as the similarity between the vertex u and the center point of its block, which is approximately given as

$$s(C_i, u) = \frac{1}{|C_i|} \sum_{q \in C_i} s(u, q) \tag{9}$$

that is, we use the mean of the similarity of u and all the vertices in its block to estimate the similarity between u and the center of the block.

The similarity between blocks calculated by algorithm 1 is converged with the number of iterations [1], and the SimRank similarity calculation process within vertex pairs is also converged [14], then the similarity of vertex pair defined by the above formula also converges with the number of iterations. Therefore, it is possible to separately calculate the similarity between blocks and the similarity of vertex pairs within a block, and finally calculate the global similarity between vertex pairs based on them. In summary, the main steps of our algorithm are as follows:

1. First we partition the original graph G according to the method explained before, and we can get several blocks $P = (C_1, C_2, \ldots, C_n)$.
2. Each block is collapsed as a vertex to obtain a weighted directed graph G'. The SimRank++ algorithm applied to the weighted graph is run on G' to obtain the similarity between blocks.
3. Run the serial full-pair SimRank algorithm directly on each block C_i to obtain the vertex pair similarity within the block.
4. Use Formula 8 to compute the similarities of vertices belong to the different blocks.
5. Return the global similarities in the end.

4   Experimental Results

4.1   Experimental Environment

The cluster consists of six computing nodes. Each node processor is a 12-core Intel Xeon E-2650 with a frequency of 2.1 GHz, 64 GB of memory, and 1 TB of hard disk. The nodes are connected by Gigabit Ethernet. The operating system is Ubuntu 16.04. The Spark running version is 1.6.2 and the underlying distributed file system HDFS version is 2.6.0. All nodes are configured as slave nodes, one of which is additionally configured as a master node. When we run in Spark, we allocate 10 GB of memory for each executor.

4.2   Datasets

We used a total of four real datasets, which are eu-2005, ljournal-2008, arabic-2005 and wiki-topcats. Details of the first three datasets are shown in Table 1, eu-2005 is a small part of webpage link data crawled from .eu domain name, ljournal-2008 is a virtual social network. Wiki-topcats[1] is a directed graph that records the references between various WEB hyperlinks in Wikipedia, whose entries are divided into 17364 different categories. We select four largest categories to obtain our wiki-topcats graph (we call them C1, C2, C3, C4), with vertices in these categories and the edges between them. The details of wiki-topcats are shown in Table 2.

Table 1. Details of datasets.

Dataset	Vertex number	Edge number	Average vertex degree	Size
eu-2005[a]	862, 664	19, 235, 140	22.29	256.4 MB
ljournal-2008[b]	5, 363, 260	79, 023, 142	14.73	1.2 GB
arabic-2005[b]	22, 744, 080	639, 999, 458	28.14	10.9 GB

[a]http://law.di.unimi.it/webdata/eu-2005/
[b]http://law.di.unimi.it/webdata/ljournal-2008/
[c]http://law.di.unimi.it/webdata/arabic-2005/

Each graph data begins as a normal text format, with each row representing an edge of the graph. Before starting the experiment, all datasets were pre-loaded onto the distributed file system HDFS.

4.3   Effectiveness

Strictly speaking, the similarity calculation method proposed in this paper is an algorithm for calculating approximate SimRank similarity. For vertex pairs within the same block, our results do not differ substantially from the strict

---

[1] https://snap.stanford.edu/data/wiki-topcats.html.

Table 2. Details of wiki-topcats.

(a) Vertex numbers of four categories.

Category	Vertex number
C1	34,722
C2	22,700
C3	15,303
C4	11,662

(b) Edge numbers between four categories.

	C1	C2	C3	C4
C1	9,653	14,321	15,678	18,323
C2	9,804	82,767	32,130	135,480
C3	13,098	21,104	51,092	11,523
C4	15,431	28,873	9,522	73,564

SimRank similarity, but for vertex pairs from different blocks, it is clear that there are differences in the values. Our experimental results on wiki-topcats show that their numerical results do not differ by more than ±5%. In order to test the effectiveness of the algorithm at the semantic level in practical applications, we use PAM [18], a classical k-medoids graph clustering algorithm based on vertex similarity to cluster wiki-topcats as a standard result. We run the SimRank algorithm and our algorithm separately, and take the ratio of the number of vertices correctly classified to the total number of vertices as the accuracy rate. The results show that the accuracy of SimRank is 0.6218 and the accuracy of our algorithm is 0.6221. From the results, our accuracy rate is generally the same as or slightly higher than that of SimRank. We think this may be because we have used the graph partition preprocessing process to extract the dense subgraph in the original graph to some extent so have eliminated the noise.

4.4 Computational Efficiency

We compare the computational efficiency of our algorithm partitionSimRank with matrixSimRank calculation method based on sparse matrix calculation and DeltaSimRank algorithm based on data transmission optimization. Among them, the SimRank process based on the sparse matrix calculation directly performs a large-scale matrix multiplication according to Formula 2. DeltaSimRank [5] uses an incremental calculation method, and does not directly update the similarity between vertex pairs but rather calculates the increment relative to the previous iteration, and finally aggregates the previous increments to get the final solution. All three algorithms are written as distributed programs based on Spark. The operating environments and the related parameter settings are exactly the same. The number of partition blocks set in the partitionSimRank preprocessing process is 300. The partition time of the graph accounts for the total time cost of the algorithm. Table 3 shows the running time of three algorithms. As can be seen from the table, DeltaSimRank has about tens of times improvement in computational efficiency compared to matrixSimRank. This is due to the fact that DeltaSimRank greatly reduces the amount of intermediate data generated during the iteration process. Compared to DeltaSimRank, partitionSimRank has several times or even ten times improvement in computing efficiency too. This is because the running time of calculations of similarities within the blocks that take the most time in the algorithm process is reduced by $(n/m)^2$ times in comparison to the previous global all-pair calculations.

Table 3. Running time (min) of three algorithms.

	matrixSimRank	DeltaSimRank	paritionSimRank
eu-2005	1278.20	51.95	16.38
ljournal-2008	6523.14	402.03	32.38
arabic-2005	-	2045.50	126.32

Figure 4 inspects the relationship between the number of blocks obtained from the preprocessing and the overall running time of the algorithm, the time here also includes the running time of the graph partition. The input data of the algorithm is the largest graph arabic-2005 of the three graphs. The number of iterations of SimRank calculation is set to be $k = 6$. All cluster computing nodes are used during the operation. Other parameters are fixed and only the number of partition blocks α can be changed. It can be seen from the figure that the running time curve shows a pronounced convexity. A smaller number of blocks means that the graph partition algorithm has been iterated more because only a sufficiently iterated partition algorithm can obtain a sufficiently small number of blocks. As the number of partition blocks gradually increases, the number of iterations of the partitioning algorithm decreases. However, at this time, SimRank similarity in each block is highly costly to calculate, because only about 144 cores are available for our cluster, which is the upper limit of the degree of parallelism. More computing tasks make limited CPU resources a bottleneck. It can also be seen from the figure that the optimal setting of the number of blocks is around 300–350.

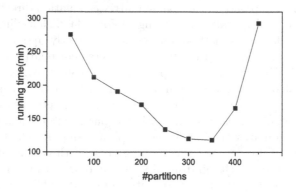

Fig. 4. The relationship between the number of blocks and the running time on arabic-2005.

4.5   Scalability

Figure 5 shows the scalability of our algorithm. First, we investigate the relationship between the running time of the algorithm and the size of the input graph, the results are shown in Fig. 5(a). The figure shows that when the number of cluster computing nodes is fixed, the running time varies with the size of the input graph for different graph data. We run the algorithm with block number $\alpha = 300$, iteration number of SimRank calculation $k = 6$ and other parameters fixed. It can be seen that the input map size increases from 256 MB to 10.9 GB, and the corresponding running time generally changes approximately linearly with the input size, which indicates that our multi-level partitioning model has good data scalability. We also examined how the efficiency of the algorithm varies with the number of compute nodes in the cluster when the scale of the input graph is fixed. The input graph is the largest arabic-2005 of the three graphs, with all parameters fixed at runtime, and the number of computing nodes increased from 2 to 6. The experimental results are shown in Fig. 5(b). From the figure, we can see that, for input graphs of different sizes, the running time of the algorithm decreases almost linearly with the increase of cluster computing nodes, which indicates that the algorithm has good node scalability in a distributed environment.

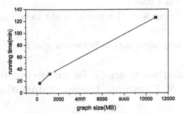
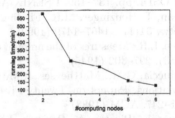

(a) The relationship between the running time and the size of input graph.

(b) The relationship between the running time and the number of computing nodes.

Fig. 5. The scalability of the algorithm.

5   Conclusion

In this paper, we study the problem of full-pair SimRank similarity calculation on large-scale graph data. In real-life large-scale graph data has millions of nodes, the element size of its adjacency matrix reaches trillion level ($|V|^2$), and existing methods cannot effectively calculate it. In order to effectively reduce the complexity of the problem, we propose an algorithm based on the concept of divide and conquer, in consideration of the fact that the dense blocks in the graph often contain the most information that people are interested in, to decompose the problem of one-to-all similarities calculation from two levels: similarity between the affiliated blocks and the similarity of vertex pairs within the block, and then calculate the global similarity between any vertex pair based on these. Experiments have shown that our algorithm has high efficiency and good parallelism.

References

1. Antonellis, I., Garcia-Molina, H., Chang, C.: SimRank++: query rewriting through link analysis of the click graph. PVLDB **1**(1), 408–421 (2008)
2. Baeza-Yates, R., Ribeiro-Neto, B., et al.: Modern Information Retrieval, vol. 463. ACM Press, New York (1999)
3. Bhattacharya, I., Getoor, L.: Entity resolution in graphs. In: Mining Graph Data, p. 311 (2006)
4. Bui, T.N., Moon, B.R.: Genetic algorithm and graph partitioning. IEEE Trans. Comput. **45**(7), 841–855 (1996)
5. Cao, L., Cho, B., Kim, H.D., Li, Z., Tsai, M.H., Gupta, I.: Delta-SimRank computing on MapReduce. In: Proceedings of the 1st International Workshop on Big Data, Streams and Heterogeneous Source Mining: Algorithms, Systems, Programming Models and Applications, pp. 28–35. ACM (2012)
6. Dean, J., Ghemawat, S.: MapReduce: simplified data processing on large clusters. In: OSDI, pp. 137–150. USENIX Association (2004)
7. Dean, J., Henzinger, M.R.: Finding related pages in the world wide web. Comput. Netw. **31**(11), 1467–1479 (1999)
8. Dice, L.R.: Measures of the amount of ecologic association between species. Ecology **26**(3), 297–302 (1945)
9. Fiduccia, C.M., Mattheyses, R.M.: A linear-time heuristic for improving network partitions. Papers on Twenty-Five Years of Electronic Design Automation, pp. 241–247. ACM (1988)
10. Fouss, F., Pirotte, A., Renders, J.M., Saerens, M.: Random-walk computation of similarities between nodes of a graph with application to collaborative recommendation. IEEE Trans. Knowl. Data Eng. **19**(3), 355–369 (2007)
11. He, G., Feng, H., Li, C., Chen, H.: Parallel SimRank computation on large graphs with iterative aggregation. In: Proceedings of the 16th ACM SIGKDD International Conference on Knowledge Discovery and Data Mining, pp. 543–552. ACM (2010)
12. Hendrickson, B., Leland, R.W.: An improved spectral graph partitioning algorithm for mapping parallel computations. SIAM J. Sci. Comput. **16**(2), 452–469 (1995)
13. Jaccard, P.: Etude comparative de la distribution florale dans uneportion des Alpes et du Jura. Impr. Corbaz (1901)
14. Jeh, G., Widom, J.: SimRank: a measure of structural-context similarity. In: Proceedings of the Eighth ACM SIGKDD International Conference on Knowledge Discovery and Data Mining, pp. 538–543. ACM (2002)
15. Johnson, D.S., Aragon, C.R., McGeoch, L.A., Schevon, C.: Optimization by simulated annealing: an experimental evaluation; part I, graph partitioning. Oper. Res. **37**(6), 865–892 (1989)
16. Kamvar, S., Haveliwala, T., Manning, C., Golub, G.: Exploiting the block structure of the web for computing PageRank. Technical report 2003-17, Stanford InfoLab (2003)

17. Karypis, G., Kumar, V.: METIS - unstructured graph partitioning and sparse matrix ordering system, version 2.0. Technical report (1995)
18. Kaufman, L., Rousseeuw, P.: Finding Groups in Data: An Introduction to Cluster Analysis. Wiley, Hoboken (1990)
19. Kernighan, B.W., Lin, S.: An efficient heuristic procedure for partitioning graphs. Bell Syst. Tech. J. **49**(2), 291–307 (1970)
20. Kusumoto, M., Maehara, T., Kawarabayashi, K.I.: Scalable similarity search for SimRank. In: Proceedings of the 2014 ACM SIGMOD International Conference on Management of Data, pp. 325–336. ACM (2014)
21. Li, C., et al.: Fast computation of SimRank for static and dynamic information networks. In: Proceedings of the 13th International Conference on Extending Database Technology, pp. 465–476. ACM (2010)
22. Li, L., Li, C., Chen, H., Du, X.: MapReduce-based SimRank computation and its application in social recommender system. In: BigData Congress, pp. 133–140. IEEE Computer Society (2013)
23. Li, Z., Fang, Y., Liu, Q., Cheng, J., Cheng, R., Lui, J.C.S.: Walking in the cloud: parallel SimRank at scale. PVLDB **9**(1), 24–35 (2015)
24. Lizorkin, D., Velikhov, P., Grinev, M., Turdakov, D.: Accuracy estimate and optimization techniques for SimRank computation. Proc. VLDB Endow. **1**(1), 422–433 (2008)
25. Maehara, T., Kusumoto, M., Kawarabayashi, K.: Efficient SimRank computation via linearization. CoRR abs/1411.7228 (2014)
26. Newman, M.E.: Modularity and community structure in networks. Proc. Nat. Acad. Sci. **103**(23), 8577–8582 (2006)
27. Page, L., Brin, S., Motwani, R., Winograd, T.: The PageRank citation ranking: bringing order to the web (1999)
28. Rothe, S., Schütze, H.: CoSimRank: a flexible & efficient graph-theoretic similarity measure. In: ACL (1), pp. 1392–1402. The Association for Computer Linguistics (2014)
29. Yu, W., Lin, X., Zhang, W.: Towards efficient SimRank computation on large networks. In: 2013 IEEE 29th International Conference on Data Engineering (ICDE), pp. 601–612. IEEE (2013)
30. Yu, W., Zhang, W., Lin, X., Zhang, Q., Le, J.: A space and time efficient algorithm for SimRank computation. World Wide Web **15**(3), 327–353 (2012)
31. Zaharia, M., Chowdhury, M., Franklin, M.J., Shenker, S., Stoica, I.: Spark: cluster computing with working sets. In: HotCloud. USENIX Association (2010)
32. Zhao, P., Han, J., Sun, Y.: P-rank: a comprehensive structural similarity measure over information networks. In: CIKM, pp. 553–562. ACM (2009)
33. Zhu, R., Zou, Z., Li, J.: SimRank computation on uncertain graphs. In: ICDE, pp. 565–576. IEEE Computer Society (2016)

CLDM: A Cache Cleaning Algorithm for Host Aware SMR Drives

Wenguo Liu, Lingfang Zeng$^{(\boxtimes)}$, and Dan Feng

Key Laboratory of Information Storage System, MoE Wuhan National Laboratory
for Optoelectronics School of Computer,
Huazhong University of Science and Technology, Wuhan 430074, China
liuwenguo_hust@163.com, {lfzeng,dfeng}@hust.edu.cn

Abstract. Host aware SMR (HA-SMR) drives can effectively increase
the capacity of hard disk drives. However, the cache cleaning algorithms
implemented in the HA-SMR drives need to be improved. Current cache
cleaning algorithms do not consider the characteristics of applications
and usually bring too much data migration. In this paper, we propose
a new cache cleaning algorithm called CLDM, which takes the characteristics of applications into account. It uses the "zone heat" to reflect
the access frequency in the disk cache of a zone, and the "zone data
migration" to reflect the data migration of a zone when cache cleaning
is performed on the zone. When CLDM is performed, it first computes
the "zone heat" for each zone which is currently buffered in the disk
cache, and then computes the "average zone heat" for all the buffered
zones. After that, CLDM computes the "zone data migration" for each
buffered zone, and sorts all the buffered zones in the ascending order of
their "zone data migration"s. CLDM first cleans the zones which satisfy
the condition "the zone heat of a zone is less than the average zone heat".
And then it cleans the zones with less "zone data migration"s. Experimental results show that CLDM can effectively reduce the amount of
migrated data during both the cache cleaning process and garbage collection process, and improve the performance of HA-SMR drives.

Keywords: Host aware SMR · Disk cache cleaning · Zone heat
Zone data migration

1 Introduction

Although the areal density of traditional HDDs will reach a limit [1], SMR can
effectively solve this problem through a stronger write head with asymmetric

This work was supported by the National High Technology Research and Development
Program (863 Program) No. 2015AA016701, No. 2015AA015301; NSFC No. 61472153,
No. 61402189, No. 61303046; State Key Laboratory of Computer Architecture, No.
CARCH201505; Wuhan Applied Basic Research Project (No. 2015010101010004); This
work was also supported by Key Laboratory of Information Storage System, Ministry
of Education, China.

© Springer Nature Switzerland AG 2018
J. Vaidya and J. Li (Eds.): ICA3PP 2018, LNCS 11334, pp. 608–620, 2018.
https://doi.org/10.1007/978-3-030-05051-1_42

magnetic field [2,3]. However, when SMR updates data on a track, the data on adjacent tracks often needs to be read out first, resulting in performance degradation of SMR drives [4].

Based on different data management models, SMR drives can be classified into three types: drive managed SMR drives, host managed SMR drives and host aware SMR drives [5]. HA-SMR drives support both sequential writes and non-sequential writes, and can expose the internal information to the host, making it more popular than drive managed and host managed SMR drives [6,7]. However, HA-SMR drives often show poor performance under write-intensive applications mainly because of data migration during the cache cleaning process [8]. When the free space in the disk cache of the HA-SMR drive falls bellow a threshold, disk cache cleaning is performed to migrate data blocks from the disk cache to their target zones. The basic cache cleaning algorithm used in the HA-SMR drive is the zone-oriented FIFO algorithm. When this algorithm is performed, it first cleans data blocks belonging to the zone which first appears in the disk cache. However, the zone-oriented FIFO algorithm does not consider the characteristics of applications, and usually brings a lot of data migration under write-intensive applications, resulting in severe performance degradation of HA-SMR drives [9].

In this paper, we propose a new cache cleaning algorithm called CLDM, which takes the characteristics of applications into account and cleans Cold zones and the zones with Less Data Migration with higher priorities. CLDM uses the "zone heat" to reflect the access frequency of a zone when its data blocks are buffered in the disk cache, and the "zone data migration" to reflect the data migration of a zone when cache cleaning is performed on the zone. It combines the "zone heat" and the "zone data migration" together. When CLDM is performed, it first computes the "zone heat" for each zone which is currently buffered in the disk cache, and then computes the "average zone heat" for all the buffered zones. After that, CLDM computes the "zone data migration" for each buffered zone, and sorts all the buffered zones in the ascending order of their "zone data migration"s. CLDM first cleans the zones which satisfy the condition "the zone heat of a zone is less than the average zone heat". And then it cleans the zones with less "zone data migration"s. Experimental results show that CLDM not only can effectively reduce the amount of migrated data during the cache cleaning process, but also can effectively reduce the amount of migrated data during the garbage collection process, and finally improves the performance of HA-SMR drives.

The rest of the paper is organized as follows. The background and motivation are presented in Sect. 2. We describe the design of CLDM in Sect. 3. The experimental results are presented in Sect. 4. We review the related work in Sect. 5 and conclude this paper in Sect. 6.

2   Background and Motivation

2.1   Host-Aware SMR Basics

Figure 1 shows the architecture of a HA-SMR drive. Because the write head width is much wider than the track width in a SMR drive, when data on a track is updated, the data in subsequent tracks should be read out first to avoid being damaged [10]. A set of consecutive tracks constitute a zone, which is also a range of consecutive LBAs. In a HA-SMR drive, some zones build the disk cache, which is used to buffer non-sequential writes. The other zones are used as sequential write preferred zones, each of which maintains a write pointer [6,7]. When there is not enough free space for incoming non-sequential writes, the cache cleaning process is triggered to migrate non-sequential data from the disk cache to the corresponding zones through read-modify-write operations. And then garbage collection is implemented to obtain more free space in the disk cache through read-modify-write operations, too [4,8,9].

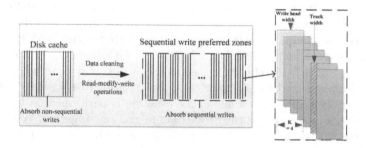

Fig. 1. The architecture of a HA-SMR drive.

In addition to read-modify-write operations, another main type of operations in a HA-SMR drive is "synthesized data" - generated operations [9]. When data blocks are migrated from the disk cache to their corresponding zones, if these data blocks are not consecutive, then the LBA "holes" are filled by "synthesized data".

2.2   Motivation

Data migration between the disk cache and sequential write preferred zones is the main reason causing the performance degradation of a HA-SMR drive. Thus reducing the data migration can effectively improve the performance of a HA-SMR drive. Each time cache cleaning is performed, data blocks belonging to the same zone are selected to be migrated from the disk cache to their target zone [8,9].

Because an application has different spatial localities on different zones, the numbers of non-overlapping data blocks buffered in the disk cache belonging to different zones are usually different. In addition, two non-overlapping data blocks usually have different access frequencies in the disk cache. Thus different zones have different "zone heat"s in the disk cache. Cleaning cold zones can result in less data migration and better garbage collection performance than cleaning hot zones. In addition, each time data cleaning is performed, cleaning different zones can result in different "zone data migration"s.

In this paper, we propose a cache cleaning algorithm called CLDM, which takes both "zone heat" and "zone data migration" into account. CLDM first computes the "zone heat" for each zone which is currently buffered in the disk cache, and then computes the "average zone heat" for all the buffered zones. After that, CLDM computes the "zone data migration" for each buffered zone, and sorts all the buffered zones in the ascending order of their "zone data migration"s.

CLDM checks the first zone in the ordered zone list. If its "zone heat" is less than the "average zone heat", then cache cleaning is performed on this zone; if not, CLDM checks the next zone. CLDM keeps implementing this process until at least one cache zone can be reclaimed. After cleaning all the zones that satisfy the condition "the zone heat is less than the average zone heat", if no cache zones can be reclaimed, then CLDM selects to clean the remaining zones in the ordered zone list until at least one cache zone can be reclaimed.

3 Design and Implementation

In this part, we first introduce the key data structure designed for CLDM, and then describe how to compute the *zone_heat* and *zone_data_migration*. At last we present the details of CLDM.

3.1 Key Data Structure

The key data structure shown in Fig. 2 is designed to collect the relative information for CLDM. When a data block arrives in the disk cache, it first checks whether the zone the block belongs to is buffered in the disk cache. If not, the zone is added to the *buffered_zone_list*. If the data block is not a update block, it will be added to the *buffered_valid_blk_list* of the corresponding zone. If the data block has not ever accessed the disk cache, it will be added to the *history_buffered_blk_list* of the corresponding zone. When the disk cache cleaning is implemented, the *zone_heat*, *Data_Rcache*, *Data_Rzone* and *Data_Fill* for each buffered zone are computed based on the information collected by the key data structure.

The main variables in the key data structure are explained as follows.

buffered_zone_count: the number of zones which are currently buffered in the disk cache.

ave_zone_heat: the average access frequency of all the zones currently buffered in the disk cache.

buffered_zone_no: the zone number of a buffered zone.

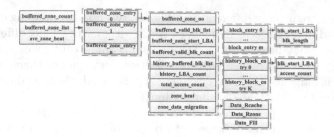

Fig. 2. Key data structure

buffered_zone_start_LBA: the lowest start LBA among all the start LBAs of data blocks belonging to the same zone, which are buffered in the disk cache.

history_buffered_blk_count: the number of data blocks that have ever been buffered in the disk cache belonging to the same zone.

history_LBA_count: the number of non-overlapping LBAs of the data blocks that have ever been buffered in the disk cache belonging to the same zone.

blk_start_LBA: the start LBA of a data block.

blk_length: the length of a data block.

access_count: the access count of a data block when it is buffered in the disk cache.

total_access_count: the sum of *access_count*s of all the data blocks that have ever been buffered in the disk cache belonging to the same zone.

zone_heat: the access frequency of a zone reflected by the data blocks which have ever been buffered in the disk cache.

zone_data_migration: the size of migrated data when cache cleaning is performed on a zone.

Data_Rcache: the size of data read from the disk cache when cache cleaning is performed on a zone.

Data_Rzone: the size of data read from a zone when cache cleaning is performed on the zone.

Data_Fill: the size of synthesized data when cache cleaning is performed on a zone.

3.2   The Calculation of the Zone Heat and Zone Data Migration

Different zones have different access frequencies in the disk cache under an application. The more frequently it cleans a zone, the more data is migrated during the cache cleaning process. We use the "zone heat" to indicate whether a zone is "hot" or not when its data blocks are buffered in the disk cache. Cleaning different zones usually brings different sizes of migrated data, and we use the "zone data migration" to reflect the data migration of a zone when cache cleaning is performed on this zone.

The larger number of non-overlapping data blocks belonging to a zone are buffered in the disk cache, and the more frequently data blocks are accessed in the disk cache, the hotter is the zone. To compute the "zone heat" for a zone, we maintain an *access_count* for each data block, which records the access frequency of the data block in the disk cache, and use *history_LBA_count* to record the number of non-overlapping data blocks which have ever been buffered in the disk cache belonging to the same zone. Assume a zone consists of N non-overlapping LBAs, and each LBA corresponds to a data block, then the *zone_heat* can be calculated as

$$zone\_heat = \frac{total\_access\_count}{history\_LBA\_count}$$
$$= \frac{access\_count\ 0 + ... + access\_count\ N}{history\_LBA\_count} \tag{1}$$

When cache cleaning is performed on a zone, the migrated data of the zone is composed of four parts: *Data_Rcache*, *Data_Rzone*, *Data_Fill* and *Data_Wzone*, in which *Data_Wzone* represents the size of data written to the zone. The *Data_Rcache* depends on the *buffered_valid_blk_count*, and the *Data_Rzone* can be calculated according to the *buffered_zone_start_LBA* and the number of valid blocks in the zone with LBAs higher than the *buffered_zone_start_LBA*. The *Data_Fill* depends on the number of "synthesized data" blocks. Based on the *Data_Rcache*, *Data_Rzone* and *Data_Fill*, *Data_Wzone* can be calculated as

$$Data\_Wzone =$$
$$Data\_Rcache + Data\_Rzone + Data\_Fill. \tag{2}$$

Then when cache cleaning is performed on a zone, the *zone_dulu_migration* can be calculated as

$$zone\_data\_migration = Data\_Rcache+$$
$$Data\_Rzone + Data\_Fill + Data\_Wzone \tag{3}$$
$$= (Data\_Rcache + Data\_Rzone) * 2 + Data\_Fill.$$

3.3   CLDM: The Cache Cleaning Algorithm

When the HA-SMR drive is idle or there is not enough free space in the disk cache, cache cleaning is performed to migrate data blocks from the disk cache to their target zones. Selecting different zones to perform cache cleaning can result in different sizes of data migration. The more data is migrated, the poorer the performance of the HA-SMR drive will be. We propose CLDM, a cache cleaning algorithm which can reduce the data migration by combining the *zone_heat* and *zone_data_migration* together, which is described in Algorithm 1.

Assume data blocks belonging to *zone* 3, *zone* 56, *zone* 300, ..., *zone M* are currently buffered in the disk cache. When cache cleaning is performed, CLDM first computes the *zone_heat* and the *zone_data_migration* for each buffered zone. The *zone_heat* is computed based on the *total_access_count* and *history_LBA_count*, and the *zone_data_migration* is computed based on the *Data_Rcache*, *Data_Rzone* and *Data_Fill*. Then CLDM computes the

---

Algorithm 1. CLDM: the cache cleaning algorithm for the disk cache

---

1: //*gc_state*: if at least one cache zone can be reclaimed, meaning garbage collection can be performed in the disk cache, the value is set as 1; otherwise the value is set as 0.

2: //*invalid_zone_count*: indicates how many cache zones can be reclaimed when implementing garbage collection operations.

3: $gc\_state = 0$;

4: **for** $k \in \{3, 56, 300, ..., M\}$ **do**

5:
$$zone[k].zone\_heat = \frac{zone[k].total\_access\_count}{zone[k].history\_LBA\_count} \qquad (4)$$

6:
$$\begin{aligned} zone[k].zone\_data\_migration = \\ (zone[k].Data\_Rcache \\ + zone[k].Data\_Rzone) * 2 \\ + zone[k].Data\_Fill. \end{aligned} \qquad (5)$$

7: **end for**

8:
$$ave\_zone\_heat = \frac{zone[3].zone\_heat + ... + zone[M].zone\_heat}{cached\_zone\_count}. \qquad (6)$$

9: $cache\_cleaning\_sort(\{3, 56, 300, ..., M\})$;

10: **for** $k \in \{300, 3, 56, ..., M\}$ **do**

11:     **if** $(zone[k].zone\_heat \leq ave\_zone\_heat)$ **then**

12:         $cache\_clean(zone[k])$;

13:         $invalid\_zone\_count = compute\_invalid\_ratio()$;

14:         **if** $(invalid\_zone\_count \geq 1.0)$ **then**

15:             $gc\_state = 1$;

16:             break ;

17:         **end if**

18:     **end if**

19: **end for**

20: **if** $(gc\_state == 0)$ **then**

21:     //After the preceding cache cleaning, assume the order of the remaining buffered zones in the ordered list is *zone 42, zone 13, ...zone M*;

22:     **for** $k \in \{42, 13, ..., M\}$ **do**

23:         $cache\_clean(zone[k])$;

24:         $invalid\_zone\_count = compute\_invalid\_ratio()$;

25:         **if** $(invalid\_zone\_count \geq 1.0)$ **then**

26:             break;

27:         **end if**

28:     **end for**

29: **end if**

---

ave_zone_heat based on the the *zone_heat*s of all the currently buffered zones. After that CLDM uses the *cache_cleaning_sort()* function to sort all the currently buffered zones in the ascending order of their *zone_data_migration*s. CLDM checks the first buffered zone in the ordered list. If the *zone_heat* of the first buffered zone is less than the *ave_zone_heat*, which means that this buffered zone is a cold zone and will bring the least data migration, then cache cleaning will be performed on this zone. If the *zone_heat* of the first buffered zone is not less than the *ave_zone_heat*, then CLDM moves to check the next buffered zone in the ordered list. Each time the cache cleaning is finished on a zone, CLDM invokes the *compute_invalid_ratio()* function, which first computes the ratio of invalid data blocks for each cache zone, and then returns the value of *invalid_zone_count* which represents the number of cache zones that can be reclaimed by garbage collection operations. If the value of the *invalid_zone_count* is not less than 1.0, which means that at least one cache zone can be reclaimed to hold new arriving data blocks, then the cache cleaning stops. If the value of the *invalid_zone_count* is less than 1.0 after all the buffered zones satisfying the condition $zone[k].zone\_heat \leq ave\_zone\_heat$ have been cleaned, CLDM selects the remaining buffered zones from the beginning of the ordered list to perform cache cleaning. Once the value of *invalid_zone_count* is not less than 1.0, the cache cleaning stops.

4   Experimental Results

4.1   Experimental Setup

We use Disksim [11] to simulate the HA-SMR drive, and the disk model used is Maxtor Atlas 10K IV disk. The whole capacity of the HA-SMR drive is 146 GB, and the zone size and the disk cache size are set to 16M and 512M respectively. A greedy garbage collection algorithm is implemented in the disk cache [9]. CLDM and the zone-oriented FIFO algorithm are two cache cleaning algorithms implemented in the disk cache. Three write-intensive enterprise traces are used as input traces, which are collected from enterprise servers at Microsoft Research Cambridge [12]. The main characteristics of these traces are listed in Table 1, and in particular, the "Non-sequential ratio" represents the ratio of non-sequential writes to all the writes of a trace.

Table 1. Characteristics of traces

Trace	Total write size (GB)	Avg. write size (KB)	Write ratio (%)	Non-sequential ratio (%)
proj_0	144.27	34.78	87.52	93
src1_2	44.15	32.51	83.41	88
prn_0	45.19	8.50	89.21	92

4.2   Results

In this part, we first show the variations of data migration during the cache cleaning process in the HA-SMR drive, and then shows the variations of data migration during the GC process. At last we compare the average response times of the HA-SMR drive when adopting FIFO and CLDM respectively.

Data Migration During the Cache Cleaning Process in the HA-SMR Drive. The migrated data during the cache cleaning process consists of four parts: data read from the disk cache, data read from zones, data synthesized because of "LBA gaps", and data written to zones. Figures 3, 4, 5 show the variations of the four parts of data respectively when the HA-SMR drive adopts different cache cleaning algorithms under proj_0, src1_2 and prn_0.

From Fig. 3(a) we can see that, when CLDM is implemented in the HA-SMR drive, the sizes of data read from the disk cache are about 23.17% smaller under proj_0, 25.52% smaller under src1_2 and 44.17% smaller under prn_0 respectively than that when FIFO is implemented. The main reason is that CLDM cleans colder zones with higher priorities, which reduces the access frequencies to the disk cache, and also gives higher priorities to zones with less "zone data migration"s, which reduces the amount of data read from the disk cache. Because of the same reason, Fig. 3(b) shows that when CLDM is implemented in the HA-SMR drive, the sizes of data read from zones are about 71.79% smaller under proj_0, 75.19% smaller under src1_2 and 72.98% smaller under prn_0 respectively than that when FIFO is implemented in the HA-SMR drive.

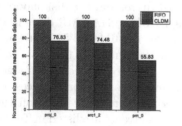 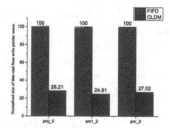

(a) Comparison of data read from the disk cache.   (b) Comparison of data read from the zones.

Fig. 3. Comparisons of data read from the disk cache/zones during the cache cleaning process under proj_0, src1_2, and prn_0.

Figure 4 shows the variations of synthesized data generated during the disk cache cleaning. When CLDM is implemented in the HA-SMR drive, the sizes of synthesized data are about 82.49% smaller under proj_0, 89.77% smaller under src1_2 and 60.56% smaller under prn_0 respectively than that when FIFO is implemented. The main reason is that synthesized data mainly comes from small random writes, and CLDM can effectively reduce the number of small random writes.

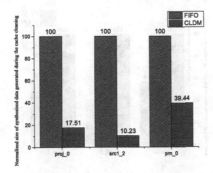

Fig. 4. Comparison of data synthesized during the cache cleaning process under proj_0, src1_2, and prn_0.

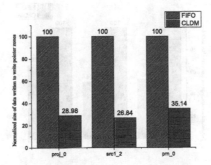

Fig. 5. Comparison of data written to the zones during the cache cleaning process under proj_0, src1_2, and prn_0.

The data written to zones is composed of the data read from the disk cache, the data read from zones, and the data synthesized during the disk cache cleaning. From Fig. 5 we can see that, when CLDM is implemented, the sizes of data written to the write pointer zones are about 71.02% smaller under proj_0, 73.16% smaller under src1_2 and 64.86% smaller under prn_0 respectively than that when FIFO is implemented in the HA-SMR drive.

Data Migration During the GC Process in the HA-SMR Drive. Different cache cleaning algorithms can result in different sizes of migrated data when GC operations are performed in the HA-SMR drive. This is because different algorithms select to clean different buffered zones and cause different numbers of valid data blocks and invalid data blocks in the disk cache. Figure 6 shows the variations of data migrated by GC operations. When CLDM is implemented in the HA-SMR drive, the sizes of migrated data are about 42.76% smaller under proj_0, 58.22% smaller under src1_2 and 40.35% smaller under prn_0 respectively than that when FIFO is implemented. The main reason is that, the main task of GC operations is to compact valid data blocks together, and when CLDM is implemented, it cleans hotter zones with lower priorities, which can increase the number of invalid data blocks and reduce the number of valid data blocks.

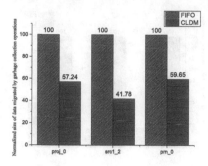

Fig. 6. Comparison of data migrated during the GC process under proj_0, src1_2, and prn_0.

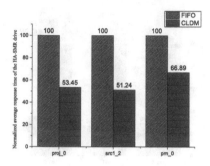

Fig. 7. Comparison of average response times of the HA-SMR drive under proj_0, src1_2, and prn_0.

Comparison of Average Response Times of the HA-SMR Drive.
Figure 7 shows the comparison of average response times of the HA-SMR drive under proj_0, src1_2 and prn_0 when adopting FIFO and CLDM. From Fig. 7 we can see that when CLDM is implemented in the HA-SMR drive, the HA-SMR drive performs about 46.55% better under proj_0, 48.76% better under src1_2 and 33.11% better under prn_0 respectively than that when FIFO is implemented. The main reason is that CLDM can effectively reduce the data migration during the cache cleaning process and then improve the performance of the HA-SMR drive.

5 Related Work

Mitigating the write amplification caused by the SMR technology can improve the performance of SMR drives. Cassuto ea al. proposed to use indirection systems to reduce read-modify-write operations caused by shingle writing [2]. In the DM-SMR drive adopting the set-associative STL, each data update needs a read-modify-write operation, and when the disk cache is nearly filled, it implements a FIFO cleaning algorithm [10]. To reduce long-term data migration in

HM-SMR drives, Jones et al. proposed a cold-weight garbage collection algorithm to reclaim free space, and cleaned the write buffer using a hot/cold data separation approach [13]. Wu et al. investigated the special features of HA-SMR drives such as the disk cache cleaning, and proposed an approach called H-Buffer to improve the performance of HA-SMR drives [8]. The disk cache cleaning algorithm used in a HA-SMR drive is a zone-oriented FIFO algorithm, which groups data blocks belonging to the same zone together. However, it does not take the characteristics of applications into account, and often results in severe performance degradation of HA-SMR drives under write-intensive applications [9].

6   Conclusions

The current cache cleaning algorithms implemented in HA-SMR drives didn't consider the characteristics of applications and often brought too much data migration. In this paper, we have designed a new cache cleaning algorithm called CLDM. It uses the "zone heat" and the "zone data migration" to reflect the characteristics of applications. When the cache cleaning is about to be performed, CLDM first computes the "zone heat" for each buffered zone, and then computes the "average zone heat" for all the buffered zones. After that, CLDM computes the "zone data migration" for each buffered zone, and sorts all the buffered zones in the ascending order of their "zone data migration"s. CLDM first cleans the cold buffered zones and then cleans the zones with less "zone data migration"s, aiming to reduce the cache cleaning frequency and the amount of migrated data. Experimental results show that CLDM can effectively reduce the amount of migrated data during the cache cleaning process and garbage collection process, and improve the performance of HA-SMR drives.

References

1. Wood, R., Williams, M., Kavcic, A., Miles, J.: The feasibility of magnetic recording at 10 terabits per square inch on conventional media. IEEE Trans. Magn. **45**(2), 917–923 (2009)
2. Cassuto, Y., Sanvido, M.A.A., Guyot, C., Hall, D.R., Bandic, Z.Z.: Indirection systems for shingled-recording disk drives. In Proceedings of 26th IEEE Symposium on Mass Storage Systems and Technologies (MSST), May 2010, pp. 1–14 (2010)
3. Venkataraman, K.S., Dong, G., Zhang, T.: Techniques mitigating updateinduced latency overhead in shingled magnetic recording. IEEE Trans. Magn. **48**(5), 1899–1905 (2012)
4. Amer, A., Holliday, J., Long, D.D.E., Miller, E.L., Paris, J.-F., Schwarz, T.: Data management and layout for shingled magnetic recording. IEEE Trans. Magn. **47**(10), 3691–3697 (2011)
5. Feldman, T., Gibson, G.: Shingled magnetic recording areal density increase requires new data management. USENIX; Login: Mag. **38**(3) (2013)
6. INCITS T10 Technical Committee, Information technology - zoned block commands (ZBC). Draft Standard T10/BSR INCITS 536. American National Standard Institute Inc., December 2015

7. INCITS T13 Technical Committee, Information technology - zoned device ATA command set. Draft Standard T13/BSR INCITS 537. American National Standard Institute Inc., December 2015

8. Wu, F., Yang, M.-C., Fan, Z., Zhang, B., Ge, X., Du, D.H.C.: Evaluating host aware SMR drives. In: Proceedings of the 8th USENIX Workshop on Hot Topics in Storage and File Systems, pp. 31–35. USENIX Association, June 2016

9. Fenggang, W., Fan, Z., Yang, M.-C., Zhang, B., Ge, X., Du, D.H.C.: Performance evaluation of host aware shingled magnetic recording (HA-SMR) drives. IEEE Trans. Comput. **66**(11), 1932–1945 (2017)

10. Aghayev, A., Shafaei, M., Desnoyers, P.: Skylight - a window on shingled disk operation. ACM Trans. Storage (TOS) **11**(4), 16–30 (2015)

11. Bucy, J.S., Schindler, J., Schlosser, S.W., Ganger, G.R.: The DiskSim simulation environment version 4.0 reference manual. Technical report. Carnegie Mellon University, May 2008

12. Narayanan, D., Donnelly, A., Rowstron, A.: Write off-loading: practical power management for enterprise storage. ACM Trans. Storage **4**(3), 10–23 (2008)

13. Jones, S.N., Amer, A., Miller, E.L., Long, D.D.E., Pitchumani, R., Strong, C.R.: Classifying data to reduce long-term data movement in shingled write disks. ACM Trans. Storage **12**(1), 2–17 (2016)

HyGrid: A CPU-GPU Hybrid Convolution-Based Gridding Algorithm in Radio Astronomy

Qi Luo[1], Jian Xiao[2(✉)], Ce Yu[1], Chongke Bi[2], Yiming Ji[1], Jizhou Sun[1], Bo Zhang[3], and Hao Wang[1]

[1] School of Computer Science and Technology, Tianjin University, 135 Yaguan Rd, Haihe Education Park, Tianjin 300350, China
[2] School of Computer Software, Tianjin University, 135 Yaguan Rd, Haihe Education Park, Tianjin 300350, China
xiaojian@tju.edu.cn
[3] National Astronomical Observatories, Chinese Academy of Sciences, 20A Datun Rd, Chaoyang District, Beijing 100012, China

Abstract. New-generation radio telescopes have been producing an unprecedented scale of data every day and requiring fast algorithms to speedup their data processing work flow urgently. The most data intensive computing phase during the entire work flow is gridding, which converts original data from irregular sampling space to regular grid space. Current methods are mainly focused on interferometers or have limitations on the resolutions due to the memory wall. Here we propose a CPU-GPU hybrid algorithm which accelerates the process of gridding. It employs multi-CPU to perform pre-ordering and GPU to speed up convolution-based gridding. Several optimization strategies are further proposed for reducing unnecessary memory access and maximizing the utilization of the heterogeneous architecture. Testing results demonstrate that the proposal is especially suitable for gridding large-scale data and can improve performance by up to 71.25 times compared to the traditional multi-thread CPU-based approach.

Keywords: Gridding · Heterogeneous computing · Convolution
Data pipeline · Astroinformatics

1 Introduction

In radio astronomy, the original observed data are always irregularly sampled or under-sampled because of the scan pattern. But visualizing the data on pixel-based devices requires a regular grid. Hence, gridding is applied to astronomical data for converting the data from an irregular sampling space to a regular grid space [20]. Figure 1 shows an example of original astronomical data and its output resampled data. Gridding is one of the phases in the pipeline, which involves a major data intensive computing [7,14,31]. As many new large radio telescopes have been established or are under construction, more and more observed data

© Springer Nature Switzerland AG 2018
J. Vaidya and J. Li (Eds.): ICA3PP 2018, LNCS 11334, pp. 621–635, 2018.
https://doi.org/10.1007/978-3-030-05051-1_43

are being produced. So they require significant processing capability. For example, the Five-hundred-meter Aperture Spherical radio Telescope (FAST) [27,28] will generate about 40 GB to 1 TB of raw data per hour. But gridding 1 TB of raw data with a traditional multi-thread method on a 6-core CPU takes about 550 h. To reduce storage requirements and speed up observational cosmology research, how to gridding in an efficient way has become a great challenge.

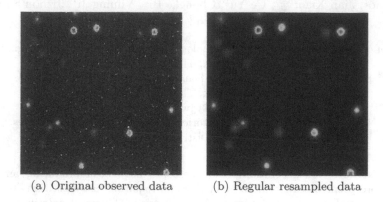

(a) Original observed data   (b) Regular resampled data

Fig. 1. An example of gridding irregular data to regular space.

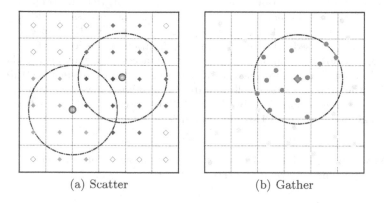

(a) Scatter   (b) Gather

Fig. 2. Two approaches of implementing convolution-based gridding. (a) Scatter: each input point (black dot) partially contributes its sampling value to all neighboring output points (rhombuses) within a kernel (dotted circle). (b) Gather: each output point (rhombus) collects its resampling value of all neighboring input points (green dots) within a kernel (dotted circle). (Color figure online)

The gridding problem has been studied extensively in both industry and academia. A number of efficient methods are developed to provide efficient performances, for example, the direct Fourier transform method [21], the back-projection method [9], the matrix inversion method [33] and so on. In radio astronomy, the convolution-based method [29] is the most commonly adopted method [8]. It divides the sampling plane into an equally spaced linear grid, then assigns each cell (i.e., output point) a value. For each output point, its value is calculated by weighted summing all neighboring sampling points (i.e., input points). To reduce the calculation, a convolution kernel is often applied to limit these potential contributors within a relatively small range. As illustrated in Fig. 2, scatter and gather are two classical approaches to implement the convolution-based gridding. A scatter traverses each original input point and computes its contributions for all output points within the kernel. Vice verse, a gather traverses each output point, finds all neighboring input points within the kernel and calculates the final result by convolving these contributors.

Many previous studies have shown that GPU-based gridding would significantly outperform the CPU-based counterpart [1,10,17,24,32]. They also found the data writing race were unavoidable when parallel a scatter, since multiple input points may contribute to the same output points (e.g., purple rhombuses in Fig. 2(a)) [23]. Although atomic operations can serialize the updates, the performance of a scatter is still fundamentally bounded by the memory wall. On the other hand, a gather will never suffer the race condition, because all operations of an output point are executed by a single thread. Nevertheless, irregular input points result in the access pattern of each output point being less predictable. To reduce unnecessary memory access of non-contributing input points, a gather always requires a pre-ordering process. The pre-ordering will generate a lookup table by hashing the input points to regular bins. Then each output point can quickly determine the bins falling within its kernel and access its neighboring input points. The Hierarchical Equal Area isoLatitude Pixelation (HEALPix) [13] is a widely adopted spherical division scheme in observational cosmology [2,11,15,36].

However, existing proposals are not designed for radio interferometers or have not well considered large-scale data situation such as FAST. To address these problems, this paper presents a CPU-GPU **Hy**brid convolution-based **Grid**ding algorithm, called **HyGrid**. Our main contributions are summarized as following:

- Firstly, a pre-ordering algorithm is presented to build an efficient HEALPix-based lookup scheme on CPU with a $O(N \log(N))$ time complexity and a low memory consumption.
- Then, a gather is further accelerated on GPU with a data layout strategy. Moreover, thread coarsening is adopted on the situation of large output resolution.
- Finally, several cases are feed into HyGrid to verify its validity and feasibility. The results show that HyGrid can solve the convolution-based gridding quickly and efficiently. Compared to the traditional multi-thread approach, it can achieve a speedup by up to 125.81 times on pre-ordering and a speedup by up to 18.63 times on gather. For thread coarsening, the performance can achieve 4.64 times improvement by using it compared to the counterpart.

This paper is structured as follows. In Sect. 2, several related works are briefly discussed. in Sect. 3, there are details about preliminaries and problem description. in Sect. 4, the HyGrid algorithm is described in detail. In Sect. 5, the test data and result are provided. Finally in Sect. 6, it is the conclusions and further work.

2   Related Work

Previous studies related to the convolution-based gridding are introduced and reviewed on three aspects: (1) GPU-based scatters, (2) pre-ordering and gathers, and (3) optimization strategies.

Due to the intrinsic data race, proposed scatters mainly focused on avoiding updating device memory simultaneously. Van Amesfoort et al. [1] developed a scatter on GPU by assigning a small private grid to each input point. Although it can avoid data race fundamentally. It limits the resolution of the output grid and cannot be applied to the latest large radio telescopes. Based on memory copy, Humphreys and Cornwell [5,6,17] also implemented a scatter for the Australian Square Kilometre Array Pathfinder (ASKAP) [16] on GPU. To reduce device memory access, Romein [32] designed anther GPU-based scatter. For each antenna pair in a radio telescope interferometer, its sampling coordinates changes slowly in the sampling space. Hence, using a dedicated thread to iterate over the sampling trajectories will lead to tiny shifts in the kernel. So the thread can accumulate weighted sums in its register as long as possible and write the sums to device memory when necessary. Merry [24] further improved Romein's algorithm by using thread coarsening [26]. The improved version significantly reduces the addressing overhead of device memory. However, both methods heavily depend on the spatial coherence of the interferometers' data and cannot be adopted by single dishes.

Proposed gathers are mainly aiming at reducing unnecessary memory access of non-contributing input points. Edgar et al. [10] designed a gather for the Murchison Widefield Array (MWA) [37] on GPU. It uses Thrust [3] to pre-order input points into 24×24 bins. Then each output point can only search the neighboring input points within the bin it falls in and its adjacent eight bins. Although the pre-ordering leads to an efficient device memory access, the coarse binning strategy makes that a big part (i.e., 8/9) of searched input points still cause unnecessary memory addressing overheads and convolving calculations. Gai et al. [12] presented a gather for magnetic resonance imaging data [18] on GPU by pre-ordering data with a compact binning method. Winkel et al. [40] proposed another compact binning method based on HEALPix. Their implementation is on CPU, called cygrid. It pre-orders astronomical data by using the C++ STL vector [30] to convert an input-output hash map to an output-input hash map. For large-scale data, the data layout and the pre-ordering strategy will significantly increase time overhead and memory consumption. Hence, it is not suitable for gridding large-scale data.

In addition, researches also focused on improving GPU's efficiency and allowing synergies between the CPU and GPU. Amesfoort's scatter [1] accesses the convolution kernel as a 1D texture and loads common data into shared memory for all threads in a block only once. It can efficiently utilize memory bandwidth. But it is not appropriate for neither large kernels nor varying kernels, because different input points may use an identical convolution kernel. Merry [24] adopted a trade-off method between thread coarsening and parallelism efficiency. While Gai et al. [12] improved load balance by partitioning the gridding operators evenly between GPU and CPU.

3 System Model

3.1 Preliminaries

When applying the FITS World Coordinate System (WCS) [25,39], HEALPix is suitable to bin the spherical sampling space [4]. Given a grid resolution (denoted by $N_{side} \in \{1, 2, 4, 8, \cdots\}$), HEALPix hierarchically subdivides the sphere surface into $12N_{side}^2$ equal-area pixelization. As illustrated in Fig. 3, all pixel centers are placed on $4N_{side} - 1$ rings of constant latitudes, and are equidistant in azimuth (on each ring). Then, these pixels can be simply indexed by moving down from the north to the south pole along each ring.

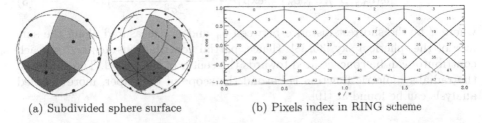

(a) Subdivided sphere surface   (b) Pixels index in RING scheme

Fig. 3. The HEALPix partition [13]. (a) It is hierarchically subdivided with resolution $N_{side} = 1$ and 2 respectively; (b) $12N_{side}^2$ pixels are located at $4N_{side} - 1$ isolatitude rings with resolution $N_{side} = 2$.

HEALPix software libraries[1] support spherical transformations. For instance, the WCS coordinates (denoted by (α, β) with α being the longitude and β being the latitude) of any pixel center (denoted by pix) can be computed by $(\alpha, \beta) \leftarrow Pix2Loc(pix, N_{side})$; the reverse transformation is $pix = Loc2Pix(\alpha, \beta, N_{side})$; the ring (denoted by rix) to which pix belongs can be calculated by $rix = Pix2ring(pix, N_{side})$; the lowest numbered pixel which is located at rix can be calculated by $pix = Ring2Start(rix, N_{side})$.

3.2 Problem Description

Suppose N input points $\mathbb{S} = \{s_1, s_2, \cdots, s_N\}$ are distributed on a sampling plane, where each input point $s_n \in \mathbb{S}$ is located at coordinates (α_n, β_n) with a

---

[1] http://healpix.sourceforge.net/.

value $V[s_n]$ representing its sampling value. After dividing the plane into $I \times J$ regular grid cells (denoted by $\mathbb{G} = \{g_{1,1}, g_{1,2}, \cdots, g_{I,J}\}$), where the center of each grid cell $g_{i,j} \in \mathbb{G}$ is located at coordinates $(\alpha_{i,j}, \beta_{i,j})$, convolution-based gridding will assign $g_{i,j}$ an resampling value (denoted by $V[g_{i,j}]$) and an overall weighting value (denoted by $W_{i,j}$).

Given a weighting function (denoted by w), the convolution kernel of $g_{i,j}$ will be,

$$V[g_{i,j}] = \frac{1}{W_{i,j}} \sum_n V[s_n] w(\alpha_{i,j}, \beta_{i,j}; \alpha_n, \beta_n), \tag{1}$$

where

$$W_{i,j} = \sum_n w(\alpha_{i,j}, \beta_{i,j}; \alpha_n, \beta_n). \tag{2}$$

Here, s_n be a contributed input point, $w(\alpha_{i,j}, \beta_{i,j}; \alpha_n, \beta_n)$ be a weight that s_n contributes to $g_{i,j}$, $W_{i,j}$ be the overall weight of all contributors. $W_{i,j}$ be used to conserve flux density, because different output points will be influenced by different contributors in varying degrees. In most cases, w be a radially symmetric function, for example, a Gaussian kernel with standard deviation σ. Such that,

$$w(\alpha_{i,j}, \beta_{i,j}; \alpha_n, \beta_n) = \exp\left[\frac{-d^2(\alpha_{i,j}, \beta_{i,j}; \alpha_n, \beta_n)}{2\sigma^2}\right], \tag{3}$$

where d be the shortest distance between s_n and $g_{i,j}$ measured along the surface of the spherical sky [35,38]. Hence, partial contributions denoted by each contributor can be concentrated towards the center of the kernel. The chosen of the radial-symmetric function is beyond the scope of the paper, more detailed analysis can be found at [19].

4 HyGrid Algorithm

In this section, we present a CPU-GPU hybrid gridding algorithm. To limit the search space, the algorithm first pre-orders the input points using multi-CPU. Then the proposal parallelizes the convolution by assigning each output point a dedicated thread on GPU. It further optimizes gridding using data layout and thread coarsening.

4.1 Pre-ordering

4.1.1 Ring-Based Lookup Strategy

$\forall s_n \in \mathbb{S}$, given $S_{pix}[n] = Loc2Pix(\alpha_n, \beta_n, N_{side})$ be the pixel to which s_n belong, $rix_n = Pix2ring(S_{pix}[n], N_{side})$ be the ring at which $S_{pix}[n]$ be located. Different pixels may located at the same ring, i.e., $rix_i = rix_j$ with $i \neq j$. Let $rix_1 = r_1$ and $rix_N = r_{total}$, we have $\mathbb{R} = \{r_1, r_2, \cdots, r_{total}\}$ be a set of rings at which S_{pix} be located.

Since guaranteeing the output grid image resolution requires a considerable number of pixels. The rearranged input points (denoted by $\mathbb{S}'$) will be stored in

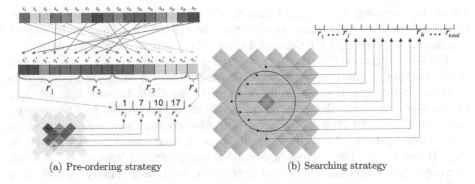

(a) Pre-ordering strategy   (b) Searching strategy

Fig. 4. Ring-based lookup table. (a) It sorts input points by their pixels (i.e., boxes in different colors) and generates a lookup table based on their rings; (b) it searches the neighboring input points for a given pixel by using the lookup table. (Color figure online)

a compact way on GPU's device memory. Hence, we cannot afford to directly search a pixel among $\mathbb{S}'$. To address the problem, we propose an efficient ring-based lookup table (denoted by R_{start}). It records the lowest indexed pixels which are located at each ring. Specifically, $S_{pix}[R_{start}[k]]$ be the lowest indexed pixel in S_{pix} which also be located at ring $r_k \in \mathbb{R}$. Such that $R_{start}[k] = n$ if and only if $rix_{n-1} < r_k$ and $rix_n \geq r_k$.

Therefore, given pixel pix with $rix = Pix2Ring(pix, N_{side})$, the problem of finding its contributors within a kernel radius (denoted by rad) becomes how to calculate the rings which are rad distant from rix, where $r_l = Loc2Pix(\alpha_{i,j}, \beta_{i,j} - rad, N_{side})$ and $r_h = Loc2Pix(\alpha_{i,j}, \beta_{i,j} + rad, N_{side})$ denote lowest and highest indexed rings, respectively. Then, for each r_k between r_l and r_h, we can binary search the lowest indexed neighboring pixel within the range $[R_{start}[k], R_{start}[k+1]]$ in S_{pix}. Due to the compact relationship among pixels, the following elements in S_{pix} will be continuously contributed to pix. Such that, if $S_{pix}[n]$ and $S_{pix}[n+2]$ are contributors and $rix_n = rix_{n+2}$, then $S_{pix}[n+1]$ will also be a contributor with $rix_{n+1} = rix_n$. So performing lookup only once, we can find all contributors located at rix_n and access them by sequential scanning $\mathbb{S}'$.

Figure 4(a) shows an example of generating R_{start}. In this example, 17 input points are binned into 9 pixels and rearranged according to the pixels' indexes in RING scheme. Then we have $R_{start}[1] = 1$, $R_{start}[2] = 7$, $R_{start}[3] = 10$ and $R_{start}[4] = 17$. Figure 4(b) illustrates an example of lookup with R_{start}.

4.1.2 Pre-ordering Algorithm on Multi-CPU

Given N_{side} and S_{pix}. The HEALPix-based Pre-ordering Algorithm (denoted by $HpxPreOrdering$) applies a parallel block indirect sort algorithm[2] to rearrange input points. The sort algorithm is represented by

---

[2] https://boost.org.

$BlockIndirectSort(S_{pix}, S_{val}, N)$ with $S_{val}[n] = n$ being the sort value. In addition, our early attempts have shown that the CPU-based block indirect sort algorithm outperformed GPU-based Thrust [3] on sorting large-scale data.

Details of $HpxPreOrdering$ are described in Algorithm 1. There are two steps: sorting (Line 1–4) and lookup-table-generating (Line 5–13). In step 1, $BlockIndirectSort$ is performed on multi-core CPU to sort S_{val} by S_{pix} in parallel (Line 1), then we rearrange $\mathbb{S}$ to $\mathbb{S}'$ according to the ordered S_{val} (Line 2–4). In step 2, the algorithm first computes r_1 and r_{total} (Line 5–6), then updates R_{start} by iterating over $\mathbb{R}$ and doing binary search in S_{pix} (Line 7–13). Here, given a non-decreasing array (denoted by $Array$), $BiSearchLastPosLessThan(Array, left, right, key)$ will binary search key within the range of $[left, right]$ in $Array$ and return an index i satisfying $Array[i] < key$ and $Array[i + 1] \geq key$.

The complexity of $HpxPreOrdering$ is decided by the block indirect sort algorithm, which is $O(N \log(N))$ at the worst time and $O(N)$ at the best time.

4.2   Gather Algorithm on GPU

Algorithm 2 illustrates the GPU-based Gridding Gather (denoted by $GPU\text{-}GridGather$). The entire computation of $V[g_{i,j}]$ is executed by a single thread. The thread iterates from r_l to r_h for finding all contributors of $g_{i,j}$ and performing Eq. 1 to obtain $V[g_{i,j}]$ and $W_{i,j}$ (Line 1–17). For each ring (denoted by $cntRix$), the thread calculates its latitude β (Line 2–3) to obtain the lowest and the highest indexed neighboring pixels (denoted by p_l and p_h, respectively) located at $cntRix$ (Line 4–6), where $tanRad$ is the great-circle distance between $(\alpha_{i,j}, \beta)$ and p_l (or p_r). Secondly, the thread binary searches p_l in S_{pix} with the search space restricted by R_{start} (Line 7–9). Finally, the thread can sequential scan $\mathbb{S}'$ and apply Eq. 1 (Line 10–16).

The calculation of Function GPUGRIDGATHER$g_{i,j}$ is actually linear to the number of contributors, although there exist double nested loops.

4.3   CUDA Optimization Strategy

We further propose two optimization strategies while implementing HyGrid in CUDA 8.0 [34]: (1) using different device memory types to optimize the data layout; (2) using thread coarsening to accelerate gather in the situation of the larger output resolution.

To optimize memory access, the data layout strategy manipulates $\mathbb{S}$ and $\mathbb{G}$ in the structure of an array format, accesses the lookup table as a 1D texture memory, as well as accesses global parameters (such as N, I, J, N_{side} and so on) as constant memory. Furthermore, partial convolving results of a thread are maintained in a register and only flushed to global memory once after all calculation.

In the situation of a large output resolution, although the same scale of threads could be generated by GPU processors. But these threads cannot be

---

Algorithm 1. HEALPix-based Pre-ordering Algorithm: *HpxPreOrdering*

    Parameter: N_{side}
    input: $\mathbb{S}, S_{pix}, S_{val}$
    output: $\mathbb{S}', S_{pix}, R_{start}, r_1, r_l, r_h$
    Initialize: $\mathbb{S}' \leftarrow \varnothing, R_{start} \leftarrow \varnothing$

                                                           ▷ sort input points
1: $BlockIndirectSort(S_{pix}, S_{val}, N)$
2: **for** $n = 1$ **to** N **do**
3:     $\mathbb{S}'[n] \leftarrow \mathbb{S}[S_{six}[n]]$
4: **end for**

                                                 ▷ generate lookup table
5: $r_1 = Pix2Ring(S_{pix}[1], N_{side})$
6: $r_{total} = Pix2Ring(S_{pix}[N], N_{side})$
7: $R_{start}[0] \leftarrow 1, idx = 1$
8: **for** $cntRix = r_1 + 1$ **to** r_{total} **do**
9:     $pix = Ring2Start(cntRix, N_{side})$
10:    $cntIdx = BiSearchLastPosLessThan(S_{pix}, idx, N, pix)$
11:    $R_{start}[cntRix - r_1] = cntIdx + 1$
12:    $idx = cntIdx$
13: **end for**

Algorithm 2. GPU-based Gridding Gather: *GPUGridGather*

    Parameter: N_{side}, rad
    input: $\mathbb{S}', S_{pix}, r_1, R_{start}, r_1, r_l, r_h$
    output: $W_{i,j}, V[g_{i,j}]$
    Initialize: $W_{i,j} = 0, V[g_{i,j}] = 0$
1: **for** $cntRix = r_l$ **to** r_h **do**

                                           ▷ iterate each neighboring ring
2:    $pix = Ring2Start(cntRix, N_{side})$
3:    $(\alpha, \beta) \leftarrow Pix2Loc(pix, N_{side})$
4:    $tanRad = Rad2Tan(\beta_{i,j}, \beta, rad)$
5:    $p_l = Loc2Pix(\alpha_{i,j} - tanRad, \beta, N_{side})$ ▷ lowest pixel
6:    $p_h = Loc2Pix(\alpha_{i,j} + tanRad, \beta, N_{side})$ ▷ highest pixel
7:    $lIdx = R_{start}[cntRix - r_1]$
8:    $rIdx = R_{start}[cntRix - r_1 + 1]$
9:    $n = BiSearchLastPosLessThan(S_{pix}, lIdx, rIdx, p_l) + 1$

                                              ▷ calculate Equation 1
10:   **while** $S_{pix}[n] \leq p_h$ **do**
11:     **if** $d(\alpha_{i,j}, \beta_{i,j}; \alpha_n, \beta_n) \leq rad$ **then**
12:       $W_{i,j} = W_{i,j} + w(\alpha_{i,j}, \beta_{i,j}; \alpha_n, \beta_n)$
13:       $V[g_{i,j}] = V[g_{i,j}] + w(\alpha_{i,j}, \beta_{i,j}; \alpha_n, \beta_n) * V[s'_n]$
14:     **end if**
15:     $n = n + 1$
16:   **end while**
17: **end for**

---

executed simultaneously due to the limited processing capability on each GPU processor. We also notice that output points located at the same ring usually have similar neighboring rings. Accordingly, we apply thread coarsening to collaborate the computations of several continuous output points located at the same ring into one thread. In particular, each thread executes *GPUGridGather* only once and its corresponding output points share the same p_l, determined by the "first" output point. Furthermore, partial convolving results of different output points would be remained on the different registers. The performance of the thread coarsening strategy will depend on the number of output points calculated by each thread, called coarsening factor (denoted by γ).

5   Benchmarking

Let output resolution (denoted by O_r) be the width of each output point. For a given sampling field, a small output resolution indicates a big I (or J). For instance, let $O_r = 200''$ and the sampling field be $5° \times 5°$, we have $I \times J = (5°/200'') \times (5°/200'') = 90 \times 90$. Several experiments are conducted to evaluate the performance of HyGrid with different N and O_r. To better illustrate the performance of HyGrid, we compare it against cygrid [40], which is one of the fastest gridding implementations to the best of our knowledge. The experimental environment is shown in Table 1. Specifically, cygrid and *HpxPreOrdering* are executed on a 6-core CPU with 12 threads per core. *GPUGridGather* is executed by $I \cdot J/\gamma$ threads on GPU with each thread being responsible for γ output points.

Table 1. Experimental environment

	Brand	Model	Cores	SMs	Tflops	RAM (GB)	Freq. (GHz)	Cache (MB)	Thread pre core
GPU	NVIDIA	Tesla K40	2880	15	1.4	12	-	-	-
CPU	Intel	Xeon E5-2620	6	-	-	-	2.5	15	12

5.1   Performance vs. Input Size

Figure 5(a) illustrates the performance of gridding as a function of N, where the sampling field is $5° \times 5°$ with $O_r = 600''$ (i.e., $I \times J = 90 \times 90$) and $\gamma = 1$. The results indicate that HyGrid outperforms the multi-thread cygrid with a speedup of 125.81 times on pre-ordering, a speedup of 18.63 times on gather and a speedup of 71.25 times on the gridding process overall. As N increasing, the pre-ordering strategy of cygrid is strictly limited by the memory wall. The number of contributors and convolving computations of each thread are also significantly increased. Thereby, *GPUGridGather* can obtain higher performance and data throughput, especially when $N > 10^8$.

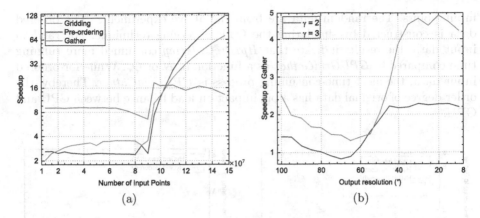

Fig. 5. The speedup of performance. (a) Gridding a different number of input points to a $5° \times 5°$ sampling filed with $O_r = 200''$ ($I \times J = 90 \times 90$); (b) gridding 1.5×10^8 input points to a $5° \times 5°$ sampling filed with different O_r.

5.2 Performance vs. Thread Coarsening

To analyze the efficiency and the feasibility of the thread coarsening strategy, we select a benchmark model of a fixed N and different O_r. Figure 5(b) shows the performance as a function of O_r with 1.5×10^8 input points and a $5° \times 5°$ sampling field. The results show that the strategy can achieve significant performance improvement even if I (or J) is very large. Compared to executing *GPU-GridGather* with $\gamma = 1$, we find that thread coarsening can achieve a speedup of 2.28 times with $\gamma = 2$, $O_r = 30''$ ($I \times J = 600 \times 600$) and a speedup of 4.64 times with $\gamma = 3$, $O_r = 20''$ ($I \times J = 900 \times 900$).

We also found that the trade-off between thread coarsening and parallel efficiency partly depends on the output resolution and the hardware. Hence, γ should be well-chosen in actual use. For example, a good γ should be 2 when gridding onto 327×327 ($O_r = 55''$) output grid cells, while 514×514 ($O_r = 35''$) output grid cells prefer $\gamma = 3$. In addition, because the shape of the convolution kernel is actually rectangular in thread coarsening strategy, the experiments with $\gamma = 4$ and 5 may result in "bad" output images. Such that original circular astronomical sources (as showed in Fig. 1) become rectangular sources after the gridding process. Therefore, we do not recommend a big γ, although it can bring about a high speedup of performance.

5.3 Performance vs. Order Degree

In practice, radio astronomical observations are usually taken by using the On-The-Fly (OTF) observing technique [22], where sampling value and position information are recorded continuously. Hence, some original astronomical data should be partial ordered. Some experiments are conducted to demonstrate the performance at such situation. Figure 6 shows the time overhead ratio of pre-ordering to gather, when respectively gridding random input points and ordered input points. The random data are from the above experiments. The ordered data is constructed by simulating the OTF observing technique. For random input data, the results indicate that *HpxPreOrdering* consumed more running time compared to *GPUGridGather* as a function of N or O_r. While for ordered input data, the most time-consuming process is *GPUGridGather*. Thereby, the order degree of original data has a big impact on load balance between CPU and GPU.

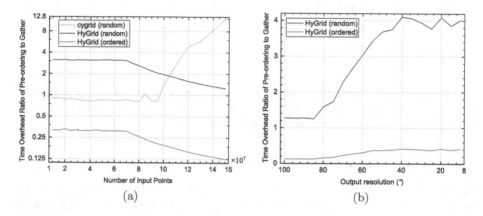

Fig. 6. The time overhead ratio of pre-ordering to gather. (a) Gridding a different number of input points to a $5° \times 5°$ sampling filed with $O_r = 200''$ ($I \times J = 90 \times 90$); (b) gridding 1.5×10^8 input points to a $5° \times 5°$ sampling filed with different O_r.

5.4   Performance in Practice

In addition, the time overhead of using HyGrid (with $\gamma = 3$) to gridding 1.7 GB of ordered (or random) data (nearly $N = 1.5 \times 10^8$) onto a 900×900 grid image is within 8 s (or 32 s). Approximately, gridding 1 TB of ordered (or random) data takes about 1.34 h (or 5.35 h). Accordingly, executing HyGrid on a single workstation is qualified for small-scale data, while a small cluster is enough for large-scale data by running multiple HyGrid simultaneously. In order to achieve a best trade-off between performance and power saving, the number of CPU and GPU should be well-chosen according to the order degree of input data.

6   Conclusion and Future Work

Due to the irregularity and the large-scale astronomical data, simply transferring the convolution-based gridding to GPU cannot obtain a good performance. Here we propose a hybrid approach. First an efficient lookup table based on HEALPix is introduced in the pre-ordering step. Then a GPU-accelerated gather is implemented by utilizing data layout and thread coarsening in a proper manner.

Experiments have shown that our proposal provides a significant improvement in performance, and can be applied in practical data pipelines for both large interferometer and single dish.

However, current implementation has not yet supported auto-tuning to find the optimized coarsening factor. Also, there need some improvements in load balance between CPU and GPU. Future research will mainly focus on extending the gridding approach to multiple GPUs platform, adapting it to real-time data stream, as well as integrating it into the data pipeline of FAST.

Acknowledgments. The authors would like to thank Benjamin Winkel for providing the Cython code of the *cygrid* method.

This work is supported by the Joint Research Fund in Astronomy (U1731125, U1531111) under a cooperative agreement between the National Natural Science Foundation of China (NSFC) and Chinese Academy of Sciences (CAS). This work is also supported by the Young Researcher Grant of National Astronomical Observatories, Chinese Academy of Sciences.

References

1. van Amesfoort, A.S., Varbanescu, A.L., Sips, H.J., van Nieuwpoort, R.V.: Evaluating multi-core platforms for HPC data-intensive kernels. In: Proceedings of the 6th ACM conference on Computing frontiers, CF 2009, pp. 207–216. ACM, New York (2009)
2. Baron, F., Kloppenborg, B., Monnier, J.: Toward 5D image reconstruction for optical interferometry, vol. 8445. Amsterdam, Netherlands (2012)
3. Bell, N., Hoberock, J.: Thrust: a productivity-oriented library for CUDA. In: Hwu, W.W. (ed.) GPU Computing Gems. Applications of GPU Computing Series, Jade edn, pp. 359–371. Morgan Kaufmann, Boston (2012)
4. Calabretta, M.R., Roukema, B.F.: Mapping on the healpix grid. Mon. Not. R. Astron. Soc. **381**(2), 865–872 (2007)
5. Cornwell, T.J., Golap, K., Bhatnagar, S.: W projection: a new algorithm for wide field imaging with radio synthesis arrays. In: Astronomical Data Analysis Software and Systems XIV. Astronomical Society of the Pacific Conference Series, vol. 347, p. 86 (12 2005)
6. Cornwell, T.J., Golap, K., Bhatnagar, S.: The noncoplanar baselines effect in radio interferometry: the W-projection algorithm. IEEE J. Sel. Top. Signal Process. **2**(5), 647–657 (2008)
7. De, K., Gupta, Y.: A real-time coherent dedispersion pipeline for the giant metre-wave radio telescope. Exp. Astron. **41**(1), 67–93 (2016)
8. Dickey, J.M.: Spectral line advanced topics. In: Single-Dish Radio Astronomy: Techniques and Applications. Astronomical Society of the Pacific Conference Series, vol. 278, pp. 209–225 (2002)
9. Dudgeon, D.E., Mersereau, R.M.: Multidimensional Digital Signal Processing. Prentice Hall Signal Processing Series. Prentice-Hall (1984)
10. Edgar, R., et al.: Enabling a high throughput real time data pipeline for a large radio telescope array with GPUs. Comput. Phys. Commun. **181**(10), 1707–1714 (2010)

11. Fernique, P., Durand, D., Boch, T., Oberto, A., Pineau, F.: HEALpix based cross-correlation in astronomy. In: Astronomical Data Analysis Software and Systems XXII. Astronomical Society of the Pacific Conference Series, vol. 475, p. 135 (2013)

12. Gai, J., et al.: More IMPATIENT: a gridding-accelerated Toeplitz-based strategy for non-Cartesian high-resolution 3D MRI on GPUs. J. Parallel Distrib. Comput. **73**(5), 686–697 (2013)

13. Górski, K.M., et al.: HEALPix: a framework for high-resolution discretization and fast analysis of data distributed on the sphere. Astrophys. J. **622**(2), 759 (2005)

14. Giovanelli, R., Haynes, M.P., Kent, B.R., et al.: The arecibo legacy fast ALFA survey: I. Science goals, survey design, and strategy. Astrophys. J. **130**(6), 2598 (2005)

15. Hong, Z., Yu, C., Wang, J., Xiao, J., Cui, C., Sun, J.: Aquadexim: highly efficient in-memory indexing and querying of astronomy time series images. Exp. Astron. **42**(3), 387–405 (2016)

16. Hotan, A.W., et al.: The Australian square kilometre array pathfinder: system architecture and specifications of the boolardy engineering test array, vol. 31, p. e041. Publications of the Astronomical Society of Australia (2014)

17. Humphreys, B., Cornwell, T.: SKA memo 132: analysis of convolutional resampling algorithm performance (2011)

18. Hwu, W.M.W., et al.: Accelerating MR image reconstruction on GPUs. In: 2009 IEEE International Symposium on Biomedical Imaging: From Nano to Macro, pp. 1283–1286 (2009)

19. Jackson, J.I., Meyer, C.H., Nishimura, D.G., Macovski, A.: Selection of a convolution function for Fourier inversion using gridding. IEEE Trans. Med. Imaging **10**(3), 473–478 (1991)

20. Léna, P., Rouan, D., Lebrun, F., Mignard, F., Pelat, D., Lyle, S.: Observational Astrophysics. Astronomy and Astrophysics Library, 3rd edn. Springer, Heidelberg (2012). https://doi.org/10.1007/978-3-642-21815-6

21. Maeda, A., Sano, K., Yokoyama, T.: Reconstruction by weighted correlation for MRI with time-varying gradients. IEEE Trans. Med. Imaging **7**(1), 26–31 (1988)

22. Mangum, J.G., Emerson, D.T., Greisen, E.W.: The on the fly imaging technique. A&A **474**(2), 679–687 (2007)

23. McCool, M., Reinders, J., Robison, A.: Structured Parallel Programming: Patterns for Efficient Computation, 1st edn. Morgan Kaufmann Publishers Inc., San Francisco (2012)

24. Merry, B.: Faster GPU-based convolutional gridding via thread coarsening. Astron. Comput. **16**, 140–145 (2016)

25. Mink, D.: WCSTools 4.0: Building Astrometry and Catalogs into Pipelines. In: Astronomical Data Analysis Software and Systems XV. Astronomical Society of the Pacific Conference Series, vol. 351, p. 204 (2006)

26. Muscat, D.: High-performance image synthesis for radio interferometry (2014)

27. Nan, R.: Five hundred meter aperture spherical radio telescope (fast). Sci. China Ser. G **49**(2), 129–148 (2006)

28. Nan, R., et al.: The five-hundred-meter aperture spherical radio telescope (fast) project. Int. J. Mod. Phys. D **20**(06), 989–1024 (2011)

29. O'Sullivan, J.D.: A fast sinc function gridding algorithm for Fourier inversion in computer tomography. IEEE Trans. Med. Imaging **4**(4), 200–207 (1985)

30. Plauger, P., Lee, M., Musser, D., Stepanov, A.A.: C++ Standard Template Library, 1st edn. Prentice Hall PTR, Upper Saddle River (2000)

31. Reynolds, C., Paragi, Z., Garrett, M.: Pipeline Processing of VLBI Data. Physics (2002)

32. Romein, J.W.: An efficient work-distribution strategy for gridding radio-telescope data on GPUs. In: Proceedings of the 26th ACM International Conference on Supercomputing, ICS 2012, pp. 321–330. ACM, New York (2012)

33. Rosenfeld, D.: An optimal and efficient new gridding algorithm using singular value decomposition. Magn. Reson. Med. **40**(1), 14–23 (1998)

34. Sanders, J., Kandrot, E.: CUDA by Example: An Introduction to General-Purpose GPU Programming, 1st, edn. Addison-Wesley Professional, Boston (2010)

35. Sinnott, R.W.: Virtues of the Haversine, vol. 68, p. 158 (1984)

36. Sum, J., Leung, C.S., Cheung, R.C.C., Ho, T.Y.: HEALPIX DCT technique for compressing PCA-based illumination adjustable images. Neural Comput. Appl. **22**(7), 1291–1300 (2013)

37. Tingay, S.J., et al.: The Murchison widefield array: the square kilometre array precursor at low radio frequencies. Publications of the Astronomical Society of Australia, vol. 30, no. 30, pp. 109–121 (2013)

38. Vincenty, T.: Direct and inverse solutions of geodesics on the ellipsoid with application of nested equations. Surv. Rev. **23**(176), 88–93 (1975)

39. Wells, D.C., Greisen, E.W.: Fits: a flexible image transport system, vol. 44, p. 363 (1981)

40. Winkel, B., Lenz, D., Flöer, L.: Cygrid: a fast cython-powered convolution-based gridding module for python. Astron. Astrophys. **591**, A12 (2016)

COUSTIC: Combinatorial Double Auction for Crowd Sensing Task Assignment in Device-to-Device Clouds

Yutong Zhai[1]([⊠]), Liusheng Huang[1], Long Chen[2], Ning Xiao[1], and Yangyang Geng[1]

[1] School of Computer Science and Technology,
University of Science and Technology of China, Hefei, China
{zyt1996,xiaoning,geng325}@mail.ustc.edu.cn,
lshuang@ustc.edu.cn
[2] School of Computer Science and Technology,
Guangdong University of Technology, Guangzhou, China
lonchen@mail.ustc.edu.cn

Abstract. With the emerging technologies of Internet of Things (IOTs), the capabilities of mobile devices have increased tremendously. However, in the big data era, to complete tasks on one device is still challenging. As an emerging technology, crowdsourcing utilizing crowds of devices to facilitate large scale sensing tasks has gaining more and more research attention. Most of existing works either assume devices are willing to cooperate utilizing centralized mechanisms or design incentive algorithms using double auctions. There are two cases that may not practical to deal with, one is a lack of centralized controller for the former, the other is not suitable for the seller device's resource constrained for the later. In this paper, we propose a truthful incentive mechanism with combinatorial double auction for crowd sensing task assignment in device-to-device (D2D) clouds, where a single mobile device with intensive sensing task can hire a group of idle neighboring devices. With this new mechanism, time critical sensing tasks can be handled in time with a distributed nature. We prove that the proposed mechanism is truthful, individual rational, budget balance and computational efficient.

Keywords: Mobile crowd sensing · Device-to-Device clouds
Combinatorial double auction · Task allocation

1 Introduction

Nowadays, mobile devices like smart phones, laptops and ipads have become proliferation in people's daily life. They can generate massive information about the environment by themselves for sensing the physical world. Mobile crowd sensing [1], which means sharing data collectively in both sensing and computing devices and measuring and mapping phenomena of common interest through extract information, is becoming more and more popular in the evolution of the Internet of Things (IoT).

© Springer Nature Switzerland AG 2018
J. Vaidya and J. Li (Eds.): ICA3PP 2018, LNCS 11334, pp. 636–651, 2018.
https://doi.org/10.1007/978-3-030-05051-1_44

In general, mobile crowd sensing classifies as personal sensing [2] and community sensing [3]. Personal sensing always senses one simple task, like the monitoring of movement patterns of an individual for personal record-keeping or health care reasons. Community sensing is a cognitive sensing mode which requires many individual devices to conduct cooperative sensing. This mode is suitable for the case when a single device has to perform complex sensing tasks, such as air quality monitoring [4], traffic information mapping [5] and public information sharing [6]. However, the complicated sensing tasks are constrained by the limited computational, energy and data resources. In order to ensure the normal operation of sensing applications, we can consider a set of mobile devices forming what we called Device-to-Device (D2D) Clouds [7]. Device-to-device cloud are consisted of a set of mobile devices and a cluster head or an access point (AP), shown in Fig. 1.

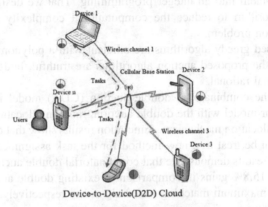

Fig. 1. One example of device-to-device (D2D) cloud. The red (blue) color portion represents the available bandwidth (computation) resource. (Color figure online)

Users or mobile devices may generate many large scale sensing tasks which is difficult to process in a short time efficiently by a single device. By the use of crowdsourcing, we can offload the computation incentive task to nearby devices. Inefficient allocation of large scale sensing tasks will tremendously influence the performance xxx. Therefore, task allocation is a key issue in mobile crowd sensing. Most of the crowdsourcing algorithms can be classified as centralized algorithms and distributed algorithms. In the distributed algorithm, auction has become a popular tool to solving task allocation problem in mobile crowd sensing [8]. In general, there are four types auction—single auction, double auction, combinatorial auction and combinatorial double auction. An auction involving both buyers and sellers is called double auction [9], combinatorial auction mechanism is first used for airport time slot allocation [10], combinatorial double auction is first proposed in [11] for a market with public goods. Existing studies for crowd sensing such as [12, 13] and [14] are double auction mechanisms. Several double auction mechanisms [9, 15] assume one task can only be offloaded to one device, this may cause big delay while processing a large scale tasks. Therefore, it is necessary to use a combinatorial double auction (CDA) mechanism for the task allocation by the use of crowdsourcing.

Designing a CDA mechanism for mobile crowd sensing has three major challenges. **Which sensing tasks should be offloaded? How much monetary compensation should be paid by mobile users to simulate the offloading? The third challenge is how to allocate the sensing tasks, finding the optimal task allocation solution is a NP-hard problem that cannot be solved in polynomial time.**

In this paper, we mainly consider a Combinatorial dOuble aUction for taSk assignmenT in device-to-device Crowdsourcing clouds (COUSTIC) problem. To tackle the problem and the three challenges mentioned above, we try to design an efficient combinatorial double auction mechanism for task allocation in D2D clouds. The major contributions of this paper can be summarized as follows:

- We first analyze the case when there are several tasks and several mobile devices in the D2D clouds, then we formulate the task assignment as a combinatorial double auction problem into an integer programming. That we design a polynomial time greedy algorithm to reduce the computational complexity and solve the utility maximization problem.
- The proposed greedy algorithms are efficient with a polynomial running time. We prove that the proposed auction algorithms are truthful, budget balanced and they are individual rational.
- We build the combinatorial double auction (CDA) model in a D2D cloud, and compare our model with the double auction, random allocation, and the maximum matching allocation mechanism. Simulation results show that our model gets a good result, it can be treat as a new method for the task assignments in D2D clouds.
- Simulation results demonstrate that combinatorial double auction mechanism gets a 26.3% and 15.8% gains in comparison to existing double auction scheme and the centralized maximum matching based algorithm respectively.

The rest of the article is organized as follows. Section 2 introduces the related works. Section 3 describes the system model and formulate the problem. Section 4 presents the algorithm for task assignment and pricing payments, then prove the several properties of the auction. Section 5 presents the simulation results. Finally, we conclude the paper in Sect. 6.

2   Related Work

In the following, we summarize and compare the related work on the centralized mechanisms and distributed mechanisms.

2.1   Centralized Mechanisms

There have been some works on the crowd sensing in D2D cloud based centralized mechanisms [16, 17]. The centralized mechanisms sense data or assign tasks by a central controller or a central platform. Xiao et al. [16] designed an energy efficient mode selection and user association scheme which the marco cell base station as a central controller. They aimed to maximize the energy efficiency of uplink transmission while guaranteeing the quality-of-service (QoS) requirement of users via a joint optimization of access point selection, mode switching, and power control. Song et al. [17]

announced a crowdsensing-based system which comprised of a central platform and a collection of smartphones. They assumed the smartphones are cooperative and willing to take sensing tasks and provide sensing services to the system.

Although the Centralized mechanisms are successful and inexpensive methods in sensing task assignment scenarios, they are not suitable for the case when a central controller missing.

2.2 Distributed Mechanisms

Except the centralized mechanism, the distributed mechanism can still work efficiently in the absence of a central controller. Auction, as an incentive mechanism, has been studied in various specific fields to improve the efficiency such as spectrum allocation [18], resource allocation [19, 20] and cooperative communication [9]. Most of the studies are focused on the double auction mechanisms in the mobile crowd sensing scenarios. Chen et al. [12] proposed a strategy-proof double auction model for mobile participatory sensing. They considered the mobile participatory sensing system between a number of smartphones and sensing tasks in an open market. However, they did not handle the collusion between all these participates. Tang et al. [13] designed a double-sided bidding mechanism for resource sharing in mobile cloud. In their mobile cloud model, each supplying user submitted a bid to reveal the amount of sharing resources "supplied" to the mobile cloud given a price to be paid, and each demanding user submitted a bid to reveal the amount of resources "demanded" from the mobile cloud given a price to pay. H. Huang announced a truthful double auction mechanism which can achieve the max-min fairness. They maximize the minimum utility among all the data consumers. However, none of the above mentioned works consider the case of collaborating one large scale sensing task by several participants.

A large scale sensing task is produced through the device which is too inefficient to process the task on itself. However, some adjacent devices are idle. Thus, we consider the combinatorial double auction. Similar to the existing incentive mechanisms mentioned above, combinatorial double auction is also an incentive and distributed mechanism and more efficient by comparing with double auction mechanisms. Samimi et al. [20] proposed a combinatorial double auction model and a CDARA algorithm for the task allocation. However, the CDARA algorithm can't guarantee individual rational. So we design our task allocation scheme by the combinatorial double auction model to tackle the COUSTIC problem.

3 Problem Definition

3.1 Device-to-Device Cloud Model

We consider in a Device-to-Device (D2D) cloud, combined with an access point (AP) and a set of mobile devices. In a D2D cloud, we suppose that $D = \{d_1, d_2, \ldots d_n\}$ are the mobile devices willing to participate in task assignments. Each device in D may carry the task by itself, or it may be idle, or it can participate in the task assignment.

In general, we assume that m tasks $T = \{T_1, T_2, \ldots T_m\}$ are created during the use of mobile devices, each task are consisted of multiple subtasks. For each sub-task $T_i, i \in \{1, 2, \ldots m\}$ is denoted by $T_i = \{\theta_{i,1}t_1, \theta_{i,2}t_2, \ldots \theta_{i,k}t_k\}$, $\theta_{i,j}$ denotes the demand for each type of tasks. And v_i is the true valuation for the computing process of the sub-task T_i. The problem we need to solve is the allocation of these tasks.

For a group of mobile devices in a D2D cloud network, due to the heterogeneity of mobile devices, different mobile devices have different computing resources, storage capacity, and so on. We assume as follows: each devices j has its own free resources R_j, the total free resources of n devices are represented as: $\vec{R} = \{R_1, R_2, \ldots R_n\}$.

3.2   Combinatorial Double Auction Model

In this system, there are several sensing tasks (buyers) which need to be processed efficiently and devices (sellers) which have a large amount of computing resources, and the access point serves as an auctioneer. Each task submits a bid to the access point, denoted as $B_i = \left\{ \vec{\theta_i}, v_i \right\}$ where $\vec{\theta_i} = \left\{ \theta_{i,1}, \theta_{i,2}, \ldots \theta_{i,k} \right\}$ represents the demand amount of every subtask. v_i denotes the truthful value evaluated by the ith task.

Consider about all mobile devices (sellers), each device submits a bid S_j to the auctioneer, $j \in \{1, 2, \ldots n\}$. $S_j = \{\vec{s_j}, w_j, c_j\}$ where $\vec{s_j} = \left\{ s_{j,1}, s_{j,2}, \ldots s_{j,k} \right\}$. $s_{j,i}$ represents the ith type resource owned by device j, $\vec{s_j}$ denotes a combination of resource provided by device j. w_j represents the maximum number that can provide this type of service. c_j denotes the truthful value evaluated by the ith device's cost.

While the access point get all bids from buyers and sellers. It acts as an auctioneer to determine who has wined (failed) in the auction, and expresses a task assignment scheme at the same time. The scheme includes one task offloaded to which device and each device offload how many. At the same time, the auctioneer computes the charge and payment by a pricing model. Then get charge from tasks and pay corresponding money to the sellers. The flow of the proposed CDA model shows in Fig. 2.

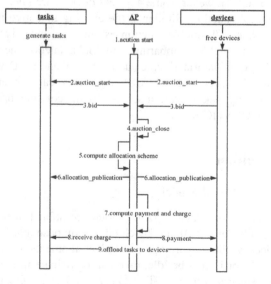

Fig. 2. The flow of communications among the combinatorial double auction model in MDCs.

3.3 Problem Formulation

In this work, one application is consisted of multiple tasks capable to be divided and to be distributed to multiple mobile devices for parallel computing in the auction model. And the extra cost of distributed computing denoted as $e_i = \alpha * t_i + \beta$ where α and β are constants.

Let M denote the set of tasks in the D2D cloud and $|M| = m$. Let N denote the set of mobile devices in the D2D cloud and $|N| = n$. Obviously, the access point (AP) formed an allocation matrix. The matrix is a M * N matrix and is denoted as x_{mn}.

Each element in matrix X can be denoted as

$$x_{ij} = \begin{cases} 1, & \text{if device } j \text{ offload part of the ith task} \\ 0, & \text{otherwise} \end{cases} \tag{1}$$

Since the task is offloaded to each device, the sum of the requested resources cannot exceed the maximum resources of the device. Thus

$$\sum_{k=1}^{m} m_{kj} \leq w_j, j \in \{1, 2 \dots, n\} \tag{2}$$

At the same time, each task gets enough resources from several devices. Hence

$$\sum_{k=1}^{n} x_{ik} * \vec{s_k} \geq \vec{\theta_i}, i \in \{1, 2 \dots m\} \tag{3}$$

Let $trade\,price_i$ denotes the final payment for the ith task. And $trade\,price_j$ denotes the final payment for the jth device. Then we can get the utility for both the buyers and the sellers. The utility of ith task (buyer) is:

$$utility_i^b = \begin{cases} (v_i - e_i) - trade\,price_i, & \text{if ith task win the auction} \\ 0, & \text{if ith task lose the auction} \end{cases} \tag{4}$$

The utility of jth device (seller) is:

$$utility_j^s = \begin{cases} trade\,price_j - \sum_{k=1}^{m} x_{kj} * c_j, & \text{if jth device win the auction} \\ 0, & \text{if jth device lose the auction} \end{cases} \tag{5}$$

Therefore, given the bids from the tasks and the devices, firstly the access point (AP) needs to determine the allocation matrix X, by the allocation matrix, we can also get the payment and the charge for the buyers and sellers. The problem to determine X can be formulated as follows:

$$\max \left(\sum_{i=1}^{m} utility_i^b + \sum_{j=1}^{n} utility_j^s \right) \tag{6}$$

subject to:

$$\sum_{i=1}^{m} x_{ij} \leq w_j, \forall d_j \in D \tag{7}$$

$$\sum_{j=1}^{n} x_{ij} * \vec{s_j} \geq \vec{\theta_i}, \forall t_i \in T \tag{8}$$

$$x_{ij} \in \{0,1\}, i \in \{1,2\ldots m\} \ and \ j \in \{1,2\ldots n\} \tag{9}$$

Refer to the work in [21], the above problem of determine allocation matrix is an NP-hard problem. The optimal solution is unable to be obtained in polynomial time. The problem has both capacity constraint and deadline limitation. Unlike traditional double auction model [15, 9], the use of multiple combinations increases the complexity and difficulty. It is proved that the problem ((4) to (9)) is NP-hard in the following theorem.

Theorem 1: The problem ((4) to (9)) is NP-hard.

Proof 1: In order to prove its NP-hardness, we then show that the above problem can be reduced to the 0-1 knapsack problem: given n items, each with a weight s_j and a value c_j, find a set of items so that the total weight does not exceed S and the total value is maximized [22]. We assume there are n items, the value of each item is c_j. According to (4) to (6), our goal is to maximize (6), the same as minimize $\sum_{k=1}^{m} x_{ik} * c_k$, subject to (7) to (9). We define the x'_{ik} equals to $1 - x_{ik}$. Then our goal is to maximize $\sum_{k=1}^{m} x'_{ik} * c_k$, and subject to following formulation:

$$\sum_{k=1}^{n} x'_{ik} * \vec{s_k} \leq \sum_{k=1}^{n} \vec{s_k} - \vec{\theta_i}, \forall t_i \in T \tag{10}$$

$$x'_{ik} \in \{0,1\}, i \in \{1,2\ldots m\} \ and \ k \in \{1,2\ldots n\} \tag{11}$$

We let S be the right value of (10), then our goal is reduced to the 0-1 knapsack problem mentioned above. Therefore, the problem defined by (4) to (9) is also NP-hard.

3.4   Economic Properties

Our goal is to design a combinatorial double auction mechanism, and the mechanism is able to achieve the three economic properties in polynomial time: individual rationality, budget balance and truthfulness.

Individual Rationality. A combinatorial auction is individually rational if no winner's utility is negative.

Budget Balance. The auctioneer's revenue is not negative. The property is utilized to motivate the auctioneer to participate in the auction.

Truthfulness. The bid submitted by each buyer and seller should be truthful. No one can get more utility by submitted a fake bid.

Computational Efficiency. The mechanism or algorithm we propose should be solved in polynomial time.

4   Greedy Allocation Mechanism

In this section, we present a greedy algorithm to solve the NP-hard problem ((4) to (9)). Although the optimal solution of an NP-hard problem is impossible to get in polynomial time, it is feasible to get an approximate optimal solution. The bid density is utilized to push bids for an efficient allocation, and the bid density must be a monotonic function. The bid density should reflect the value of sub-tasks and resources, which is a function about v or c. Different from the bid density used in [21], we define the bid density of tasks and devices as follows:

$$bd\_task_i = \sqrt{\sum\nolimits_{j=1}^{k} \theta_{i,j}^2 + v_i^2}, i \in \{1, 2 \ldots m\} \tag{12}$$

$$bd\_device_j = \sqrt{\sum\nolimits_{j=1}^{k} 1/s_{i,j}^2 + c_j^2}, j \in \{1, 2 \ldots n\} \tag{13}$$

Therefore, we have

$$\sqrt{v_1^2 + \sum\nolimits_{j=1}^{k} \theta_{1,j}^2} \geq \sqrt{v_2^2 + \sum\nolimits_{j=1}^{k} \theta_{2,j}^2} \geq \ldots \geq \sqrt{v_m^2 + \sum\nolimits_{j=1}^{k} \theta_{m,j}^2} \tag{14}$$

$$\sqrt{c_1^2 + \sum\nolimits_{j=1}^{k} 1/s_{1,j}^2} \geq \sqrt{c_2^2 + \sum\nolimits_{j=1}^{k} 1/s_{2,j}^2} \geq \ldots \geq \sqrt{c_n^2 + \sum\nolimits_{j=1}^{k} 1/s_{n,j}^2} \tag{15}$$

Then, we design the allocation model and the pricing model are shown in algorithm 1 and algorithm 2, and the complexity of two models are both $O(mn)$. And prove the pricing and the allocation model satisfy several economic properties.

4.1   Allocation Model

The allocation model is an algorithm to determine which task should be assigned to which device. In a D2D cloud, bids of tasks and mobile devices are submitted to the access point (AP). According to the definition of bid density (12) (13), the bids are sorted in ascending order and descending order by the access point (AP). The AP determines the allocation matrix by a greedy strategy which describes in Algorithm 1 (see Fig. 3).

Algorithm 1

Input: M, N, B, S //The number of tasks M, the number of devices N, bids of the tasks B
// bids of the devices S
Output: X //allocation matrix X
1: Calculate and sort the bids of tasks and devices
2: $E = \{\emptyset\}$
3: Normalized v and θ between (0,1)
4: for i $=$ 1 to M do
5:    $bd\_task_i = \sqrt{\sum_{j=1}^{k} \theta_{i,j}^2 + v_i^2}$
6:    $E = E \cup \{bd\_task_i\}$
7: end for
8: sort bid densities in E in descending order
9: $F = \{\emptyset\}$
10: Normalized s and c between (0,1)
11: for j $=$ 1 to N do
12:    $bd\_device_j = \sqrt{\sum_{j=1}^{k} 1\big/s_{i,j}^2 + c_j^2}$
13:    $F = F \cup \{bd\_device_j\}$
14: end for
15: sort bid densities in F in ascending order
16: initialize allocation matrix X
17: $X_{mn} = 0$
18: for e $=$ 1 to |E| do
19:    for f $=$ 1 to |F| do
20:       if w > 0 and v > c and θ > 0: // enough cost and enough resources
21:          $X_{ef} = 1, w = w - 1, \theta = \theta - s$
22:       end if
23:    end for
24:    if θ < 0: //announce the eth task win the auction
25:    end if
26: end for
27: get allocation matrix X

Fig. 3. The greedy allocation algorithm

4.2   Pricing Model

We then introduce the pricing model which decides the payment of buyers and the charge of sellers. Similar to the work of [19], while the allocation matrix is fixed, the winning resources of each buyer is also fixed as follows:

$$resource_i = \sum_{j=1}^{n} x_{ij} * s_j, i \in \{1, 2 \ldots m\} \tag{16}$$

We define the per unit price for resources as follows:

$$perprice\_task_i = \frac{v_i}{\sum_{j=1}^n x_{ij} * s_j}, i \in \{1, 2 \ldots m\} \tag{17}$$

$$perprice\_device_j = \frac{c_j}{\sum_{j=1}^n s_j}, j \in \{1, 2 \ldots n\} \tag{18}$$

Next, the average price matrix P was calculated based on the average value of (17) and (18), then we use the algorithm 2 (see Fig. 4) to calculate corresponding payments by the price matrix, then the auctioneer would send the payment and the charge to both buyers and sellers.

Algorithm 2

Input: X, B, S //The allocation matrix X, bids of the tasks B, bids of the devices S
Output: P, $trade\ price\_task_i$, $trade\ price\_device_j$

1: Calculate the per unit pricing matrix
2: for the winner of the buyers
3:   $per\ price\_task_i = \frac{v_i}{\sum x_{ij} * \sum s_j}$
4: end for
5: for the winner of the sellers
6:   $per\ price\_device_j = \frac{c_j}{\sum s_j}$
7: end for
8: initialize pricing matrix P
9: for the winner of the buyers
10:    for the winner of the sellers
11:       $P_{ij} = (per\ price\_task_i + per\ price\_device_j)/2$
12:       if $per\ price\_device_j \le P_{ij} \le per\ price\_task_i$
13:       end if
14:       else $P_{ij} = per\ price\_device_j$
15:    end for
16: end for
17: calculate the payment and the charge
18: for the winner of the buyers
19:    $trade\ price\_task_i = \sum_{m=1}^k P_{im} * \vec{s}_j * x_{im}$
20: end for
21: for the winner of the sellers
22:    $trade\ price\_device_j = \sum_{i=1}^k P_{kj} * \vec{s}_j * x_{kj}$
23: end for
24: get $trade\ price\_task_i$, $trade\ price\_device_j$

Fig. 4. The greedy allocation algorithm

4.3   Algorithm Analysis and Auction Properties

We now analyze the properties of the allocation and pricing model, including computational efficiency, individual rationality, budget balance and truthfulness.

Time complexity analysis

Theorem 2: The time complexity of the allocation model is $O(m\log m + n\log n + mn)$ and the pricing model is $O(mn)$.

Proof 2: For the allocation model, according to Algorithm 1, the complexity for sorting the bid density is $O(m\log m + n\log n)$, and the generate allocation matrix phase is $O(mn)$. Therefore, the complexity of the allocation is $O(m\log m + n\log n + mn)$. There are two loops in Algorithm 2, thus the complexity of the pricing model is $O(mn)$ obiviously. Both of them can be completed in polynomial time.

Individual Rationality

Theorem 3: For each buyer and seller, its utility is not negative.

Proof 3: According to (4), the utility of the winner of the buyer is equal to the valuation plus the trade price (payment), and the utility of the buyer lose the auction equals to zero. In algorithms 1, if the buyer has no extra value to support the cost, it will lose the auction. Therefore, the winner has enough value to support the cost, and the final payment of buyers is higher than the cost but lower than the valuation, so the utility of each buyer is not negative.

According to (5), for the winner of the seller, because of the per unit pricing is more expensive than the cost, the per unit utility of each seller is not negative, then the utility is also not negative. And the utility of the seller loses the auction equals to zero. Therefore, the utility of each seller is not negative.

Budget Balance

Theorem 4: The auctioneer in the auction is budget balanced.

Proof 4: When the auctioneer gets all the bids, it will determine the winner and payment of the auction by the allocation model and pricing model, the value of utility of the auctioneer equals to the difference between the payments received from all buyers and the charges payed to all sellers. Therefore, we have

$$utility_{auctioneer} = \sum_{i=1}^{m} trade\,price\_task_i - \sum_{j=1}^{n} trade\,price\_device_j$$

Because of the per cost of buyers is higher than sellers, so the buyer's sum of payments is greater than the seller's sum of payments, and the utility of the auctioneer is not negative, in other words, the auctioneer in the auction is budget balanced.

Truthfulness

Theorem 5: The greedy allocation and pricing mechanisms are truthful.

Proof 5: While the allocation matrix X is fixed, both the winner of buyer and the seller in the auction get the most efficient allocation. By the pricing strategy, the revenue is fixed and maximized. Buyers (sellers) cannot improve their own utility by submitting a fake bid.

For the lose buyer failed in the auction. If the buyer submits a lower bid, he will still cause his own auction to fail. In this case, the utility is still zero, if a higher bid is submitted, it will cause you to obtain resources, but the resulting utility is negative.

For the lose seller failed in the auction. If a higher bid is submitted, it still fails and the utility is still zero, if the bid is submitted with a lower bid, it will cause him to obtain the buyer, but the actual cost is too large and the utility will be negative.

Therefore, the greedy allocation and pricing mechanisms are truthful.

5   Simulation Setup and Experimental Results

In this section, we evaluate the performance of our algorithms.

The presented evaluation metrics are (1): the individual rationality of applications and mobile devices; (2): the percentage served users, which is the ratio of the number of winning participants to the total number of participants and the (average) utility of tasks and devices. For comparison purpose, we also implement the random allocation method and maximum matching algorithm.

We assume there are six sensing applications and five devices in a device-to-device (D2D) cloud. Each task can be divided into two different types of subtasks, task1 and task2. We list the task amount and the corresponding bid in Table 1, each mobile device has own unused resources, as shown in Table 2. According to the evaluation function (12) (13), we compute the bid density for tasks (buyers) and devices (sellers). And we set = 0.01 and = 0.05 for the extra cost of parallel computing.

Table 1. Bid density of the tasks (buyers)

Tasks	Task1 (θ_1)	Task2 (θ_2)	v	Bid density
T1	30	30	13	1.732051
T2	30	20	12	1.563472
T3	25	25	12	1.545603
T4	30	20	11	1.511530
T5	15	15	10	1.092906
T6	10	15	9	0.961047

Table 2. Bid density of the devices (sellers)

Devices	Resource1	Resource2	W	v	Bid density
D1	3	6	6	1	0.885689
D2	5	5	6	1.2	0.958458
D3	8	6	6	1.5	1.283333
D4	10	8	5	2	1.670366
D5	9	9	4	2	1.676305

We implement our CDA algorithms using Python 3.6 to test the performance. The default parameters of the tasks and the devices used during the simulation are listed in Tables 1 and 2 respectively. We run our program 1000 times and calculate the average value under each condition.

5.1 Performance on Individual Rationality

We first investigate the performance of the proposed mechanisms on individual rationality. As shown in Fig. 5, the first experiment observes the submitted bid of the tasks (buyers) are more than the final payment and the submitted bid of mobile devices (sellers) are less than the final payment. As shown in Figs. 6 and 7, both the sellers and the buyers get positive utility. In other words, the algorithms we proposed can achieve the individual rationality.

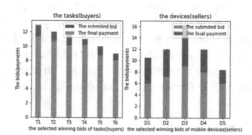

Fig. 5. Performance on individual rationality

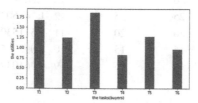

Fig. 6. Utility of tasks (buyers)

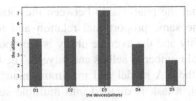

Fig. 7. Utility of mobile devices (sellers)

5.2   Percentage Served and Total Utility

For comparison purpose, we second compare our model with the double auction model in [15], the random allocation scheme, and the maximum matching scheme by the percentage served, total utility and average utility. Results for the three metrics are illustrated in Fig. 8(a), (b) and (c), respectively.

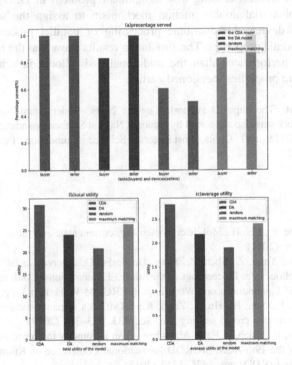

Fig. 8. Total utility and average utility

As shown in Fig. 8(a), the second experiment observes the CDA get a better percentage served than the double auction. In the CDA model, six buyers and five sellers win the auction. However, only five buyers and five sellers win the auction in the double auction model. We run the random allocation model two thousand times, the results show the random scheme get an average of 3.686 tasks and 3.074 devices get the task offloading. And the maximum matching schemes also can't get full use of tasks or devices.

Then we consider about the relationship between the total utility and the average utility. Figure 8(c) has the same proportional relation and tendency with Fig. 8(b), which means the total utility and the average utility is a proportional relationship, and the ratio of them is the total number of sellers and buyers. The CDA model get a 26.3% and 15.8% benefits than the DA model and maximum matching mechanism respectively. In the CDA model, a task is divided into multiple subtasks and offloaded to different device to execute, and a device is able to offload multiple tasks synchronously, this accelerates the auction process and improve the efficiency of the devices.

From the above mentioned discussions, we can now draw the conclusion that the CDA model are efficient to allocate tasks in a D2D cloud.

6 Conclusion

In this paper, we discuss sensing task assignment problem in D2D clouds and we propose a combinatorial double auction mechanism to assign the sensing tasks to different mobile devices for distribute processing or parallel processing. Then we analyze the economic properties. The simulation results show that the mechanisms can achieve a fairy performance than the traditional task allocation schemes and also achieve economic properties mentioned earlier.

Acknowledgement. The paper is supported by the NSFC under Grant No. U1709217 and 61472385. This work was also supported by National Natural Science Foundation of China under Grant No. 61702115 and China Postdoctoral Science Foundation Fund under Grant No. 2017M622632.

References

1. Ganti, R.K., Ye, F., Lei, H.: Mobile crowdsensing: current state and future challenges. IEEE Commun. Mag. (2011)
2. Dai, J., Bai, X., Yang, Z., Shen, Z., Xuan, D.: PerFallD: a pervasive fall detection system using mobile phones. In: Proceedings of the 8th IEEE International Conference on Pervasive Computing and Communications Workshops (PERCOM Workshops), pp. 292–297 (2010)
3. Wang, F., Hu, L., Sun, R., Hu, J., Zhao, K.: SRMCS: a semantic-aware recommendation framework for mobile crowd sensing. Inf. Sci. **433**, 333–345 (2017)
4. Zheng, Y., Liu, F., Hsieh, H.P.: U-Air: when urban air quality inference meets big data. In: Proceedings of the 19th ACM SIGKDD International Conference on Knowledge Discovery and Data Mining (KDD), pp. 1436–1444 (2013)
5. Coric, V., Gruteser, M.: Crowdsensing maps of on-street parking spaces. In: Proceedings of the 2013 IEEE International Conference on Distributed Computing in Sensor Systems (DCOSS), pp. 115–122 (2013)
6. Guo, B., Chen, H., Yu, Z., Xie, X., Huangfu, S., Zhang, D.: A mobile crowdsensing system for cross-space public information reposting, tagging, and sharing. IEEE Trans. Mob. Comput. (2015)
7. Mtibaa, A., Fahim, A., Harras, K.A., Ammar, M.H.: Towards resource sharing in mobile device clouds: power balancing across mobile devices. In: Proceedings of the Second Edition of the MCC Workshop on Mobile Cloud Computing (MCC), pp. 51–56 (2013)

8. Feng, Z., Zhu, Y., Zhang, Q.: TRAC: truthful auction for location-aware collaborative sensing in mobile crowdsourcing. In: IEEE Conference on Computer Communications (INFOCOM), pp. 1231 – 1239 (2014)
9. Yang, D., Fang, X., Xue, G.: Truthful auction for cooperative communications. In: MobiHoc 2011 Proceedings of the Twelfth ACM International Symposium on Mobile Ad Hoc Networking and Computing (2011)
10. Rassenti, S.J., Smith, V.L., Bulfin, R.L.: A combinatorial auction mechanism for airport time slot allocation. Bell J. Econ. **13**(2), 402–417 (1982)
11. Ba, S., Stallaert, J., Whinston, A.B.: Optimal investment in knowledge with in a firm using a market-mechanism. Manag. Sci. **47**, 1203–1219 (2001)
12. Chen, C., Wang, Y.: SPARC: strategy-proof double auction for mobile participatory sensing. In: Cloud Computing and Big Data (CloudCom-Asia) (2013)
13. Tang, L., He, S., Li, Q.: Double-sided bidding mechanism for resource sharing in mobile cloud. IEEE Trans. Vehic. Technol. **66**, 1798–1809 (2017)
14. Huang, H., Xin, Y., Sun, Y.-E.: A truthful double auction mechanism for crowdsensing systems with max-min fairness. In: Wireless Communications and Networking Conference (WCNC) (2017)
15. Wang, X., Chen, X., Wu, W.: Towards truthful auction mechanisms for task assignment in mobile device clouds. In: IEEE Conference on Computer Communications (INFOCOM), pp. 1–9, Atlanta, USA, (2017)
16. Xiao, S., Zhou, X., Feng, D., Yuan-Wu, Y.: Energy-efficient mobile association in heterogeneous networks with device-to-device communications. IEEE Trans. Wirel. Commun. **15**(8), 5260–5271 (2016)
17. Song, C., Liu, M., Dai, X.: Remote cloud or local crowd: communicating and sharing the crowdsensing data. In: 2015 IEEE Fifth International Conference on Big Data and Cloud Computing (BDCloud) (2015)
18. Chen, L., Huang, L., Sun, Z., Xu, H., Guo, H.: Spectrum combinatorial double auction for cognitive radio network with ubiquitous network resource providers. IET Commun. **9**, 2085–2094 (2015)
19. Baranwal, G., Vidyarthi, D.P.: A fair multi-attribute combinatorial double auction model for resource allocation in cloud computing. J. Syst. Softw. **108**, 60–76 (2015)
20. Samimi, P., Teimouri, Y., Mukhtar, M.: A combinatorial double auction resource allocation model in cloud computing. Inf. Sci. **357**, 201–216 (2014)
21. Xu, W., Huang, H., Sun, Y.: DATA: a double auction based task assignment mechanism in crowdsourcing systems. In: 8th International Conference on Communications and Networking in China (CHINACOM), pp. 172–177 (2013)
22. https://en.wikipedia.org/wiki/Knapsack_problem

Author Index

Printed in the United States
By Bookmasters